Scripting Revolution

Scripting Revolution

A Historical Approach to the

Comparative Study of Revolutions

Edited by Keith Michael Baker

and Dan Edelstein

Stanford University Press

Stanford, California

Funding for this volume was made possible thanks to generous support from The Europe Center at the Freeman Spogli Institute for International Studies

Stanford University Press
Stanford, California

Printed in the United States of America
on acid-free, archival-quality paper

Library of Congress Cataloging-in-Publication Data

Scripting revolution : a historical approach to the comparative study of revolutions / edited by Keith Michael Baker and Dan Edelstein.
       pages   cm
    Includes bibliographical references and index.
    ISBN 978-0-8047-9396-4 (cloth : alk. paper) —
    ISBN 978-0-8047-9616-3 (pbk. : alk. paper)
    1. Revolutions—History. I. Baker, Keith Michael, editor.
 II. Edelstein, Dan, editor.
 JC491.S38   2015
 321.09'4—dc23   2015005110

 ISBN 978-0-8047-9619-4 (electronic)

 Typeset at Stanford University Press in 10/13 Galliard

Acknowledgments

The editors would like to thank the following entities at Stanford University for their support: The Europe Center at the Freeman Spogli Institute for International Studies; the School of Humanities and Sciences; the Division of Literatures, Cultures and Languages; the Department of History; the Stanford Humanities Center; and the France-Stanford Center for Interdisciplinary Studies. They are also grateful to Andrew Schupanitz for his editorial assistance.

Contents

KEITH MICHAEL BAKER

DAN EDELSTEIN

Introduction

"Is this a revolution?" Shortly after massive popular protest in Egypt on 25 January 2011 unleashed the flood of events that would sweep Hosni Mubarak from the presidency, an interviewer put this question to a principal Internet animator of the uprising, Google employee Wael Ghonim. He thought briefly before proclaiming the advent of "Revolution 2.0."

Ghonim repeated this formulation frequently in interviews during the following days and in the fascinating memoir, *Revolution 2.0,* he published a year later. "Revolutions of the past have usually had charismatic leaders who were politically savvy and sometimes even military geniuses," he concluded in this book. "Such revolutions followed what we can call the Revolution 1.0 model. But the revolution in Egypt was different: it was truly a spontaneous movement led by nothing other than the wisdom of the crowd." This Revolution 2.0, Ghonim wanted to insist, was essentially leaderless: "no one was the hero because everyone was the hero." It was "like an offline Wikipedia, with everyone anonymously and selflessly contributing efforts toward a common goal.[1]

One has to say that Ghonim's characterization of Revolution 1.0 is as radically attenuated as the accompanying conceptualization of Revolution 2.0 is thin. But his title, and the events unleashed by the Arab Spring, invite us to think again about the longer history of the revolutionary tradition. To speak of Revolution 2.0 suggests a significant revision of an ongoing project, an upgrading of a revolutionary program through conceptual elaboration and technical innovation. Clearly, the Internet has placed an immensely more powerful technology of communication in the service of social and political change. But has the conceptualization of revolution been updated along with the technology? Has Facebook revolutionized revolution itself? To consider this question, we need to think about revolution again. This volume of essays proposes to do so by exploring the possibilities of a new historical approach to the comparative study of revolutions.

Approaching Revolution as Script

Until now, a curious division of labor has prevailed among scholars of revolution. Historians have mostly studied revolutions as distinct and separate events, leaving the comparative study of revolutions to sociologists and political scientists. Methodologically, these two approaches to revolution could hardly be more opposed. Where historians emphasize the specificity of historical context, social scientists point to comparable structural social and institutional imbalances in their analyses. Historians such as William Sewell and Martin Malia have long pointed out the flaws with the sociological analysis of comparative revolutions. But historians have been reluctant to propose an alternative method, in large part because the comparative study of revolutions requires a close familiarity with many different cultures, languages, and historical traditions.

The guiding insight of the essays in *Scripting Revolution* is that at least one feature of revolutions transcends these cultural differences—and this is the notion of a revolutionary "script." Revolutions do not occur ex nihilo. Revolutionaries are extremely self-conscious of (and often highly knowledgeable about) how previous revolutions unfolded. These revolutionary scripts offer frameworks for political action. Whether they serve as models or counterexamples, they provide the outlines on which revolutionary actors can improvise. And revolutionaries, in turn, can transform the scripts they inherit. Marx rewrote the script of the French Revolution; Lenin revised Marx; Mao revised Lenin; and so on and so forth.

It is our contention that an historical approach of this kind is better suited than a sociological method to reveal the similarities (and differences) between revolutionary origins and outcomes. To advance this claim, and to address the added difficulty of navigating between different linguistic and cultural traditions, we have assembled a group of leading historians to explore how the revolutions on which they are experts modeled themselves on—or actively transformed—preexisting revolutionary scripts.

To take the notion of script in its fairly straightforward literary or dramatic sense, we might say that a script creates a situation and sets out the manner of its unfolding. It requires the setting of a scene and the character-ization of those acting within it, in relationship one to another and to the situation more broadly construed. Its initial definition of the situation implies a narrative (or possible narratives) to be enacted in subsequent scenes, which in turn introduce actions and events that offer its characters choices among possible courses of action. A script, in other words, constitutes a frame within which a situation is defined and a narrative projected; the narrative, in turn, offers a series of consequent situations, subject positions, and possible moves to be enacted by the agents within that frame. Once known and enacted, the script can be replayed indefinitely; but it can also be changed, adapted, or even subverted by the introduction of new events, characters, or actions. The actors—or even the audience—can take over the stage.

In politics, as in the theater or on the screen, scripts generate events. They do so in the obvious sense that a script suggests positions to be taken, actions to be carried out, incidents to be anticipated. They do so, less obviously, in the sense that positions that have been taken, actions that have been carried out, or incidents that have occurred are necessarily configured (or reconfigured) to give them meaning within a script—or within competing scripts. They do so, further, as scripts thus become subject to interpretation or improvisation, leading to conflicts among those competing to define and enact their own claims in relation to a particular script, or to resist the characterizations forced upon them within a script imposed by others. Competition to impose a script, or to control a script that has been imposed, is a fundamental fact of politics, though perhaps never more in evidence than in a situation that has been declared revolutionary.

Extending this notion of script to the phenomenon of revolution, we might begin by postulating that all politics is about the definition of the situation. To declare that a revolution has occurred or is imminent, or that a revolution is underway; to act in the name of revolution, or to invoke its necessary logic as a form of legitimation or justification: these are ways of defining a political situation. There is, though, a very significant difference between seeing a revolution as an event—a significant change that has occurred, might be anticipated, or might even be passively experienced or undergone—or conceiving it as a dynamic and ongoing process of contestation and conflict, or as a mode of collective action directed toward the goal of radical transformation. This latter conceptualization, we think, is an invention that appeared first in France in the years following 1789. It is best described, in our judgment, as the first modern revolutionary script. Our contention is that it was elaborated in France in the years between 1789 and 1815. Thereafter, revolution became an action frame providing a repertory of situations, subject positions, political options, historical narratives, and social logics invoked and enacted, adapted and extended throughout the nineteenth and twentieth centuries, and into the twenty-first. To declare a particular collective political action a Revolution, to pronounce a particular situation revolutionary, to become oneself a revolutionary, to justify one's deeds in the name of the Revolution, to insist upon, or impose, what the Revolution requires: these are all performatives—performances made possible (whether made successfully or not) within or upon the revolutionary script.

One methodological advantage of thinking about revolution in these terms is that it offers a middle ground between the generalizable empirical description of phenomena for which social scientists aim and the close characterization of unique actions and events in specific time and place to which historians aspire. Revolutions are neither identifiable and independent unit phenomena to be sequenced comparatively nor unique historical occurrences to be understood solely in terms of their particular time and place. One can think of them historically—and transhistorically—as variations on a script for political action and understanding invented at a particular moment and in specific circumstances, a script played and replayed, improvised upon and extended in different times and places, but nevertheless possessing a degree of narrative continuity and analytical identity.

The suggestion that the concept of "scripting" could offer a useful handle on revolutionary events was first made by one of us some years ago in an essay on the French Revolution.[2] Here we propose this concept as a way to think about the comparative study of revolution. More specifically, we argue that scholars who engage in this study have largely overlooked a defining feature of revolutions and of revolutionary history—namely, the self-conscious awareness with which revolutionaries model their actions on those of revolutions past. Marx famously mocked this tendency in his *18th Brumaire of Louis Napoleon*; we consider it more seriously. In fact, we argue that it offers a better approach to the comparative study of revolution than Marx's own method, which has provided the basic framework for most of the sociological studies on this topic. We consider the problems with this framework in the following section, before examining how our own approach compares with current trends in global and intellectual history.

Against Sociological (and Deterministic) Accounts of Revolution

As noted above, the comparative history of revolutions, with a few notable exceptions (which we discuss below), has traditionally been left to sociologists and political scientists. The heyday of this social-scientific school occurred in the late 1970s, with the publication of such classics as Charles Tilly's *From Mobilization to Revolution* (1978) and Theda Skocpol's *States and Social Revolutions: A Comparative Analysis of France, Russia, and China* (1979). Its roots, however, extend back to Crane Brinton's 1938 *The Anatomy of Revolution*, and more directly to Barrington Moore's 1966 *Social Origins of Dictatorship and Democracy* (both Skocpol and Tilly studied with Moore at Harvard). Nor has this school run out of steam, as evidenced by Jack Goldstone's *Revolution and Rebellion* and Steve Pincus's *1688: The First Modern Revolution*. Pincus himself owes a great deal to Moore (to whom he pays homage in *1688*), as does Jack Goldstone, one of Skocpol's students and author of numerous works on the comparative history of revolutions.[3]

The basic methodological framework for this sociological approach, however, can be traced back to Marx himself. Moore had made class struggle the motor of social change, and by extension of revolution, even going so far as to adopt Marx's concept of "bourgeois revolution."[4] Even when it sheds such explicitly Marxist categories, the sociological school remains indebted to Marx's fundamental view that the true causes of revolutions are to be found in socioeconomic conflicts (the "infrastructure"). Skocpol herself calls attention to this problem, pointing out how "everyone who writes about social revolutions recognizes that they begin with overtly political crises," and yet when it comes to studying these revolutions, "most theorists [...] tend to regard the political crises that launch revolutions as incidental triggers or as little more than epiphenomenal indicators of more fundamental contradictions or strains located in the social structure of the old regime."[5] While Skocpol makes the case for recognizing the state as independent from "socioeconomic forces and conflicts," she ultimately views the state as a "macro-structure" as well (29), hence extending the structural analysis of revolutions to another level. It is unclear how this methodological innovation resolves the problem she identified, which is to explain how political crises can trigger revolutions. In the end, revolutions in this model still appear as fated to occur, due to structural conflicts, at either the social or state level.

Historians have long treated these sociological arguments with a strong dose of skepticism.[6] The problems with the sociological method can be divided into two categories: those that concern revolutionary beginnings, and those that appear in the middle or the end.

Revolutionary beginnings. There are a number of problems with the assumption that political crises are just "incidental triggers," to be discounted in favor of structural conflicts. To begin with, it rests on an overly schematic distinction between "good," stable states (that is, those that do not suffer from any "fundamental contradictions") and "bad," unstable ones.[7] Leaving aside the fact that just about every state exhibits structural imbalances of some sort, it is the teleological conclusion that sociologists draw from this distinction that is most questionable. In their view, these intrinsically unstable states are fated to succumb to revolutions, while their happy, stable neighbors sail smoothly through the choppy waters of history. Here again we may glimpse the specter of Marxism that haunts the sociological school: Marx had similarly argued that the "contradiction between the productive forces and the form of intercourse [between individuals in society] . . . *necessarily* on each occasion burst out in a revolution."[8]

But this claim does not hold up very well to historical scrutiny. Indeed, there are plenty of counterexamples of states that exhibited "fundamental contradictions" but that muddled through all the same: think of the United States, or many Western European nations, during the Great Depression. If anything, it is often those states that should be ripe for revolution that outlast most analysts' expectations: for instance, the USSR, the People's Republic of China, Belarus, or many Middle Eastern and African autocracies.[9] If some of these states did eventually witness revolutions, there are usually proximate causes that played important roles: *perestroika*, in the Soviet case, or the self-immolation of Mohammed Bouazizi, for the Tunisian Revolution.

It is this tension between proximate and indirect causes of revolution that poses a second major problem with the sociological method. In his Moore-inspired theory of revolutionary origins, for instance, Pincus claims that state-sponsored modernization projects are the true cause of revolutions, yet also acknowledges that these same projects can result in the creation of "a stable and efficient state."[10] But if the same cause can produce completely opposite effects, clearly there must be other, more proximate causes for the revolutionary outcome. And if there are other causes, why focus exclusively on modernization? Without supplying the missing links connecting a structural conflict to the outbreak of revolution, there is no obvious reason to place greater emphasis on one cause over another.

This difficulty with evaluating the different potential causes of a revolution, finally, extends to the competing sociological theories themselves. On what basis is the reader, even one sympathetic to the authors' methodology, to decide whether, say, demographic tensions (Goldstone), intrastate conflicts (Skocpol), or risky modernization projects (Pincus) were *the* critical factor in bringing down a regime? Each of these structural imbalances may well have played a part; but by dismissing the causal relevance of those immediate crises that precipitate revolutions, sociologists deny us the ability to cross-evaluate their different hypotheses.[11] Sociological accounts of revolutionary causes end up resembling the story of the blind men and the elephant: for one, it's all about the trunk; for another, the belly's the thing; for the third, the legs hold the answer.

To be sure, we do not mean to suggest that structural conflicts play no role whatsoever in the outbreak of revolutions. Without certain preconditions, no revolution is possible. But preconditions are not conditions: some human assembly is still required. It is here, we argue, that scripts come into play. When a crisis occurs, a sufficient number of individuals may decide that the time is right to enact a revolutionary script. The factors that brought about the crisis can vary from case to case: it was a financial crisis that brought France to the brink of revolution in 1789, a political one that triggered the July Revolution of 1830, and a military conflict that led to the Paris Commune of 1871. The sociological search for a "single basic process" that can explain "the periodic state breakdowns in Europe, China, and the Middle East from 1500 to 1850" is a quixotic pursuit.[12] But once the crisis has occurred, and a critical mass of actors opts for a revolutionary diagnosis and revolutionary action, events tend to unfold in a very similar — even scripted — fashion.

Revolutionary middles and ends. Sociologists have not ignored these recurrent patterns in revolutionary activity, but they tend to analyze them in terms of "phases," often modeled on emblematic revolutionary moments.[13] The problem with this approach is that it conflates description with explanation. Goldstone, for instance, collapses the first five years of the French Revolution into a single "phase," arguing that a causal chain connects the collapse of the Bourbon monarchy, the civil war, and the Terror.[14] Teleology becomes his only explanatory model: the French revolutionary wars are "a natural outcome of this revolutionary struggle," while complex historical outcomes are judged "inevitable."[15] Almost needless to say, historians would beg to differ.[16]

This teleological temptation seeps through a number of sociological accounts of revolution, including Moore's.[17] But simply because similar events took place in succession in multiple revolutions does not mean that they were fated to do so. Revolutions do not occur in isolation: the Russian revolutionaries, for instance, were extremely self-conscious about the history of the French Revolution, and sought to emulate (or avoid, in the case of the Napoleonic period) its path. Hence, if there was a "Terror" after the Bolsheviks seized power, it was not because, according to sociological theory, that's when the Terror phase occurs, but rather because the Bolsheviks were consciously modeling their actions on the Jacobin script. To be sure, they faced intense opposition, which culminated in civil war, but they perceived their situation through a Jacobin lens. They moved rapidly to create a "revolutionary tribunal" to try "enemies of the people," just as the Montagnards had; Lenin even expressed his satisfaction that a Russian Fouquier-Tinville could be found to serve as its prosecutor.[18] Accordingly, Terror occurred in the French and Russian Revolutions for different reasons, but the end results bear a resemblance.

It is somewhat ironic that the dominant approach to the comparative study of revolutions should remain so indebted to Marx, given that Marx's own followers came to abandon it in the late nineteenth century. At that time, it had become painfully apparent that the revolution, judged "inevitable" by Marx's doctrine of historical materialism, was not just around the corner.[19] "Socioeconomic forces and conflicts," in Skocpol's words, had failed to produce the "political crises that launch revolutions." It was precisely this realization that led to the various revisions of Marxism, from Eduard Bernstein's rejection of violent revolution in favor of parliamentary reform, to Lenin's abandonment of Marx's structural model in favor of a system of professional revolutionaries who could inculcate a "political consciousness" in the proletariat. The first successful Marxist revolution, in October 1917, was brought about by a political party that explicitly *reversed* Marx's relation between historical conditions and ideology.[20]

Global History in a Different Key

One of the major shortcomings of the sociological approach to the study of revolutions is that it does not consider the impact that different revolutions had on each other. With the rise of interest in global history, historians are once again exploring these interrelations between revolutions—"once again," since this was the approach pioneered by R. R. Palmer, Eric Hobsbawm, and Jacques Godechot in the 1950s and 1960s.[21] To be sure, the current global historians expand the geographic scope of these earlier scholars, who focused exclusively on the European and North Atlantic theater. But they largely maintain their predecessors' chronological focus on an "age"—1760 to 1840, in the case of the volume edited by David Armitage and Sanjay Subrahmanyam; or "the global imperial crisis of the eighteenth century," for the essays in a recent volume on *The French Revolution in Global Perspective*.[22]

Within these chronological confines, these historians seek primarily to draw attention to the "interconnectedness" of revolutions during this period.[23] They remind us that the "increasingly globalized circuits of economic exchange and worldwide geopolitical competition" determined to a large degree both foreign and domestic policies.[24] Commodities, but also ideas, circulated throughout these networks, which were, moreover, multidirectional: the inward flow from the margins of empire to the capital was as determinant as the flow out.

This "synchronic" model goes some way toward explaining how revolutionary scripts circulated as well. Their circulation was truly global: the publication of Lamartine's *Histoire des Girondins* in 1847, for instance, so inspired a group of Chilean revolutionaries that they each chose a *nom-de-guerre* from one of Lamartine's political idols.[25] And the circulation could go in many directions: as the essay by David Como in this volume informs us, the nascent seventeenth-century script of revolution in England had Spanish and southern Italian elements to it.[26]

There are some limits, however, to what this synchronic model can offer. In a recent review essay, David A. Bell notes how historians eager to highlight the impact of global events on the French Revolution have mostly had to content themselves with gesturing to the need for further research.[27] He also points out how very difficult it can be to measure the "impact" of global affairs on national events. There is no denying, for instance, that deputies to the National Assembly paid considerable attention to colonial issues in the first year of revolution, but they paid attention to a great number of issues. It would be nearly impossible to demonstrate, and is moreover highly unlikely, that colonial issues mattered more than other red-button questions, such as the Civil Constitution of the Clergy. Accordingly, Bell concludes that "despite the best efforts of several talented historians, conditions and events in France's own colonies . . . seem to have had little impact on metropolitan political developments."

One reason the historians Bell discusses have found it challenging to connect French Revolutionary history with events occurring outside of metropolitan France may also have to do with the synchronic time frame they adopt. Contemporaneous events do not always have the largest impact: it sometimes takes the repeated transmission and reworking of past events to make them influential. The beheading of Charles I arguably mattered more for the French in 1792 than in 1649. Similarly, it was only after the king's flight to Varennes (in June 1791) that French political actors and theorists became receptive to English republican arguments from the late seventeenth and early eighteenth centuries.[28]

We have accordingly privileged a more "diachronic" model of revolutionary transmission, one that considers the impact of revolutions on each other over the *longue durée*.[29] As the Catalonian and Neapolitan examples cited above indicate, many elements of what would become the modern script of revolution began to coalesce well before the "age of revolutions" might be said to have begun. Our approach challenges the logic of imposing chronological bookends on the study of revolution: on the contrary, the essays collected here underscore the importance of analyzing the continuity (and the ruptures) between, say, seventeenth-century English revolutions and the eighteenth-century American and French revolutions. They also look forward to appreciate the lasting reverberations of 1789–94 on the Bolshevik Revolution, and even in the ongoing Arab uprising.

Adding a Fourth Dimension to Intellectual History

Over the course of this *longue durée*, the meaning and connotations of "revolution" of course changed considerably. Far be it for us, indeed, to suggest that a revolutionary script is a "unit idea" that plows through history untouched. On the contrary, our essays call attention to the manner in which revolutionary scripts are always mutating. This perpetual transformation has not occurred uniformly in time and place: at different points in history, there have been a variety of scripts to choose from. The Spanish American revolutions of the early nineteenth century (which, for reasons of space, are not otherwise discussed in this volume) offer a striking example of how most revolutionaries sought to perform an "American" script, rather than a "French" one.[30]

To examine these transformations of revolutionary scripts over time, we pay particular attention to the evolving meaning of the term "revolution" itself. A considerable amount of scholarship has already charted the evolution of this term, from a general designation (usually in the plural) of political troubles, to the modern sense of a political and social transformation of a state along constitutional lines.[31] The essays here draw and build on this body of work, shedding new light in particular on the seventeenth-century emergence of the term and its eighteenth-century modifications.

From a methodological point of view, this study of the changing values and connotations of the term "revolution" owes a debt to the intellectual historical approach known as *Begriffsgeschichte*, or "conceptual history." Practitioners of this methodology examine how certain "basic concepts," mostly of a political nature, become the objects of definition wars between different social groups.[32] Because of this contestation, the meanings of these terms tend to vary significantly over time. *Begriffsgeschichte* traces these variations both synchronically (exploring the range of meanings available at a given moment) and diachronically (often over the *longue durée*). Not surprisingly, the historian most closely associated with the school, Reinhart Koselleck, chose "revolution" as one of the important political keywords of modernity.[33]

Despite our appreciation of this historiographical method, our scripting approach varies from it in one critical fashion. Koselleck and his colleagues essentially consider the meaning of political keywords to stem from different structural arrangements of other concepts. In his article on the "Historical Criteria of the Modern Concept of Revolution," for instance, Koselleck notes how the early-modern understanding of revolution combined different concepts of time (46–47). But where he adopts an implicitly spatial metaphor, we again wish to highlight the diachronic relations between constitutive elements of revolution. To use a different metaphor (explicitly, this time), political keywords can be "scripts" in a programming sense: they entail a certain number of actions, to be executed in a certain order. Our approach therefore emphasizes how debates over the meaning of revolution take the form of competing narratives.

A View of the Essays

The volume of essays we present grew from a conference on "Scripting Revolution" organized at Stanford University in November 2011. In the year or so between the conference's initial planning and its eventual occurrence, there came the surprise of the Arab Spring, triggering a sequence of revolutions that are still ongoing and engaging both public and scholarly interest in their nature and progress. In that context, we found colleagues more than ready to address the notion of revolution as script. Their essays do not all engage the notion in the same way or to the same degree, nor do they necessarily agree on every aspect of the still incomplete and patchy history of scripting revolution that emerges from the essays taken as a whole. We offer them as an exploration of an approach and an invitation to debate, and as an effort to reconsider the history of a form of collective political action recently thought dead but now dramatically replayed before our eyes.

Part I: Genealogies of Revolution

Our opening section takes readers to the locus classicus for discussion of the early history of modern revolutions: the seventeenth century and, more particularly, seventeenth-century Britain, with its contrasting conventional images of revolution as civil war and revolution as gloriously peaceful political change. What did it mean to speak or write of "revolution" during this period, and can it be said that meanings of the term then current allowed possibilities for imagining a script for revolution in the sense we have defined above? Tim Harris opens the discussion by emphasizing a common theme in this first section: the erroneousness of the long-accepted and still frequently repeated assumption that "revolution" derived its initial sense as a political concept from the more traditional notion of a return to a status quo ante, as exemplified by the movement of the stars. "Revolution" did not mean "Restoration" in the seventeenth century. It could describe that outcome, but only as a specific case of a more general phenomenon of change and transformation, often experienced negatively as disruption, disorder, and upheaval. "Revolution" in this sense could signify a radical and abrupt transformation of political regime occurring as an outcome of human action; but could such an outcome be instigated or planned in advance? Could there be a script for revolution in this sense?

Harris suggests two discursive possibilities to this end—and two notions frequently seen as implied in the idea of revolution—one theoretical, the other empirical. Theoretically, the right to resistance could justify action to produce political change (though there was always the counter claim that all power came from God and must be accepted as such). One might argue, however, that early-modern resistance theory still required recourse to some principle of legitimacy within the existing political order rather than validating its complete overthrow. The empirical reasoning was more straightforward: it recognized the simple fact that tyranny frequently provoked rebellion. God, in this case, could be seen to be working through human agency to overthrow tyrannical regimes. Can this be seen as a script for revolution? One could object that waiting for revolution to occur is scarcely a script for bringing it about. Locke, in effect, resorted to both the theoretical and the empirical argument, combining the right of resistance with recognition of the fact of rebellion (though he insisted that the latter usually appeared infrequently and only after "a long chain of abuses"). Did this combination thereby turn his *Second Treatise* into a script for revolution?

To resistance and rebellion, David Como adds a third related notion: civil war. Noting the shift in historiographical fashion that led what was once called "the English Revolution" to be renamed "the English Civil War," Como shows that it was precisely during the upheavals of the 1640s and (more precisely) the 1650s that "revolution" became a more markedly political term in English. The usage came from abroad as expanding circuits of communication brought news of rebellion and disruption in accounts of the "revolutions" occurring most remarkably in Catalonia, Sicily, and Naples. The most notable of these accounts, that of Alessandro Giraffi, translated by the royalist James Howell in 1650 as *An Exact Historie of the late Revolutions in Naples,* offered a dramatic description of popular revolt forcing political change. As its translator doubtless intended, it succeeded (along with similarly entitled accounts) in provoking reflection on the stormy course of English affairs. Como shows that participants in the English political conflicts of the 1650s reached increasingly for the still fluid term "revolution" to characterize the shifts and upheavals in the events engulfing them. But they shrank from claiming full agency in producing these events; "revolution" was not yet a frame for action. "Revolutions," for better or worse, remained the work of providence. To embrace them meant accepting a gift from God. To lament them meant acknowledging the fact of divine punishment for human fractiousness. The empirical was ultimately the theological.

In the wake of the Wars of Religion, there were strong claims to be made for absolute monarchy as the essential bulwark of peace and stability against the disorders and upheavals of civil war. But these claims could be contested on the grounds that monarchy was the cause of political instability, not its cure, and that the needs of citizens were better served by popular or republican government. The argument drew, David Armitage shows, on the Roman republican tradition celebrated by Algernon Sidney and other Commonwealthmen. Turning the Roman narrative to other purposes, Sidney saw the history of monarchy in England as an endless succession of civil wars. Thomas Paine saw the same, going so far as to include the Glorious Revolution in this category. So, indeed, did Edmund Burke, though in an entirely different register. In this strain of thinking, Armitage posits, the modern script for revolution may simply have absorbed the older notion of civil war and rebranded it successfully.

Part II: Writing the Modern Revolutionary Script

The appearance of this modern script provides the topic for our second section. In its opening essay, Keith Michael Baker argues that "revolution" was slow to acquire its modern meaning as an action category. He draws on evidence offered by digitized databases to show the continued dominance of the seventeenth-century meanings of the term in English, French, and American usage. In the conventional eighteenth-century lexicon, he argues, "revolutions" still happened; they were not yet thought of as consciously made. Enlightenment gave "revolution" a more positive valorization, and the abbé Raynal's *Révolution de l'Amérique* described one as unfolding. But it was only as the French Revolution unleashed political energies with terms like "revolutionary" and "revolutionize," Baker contends, that "revolution" was decisively scripted as an act rather than a fact.

The American insurgents may not have called themselves "revolutionaries," and they may have preferred to present their "American Revolution" as an accomplished fact, as Baker argues, but Jack Rakove finds some of them already pressing upon the conventional limits of the term. John Adams speculated in a letter of 1774 that "our Children, may see Revolutions, and be concerned and active in effecting them of which we can form no conception," and Benjamin Rush was ready in 1786 to declare the "American revolution . . . far from over" and independence only "the first act of a great drama." The script the Americans thought they were following, however, was a Lockean script for resistance issuing in an "appeal to Heaven." Locke had stipulated that rebellion need not lead to an endless series of "revolutions." But what should come next? Here Locke was of little help. The Americans improvised by restricting "revolution" to an accomplished fact and binding it as closely as possible to the founding act of constitution-making. This distinctively American script, Rakove argues, merged revolution and constitution-making into a single story.

The French story proved to be quite the contrary. There, in Dan Edelstein's analysis, revolution escaped the constraints of constitutionalism. It became transcendent, a source of authority in and of itself. Edelstein goes back to the Levellers to uncover the origins of an early-modern discourse linking the natural right of resistance, popular sovereignty, and the creation of a constitution as the outcome of an act of political will. This tight combination, he argues, was articulated in the American Revolution and in the early phase of the French Revolution. But it was dismantled by the Jacobins in a series of moves after the overthrow of the constitutional monarchy by popular insurrection on 10 August 1792. Robespierre defended as revolutionary the authority of the Paris Commune to act against enemies of the people in the interim period following the fall of the king; he argued for the monarch's execution not on constitutional grounds (since there were none) but as a necessary choice between the legitimacy of Louis XVI and that of the Revolution itself. Saint-Just extended this same logic a year later by declaring French government "revolutionary until peacetime," which was to say that it was now unfettered by the restraints of the constitution ratified two months earlier and ultimately free to remodel the people from whom it had once derived its authority. Assuming a transcendental power in Jacobin discourse, Revolution now authorized continuation of . . . the Revolution. The Jacobin moment was brief, but its sanctification of revolution was to enjoy a long life.

"Revolution" had a twin called "Counter-Revolution." They grew together, as demonstrated by the displays of co occurrences of the two terms in the *Archives parlementaires* in Baker's essay. Revolution became more powerful as Counter-Revolution became more dangerous, and vice versa. Each assumed transcendental force in the Manichean political universe revealed by Guillaume Mazeau's account of the assassination of Jean Paul Marat by Charlotte Corday in July 1793. Mazeau charts the tourbillion of facts and fantasies, conspiracies and denunciations, ideas and opinions that swirled around this famed event, making it symbolic of a war to the death that would escalate into the Terror. We should not forget that Marat was a journalist, one of the tribe of scribes that endowed the Revolution with its awful eventfulness by endlessly repeating that each and every day must decide the fate of republican France—and of all humanity. Marat in death exemplifies the power of the French Revolution as it became a modern political script: a sequence of defining moments to be replayed, an agonistic struggle of iconic personalities and fundamental principles to be re-enacted, and a repertory of political situations, rhetorical strategies, and subject positions to be rehearsed and refashioned. (Even today his image haunts the Internet.)

Marat plays a minor but telling role in Malick Ghachem's chapter on "The Antislavery Script: Haiti's Place in the Narrative of Atlantic Revolution," this time as the author of *Chains of Slavery*, the work published in

London in 1774 that fueled his politics until his death. This radical warning of encroaching despotism in England, and the inevitable loss of political liberty everywhere, contained not a word about the enslavement of Africans in the Americas. In this regard, it epitomizes Ghachem's central question: was there, could there be, a script for a revolutionary destruction of plantation slavery? The classical republican tradition upon which Marat and the American revolutionaries drew in opposition to political enslavement turned out to be insufficiently capacious to embrace the overthrow of chattel slavery. The promise of universal emancipation offered within the French Revolutionary script proved problematic, too, in the face of countervailing property claims of planters and French economic interests. Ghachem emphasizes that, in any case, some of the demands for the rights of slaves and free people of color drew on the Old Regime provisions of the infamous *Code Noir* itself. There remained the oldest script for an antislavery revolution, the prospect of a Spartacist revolt against which Raynal had warned in a famous passage of the *Histoire philosophique et politique . . . des Deux Indes* mentioned by Baker. This nightmare scenario terrified whites across the Atlantic world, fueled the abolition of slavery in Saint Domingue in 1793 (though that proved transitory), and found its strongest resonances in the bloody liberation of Haiti. In the Declaration of Haitian Independence in 1804, repudiation of the *Code Noir* became entwined with another element of the French Revolutionary script, the new modern language of national sovereignty. That language was now turned against French rule, racial domination, and chattel slavery, Ghachem argues, but at the cost of leaving ambiguous the legal status of coerced labor.

Part III: Rescripting the Revolution

Our third section opens with Gareth Stedman Jones's analysis of the historical context of the *Communist Manifesto*. As in Saint Domingue, this context was defined by the failure of the French Revolution to deliver on its promise of universal emancipation. Hegel had imagined a Germany peacefully transformed in the light of Universal Reason; his reform-minded disciples found local political realities more irrational, and more obdurate. Lacking popular energy and a compliant alternate monarch waiting in the wings, the young Hegelians had watched from afar as the French replayed their revolution in 1830. Among them was the journalist Karl Marx, who found his republican *Rheinische Zeitung* abruptly closed down by the Prussian authorities in 1843. Exiled in Paris, Marx famously adapted the revolutionary script for a new age of industrial transformation and capitalist exploitation. The irony of the *Communist Manifesto* in Stedman Jones's analysis, though, is that it moved even further from the local political realities it was meant to address. Its categories—"the modern state," "the class struggle," "the bourgeoisie," and "the proletariat"—were abstract and largely fictive; they had little explanatory purchase and fleeting correspondence to any contemporary situation. Its realist, materialist rhetoric decked out a fantasy that was, Stedman Jones insists, "to a considerable extant an expression of the pathology of exile." A fiction, though, that would ultimately produce some powerful facts.

The French, meanwhile, had more frequent opportunity to replay and extend the revolutionary script. They added the barricades in 1830, overt class struggle and the dream of a socialist republic in 1848, and the bloody experience of the Commune in 1871. But did they still hew too closely to the memory and mythology of the originary revolutionary drama of 1789–95? Many thought so, as Dominica Chang shows in "Reading and Repeating the Revolutionary Script: Revolutionary Mimicry in Nineteenth-Century France." "The second time as farce," Marx famously remarked of 1848; Proudhon and Tocqueville, among others, found their different ways of expressing the same judgment. So did Flaubert, whose *Education sentimentale* was, as Chang shows, directed specifically against the imitation of French Revolutionary figures its author deplored as empty, futile mimicry. Flaubert reportedly said of the slaughter of 1871 that "none of this would have happened if they had understood *L'Education sentimentale*." Chang's analysis reveals how deeply divided (and possibly weakened) the Communards were as they fought over the deployment of language and actions they valorized or repudiated as a re-enactment of the Terror of 1793–94.

The Third Republic that emerged from the revolutionary violence of 1871 nonetheless declared itself the realization of the script announced in 1789. The French Revolution became its myth of origin. Observers elsewhere saw 1871 as marking the final failure of a script now exhausted. Claudia Verhoeven analyzes the reaction of one such group, the radical Russian intelligentsia, in "'Une Révolution Vraiment Scientifique': Russian Terrorism, the Escape from the European Orbit, and the Invention of a New Revolutionary Paradigm." In her account, disillusionment with the revolutionary script they saw failing so miserably (and bloodily) in France, and recognition of the backwardness of their country in relation to European social and political development, led these intellectuals toward Terrorism as a substitute for Terror. The path was not a straight one. For Herzen, after

1848, there was no longer a *libretto;* revolution no longer consummated the logic of history. Zaichnevsky, in 1862, still imagined that historical progress could be accelerated in Russia by doubling down on revolutionary violence, unleashing civil war, and establishing the dictatorship of a revolutionary party. For their successors, from Karakozov in 1866 to Morozov in 1880, revolution triggered history rather than accelerating it. Historical development could be leapfrogged, autocracy shattered, and massive violence avoided, by the precise and "truly scientific" terroristic application of the assassin's pistol. Russia could choose a new door to the future.

The portal eventually opened in Russia in 1917 involved a very different rethinking of the European script, as Ian Thatcher shows in "Scripting the Russian Revolution." As he points out, the Bolshevik script was certainly not the only one in play in 1917, nor was it fated to dominate the others. It had to jockey with a liberal script emphasizing freedom (particularly that of the gentry to keep their land); a socialist script that promised the "re-allocation of Russian national resources"; an extreme left, Menshevik script that ruled out collaboration with bourgeois parties but nonetheless accepted a brief period of bourgeois rule; national scripts that sought the breakup of the Russian empire; and finally, popular scripts that were not theorized to the same extent as the others but contained a powerful hope for basic living improvements. If the Bolshevik script ultimately won out, Thatcher argues, it was because it was the one that could most easily absorb the popular script, and appear to reflect the true demands of the people.

Part IV: Revolutionary Projections

After 1917, revolution became institutionalized in a government whose very authority derived from its revolutionary promise. But the script of communist revolution could no longer be controlled and finessed in Moscow alone: competing versions emerged in Hungary, Poland, and Cuba in 1956, in Czechoslovakia in 1968, and more regularly in China. How did this bureaucratization (on the one hand) and rapid mutation (on the other) affect the revolutionary script?

The Soviets saw China as a revolutionary latecomer, but in fact their southeastern neighbor had a long history of revolutionary action. In their paper on revolutionary scripts in China, Jeffrey Wasserstrom and Wu Yidi focus on two moments in this history. First, they examine the period, from the late nineteenth century to the 1911 revolution, when opponents to the Qing dynasty revived a classical Chinese term for "revolution" (*geming*) to express their desire for an American- or French-inspired upheaval. In opposition to these would-be revolutionaries, others looked to the Meiji Restoration for a more reformist script. Both sides believed that change was necessary, however, and this shared belief made their positions more fluid (compared with the fierce debate over Marxist revisionism occurring at the same time in Germany and Russia). Wasserstrom and Wu then show how current Chinese political debates, going back to 1989, echo this earlier moment, with some dissidents looking to the revolutionary scripts that emerged from Eastern Europe, the color revolutions, and (more recently) the Arab Uprising, while others, more fearful of China's own violent revolutionary past, continue to advocate for some kind of slower moving reform. Both of these moments demonstrate how political conflicts in China have often taken the form of arguments over which foreign script was most applicable to the domestic situation.

Between these revolutionary bookends, however, we find a script that was more defiantly Chinese: Mao's *Little Red Book*. Alexander Cook offers a study of this work's reception, taking seriously Lin Biao's claim that this work was a "spiritual atom bomb." This was a very deliberate metaphor in the 1960s, when the fear of nuclear destruction ran high. Cook uses the fable of "The Foolish Old Man" (which appears in the *Little Red Book*) to explain Lin Biao's claim. This is a curious fable, in that it involves the appearance of supernatural forces to move mountains. For Cook, this oddity reflects the fact that Mao's revolutionary script relied just as much on spiritual — that is, ideological — devotion to revolution as on material efforts. But spiritual power was, in Mao's view, akin to the atom: if it could be released, its power would be overwhelming. This vision was not limited to economic transformation: like the atom bomb, it had a military point as well, which was the pursuit of a "people's war." In the face of nuclear catastrophe, Mao upheld that this force was greater than any bomb.

We follow this focus on China with three in-depth case studies, each placed a decade apart, of how revolutionary scripts were transformed across the globe. Lillian Guerra examines how cinema was instrumental in shaping the dominant script of the 1959 Cuban Revolution. The central villain of this script was, of course, the United States, portrayed as being responsible for every problem facing Cuban society. Cinema was a key medium for disseminating this script, since it allowed people literally to see themselves as part of the revolutionary transformation of Cuba. The official film industry accordingly exercised strict censorship over films to ensure that the "correct" script was being represented. Guerra turns to the much-censored films of Nicolás Guillén Landrián to explore the ways in which his "counter-scripts" challenged the privileged narrative of the Cuban regime.

Julian Bourg zooms in on the watershed year of 1968, and more particularly on the revolutionary upheaval that rocked France, to underscore a paradox: the students were acutely self-conscious about recycling scripts from revolutions past, but curiously, the events in Paris had an unscripted feel. Students were acting out revolution, but everyone was also taken by surprise by the rapid pace and breadth of events. Indeed, '68 led many philosophers to reconceptualize it as an *event*—that is, something unplanned, with unforeseeable consequences.

What this meant, however, is that "1968" could become the keystone of a plethora of different revolutionary scripts, be they political, economic, social, or cultural. As Bourg points out, the very concept of revolution was very much in flux at this time, as the contrast between student protesters in Berkeley and, say, the Red Army Faction in Germany indicates. In the end, however, he shows how '68 can be seen as marking the demise of the Leninist script of party-led revolution, and a return to the boisterous, disorganized, popular script of revolution.

Ten years later, in Iran, it certainly seemed at first that this "democratic" script was triumphing. In his reading of the 1979 Revolution, Abbas Milani points to how it largely stemmed from the frustrations of the Iranian middle class: the shah's rapid modernization and secularization program had produced a new, urban, more worldly society, but it had not opened up the political process. By 1979 he was an incredibly unpopular figure, and, what's more, an erratic ruler. But the Iranian Revolution is perhaps most fascinating as a case study of how a revolutionary script that was expected to conclude with the establishment of a constitutional republic was instead rewritten, at the last minute and through remarkable strategic planning, by Khomeini and his clerical allies. For Milani, this high-wire act of political manipulation underscores the unplanned, even unscripted nature of the Iranian revolution. But he also notes how Ayatollah Khomeini's appropriation of the revolutionary process was itself part of a clerical, messianic script to accomplish a divine order in history.

Finally, we close this part by bringing our narrative up to the present, thus also highlighting the continuing relevance of the revolutionary scripts discussed here. Silvana Toska focuses on how revolutionary scripts, in the recent Arab revolutions (as in others before them), became progressively more radical. In so doing, however, they also opened up splits between political groups that no longer agreed on the meaning of revolutionary goals.

In her examination of the Egyptian and Yemeni revolutions of 2011, Toska ends up highlighting a paradox. On the one hand, revolutionary groups in both countries shared little in common beyond a desire to overthrow the regime in place; hence, as these revolutions went on, dissensions among revolutionaries became increasingly visible. At the same time, these open disagreements were also what made it impossible for one group to impose its point of view on the others, thereby making the likelihood of a democratic outcome higher. Recent developments have added new chapters to the history of the Arab uprising, transforming Ghonim's fantasy of a leaderless revolutionary script into an ongoing struggle for leadership.

As David Bell notes in his "Afterword," the contributions in this volume do not all deploy the concept of a revolutionary script in exactly the same fashion. It is our hope that these methodological variations on a theme will be seen as evidence of the usefulness and flexibility of the "scripting" concept. Our goal with this volume is primarily to outline a more promising, historically grounded method for the comparative study of revolutions. We certainly do not claim, with one volume, to have exhausted such a study, and hope that other historians will pursue this investigation, exploring the revolutions that we left out, and uncovering other ways in which revolutions are produced by, and in turn produce, scripts.

PART I

Genealogies of Revolution

Did the English Have a Script for Revolution in the Seventeenth Century?

The seventeenth-century English joked about themselves being a rebellious people. "The King of Spain," ran a common adage, was "said to be Rex Hominum, the king of men, his subjects being generally well affected towards him: the King of France, Rex Asinorum, the king of asses, whose subjects are forced to bear whatsoever taxes he is pleased to lay on their backs: the King of England, Rex Diablorum, the king of Devills, by reason of their many rebellions."[1] The historiographer royal James Howell, writing in 1661 just after the restoration of the monarchy, asserted how England "hath bin fruitfull for Rebellions," there having "hapned near upon a hundred" since the Norman Conquest in 1066.[2] Yet despite such self-awareness, and despite the fact that the English had two revolutions over the course of the seventeenth century, it has traditionally been thought that the English did not possess the modern concept of revolution in this time period. The first historian to write of "the English Revolution" was François Guizot in his *Histoire de la révolution d'Angleterre* of 1826, the preface of which contained an extended comparison between affairs in England and the French Revolution.[3] In the seventeenth century, the word "revolution"—so we have been told—possessed a "mainly non-political meaning," and was used predominantly in an astronomical sense, as in the revolution of the planets; if it was ever applied to politics, it carried a conservative meaning, as bringing "the situation back to what it had been before—to complete the historical cycle": in short, a return to the status quo ante. Hence, contemporaries called the restoration of monarchy in 1660 a revolution, but referred to what we now call the English Revolution as "the Great Rebellion." The Glorious Revolution of 1688–89, on the other hand, was indeed styled a revolution at the time, but this was supposedly "because so much of it was not in the modern sense revolutionary," but rather an attempt to restore the old system.[4]

Such a view has proven remarkably resilient. It is, however, seriously misleading. Christopher Hill demonstrated more than a quarter of a century ago that the word "revolution" underwent a transformation in meaning over the course of the seventeenth century as a result of the profound political changes of the 1640s (though he did also note earlier usages of revolution not implying circularity), and concluded that the term had certainly acquired its modern political meaning well before 1688.[5] David Cressy has likewise seen a key shift in meaning occurring in the mid-seventeenth century, suggesting that "under the pressure of events" the word "acquired new political and constitutional shadings" and came to be employed "metaphorically to signify a sudden and dramatic change, or significant and abrupt turnover in the politics and religion of the state."[6] Yet even this might put the emergence of these allegedly "new" shades of meaning too late. The *Oxford English Dictionary* dates the first known use of "revolution" to mean the "overthrow of an established government or social order by those previously subject to it" and the "forcible substitution of a new form of government" to 1521, in a letter written by Thomas More to Cardinal Wolsey. In fact the letter is from 1526, although the five-year time difference is hardly significant; as the context makes clear, More presumed that Wolsey would have no trouble grasping his meaning, and thus he could not have been using the word in a novel way. Writing with regard to the internal conflict in Scotland during the minority of James V and the battle among rival Scottish factions for control of the young king's body (the letter was written in the aftermath of the slaying of the Earl of Lennox at the Battle of Linlithgow on 4 September 1526), More reported how Henry VIII was pleased that the heads of the regency council, the Earls of Angus and Arran, seemed to be prospering "against theire enemyes," but nevertheless remained concerned that the Chancellor, the Archbishop of Saint Andrews James Beaton, was using "all his possible power to procure [the Earls'] destruction, and to rere broilerie, warre and revolution in the Realme to the no little perell of the yong King."[7] The *OED* also notes a usage from 1569, in an English translation of a French work by Pierre Boaistuau (d. 1566), in which in reference to the turbulent history of Naples and the frequent overthrow of its kings by war it is observed: "of al the kingdoms of the earth, only this state of Naples hath exceeded in revolution, mutation, persecution and losse of blood."[8] One certainly should not attempt to make inferences about typical usage from two isolated examples; moreover, the *OED* also cites numerous usages from this time of the term "revolution" in a cyclical sense. Nevertheless, what we can say is that already in the sixteenth century there was available the concept of a revolution that involved the forcible overthrow of a reigning monarch by violence and bloodshed and the erection of a new regime, and that English readers would have recognized—and have been familiar with—the meaning of this term when used in this manner.

How, then, did the English use the term "revolution" in the seventeenth century, during their century of revolution? Clearly, the word possessed an array of closely related though ultimately discrete meanings, and we find it being used in a variety of ways. The problem facing the modern reader is that when the sense of a word transforms over time, the new meaning emerges gradually out of what was already implied in the old, as the word comes to be applied to new or altering circumstances; there is thus the risk that we can read our modern assumptions back into a word and see modern overtones when such overtones might not yet have been apparent to contemporaries. There was something about the imagery of revolving around that made it ultimately possible for revolution to come to designate the sort of radical rupture that we now associate with the term. When considering seventeenth-century usage, therefore, one must exercise extreme caution; it is often possible to detect alternative resonances that the term "revolution" might conceivably have held for contemporaries without being sure precisely how contemporaries would have understood the term in any given context. What we can say with confidence is that when the seventeenth-century English invoked the term "revolution" in a political context they invariably did *not* mean a return to the status quo ante. Most typically, they used the word to designate a sudden and dramatic change, or "a turning quite round," to cite the definition Elisha Coles provided in his English-Latin dictionary of 1677, rather than "a turning round to the first point" (as in "the revolution of heaven").[9] This sudden and dramatic change might simply involve a change in personnel: we find the word "revolution," for example, being used to describe what a later age might have thought of as a ministerial coup. But it could be a more fundamental alteration, such as a change in the political system itself. Often the term "revolution" was employed to refer to what we would think of as a "regime change." Such a regime change might not necessarily have radical implications or involve what we would think of as being "revolutionary upheavals," but it could do. Did the seventeenth-century English, then, have a script for revolution? If revolution meant in essence regime change, then the question "How to effect a revolution?" essentially translated into "How did one bring about a change of regime?" and this was something to which the seventeenth-century English certainly did give much thought. Since the monarchy in seventeenth-century England was deemed to be absolute and irresistible, the crucial question in the first instance became how could one resist an absolute regime. The question of what to replace that regime with once it had been effectively resisted came up later.

⤳

The word "revolution" and its plural "revolutions" were employed frequently in a political context in seventeenth-century England. One of its usages certainly was in the literal sense of things turning or revolving around, though without necessarily implying turning full cycle. Sir John Davies, in his history of Ireland written in 1612, observed how the conquest of Ireland was made "by slow steps and degrees, and by several attempts" across the ages, and that "there were sundry revolutions, as well of the English fortunes, as of the Irish"—"revolution" here carrying perhaps the sense of reversal (as well as overturning) but not quite putting things back to where they had started.[10] When the Warwickshire-based doctor and translator Philemon Holland delivered a speech before James I at Coventry in 1617, he observed how this once-flourishing city, "by sublunary changes, and fatall revolutions," had "falln to decay"; Holland brought this up precisely because he hoped that James might do something to reverse these "fatall revolutions" and help return Coventry to its status quo ante.[11]

It is true that contemporaries did sometimes refer to the restoration of monarchy in 1660 as a revolution. The royalist astrologer George Wharton styled it "this happy, and (by many, almost) unexpected Revolution of Government; viz. of turning from Anarchy, to the most natural of all Governments, MONARCHY."[12] The Anglo-Irish Protestant Richard Cox, in his history of Ireland written in the aftermath of the Jacobite war of 1689–91, observed how the Irish Catholics, although they welcomed the return of monarchy, nevertheless "sat still" during the spring of 1660 "and contributed nothing to this great Revolution."[13] Yet if 1660 was a revolution, it was because it involved a change or turnover in government; the fact that this particular change marked a restoration of the old system of government was incidental. The contemporary Scottish lawyer Sir George Mackenzie could call both the Restoration of 1660 and the far-reaching ministerial changes of 1663 in Scotland a "revolution."[14] Even Thomas Hobbes's oft-quoted ascription of the Restoration as a revolution in his

Behemoth (written c. 1668, though not published until 1679)—"I have seen in this revolution," Hobbes wrote, "a circular motion, of the Sovereigne Power through two Usurpers Father and Son, from the late King to this his son"—makes it clear that he thought of a revolution as being a regime change and that other revolutions (besides "this" one) might not entail such a circular motion.[15] One individual, writing in his commonplace book in the late 1690s, described as a "Revolution" both "the Return of Charles the Second" and "the coming of the Prince of Aurenge now King William the 3d," yet this commonplacer made it clear that the term referred to "all Changes or Alterations of Government."[16]

The congratulatory addresses delivered to Charles II from up and down the country in May 1660 frequently invoked the notion of revolution (or rather, the plural revolutions), but principally to refer to developments prior to the actual Restoration itself. For instance, when a group of twenty Puritan ministers from London and Westminster rejoiced how God had, "after many great revolutions, and wonderfull providences," brought His Majesty to "so peaceable possession of [his] imperial throne," they were clearly alluding to the numerous regime changes and upheavals that had happened since the execution of Charles I in January 1649, though they perhaps also saw the Restoration itself the last of these revolutions.[17] Likewise, the inhabitants of Totnes in Devon announced how they rejoiced at "the eminent appearing of the hand of God for your Majestie in such late miraculous revolutions by overturning and overturning and overturning even untill he hadd as itt were with his owne Finger chalk'd out a pathe for your Majestie's happy restauration to your Father's throne"—the triple emphasis on "overturning" leaves us in no doubt about the essential meaning of the term for the framers of this address, albeit the Restoration itself was the outcome of this process of overturning.[18] The inhabitants of Lyme Regis, Dorset, by contrast, saw the revolutions and the Restoration as distinct: their address stated how they admired and adored "That Stupendious Providence of Almighty God," whereby after "all these Illegal Changes and Revolutions of Government, by which we have been hurried to and fro, since the Foundations were overthrowne," they were "now at last mercifully reduced to An Hopefull Condition of Ease and Settlement, By the miraculous Restitution" of Charles "to the Possession and Exercise of [His] Royall Rights and Government."[19]

To think of the upheavals in the three kingdoms in the 1640s and 1650s as being revolutions was therefore already common by the time of the Restoration.[20] Charles II invoked this vocabulary himself. In his Declaration of Breda, issued in April 1660 on the eve of his return, he made reference to "the continued Distractions of so many Years, and so many and great Revolutions," and he used this language again in letters subsequently written to the House of Commons, the Lord Mayor of London, and General George Monck (the military leader who was in effect the architect of the Restoration).[21] Historiographer royal Howell likewise did so in his *Twelve Several Treatises, of the Late Revolutions in These Three Kingdoms*; revealingly, this work was also published under the variant title *Divers Historicall Discourses of the late Popular Insurrections in Great Britain, and Ireland*. Similarly, John Paterson (the future bishop of Edinburgh and archbishop of Glasgow), preaching a thanksgiving sermon in Scotland for the restoration of monarchy in 1660, condemned the types of arguments that had been used to justify the usurpation of royal authority "in these late Troubles and Revolutions."[22]

Interesting insight into the multiple resonances of the term "revolution," as well as the potential for unintended slippage, can be gleaned from the reflections of Nicholas French, the Catholic Bishop of Ferns, on the Irish Rebellion of 1641 in a tract published in 1675. French's objective was to clear the majority of the Catholic population of Ireland from the charge of rebellion. Some evil men, he alleged, had misled Charles I by informing him "that the Catholics of Ireland without discrimination had entered into a Rebellion," when "only some discontented men began a Revolution in the North [Ulster]." In fact, French affirmed, the Catholics of the other three provinces, as well as those of Ulster who did not join this "first rysing in the North"—note this revolution is seen as being the same as a "rising" of "discontented men"—"lived in soe happy a state and soe opulent and rich, that they would never abett a Revolution for gaining other men's estates." Indeed, French continued, "all those . . . and theire Fathers before them" had remained "faithfull to the Crowne," as was shown "in the warrs of Desmon[d], Tyron[e], and other smaller Revolutions" (an allusion to rebellions in Ireland under Elizabeth in the later sixteenth century). By "Revolution for gaining other men's estates" French presumably meant an uprising or a war intended to achieve this objective. There is possibly an implication of a revolution in estate ownership, in the sense of a sudden and dramatic forcible change or even "a turning round to the first point," since in the North the rebels wanted to undo the Protestant Plantation of Ulster and seize back lands they had lost following the Flight of the Earls in 1607; but was French hinting at that, could other people have seen that as an implication even if French did not intend to imply it, did the word subconsciously seem to him suitable to use in this context because of these various resonances even if he was not consciously aware of this when he first inked the word on the page, or are we reading too much into this because of our own knowledge of the issues at stake in the Irish rebellion, as well as our awareness of how the term "revolution" in modern times has come to be associated with a radical redistribution of land ownership? Having used language that seems to associate revolution with rebellion—"rysing in the North," "warrs of Desmond and Tryone"—French later sought to distinguish revolution from rebellion, as part of his effort to insist that the Catholics of Ireland had not been disloyal to the Stuart monarchy: "in case our Revolution hath bin Judg'd a Rebellion," he wrote, people should remember the Irish had an act of oblivion granted to them by Charles I in 1648 and subsequently confirmed by Charles II.[23]

A revolution did not have to involve a change at the top, and it certainly did not have to have radical implications. As late as 1688 the author of a "Short Account of Sweden" could describe Charles XI's rebuilding of the powers of the Swedish monarchy so as "to lay the foundations of a Soveraignty as absolute as any Prince in Europe professes" as "this great Revolution."[24] Yet when used to describe events in seventeenth-century England (or in the three kingdoms more broadly), the word "revolution" often carried with it the implication of far-reaching change, including a fundamental challenge to the traditional power structures in the state (and ultimately the overthrowing of those power structures). Whether this was seen in a positive or negative light, of course, depended on where one's sympathies lay. We can certainly find radicals welcoming the revolutionary changes of the 1640s and 1650s. Others invoked the term "revolution" in a more neutral sense, to recognize the reality of what had come to pass, as a result of God's providence, without passing judgment upon it, or as an alternative to rebellion, which carried with it the implication of "illegitimacy." Those who condemned the "innovations" and "transgressions of government" of the 1640s and '50s, by contrast, tended to abstain from using the word "revolution," precisely because of its neutrality; they preferred to talk of rebellion.[25] Hence why those who welcomed the return of monarchy in 1660 found it easier now to embrace the term, since the many great revolutions and wonderful providences had ended up giving them the outcome they desired: there were "miraculous revolutions" to follow on from the earlier "Illegal Changes and Revolutions of Government." In the Restoration period, when the word "revolution" (or "revolutions") was employed to refer to what had taken place in the 1640s and 1650s, it tended to carry negative connotations. A loyal address from the corporation of Ripon of April 1682, for instance, recalled "the Miseries, Calamities and direful Revolutions of the late Times, occasioned by the Hellish and Traiterous Practices of evil Men" who overthrew the Church of England and usurped royal authority.[26] But we see a shift again with the Glorious Revolution of 1688–89, when revolution once more came to be seen as potentially positive. One individual, summarizing the argument of William Sherlock's *Case of Allegiance* (an anti-resistance tract of 1684) in his commonplace book in ca. 1691, for example, noted: "Revolutions of Government will happen since God has power to remove Kings and set up Kings and since it may be for the Punishment for either King or People and the deliverance of good men from oppression and Tyranny."[27]

Whether contemporaries opposed them or welcomed them, they recognized that revolutions could involve radical change. In 1689 one English Jacobite complained how "this Revolution" had established a "New Fabric," "breaking the very Constitution" by making "Our Monarchs [who] were ever Sovereign and Imperial" little more than "Dukes of Venice; the meer Puppets of the People," and forcing us "to Dance after the Pipe of a Common-wealth."[28] A satirical tract of that same year recalled how, when an Anglican clergyman asked a dissenter his opinion of the times, he was regaled with a story about a gentlemen who, on the verge of death, instructed his relations to bury him face downward, saying "That in a short time the World would be turned upside down, and then he should be the only Person who lay decently in his Grave." The Anglican cleric could only retort, "Why, I must confess there has been a considerable Revolution."[29] In June 1693 the Scottish Parliament, the body that had introduced far-reaching reforming legislation north of the border since 1689, wrote to William III urging him to confer a Scottish title upon William Bentinck, now Earl of Portland in the English peerage, "in consideration of the many good offices done by the earl" to those Scots "who during the violences of the late reigns" had taken "shelter in the United Provinces, but especially in consideration of the obligations that this nation [Scotland]" had "for his care of their concerns in the carrying on of the late happy revolution." The reference to "carrying on" perhaps even suggests that contemporaries by now possessed the notion that revolutions could be made and did not just happen.[30]

By the time of the Glorious Revolution, then, the term "revolution" could refer to establishing a "new fabric," even to turning the world upside down. Undoubtedly the experiences of the 1640s and '50s—as David Como explores more fully below—played an important role in shaping the political shadings that the term would come to possess as it entered the mainstream of English political vocabulary in the second half of the seventeenth century. Yet we should not conclude that the English in the early seventeenth century were therefore not able to imagine a revolution involving fundamental change and radical upheaval. Even if England had yet to have its own experience of revolution, the English were nevertheless deeply worried about the potential threat to the peace and stability of the church and state in England posed by political and religious dissidents, threats that were viewed against the backdrop of the wars of religion that afflicted much of Europe during the age of reformations and which provided concrete illustration of the sort of miseries and calamities that could befall a state torn apart by religious and political upheaval. In a tract commemorating "Great Britain's Great Deliverance" from the Gunpowder Plot of 1605—a Catholic plot to blow up James I and leading members of the political establishment when the king opened Parliament on 5 November—William Leigh (tutor to the young Prince of Wales) observed that if the conspiracy had succeeded, 5 November would have become "the day of the dissolution of so blessed an estate" (that is, the Stuart monarchy), and the "yeare 1605 had beene a yeare of Revolution."[31] Preaching at court in 1606 on the supposed dangers posed by Puritan schismatics, royal chaplain Anthony Maxey urged the need for magistrates and MPs to enforce religious conformity in order to preserve order, to prevent popular upheaval and "revolution," to guard against being infected by Presbyterian practices north of the border (a particular concern of many English Church conformists in the aftermath of the union of the crowns), and to maintain the authority of the crown. The "common people," Maxey continued, were "soone stird up" and "quickly led awry"; it therefore betrayed "a vaine and proud spirit for any, especially men of religion and understanding, to . . . seeke to win unto themselves the applause of common people," since "the braine-sicke humour of the multitude" was "subject and pliable to every change and revolution." It was not many years ago, Maxey recalled, alluding to the Puritan challenge to the Elizabethan Church settlement in the 1580s, that "divers personages of great credit and countenance . . . invegled many weake men, young divines, trades-men, artificers, and such like" to cry out "for the Geneva discipline, and Scottish reformation in the Church." The result was disastrous: "the ignorant multitude once stirred up, the whole land was in sects, and tumults, the state was troubled, the Prince was disobeyed, good lawes were neglected, by Libels, Pamphlets, by consealements, by treacheries, by sundry foule disorders, violence and

disgrace was offered, to many societies and worthy callings in this land."
This was Maxey's nightmare world of "revolution"—exactly the sort of
thing that was to happen in England in the 1640s—even if he was using the
term to mean an overturning ("change and revolution").[32] Contemporaries
even anticipated that the political and religious crisis of 1642 that led to
the outbreak of the English civil war would bring in its wake revolutions.
Thus the moderate Puritan Edward Reynolds, a man also deeply concerned
about the threat posed by the sects, could observe in November 1642 how
"some strange revolutions, and portending Comets seeme to affright thy
[his readers'] tender sences, threatning the speedy annihillation of all things
with their streaming flashes"—"revolutions" that Reynolds associated with
"raging seas" exceeding "their bounds" and "bending their swelling tydes
against the Christal Heaven" and "warlike allarums of beating Drums and
sounding Trumpets" sending "death to summon thee."[33]

⌐

Revolution, a change in the existing political ordering, a regime change
that brought with it fundamental and far-reaching reform, was recognized
by seventeenth-century English people as something that could and did
happen, and by the later seventeenth century as something that had happened in England (and indeed Scotland and Ireland). Revolution could be
seen as calamitous, it could have direful consequences; but it could also be
deemed desirable, it could certainly bring an outcome that was seen as positive, and could even be welcomed as delivering good people from tyranny.
Yet if the seventeenth-century English possessed the concept of revolution,
did they have a script for revolution? If revolution could be positive, did
they imagine how it might be possible to bring one about? The Church of
England, following Romans 13, had always taught that "the powers that
be" were ordained of God, and that if one resisted those in authority one
was resisting God and would be damned. The monarch was said to rule
by divine right and was deemed to be "absolute" and thus not accountable
to his subjects. Even a tyrant could not be resisted: tyranny was seen as a
punishment from God for a nation's sins, though God might also choose
to deliver a penitent nation from tyranny. Hence why great transformations, when they happened, were so often seen as the result of divine will.
The Restoration was seen in providential terms, as also was the Glorious
Revolution—by many, though not by all. Indeed, many staunch royalists
accepted the regicide and the subsequent establishment of a republic precisely because they saw it as a divine judgment. Such theorizing seems to
leave little room for human agency in effecting a regime change.

To conclude, then, I wish to consider briefly what options there were for effecting regime change in a monarchy that proclaimed itself to be absolute and to rule by divine right. Was instigating revolution even imaginable? This is a large and complex topic that there is not the space to treat fully here. My remarks will necessarily be brief and somewhat schematic.

One way to answer this question is to point out that there were some who did not think that the English monarchy was absolute but rather that it was limited in certain ways. And if it was limited, then those limitations had to be enforceable: there had to be some means of holding a monarch accountable if he (or she) abused his (or her) power. A fairly sophisticated theory of resistance had emerged in Europe by the second half of the sixteenth century, articulated by the likes of Christopher Goodman and John Ponet in England and John Knox and George Buchanan in Scotland.[34] Indeed, the theory of royal absolutism in the late sixteenth and seventeenth centuries was an ideological counterblast to the theory of resistance that had emerged during the European wars of religion. The Scottish Covenanters who rebelled against Charles I's religious reforms in Scotland in 1638 had a pre-existing theory of resistance to which they could appeal; indeed, they reprinted Buchanan's *De Jure Regni Apud Scotos*, justifying the revolution against Mary Queen of Scots, to remind Scots how they were entitled to respond to royal tyranny.[35] The parliamentarians on the eve of the English civil war likewise developed a theory of limited resistance in certain circumstances, their key ideological spokesman being the Oxford-trained lawyer Henry Parker.[36] If we jump forward to the later seventeenth century, the Whigs under Charles II and James II certainly believed that the monarchy was limited and could, under certain circumstances, be resisted.[37]

However, such an answer takes us only so far. Those who led the resistance to Charles I in the late 1630s and early 1640s tended to acknowledge that the king ruled by divine right. The Scottish Covenanters, for example, insisted that they never had "the least intention" of calling off their "duetifull obedience unto his Majestie's most lawfull authoritie" and agreed that Charles was "the Lord's Vicegerent"; they had merely proceeded by humbly "petitioning his Majestie for legall redresse" against innovations "pressed upon the whole Church here."[38] John Pym, the man who was to lead Parliament to war against Charles I in 1642, likewise accepted that the king was God's agent on earth.[39] The train of events that were to culminate in the Glorious Revolution of 1688–89 in England was set in motion by Tory Anglicans who had long been proclaiming, from the pulpit and in the press, that the king was absolute and could not be resisted.[40] We return to the question, then, of how it might be possible to resist a monarchy that was divinely ordained and absolute.

There are some initial confusions that need to be cleared up here. Divine-right monarchy was not the same thing as absolute monarchy, although they are sometimes discussed as if they were equivalents. All monarchs ruled by divine right, because it said so in the Bible: but that was true if monarchy was limited or absolute, elective or hereditary. A monarch was absolute if he had complete (absolute) power and did not share his power with anyone else: not the pope (even Puritans were happy to recognize the king's power as absolute in this regard), but also not with Parliament. An absolute king was above the law in the sense that he could not be held accountable by his subjects: he could not be tried by his peers because he had no peers, and was in that sense *ab legibus solutus* (absolute). Yet this did not mean that he did not have to rule according to law; in fact he was obliged to do so, as all theorists recognized—even James I said that kings were obliged to rule according to law and degenerated into tyrants and were no longer legal kings if they did not.[41]

What recourse, then, did one have against an absolute and irresistible monarch if he chose not to rule according to law? Even if the king could not be held accountable by his subjects, those who ruled in the king's name—the king's ministers—could. This was the logic of the axiom "the king could do no wrong": it did not mean that the king was free to do as much wrong as he liked, but rather that if wrong were done in the name of the crown the king's ministers were to blame. Ministers could be held accountable by Parliament, hence the logic of impeachment; they could be prosecuted at law. Yet in fact all subjects had the duty to uphold the law in the king's name. What was a subject supposed to do, then, if asked to commit an illegal act? One certainly had to obey God rather than man: if asked to break a moral law (for example, commit murder, or perjury), one was obliged not to do so, although one was supposed to accept passively the consequences of noncompliance—the theory of passive obedience. Yet what if one were asked to break a law that was not a moral law? For example, in 1687 James II issued a Declaration of Indulgence suspending the laws prohibiting Catholics and Protestant nonconformists from holding their own religious meetings. Such meetings were not intrinsically evil; they were illegal only because they had been declared such by the state. It is unclear how a higher moral law might oblige one to disobey the king over his indulgence. Having said that, local magistrates had taken an oath to enforce the law; it was their duty to do so and could be held accountable if they did not, so what were they supposed to do? In the circumstances, some Anglicans felt they were obliged to continue to suppress Catholic and nonconformist meetings, not in spite of the theory that the king could do no wrong but precisely because the king himself could do no wrong.[42]

Thus even those who denounced resistance, and who held that the king ruled by divine right and was absolute, believed in the obligation to rule according to law and allowed for some degree of accountability in the system. They would nevertheless have insisted that one could not actively resist a king who acted tyrannically: one could not touch the body of the Lord's anointed. The only remedy, the church preached, was prayers and tears, in the hope that God might be induced to deliver a penitent people from tyranny. But how did God do this? People did not think that a tyrant would be zapped from the sky by a thunderbolt. God would work through human agency. It was in this way that an acknowledgment of resistance as a check to tyranny crept into the theory of divine-right, irresistible monarchy through the back door. Preaching in 1610, the Church of England cleric David Owen insisted that "God hath forbidden Christian subjects to resist," who were to endure tyranny with patience; nevertheless, he conceded that God did sometimes "permit rebels . . . to prevaile against Kings" who showed contempt for the law and neglected their duty.[43] James I, in his *Trew Law of Free Monarchies*, published originally in Scotland in 1598 and reprinted in England in 1603, insisted that God, "as the great Judge, may justly punish his Deputie, and for his rebellion against him, stir up his rebels to meet him with the like." These rebels would still be playing "the divel's part." Yet in concluding his discussion of non-resistance, James explained that he did not think "by the force and argument of this . . . discourse so to perswade the people, that none will hereafter be raised up, and rebell against wicked Princes."[44]

The view that tyranny was likely to provoke rebellion appears to have been widespread. One man recorded in his commonplace book in about 1625 the saying from Tacitus that "Tyrannie is a violent rule against the lawes and customes; which causeth rebellion, which is an insurrection against the prince to pluck him from his throne."[45] Another, writing in about 1698 (his views undoubtedly colored by the revolutions of the seventeenth century), saw fit to recall how Machiavelli, despite regarding "risings in arms and clandestine conspiracies" as "the greatest crime that can be committed among men," nevertheless saw them as likely to occur "as often as Princes Tyrannize," since it was "impossible, that Humane Nature . . . can support with Patience and Submission, the greatest Cruelty and injustice."[46] Thus ironically the biggest check on tyranny was the threat of rebellion, even though rebellion was deemed illegitimate. Asked once at dinner "whether there could be no Case in which Defensive Arms were Lawful," the principal of St. Mary's College, St. Andrews, Dr Alexander Colville (d. 1666), replied: "It was fit for the People to believe them unlawful, and for Kings to believe them lawful."[47]

If prayers and tears could induce God to deliver people from tyranny, then when successful resistance had taken place—when a regime had been overthrown and replaced by something that was deemed preferable—contemporaries often explained the resultant revolution in providential terms, as we have seen already. But what about those who did engage in overt acts of resistance, either on the eve of the English civil war or at the time of the Glorious Revolution? What options were there available to them when seeking to justify their actions? How did one argue for a revolution, for a regime change, in advance?

There are two things to distinguish here: resisting tyranny and oppression, and actively seeking to replace an existing regime with another deemed more desirable. Neither the Scottish Covenanters of 1638 nor the English parliamentarians of 1642 claimed to be seeking a revolution of the second type. They positioned themselves as acting defensively, as seeking to uphold the rule of law and the true religion against violations and innovations introduced by the crown. This was tactical positioning: Charles I tended to do the same, to claim that it was he who was upholding the rule of law and the true religion and that it was his enemies who were violating the law and seeking to introduce innovations in the church. It is not my intention here to reflect on who might have been right; rather, my point is that the way the early Stuart monarchy was theorized as absolute and irresistible dictated that those who sought to justify resistance couch it as defensive action against innovation and aggression by the crown, and not as looking forward to creating a new type of political "fabric." Hence why the Scottish National Covenant of 1638, for instance, was couched in conservative rhetoric; within it, however, was embedded a revolutionary ideology.[48]

We do see attempts in the 1650s and the Restoration period actively to bring about a regime change. Most of these failed: the radical and the monarchist plots of the 1650s; the republican plots of 1660s; the Rye House Plot of 1682–83; the Monmouth rebellion 1685. But of course 1688–89 succeeded. How were these attempts justified? A number of typologies of "imagined revolution" suggest themselves. One is the utopian—such as the Fifth Monarchist plots of 1657 and 1661. Another is a revolution to restore the former regime—one thinks here of the various royalist conspiracies of the 1650s, and the ultimate restoration of monarchy in 1660. Then there is a revolution in the name of a pretender, someone who has a legitimate alternative claim to the throne: the duke of Monmouth, for example (the eldest but illegitimate son of Charles II) in 1685, and William of Orange, of course (the nephew and son-in-law of James II) in 1688.

Contemporaries did imagine revolution against James II in 1687–88—they actively conspired for regime change. How did they justify this? James helped people in the end by running away. So it was possible to claim that no resistance had taken place—that the revolution was the result of a desertion by the king and a resultant vacancy in the throne. Alternatively, one might argue that God had raised up William of Orange as a deliverer—and as a foreign prince William could legitimately take action against James II in a just war. English subjects who opposed James II tended to insist that they were acting defensively, in defense of the rule of law against violations by the crown—and this included some Tories, not just Whigs. The Whigs did embrace contract theory, though they tended to the view that James II, by refusing to rule according to law, had unkinged himself. It was only a handful of the most radical Whigs who were prepared to argue that Parliament, or the people, had the right to unking James, because he had ruled unconstitutionally.[49]

The modern concept of revolution carries with it the idea not just of a regime change but of a radical restructuring of political (and social and economic) power. Finally, then, when did seventeenth-century Englishmen think you could "new model" the state? Although there were republican conspiracies in the seventeenth century, what we think of as the revolutions of the seventeenth century did not start out as attempts by those who opposed the crown to radically restructure the state. As already noted, the Covenanters of 1638 saw themselves as undoing innovation, not as creating something new. The English parliamentarians in 1642 claimed to be acting in defense of the King and Parliament. Those who actively conspired to frustrate James II's policies in church and state or to put William of Orange on the throne regarded themselves, in the main, as seeking to vindicate and assert ancient rights and liberties. It is not quite that straightforward, however. The parliamentarians in 1640–41 were already arguing for root and branch (that is, radical)[50] reform in the church—the abolition of episcopacy—and they put forward a number of proposals for constitutional reform over the course of 1641–42 that would have severely eroded the prerogatives of the crown and reduced the king, as Charles I saw it, to little more than a doge of Venice. Certainly once Charles I was defeated in war in 1646 we see serious reflection upon whether and to what extent it might be desirable to new model the state, although it was not until after Charles was defeated in a second civil war in 1648 that the prospect of regicide and establishing a republic was really put on the political agenda.[51] In 1688–89 it was argued that, given that James had unkinged himself—whether he had done so by breaking his contract or deserting the throne—one could either simply restore the old regime with a new king or set up an entirely new system of government (a position taken by the so-called True Whigs).[52] These potential paths forward were famously outlined by John Locke at the end of his *Second Treatise of Government* (first published in 1689, though written in the period 1681–83), itself a work of resistance theory—a script for revolution, one might justifiably style it. Indeed, Locke described the people's efforts to secure themselves from tyranny as resulting in "revolutions," though he was at pains to reassure his readers that "such revolutions" were unlikely to occur often.[53]

⤸

In short, not only did England experience two revolutions in the seventeenth century, but the English possessed a concept of revolution, and arguably there existed a script, or at least a discourse, of how it might be possible to bring such a revolution about. When they invoked the term "revolution," the seventeenth-century English essentially meant a regime change, and thus in a monarchy that was theorized as absolute and irresistible the crucial issue became how one could legitimize resistance so as to bring about the desired changes in the regime. The script for revolution in seventeenth-century England was intrinsically tied up with the articulation of resistance theory, rather than the drawing up of blue prints for a radically different political order. Indeed, in resisting an absolute monarchy it invariably made most sense to position oneself as acting defensively to conserve a traditional order that was under threat—that is, to deny that one was seeking to new model the state. This did not mean, of course, that the English had no desire to new model the state, or that they did not succeed in doing so over the course of the seventeenth century. As I have argued elsewhere, they most definitely did succeed in doing this in this time period, which is why the seventeenth century deserves to be styled England's century of revolutions.[54]

DAVID R. COMO

God's Revolutions

*England, Europe, and the Concept of
Revolution in the Mid-seventeenth Century*

Not so long ago, the events that rocked England during the 1640s and
1650s were habitually described as an "English Revolution." The phrase
was coined by the French politician and historian Guizot, who saw in the
execution of King Charles I and the establishment of the English Republic a clear parallel to the revolution he had lived through as a young boy.
Guizot's conceit was adopted by some of the nineteenth-century pioneers
of the field of Tudor-Stuart history, notably the great Whig-liberal scholar
S. R. Gardiner, who dubbed England's tumults "the Puritan Revolution."[1]
The revolutionary paradigm dominated into the 1960s, when a revisionist school of historiography rose to question the framework. Revisionism
challenged the edifice of Whig history, with its stress on progress, the rise
of parliamentary democracy, and the victory of religious toleration, all of
which were scorned as artificial teleologies that obscured the true nature of
the period. One of the casualties of this process of historiographical reaction was the concept of an English Revolution, in part because revolution
itself was taken to be an anachronistic and ultimately misleading category,
one not recognized by contemporaries. The term came to be contested,
even dropped, usually in favor of the more neutral "civil war." The historiographical sea-change was dramatic: in 1972, Lawrence Stone entitled his
widely read interpretive essay *The Causes of the English Revolution*; eighteen
years later, with a sly allusive nod, the leading revisionist Conrad Russell
published his Oxford Ford Lectures as *The Causes of the English Civil War*,
calling into question the utility of the concept, not just in the English case,
but at a more global level: "[It] is worth asking," he mused, "whether the

idea of 'revolution' is one of those universals invented for the purpose of demonstrating the merits of nominalism."[2]

There were good reasons for skepticism with respect both to the concept of an English Revolution, and indeed to the category of "revolution" more generally. Nevertheless, partly prompted by this revisionist challenge, a number of scholars have in recent decades focused their attention on the problem, offering a much more elaborate and sophisticated picture of how the word was used in England and Europe during the period. The most important contribution has come from Ilan Rachum, who has provided an able survey of the etymological and conceptual history of the term "revolution" from its beginnings in Italy through to the French Revolution.[3] In the present volume, Tim Harris carries the project further, powerfully demonstrating the ubiquity of the word in seventeenth-century British political discussion. Where Harris furnishes a broad overview of the seventeenth century as a whole, the present article builds on these previous studies and examines more explicitly the use of the term during the 1640s and 1650s. It should be emphasized at the outset that the goal of this essay is not to assert that seventeenth-century contemporaries possessed a concept of revolution identical to our own; nor is the point to suggest that events in the 1640s and 1650s should be understood as, in some sense, a modern revolution. Rather, the purpose of this article is to examine the process whereby the vocabulary of revolution, or rather revolutions, became normalized over time during the seventeenth century. Any attempt to grapple with the emergence of revolution as a "script" or template for action must reckon with the intriguing, if halting, process through which Europeans came to adopt the conceptual framework of revolution, and indeed to apply it to their own experience. This essay seeks to reveal the course of that process in England, and in so doing to shed light on how English observers made sense of the deeply disruptive events of the 1640s and 1650s.

To begin this investigation, it might be useful to start with a brief overview of the military and political tumults of the period. As in the French Revolution, and other analogous moments of upheaval, the events of the English midcentury crisis unfolded over a protracted period and involved different phases. The immediate standoff in England began with the Long Parliament in 1640 (although this crisis was itself prompted by King Charles I's loss of control of his northern realm of Scotland). The Long Parliament quickly descended into political deadlock, which was followed by political breakdown, an uprising of Catholics in Ireland, and the outbreak of open civil war between parliamentarians and royalists in England in 1642, war that lasted until the king's surrender in 1646; in 1647, as different parliamentarian factions jockeyed for position in the aftermath of the war, a politicized, indeed radicalized, army seized control of the political initiative, then seized control of the king; a brief second civil war ensued in 1648; this was followed by the purge of Parliament by the army, the trial and execution of the king in 1649, and the establishment of an English republic under the leadership of this so-called Rump of the Long Parliament. However, this was hardly the end of the drama; in 1653, angry over what were taken to be the failings of the Rump Parliament, the army stepped in again, dissolved the Rump, and established a short-lived assembly of parliamentarian extremists, generally known as the Barebones or Nominated Parliament. Before the year was out, the army once again intervened, dissolved this assembly, and promulgated a new constitution, composed of a Lord Protector (that is, Parliament's Lord General, Oliver Cromwell), a Council of State, and periodic parliaments. This government, with emendations, survived until Cromwell's death in 1658. When the reins of power were passed to his son Richard, the whole edifice crumbled, and in 1659 England was swept by a dizzying series of unstable regimes as the Protectorate collapsed and the Rump was restored by the army, only to be dissolved again and replaced by overt military rule. Amid this instability the republican coalition fell apart, and ultimately a fragment of the army, led by General George Monck, intervened to put Charles Stuart, son of the executed king, back on the throne—the so-called Restoration of 1660.

A number of observations are in order at the outset. First, the words "revolution" and "revolutions" in their more political guises remained rare in England through the 1640s. The word appeared occasionally during the decade, but it was typically invoked in one of several more traditional senses, most of which had no specific political connotation: first, it was sometimes used in its astronomical or astrological sense, to describe the revolutions of stars and planets; secondly, a related usage sometimes saw the word employed to describe the passage of time, or the changing of the seasons; a third usage, which in some ways flowed naturally from this last, deployed the word to refer to the ineluctable changes, mutations, and alterations that attended the passage of time. It was in this context that the word was sometimes invoked in a more political guise (and usually in its plural form of "revolutions") to describe the ebb and flow of political fortune and the inevitable changes that were taken to characterize human political society. Used in this sense, the word comported other shades of meaning, not just by invoking the astronomical connotation of the word—

with its implication of circular or repetitive motion—but also by gesturing toward widely shared canons of political thought, which following Aristotle and later interpreters such as Polybius, viewed the rise and degeneration of polities as a regular or cyclical process. It was this valence of the word—with its implication of cyclical return to a starting point—that led earlier scholars to suggest that "revolution," in its early modern sense, was in essence different from our more modern conception of revolution.[4] Yet it was also this last usage that paved the way for the more specific, modern meaning of the word "revolution" in English, deployed as a concept to describe the overturning of a political order, and its replacement by another. As Harris's contribution to this volume suggests, that process of etymological and conceptual change was already in embryo in the early part of the century; but it was only toward the end of the 1640s, and then, much more impressively in the 1650s, that more familiar political usages of the word intruded into the English language.

The relative absence of the word in the 1640s serves to underscore a curious but significant point: the chain of events that has impressed modern observers as the archetypal revolutionary moment of the era—the execution of Charles I and establishment of a republic—was only rarely described as a "revolution" by English contemporaries at the time. This irony is encapsulated by the fact that perhaps the most spectacular contemporary application of the word to the English situation derives not from a native observer, but from a Frenchman. In June 1647, a French diplomat in London reported to his superiors that "in history we have never seen a similar revolution happen, nor ever has there ever been a Prince more tossed about than the King of Great Britain is today." The French agent was writing, interestingly, not of the regicide, but of the seizure of Charles I by the army, and the political upheaval this portended. His words suggest some of the nuances of meaning that characterized the standard use of the word in its political form during the period, conveying a sense of dramatic reversal of political fortune. Yet his use of the term also hinted at a more novel and significant shift in conceptual register, for it is clear that he also intended to convey to his political masters a sense not simply that what was taking place in England was a major change, or even an alteration of government, but that it represented a startling inversion of the political order. His comments likewise hint at the considerable significance that contemporaries outside of England attached to what was happening there in the 1640s.[5] Writing two years later, just after the execution of the king, the Franco-Scottish priest Robert Mentet de Salmonet would echo these sentiments, describing his own chronicle of the English upheavals as "the History of the strangest revolution that ever happened in the world."[6]

The French case should alert us to an important feature of the history of the concept during this period. As earlier work by Vernon Snow and Rachum has highlighted, the concept of revolution, or revolutions, was more robustly developed—and more familiarly modern—in some other European cultural zones at this point.[7] It is only by examining the ways in which the word and its attendant conceptual baggage moved across borders, to be redeployed and reconfigured in different languages and contexts, that the shifting history of the term can be understood. As Rachum demonstrates, the word had long been an ephemeral feature of Italian political vocabulary, and had seen a revival in use beginning in the 1630s; mutual intercommunication appears to have injected the word into French political discourse around the same time, helping to explain its presence in French diplomatic circles during this period.[8] As yet, however, this shift in political vocabulary had not yet caught firm hold in England. This leads to an interesting paradox, exemplified by the French agent's words: the events in England were being dubbed a revolution—even somewhat hyperbolically, the most dramatic revolution in history—but not by the English (at least not yet).

To trace the eruption of the word "revolution" into the English political lexicon, we need to look not at the spectacle of war and political contestation in the British Isles, nor to French comment on it, but rather to more distant locales on the Mediterranean basin—the Spanish principality of Catalonia and the Spanish dependencies in Southern Italy. In 1640, Spain was rocked by nearly simultaneous uprisings in Catalonia and Portugal, the latter of which succeeded in evicting Philip IV from the Portuguese throne. In 1647 and 1648, meanwhile, as England was buckling under its own dramatic political crisis, the Spanish monarchy was again gripped by fierce uprisings, first in Sicily and then in Naples, brought about by heavy taxation coupled with economic difficulties.

These remarkable events quickly generated intense interest throughout Europe. But it was in Italy that the disparate uprisings received a novel taxonomic stamp. In 1644, Luca Assarino published *Delle Rivolutioni di Catalogna*, marking, it seems, the first time the word was utilized in the title of a book; in the next decade, Assarino's history went through multiple editions, published in Genoa and Bologna.[9] The nomenclature proved appealing. In 1648, on the heels of the risings in Sicily, Placido Reina brought out *Delle Rivolutioni della Città di Palermo* in Verona. More popular, and more widely disseminated, was a second tract, published almost simultaneously, Alessandro Giraffi's *Le Rivolutioni di Napoli*, published first in Venice. Perhaps because of the sanguinary and dramatic events in Naples, and the colorfully magnetic centrality of the fisherman turned political leader, Masaniello, Giraffi's book proved to be an international bestseller. Before the end of 1648 it had been printed in Italian editions at Ferrara, Padua, Gaeta, and Geneva, and had been translated into German. Interestingly, the Padua edition bore the even more sensationalistic title *Relatione Delle Rivolutioni Popolari Successe nel Distretto, e Regno di Napoli*. Here we have an image of "popular revolutions," a phrase that to modern ears will sound eerily familiar. Moreover, Giraffi's book did not simply use the term in the title, but also invoked it repeatedly in its text, sometimes in its singular form, *rivolution*, to describe what happened in Southern Italy.[10] There is good reason to believe that Giraffi's work would be instrumental in the diffusion of a more starkly political conception of "revolution" throughout Europe.

The popularity of the book owed much to the fact that news of the Neapolitan uprising had quickly spread across the continent, whetting appetites for more information. In England, events in Naples were widely known within weeks.[11] Here, contemporaries quickly assimilated the Neapolitan experience to their own. Word of the Naples rising arrived, in fact, just in time to coincide with the emergence of the popular groundswell usually known as the Leveller movement, which began in 1647 to push for dramatic, indeed essentially republican, constitutional change, floating the idea for the first time that the king might be subject to execution for treason.[12] At an early assembly organized to push forward this agenda, a gathering of hundreds of weavers outside the city of London in November 1647, one firebrand allegedly rose and declared, "Gentlemen, the same busines wee are upon is perfected in Naples, For if anie person stand upp for Monarchie there hee is ymediatly hanged at his doore."[13] Four months later, the Puritan George Downing, writing to Governor John Winthrop of Massachusetts, described the fragmented but ultimately promising political situation on the eve of the second civil war: "[W]hat the issue will be the Lord only knowes, only he seems to be shaking the great ones of the earth. in Fraunce have lately been practises in this kind. the story of Naples with their successe I suppose you have."[14] Here, not only Naples but also the prelude to the Fronde were assimilated into a single, emerging story of God shaking the mighty, and unsettling kings throughout Christendom. Tellingly, Downing simply assumed that Winthrop, in New England, already knew what had occurred in Naples.

Still, although there is something unnervingly revolutionary about

Downing's thinking here, he did not use the word itself. Shortly after Downing wrote, the term began to creep into the English political lexicon in a more substantive way. As historians have long recognized, there were two chief culprits here. First, during the brief second civil war of 1648, Anthony Ascham published *A Discourse: Wherein is Examined, what is Particularly Lawfull during Confusions and Revolutions in Government*, a tract urging people to submit to the authority of Parliament. This marked the first appearance of the word, in its political guise, in the title of an English book. Ascham's use of the term in his text was sparing, and cleaved to a more traditional use, which configured "revolutions" as a synonym for tumults or unruly political events, rather than to denote specific and clear transformations of the political order.[15] Nevertheless, the book quickly went through three editions and elicited at least one printed refutation, ensuring that the word in its political form received a wider exposure than had yet been the case.

It was in 1650 that a more dramatic appropriation of the word took place. That year, James Howell brought out a translation of Alessandro Giraffi's account of the Neapolitan tumults, which Howell entitled *An Exact Historie of the late Revolutions in Naples*. Howell was a well-traveled polyglot, with a pronounced taste for Italian culture, which helps to explain his attraction to this exotic fare; yet he was also a royalist sympathizer who had spent a considerable amount of time in prison for his allegiances.[16] Although his motives for publication are uncertain, it seems likely that the book was intended as a sotto voce commentary on events in England, an invitation to readers to draw parallels between events in the two polities. Of course, by the time Howell went to press, the Neapolitan republic had collapsed and Spanish authority had been reasserted, thus perhaps rendering the analogy more poignant and, for Howell at least, exemplary. Whatever his motivation, Howell tapped into widespread popular fascination with the events in Naples. His rendition of Giraffi's book, with its crude woodcut of the plebeian rebel leader Masaniello, was an instant success, going through at least three editions in a single year and prompting Howell to bring out a translation of the second part of Giraffi's work shortly thereafter. Unlike Ascham's treatise, with its relatively innocuous use of the word, Howell's translation brought Giraffi's more novel deployment of the term—to signify not just popular tumults but tumults that resulted in the dramatic overturning of a political order—to a broad English audience.

These bestsellers, provoked by the furious changes overtaking England in 1648–49, appear to have catapulted both the word and the concept of "revolution" into wider circulation in the English language. Yet the concept was partly an import: in this case, the more sharply developed idea, as seen in Italy, was transplanted into an English context by Howell. This reinforces a fundamental supposition that holds together all of the essays in this volume: the need to think about the concept and "scripts" of revolution in a genuinely European manner. In its initial incarnation, the word, and the amorphous and shifting set of concepts attached to it, spread back and forth through Europe by way of a series of borrowings, appropriations, and refashionings that cannot be understood in any single national framework.

This hints at a pair of broader contexts, both of which are crucial to understanding the story being told here. The first is that this sort of transnational lexical drift was enabled by the emergence of a robust culture of news and information that had gradually over the previous decades come to knit Europe together in an ever tighter discursive community. Of course, the cultural and political patchwork of Europe had always been porous, and books and ideas had traveled easily from one place to another, aided and abetted by the existence of a transcontinental Latinate scholarly community. But there are clear signs that, by the early seventeenth century, the outlets and pathways for this sort of borrowing and intellectual transmission were becoming more numerous and more open. Increasing volumes of trade, along with the cultural and material infrastructure that came along with such commerce, played a part in this development, as did the emergence in many parts of Europe of vibrant and formidable printing industries (which were themselves to an extent dependent on the wealth generated by intensifying trade). The most obvious symbol of this burgeoning culture was the periodical newspaper, which from humble beginnings at the close of the sixteenth century had become an established fixture in several parts of Europe by the 1640s, energized in particular by hunger for news about the interlinked and indeed pan-European struggle we know as the Thirty Years' War.[17] It was this infrastructure for news and information which meant that large numbers of English people learned of the Neapolitan uprising scarcely a month after it had happened, news that in short time made its way across the Atlantic to English settlers in the Americas. Similar forces ensured that Giraffi's account of the uprising was translated into German, Dutch, and English within four years of its composition, and that it had appeared in no fewer than ten separate editions by 1652. The enfolding of Europe into a more integrated network of trade and news meant not simply that people knew what was happening elsewhere with surprising speed, but also that concepts and language could and did make very rapid migrations from one context to another.

Yet it is not just that we are seeing here a case of linguistic transmigration. There is also a sense in which events taking place in England and Naples were, in a very loose way, linked together. The English crisis was the product of long-standing and complex forces, but chief among them were attempts by the Stuart kings to assert something more like respectably continental monarchical authority over their subjects, most obviously by extracting greater taxation through ever less consensual means. This was not simply a matter of self-aggrandizement; it was also prompted by the need to wage increasingly expensive warfare, in this case the Thirty Years' War, and it was partly Charles I's unsuccessful bids to intervene in that conflict that destabilized his regime. Onerous taxation, demands for troops, and other burdensome exactions that attended the Thirty Years' War were also crucial in driving Spanish subjects in Catalonia, Portugal, Sicily, and Naples into rebellion in the 1640s.[18] Such maneuvers were particularly destabilizing for rulers, such as the Stuarts and Habsburgs, who presided over composite monarchies and thus governed peoples of greatly varying political, cultural, or institutional character, often at considerable distance. Without resurrecting the thesis that Europe experienced during this period some form of "General Crisis," it might reasonably be suggested that the events described as "revolutions" in Naples and in England did not merely coincidentally unfold at the same time, but at a deep level were conjured by shared structural forces.[19] On this reading, then, the concept of revolution, as an emerging European discourse for discussing political change, was perhaps being brought into being on the back of the same parallel, and intertwined, political developments. Moreover, this process of conceptual codevelopment was powered by a new informational infrastructure—again, one that had initially been energized in no small measure by the Thirty Years' War—that carried news swiftly from one end of Europe to the other in a matter of weeks.

Whether or not such overarching forces were at work, it is clear that the word had now made a much more lasting entrance into the English political vocabulary. That reality became apparent when England experienced its next moment of dramatic constitutional upheaval. In April 1653 the army intervened to shut down the Rump Parliament and set up a new assembly of hand-selected godly extremists, the Nominated Parliament. The newly fashionable language of "revolution" can be traced in the semi-public correspondence of regime insiders, who were quick to brandish the novel conceptual apparatus to describe the sudden reversal. Two days after the dissolution of the Rump, the naval secretary and Fifth Monarchist John Poortmans remarked upon "this late revolucion" and declared that "my heart rejoyces within mee to heare of it." On the same day Poortmans's commander, General Richard Deane, likewise wrote a letter in which he referred to the dissolution of the Rump as "this great revolucion." Rear Admiral John Lawson informed his correspondents a few days later: "I trust the Lord will Bring Glory to himselfe and good to his people by all these Revolutions."[20] Those who were less certain of the hidden hand of providence nevertheless fully embraced the novel taxonomy: one member of the Rump, who objected to the breaking of the Parliament, nevertheless referred to "this and all other revolutions."[21]

Shortly thereafter, the new terminology found another advocate in John Ward, a former soldier and defender of the regime, who in the aftermath of the dissolution of the Rump wrote a poem entitled "The Changes Or A Vicessitude of Change of Goverment Being A Vindication of the present Actings of the Army in dissolving the late Parliament Wherein divers Objections are answerde Relating to the severall translations and Changes of Goverment since the yeare on thousand six hundred fourty and two unto this Present Revolution." Although this theme unsurprisingly made for appalling poetry, David Norbrook has shown that the content of the verse was in many respects remarkable. Ward's work attested to a recognition of the necessity of dramatic change, but it also revealed the fundamental and underlying premise that imbued much of the discourse of "revolution" during this period: as Ward put it: "doubtlesse there will now (since the Lord is risen to that purpose) be an Intercourse of Changes untill Justice and Righteousnesse bee risen in the Earth."[22] The abolition of monarchy, and then the dissolution of the Rump for its failure to make good on the promised transformation that was supposed to follow, were seen as part of string of profound changes—revolutions—through which God would establish some more purified order. Whether that order would be accompanied by Christ returned and ruling over his people, and by the establishment of the Fifth Monarchy foretold in the book of Daniel, or whether it would have a more modest, secular, and less overtly apocalyptic status, was a matter of dispute among the defenders of England's revolutions; where they agreed, however, was in seeing the changes gripping England as emanating from the providence of God, whereby the powers of the earth would be shaken and the forces of oppression removed.[23]

As all of this suggests, the valence of the word "revolution" was itself shifting in England during the 1650s. For some, it was coming both to signify a dramatic change in the nature of government, and also to be given, at least by its boosters, a positive interpretation, seen as part of an unfolding divine plan in which England was at the very center. This tendency to embrace "revolutions," and indeed to own them as events in which one was a participant, is quite arresting, and represents a departure from prior historians and commentators, such as Assarino and Giraffi, who had popularized the word, but always in order to describe something unfortunate, carried out by desperate outlaws. Also striking, however, was a reluctance to claim agency: these were God's revolutions, worked out through the instrumentality of humble men. Indeed, it might be argued that it was precisely this displacement of agency to the realm of divine providence that allowed people increasingly to overcome ingrained and conservative habits of thought in order to appropriate "revolutions" as positive, even desirable, confluences of events.

Despite the high hopes that preceded it, the Nominated Parliament of 1653 proved to be a failure, and at the end of the year, the army once again stepped in to bring forth still another constitutional arrangement—the Protectorate, which vested quasi-regal powers in Oliver Cromwell as Lord Protector, backed by a council of state. Not surprisingly, the language of "revolutions" was once again used to describe this great shift, most famously by the chief public cheerleader of the new regime, Marchamont Nedham. The currency of the term may be gauged by the fact that Oliver Cromwell, dissolving the first protectoral Parliament in 1655, took the opportunity to extol the "revolutions of Christ himself," and (significantly) to warn against the temptation to ascribe these acts of providence to the power of man.[24] Cromwell's admonition was necessary, however, precisely because the Protectorate was not widely embraced as a permanent solution. Challenged in Parliament, the army, and the countryside, the Protectorate from the beginning was subjected to persistent and partially successful attempts at revision or total overhaul, which meant that during the five years of its existence, England saw little sense of constitutional fixity.[25] This atmosphere of flux and insecurity only served to give further purchase to the emergent concept of "revolution," since England seemed to have entered a churning state of constitutional upheaval. Contemporaries reached for a new vocabulary to describe the resulting sense of political turbulence and disorientation.

Some, including Cromwell, were able to attach a comfortably providentialized gloss to the new terminology. But this move was not universal; as the term became more commonplace, it opened itself up to more neutral appropriations. In May 1656, for instance, Charles Longland, the English agent at Livorno, wrote a letter of intelligence to John Thurloe, Cromwell's secretary and spymaster. Longland relayed rumors from Rome: "The pope, 'tis sayd, wil now receiv the Portugal ambassador, but demands the revenues of al the vacancyes in that kingdom since it's revolution, which wil amount unto a vast sum abov 10 millions of crownes." Here, it seems, Longland deployed the word in an entirely casual and dispassionate manner, to describe the successful revolt of the Portuguese against their Spanish king, a usage that looks to all intents and purposes indistinguishable from modern senses of the word.[26] Lurking behind Longland's casual use of the term, however, we see some of the same embedded, indeed eschatological, assumptions of political thought: the Portuguese king, he opined, was poised to accept the pope's hard bargain, "of so great use is the papacy for monarchical government." Here, popery and monarchy were linked together in an unholy duality that points toward the ideological foundations of English interregnum republicanism.

Longland's words also hint at dissensions that plagued the new Cromwellian order. The collapse of the Nominated Assembly and the rise of the Protectorate proved deeply troubling for more extreme partisans of the cause, who resented the attempt to reconfigure the republic along more familiarly monarchical lines. The disappointment felt by more zealous republicans was palpable, made worse when Cromwell in 1657 was offered the Crown by Parliament; although pressure from the likes of Poortmans and others in the military helped to convince Cromwell to reject the offer, once again the constitution was reshaped, allowing for the reintroduction of a new House of Lords (euphemistically known as "the Other House"), and bringing the polity closer than ever to a restoration of the ancient constitution.[27]

The entire political order was once again plunged into chaos by Cromwell's death in September 1658. His demise brought on a rolling crisis and led to the collapse of the Protectorate, as Cromwell's son Richard proved incapable of holding together the coalition of interests that had propped up the Cromwellian regime. What followed in 1659 was a dizzying train of political intrigues and shifts, outlined at the outset of this article. It was of course this rampant instability that shattered the republican coalition, divided the army, and created the conditions for the triumphal return of Charles II and the Restoration of the Monarchy in 1660. But it was not at all clear that this would be the case in 1659; indeed, many devotees of the republican solution—which by this time had been consolidated under the slogan "Good Old Cause"—now came forward to agitate for a renewed push to wipe away the stain of Cromwell and to create a purified republican order. It was in this environment of almost weekly change and disorder that we really see the word "revolution," in its new and ambidextrous forms, trundled out to describe what might justly be called the "year of revolutions."[28]

Thus, for instance, when the restored Rump convened in May 1659, it quickly received a petition from the "well-affected" inhabitants of Hampshire. The petition began with a preamble extolling "the wonderfull Providences of God in the Revolutions of late years" and called for the Rump to establish "a Happy Free-state," purged of the pernicious traces of Protectoral backsliding toward monarchical and lordly oppression.[29] Somewhat earlier in the year, an obscure figure called R. Fitz-brian had published a pamphlet called *The Good Old Cause Dress'd In It's Primitive Lustre, and Set Forth to the View of All Men. Being a short and Sober Narrative of the great Revolutions of Affairs in these later times.* Fitz-brian offered a comprehensive defense of the English Commonwealth against detractors at a moment of growing tension. In the process, he formulated not only a historical interpretation of the series of revolutions that had swept England since 1640, but even something like a theory of revolution (or rather revolutions) more generally. As he wrote: "When States are at the worst; when vitious, and peccant humours are every where predominant; when the prevalency of evil Counsells do'es take place to the introducing of new, and Arbitrary impositions, contrary to the established Constitutions; They must then either necessarily sinke under their own weight, and crumble into disorder, Anarchy and ruine; Or else there will follow some notable alterations: And the distempers being so great, and enormous, that they cannot possibly admit of a redresse, and healing, and conserve still their old frame, Things must unavoydeably wheele about, and fix themselves upon another Basis." Here, in the image of "wheeling about," we can see the vestiges of that older understanding of revolution, construed as a return to a starting point. But Fitz-brian's inquest into "The true Sources of our Late Revolutions" also left no doubt that he saw those revolutions in terms of an escalating providential drama: although the shifts in England "were small in their beginnings, yet have they by severall steps, and progressions been advanced to a considerable height: And I may say, there have been such interweavings of stupendious Providences; such glorious exertings of power, and goodness, such astonishing successes, and such legible characters of divine ownings,

That we are now bigg with just hopes of arriving in the end unto some em-
inient establishment, even above the magnificense of all those forms, which
meerely have the worldly stamp upon them." Again, the words imparted
a sense of divine revolutions and eager anticipation that God's design in
bringing about the vertiginous changes of recent years might soon be fulfilled. The remainder of the tract was laced with many of the characteristic radical Puritan aspirations as to what such an order might look like: it
would be purged of religious persecution, reformed in its laws, secured
against arbitrary imprisonments and the oppression of the poor. Yet part of
that framework was indisputably its pure republican constitution. Nothing
good could be "erected upon a rotten decrepit foundation" of monarchy:
"the single Person, the Lords, and the corrupt Interests . . . were necessary
to be shaken and abridged in their illegal usurpations," and "Kingship being laid aside as . . . dangerous," the government had justly been "divolved
into a Commonwealth," which was the only constitution that could uphold
"the interests of the People."[30]

Yet Fitz-brian's account also exposed the tensions inherent in this radical republican discourse: while the government was supposed to serve the
"interests of the People," it was also to serve principally the people of God:
indeed, "it was peculiarly for their sakes that he had brought about those
unexpected Revolutions."[31] This friction between the desire to create a popular state on the one hand, and on the other to protect and exalt the interests of the godly was evident in other invocations of the concept in 1659.
In September, a set of Fifth Monarchist leaders, including the naval official
John Poortmans, issued a declaration witnessing "against the setting up
or introducing any Person whatsoever, as King, or chiefe Magistrate; or
a House of Lords . . . upon the old corrupt and almost ruinated constitution." They exclaimed "that the great work of taking the Kingdome from
Man, and giving it to Christ, hath had its beginning in the revolutions wee
have been under."[32] Again, the revolutions of the times were posited merely
as a beginning; again, too, we have a strange tension between a virulent opposition to monarchy and the House of Lords as constitutional forms, and
a sense of apocalyptic expectation, in which the true goal of these upheavals
was the establishment of Christ's kingdom on earth. This influential manifesto provoked copycat declarations from regional sectarian congregations,
which rejected monarchism and lordly domination, and celebrated what
the saints of the East Midlands called God's "still continued Revolutions
and Over-turnings."[33]

As all of this should make evident, while we see here the indubitable explosion of the word "revolution" into the political argot of the time, its definition remained plastic, as subtly different uses of the term jostled with one another. At one extreme, the reader can occasionally find the word deployed in a sense almost identical to our own, modern conception of revolution, as a calculated and violent displacement of one political order by another; at the other end of the spectrum, the word continued some-times to be used as little more than a synonym for a major event or tumult of some sort. The declarations and manifestos of 1659 reveal, however, the most interesting and newly fashionable use of the word during this pe-riod, as a way of describing the tortuous but ultimately triumphant chain of ruptures, reversals, and political upheavals that had convulsed England in recent years. This meaning was certainly distinct from our own modern conception. In particular, the manifest providentialism of these declara-tions, their insistence that the recent revolutions were the work of God, is quite alien to later constructions of the concept. Nevertheless, we can see in these statements many of the outlines of later and more familiar notions. Here, revolution or revolutions (because the word was most frequently used in the plural to describe a series of changes) were viewed as progres-sive, deeply transformative, and frankly positive occurrences that denoted a radical break from the past. Even more clearly than in 1653, partisans came forward to embrace England's "revolutions," to see in recent political up-heavals a welcome and providential gift of God, auguring an even more final and rapturous transformation.

There were of course those who felt otherwise, and who saw the roil-ing instabilities of the 1659 as still more evidence that what was necessary was some kind of conservative retrenchment. Yet interestingly, even these alarmed commentators adopted and expropriated the new terminologi-cal apparatus for their own purposes. Hence, in late 1659, one group of Londoners petitioned the government of the city of London "That the sad and sinfull Revolutions to which God hath of late years subjected these Nations, doth provoke us, seriously to reflect upon the Fundamentall Government thereof, transmitted to us by our Progenitors; under which we long flourished, to the Envy of Neighbour Nations, enriching of our selves, and the great encouragement of the *Protestant* Religion"; they called for the return to Westminster of those members of Parliament who had been purged in 1649; another similar petition to the city authorities in De-cember deplored "the frequent Revolutions of Government and intolerable Taxes and Excizes incessantly continued upon us, through the Ambition and Avarice of self-seeking men."[34] A rather more complicated petition from the county of Warwickshire a few weeks later declared: "The cause of our present calamities . . . proceeds from the many Revolutions, through Male-Administration of Government, and want of the right Constitution of Parliaments."[35] Many of these petitioners, although they did not say so, no doubt understood that their proposals tended toward the restoration of the Stuart monarchy. And this, of course, was the ultimate upshot of the year of instability, as a faction of the army, under George Monck, seized the reins of power and engineered the return of Charles II from exile.

Predictably, given what we have seen here, the Stuart Restoration would not infrequently in the months after April 1660 be described by contemporaries as the latest and most decisive revolution of all. In 1661, for instance, one commentator referred to the revival of the Stuart monarchy as "this glorious Revolution," a turn of phrase, which, as Keith Baker shows elsewhere in this volume, occasionally recurred in later years to describe the return of Charles II.[36] Here, perhaps, the word was being used in its more traditional sense, as signaling a return to an origin or starting point. If this points toward the multiple connotations of the term, and the fact that it occasionally retained some of its older associations, the example also serves to demonstrate that the word and nascent concept of revolution—understood as a pivotal political turning point and overturning of an existing constitutional order—had infiltrated English political discourse at a deep level during the 1650s. Remaining flexible, and deployable with different shadings of meaning, most of which were subtly different from our own more modern iterations of the concept, its prevalence by 1660 cannot be denied. The relentless, violent, and protracted nature of England's political upheavals meant that the protean concept found ready acceptance as an apt way of interpreting the disorienting experience of political instability and constitutional change. Unsurprisingly, the vocabulary proved durable. One can find the word being used in different ways by the likes of John Locke and Sir Isaac Newton during the Restoration decades. And it is no surprise that in 1688–89, when the Stuart monarchy once again descended into crisis, and James II fled with William of Orange's army at his heels, the transformation would immediately be dubbed a revolution; indeed, it would quickly receive fixity and reification not just as "the Revolution," but as "the Glorious Revolution."[37]

DAVID ARMITAGE

Every Great Revolution Is a Civil War

Originality and novelty define the modern script of revolution. That script was original in the sense that it had identifiable beginnings that have been precisely located in France in 1789 when "revolution was revolutionised." And it was novel because in that year "the French imagined a radical break with the past achieved by the conscious will of human actors, an inaugural moment for a drama of change and transformation projected indefinitely into the future." After 1789, "revolution" in the singular replaced "revolutions" in the plural. What had been understood before 1789 as unavoidable features of nature, as predetermined astronomical cycles, or as eternal recurrences in human affairs became instead voluntary, transformative, and repeatable: revolution as fact gave way to revolution as act. With that daring feat of collective imagination, revolution became ineluctably political, covering primarily but not exclusively fundamental changes concerned with the distribution of power and sovereignty. In the years after 1789, revolution also developed into an authority in its own right, in whose name political violence could be legitimated. Taken together, these features made up "the script for modern politics invented in 1789."[1]

These elements constituted the originary conception of revolution as a process by which the world could be made over again. "[E]very revolution," noted François Furet, "and above all the French Revolution itself, has tended to perceive itself as an absolute beginning, as ground zero of history": paradoxically, the uniqueness of each successive revolution became an index of its universality.[2] The modern script of revolution may have been new in 1789, but it has been frequently replayed on stages around the world. The authors of later revolutions adapted it to their purposes and added new properties for each performance. Their revolutionary dramas borrowed lines and gestures, symbols and costumes, from previous productions. Such borrowings could constrain the actors, as Karl Marx classically noted in the *Eighteenth Brumaire of Louis Bonaparte*: "Thus Luther donned the mask of the Apostle Paul, the Revolution of 1789 to 1814 draped itself alternately as the Roman republic and the Roman empire, and the Revolution of 1848 knew nothing better to do than to parody, now 1789, now the revolutionary tradition of 1793 to 1795."[3] But they could also justify revolutionaries' actions, as each attempt to overthrow tradition contributed to the creation of a new tradition. In this manner, from 1789 to 1989 and beyond, a consciously accumulating revolutionary repertoire came to form the scarlet thread of modernity itself.

In this chapter, I want to suggest that the modern revolutionary script was not entirely original or novel. I will argue instead that it adapted a much older narrative of violent political change. That script also depended on the exercise of human will. It too featured contestations over sovereignty. And it was likewise shadowed by the specter of repetition with variation. The palimpsest over which self-conscious revolutionaries wrote their script was a conception of history not as a sequence of revolutions but as a series of civil wars. The earliest version of this script came from republican Rome in the first century b.c.e., but it reached its full flowering between the first and fifth centuries c.e. This originally Roman narrative of political violence informed the emerging scripts of revolution in the seventeenth, eighteenth, and nineteenth centuries. Traces of it remain in the twenty-first century, embedded in the assumptions of formal social science and informal political analysis, and in the historiography of modern revolutions.[4]

At first sight, assimilating the modern script of revolution to the ancient script of civil war might seem counterintuitive, even counter-revolutionary. The two forms of forcible political transformation are usually assumed to be distinct both morphologically and genealogically. According to Reinhart Koselleck, revolution emerged across the course of the eighteenth century "as a concept in contrast to that of civil war." At the beginning of the century, he argued, the two expressions "were not interchangeable, but were not at the same time mutually exclusive." Civil war raised memories of destructive confessional conflict across Europe, the very kinds of events in the past that proponents of Enlightenment hoped to prevent in the future. By contrast, revolution would be the leading edge of positive transformation across all domains of human activity: education, morality, law, politics, and religion. The irrational, atavistic, and destructive activity of civil war would wither away and gradually become impossible. A practical desire to expunge civil war thus gave way to a positive program for promoting revolution. The result was the final separation of the two concepts by the late eighteenth century. "In many respects," Koselleck concluded, "'civil war' had now acquired the meaning of a senseless circling upon itself, with respect to which Revolution sought to open up a new vista."[5]

This conceptual opposition between revolution and civil war generated a set of preconceptions, even prejudices, that still endure. Civil wars appear sterile and destructive, while revolutions are fertile with innovation and productive possibility. Civil wars hearken back to ancient grievances and deep-dyed divisions, while revolutions point the way toward an open and expansive future. Civil wars are local, time-bound, and rooted in history, while revolutions have occurred across the world in a universal sequence of human liberation. Revolutions mark the unfolding and realization of the emancipated human spirit; civil wars herald only its blighting and collapse. Such contemporary conceptions have their own histories, but they should not be projected back onto the past as natural facts and should be understood rather as ideological constructions. As self-conscious revolutionaries from Thomas Paine to V. I. Lenin were well aware, the scripts of civil war and revolution had much in common and were difficult to disentangle. Uncovering some of those commonalities will be the task of the second part of this chapter; firstly, however, we need to reconstruct the classical script of civil war that later helped to shape modern conceptions of revolution. In light of that reconstruction, the reign of revolution appears to be relatively brief—perhaps two or three centuries at most—while the sequence of civil wars was much longer, stretching back over two thousand years.

The Romans were the first to experience political violence and internal discords as civil wars, because they were the first to conceive of them as "civil" even if they were not the first to describe them as "wars." Such upheavals were civil in the sense that they were fought between fellow citizens (*cives*), within the bounds of a single political community. This distinguished them from *staseis*, the various forms of sedition and rebellion that divided the Greek *polis* in which social and political rupture was sometimes understood to be a war (*polemos*) but where the community was conceived ethnogenetically, even racially, rather than in terms of a common legal or political status as citizens.[6] As Cicero noted in *On Duties*, "among the Athenians there were great discords but in our commonwealth there were not only seditions but even accursed civil wars" (*pestifera bella civilia*).[7] At least since Cicero himself had first used the term, in 66 b.c.e., the Romans identified a disturbing and increasing number of their conflicts as fought not against foreigners, allies, pirates, or slaves: these were instead wars *by* the people of Rome *against* the people of Rome.[8] Because the standard Roman conception of war defined that condition as both just and directed against an external enemy, the idea of a civil war—*bellum civile*—was deliberately paradoxical, even oxymoronic. It was nonetheless a distinctively Roman invention.

By general agreement, the first instance of full-blown *bellum civile* in Roman history had occurred in 88 b.c.e., when the consul Lucius Cornelius Sulla had marched on Rome at the head of his army. Sulla thereby broke the ultimate taboo for any Roman magistrate or commander by breaching the absolute threshold established between the spheres of military and civilian authority, just as Julius Caesar would do still more notoriously four decades later, when he crossed the river Rubicon in 49 b.c.e. Sulla's opponents, Gaius Marius and P. Sulpicius, confronted him with similar forces inside the bounds of the city itself. At that moment, wrote the Greek-speaking historian Appian in the second century c.e., the peculiar elements of civil war could be clearly seen: "there took place a struggle under the guise of civil dissension, but nakedly as a war, complete with trumpets and military standards. . . . In this way the episodes of civil strife escalated from rivalry and contentiousness to murder, and from murder to full-scale war; and this was the first army composed of Roman citizens to attack their own country as if it were a hostile power."[9]

It may have been the first, but it would be far from the last: over the course of almost a century, from Sulla's march to the succession disputes following the death of the emperor Nero in 69 c.e., Rome would be racked by a series of citizens' wars. Trumpets and standards were the visible signs, conventional warfare was the means, and control of the city of Rome was the aim: all told, these were the identifying marks of the script of civil war rather than signs of mere tumult, dissension, or sedition. Tumults and seditions—like later conceptions of rebellion or revolt, for instance—implied to the Romans episodic and nonrecurrent expressions of political violence. Civil wars, by contrast, increasingly came to appear sequential and cumulative across the course of Roman history. Sulla's first war against Marius in 88–87 b.c.e. led to a second in 82–81 b.c.e. Catiline's conspiracy was quashed before Caesar had brought his army from Gaul to confront Pompey. That led in turn to the cycle of intermittent and transnational violence that spanned the Mediterranean (and beyond) in the years from 49–31 b.c.e. In these decades, it became increasingly easy to believe that Rome was cursed by civil war, and that it was doomed to reiterate citizens' conflicts cumulatively and endlessly in a deadly and debilitating series.[10]

After the death of Augustus, the cycle of civil war—and the sequence of civil war writing—remained unbroken. Of making books about civil war, there would be no end. The greatest surviving treatments of Rome's civil wars were written between the 60s and the 160s c.e.: most notable were Lucan's epic poem, the *Bellum Civile* (60–65), Tacitus's *Histories* (ca. 109), Plutarch's Roman lives of the Gracchi, Marius, Sulla, Caesar, Pompey, and Antony (ca. 100–125), Florus's *Epitome* (ca. 117–138 or 161–169), and the surviving books of Appian's *Roman History* treating the *Civil Wars* (ca. 145–165). Tacitus covered the wars of succession that followed the death of the emperor Nero, in the so-called Year of the Four Emperors (69), which he opened with a warning: "I am entering on a work full of disasters, terrible in its battles, riven by seditions, in which even peace was savage. Four emperors were cut down by the sword; there were three civil wars, more foreign wars and many that were mixed" (*trina bella civilia, plura externa, ac plerumque permixta*).[11] Florus's *Epitome* told Rome's history in the seven centuries from Romulus to Augustus as a sequence of wars foreign, servile, social, and civil. And Appian made his comprehensive attempt to encompass all Rome's civil wars from Sulla to Octavian in the surviving books of his *Roman History*. Their accounts formed the matter of Rome's civil wars into sequences both genealogical and teleological that probed Romans' moral failings, diagnosed civil war as the city's seemingly unshakeable curse, and prescribed remedies for the disease or condemned its victims.

Civil wars appeared to be successive and cumulative across the course of Roman history. They came not singly but in battalions, and left wounds that would not heal, heirs who demanded vengeance, and divisions that split first the city itself and then the entire Roman empire in the Mediterranean and beyond. These were unforgettable traumas, seared in the memory and likely to recur at any time. A grieving parent who had lived through Sulla's and Marius's civil wars and then suffered through Caesar's and Pompey's contentions forty years later lamented this cycle in Lucan's poem *The Civil War*: "These sufferings await, again to be endured, this will be the sequence / of the warfare, this will be the outcome fixed for civil strife."[12] This was a sequence that looked like it might become a cycle, a repetitious and destructive series of events that closely tracked and decisively informed the pivotal moments in Roman politics.

The Roman narratives of civil war took three broad forms, each of which would inform later understandings of internal violence in the West

and help variously to inspire both revolutionary ideologies and counterrevolutionary ideologues. First, there was what might be called the republican
narrative of seemingly endless and repeated civil wars arising from the very
fabric of Roman civilization itself: to be civilized at all was to be prone to
civil war, and to suffer one civil war opened the way for further destructive
dissensions within the commonwealth: "'Tis in vain to seek a Government
in all points free from a possibility of Civil Wars, Tumults, and Seditions,"
warned the aristocratic English republican Algernon Sidney in the early
1680s: "that is a Blessing denied to this life, and reserved to compleat the
Felicity of the next."[13] Then there was a parallel imperial or Augustan narrative that followed much the same pattern but held that the only cure for
the pathology of civil war would be the restoration of monarchy or the
exaltation of an emperor. "In this way," wrote Appian, "the Roman polity
survived all kinds of civil disturbances to reach unity and monarchy": "an
evident demonstration," agreed his late-sixteenth-century English translator, "That peoples rule must give place, and Princes power prevayle."[14]
And finally there was a Christian narrative, constructed most famously by
Augustine, which presented Rome's pagan history as a catalogue of "those
evils which were more infernal because internal" (*quanto interiora, tanto
miseriora*), a series of "civil, or rather uncivil, discords" (*discordiae civiles vel
potius inciviles*). "How much Roman blood was shed, and how much of
Italy destroyed and devastated," Augustine lamented, "by the Social War,
Servile Wars and Civil Wars!" (*bella socialia, bella servilia, bella civilia*). The
contrast with that peaceable *civitas*, the City of God, could hardly have
been greater.[15]

These narratives of civil war would not, and could not, be forgotten as
long as the Roman historians and poets continued to be read and imitated.
There has been much debate among historians whether books made revolutions in the early modern period, but there can be little doubt that civil
conflicts were good for book sales. The reputations of Roman writers on
civil war closely tracked the prevalence of civil conflict. Between 1450 and
1700, Roman historians greatly outnumbered their Greek predecessors in
the number of editions of their works: five of the top ten were histories
of civil war or by historians of civil war, as Sallust's *Catiline* and *Jugurtha*
were the two most frequently printed texts, with Caesar, Tacitus, and Florus, who portrayed the seven centuries from Romulus to Augustus as a sequence of wars, not far behind. Florus became a mainstay of early modern
school and university curricula: editions of his *Epitome* appeared almost
annually across Europe during the eighteenth century. Through his text

and that of his fellow epitomist, the fourth-century historian Eutropius, many canonical thinkers derived their first immersion in Roman history from Florus: Hobbes knew his work well—it partly inspired his "Epitome" of the English civil wars, *Behemoth* (1679)—and Locke would have read him at Oxford, as Adam Smith later studied Eutropius.[16]

Such synoptic and serial accounts of Rome's civil wars inspired the genre of European historical writing that presented the histories of particular nations or peoples as a narrative of their "revolutions"—meaning their external invasions, succession disputes, and civil wars. Late-seventeenth- and early-eighteenth-century historians such as Laurence Echard, in *The Roman History from the Building of the City to the Perfect Settlement of the Empire by Augustus Cæsar* (1695, and later editions), and the Abbé René Aubert de Vertot, in his *Histoire des révolutions arrivées dans le gouvernment de la république romaine* (1719, and later editions), represented Roman history as a sequence of disruptive "revolutions" by which Rome had moved over the centuries from monarchy to empire via the republic. Vertot capitalized on the success of his Roman revolutionary history with sequels on the histories of revolutions in Portugal and Sweden, and his imitators anatomized revolutions throughout European history and in the wider Eurasian world.[17] Throughout the life-span of this genre, civil wars were included among the roster of revolutions, and revolutions could not be distinguished conceptually from civil wars. "Revolutions" also became the standard European description for violent upheavals in Asia, such as the fall of the Ming dynasty in China in 1644. Only toward the end of the eighteenth century did Europeans cease to call these Asian struggles "revolutions," as they reserved that term for their own political transformations.[18]

Most of these histories of revolutions served absolutist purposes by showing the advantages of monarchy over other regimes.[19] But the republican narrative of civil war also survived to provide a counterpoint to the broadly Augustan account of the unsettling effects of revolutions. In this version of events, monarchy was not the cure for political instability: it was its cause. And civil war, like other manifestations of revolution, might therefore be welcomed as a purge rather than feared as a scourge. As the Commonwealthman noted in the Abbé de Mably's *Des droits et des devoirs du citoyen* (1758), the oppressors of society have a magical ability to persuade their citizens not to disturb the progress of their usurpations and injustices, "and that civil war, for a people still virtuous enough to profit from it, is nonetheless a greater scourge than the tyranny which threatens it." It was the duty of a people—in this case, the French people—to resist such mystifications about both tyranny and civil war and to follow instead the path of constitutional reform and political resistance. Mably's "script for a French revolution" therefore sprang from the Roman tradition of narrating history as a sequence of civil wars. And it did so in dialogue with a British version of that narrative whose roots lay in the Exclusion Crisis of the late seventeenth century. Both would come to inform an early version of the so-called democratic peace argument in the late-eighteenth-century age of revolutions—and civil wars.[20]

The transformation of the ancient story of civil war into a modern script for revolution began with the staunchly monarchist writing of Sir Robert Filmer and proceeded via Algernon Sidney's equally vehement republican refutation of Filmer to the work of the Abbé Mably, Thomas Paine, and Edmund Burke. In order "to manifest the Imperfection of Popular Government," Filmer in his *Patriarcha* (ca. 1628; pub. 1680) had portrayed Rome's "Democratie" as turbulent and short lived: a mere 480 years, from the expulsion of Rome's last king, Tarquinius Superbus, to the rise of Julius Caesar. Conflict between the nobility and people led to seditions; these seditions then spawned a destructive sequence of civil wars: "the *Social* War was plainly Civil; the Wars of the Slaves, and the other of the Fencers; the Civil Wars of *Marius* and *Sylla*, of *Cataline*, of *Caesar* and *Pompey* the *Triumvirate*, of *Augustus*, *Lepidus* and *Antonius*: All these shed an Ocean of Blood within *Italy* and the Streets of *Rome*." These wars continued even while Rome expanded, as its citizens turned their conquering arms upon themselves, until the "Civil Contentions at last settled the Government again into a Monarchy." To prove the necessity of monarchy and the instability of "*Democratical* Government," Filmer turned the republican narrative of civil war on its head in the service of an Augustan account of the benefits of monarchy for securing peace.[21]

Algernon Sidney returned to the Roman republican narrative of civil war—and in particular to Sallust's version of it—to refute Filmer's defense of patriarchal monarchy. He argued that it was not adherence to a republican constitution that had caused Rome's seditions and ultimately its civil wars: it was straying from that constitution and allowing the spoils of empire to foster inequality and to corrupt private life. Sidney also took Filmer to task for his overexpansive application of the term "civil war": "'tis most absurdly applied to the servile and gladiatorian Wars; for the Gladiators were Slaves also, and Civil Wars can be made only by those who are Members of the Civil Society, which Slaves are not. Those that made the *bellum Sociale*, were Freemen, but not Citizens; and the War they made could not be called Civil." When Caesar and Pompey, the members of the triumvirate, and the four emperors who followed Augustus engaged in what were rightly called "civil" wars, their armed contentions could not be used to discredit popular government. The civil conflicts of the republican era were "the last Struglings of expiring Liberty," while those under the empire, and "all the Mischiefs that accompanied them, are to be imputed wholly to the Monarchy for which they [Nero, Galba, Otho, Vitellius, and Vespasian] contended."[22]

This difference between republican and monarchical government was universal in the Latin West, not simply a contingent feature of Roman politics. Sidney argued: "All monarchies are subject to be afflicted with civil wars . . . . But commonwealths are less troubled with those distempers": indeed, as the title of his chapter on the subject had it, "Popular Governments are less subject to Civil Disorders than Monarchies; manage them more ably, and more easily recover out of them." This was in large part because nonmonarchical regimes did not suffer from the destructive disputes over inheritance and the succession that bedeviled monarchies. Sidney showed this distinction by a detailed breakdown of all the violent disturbances across history: in Israel under its kings, in the Persian monarchy, in Rome, France, Spain, and Britain. For example, the succession caused "many Revolutions" in France where, as in Rome, "the end of one Civil War has bin the beginning of another." As if the pages of evidence from the Mediterranean and northern Europe were not enough to convince his readers, Sidney concluded with the litany of civil wars that had scarred England since the Norman Conquest: "the Miseries of *England* on like occasions," he wrote, "surpass all." From the contested succession after the death of William the Conqueror to the troubles of the Tudors, English history appeared to be an almost continuous time of troubles for five centuries.[23] What more could be needed the show that it was monarchy that bred war, and republicanism that brought peace, in the ancient world as in the modern?

The most incendiary use of this argument was Thomas Paine's in *Common Sense* (1776). Writing in Philadelphia in January 1776, Paine sought to shake his colonial readers out of their complacent British monarchism by linking a plea for republican government with his larger argument in favor of independence from Great Britain. He contrasted his own attachment to republicanism with what he called the "most plausible plea, which hath ever been offered in favour of hereditary succession," in a passage that hewed closely to Sidney's arguments from almost a century earlier, not least by recalling the claims of Filmerian patriarchalists. Their justification for monarchy was

> that it preserves a Nation from civil wars; and were this true, it would be weighty; whereas, it is the most barefaced falsity ever imposed upon mankind. The whole history of England disowns the fact. Thirty kings and two minors have reigned in that distracted kingdom since the conquest, in which time there have been (including the [Glorious] Revolution) no less than eight civil wars and nineteen Rebellions. Wherefore instead of making for peace, it makes against it, and destroys the very foundation it seems to stand on. . . . In short, monarchy and succession have laid (not this or that kingdom only) but the world in blood and ashes.[24]

Paine went beyond Sidney—who had been executed in 1683—by adding the Glorious Revolution to the list of England's troubles, and by inference to its roster of civil wars. The years 1688 and 1689 were years of two kings, and thereby no doubt only half as bad as the Year of the Four Emperors chronicled by Tacitus in his *Histories*. Far from being the upheaval that secured the recovery of England's "civil and political liberties" (as Sir William Blackstone had described it), the Glorious Revolution was simply one more example of how a contested succession could lead to national instability, setting citizens against citizens in their quest to affirm their monarchical subjecthood.[25] Most wrenchingly of all, it was part of a narrative of successive civil wars like that traced by Tacitus and other Roman historians. Yet the cure for civil war was not, as the pro-Augustan writers and their heirs asserted, the imposition of monarchy. It was instead what Sidney and his readers, like the Commonwealthman in Mably's *Des droits et des devoirs du citoyen*, had recommended—namely, popular government rather than hereditary succession.

Paine would not be alone in identifying the Glorious Revolution as a civil war. Writing almost fifteen years after him in 1790, Edmund Burke noted acidly that the "ceremony of cashiering kings"

> can rarely, if ever, be performed without force. It then becomes a case of war, and not of constitution. Laws are commanded to hold their tongues against arms, and tribunals fall to the ground with the peace they are no longer able to uphold. The Revolution of 1688 was obtained by a just war, in the only case in which any war, *and much more a civil war*, can be just. *Justa bella quibus necessaria*.[26]

Why did these events constitute a "civil" war? Possibly Burke wrote here as an Irishman rather than an English politician by recalling the conflict between James II and William III on his native soil and its enduring consequences for Ireland. In this light, the Glorious Revolution was "not a revolution, but a conquest; which is not to say a great deal in its favour."[27] Or Burke may have remembered the English side of the Revolution as an invasion by one claimant to the thrones of the Three Kingdoms, backed by force and his English supporters, against another. Either way, he made an essentially Lockean argument for the exceptionality of what had happened in 1688. Dethroning a monarch could not be regulated by law or determined by right: it was a question of armed necessity and hence of war. And because it was fought between members of the same polity, it was by definition civil.

Paine and Burke saw the events of 1688–89 as both a revolution—indeed, as *the* Revolution, the only one up to that point in British and Irish history— and a civil war: a just war, in Burke's case, an unjust war in Paine's. If Paine had been right in 1776, then the Glorious Revolution was the culmination of a series of unsettling contentions over the succession, with 1688 as a year of two kings to parallel the Year of the Four Emperors chronicled by Tacitus in his *Histories*. Yet if Burke was correct in 1790, then the Glorious Revolution was an unrepeatable exception, an extreme example of necessity, and not the inevitable recurrence of an inescapable sequence: it was a civil war that transcended the repetitive compulsions predicted by Roman narratives. Despite these fundamental differences, Paine's and Burke's identifications of the Glorious Revolution as a civil war give the lie to Koselleck's argument that revolution and civil war had separated semantically and conceptually by the end of the eighteenth century. Even in the Age of Revolutions they were not mutually exclusive, even if not entirely interchangeable.

And so, indeed, they remained long after the late eighteenth century.[28] Revolutionaries redescribed what in other circumstances—or by other ideologues—had been called rebellions, insurrections, or civil wars. Indeed, one sure sign of a revolution's success is precisely that retrospective redescription. The renaming can happen relatively quickly: for example, the transatlantic conflict of the 1770s that many contemporaries saw as a British "civil war" or even "the American Civil War" was first called "the American Revolution" in 1776 by the chief justice of South Carolina, William Henry Drayton.[29] The rebranding can also come more slowly, as when the French historian François Guizot became among the first in 1826 to call the mid-seventeenth-century crisis in Britain the "English Revolution," on the grounds that "the analogy of the two revolutions is such that [the English] would never have been understood had not [the French] taken place."[30] As the English poet Sir John Harington *might* have put it in one of his late-sixteenth-century epigrams:

> Civil war doth never prosper: what's the solution?
> For if it prosper, it's called *revolution*.[31]

To recover the modern script of revolution, we need to be alert to the scripts of civil war revolutionaries followed and subsequently attempted to efface or deny. Inspiration for this task comes from some of the greatest theorists of revolution themselves. In *The Communist Manifesto*, Marx and Engels noted: "In depicting the most general phases of the development of the proletariat, we traced the more or less veiled civil war [*den mehr oder minder versteckten Bürgerkrieg*], raging within existing society, up to the point where that war breaks out into open revolution."[32] Similarly, Lenin argued in 1917 that "civil wars . . . in every class society are the natural, and under certain conditions, inevitable continuation, development and intensification of the class struggle. That has been confirmed by every great revolution."[33] Looking back on the Russian Revolution a decade later, Stalin agreed: "the seizure of power by the proletariat in 1917 was a form of civil war."[34] There is now considerable evidence in the literature on revolutions that civil war was an actors' category, as well as a revealing analytical optic for evaluating the causes, course, and consequences of such events as the American, French, and Spanish American "revolutions."[35] In light of this, when tracing the genealogy of the modern script of revolution, we should seriously consider the hypothesis that civil war was the original genus of which revolution was only a late-evolving species.[36]

PART II

Writing the Modern Revolutionary Script

Revolutionizing Revolution

I argue in this chapter that revolution was revolutionized in 1789 as the notion of revolution as fact gave way to a conceptualization of revolution as ongoing act. With this transformation, "revolution" assumed its modern political meaning and the French Revolution became the script upon which subsequent revolutionaries improvised. To state the case bluntly, there were no "revolutionaries" before the Bastille fell.

Much of the information that follows in support of this claim comes from digital searches showing the relative frequencies of co-occurrences of terms at particular periods or in specific works. To the extent that the relevant databases remain incomplete or rely on uncorrected optical character recognition (OCR), and as search capabilities are still work in progress, the analysis stands open to revision. Collocation searches yield aggregate data that can naturally miss the subtleties of individual works and arguments, though they can be supplemented (as they have been here) by closer attention to specific texts. They nonetheless provide some fascinating and revealing information relating in this case to the conceptualization of revolution in the century that separated the Glorious Revolution from the French Revolution.

Glorious Revolution

The Glorious Revolution of 1688 offers an instructive case for this research precisely because its participants and observers had no clear conceptualization of "revolution" as a collective political act. "Revolution" did not offer a script for action, nor did it provide a source of authority or legitimation. This seems clear in light of the evidence available from Early English Books Online (EEBO), the database of English books published between 1473 and 1700. That database contains 4,263 occurrences of "revolution" among 1,534 works published between 1640 and 1700; it also contains 2,932 occurrences of "revolutions" among 1,225 works published during the same period.[1] As one would expect from the term's Latin etymology, occurrences of "revolution" in this database signified any kind of rotation: the turning of wheels and circles, the rotation of heavenly bodies, of days, weeks or years, of times and epochs. By extension, they could also connote any significant turn in human affairs, whether slow or rapid, orderly or disorderly, favorable or unfavorable. Contemporary usage thus went far beyond the lagging and parsimonious definition of "revolution" in Edward Phillips, *The World of Words, or A General English Dictionary* (London, 1678): "A rowling back, the turning back of Celestial bodies to their first point, and finishing their circular course." "Revolution" did not, pace Hannah Arendt, necessarily imply a return to an original state or position, as in the astronomical sense.[2]

"Revolutions" in the plural could have a similarly broad range of connotations. But the plural usage was frequently negative, suggesting disruptions, upheavals and disorders, turns of fortune, vicissitudes of many kinds that the movement of time could bring. In this aleatory sense, "revolutions" could be tellingly paired with "confusions," especially in the uncertain 1640s and 1650s. Anthony Ascham's *A Discourse: Wherein is examined, What is particularly lawfull during the Confusions and Revolutions of Government* offered an interesting use of this term when it was published in 1648. His work asked, in effect, whether it was right to submit to whichever side exercised power during the vicissitudes of a civil war. It was republished in 1649 under a slightly different title, *Of the Confusions and Revolutions of Governments.* More remarkably, it reappeared forty years later as *A Seasonable Discourse, Wherein is examined What is Lawful during the Confusions and Revolutions of Government; Especially in the Case of a King deserting his Kingdoms: And how far a Man may lawfully conform to the Powers and Commands of those, who with Various Successes hold Kingdoms.* The 1689 title offers explicit acknowledgment of the touchy question of the role of conquest, rather than consent, in settling the political confusions of 1688 and 1689.[3] But whoever adjusted the title apparently saw no need to recalibrate the republished text to a new situation. The work continued to advocate acceptance rather than celebration. Revolution was not yet made "glorious" in its pages.

With this prevailing sense of "revolution" in mind, we might better understand its use in that other work scrolled up from the past to justify the events of 1688, Locke's *Second Treatise*. Following the common practice, Locke also used the term in the plural and to describe intermittent periods of change and disorder. Answering pre-emptively the argument that his justification of resistance would make it impossible for any government to last for long, he reasoned that the people were too set in their old ways for this fear to become a reality.

> People are not so easily got out of their old Forms, as some are apt to suggest. They are hardly to be prevailed with to amend the acknowledg'd Faults, in the Frame they have been accustom'd to . . . . This slowness and aversion in the People to quit their old Constitutions, has, in the many Revolutions which have been seen in this Kingdom, in this and former Ages, still kept us to, or, after some interval of fruitless attempts, still brought us back to our old Legislative of King, Lords and Commons.[4]

Revolutions occur, Locke acknowledged, but accepting that the frame of government rested on the consent of the governed did not make them more likely. Peoples made miserable by their governments had sought throughout history to throw off their burden when the opportunity to do so was offered by the "change, weakness, and accidents of humane affairs." Nonetheless, "such Revolutions happen not upon every little mismanagement in public affairs." Much could be borne by the people "without mutiny or murmur." This reasoning led, of course, to one of the most famous assertions of the *Second Treatise*, echoed later in the American Declaration of Independence. "But if a long train of Abuses, Prevarications, and Artifices, all tending the same way, make the design visible to the People, and they cannot but feel, what they lie under, and see, whither they are going; 'tis not to be wonder'd, that they should then rouze themselves, and endeavor to put the rule into such hands, which may secure to them the ends for which government was at first erected."[5]

These celebrated lines have often been used to make Locke appear as a theorist of revolution. Read closely, though, they seem to do rather less than that. Like his contemporaries, Locke thought of revolutions as dramatic historical changes or as periods of disturbance and disorder. He thought that such ruptures could indeed happen in the realm of politics. He thought too that they could and would, though rarely, be brought about by political resistance or popular insurrection. But he saw political change, no matter how precipitated, only as an instance of a much broader category: that of revolutions in the general sense of changes and disorders occurring in the flow of human time. Such changes might result from political resistance or popular rebellion, Locke reasoned, but were not necessarily defined in relation to them. Locke wanted to save the doctrine of resistance from association with the endless instability of constant "revolutions."

The events of 1688, nonetheless, did soon become the "Glorious Revolution." But they were not the first to do so. Ironically, an "ever-glorious and wonderful Revolution" had been celebrated in a sermon of 1676 calling upon the faithful to praise God "with joyful, and thankful hearts" for the "happy Restauration" of Charles II.[6] The "secret passages and particularities" of this same "Glorious Revolution" had been further explained in a book by one John Price in 1680.[7] Only after another remarkable turn of events in 1688 did the phrase meet its historical destiny. In 1690, as in many previous years, a sermon was preached before the House of Commons on 5 November to celebrate the frustration of the Gunpowder Plot in 1605. But William of Orange had cannily timed his 1688 landing in England to coincide with the anniversary of this earlier day of national deliverance from popery.[8] The 1690 sermon, accordingly, served double duty: it became *A Sermon preached before the honorable House of Commons at St. Margaret's Westminster on Wednesday the Fifth November, 1690 being the Anniversary Thanksgiving for the Happy Deliverance of King James the First, and Three Estates of the Realm, from the Gunpowder-treason: and also for the Happy Arrival of His Present Majesty on this day, for the Deliverance of our Church and Nation from Popery and Arbitrary Power.*

Delivered by a chaplain to William and Mary, the new sovereigns, this sermon offers a notable early use of "Glorious Revolution" to characterize the events of 1688, and it is remarkable for the way it outlines what became the canonical view. As such it is worth quoting at some length:

> No less visible was the Sword of the Lord, than the Sword of Gideon, in our late happy Happy [*sic*] and Glorious Revolution; when we consider with what an invincible Spirit of Wisdom and Courage his Majesty undertook the Cause of our Country; what general Desires and Inclinations were on the sudden kindled in Mens Hearts towards Him, their Laws, and their Religion; What a burning Zeal and Vigour, what an universal Harmony of Affections, what a perfect agreement of Councils and Endeavours inflamed the Breasts of all Men; What a strange Folly and Infatuation blinded the Councils of our Enemies; what guilty Fears and Cowardise seiz'd their Spirits; How all was brought about by a dry Victory, without the expence of the Blood either of our Friends or Enemies; We must conclude, That God was with him of a truth, and that it was he that made it to prosper.[9]

We know that the nature and outcome of the Dutch invasion of 1688 were still being contested in 1690 and years following. Matters were still far from settled. Disagreement remained as to whether James II had deserted or abdicated, whether he had been overthrown by the people for a breach of trust or contract, whether William and Mary had come to the throne by invitation, or by right of succession, or merely by force of arms. Seen in that context, the rhetorical force of this characterization of the "Glorious Revolution" becomes all the more powerful. The phrase served to portray a great shift in political fortune, but one that was emphatically over, one that had quickly become the "late" Revolution. It described "revolution" without "confusion," a change that was held to be providential, a bloodless transition ordered and stabilized by God rather than by the power of the sword. It asserted a transformation that was all the more decisive for being "happy" and "glorious." Those who celebrated the outcome of 1688 in this way wanted to make it a shift big enough to hold firm, one that would end the instabilities and uncertainties that had threatened British political life for much of a century. The rhetoric of the "late, glorious Revolution" served this purpose. Singularized, capitalized, and glorified, this late, great revolution was not just one in an endless series of ruptures time would bring. The "Glorious Revolution" meant an end to "revolutions and confusions." It meant closure. This way of celebrating it continued throughout the eighteenth century, passing eventually into historiographical convention.

To celebrate the "Glorious Revolution" as a revolution without confusion was also to declare it a revolution without rebellion. Its initial characterization as providential made it possible to acclaim the changes effected in 1688 in a way that avoided acknowledgment of any act of rebellion or endorsement of a right of resistance arising from an original contract of government. But it could also be praised or denounced, ex post facto, in more radical terms. The extent to which the events of 1688 could indeed be vindicated as a justifiable (and possibly repeatable) assertion of the collective will of the people in the face of despotism lay at the heart of the intense political maneuvering between Whigs and Tories over the course of the next two decades. The struggle to define "Revolution Principles" remained unresolved. The "Glorious Revolution," in the meantime, could be accepted as an accomplished fact without any clear agreement regarding the precise nature and implications of what had actually happened in 1688.[10]

If the "Glorious Revolution" inflected English usage of "revolution," then, it did not radically transform that usage. In the prevailing understanding, "revolutions" still occurred, they were not made; a "revolution" was still recalled, apprehended, experienced, or anticipated as a fact rather than imagined, undertaken, or projected as an act. Evidence drawn from ECCO (Eighteenth Century Collections Online), the database of works published in Britain during that period, shows that this set of meanings remained common in English for much of the eighteenth century. Although it is not yet possible to search the terms that co-occur with "revolution" or "revolutions" throughout the entire ECCO database, a collocation analysis of this kind can be generated from a smaller but more thoroughly searchable sample in ECCO-TCP, available on line at ARTFL (American and French Research on the Treasury of the French Language, a project of the University of Chicago).[11] Figures 1a and 2a show "word clouds" illustrating co-occurrences with "revolution" from 1700 to 1785 (those dates chosen, for reasons that will soon become clear, to avoid semantic effects of the French Revolution); figures 1b and 2b show tables of the ten most frequent co-occurrences during the same period.[12] In the most common usages in the singular, "revolution" is preceded by "late," "sudden," "happy," "new," "strange," "total," "glorious," "grand," "extraordinary," or "general." These descriptions form a counterpoint to the more threatening "revolutions" accompanied by "various," "changes," "wars," "history," "frequent," "state," "several," "motions," "violent," and "sudden."

In this semantic field revolution was a fact but not yet a collective act; there were revolutions but no revolutionaries. A search of the entire ECCO database uncovers no political usage of "revolutionary" in English before the 1790s, when the term begins to show up first in translations from the French and then more generally in reference to French developments. Before that date, "revolutionary" was used most frequently in English to refer to a cyclical motion of some kind (for example, "the sublime revolutionary scheme of heaven," 1777), occasionally to characterize something or someone changeable, and a couple of times to designate the principles of the constitutional settlement of 1689. Strikingly, the American rebels do not appear in this database as "revolutionaries." Nor are they described as such in works comprising the database of Early American Imprints. No occurrence of the term "revolutionary" shows up between 1770 and 1790 in Evans TCP, the more searchable (though significantly smaller) version of the Evans Early American Imprint Collection. (There is, though, a lone instance of "revolutional").[13]

If there appear to be no "revolutionaries" in English before the 1790s, however, there were indeed "revolutionists." This designation was first used in the early decades of the eighteenth century, not to describe the political

about account affirmed agreed ah alone along among annual another anti
auspicious because began blessed bloodless both brings brought called cannot
chaque charters chosroes church clemency clesiastical colonels coming commenced
confirmed considerable constant converted declared demand depended deposed determined
did diurnal dreadful during e ecclesiastical eighth either engagement etant
extraordinary famous fared fatal favorable favourable five foregoing fourth fre
future gagne general glorious grand greater grinling gular happen
happened happening happens happy hath having heart hibernian however iii
immediate important incline incredible interest internal intire itself joined k la lasted
late laurens lowering marvellous means memorable might mighty miraculous nary
national neither new next nor obliterated oldworth once ordinary p page patriotism
pected periodic periodical perpetual political portant possible power present
priestess princi principle principles principles—yet private produced professed projected
proper put re reckoning render round salutary saxon scots second secret seem seemed
seems settlement shou' si side signal signed since singular slow sometimes spicious stale
stanch stand still strange strangest sublunar successive sudden surprising takes
taking temporary tenth theatrical therefore things third though thought till tional total
transferred traordinary udden unaccountable under unexpected unhappy universal until
upwards visible went whole women wonderful wondrous worthies xi yearly
years —endeavours —their

	Within 1 Words on Either Side	Within 1 Words to Left only	Within 1 Words to Right only
1	late (43)	late (43)	principles (9)
2	sudden (17)	sudden (17)	might (7)
3	strange (13)	happy (12)	under (6)
4	happy (12)	new (11)	round (5)
5	new (11)	strange (10)	happened (5)
6	total (9)	total (9)	put (4)
7	principles (9)	glorious (9)	itself (4)
8	glorious (9)	grand (7)	strange (3)
9	might (7)	extraordinary (7)	nor (3)
10	grand (7)	general (5)	however (3)

FIGS. 1a and 1b (table). "Revolution" in the ECCO-TCP database 1700–1785.
Co-occurrences within space of one word. 1716 documents; 1263 occurrences.
(Corpus as of 8/2012)

abortions about abraham according africa al amazing among annual annually attend attends
battles because bengal bloodshed brought C came cannot cent certain cessant changes circular
common conspiracies constant continual corinth create crediting croud daily dangerous dated
delicate den des different dinary dire distant diurnal does domestic dreadful during elder
emigrations endless entire eternal ev' even exact expected external
extraordinary factions famous fatal few fewer fortunate frequent
future gained general give got gradual gratianus greater greatest happiest hath
however human hundred illegib important influences introduced inveterate josephus
lar last late les less lost memorable might mighty miserable momentary motions natural
naturally new numerous occa ordinary overturned p page particular perhaps periodic periodical
perpetual perplexed pestilence pestilences peter place portant positions present principal prising
produce produced progress proportioned public publick qui rable ral rate rebellion relate
religion repeated revolts rious round seem sequent several shining signal similar since sing
singular solemn speedy stated strange striking stupendous subsequent suc
successes successive sudden surprising taxes tend theatric theatrical think though through
ticular till trange transfer' traordinary true tumults twelve under unexpected unforeseen urnal v
various veral vid violent whimsical whose win wonderful wou' yes zing
— —the

	Within 1 Words on Either Side	Within 1 Words to Left only	Within 1 Words to Right only
1	various (12)	various (12)	however (4)
2	frequent (7)	frequent (7)	till (3)
3	several (6)	several (6)	c (3)
4	violent (5)	violent (5)	according (3)
5	important (5)	important (5)	round (2)
6	extraordinary (5)	extraordinary (5)	qui (2)
7	sudden (4)	sudden (4)	less (2)
8	strange (4)	strange (4)	even (2)
9	however (4)	subsequent (3)	does (2)
10	till (3)	singular (3)	—the (1)

FIGS. 2a and 2b. "Revolutions" in the ECCO-TCP database 1700–1785. Co-occurrences within space of one word. 1716 documents; 530 occurrences. (Corpus as of 8/2012) actors who had brought about the Glorious Revolution but to characterize those who subsequently upheld its principles against the Jacobite backlash. Rachum also cites the appearance, in Nathan Bailey's *Dictionarium Britannicum* of 1730, of "Revolutioners, those who approved of the great Turn of Affairs, after the Abdication of King James."[14] Like these "revolutioners," the "revolutionists" wanted the Revolution to remain closed; they defended the Glorious Revolution as an accomplished fact against those "anti-revolutionists" (the Jacobites) who would reopen or overthrow it, or against those who would place it at risk by pushing for extreme measures in its support.[15] The term still had this connotation of commitment to the principles of 1688 when it was taken up by Wilkes and his supporters in the 1760s. It was, though, also beginning to convey something beyond resolute acceptance and support of those principles. Usages from the 1770s and 1780s do suggest a tendency toward activation of the meaning of "revolutionist" to describe persons implementing or pressing for political change.[16]

It is tempting to think that this tendency might be linked to the events unfolding in America during these same decades. But there seems to be no direct semantic link. Early American Imprints TCP throws up only two usages of "revolutionist" there before 1790, both referring simply to persons who held true to the principles of the Glorious Revolution. In fact, well into the 1770s, Americans on either side of their political conflict continued, as did their English cousins, to appeal for justification to "The Revolution," by which they meant the constitutional settlement of 1688. Only gradually did loyalists begin to denounce their opponents for "proposing" or "projecting" a new revolution, or as determined to persist "till a complete political revolution is effected."[17] In rejoinder came talk of the need for "another glorious and necessary revolution."[18]

There also came a bold effort to rewrite Locke, and to radicalize the meaning of the Glorious Revolution, in *An Essay upon Government. Adopted by the Americans: Wherein the Lawfulness of Revolutions, are demonstrated in a Chain of Consequences from the Fundamental Principles of Society*. This pamphlet is particularly intriguing in the way it purports to be a contemporary justification of the Revolution of 1688 that "gives us a Right Notion of Revolutions in Government, and as it shews us how far Revolutions may be Lawful, so it teaches us how they are to be regularly managed."[19] In effect, it appears closer than any other American work of the time to redefining "revolution" as an action (an act of legitimate resistance) rather than an outcome.

Nonetheless, this semantic opening was quickly closed; revolution soon became again a fait accompli, a fact rather than a project. *American Independence Vindicated,* a sermon explaining the Declaration of Independence, was by September 1776 announcing that "since this mighty revolution has taken place in America, there must of necessity be a change in our modes of government."[20] Within a year, *The Genuine Principles of the Ancient Saxon or English Constitution* could speak of the "events which have given birth to this mighty revolution"; and Benjamin Rush, in his *Observations upon the Present Government of Pennsylvania,* could remark on "the suddenness of the late revolution."[21] By 1778, *An Oration on the Advantages of American Independence* would contemplate the "fruits of our glorious revolution"; and Paine, in *The American Crisis, no. V,* could celebrate "the most virtuous and illustrious revolution that ever graced the history of mankind."[22] In America, "The Revolution" now no longer referred to the change of affairs that had occurred in 1688, but it retained its retrospective character. It meant a great change that had occurred, the "American Revolution" now explained to the world by Congress in its *Observations on the American Revolution* (1779).[23] It meant the political transformation celebrated in 1782, in *A Memorial of Lexington Battle, and of Some Signal Interpositions of Providence in the American Revolution,* as "the glorious American Revolution which, in the course of nature, and by the will of Heaven, has opened in our day."[24]

It thus seems to be a remarkable aspect of the American Revolution that "revolution" went so rapidly in early American imprints from connoting a change that was anticipated to one that had already occurred. Semantically, it was "the late Revolution" almost as soon as it was "the present Revolution"; in this, 1776 remained very similar to 1688. "Revolution" continued to connote dramatic change, but change as an effect far more than change as a process, change as an established fact far more than change as a continuing collective act. Only with the French Revolution did the term come to designate a domain of ongoing struggle, a space of action expanding toward an indefinite political horizon, a moment of rupture constantly extended and energized by the urgency of a new conception of time.

Rethinking Revolution

In French as in English, at least from the mid-seventeenth century onward, *révolution* was commonly invoked to refer to vicissitudes of fortune, to mutations in human affairs, to instabilities and disorders within the flow of human time. The presence of this usage, alongside the astronomical metaphor, is abundant in the French dictionaries of the period. From 1680 on, Pierre Richelet's dictionary gave a succinct definition: "Revolution. Trouble, disorder and change," omitting the astronomical definition completely. Antoine Furetière supplemented the astronomical definition by adding "'revolution,' also used of extraordinary changes that occur in the world." The 1694 dictionary of the French Academy followed suit with *révolution* in this sense defined as "vicissitude, great change in fortune, in the things of this world," suggesting "great, prompt, sudden, unexpected, strange, marvelous, astonishing" as appropriate adjectives. Some twenty years later, in 1717, the academy offered a more specifically political dimension to its definition, adding "change which occurs in public affairs, in the things of this world." This specification was carried further by the *Encyclopédie* of Diderot and d'Alembert: "Revolution . . . in political terms, signifies a considerable change in the government of a state." In the meantime, the Jesuits' deeply conservative *Dictionnaire de Trévoux* continued to emphasize the negative connotations of the term by recording its use to describe "extraordinary changes that occur in the world: disgraces, misfortunes, collapses."[25]

This same pattern of meanings is echoed in collocation analyses generated from the ARTFL database. They show "great" to be the word used most frequently to characterize *révolution* between 1650 and 1787. Next came "happy," though it should be noted that almost all of these occurrences appeared after 1750 and referred to psychological rather than political changes (a warning of the dangers of accepting aggregate data too uncritically).[26] Other favored terms were "sudden (*subite*)," "new," "strange," "general," "sudden (*soudaine*)," and "latest" (see Figures 3a and 3b). This pattern was largely repeated (though without "happy") in occurrences of *révolutions* that were "great" most often but also commonly "different," "occurred," "frequent," "sudden," "terrible," "new," "diverse," and "continual" (see Figures 4a and 4b). Whether plural or singular, *révolution* in the prevailing eighteenth-century sense was an ex post facto category of historical understanding. It was the name for something that happened, often abruptly and without the conscious choice of human actors; it was not a script for political or social action. Revolutions occurred, they could perhaps be anticipated, but they were viewed from the outside rather than the inside, observed as a past or experienced passively as a present. [27] Even as late as 1798, the dictionary of the French Academy harked back to this tradition by observing that "one says, the Roman revolutions, the revolutions of Sweden, the revolutions of England for the memorable and violent changes which have agitated these countries."[28]

« acquaviva affreuse afin agréable ait alors amène annuelle antipater apparente apportera arriva arrivât arrivée assez aucune auquel autour avantageuse avoit beaucoup bientôt brusque capable certaine chapitre chaque chasse chez combien comment commença composée considerée c'est dangereuse depuis derniere dernière derniére desirable deviennent devoit dites diurne doit domestique double douloureuse douze durable dut décisive développement d'angleterre d'environ d'une effrayante empêcha enfin entiere entière entiére entraîna extraordinaire eût fabrice faisoit fameuse fatale favorable focs forte française françoise funeste furent furieuse future gisler glorieuse grande générale henri heures heureuse hélas imaginaire importante imprévue incroyable inouie insensible intérieure inévitable joignez journaliere journalière lorsqu' lorsque louis lucile lunaire légére malheureuse met moindre morale musicale naissante notre nouvelle nulle nécessaire opérée ordinaire outre oëcette parce pareille parmi paroîtroit particulière passagère periculosa perpétuelle petite physique pitoyable politique porte pouvoit première presque probable prochaine prodigieuse prompte prédite présente prétendue puisqu'il périodique quelconque quelle quelques ramene ramenera rapide remarquez remet rendent renversa révolution salutaire sanglante seconde semblable sensible sera serait seul seule signifie simple singulière soit solaire soudaine sourde subite supposé surnaturelle sérieuse sûre s'il t' tacite tantôt telle tels terrible tibère totale trop universelle venait venoit vient voilà vraie whig xi éclatante éternelle étoit étonnante étrange ô

	Within 1 Words on Either Side	Within 1 Words to Left only	Within 1 Words to Right only
1	grande (67)	grande (67)	subite (24)
2	heureuse (30)	heureuse (28)	générale (14)
3	subite (25)	quelle (20)	soudaine (9)
4	quelle (21)	nouvelle (16)	arrivée (9)
5	nouvelle (16)	étrange (15)	prochaine (8)
6	étrange (15)	dernière (10)	autour (5)
7	générale (14)	aucune (10)	universelle (4)
8	d'une (13)	d'une (9)	journalière (4)
9	soudaine (12)	telle (6)	extraordinaire (4)
10	dernière (10)	fameuse (5)	d'une (4)

FIGS. 3a and 3b. "Révolution" in the ARTFL database 1650–1787. Co-occurrences within space of one word. 1005 documents; 120 occurrences. (Corpus as of 8/2012)

admirables affreuses aigris ait amenées amortirent analogues **anciennes**
antérieures apparentes appuyée aristobule arrivent **arriveront** arrivoient
arrivées assez astronomiques ausquelles **autour** auxquelles avant
avantageuses avançoit avoient ayant beaucoup belles bretagne cachées capricieuses carthage
causes causées celles **cent** certaines chacun **chaque** chose **cinq** comment communes
continuelles contraires correspondantes cruelles célestes césar **c'est**
dangereuses demi depuis **dernières** derniéres differentes
différentes dis dissolvent **diverses** diversités doivent
domestiques douze dès déjà désastreuses dévasté d'angleterre d'autres effroyables
enfin entières eussent **extraordinaires fameuses fatales** faute favorables
florissante font fortes frappantes **fréquentes funestes furent** futures
galantes grammaticales **grandes** générales **heureuses** histoire
humaines immuables imprévues inespérées infiniment injustes **innombrables** inopinées
intéressantes **inévitables** journalières jupiter lisette locales longues lorsqu' l'esprit
mahmoud maintes **mille** monastiques **monsieur** morales multipliées **mêmes**
nouvelles nul néanmoins occupés paralléles paraît **pareilles** parmi paroît
particulières **passées** pepin perdicas **perpétuelles** perpétuoit petites peuvent
physiques plusieurs politiques populaires pouvoit **presque** principales
prodigieuses produisent puissent **périodiques** quarante **quelles** quelques
qu'éprouva rapides reglées **remarque** respectives **romaines** rosbac ruinent
ruineuses répartit saintes salutaires **sanglantes** sanguinaires secretes **semblables**
serait seront singuliéres **solaires subites** successives suivant suivra supposez
surprenantes survenues survenuës sûres tantôt telles **terribles** chamas totales
tristes **trois** trop tumultueuses venues versatiles **violentes** vives **voici** voyez égales
énormes épouvantables éternelles étoient étonnantes **étranges**

		Within I Words on Either Side	Within I Words to Left only	Within I Words to Right only
I		grandes (59)	grandes (59)	arrivées (16)
2		différentes (16)	différentes (15)	subites (11)
3		arrivées (16)	nouvelles (10)	périodiques (8)
4		fréquentes (12)	mêmes (9)	continuelles (8)
5		subites (11)	mille (9)	physiques (6)
6		terribles (10)	fréquentes (8)	terribles (5)
7		nouvelles (10)	diverses (8)	solaires (4)
8		mêmes (10)	étranges (7)	sanglantes (4)
9		diverses (10)	terribles (5)	passées (4)
10		continuelles (10)	plusieurs (5)	furent (4)

FIGS. 4a and 4b. "Révolutions" in the ARTFL database 1650–1787. Co-occurrences within space of one word. 1005 documents; 995 occurrences. (Corpus as of 8/2012)

Much changed from 1789, however, as the moment of revolution was opened up and extended from within to become a domain of lived experience with its own dynamic and its own chronology. No longer viewed solely from without or through the lens of historical hindsight, *révolution* emerged as an immediate present in a frame of action opening up to the future. *Révolution* became the name for a collective political act ushering in the birth of a new world. It is difficult not to see the role of the Enlightenment in creating conditions of possibility for this shift. If we look at usages of "*révolution*" in the *Encyclopédie* overall, we see—here as in other respects—the heavy weight of the past. The semantic field of *révolution* in the entire work does not differ significantly from that in ARTFL as a whole. D'Alembert himself resorted to a conventional use in expressing the hope that the *Encyclopédie* would grow into a sanctuary that would safeguard human knowledge from the ravages of "time and revolutions." But he also celebrated the Renaissance in terms that gave *révolution* a more beneficent gloss: "to escape barbarism, the human race needed one of those revolutions that give the universe a different face."[29] Diderot's article describing the nature and purposes of the work they had edited hints further at a change that might be underway.

In this article defining its entire philosophical project, the *Encyclopédie* looks forward to its own superannuation in consequence of "the revolution that will occur in the minds of men and the national character" as the result of the advance of reason. Because human knowledge is limited, Diderot argued, it can and must progress. It follows that "revolutions are necessary; there have always been revolutions, and there always will be."[30] From this philosophical perspective, revolutions cease to be mere vicissitudes; they provide the mechanism of change for the indefinite transformation of knowledge—and thereby of society.

Diderot's definition of an encyclopedia points to a revalorization of change, and of "revolution" as its manifestation, that lay at the heart of the Enlightenment. Proponents of absolute monarchy and classical republicanism shared a common conviction that disorder and vicissitude (the natural state of human existence, deriving from the unstable play of the passions) were a dangerous state to be contained only by the imposition of order— either through the authority of an absolute monarch or by the inculcation of that civic virtue by which individual interests were artificially identified with the common good. Enlightenment thinkers, by contrast, began to offer a competing vision of human existence as grounded in the progressive order of society—society now increasingly imagined as at once the creation and the frame of human activity, as an autonomous entity endowed with a mechanism producing stability through the very process of constant transformation.

Society understood in this way had to have a history and a logic far different from the endless vicissitudes of historical time implied in the conventional use of the term "revolution." Against the traditional succession of revolutions introducing abrupt changes or political disruptions, usually negative in their effects, Enlightenment philosophy therefore set other revolutions taking form as longer-term social and cultural transformations, at once more profound and more beneficent. Moreover, to the extent that Enlightenment historiography took as its object world history—the history of human civilization as a whole—the revolutions it identified as dynamic processes of transformation had universal implications. They were not merely local events but phenomena of world-historical significance. Fundamental to the mechanism of human progress, they were "wheels in the machine of the universe," to quote Voltaire's remarkable phrase.[31] The philosophical manifesto Condorcet offered the French Academy in his reception speech of 1782 assured contemporaries that they could "expect everything from time, the infallible effect of which is to bring happy revolutions and great discoveries." A note for a revised edition set this view of social change against the (classical republican) notion "that the human race can only hope to achieve happiness by violent revolution in a country where it is oppressed, that societies tend to corruption unless legislation gives men that restless love of liberty which excites factionalism and quarrels and divides them into mutually suspicious parties, and that a peace which is not a shameful servitude, a true political death, can only subsist as the result of equilibrium between contrary efforts, each tending to break it." The first conception, Condorcet insisted, would lead to progress through the indefinite advance of enlightenment; the second would result in "disorder or general discouragement."[32]

Thus, in the idiom of Enlightenment, "revolutions" as the disorder of events in the flow of human time, expression of the instability of all things human, began to give way to "revolutions" as expressions of the dynamic transformational process advancing the progress of the human mind and of society. "Everything I see is sowing the seeds of a revolution that is bound to occur and that I shall not have the pleasure to witness," Voltaire rejoiced in 1764. "Enlightenment is being spread to such a point that at the first chance there will be a great outburst, and then there will be a fine to-do. Our young people are very fortunate, they will see great things."[33] The philosophes not only expanded the concept of revolution to universal significance; they began to shift the chronological inflection of the term. Extended as process, revolution constituted a domain of lived experience and offered a new horizon of expectation. Seen in this light, events in France, too, began to take on a new coloring. "The revolution is being prepared, the happy epoch is already being announced when the august monarch who governs France is going to recognize all his subjects as his children," proclaimed the Huguenot leader Rabaut Saint-Etienne in 1779 as he contemplated the possibility of a reform granting civil rights to Protestants.[34] When, a decade later, the editor of the section of the *Encyclopédie méthodique* devoted to local government, Jacques Peuchet, declared that "the good old times is a chimera and the rallying cry for ignorance and imbecility," he expressed a mood increasingly pervasive in the last years of an enlightened, reforming monarchy. These years saw a cascade of proposals for legal, fiscal, and constitutional reforms. Each was celebrated as offering another "happy revolution." Discussing the provincial assemblies introduced in France by Loménie de Brienne in 1787, Peuchet cast this change as the fruit of the intellectual progress that had brought Europe to its "present state of civility and enlightenment."[35] His work epitomized the belief in human progress as a succession of beneficent revolutions in the human mind culminating in the universal transformation of civil society that was the Enlightenment. The mood of the *cahiers de doléances* submitted to Louis XVI by his subjects in 1789 is revealing here. They made "happy" by far the most frequent term to qualify "revolution," the change of affairs for which they hoped (see Figure 5).

In Enlightenment discourse, then, the notion of "revolution" was being universalized and reoriented from past to future, taking on an entirely new set of meanings as it came to designate a process of transformation within modern society.[36] It goes without saying, though, that the Enlightenment conception of society had its eighteenth-century critics; nor is it surprising that in indicting society these critics also gave "revolution" a rather different valence.

accepter annuelle arrêter aussi certaine cornp désastreuse

extraordinaire française glorieuse grande **heureuse**

longue notre nous opérée prompte préparée salutaire sauf seconde subite survenue ta tandis troisième voua également

FIG. 5. "Révolution" in the *Cahiers de doléances* 1789. Archives parlementaires ARTFL (uncorrected OCR). Co-occurrences within space of one word. 114 occurrences. (Corpus as of 8/2012)

The critical tone was sounded by that great Enlightenment heretic, Jean-Jacques Rousseau. "You trust in the present order of society without imagining that this order is subject to inevitable revolutions, and that it is impossible for you to foresee or prevent the one that can affect your children," he wrote in a celebrated passage of *Emile*. "The great become small, the rich become poor, the monarch becomes subject: are the blows of fortune so rare that you can count yourself as exempt from them? We are approaching the state of crisis and the century of revolutions? Who can tell you what you will become then? All that men have made, men can destroy."[37] The classical republican themes in this passage are readily recognizable. But there was a new prophetic note in Rousseau's warning. Revolution as extended crisis—a "century of revolutions"—here became the negative image of the philosophes' conception of revolution as extended transformational process.

This negative prognosis was taken up nowhere more vociferously than in Linguet's *Annales politiques*, perhaps the most compelling French-language journal of the entire prerevolutionary period. Linguet's vision of the "singular revolution threatening Europe" turned the Enlightenment theory of the progress of civil society on its head. While others were celebrating the emergence of modern commercial society from the collapse of feudalism, he lamented its exploitation of the masses. He saw only two possibilities. Either the oppressed, contained by military force, would expire in silent misery, destroying European prosperity through inanition. Or they would throw up "some new Spartacus, emboldened by despair, enlightened by necessity, calling his comrades in misery to a true liberty through the destruction of the murderous and deceitful laws that make it misunderstood."[38]

The idea of a new Spartacus was scarcely a fresh thought. Raynal's *Histoire philosophique et politique des établissements et du commerce des Européens dans les deux Indes,* in its 1774 version, conjured up a nightmare scenario of massive slave revolt that might ensue if the sovereigns of the earth failed to begin the abolition of African enslavement in the New World. The enslaved, it warned, lacked only "a leader courageous enough to lead them to vengeance and slaughter."

> Where is he, this great man whom nature owes perhaps to the honor of the human species? Where is he, this new Spartacus who will not find a Crassus? Then will the black code be no more; and how frightful will be the white code if the conqueror considers only the right of reprisal.
>
> Until this revolution takes place the Blacks groan under the yoke of their labor, description of which cannot fail to interest us increasingly in their fate.[39]

This language was alarming enough. But a few years later, in the 1780 revision of the *Histoire philosophique et politique,* the warning of impending insurrection had become sharper and even more terrifying. The passage in its revised form demands quotation in full, even at the risk of some repetition.

> Where is he, this great man whom nature owes its afflicted, oppressed, tormented children? Where is he? He will appear without a doubt, he will reveal himself, he will raise the sacred standard of liberty. This venerable signal will gather around him the companions of his misfortune. More violent than a torrent, they will leave everywhere behind them indelible traces of their righteous resentment. Spaniards, Portuguese, English, French, Dutch, all their tyrants will fall victim to fire and sword. The plains of America will drink in exaltation the blood they have long awaited, and the bones of so many wretches, heaped together for three centuries, will leap for joy. The Old World will join in applause with the New. The name of the hero who has restored the rights of humanity will everywhere be blessed; everywhere monuments will be raised to his glory. Then will the black code be no more: and how frightful will be the white code if the conqueror considers only the right of reprisal.
>
> Until this revolution takes place the Blacks groan under the yoke of their labor, description of which cannot fail to interest us increasingly in their fate.[40]

What then does *révolution* now mean for Raynal and his collaborators? Has it become synonymous with insurrection—a violent collective act in and of itself—or does it still refer to the radical change that will result de facto, once an insurrection has occurred? Is *révolution* now a process rather than an event, is it now an action or an outcome? To answer these questions, and for further evidence of the meanings of the term on the eve of the French Revolution, we might look at its presence in the *Histoire philosophique et politique* more broadly. This work was, after all, the publishing phenomenon of the 1770s and 1780s, exploding in a series of increasingly radical versions, proliferating through a host of editions, re-editions, supplements, selections, and extracts, and rapidly translated into many languages. As official condemnations supplied additional publicity, and rival publishers competed to satisfy a greedy public demand, its various manifestations fed a market almost impossible to saturate. Conceived and directed by Raynal but shaped over the years of its publication by a number of collaborators, Diderot most notable among them, this work defined and exemplified a shifting political horizon. The book's popularity makes it an obvious site to explore further the meanings of the term *révolution* during these last decades of the Old Regime.[41]

Raynal's "*Révolution de l'Amérique*"

Searching *révolution* in volumes of the initial version of the *Histoire philosophique et politique* published in 1770 reveals a conventional usage to describe many different kinds of changes, shifts in fortune, unanticipated events, and transformational processes. Significantly, the most common (and the only really strong) co-occurrence of the term in the plural is with "frequent" (see Figures 6a and 6b; note that only vols. 1 and 6 of the 1770 version are available in ARTFL for collocation analysis). The *Histoire philosophique et politique* teems with *révolutions*, discovering ever more of them as its successive editions grow in length. It finds revolutions present and revolutions past, accidental revolutions, necessary revolutions, happy revolutions, disastrous revolutions, revolutions to be anticipated, revolutions to be hastened, revolutions to be feared. At the same time, the use of *révolution* in the singular points to the importance of the term in also characterizing broad transformational process: revolution in commerce, in manners, in minds (Figures 7a and 7b). Indeed, as its very first sentences suggest, the *Histoire philosophique et politique* can be seen as structured precisely around the question of the relationship between two types of revolution: revolution qua vicissitude and revolution qua long-term transformation.

The book opens, throughout its various editions, by positing the global transformation that has resulted from the European discovery of the East and West Indies, an event more significant than any other "for humankind in general and for the peoples of Europe in particular:"

> Thus began a revolution in commerce, in the power of nations, in the manners, industry and government of all peoples. At this moment individuals in the most distant countries became necessary one to another; the products of equatorial climates are consumed in those close to the pole; the industry of the north is transported to the south; oriental fabrics clothe the west, and people everywhere share their opinions, their practices, their remedies, their virtues and their vices.

Was this transformation stable? Would it, could it, be beneficent? No sooner was it inscribed as a *révolution* on the very first page of the *Histoire philosophique et politique* than it conjures up the specter of "revolutions" in general, *révolutions* as no more than endless, meaningless variation.

> Everything has changed and must change again. But have revolutions past been—and can those that must follow be—useful to human nature? Will humanity owe them one day more tranquility, virtue and pleasure? Can they make its state better, or will they merely change it?[42]

abri appuyée arméniens arrakan arrivât arrivées asie assez atar aucune autrefois avançoit
avoit base bengale bouleversent celles cent changer chaque chose commencement
commerce communes contrées couvroit depuis despotisme doit doivent doux douze
défiance efforts empires espérance fixés fois foule frappent fréquentes
globe grandes grands gustave général histoire incroyable indostan ineptie koulikan
marquées milieu murs nombre nourriture nouveaux orient paroît parvenu passées pavillons
penser perpétuoit perse peuple progrès rendit riches ruine répetent sera siam siecle
soutenir suivi supposent thamas turcs tyrannie vaza vers yeux égorgent éprouvassent établie
état étoit

	Within 5 Words on Either Side	Within 5 Words to Left only	Within 5 Words to Right only
1	fréquentes (4)	siecle (2)	fréquentes (4)
2	état (2)	depuis (2)	étoit (1)
3	siecle (2)	état (1)	état (1)
4	depuis (2)	établie (1)	égorgent (1)
5	étoit (1)	éprouvassent (1)	yeux (1)
6	établie (1)	vers (1)	turcs (1)
7	éprouvassent (1)	vaza (1)	thamas (1)
8	égorgent (1)	tyrannie (1)	supposent (1)
9	yeux (1)	suivi (1)	soutenir (1)
10	vers (1)	siam (1)	répetent (1)

FIGS. 6a and 6b. "Révolutions" in Raynal's *Histoire* 1770. Vols. 1 and 6 only; ARTFL database. Co-occurrences within space of five words. 22 occurrences. (Corpus as of 8/2012)

The *Histoire philosophique et politique* thus presents a transformation of the modern world that pivots around an accidental occurrence: Europe's discovery of unknown lands beyond the seas. It offers a history of the present and the present as history. It looks to the past to grasp the present and to the present to imagine the possibilities of the future. It is a world history, not only in its vision of social processes of globalization that are integrating the fortunes of far-flung peoples but also in the perspective of universality it adopts. As a "philosophical history," it is a history of humanity, the work of the philosopher who can free himself of personal considerations

accorda affaires alors amenoit ancienne angleterre anglois arma
arrivée asie assurer attachés attention attestent aucun aujourd' avant avoit bengale
bientôt bons bénédiction cafier calme calmés cas cet changea chaque chartre chef chéri
clandestins commencerent commencé commerce compagnie conquérant
corruption courte crainte derniere devenu devoit diminua discours dissiper diviser dix
doit délivreroit démonstrations effet enfin esprits espérance europe eut exerce
extraordinaire face fermenter firent fit fleur fortunés frappante globe gouvernement
grande grandes hui imprudence influence intérêt isle jour jusqu' libres loin
long lors lorsque malheur malheureuse milles moeurs moine monde monnoie
monopole montroit méditoit méritoit naick naissante nouveau opérer originairement ouvrage
pensilvanie petite possesseur postes pouvoit principale procurer produire produisit préparer
préparoit préparée présumer ramenera renaissance rendit rendu resta rivieres royaume
récente réduiroit réparoient secours semblable seul singuliérement soit subite sujet telle
temps terre tirerent titres touchante tourna turbulent tyrans utilité vaisseaux vient
vingt voyoit éleva étoient étoit

	Within 5 Words on Either Side	Within 5 Words to Left only	Within 5 Words to Right only
1	grande (4)	grande (4)	commerce (3)
2	temps (3)	jour (2)	temps (2)
3	esprits (3)	amenoit (2)	moeurs (2)
4	commerce (3)	étoient (1)	esprits (2)
5	moeurs (2)	vingt (1)	arrivée (2)
6	lorsque (2)	vaisseaux (1)	étoit (1)
7	jour (2)	utilité (1)	éleva (1)
8	fit (2)	titres (1)	voyoit (1)
9	firent (2)	tirerent (1)	vient (1)
10	doit (2)	terre (1)	tyrans (1)

FIGS. 7a and 7b. "Révolution" in Raynal's *Histoire* 1770. Vols. 1 and 6 only;
ARTFL database. Co-occurrences within space of five words. 37 occurrences.
(Corpus as of 8/2012)

and particular attributes, thus elevating his mind's eye to judge human affairs as if from a point above the atmosphere (the point once occupied by the deity).[43] But it is also a political history, a story of a world in constant play, of change and contingency, action and interaction, vulnerability and opportunity, shifting fortunes, strategic calculations. It offers an unfolding narrative of states and peoples, of global competition, of liberty and oppression, of rights achieved and rights denied.

Within this history contemporaneity, immediacy, and universality come together at the joint between humankind's shameful past and its still uncertain future. And as the work extends through successive versions, it gives its readers, almost as if in a newsreel, perhaps the most widely influential early account of the American Revolution. The first version of the text, when it appears in 1770, begins with the European discovery of America; it concludes its account of the ensuing centuries by declaring inevitable the ultimate separation of the American continent from its European masters. But if it supports the North American colonists' demands for representation as essential to their liberty, it nonetheless warns of the risks to them of seeking absolute independence. It points, too, to the dangers European powers would invite in accelerating "a revolution that would deliver them from a neighboring enemy only to give them a more formidable distant one. Why hasten an event that must arise from the inevitable concurrence of so many others? . . . Everything conspires to the great dismemberment the precise moment of which cannot be foreseen. Everything leads to it, the progress of the good in the new hemisphere and the progress of evil in the old."[44]

Five years later, this closing section of the *Histoire philosophique et politique* appeared in Philadelphia as *The Sentiments of a Foreigner, on the Disputes of Great-Britain with America. Translated from the French.* It does not appear to have slowed the momentum of the American colonies toward the complete independence against which it had warned. Nor did it discourage Britain's European enemies, and more especially the French, from supporting colonial resistance. By the time the final version of the *Histoire philosophique et politique* appeared in 1780, there was an American Revolution, a War of Independence, and the military intervention of France and Spain in the conflict against Britain to account for. The result was the expanded discussion of American affairs that also appeared separately in 1781 as *Révolution de l'Amérique.* Editions and translations of this separate work, into English and other languages, rapidly followed.

Révolution de l'Amérique is remarkable in the way that it represents a collective act in an immediate present. It opens with an evocation of Britain in "a moment of crisis," exhausted by long and bloody war, overextended abroad as a result of new territorial acquisitions, crushed at home by unprecedented taxes.[45] In this condition, the metropole had to call upon the help of its colonies. But its leaders did so tyrannically, disregarding customary practice and their constitutional inheritance of the colonists as Englishmen: the principle of consent to taxation, that right "which should belong to all peoples, since it is founded on the eternal code of reason."[46] Heedless of the delicate art of maintaining authority, the British created a situation that could only place the legitimacy of its rule at risk. Raynal's candid summary of the conditions of successful rule is succinct:

> Never forget that the lever of power has no other fulcrum than opinion; that the force of those who govern is really only the force of those who let themselves be governed. Never prompt peoples distracted by their labor, or asleep in their chains, to open their eyes to truths too frightful for you. When they obey don't let them remember they have the right to command. Once this moment of terrible awakening arrives; once they think they are not made for their rulers but their rulers are made for them; once they have been able to gather together, to communicate, and to pronounce with one voice that We do not want this law, this practice displeases us, there is no middle ground. You will be constrained, by an unavoidable alternative, either to yield or to punish, to be weak or tyrannical; and your authority, henceforth detested or despised whatever action it takes, will have no choice but the open insolence of the people, or their hidden hate.[47]

This is the perspective from which *Révolution de l'Amérique* follows the escalation of the conflict in North America as increasingly despotic measures by the British incite the growing determination of the colonists to resist. With news of the closing of Boston harbor circulating throughout the colonies in 1774, "dispositions to a general insurrection grow . . . . Soon the disquietude communicates itself from house to house. The inhabitants assemble and converse in public places. Writings full of eloquence and vigor are published everywhere." The moment of decision has arrived, these publications announce. The colonies, they say, "have now nothing left them but to choose between fire and sword, the horrors of death or the yoke of passive, slavish obedience. Behold the time of an important revolution has finally arrived, the outcome [*événement*] of which, happy or disastrous, will fix for ever the regret or admiration of posterity." Readiness for resistance was now the common mood, but the step from general outrage to concerted action remained a critical one:

> the important object, the difficult thing, in the midst of a general tumult, was to introduce calm that would allow the formation of a union of wills giving resolu-

tions dignity, force, and consistency. This is the concert that, from a multitude of scattered parts easy to break, composes a whole not to be brought down unless it be divided by force or policy.

The Continental Congress once founded, "the ferment of animosity increases. All hope of reconciliation vanishes. The two sides sharpen their blades . . . . The combustibles are collected; the conflagration is about to blaze."[48]

With this introduction, *Révolution de l'Amérique* invites its readers to enter into the narrative of an unfolding present played out within a dramatic frame of collective political action and decision-making. They are treated to arguments drawn from prerevolutionary pamphlets. They are taken into the House of Commons to hear speeches for and against severe action against the American rebels (there are shades here of the speeches Thucydides composed to bring alive the debate over the fate of Corcyra at the hands of the Athenians). They are instructed (in language Thomas Paine later denounced as plagiarism) in the cardinal distinction between society (born of men's needs and "always good") and government (born of men's vices and "only too often bad").[49] They are treated to lengthy paraphrases of *Common Sense* as it radicalizes the meaning of the conflict ("The tribunal of war is from now on the only tribunal that exists for us").[50] They follow the Declaration of Independence, the creation of a constitution, the vicissitudes of a war. They ponder the future of the new state as it is urged to avoid luxury, corruption, inequality, the spirit of conquest and intolerance, and to "let liberty be an unshakeable basis of your constitutions."[51]

In all this, revolution as an event becomes revolution imagined, enacted, and narrated as dynamic process. The success of Washington's army in driving the English back onto Boston in March 1776 becomes "the first step of English America toward the revolution." The English grasp, in response, that "to snuff out revolutions, there is an initial moment that has to be seized." Paine's *Common Sense* announces that "one day has given birth to a revolution. One day has transported us into a new century"; that America is blessed by its lack of a nobility for whom "in times of revolutions and crisis, the people is only an instrument"; that "souls expand in revolutions, that heroes emerge and assume their place." As independence is declared with an eloquence worthy of the great days of Greece and Rome, and as an initial constitution is formed, readers are reminded that "in these moments of revolution the public will cannot be too well known, too literally pronounced." They are later asked whether enough has been done to "consolidate (*affermir*) the revolution," and to allow the French the pride of "sharing with an ally the honor of this important revolution." Despots, too, are readers; they too are instructed that nothing privileges tyranny over liberty. "These great revolutions of liberty are lessons for despots. They warn them not to count on the too-long patience of peoples or on an eternal impunity."[52]

In this reenactment of the American Revolution, a space has been opened for imaginative investment in collective action. "Thus when society and the laws take vengeance against the crimes of individuals the man of good will hopes that punishment of the guilty can prevent new crimes. Terror sometimes takes the place of justice for the brigand or conscience for the assassin. This is the source of the keen interest all wars for liberty awaken in us. This has been the interest the Americans have inspired. Our imaginations have been inflamed for them. We associate ourselves with their victories and their defeats."[53] Readers of *Révolution de l'Amérique* are invited to contemplate that revolution as a collective act. They are urged to embrace its promise on behalf all humankind.

Revolution Revolutionized

The evidence discussed in the previous sections suggests several conclusions regarding the notion of revolution in France in the century before 1789. First, in the French database as in the English, "revolution" retained a broad range of meanings while remaining largely an ex post facto category, the expression of the instabilities of human existence and the vicissitudes wrought by time. Revolution was a fact rather than an act, an event that occurred or could be anticipated, a change in public life that could be celebrated or decried, not a collective political process demanding engagement. Revolutions happened, they were not made; they prompted anxiety rather than hope. They were better celebrated than anticipated.

Second, nonetheless, there were signs that "revolution" was being revalorized within Enlightenment thinking. Revolutions in knowledge could be seen as contributing to the general advance of the human understanding. Revolutions in society could be welcomed as beneficent transformations of the conditions of human existence. Political changes could be demanded or anticipated as "happy revolutions."

Third, as expectations of social progress expanded so did countervailing fears of cataclysmic social collapse. The specter of revolution as political crisis and social apocalypse, not the expression of the beneficent march of modern civilization but the inevitable explosion resulting from its accelerating evils, was the dark side of eighteenth-century social thought. Raynal's *Histoire philosophique et politique* is particularly striking in the way it fostered both understandings of revolution, sustaining a profound dichotomy between hopes for social transformation and warnings of impending disaster.

Fourth, the *Histoire philosophique et politique* is particularly striking, too, for the conceptualization of the American Revolution it offered the many readers of its expanded final version. That work, with its offshoot, *Révolution de l'Amérique,* was reimagining revolution as a collective act and as a political dynamic unfolding in time. It was expanding the moment of change and revealing a horizon of choice and engagement. Read from this perspective, it was already opening a conceptual space for a French Revolution that sought the achievement of universal values while finding them constantly at risk in the immediacy and contingency of political time.

In an earlier analysis, I used the example of the *Révolutions de Paris,* the most widely read of the new political journals that sprang into existence in 1789, to suggest the initial scripting of the French Revolution in the months following the fall of the Bastille. The title of the journal itself pointed to older understandings of "revolutions" as sudden occurrences and dramatic events bringing unanticipated changes in the affairs of a state. Appearing first as a succession of brochures reporting particular incidents, it was soon transformed as political crisis continued into a periodical publication feeding the revolutionary dynamic. As it took form, so did the conception of revolution in its pages. A succession of "revolutions" became "a revolution" and then "the astonishing revolution that has taken place"; "these revolutions" turned into "this revolution forever memorable in the annals of our history," which soon assumed its title as "The Revolution."[54] In the light of the present research, this evolution seems to parallel the semantic pattern of "The Glorious Revolution" and "The American Revolution" in which a series of events rapidly became a great event singularized, capitalized, and celebrated.

But "The French Revolution" was not to be recognized and understood ex post facto—which is to say that it was not to be stopped. It found force as an act rather than legitimacy as a fact. The revolutionary moment was opened up and extended from within to become a frame of action with its own dynamic, its own logic, its own immediacy, its own accelerated conception of time. In this respect, the parallel between the *Révolutions de Paris* and the *Révolution de l'Amérique* is striking. But it is not irrelevant here that the *Révolutions de Paris* was a newspaper, its editors intent on convincing readers that no issue could be left unpurchased or unread. The narrative time of the French Revolution was at once driven and reflected by the periodicity of its press. Time itself was to be experienced as a succession of moments in which life and death hang in the balance. Each day was to offer a new combat between the Revolution and its enemies. Each day was to decide whether France is to be "enslaved or free," whether its inhabitants will be "the happiest of peoples" or the most miserable. Each day—and each issue of the journal—counted.

Remarkably, then, the conception of revolution we see taking form in the *Révolutions de Paris* combined the meanings of revolution as crisis and revolution as transformational process. The French Revolution was a crisis, a moment of life or death in the social body, experienced as a terrifying moment of violence and danger, a period of agitation and anguish. But this version of a classical republican script was presented in Enlightenment tones. A local crisis was being raised to the level of a world-historical process to effect the transformation of humanity. Each day would decide not only the fate but that of all humankind. The French were carrying out a universal historical mission, acting on behalf of "all the nations that have not yet broken the chains of despotism."

There is no reason to repeat here an earlier analysis of the *Révolutions de Paris*. Understanding of the revolutionary conceptualization of revolution has in any case been extended by William Sewell's discussion of the link between revolution and popular violence forged at the Bastille, by Mary Ashburn Miller's analysis of metaphors of revolutionary violence as natural phenomena, and by Dan Edelstein's account of the emergence of revolutionary authority in 1793.[55] Instead, we can consider briefly the aggregate picture now made possible by digitization of the first eighty volumes of the *Archives parlementaires,* the omnibus basic collection of reports of the sessions of the revolutionary national assembly and of materials relating to them. It should be emphasized that the data available so far is "dirty OCR," the product of an initial optical scanning that provides still messy results. But these results are nonetheless quite fascinating and suggestive.

Figures 8a and 8b show co-occurrences with *révolution* for the year 1789. The change is dramatic: "happy" is now the most common descriptor followed by "great" and "present *(actuelle)*." Also favored are "certain," "against or counter *(contre)*," "sudden," "present *(présente)*," "our," and "salutary." But the revolution is happy but briefly: by 1790 *heureuse* has been displaced by *contre* (Figures 9a and 9b). The collocation analysis for 1791–93 shows the continuation of this trend. "Counter" dominates, followed by "our" and "French"; "we," "great," "you," "happy," "violations," "your," abandonneraient absolue **actuelle** adresse alors amalgamez amène and anglaise annuelle approche arreter art aucune aujourd' aurait **aussi** autre avantageuse avons belle bien car cela celte cependant **certaine** cessent changes chaque citoyens com commandait constante contraire **contre** contribuassent contré conçut **courte** croit cultivateur **delà** dernière desdenrees desdites **desquelles** destinée difficile doit dure dé défiez dépouillés désastreuse **désirée** désormais détournons effrayante eh elles entière especede etc eurent extraordinaire faite fameuse fatale favorable favorise **française** fu fut fâcheuse **fût** ge glorieuse gnnde **grande** guidés **générale** h **heureuse** hommage ia' immense importante impossible imprévue in inattaquable inattendue inespérée inouïe inspire inspirée intérieure inévitable iâ **jamais** jusqu' lettre lorsqu' lorsque lâ légitime majeure manqué me misère moindre morale motion murmures mécontente **mémorable** necker non **notre** nouvelle nécessaire obser operee or ɔrganisons osent **pareille** partielle passant peuvent pheureusè porte pourrait pouvait. ppfpplip prepare prochaine profonde proposée **présente** présenté puisqu' puisse pure pèsent quel quelconque **quelle** quoique ramènera rapport reuse saisit **salutaire** sauf seconde semblable **semble** sena seraient serait si' soudaine **subite** superbe surprenante surtout survenue tandis **telle** the tient toute **troisième** trouvent **très** témoignage unç uoe **utile** uûecertainè violente voici voilà vâ également étaient étend **étonnante** ët iâ

	Within 1 Words on Either Side	Within 1 Words to Left only	Within 1 Words to Right only
1	heureuse (47)	heureuse (42)	actuelle (17)
2	grande (24)	grande (24)	subite (5)
3	actuelle (17)	contre (9)	présente (5)
4	contre (10)	certaine (9)	heureuse (5)
5	certaine (9)	notre (5)	générale (4)
6	subite (7)	étonnante (4)	française (4)
7	présente (5)	delà (4)	aussi (4)
8	notre (5)	telle (3)	fût (3)
9	étonnante (4)	pareille (3)	très (2)
10	telle (4)	jamais (3)	semble (2)

FIGS. 8a and 8b. "Révolution" in *Archives parlementaires* 1789 ARTFL (uncorrected OCR). Co-occurrences within space of one word. 687 occurrences. (Corpus as of 1/2013)

actuelle adoption adresse adresses ae affectent ah alors annonçaient anéantit août appelez arrivait arrivée art article assure attaquant attendent attestée aucun auraient aurait aussi avaient avait avril batave belle bientôt bous brillante car celui cependant chaque cherchaient cherchent choisi conirib conlre contenus contre contrë conversation coupable côntre daos daus delà dernière devaient devait devenue disposé dit do doit doivent domine donc durable désastreuse désirable dévoile e ele enfin entre eontré es estaussiimpossibleque etat eussent exige f farcy fatale favorable finissent fournir française funeste fut fût g' glorieuse gothique graduée grande grandie grándé heureuse hollandaise honneurs honore hëlirëusé ils' imaginaire imaginée imprévue inattendue incendient ineffable innover inverse ja jd juin juste lequel lettre lit livres lors lorsqu' lu lâ machinée malgré mes mettent moi mots mémorable mérite méritent non notre nouvelle nécessaire nécessite opérée orageuse paisible parce partout pendant pleins plusieurs politique pourquoi pourraient pouvait prescrite pressés privés procurait projetée prédiction préparée présente présenter publient pure put qpi quand quant quel quelle quelque quelquefois quelë quoiqu' religieuse relise respectent retentit rpusp réunis sagement salutaire seconde semblable serait solide subite sublime survenue telle tels tqiljop tramé triomphant trouveront tu universelle uoe uqe viendront vient voilà voir votre voulez étaient étant étonnante ët

	Within 1 Words on Either Side	Within 1 Words to Left only	Within 1 Words to Right only
1	contre (137)	contre (135)	française (11)
2	notre (29)	notre (29)	actuelle (10)
3	heureuse (28)	heureuse (27)	présente (7)
4	grande (16)	grande (16)	car (7)
5	française (11)	glorieuse (8)	parce (3)
6	actuelle (10)	delà (5)	cherchent (3)
7	glorieuse (9)	nouvelle (3)	cependant (3)
8	présente (8)	ja (3)	vient (2)
9	car (7)	dernière (3)	telle (2)
10	delà (5)	mémorable (2)	serait (2)

FIGS. 9a and 9b. "Révolution" in *Archives parlementaires* 1790 ARTFL (uncorrected OCR). Co-occurrences within space of one word. 1011 occurrences. (Corpus as of 1/2013)

actuelle adresse afin aient ait alors américaine août applaudissements archives arrivée art aucune aujourd' auraient aurait aussi autant autre avaient avait avant avignonaise ayant belle bien bienfaisante car cela celui cependant certes chacun chaque chez citoyens combien comité commencée comment commis complète considérant contre contré delà depuis dernière devait devient disent dit doit doivent donné dès déhts déjà délits députés e eh elles encore enfin entière eontre etait etc eût fa faite faites finisse font fran française française frimaire furent fut fût glorieuse grande générale heureuse hâtez ici ii immortelle ja jamais juillet juin jusqu' livres longue lorsqu' lorsque là ma mai maintenant malgré marat marche marseille me mention mes messieurs mon morale mots murmures mémorable naire nairement naires nationale noire non notre nouvelle nécessaire opérée or ouverte paisible parce pareille paris partout plusieurs politique pourquoi pouvait première presque prochaine procès précédente présente prétendue puisqu' puisque puisse quand quant quel quelle quelques quoiqu' quoique r rapport recevez religieuse rien royale rue républicaine sainte salutaire seconde sectionnaire semblait semble septembre seraient serait soient subite sublime surtout ta tandis tant telle tels toujours toute tre tribunal troisième trop universelle veulent veut vient violente voilà voir vos votre véritable ❖❖ étaient étant étonnante

	Within I Words on Either Side	Within I Words to Left only	Within I Words to Right only
I	contre (1868)	contre (1855)	française (327)
2	notre (562)	notre (554)	délits (149)
3	française (328)	grande (130)	naires (58)
4	délits (149)	heureuse (100)	naire (51)
5	grande (132)	votre (46)	jusqu' (40)
6	heureuse (105)	dernière (44)	depuis (36)
7	naires (58)	nouvelle (36)	car (35)
8	votre (57)	glorieuse (33)	parce (32)
9	nouvelle (57)	sainte (31)	doit (29)
10	naire (51)	seconde (27)	serait (27)

FIGS. 10a and 10b. "Révolution" in *Archives parlementaires* 1791–1793 ARTFL (uncorrected OCR). Co-occurrences within space of one word. 7461 occurrences. (Corpus as of 1/2013)

activité adresse afin alors annonce anti août applaudissements ardeur armée armées art auprès aussi autorités auxquelles avaient avait avant avril ayant bataillon bien bunal car caractère carrière cavalerie central chargé chez citoyennes citoyens club code comite comité comités commandée commandées commission commune composé composée considérant contre convulsions corps criminel crise culottes demande depuis devant disant dispositions dit doit doivent dès décidé décidés décret décrets déguisés déjà eh elles eontre er esprit etc faites faits femmes fera force français furent fut fût garde gouvernement génie hache hommes ii imprimé insertion institutions instruction instrument janvier juger juillet juin jusqu' ligne loi lois lorsque légion législateurs mai marche mars mention mesure mesures militaire moi monnaie mouvement mouvements moyens murmures nal nivôse nom nommé non oomité opinions opérations or orages parce parmi parti pendant peu peuple peuvent plusieurs pourrait pouvoir pouvoirs principes pris prises procès provisoire prétendu prétendues public puisqu' puisque puisse quand quelques rabaut res régime républicaines républicains section sentiments septembre serait société sociétés soient soyez suit surtout surveillance système séant tandis taxe taxes taxés tel temps torrent toujours travaux tre tribunal tribunaux trop très ultra va vie viennent vient vigueur ville voici voilà vraiment véritablement écrit énergie établi établie étaient état événements

	Within 1 Words on Either Side	Within 1 Words to Left only	Within 1 Words to Right only
1	contre (2809)	contre (2795)	mai (47)
2	tribunal (1473)	tribunal (1473)	art (45)
3	comité (343)	comité (342)	août (43)
4	armée (299)	armée (296)	juillet (36)
5	comités (218)	comités (218)	nivôse (23)
6	mesures (168)	mesures (168)	avril (23)
7	gouvernement (91)	gouvernement (91)	établi (22)
8	mouvement (89)	mouvement (89)	séant (19)
9	lois (77)	lois (77)	parce (19)
10	pouvoir (73)	pouvoir (73)	jusqu' (19)

FIGS. 11a and 11b. "Révolutionnaire(s), révolutionnairement" in *Archives parlementaires* 1791–1793 ARTFL (uncorrected OCR). Co-occurrences within space of one word. 1011 occurrences. (Corpus as of 1/2013)

"their." The revolution is defined more in terms of antagonism than of cele-bration (Figures 10a and 10b). And the embattled revolution needs "revolu-tionaries" to struggle, above all, against "counter" revolutionaries; it needs a "revolutionary tribunal," "revolutionary committees," a "revolutionary army," "revolutionary measures," a "revolutionary movement," more than one "revolutionary society," a "revolutionary government," and "revolu-tionary laws"(Figures 11a and 11b). The presence of these terms will scarcely surprise specialists of the French Revolution, but their abrupt appearance in the collocation tables will perhaps remind historians not to take them for granted. They offer a dramatic demonstration of the ways in which revolu-tion was transformed into a political script and a domain of action.

As this happened, *révolution* was endowed by the French with adjectival and verb forms delineating a frame of action and those within it: *révolution-naire* ("revolutionary") to characterize a certain kind of situation, or the actors or deeds producing or engaging it; *révolutionner* ("revolutionize") to designate what these latter did. With the meaning of these same terms quickly sharpened by the appearance of their opposites, *contre-révolution* and *contre-révolutionnaire*, "revolution" shifted from fact to act, becoming a dynamic, violent process with no clear end in sight.[56] Revolution, in short, was revolutionized.

Constitutionalism

The Happiest Revolutionary Script

"There is nothing more common than to confound the terms of the American revolution with those of the late American war," wrote Benjamin Rush, who ranked, after Benjamin Franklin, as Philadelphia's most enlightened citizen, in June 1786. "The American war is over: but this is far from being the case with the American revolution." Securing political independence concluded only "the first act of the great drama," Rush suggested. What yet remained to be done was to "perfect our new forms of government; and to prepare the principles, morals, and manners of our citizens, for these forms of government, after they are established and brought to perfection."[1]

Whether this often-cited passage is read in isolation or quoted out of context, Rush's injunction sounds like a chant for political zeal familiar to the votaries of modern revolutions. One part of a struggle, certainly important in itself, has been won. But a grander project of revolutionary transformation, involving the perfection of both institutions and citizens, remains to be pursued and attained, at some indefinite point in the future. The cause of revolution cannot be limited to its manifest original object in the mid-1770s: securing rights of provincial autonomy against a distant empire, an arbitrary Parliament, and a monarch who had failed to serve as a patriot king or an impartial ruler of *all* of his subjects. Essential as these original purposes were, the revolution transcends them.

Alas for exponents of revolutionary zeal, the remainder of Rush's essay takes a decidedly more prudent and prosaic form. It is, first and foremost, a constitutionalist document, comprising a set of sensible recommendations that are designed to address "the weakness and other defects of our governments." What kinds of innovations does Rush endorse as objects of revolutionary reform? Allowing the national government to emit money and create a uniform currency. Converting the existing unicameral Congress into a bicameral legislature, and creating an independent executive to operate with a privy council. Replacing the republican principles of annual elections and rotation in office with the recognition that "Government is a science; and can never be perfect in America, until we encourage men to devote not only three years, but their whole lives to it." Removing the popular prejudice that sovereign authority "'is seated *in* the people'" and replacing it with the idea that they exercise it "only on the days of their elections," after which it becomes "the property of their rulers."[2]

To make the American people suitable for their republican governments, Rush continued, two other measures seemed desirable. One was to create "a federal university" in the new "federal town" that might eventually serve as a national capital. Its faculty would include professors of history, law, commerce, the military arts, and most important, a position reserved for "what is called in the European universities, œconomy." Its occupant would be charged with studying "agriculture and manufactures of all kinds," to be assisted by "a travelling correspondent" in Europe, monitoring improvements Americans could adopt. At some point, after this university was established, it should anticipate the workings of *les grandes ecoles* in modern France, so that "the honours and offices of the united states" would "be confined to persons who had imbibed federal and republican ideas in this university." To improve the civic capacity of citizens, Rush concluded, the key institution of revolutionary improvement would be—sound the tocsin—"the post-office. This is the true non-electric wire of government."[3]

A clarion call for a post office, a national university, and the benefits of incumbency can hardly scale the summits of modern revolutionary zeal. Of course, there were other political voices in America whose notion of political change struck more radical notes than Rush sounded, and whose writings accordingly appeal to modern scholars. Many historians, justifiably fatigued with endless publications about the major Founders, still search for alternative voices on the Revolution, producing works that complicate the central story or illustrate the range of meanings that the Revolution had, either for individuals or for distinct communities. Thus in one recent book, Christian Fritz valiantly struggles to demonstrate that appeals to the reserved right of a people to alter and abolish governments continued to resonate in American politics, not only in the context of colonial resistance in the mid-1770s but also during Shays's Rebellion (1786–87), the Whiskey Rebellion (1793), and Rhode Island's obscure Dorr War of the early 1840s (which ended with the adoption of a document known as the Algerine Constitution—which would be a great trivia question).[4] Here, in theory, might be a basis for the idea that the American Revolution did produce a "script" that its inheritors could follow.

Yet the ease with which Rush merged the idea of revolution with an agenda for constitutional reform identifies a persisting problem in applying the concept of a pre-existing revolutionary script to the American case. The most striking feature of the American experience, and perhaps the one that makes this revolution so hard to compare with other cases, is that the cause of constitutionalism superseded and subsumed the idea of revolution. It did so not only in the climactic debates of 1787–88, which are customarily seen as the culmination of the Revolution, but also much earlier, at the moment of independence itself. Starting in the early months of 1776, individual colonies, notably acting with the permission of the Continental Congress, began writing new constitutions of government. Of course, independence from British tyranny, rather than loyalty to particular state constitutions, remained the banner under which Americans marched. Yet the idea that this was a republican revolution, with aspirations of a fundamental transformation of American governance, took place concurrently with the decisive movement toward independence.[5] Other revolutions have favored preserving the apparatus of resistance—committees and conventions and *soviets*—because they maintain not only popular enthusiasm but also more efficient means of pursuing the cause, unconstrained by the forms of legality. The Americans took a different course, making a new form of constitutionalism a distinguishing feature of their revolution almost as soon as it became possible to do so.

Among those who grasped this point first were John Adams and Thomas Jefferson. "The Time is now approaching, when the Colonies, will find themselves under a Necessity, of engaging in Earnest in this great and indispensible Work," Adams wrote Mercy Otis Warren in mid-April 1776, which would prove, he predicted, "the most difficult and dangerous Part of the Business." This perception was growing rapidly, and "Measures are taking which must terminate in a compleat Revolution."[6] Jefferson expressed similar enthusiasm a month later. In May 1776, when he was marooned attending Congress in Philadelphia, Jefferson wrote almost wistfully of his desire to be able to return to Virginia, there to join the task of writing its new constitution. This would be "a work of the most interesting nature and such as every individual would wish to have his voice in," he wrote a correspondent at home. "In truth it is the whole object of the present controversy; for should a bad government be instituted for us in future it had been as well to have accepted at first the bad one offered to us from beyond the water [that is, from Britain] without the risk and expence of contest."[7] Jefferson longed to participate directly in Virginia's constitution-making venture back in Williamsburg; instead he was stuck in Philadelphia, sentenced to earning his global fame as author of the Declaration of Independence.

The logic of the American script was thus to terminate one defining condition of revolutionary spontaneity as quickly as possible and instead to restore legal rule under constitutional authority. The question of determining precisely how that could be done became one of the great challenges the Americans faced, and it was not definitively solved until the late 1780s. Part of the difficulty in scripting this revolutionary story was that Americans initially lacked an adequate mechanism for bridging the gap between a constitutional form of resistance and the right to complete a constitutional revolution. The existence of a *right* to alter or abolish governments was not a novelty; but the question of how that right could be exercised required some measure of improvisation before a definitive set of procedures was finally created. The real story of how the American Revolution was scripted—assuming that constitutionalism was indeed its true and proper end—was thus a matter of conceptual creativity and political innovation. Here the Founding generation deserves a degree of credit that goes beyond the customary reverence that Americans routinely pay them. The story of how to bring a revolution to a successful close may be the most difficult script of all to write, yet it also became one that the American revolutionaries brought to a successful conclusion. Given the absence of precedents for what they were attempting, the American success in distinguishing a constitution from ordinary law and in developing a method to make the adoption of a national constitution the result of an unambiguously clear and definitive deliberative process—and this within the space of fourteen months!—arguably deserves more credit than it ordinarily receives, perhaps because we naturally take it too much for granted.

Two reservations initially weigh against the idea of understanding colonial resistance to British imperial policy before 1776 as a scripted revolutionary story. One is that the leaders of colonial resistance did not actively believe that their protests were conceived to produce a radical transformation of a political regime or a historically unprecedented movement for national liberation. True, even during the Stamp Act controversy of 1765–66, some observers began worrying whether the conflict over Parliament's colonial jurisdiction might lead to a revolt against all British authority.[8] Yet the idea that independence was the real goal of resistance came to Americans only fairly late in the struggle—which is one reason why Thomas Paine's *Common Sense* became the political sensation it has always been understood to be. The history of the prerevolutionary decade 1765–75 was not a simple story of one grievance piling upon another in an ever upward-sloping graph of colonial resentment until independence became the Americans' sole choice. A better case can be made that most colonists in the early 1770s thought that the Stamp Act controversy of 1765–66, and its sequel, the Townshend duties dispute of 1767–70, were episodes from which a reasonably informed British government would draw the appropriate lessons. Rather than imagining they were on the eve of a revolutionary upheaval, Americans plausibly hoped that the government of Lord North would realize that the costs of reforming imperial policy were simply too high to pursue.[9]

One noteworthy statement of this came from John Adams, writing four months after the Boston Tea Party and bare weeks before texts of the Boston Port Act reached America in mid-May 1774. In his view, the imperial controversy "shall oscilate like a Pendulum and fluctuate like the Ocean, for many Years to come," with no determinate conclusion. "Our Children, may see Revolutions, and be concerned and active in effecting them of which we can form no conception." Adams offered no definition of "revolution," but he saw the contest as a struggle between "American Grievances" on the one hand and "an absolute Establishment of Parliamentary Authority."[10] Well into 1775, a working definition of independence for many American colonists still meant independence from Parliament, not the larger empire within whose governance its role remained disputed.[11] When Adams occasionally used the word "revolution" in his correspondence, he remained linguistically and conceptually ahead of nearly all of his countrymen; even then, his usage connotes more of a radical change in circumstances and expectations than a political revolution in the substantive sense of the term.[12] The phrase "revolution principles" that occasionally appears in correspondence was a reference to 1688, not an anticipation of 1776.[13]

The second reservation against a revolutionary script comes from the dynamics of the political struggle between Britain and America. Here the patriotic biases that inhere even in modern scholarly analyses of the coming of the Revolution may distort our judgment. Still, having thought about this issue for a modest four decades, I remain convinced that colonial leaders—whether militants like the Adamses of Massachusetts, or moderates like John Dickinson and Robert Morris of Pennsylvania—believed that the animus for escalation came primarily from the other side. In their view, the British government had repeatedly taken the critical initiatives that worked as a one-way ratchet for colonial resistance, making possible, over time, a degree of intercolonial agreement and coordination that brought America to the brink of independence. In the early 1770s, ostensible colonial radicals—the ideologically driven leaders who did believe that the British government was committed to reducing the realm of American liberties—agreed that they could do little more than vigorously monitor British policy. Only in Massachusetts did the group around Samuel Adams and the Boston Committee of Correspondence discover an effective means of reviving the issues of the previous decade. Even then they depended primarily on the activities and miscalculations of Governor Thomas Hutchinson to create the explosive situation from which the Boston Tea Party and the government's reaction with the Coercive or Intolerable Acts of 1774 emerged.[14] Samuel Adams, the closest case we have to a proto-quasi-Trotskyite, stated the point well in April 1776, when independence was becoming a mere matter of timing. "We cannot make Events," Adams observed. "Our Business is wisely to improve them."[15] Other delegates, including those who mistrusted the failed Boston brewer's motives, essentially agreed. "Great Britain may thank herself for this Event," Robert Morris wrote a month before independence was declared. "Whatever may have been the original design of some men in promoting the present Contest," he wrote, with the Adams cousins clearly in mind, Americans had never intended to create "an Independent Empire. They have been driven into it step by step with a reluctance that has been manifested in all their proceedings, yet I dare say our Enemies will assert that it was planned from the first movements."[16]

Perhaps the better script to be proposed here, then, would be set in London rather than Boston, Philadelphia, or Williamsburg. Scripting the story of imperial reaction, in other words, might be just as engaging as writing about the rights and rites of revolution—and for revolutionary screen-writers, the manners, costumes, and metropolitan settings back in the imperial central world of London would also provide far more attractive material with which to work than patriots masquerading as Indians at the Boston Tea Party.

Yet even if the colonists might have had a hard time grasping that they were somehow conforming to a revolutionary script in the full sense of the term, they would have found it much easier to agree that they were adhering to a reasonably well settled story about the nature of their resistance to British authority. The idea that proper resistance to the abuse of legal authority had to follow a well-defined set of steps was a staple theme of Anglo-American political thinking, and arguably practice, between the Glorious Revolution of 1688 and the rise of colonial opposition to Britain. In the dominant "neo-whig" account of the origins of the revolution, this theme stresses how closely the leaders of colonial resistance followed a defined set of steps that carried Americans "from resistance to revolution," in the late Pauline Maier's apt title for her first book, in the decade after 1765. Maier's book remains an essential account for retracing the ordered sequence of steps that a community must take to vindicate its rights against the abuse of public authority.[17] Disputing "progressive" accounts of the Revolution, which saw popular protests as the manifestation of class-based tensions within colonial society, Maier argued that Americans had significant prior experience of taking "extra-legal" actions to counteract improper acts of government. At the extreme end, these actions could devolve into scenes of apparent violence, protests of the kind that, in Britain, would lead to the reading of the Riot Act and resulting measures of enforcement. When overt opposition to the Stamp Act first erupted in August 1765, it took two immediate forms. One was for crowds to assemble outside the homes of the appointed stamp distributors, strongly urging them to resign their commissions and thereby prevent the stamp tax from being collected. This proved remarkably effective, in the "make you an offer you can't refuse" category of resistance. The other method proved more problematic. Riots broke out in several ports, spinning out of control in ways that alarmed colonial leaders. The most famous led to the destruction of the Boston house of Lieutenant Governor Thomas Hutchinson in August 1765.

In response to these events, colonial leaders made sustained efforts to bring resistance back to the rules that political tradition and the writings of Real Whig polemicists laid down for an oppressed people. Some of the tactics deployed in the cause of colonial resistance certainly intimidated its opponents, such as the handful who were tarred and feathered, or a larger group of imperial loyalists whose likenesses were burned in effigy, whose homes were picketed by the crowd, or whose shops were later smeared with the mixture of feces and other foul substances known as "Hillsborough paint," in homage to the Earl of Hillsborough, the first secretary of state for the American colonies. But precisely because complaints against these tactics became well known, resistance leaders worked hard either to challenge accusations of improper violence, or to keep the conduct of American protests within the rules. Acts of resistance had to follow a pattern, with peaceable means of expressing the grievances of a community precluding more militant tactics. The latter could be adopted only after the peaceable means that relied on petitions, resolutions, and symbolic forms of protest had been exhausted. More radical steps could be adopted only after legal authorities refused to respond to grievances. Imperial officials could be excused for believing that the real provocateurs were the factious demagogues who led the colonial crowds. "For most royal observers," Maier observed, "the careful legal distinctions that colonial leaders tried to maintain were of no significance."[18] But to the colonists, these steps were never perceived as provocations or matters of escalation, but only as responses justified by failures of public authority.

Over the course of the five years between the adoption of the Stamp Act in 1765 and the repeal of the Townshend duties in the spring of 1770, the Americans developed a set of tactics that enabled them to believe that they were conforming to the approved set of procedures. Not all steps were equally harmonious or effective. Effective commercial resistance to the Townshend duties of 1767 took much longer to become cohesive than had been the case with the Stamp Act protests. Actions directed against loyalist merchants charged with importing British goods were met by countercharges that some patriot traders were evading the boycott as well. There were fits and starts to the colonial movement. After 1770, particularly outside Massachusetts, many observers plausibly believed that the episodes of the past five years were just that: a rocky period in imperial politics from which sensible observers in Britain would draw appropriate lessons and therefore refrain from imitating.[19] Indeed, the story of how the government of Lord North chose to make the Tea Act of 1773 a potential test of American loyalties is *not* a simple case of a government looking to foment a decisive challenge to colonial resistance. When opposition voices in Parliament asked why North did not simply eliminate the reduced duty on tea rather than risk an American reaction, his reply expressed less of a determination to challenge the Americans than a reluctance to abandon the symbolic affirmation of parliamentary supremacy previously expressed in the Declaratory Act of 1766.[20]

Only after the government's reaction to the Tea Party took the form of a sweeping assertion of parliamentary supremacy in the Coercive Acts of 1774 did the revolutionary script the Americans were now following become transparent. Retrospectively, what Bernard Bailyn labeled "the logic of rebellion" now became evident.[21] Rather than demonstrating that the government's miscues toward America were the function of legitimate policy concerns, political miscalculation about the true character of American commitments, and the misinformation provided by loyalists—most notably Thomas Hutchinson—the case made by the colonial "radicals" now appeared to be confirmed. British policy was not the result of a random walk of political misjudgment. The extent of the government's over-reaction to events in Massachusetts exposed the policy for what it was: a systematic effort to reduce the colonists to a state of slavery, guided by a group of ministers with the willing support of a docile Parliament. Yet even within this script, as colonists might have understood it, the sources and dynamics of action lay in London, not America. As Samuel Adams's April 1776 remark about "improving events" that the colonists could not create on their own suggests, the script the colonists were following was one that authors elsewhere were writing.

Once the colonists grasped that complete independence from Britain, rather than mere independence from Parliament, was becoming their true destination, they did begin to develop a more refined notion of exactly how they should proceed. That story began to take coherent form in the late fall and winter of 1775–76, with an extremely powerful boost in January from Thomas Paine, and then was in full cry by the spring of independence. In this scheme, a decision for independence should become the culmination of a series of prior measures, notably including the opening of discussions with potential foreign supporters; the establishment of legal governments to replace the potent yet extralegal apparatus of committees, conventions, and congresses that had quickly appeared in 1774; and arguably the completion of a formal confederation to give a permanent structure to the intercolonial union represented by the Continental Congress. Then, too, many moderates insisted that Britain should have one more chance to indicate whether it was open to a negotiated reconciliation. Well into the spring of 1776, moderate leaders like John Dickinson and Robert Morris desperately hoped that the rumored peace commission would be announced and promptly dispatched to America, with instructions enabling genuine negotiations to take place.[22]

That opening never came, and most moderates instead accepted the decision for independence as the conclusive step the Americans could justifiably take. That does not mean that they wholly agreed that July 1776 was indeed the appropriate moment for independence. Many continued to think that the newly United States should have held off until assurances of foreign support for "the cause" were far more advanced than they yet were. When the war took a pronounced turn for the worse in the second half of

1776, their doubts remained far more compelling than their grudging recognition that British intransigence at least morally justified the decision for independence. How and why the moderates remained committed to the cause in the final months of 1776 itself remains a crucial yet arguably underappreciated passage in the larger story of the Revolution—in part, perhaps, because many historians are uncomfortable ascribing genuinely revolutionary sentiments to the men of property who constituted the moderate wing of American political leadership.[23]

In any case, this account of how one explains the decision for independence as the defining moment of the American struggle is less about the fulfillment of a script about how a revolution ought to proceed than a matter of strategic calculations about political activity and necessity. In the end, as events tumbled upon themselves in 1776, open advocates for independence—those who putatively might have been most conscious of how the script ought to unfold—recognized that any preconceived sequence was breaking down amid the press of events. That, for example, clearly became the view of John Adams, the one member of Congress who spoke most forthrightly about how the logic of independence should be detailed. Like any one swimming in the current of daily decisions, shuttling between committees, daily sessions of Congress, and all those private conversations that the documentary record rarely records, he came to understand that it was hard enough to keep one's head above the water without being able to look too far downstream.

In the end, however one characterizes the precise nature of their script, the revolutionaries of 1776 essentially followed the treatment laid down by John Locke nearly a century earlier. Locke's notion that the "appeal to heaven"—curiously modeled (if not quite scripted) on Jephthah's appeal to a divine judge in *Judges* 11—becomes possible only after a "long train of abuses" drives a people to resistance, may still provide the best story of how resistance becomes possible. Revolution does not occur for light and transient causes, but only when a chain of events dislodges a people from its inherent political inertia. Jefferson's detailed resounding of a Lockean train of abuses against George III may well overstate just how many abuses were really necessary to move the Americans to independence, as many scholars suggest, and we can quibble about the political significance of each of the charges. Few scholars today seriously credit Jefferson's effort in the Declaration to foist responsibility for the slave trade primarily or solely on the king, and other charges in the indictment seem obscure or faulty as well. But the overall Lockean paradigm, if something less than a script, remains a sound way to reconstruct how the first phase of revolution reached its climax in 1776. We can theorize about distinguishing different types and levels of revolutionary causation—from social dysfunction down to precipitants and triggers—as Lawrence Stone did in his influential essay almost half a century ago.[24] But to the American revolutionary performers, Locke's cumulative train of abuses, interpreted through the skeptical view of British politics that the colonists had shared for decades, did all the work they needed it to do.

Serious Locke scholars can well wonder how he would have handled the ongoing process of revolution *after* the appeal to heaven has been raised and succeeded. The late Richard Ashcraft saw Locke as a radical who would have welcomed political reforms going well beyond what the Convention Parliament attempted to do during the Glorious Revolution.[25] Locke's biography and the development of his epistemological, religious, and political ideas are a rich and complicated subject, and there is no need here to render an amateur judgment in this realm. It is enough to say that the *Second Treatise* does little to explain how a modern society might conduct the deliberations required to complete a revolutionary transformation on the terrain that the American colonists began to pioneer in the long decade after 1776.[26] In the *Second Treatise*, Locke never resorted to the Enlightenment ideal of the rational lawgiver in the handy form of Moses, Solon, or Lycurgus, as the alternative solution to the challenging problem of imagining how a society could engage in a process of collective deliberation and approval to produce a constitution—although of course in his collaborative role with Shaftesbury in drafting and revising the fundamental laws of Carolina, he had just that experience itself. The ideas developed in the *Second Treatise* focus instead on the origins of political authority in primitive society, beginning with the motives created in the state of nature and the transition from patriarchy and captaincy to kingship.[27] Beyond hoping that the Convention Parliament might do more than it chose to do, Locke does not puzzle about the equivalent modern version of constitutional formation.

The idea of the convention as a legally deficient yet politically effective source of revolutionary authority was one of the crucial ideas that the colonists inherited from English practice. In virtually every colony other than the corporate regimes of Connecticut and Rhode Island, which were too minor to merit royal officials of any kind, provincial conventions became the chief institutions of extralegal governance in 1774–76. In some colonies they supplanted the legal assemblies, which never reconvened after 1774. In others they coexisted with legislatures that royal or proprietary governors thought might be induced to depart from the central guidance of the Continental Congress. The decisions of these bodies had to be described not as legislative acts, which properly they were not, but as *ordinances*, a term denoting a lesser degree of legal authority.[28] Yet no one doubted the real authority these bodies and their actions commanded. Indeed, royal officials and loyalists conceded that revolutionary institutions were better known and more deeply respected than ordinary government.[29]

The evolution of the American understanding of conventions from *extra-* to *super*-legal institutions not only marked a key departure in American constitutional thinking; it also created a new script or story with implications beyond 1787. This story has been told by historians as part of the larger transformation in our understanding of the revolutionary origins of American constitutionalism.[30] For our purposes, the basic account can be summarized succinctly. The state constitutions of 1776 were drafted by provincial conventions that were simultaneously charged with implementing other acts of resistance. These conventions were thus acting in a quasi-legislative nature, and because that was the case, it was conceptually difficult if not legally impossible to distinguish a constitution from other acts. Call a charter of government what one will, an instrument drafted by a legislative body could only be legislative in nature, and it could therefore not bind or prohibit later legislative acts that seemed to deviate from or even violate a constitution proper.[31] Indeed, under the accepted legal notion of *quod leges posteriores priores contrarias abrogant*,[32] the later act has superior authority to the prior one. Had the 1776 conventions submitted the original state constitutions to the people for some explicit form of ratification, that might have obviated the objection and provided a basis for distinguishing a constitution from ordinary legislation. But that option was seriously considered only in Pennsylvania, and then not applied.

There was, however, one noteworthy exception to this story: Massachusetts. There, after the outbreak of hostilities in 1775, the Continental Congress allowed legal government to resume, not under the detested Massachusetts Government Act adopted by Parliament in 1774, but under the second royal charter of government of 1691. The one noteworthy change was to allow the provincial council appointed by the lower house to act as a collective executive. In 1776 the General Court (the legislature) proposed a new constitution to the towns, but that proved problematic on at least two fronts. One line of objections, indeed the more important one, ran against any of a number of specific provisions, assessed on their merits. The second, more intriguing objection went to the substance of the procedures for adopting a constitution. Here a leading role was appropriately played by Concord, which objected that "the Same Body that forms a Constitution have of Consequence a power to alter it," which in turn meant that "A Constitution alterable by the Supreme Legislative is no Security at all to the Subject against any Encroachment of the Governing part on any, or on all of their Rights and priviliges."[33] This, in a sense, was a popular or even populist rendering of the *leges posteriores* doctrine, but no less salient for that. Deterred, the legislature relented on the 1776 constitution but tried the project again two years later, only to elicit stronger objections on the procedural front. Only then did it develop the innovation that defined the emerging edge of American constitutional theory by calling, first, for the popular election of a convention that would have one mission only, to draft a constitution, and second, for requiring that document to be submitted to the towns for their ratification. A constitution adopted in this way would be legally distinct from other acts of government resting on mere legislative approval, and thus capable of operating as supreme law in the new definition of a constitution that Americans were in the process of developing.[34]

In practice, the theory did not work quite as elegantly as might have been hoped. The convention appointed to frame the constitution was far too large to pursue that task by itself. It appointed a committee of thirty to do the work, which in turn appointed a subcommittee of three—Samuel Adams, James Bowdoin, and John Adams, just returned from his first diplomatic stint in Europe—the first two of whom agreed that the lawyer from Braintree was the right man for the task. Back in 1776, John Adams had exulted at being "thrown into Existence at a Period, when the greatest Philosophers and Lawgivers of Antiquity would have wished to have lived."[35] Now he was as close to being a lawgiver as he could possibly be—except that the draft he left behind when he returned to Europe late in 1779 was still subject to revision by the convention and ratification by the people. Indeed, when that draft went out, the exact rules for ratification remained sufficiently vague that the towns did not act on the constitution in a uniform way. When the convention reassembled in 1780, the delegates reviewed the returns from the towns, made the best sense of them that they could, and agreed that the constitution had been ratified.

The idea of a provincial convention, appointed by an electorate larger than the ordinary voting pool for legislators, remained something of a legal fiction, but in the best sense of the term. How different really was a popularly elected convention from an ordinary legislature, especially when large numbers of legislators saw themselves as occasional delegates who rarely served more than a term or two before giving up the pleasure of popular office? But this idea of a convention marked a major conceptual advance, not least by providing a basis for converting popular sovereignty from an abstract idea into a specific, workable form. The convention was no longer a surrogate legislature, called to act in circumstances when a fully legal assembly was not possible. Now it had become an essential element of a higher form of lawmaking, superior to an ordinary legislature because its actions were not merely legislative.

Exactly how workable it was became far more evident in 1787–88, when the Federalist supporters of the proposed national Constitution managed its ratification in a remarkably adroit way. In its origins, beginning with the failed Annapolis conference of September 1786, the idea for the Philadelphia convention was the response of political entrepreneurs (including James Madison and Alexander Hamilton) to all the difficulties created by the amendment rule of the Articles of Confederation, which required unanimous approval by all thirteen state legislatures. But once twelve of the thirteen state legislatures had elected delegates to the convention—with only minuscule, antifederal Rhode Island opting out—the basis for thinking of the Philadelphia meeting in the terms set by the Massachusetts precedent became convincing. That potential was enhanced by the expectation that the convention could only propose, not promulgate changes to the Confederation. Whatever changes the convention proposed would still require subsequent ratification, which "must be obtained," in Madison's strategic calculation, "by the people, and not merely from the ordinary authority of the legislatures."[36]

Many accounts of the ratification process emphasize the extent to which the Anti-Federalists managed to manipulate it for their own ends, ultimately gaining a reasonable assurance that the First Congress would seriously consider the amendments the various state conventions recommended as they agreed to ratify. But that tribute ignores an equally fundamental point. It was the Federalists' great success to insist that the state conventions could only *recommend* amendments, and not allow the prior adoption of these changes from becoming a contingent basis for ratification. In the end, the most remarkable aspect of the ratification process was that the final decision was so clear and unambiguous.[37] Only modern legal scholars would prove ingenious enough to realize that the Constitution had been adopted illegally.[38]

Here, then, was a distinctively American script that emerged from the early American conviction that revolution and constitution-making should converge into one story, not two. Perhaps that is why there are not now, and probably never will be, good films about the American Revolution. One simply cannot understand the Revolution without taking constitutionalism quite seriously. But whatever its other merits, constitutionalism deadens the dramatic voice with too many talking heads.

Yet this convergence between revolution and constitution did not wholly close off the revolutionary story. Inadvertently and perversely, the definitive example of 1787–88 set a precedent that the protagonists of states' rights would follow later, first in the nullification controversy of 1832–33 and then in the secession crisis of 1860–61. For the precedent that gave American constitutionalism its distinctive character could run backward as well as forward. It could be used to devolve political authority from the Union to the states, not by mere legislative acts but by reviving the convention as a superlegal expression of the sovereignty of the states. Nullification and secession were not legal acts in the ordinary sense of the term. They were to be done by conventions, not legislatures, following the original constitutional precedent. To pursue such a course, as Madison himself observed in 1830, would not represent the use of recognized methods of constitutional governance. It would instead become "an appeal from the cancelled obligations of the constitutional compact, to original rights & the law of self-preservation. This is the ultima ratio under all Govt. whether consolidated, confederated, or a compound of both," which a lone state could exercise "as an extra & ultra constitutional right, to make the appeal."[39] Constitutionalism is a much happier story, but it can never preclude retelling a revolutionary story, even if the reel runs backward.

From Constitutional to Permanent Revolution

1649 and 1793

Facing the High Court of Justice that had been convened to try him as a "tyrant, traitor, and murderer, and public enemy to the Commonwealth," Charles I issued a blunt challenge: "I would know by what power I am called hither . . . . I would know by what authority, I mean lawful."[1] It was meant to be a rhetorical question, of course: under existing English law, there was no procedure for trying a king. But his stumble ("I mean lawful [authority]") is revealing. The prosecutor, John Cooke, did in fact appeal to a number of authorities—some constitutional, some philosophical, others theological—in his justification of the criminal proceedings. Whether or not they were "lawful" is less a legal than a political question—indeed, it is the very question that lies at the heart of a revolution. "A revolution usually involves a new source of legitimacy, or a new perception of an old source of legitimacy," writes an influential theorist of revolution, Gene Sharp, in a recent text.[2] Inadvertently, Charles had called attention to the fundamental struggle that defines revolution, the struggle between conflicting forms of political authority. It is in the name of a new political authority that revolutionaries justify actions that would be considered unlawful under the old; and it is also in the name of this new authority that revolutionary governments reorganize the state, and in some cases, the economy, society, and culture.[3]

Throughout the early modern period, political theorists, jurists, and theologians developed new authoritative arguments that seventeenth- and eighteenth-century revolutionaries would use to challenge monarchic regimes across the Atlantic world. These arguments, which combined elements of natural right and social contract theory, along with theories of resistance and classical republicanism, provided expansive enough powers to justify such radical actions as executing a king. But they did not present revolutionaries with a blank check. In fact, they delimited a fairly narrow sphere of conduct, demanding a swift close to revolutionary disorder and a rapid return to constitutional stability. We can see here how revolutionary scripts—the focus of this volume—ultimately reflect underpinning concepts of revolutionary authority. Depending on the authority revolutionaries invoked, they could or could not perform certain actions. Until 1789 (if not 1791), the dominant script of revolution may best be described as "constitutional" (see Jack Rakove's essay in this volume).

But during the course of the French Revolution, and more specifically in the years from 1792 to 1794, a new, far more radical model of revolution emerged. Its primary goal was no longer constitutional stability but rather the refashioning of the state and of society. Because this elusive goal always lay slightly out of reach, this model of revolution may be called "permanent."[4] It could be invoked for an unlimited duration, instead of for brief, interstitial moments between political regimes. Where revolution had initially been used to justify events that had occurred during a past insurrection, it became future-oriented, and could legitimate actions not yet undertaken. Most important, it authorized completely new scripts for revolutionary action.

What occasioned this revolutionary paradigm-shift? In part, it was made possible by the evolution of the term "revolution" itself (as Keith Baker argues in this volume). But this discursive history does not tell the whole story: after all, the majority of nineteenth-century revolutions, especially in Spanish America and Central Europe, reverted back to the earlier constitutional model. It was only in the twentieth century that permanent revolutions reappeared on the historical scene.

In this essay, I argue that the decisive factor in the switch from constitutional to permanent models of revolution was a shift in sources of political authority. So long as revolutionaries justified their actions by means of an early-modern discourse mixing social contract, natural right, and popular sovereignty theories, they remained beholden to a constitutional script (which I analyze in part 1, with particular attention paid to the English civil war). But the Jacobins abandoned this script, suspending the constitution that they themselves had written and that the French people had ratified (as I examine in part 2). They appealed instead to an even higher authority than the constitution: the Revolution itself. In a dizzying move, revolution now became the authority that justified revolution. The ramifications of this decision were momentous: where it had previously been accepted, following resistance theory, that revolutionary acts were the prerogative of an oppressed people, state officials now appropriated the right to wage revolution on their own, in the name of a people often more imaginary than real. The Jacobins would not be given much time to make use of this extraordinary power, but it constituted one of the most important and lasting legacies of the French Revolution.

The Early-Modern Story of Revolution: From the Levellers to the National Assembly

The French Revolution has often been seen as marking the start of the modern revolutionary tradition: "what happened at the Bastille," William H. Sewell, Jr., suggested, "became the establishing act of a *revolution* in the modern sense."[5] With respect to French history, this claim may be correct: up until that point, the dominant interpretation of "revolution" in French political circles excluded the kind of events that took place on 14 July. Leading members of the new National Assembly had been celebrating their achievements as marking a "pure," "glorious," "happy," and most important, nonviolent revolution.[6]

As Keith Baker details in this volume, however, the "modern sense" of revolution can already be detected in various English and French texts published before 1789. Indeed, the deputies' insistence on the positive attributes of *their* revolution suggests an awareness that not all revolutions were so pure and happy. But it is also important to peel apart the discursive and conceptual layers of "revolution." Regardless of how the word "revolution" changed in the aftermath of 14 July, the concepts that were assembled to produce its new definition had long been in circulation, in virtually the exact same combination. In other words, what we might call the political discourse that French officials and journalists adopted after 14 July to authorize (what they now called) "revolution" was in no way new. This revolutionary discourse had most recently been employed in the American Declaration of Independence, as can be seen in its famous proclamation that "when a long Train of Abuses and Usurpations . . . evinces a Design to reduce them [the people] under absolute Despotism, it is their Right, it is their Duty, to throw off such Government, and to provide new Guards for their future Security."[7] All the constitutive parts of the revolutionary discourse are already here: a popular, violent insurrection, justified by a higher authority ("the Laws of Nature and Nature's God"), against a despotic power. By October 1776, some were already calling this "the American Revolution."[8]

There is a widespread tendency, particularly among American historians, to trace these arguments back to Locke's *Second Treatise*, notably to his claim that if kings "grow exorbitant in the use of their power, and employ it for the destruction, and not the preservation of the properties of their people," then under these circumstances "it is lawful for the people . . . to resist their king."[9] But as Quentin Skinner argued many years ago, the intellectual origins of this claim extend back much further, to the sixteenth century, at least.[10] It was during these troubled times that predominantly French Huguenot authors welded together neo-Thomist concepts of natural law and natural rights, with Roman law (in particular the *lex regia*) and theories of ancient constitutionalism and conciliarism to produce doctrines of popular sovereignty that foreshadow those put forward by later revolutionaries. As Skinner put it, "the theory of popular revolution developed by the radical Calvinists in the 1550s was destined to enter the mainstream of modern constitutionalist thought."[11]

Skinner's thesis presents the historian of revolutionary discourse with a challenge. Since these theories were quite widespread in the sixteenth and even seventeenth centuries, it is difficult to write a connect-the-dots sort of intellectual history of revolution.[12] For instance, when assessing his friend Etienne de La Boétie's *Discours de la servitude volontaire ou le Contr'un* (written ca. 1549), which deploys natural right and resistance theory to argue that "all men are equal" (*nous sommes tous égaux*) and therefore have a right to defend their political liberty, Montaigne downplayed its importance, saying that it merely regurgitated commonplaces that had been "hashed out in a thousand other books."[13]

Complicating matters further, natural right and social contract theory could also be put to political uses that were far from revolutionary. One need only think of the politically conservative treatises by Grotius, Hobbes, or Pufendorf to appreciate how the arguments advanced by radical Calvinists did not constitute an orthodox interpretation of natural right. It would be naive to assume that the revolutions of the eighteenth century were foreordained in the sixteenth.

These methodological difficulties notwithstanding, one is forced to acknowledge the remarkable parallels between the way in which late-eighteenth-century revolutionaries justified their actions and the arguments set forth two hundred years prior. Leaving aside genealogical questions, these resemblances are ultimately not that surprising, particularly with regard to political authority: to paraphrase a famous French revolutionary pamphlet, natural right allowed those who had nothing to demand something.[14] For those who were largely disenfranchised under monarchic regimes, it provided them with a germ of political authority. It is thus to be expected that would-be revolutionaries should repeatedly return to the same arguments—their options were limited.[15] They could of course have crafted new arguments against the rule of one, but, to paraphrase Charles I, on what authority? Arguments drawn from natural right and social contract theory were particularly effective precisely because these discourses were widely accepted as authoritative, even by defenders of the status quo.

Moving from theory to practice, the "establishing act of a *revolution* in the modern sense" appears not to be 14 July 1789 but rather the English civil war of 1642–49.[16] Glimpses of the revolutionary discourse can be seen in earlier conflicts, such as the Dutch Revolt;[17] but the English civil war marks a particularly illuminating moment in this history, since it reveals most starkly the conditions under which a revolutionary discourse could emerge, and the outcomes it could produce.

The English civil war did not start out with a modern, revolutionary intent. Parliament's declared goal was to curb Charles I's absolutist pretences; to this end, it relied predominantly on a type of authority known as ancient constitutionalism.[18] The powers bestowed by this authority were mostly negative: they allowed Parliament to place a check on royal power when the king went beyond the limits anciently recognized in the "Great Charter of the Liberties of England"—that is, the *Magna Carta*. Hence, in the 1628 *Petition of Right*, the MP and renowned jurist Sir Edward Coke chided Charles for forgetting that the *Magna Carta* guaranteed the right of habeas corpus and forbade the levying of "tallage or aid . . . without the good will and assent of the archbishops, bishops, earls, barons, knights, burgesses, and other the freemen of the commonalty of this realm."[19] For the most part, Parliament wanted a return to the status quo ante.

But these arguments and retorts were only effective up to a point. First, there was no clear procedure in place—no script—for acting on them. The king could brush away Parliament's rebukes and petitions simply by dissolving it and ruling alone, as he would from 1629 to 1640. Secondly, it was a very conservative discourse: it allowed MPs to defend past privileges but not to argue for new ones. The constitution, according to this vision, was a fixed, quasi-eternal document that could not be replaced or modified. In Max Weber's terms, its authority was more traditional than rational.[20] We are a long way here from modern constitutionalism.[21]

The limitations of ancient constitutionalism for political action quickly became apparent once the conflict between Charles and Parliament began to escalate. While Charles, desperate for money, grudgingly recalled Parliament and acquiesced to most of its demands, he drew a line when the MPs, in December 1641, narrowly passed a "Grand Remonstrance," which (among numerous other demands) would have given Parliament veto power over the king's appointments.[22] This claim went too far even for many in Parliament, who sensed that they had overstepped the bounds of their authority. But opposition leaders were in a bind: they increasingly felt the need to restrain Charles yet lacked the authority to do so. Accordingly, when war broke out in August 1642, Parliament expressed its resolve "to expose our Lives and Fortunes for the Defence and maintenance of the true Religion, *the Kings Person, Honour and Estate,* the Power and Priviledge of Parliament, and the just Rights and Liberties of the Subject."[23] The discourse of ancient constitutionalism was here stretched to its limit: Parliament was going to war with the king to save the king.

The breakdown of ancient constitutionalism as a means of authorizing resistance, then war, against the king provided an opening for other, more radical arguments to be made. One set of voices filling this void were the pamphleteers known as the Levellers, who drew on the early-modern revolutionary discourse to authorize not only their opposition to the king but also the establishment a new political system.[24] Where MPs had justified political demands with appeals to an ancient constitution, the Levellers turned mostly to theology and natural right, both of which remained very much entwined in this period. This political discourse allowed the pamphleteers to transfer the source of political authority from the (past) constitution to the (present) people. As Richard Overton claimed in *An Arrow Against all Tyrants* (1646), one of the most famous Leveller pamphlets, "To every individual in nature, is given an individual property by nature, not to be invaded or usurped by any." On this basis, he developed an argument for popular sovereignty: "each of them [the people] [have] communicated so much unto you (their *Chosen Ones*) of their natural rights and powers, that you might thereby become their absolute Commissioners, and lawful Deputies, but no more," Overton concluded, addressing himself to the MPs. This popular theory of political authority thus presented a challenge not only to the king but to Parliament as well. What's more, Overton added some bite to his bark. Any public body or official who violated its principles could be legitimately resisted: "tyranny, oppression and cruelty whatsoever, and in whomsoever, is in itself unnatural, illegal, yea absolutely anti-magisterial, for it is even destructive to all human civil society, and therefore resistible," he wrote.[25]

Replacing ancient constitutionalism with natural right as the foundation of political authority allowed the Levellers to advance a modern theory of constitutionalism that would become a hallmark feature of revolutionary discourse up through the eighteenth century (and beyond). Their constitutional ideas were perhaps most clearly on display during the Putney Debates, when Army Agitators sympathetic to Leveller ideas faced off with Army Grandees, including Oliver Cromwell.[26] One of the advisers to the Agitators, John Wildman, painted a sharp contrast between the competing theories of constitutionalism in play. In the ancient constitutional model, "our very laws were made by our conquerors," he argued, reflecting the common Leveller view that English government had been established by William the Conqueror, who put the "freemen of England" under "Bastard Norman Bondage."[27] But now that the English were "engaged for our freedom," Wildman continued, Parliament had to cast off this tainted heritage: "That's the end [i.e., purpose] of parliaments: not to constitute what is already established but to act according to the just rules of government." He concluded with a rhetorical question that would not have been out of place in Rousseau's *Social Contract*: can "any person justly be bound by law, who does not give his consent that such persons shall make laws for him?"[28]

We find here some of the basic tenets of modern constitutional theory, which include (1) a commitment to democratic rule; (2) an agreement on procedures for determining the political process; and (3) a recognition of certain core rights.[29] The very first demand formulated in *An Agreement of the People*—the text that the Agitators presented at the Putney Debates, as a rebuttal to the Grandees' *The Heads of the Proposals*—was for electoral reform, based on a more democratic division of the electorate.[30] This was also a primary point of contention between the Grandees, represented by the general Henry Ireton (also Cromwell's son-in-law), and the Agitators: Ireton refused to accept that suffrage could be extended beyond landowners.

The Levellers also argued, secondly, that government should be constrained by "a law paramount" that would be "unalterable by Parliaments":

> that the people shall of course meet . . . once in every two years upon an appointed day in their respective countries, for the election of the representers in Parliament, and that all the free-born at the age of twenty-one years and upwards be the electors.[31]

This procedural demand, finally, was supplemented by certain "rights provisions," concerning most notably the freedom of conscience, the freedom from forced military conscription, and the equality of all before the law.[32] For these reasons, historians have accordingly viewed the Leveller proposals as foreshadowing modern constitutional endeavors.[33] But their importance for the history of revolution is equally significant: the Levellers gave the discourse of revolution its modern, constitutional script.

The Levellers ultimately lost out to Cromwell and his allies. Their leaders were rounded up and imprisoned, while their supporters in the army were crushed after various mutinies. On the fundamental question of popular sovereignty and genuine democratic rule, Cromwell also balked: the 1649 Declaration of the Commonwealth explicitly recognized Parliament, rather than the people, as "the Supreme Authority of this Nation."[34] Still, many Leveller ideas ultimately persisted.[35] It was John Lilburne's lawyer, John Cooke, who leveled the charge of tyranny against Charles I, justifying his execution in the name of natural right.[36] The Rump Parliament abolished the House of Lords, in accordance with Leveller demands. And most important for the present argument, the Commonwealth issued England's first written constitution, the *Instrument of Government* (1653). As M. J. C. Vile argued, it was a propos this document that English political writers, most notably Marchamont Nedham, developed the doctrine of the separation between executive and legislative powers.[37] As the first revolution to produce a new political constitution—one which, moreover, reflects most of the principles of modern constitutionalism—the English civil war can be regarded as the starting point of a revolutionary tradition that would remain in place at least until 1789.

How the Jacobins Scrapped—and Rewrote— the Revolutionary Script

Both the script and discourse of revolution would evolve considerably over the following 150 years, but their basic tenets would remain unchanged. Resistance to a despotic ruler and the dissolution of the old polity had to be rapidly followed by the establishment of a new constitutional order; the revolutionary interregnum had to be kept as brief as possible. Even before officially declaring independence from Britain, the American Continental Congress began considering drafts for a new constitution;[38] and one of the very first actions of the newly styled National Assembly in France was to vow that it would not disband before it had "established and solidified" the French constitution.[39] There was, as Keith Baker has argued, "between revolution and constitution . . . a fundamental link."[40]

The storming of the Bastille did not fundamentally transform this script, but rather brought another dramatis persona back into the story: the people. Nonetheless, having warily accepted to share their leading role with the Parisian crowds, the deputies did not see fit to change their course of action: "the people took up arms, blood was spilt: it was the blood of the guilty," Dominique-Joseph Garat recognized, before immediately emphasizing the task at hand, which was still for the legislature to "proclaim the eternal rights of French sovereignty and the ineffaceable rights of man."[41] Granted, the official and the popular versions of this revolutionary script would often be at odds over the following three years. But even as they differed over the *content* of the new constitution (with some groups pressing for a republican government, from mid-1791 onward), there was as yet no disagreement that producing *a* constitution was still the end-goal of revolution.

But the proclamation of the new constitution, in September 1791, did not put an end to the Revolution. Instead, over the course of the next two years, the Jacobins and their allies developed an entirely new concept of revolution, one based on a different source of political authority. This transformation of revolutionary authority was gradual and largely driven by events; it was not a preplanned conspiracy to hold on to power at all costs. But its net result was to completely transform both the revolutionary discourse and script that had been in place since the seventeenth century. It is to the story of this transformation that I turn now.

The issue of revolutionary authority was thrust to the forefront of political debates after the 10 August 1792 overthrow of the monarchy. It was with respect to this "last revolution" that Robespierre delivered his 5 November famous speech against Louvet and other Girondins, who had accused him of dictatorial ambitions. A key part of his defense concerned the activities of the general council of the Paris Commune, of which he had become a member on 10 August. Yes, they had arrested and disarmed "suspicious citizens"; they had sent representatives to other *départments*; they had cracked down on royalist presses. But their authority derived from the revolutionary circumstances, during which the *code criminel* was superseded by an unwritten revolutionary law. What is most noteworthy about Robespierre's claim, however, is that it was not simply made on behalf of the *peuple* who had stormed the Tuileries (as it had been in 1789 with respect to the Bastille); it now applied to institutional powers, such as the Paris Commune, as well. Tellingly, Robespierre even renamed the executive organ of the Commune the "conseil général *révolutionnaire*."[42] This turn of phrase highlights both the new authority on which this council acted and the fact that a state institution could now assume an authority previously possessed only by the people.

This broadening of revolutionary authority was still contained, however, by a number of pre-existing factors. First, the revolutionary activity of the Paris Commune continued to fall within the limited sphere of resistance theory. The measures it took were ultimately forms of self-defense, Robespierre argued, since the royalist party was plotting its own repression. Whether or not such a conspiracy was truly in the making, it is noteworthy that Robespierre felt the need to cite this looming threat as a justification for invoking revolutionary authority.[43] Secondly, this authority continued to be viewed as resting, in the final analysis, on popular sovereignty: revolutionary leaders "should be viewed as having received tacit approval [*fondés de procuration tacite*] from the whole of society." The Paris Commune, in this account, was simply the handmaiden of the *peuple*; its authority was subservient to the will of the people.[44] Finally, the temporal window for the exercise of revolutionary authority was still very narrow. The Commune acted in a revolutionary manner only so long as no other capable institution was in place. Its revolutionary moment thus corresponded to a brief interlude in a longer constitutional script of political dissolution and reconstruction. If Robespierre was so dismissive of Louvet's criticism, it was because the National Convention was not meant to "cast the severe gaze of the Inquisition on events pertaining to the insurrection, but to secure with fair laws the liberty thus regained."[45] Constitutional rule ("fair laws") was still the *telos* toward which Revolution was directed.

This initial transfer of revolutionary authority from popular insurrection onto a governmental institution thus appears fairly limited. Even in its revolutionary incarnation, the general council of the Paris Commune never claimed to replace the state, only to act in its absence. At the same time, Robespierre's speech signaled a new willingness to appropriate for the state a power previously reserved for the people. This willingness—and the fact that it went unchallenged by his fellow *conventionnels*—marked an important step toward establishing a novel script for revolutionary action. Where the Paris Commune could not wield revolutionary authority in an unfettered manner, other, *national* state institutions were not hampered by the same restrictions. First among these institutions was the Convention itself.

The opportunity for adapting revolutionary authority for state action at the highest level was furnished by the trial of Louis XVI. A week after Robespierre brushed off allegations of dictatorship, Saint-Just stunned the Convention with a speech demanding that the king be tried—and executed—in accordance with the law of nations, rather than positive law.[46] The first speaker to demand the floor immediately after Saint-Just was Robespierre himself, who declared that he had "different views to propose." He received the chance to express these views two weeks later: while he concurred with Saint-Just on many points, Robespierre then introduced a new justification for denying legal procedures to the king. In following with the principles put forward in his 5 November speech, he declared that "to propose trying Louis XVI . . . is a counter-revolutionary idea, since it is an indictment of the Revolution itself." Either the Revolution or the king was guilty: "if Louis can be presumed innocent, what becomes of the Revolution?" As it was absurd to question the righteousness of the Revolution, the only logical conclusion was that Louis had *already* been judged by the 10 August Revolution ("Louis cannot be tried; he has already been condemned"). All that was left for the Convention to do was to carry out the people's judgment.[47]

This argument had far-reaching theoretical repercussions, even if at this point the repercussions were only theoretical. For Robespierre was essentially calling on the state to execute the king on the basis of revolutionary authority. To be sure, this demand was supported by references to popular sovereignty and natural right theory, two political discourses that continued, at this stage, to underpin such authority. Robespierre still remained faithful in this speech to the constitutional script of revolution, which was similarly shared by most deputies. But he also revised a crucial part of this narrative: now revolutionary authority could be applied even *after* the popular insurrection, to justify the actions of the new state. This argument was driven, in part, by necessity: the Convention could not draw its authority from the 1791 Constitution, since, as Robespierre wryly noted, "The Constitution forbade everything you have done." But the people were still there: in the absence of constitutional authority, why not consult them? As we know, the Montagnards refused an *appel au peuple*, thereby deepening the rift between popular and revolutionary authority. The latter could now operate independently of the former and for a much longer duration. But how much longer? Robespierre's own answer was ominous, as he warned his colleagues not to confuse "the situation of a revolutionary people, with that of a people whose government is firmly established." This comment foreshadows Robespierre's subsequent "Rapport sur les principes de morale politique" (5 February 1794), which similarly opposed a future "democracy" with the present "popular government in revolution [*gouvernement populaire en revolution*]"—without specifying *when* this transition would ever occur.[48]

While the Montagnards did not win the initial procedural skirmishes over the king's trial, these debates did offer them an opportunity to refine and combine their arguments into a reasonably coherent political theory. Even so, their understanding of revolutionary authority continued to evolve. For instance, during the spring months of 1793, one could track its expansion over other state functions, most notably in the sphere of justice, with the creation of the revolutionary tribunal. For our present purposes, however, it may be more productive to fast-forward until October 1793, since this jump in time will allow us to appreciate the vastly expanded scope that revolutionary authority came to be granted.

The decisive event that occurred at this moment was the suspension of the Constitution, ratified a mere two months prior. Its death knell was struck by Saint-Just, speaking on behalf of the Committee of Public Safety. In a speech remarkable for the fact that it mentioned the Constitution only once, and not at all in its accompanying decree, Saint-Just insisted instead on the dangers presented by a government deemed insufficiently "revolutionary": "The laws are revolutionary, those who execute them are not," he proclaimed. Because the government could not be trusted, public administration had to be "identified with the revolutionary movement." For Saint-Just, this meant that the Constitution must be suspended until the government itself has been constituted in a revolutionary fashion: "It is impossible for revolutionary laws to be executed, unless the government itself is constituted in a revolutionary fashion [*constitué révolutionnairement*]." It was in these precise terms that the decree Saint-Just presented to the Convention was couched: article 1 declared: "The provisional government of France is revolutionary until peacetime."[49] This statement euphemistically expressed the real object of the Committee of Public Safety's decree—namely, the suspension of the Constitution. But this formulation also drew attention to the source of authority on which the government thereafter resided. Revolution was now the foundation of the Revolution.

This episode has not received much attention, yet is truly remarkable. Where earlier expressions of revolutionary authority had remained at least loosely connected with both popular sovereignty and a forthcoming constitutional order, Saint-Just now severed these ties completely. There were, to be sure, political and philosophical reasons why the Montagnard-dominated Convention would not have been overly concerned about mothballing the Constitution. During the spring/summer 1793 debates over the

Constitution, for instance, the Montagnards had expressed their general opposition to voluntaristic theories of politics, arguing in favor of jusnaturalist claims instead.[50] What is striking about the reception of Saint-Just's report, however, is that the *conventionnels* were now ready to ditch constitutionalism in any shape or form; indeed, the Committee's proposed decree did not elicit any criticism and appears to have been approved unanimously.[51] This willingness reflects how dramatically the concept of revolutionary authority had expanded in the previous few months. Where revolution had until recently been anchored in a constitutional script, it had become unmoored. Instead of disappearing with the return of constitutional order, revolutionary authority was invoked by the Committee of Public Safety to overpower and extinguish the Constitution that was supposed to be its end. What this meant for the state was unclear: since Revolution was no longer tied to popular will or constitutional strictures, its signification was largely up for grabs. At the same time, it was an incredibly powerful force, all the more so that it could be used to trump claims based on any other form of political authority.

Conclusion: A Dangerous Script for the Twentieth Century

After Thermidor, this new authority was quickly abandoned. The National Convention set about once again writing a Constitution, France's third in six years. For a while it looked as though the Jacobin script was destined for oblivion: in the wave of revolutions that swept across much of Europe and Spanish America, between 1808 and 1830, all followed the constitutional script.

During this time, however, social theorists also began thinking more imaginatively about the possible end-points of revolution. Just as the Jacobins abandoned constitutionalism for a dreamy vision of a "natural" republic, utopian socialists looked past democratic institutions toward a perfected society-to-come.[52] "Real" revolution could not be accomplished at the ballot box, Marx asserted in *The Eighteenth Brumaire of Louis Bonaparte*: the peasants would always vote for a Napoleon. Instead of pining for a constitutional solution, the next wave of revolutionaries should seek instead to establish "the permanence of the revolution."[53] His call did not go unheeded: in August 1917, Lenin would dismiss out of hand what he mocked as "constitutional illusions."[54] Two months later, the Jacobin script would be back, this time to stay.[55]

GUILLAUME MAZEAU

Scripting the French Revolution, Inventing the Terror

Marat's Assassination and Its Interpretations

Debates over the origin of a "mechanism of revolutions" that would explain their diffusion, commonalities, and differences are probably as old as the existence of the phenomenon itself. The French at the end of the eighteenth century, despite their claims to exceptionality in carrying out a revolution de novo, were also tormented (as the multitude of their publications on other historical revolutions reveals) by the question of the origins and models of revolutions, particularly those from antiquity.[1] Recent French historians, too, having long defended a Gallocentric view of the French Revolution as the mother of all revolutions, have progressively enlarged their perspective. The attempts of Jacques Godechot and Robert Palmer to integrate the French revolutionary episode into the "Atlantic revolutions" have thus contributed, along with the work of François Furet, to a deconstruction of the great Jacobin discourse that had imposed itself as the dominant vision of the events.[2] The Godechot-Palmer thesis, which gave the French Revolution a more relative place at the heart of an extended "western Atlantic revolution" in a way that suggested the preeminence of the American script, has since been strongly contested, notably by the historiography of parallel revolutions.[3] Today, understood in light of other revolutionary experiences, the French Revolution remains nonetheless in a class of its own. Its difference symbolized by the Terror, it is still defined primarily by a politics of state violence that other revolutions had not known.

In this chapter I will offer a case study to show the extent to which the protagonists of the French Revolution both acted in the light of pre-existing scripts and were driven to invent new ones, never in a theoretical

---

This chapter was translated from the French by Chloe Edmonson and Keith Michael Baker.

or planned manner but rather in response to concrete issues precipitated by events. The facts I shall consider are as follows: on 13 July 1793, the journalist and Montagnard deputy Jean-Paul Marat was stabbed by a then unknown young woman named Charlotte Corday. Carried out at a time of grave political and military crisis, this political assassination provoked an immediate debate over the more global meaning of the Revolution. After analyzing this debate, I will show that Marat's death was integral to the construction of a new script to which the French Revolution fell inescapably hostage: the script of the Terror.

Inventing the Myth of 1789.

The death of Marat was first and foremost a catalyst for the French publicity machine to fabricate stories that would consolidate the young and fragile Republic. In the summer of 1793, Marat became, along with Le Peletier and Chalier, one of the three official martyrs of the Republic upon whose spilled blood the new regime was founded. At his death he was far from anonymous; his successful trial against the Girondins in the spring, had made him the most visible man of the day. The fabrication of his memory was thus a major political issue. Even if he was isolated in the midst of the Montagnards, contested by the Enragés, and criticized increasingly by the Jacobins and the Cordeliers, he remained very popular among the "plebeians of the Republic"—the sans-culottes, the revolutionary women, and soldiers. For this reason, despite their profound differences and reservations about him, the elite and spokespersons of the Revolution allowed themselves briefly to celebrate Marat during the summer and fall of 1793. The important corpus of eulogies pronounced during this period allowed for a refinement of the French narrative (or "Jacobin myth," according to Furet) of *la grande révolution*, born on a summer day in 1789 in complete rupture with the past and (as the Montagnards would later pretend, feigning repentance) destroyed in the summer of 1794 with the fall of Robespierre.[4]

L'Ami du Peuple, "The People's Friend," pure product of European oppositional politics at the end of the eighteenth century, provided choice material for this myth. He was well suited to be the "Man of the Enlightenment" his mourners tried to make him. Born in 1743 in the Prussian principality of Neufchâtel, he had constructed his career, following the model of Montesquieu to whom he paid tribute in 1785, through numerous voyages in France, England, the United Provinces, Geneva, and Spain.[5] Anxious to make a name for himself among the enlightened elite but failing to acquire institutional recognition, he had quickly set his sights on winning public opinion, throwing himself into works of popularization and offering fashionable scientific performances. Living in London from 1765 to 1777, this "citizen of the world" (as he later described himself) had forged contacts with the popular political clubs in the north of England and frequented the diaspora of political dissidents against European despotism. In 1774, at the height of the resurgence of the Wilkesite crisis in London, he had published several essays in English. Back in France, he had translated Newton and made himself known to the celebrated Benjamin Franklin.

Imagining himself the heir of the anonymous spokesmen of the people who, between the letters of "Junius" in the *Public Advertiser* and the articles by "Publius" in the *Federalist Papers*, had resorted to pseudonyms to defend causes, mobilize public opinion, and denounce abuses of power, Marat had published in June 1790 (in addition to his journal *L'Ami du Peuple*) the first of thirteen issues of the French *Junius*. Six months before Charlotte Corday stabbed this fifty-year-old man in midsummer 1793, he had polished his autobiography in his journal. Thus he was already reputed in France and Europe as a "gutter Rousseau" (*Rousseau des ruisseaux*) who had combated despotism and prophesied the revolution.[6]

Confined to an underground lifestyle for much of the years since 1789 as a result of his inflammatory articles dramatizing his own hardships, like other journalists and pamphleteers before him, Marat was now added in the panegyrics at his death to the long list of the celebrated avant-garde of the Enlightenment, from Locke to Montesquieu. The author of *Chains of Slavery*, a work first written in English and praised as a universal history of the evils of despotism, was presented as the victim of European despotism in all its forms. Yet his death was not merely integrated into the European revolutionary narrative. In several eulogies, mention of his various periods of exile before 1789 served to invent a script that made France the last and true land of revolution: his revolutionary engagement in France became the culmination of his entire career. Inaccurately portrayed as an inspiration and even a protagonist of the storming of the Bastille, Marat was found everywhere. He incarnated the French people of 1789 whose action had eclipsed the events taking place simultaneously in Brabant, and he had managed (according to the histories written after 1792) to define other contemporary revolutions as outmoded or secondary. Years before the invention of the *Grande Nation* and its Republican sisters, Marat's death, occurring at a moment of grave political and military crisis and an explosion of nationalism, was consequently used to write the script according to which the

French Revolution (henceforth capitalized), profiting from the failure of all others, became the first and above all the only revolution that could claim the power to transform the world by reducing the past to a tabula rasa and eliminating the heterogeneous group of its enemies now lumped together under the term "Counter-Revolution."

The particular circumstances of Marat's assassination, stabbed as he was in his bath by a young aristocrat, also allowed for a crystallization of the French script into a story of Manichean revolution, a binary conflict between the revolutionaries and counter-revolutionaries.[7] In the many prints inspired by the event, the fight to the death between Corday and Marat became a metaphor for a revolution that had degenerated into a civil war. This was the danger David succeeded in covering up in his painting *Marat Assassiné*, commissioned by the Convention and released, significantly enough, the same day in October 1793 as the execution of Marie-Antoinette. The *Ami du Peuple* was not portrayed by David as a corpse but rather as merely wounded, ready to pick up his quill again. The revolution remained a utopia of the tabula rasa and of the refusal to compromise. Charlotte Corday, absent from the picture, was displaced from the event just as the Counter-Revolution was to be displaced from the course of history. The message was transparent: the counter-revolutionaries would never succeed in "bringing back the past" because the momentum toward the Republic was inevitable.

This reading of the assassination gave a teleological and secular meaning to the French Revolution: that of progress and final victory, incarnated by the man of science, the doctor and physicist, the political activist and scholar that Marat embodied, in opposition to the obscurantism of the Counter-Enlightenment represented by Corday, a women raised in the counter-revolutionary milieu of the convent. For the republicans, Marat's assassination was consequently a sign that the Revolution had well and truly become a radical break, a merciless struggle between the ghosts of the past and the people who dared to look toward the future. The scripts of the British and American revolutions, as well as the Belgian, that most often integrated "revolution" into a Christian and providential perception of the historical moment, were thus thrown into question. Four years after the failed reform of the monarchy, Marat's assassination was thus used to rewrite the genealogy of one of the century's last revolutions, differentiating the French Revolution from those earlier models by presenting it as an unprecedented rupture with the past.

The Reactionary Counter-Revolution

The facts of Marat's death thus seemed to confirm the Montagnards in their conviction that what was happening in France was an unprecedented battle between "the Revolution" propelling a dynamic of progress and irreversible change, on the one side, and what the patriots called "the Counter-Revolution," constituting a brake on progress or a refusal of history on the other. The invention of the reactionary Counter-Revolution accompanied the invention of the Revolution, which was held to be radical and progressive by its very nature. In short order, Charlotte Corday's aristocratic origins, her kinship with Corneille—bard of the noble ethos inherited from the *Grand Siècle*—and her acquaintance with the royalist milieus of Normandy were obligingly released to the public. Everything for that matter seemed to evince the counter-revolutionary or, rather, archaic character of the assassination. Like an aristocrat, Marie Anne Charlotte de Corday d'Armont (to give her full name) had appeared at Marat's home dressed as a lady of quality: like an aristocrat, she had entered thanks to the kind of letter of introduction normally used in *le monde*; like an aristocrat, she had delivered her blow decisively, succeeding as would one of the greatest swordsmen in piercing Marat's heart through the ribs. In the face of the murderess's silence in asserting that she had acted alone, it quickly proved impossible to unravel the conspiratorial network believed to have been necessary to inflict such a blow.

Frightening as it was, this invisibility reinforced the Montagnard authorities in their conviction that events in France were giving rise, for the first time in the history of revolutions, to a frontal conflict between opposing camps: the public and transparent one of the Revolution and the vast underground one of the Counter-Revolution. This was the perspective from which the Montagnard authorities sought to caricature the two actors in the event in order to integrate them into an ideal narrative of the revolution. On 20 July, the Parisian general council issued a violent description of the assassin, published in the *Gazette de France nationale* and reproduced in the form of posters destined to be posted in all the municipalities. The Counter-Revolution had a territory (the Vendée), and it now had a face, that of Charlotte Corday, likened to a "female monster" or an animal. These images excluded Corday from the human race and rendered futile any possibility of her rehabilitation, and thus of clemency. As war raged within the territory and without, Corday personified an enemy incapable of all humanity, dismissive of the elementary rules of civilization, stopping at nothing to destroy the Revolution—thus placing itself beyond the domain of natural right, justifying all forms of retaliation, and authorizing all reactions. For Corday's adversaries, this *ci-devant* represented, by her very nature, the end of a society of orders and privileges, the death of a degenerate race of nobility, and the last convulsions of a world striving in vain to drag all the patriots down into its own agony. For many, the significance of the assassination of the *Ami du Peuple* thus far surpassed its immediate meaning: it became a founding myth of a revolution seen as a wrenching from the past and a combat between good and evil. Because it attained this metaphorical dimension, Marat's assassination would for two centuries be the most frequently represented event of the French Revolution, even more than the storming of the Bastille.[8]

In contrast to the British, who spoke of Civil War rather than of revolution, the French loathed the characterization of their revolution as a civil war. But Marat's assassination revealed, almost three years to the day after the apparent harmony of the *Fête de la Fédération* (14 July 1790), that discord had once more become the engine of the national history. The counter-revolutionaries willingly went along with a Manichean interpretation of the assassination. It was in their interest as well to frame events as a merciless battle between two enemy factions. They too saw in the fatal confrontation between Marat and Corday a metonym of the revolution, conceived as a dialectical process that was now bringing about the defeat of the Montagnards and the victory of Providence. Although she was, in fact, closely aligned with the Girondins and the moderate republicans, and rejected any affiliation with the Counter-Revolution, Corday was unwillingly turned into an instrument of providential history; her execution was added to the list of glorious defeats suffered by the Christian martyrs. Compared in France and also in England to Judith and Jeanne d'Arc, had she not confessed to conceiving Marat's assassination as a means to restore the glory of a prestigious family line that had nonetheless fallen into poverty and anonymity? Had her letters not contrasted the honor and dignity of her action with the vulgarity of Marat and the sans-culottes? And finally, did this young noble from Normandy not represent the resistance of the provinces to the centralism of Paris and the Jacobins, another cliché of the times?[9]

In the last analysis, these competing readings of the event imposed the same script of the French Revolution: the "Counter-Revolution," incarnated by Charlotte Corday, brought together all those who positioned themselves against the new engine of history, the "Revolution." This script, in part unprecedented by the English revolutions ("parliamentarians" against "royalists") or the American ("insurgents" against "loyalists")—events described by their contemporaries as civil wars or wars of independence—was assimilated only with difficulty to a more complex reality. Jean-Clément Martin has demonstrated that the absolute monarchy crumbled first under the attacks of those who would only later be qualified as "counter-revolutionaries" and who, by pushing the king toward intransigence from 1787 to 1789, ultimately caused the failure of the awaited reform.[10] We can thus say that, in terms of the facts, the Counter-Revolution clearly preceded the Revolution. However, a closer examination of the motivations behind Marat's assassination confirms the extent to which such discourses, invented to reassure public opinion, remained fragile and constantly put to the test in face of the complexity of the events.

Trouble in the Revolution

Contrary to the claims of Montagnard propaganda, the assassination of the *Ami du People* left the French profoundly perplexed and divided in the summer of 1793. If Marat's journalistic engagement rendered him the most beloved man of the sans-culottes, his extreme radicalism also made him hated by a large portion of the population, even within his own faction—so much so that some even accused him of working secretly for the Counter-Revolution. Had he not served as a doctor in the household of the comte d'Artois, the king's brother? Had he not spent many years living in foreign monarchies? Had he not instigated the September Massacres of 1792, which had given the sans-culottes a very bad name?[11] In contrast, if Charlotte Corday's social origins guaranteed her the admiration of conservative milieus, the manner in which she justified her act before the revolutionary tribunal, as well as the calm with which she went to the scaffold, disconcerted even the most convinced Montagnards and weakened even the best-crafted accounts. While Marat was being celebrated in grandiose funerals and admitted to the Pantheon as official martyr of the Republic, Corday was quickly adulated by a large spectrum of public opinion, from royalists to the radicals. Official propaganda notwithstanding, she became a national heroine. The script of the revolution as a binary conflict between hermetically sealed camps thus found itself called into question. Six months after the shock of the king's execution, at the height of civil war, and with the country on the brink of invasion by foreign armies, Marat's assassination damaged the reassuring *grand récit* of the Revolution that the most radical opposing factions shared an interest in sanctioning.

This vacillation found expression in a proliferation of the wildest fears and rumors. Their number, taken seriously by the police, demonstrates that the scripts shaping the revolutionaries' imagination did not come only from the political and social elites. The popular classes participated fully in the fabrication of models of action and of the intelligibility of the events. Eager to be the first to give the latest news, constantly chasing time that never ceased to unfold before their very eyes, and finding it very difficult to verify information, many journalists and pamphleteers had no choice but to rely on *l'esprit public* in writing the immediate story. With history bursting from its hinges, the script of 1789 cowritten by the revolutionaries and their adversaries—the script according to which the French Revolution resulted from a vision of rationalistic and secular rupture—now meshed poorly with the resurgence of providential and millenarian conceptions at the heart of political practice and public debate. If divinatory activities like astrology had receded from politics since the seventeenth century in the face of statistical and predictive science, the Revolution, with its bundle of fears and uncertainties, ensured the return of the prophetic mode of interpreting the present. Thus Marat had barely expired before retrospective accounts of dozens of prophecies appeared in the streets of Paris. In some, rumors that Marat would soon be killed had already been circulating; in others, he had already been assassinated, or had even died from an illness, by the time Corday arrived to stab him. On 14 July, the readers of the *Scrutateur universel*, a Montagnard newspaper, were informed that "Marat was not assassinated; he died in his bathtub, almost cold, the moment a bout of hot fever overtook him, causing a fatal stroke."[12] By finding a medical explanation for Marat's death that made it foreseeable and even inevitable, such accounts denied Charlotte Corday any importance and hoped to efface the danger represented by the Counter-Revolution. But these were only futile responses to the doubts intruding into revolutionary convictions—doubts that had already been reflected in accounts of the progression of Marat's illness published by a number of journals in June.[13]

The assassin's profile, moreover, did not correspond to the Jacobin script of the Revolution. Partisan of neither the Jacobin "Revolution" nor the monarchist "Counter-Revolution," Charlotte Corday incarnated a model of the Revolution that was scarcely "French": an eighteenth-century European model of revolution, or rather "revolutions," conceived not as breaks with the past but rather as returns to an older order, a lost golden age. Had not the majority of revolutions in the modern age been accomplished according to this script, whether the British revolutions in the seventeenth century, the American Revolution directed in the 1770s against violations of English constitutional traditions, or the revolutions of the Austrian Netherlands, Geneva, or the United-Provinces in the 1780s, executed in the name of a return to liberty for small nations? Contrary to the ultras of the Counter-Revolution, Corday wanted a simple return neither to absolute monarchy nor to a society of privileges. But in opposition to the Jacobins, she dreamed of a revolution-restoration that could extinguish the radicalization that had taken place since the execution of Louis XVI (21 January 1793) and the proscription of the Girondins (2 June 1793), while preserving the principles of 1789 and of the Republic. "Farewell my dear papa, I beg you to forget me, or rather to rejoice in my fate, its cause being beautiful," Corday wrote on the threshold of death, attempting to convince her father that she had neither derogated from her condition nor dishonored her name. To the contrary: the sudden glory of the assassin who had dispatched the man many considered a monster embellished her family's honor, which for Corday justified her gesture as an act of heroism worthy of the grandest noble tradition.[14]

Motivated by the melancholia and revanchist spirit of the declassed gentry, Corday thus believed that the monarchy, having perverted its founding principles, was partly liable for the injustices that had particularly affected the lesser country nobility; it had paid the price of its errors with Louis XVI's execution. Even if Corday was properly horrified by the king's death, she recognized the legitimacy of civil disobedience and revealed herself to be strongly influenced by theories of tyrannicide. "Do not forget this line by Corneille: 'Crime brings shame and not the scaffold,'"[15] she wrote three days after the stabbing Marat. In justifying her act she cited a classic of seventeenth-century noble literature recounting the story of the great Count of Essex, who had been deposed and condemned to death by Elizabeth I. She thus revealed her admiration for those who give their lives in the name of the fight against tyranny. "Killing is no murder." An anglophile like many members of the liberal nobility, Corday admitted her appreciation for the tyrannicidal theses of the abbé Raynal, referred often to British history, and willingly cited John Milton, who was known in part as one of the Puritan theorists of tyrannicide.

Touched by the collective fantasy of the second half of the eighteenth century (to kill the king) and failing to understand the new political culture that the republicans had been inventing since the autumn of 1792, Corday analyzed the situation in the summer of 1793 through Old Regime eyes. Persuaded that political power always concentrated in the body of a single person, she turned toward the new figure of male despotism she saw Marat symbolizing. But her regicide was mistimed. In reality, the new regime founded on the democratization of sovereignty extended this new figure of despotism to each of the elected deputies. In stabbing Marat, Corday could not thus really reclaim the symbolic force of a regicide. On the contrary, she eliminated precisely the man who symbolized a new relationship to politics for men and women alike: in 1793, Marat was not loved in terms of the traditional model of the father of the nation, but rather in the more egalitarian guise of brother, as the "friend" of the people.

A New Relation to History

A few days after the assassination, Florent Guiot, deputy of the Côte-d'Or, sent the following news to the popular club of Semur: "This event has caused little surprise. Twenty letters from Paris to the departments that have been intercepted, including a notable one destined for Strasbourg, announced a movement in Paris for the 15th of the month and asserted that on this date, Marat, Robespierre, and Danton would no longer exist." In fabricating the fiction according to which Marat's murder was a nonevent, this deputy did not merely seek to diminish the sense of insecurity haunting many of the French; he participated in the construction of a new script for the French Revolution reflecting a new relationship to time and history. For the majority of the French in 1793 who had been subjects of an absolute monarchy only a few years before, the Republic remained but a vague, almost unknown notion referring sometimes to the more or less recent European or American experiences, of which the majority of citizens knew virtually nothing.

In the second half of July, many journalists and pamphleteers soberly affirmed that Marat was in any case dying or already dead before he was stabbed, hoping thereby to nullify the shock of the event. In the context of civil war and fear of conspiracy, mastering time was fundamental to ensuring the legitimacy of the new and fragile Republic. The popular clubs that assembled before the Convention on the morning of 14 July to proclaim their lack of surprise were also striving equally to turn Marat's death into a nonevent. Similarly, at the Jacobin Club that same morning, a man declared that an employee of the Ministry of the Interior had not only predicted the murder the day before it happened, but had also forecast its exact time. This makes understandable the report by a Ministry of the Interior observer responsible for gauging public opinion, who described the calm of the population: "Saturday night, 13 July, either because the reality of the assassination was doubted or the death of the *Ami du Peuple* was anticipated—he was considered fatally ill—the report of this tragic end was received with composure."[16] Fear of seeing the enemies of the nation becoming masters of time reflected doubt regarding the legitimacy of the recent political changes, particularly the execution of the king. Moreover, the vertigo created by Marat's assassination was reminiscent of January 1793. The startling imagery inspired by the assassination shows the extent to which the Republic invented, in practice rather than in books, a new script laid over the ashes of the monarchy.

If Marat died a thousand times before 13 July, it was because in the popular imagination his body became the emblem of the people in Revolution. The daily controversies over the body of the *Ami du people*, recognized as a "normal" hero with whom the simple citizens could easily identify, became one of the bases for democratic debate, a site for the exercise of civic critique. This phenomenon pertained not only to the case of the *Ami du Peuple*. The health of the deputies, and of the people's spokespersons more broadly, turned into a barometer of events. From Mirabeau to Robespierre, passing by way of Loustalot and thus Marat, the bodies of those who henceforth incarnated the nation's hopes became a political matter.[17] Ill since 1782, Marat traversed the Revolution as a man in decline, threatened by death; he started early to construct the legend of his sacrifice for the people's cause. In the French edition of *Chaînes de l'Esclavage*, published the year preceding his death, he claimed to have prepared his work with so much ardor and coffee that he had almost lost his life to it.[18] Because it coincided with the new criteria for heroism, the fiction of Marat's willing exhaustion persuaded some of the public. Rumors of his imminent end multiplied in the autumn of 1792. By the beginning of the summer of 1793, many believed he was already in agony: "Marat is in extremis . . . . He will die in his bed."[19]

Yet this theme was not completely consistent with the revolutionary culture. These discourses evoked the well-known theme of the king's body whose fate was linked, in an organicist conception of the kingdom, to that of the many bodies of the society of orders and of all of its subjects.[20] It is thus possible to see in the shock following Marat's assassination a mere "transfer of sacrality" (to adopt Mona Ozouf's term) in which the Republic, rather than inventing genuinely new scripts in relation to the monarchy, contented itself at best to adapting preexisting political scenarios.[21] The transfer from the political culture of the ancien régime to that of the Republic could thus be symbolically situated at the moment when the royal tombs in the necropolis of Saint-Denis were violated—just as Marat's corpse was being embalmed, a privilege previously reserved for royal bodies. The continuity of the monarchical script can also be found in the horrified reactions of those who were quick, a few months after having voted or approved Louis XVI's death, to compare the killer of the *Ami du Peuple* to history's most famous regicides from Ravaillac to Damiens, not forgetting Jacques Clément.[22] Often qualified as an act of *lèse-nation*, Marat's murder was, for some, as serious as crimes of *lèse-majesté*.[23]

However, the organicist metaphor that had previously legitimized political and social inequalities by concentrating power in the body of a single person and assigning each "member" a precise place in the functioning body of the nation, was no longer exactly the same after January 1793. In a hereditary monarchy, the kingdom's stability rested on the imperative of the survival of the lineage, but also on the longevity and vitality of the king himself. In the political imagination, the nation's fate thus rested on the fate of a single family or a single body whose biological events (births, deaths) nourished the production of histories of the realm, but whose minor derailments when poorly managed could also turn into affairs of state. After 1789, this aspect of the political culture of the ancien régime did not disappear. The National Assembly was still announcing the state of the king's health in the autumn of 1791, probably in order to restore the nation's empathy after the flight to Varennes: at that point, Louis was suffering an "indisposition." Under the Republic, however, and after the death of the king, the political imaginary was democratized along with institutions and practices. Moreover, already in the second half of the eighteenth century, in a context of rising opposition and revolts, this aspect of monarchical propaganda had already been hijacked by part of public opinion, which used the "official" theme of the king's illness to speak freely about the central taboo of the regime: the death of the monarch.[24] When this fantasy of killing the king became reality in January 1793, the incarnation of the nation became ensured only by the deputies, who henceforth found themselves the sole depositaries of national sovereignty.

Unlike the king, though, the representatives of the people were no longer sacred but only inviolable.[25] This doctrine of political immunity was very different from the sanctity of the monarch, because it protected and distinguished not a particular individual but rather a collective entity.[26] The stability of the regime rested not on the fate of one man but rather on that of several hundred, each deputy being replaceable by a substitute. In theory, a simple assassination could not weaken the entire structure. But in the context of war and looming suspicions of aristocratic conspiracy, the fears that had accompanied the king's death resurfaced with Marat's. Many persuaded themselves that all the deputies who had voted for Louis XVI's execution would soon be assassinated and the entire Convention would disappear under the blows of a vast "conspiracy of the dagger."[27] Six months after 21 January 1793, the murder of the man who had incarnated the people was consequently understood as a response to the death of the king.[28]

Here again, David knew better than anyone how to express the new script the French revolutionaries were trying to construct: in his painting, destined to be hung in the National Convention's assembly hall and thus serving as an example to the deputies, Marat's smile conveyed the confidence that the citizens had to place in the new regime. Even attacked and struck down, Marat's spirit would always lift itself up, for a thousand *Amis du People* would rise to take up his torch. In the heat of the event, establishing himself as the regime's best propagandist, David succeeded in synthesizing a story of the nation that, from the martyrs of Year II to the Unknown Soldier of World War I, enabled the new regime to convert and mobilize the French: the ideal of republican continuity capable of preserving the cohesion of the nation despite the vicissitudes of history.

Marat's assassination is thus found at the heart of a promethean endeavor, specific to the French revolutionary experience, consisting no longer of just mastering time but of abolishing it by force of political will. The utopia of the tabula rasa, an escape from monarchical time accomplished by the invention of a radically new republican culture capable of regenerating the nation, was evidently destined for failure, but it also attested to the rupture with all the experiences of the past, including those of the Revolution, that the French wanted to express. For many of them, the Republic was limited neither to the disappearance of the king nor to the creation of new political institutions, and even less to imitation of preexisting models. As Dan Edelstein has emphasized, the Jacobins' "Republic-to-come" was a project never defined in advance, but one always underway and open to a future to be invented.[29] It was a profound change in the relationship of the French to history, previously cadenced by reigns of kings or the will of God. The Republic of which the Jacobins dreamed was by nature counterfactual. If they knew that 1792 had invented an ancien régime, none of them was capable of saying what the contours of the Republic would look like, at least until they were fixed in 1795. Accordingly, the expression "new regime" was never used.

Was the pretension to "cast off" expressed in the cult of the *Ami du People* therefore merely rhetoric, a political illusion resulting from nascent nationalism? Not entirely. If the French counted among the last revolutionaries of the eighteenth century, they were on the other hand the first to enact a revolution in this new sense. In previous centuries, as earlier essays in this volume show, political trouble had been designated by such terms as "revolt," "insurrection," "rebellion," *attentat* (assassination attempt), and especially "civil war," while "revolution" was most often employed pejoratively in the plural form to describe cyclical troubles or even restorations. Yet the word gradually shifted meaning, coming by the end of the eighteenth century to signify a positive, brutal, irreversible change, not only in the political order but also in the social.[30] The French script of the Republic, tied to the new meaning of the word "revolution," was consequently linked more globally to a new regime of historicity, a new relation to time inspiring discourses and action that instituted the dynamic of radicalization as the evident paradigm of the revolutionary phenomenon. The result was the formation of a new script, cowritten by the French and foreign counter-revolutionaries with help from the Thermidorians, which imposed the idea that the French Revolution was the first and only one to have given birth to Terror—still often defined, to this day, as the "French disease."[31]

The Invention of the "Terror"

For many Europeans and French at the end of the eighteenth century, the new and positive meaning of "revolution" referred to the "Glorious Revolution" of 1688, reputed to be nonviolent and limited to a simple dynastic change, hence a revolution from above without significant damage to the social hierarchies. On the contrary, the French Revolution—from 1791 for some, 1792 for others, and 1793 for everyone—seemed to break out of the rut of Atlantic history and plunge itself into a vicious circle of radicalization that would henceforth be seen as the French mechanism of revolution.

The summer of '93 was an important turning point in the creation of this dynamic. Because it was experienced as a dramatic and incomprehensible blow at a moment of exceptional crisis, Marat's assassination radicalized fears, accelerated the history of the French Revolution, and played a more important role than has been recognized in the invention of the Terror. The emotion provoked by the attack exaggerated behaviors, reinforced the sense of urgency, and favored extremism. The speech given at the Convention on 15 July by Levasseur de la Sarthe attested to a will to derive lessons from the assassination in order to accelerate the course of the Revolution: "The assassins' dagger is raised over our heads; let us double, if possible, our political existence. Public education remains to be decreed, popular laws to be made, and only then will we have lived enough."

Many popular societies called for relentless repression of counter-revolutionaries in the name of Marat's memory. On 19 July, the Cordeliers asked the General Council of the Paris Commune that the prisoners in the Temple be treated more harshly. Marat's assassination destroyed confidence in the efficacy of customary methods, seemed to prove extreme alarmists right, put the radicals in a position of power, and justified an intensification of political repression. These developments were manifested in a toughening of emergency justice, the rise of the Robespierrists, and the demand at the beginning of September to "make Terror the order of the day"[32] In the medium term, Marat's disappearance allowed the Montagnards to get rid definitively of the Girondins, now accused of having influenced Corday, and to solidify the nation around the new republican values thanks to the diffusion of the cult of republican martyrs. Although it was not in and of itself likely to destabilize the young Republic, Marat's assassination unleashed a reaction that can be qualified as overblown in comparison to the importance of the *Ami du People* and the real danger Corday could represent.

It is precisely in this gap, in this disproportion between the act and its effects, that the mechanism of the French Revolution was lodged. The radicalization and temporal acceleration, the rush toward the future for which the Jacobins are typically held accountable, was not however the consequence of a preexisting ideology. One of the historiographical gains of the last twenty years lies precisely in a pulling back from intentionalist, essentialist, and monolithic theses in favor of constructivist interpretations emphasizing the extent to which the French revolutionaries, far from being the ideologues described in the most contradictory historiographies, revealed their constant preoccupation with finding pragmatic responses to new situations by improvising as best they could.[33] Taking account of the legacy of the work on "public opinion," a certain number of historians have highlighted the development of a new regime of political action at the end of the eighteenth century. Individuals and groups, recognizing that it was more efficacious in this period of revolution to use the multiplier effect of public opinion than traditional means of championing a cause and disrupting power relations, invented modes of action that were in part responsible for the radicalization of events. In 1986, Haïm Burstin proposed the neologism "protagonism" to describe a new mode of engagement; in his view, the logic of the new enlargement of political participation pushed each individual to claim a primary role in the Revolution. By resorting to direct and spectacular action and mobilizing a public opinion that had never previously been so powerful, the most anonymous citizens could aspire not only to gaining public recognition through celebrity but also to changing single-handedly the course of events.

At least until 1794 when other norms of civic spirit imposed themselves through the figure of the rational and deliberate property-holding citizen, this regime of action, tied to the new conception of a linear and secular time in which men are no longer playthings but rather consenting actors, was notably manifested by a transformation of the modalities of political violence.[34] Hitherto associated with an abuse, a humiliation, or a usurpation of power, the word *attentat* designated increasingly the exercise of a targeted violence aiming to mobilize and terrorize—thus creating, at the end of the eighteenth century, the premises of modern political terrorism.[35] Exploiting the disproportion between an act and its multiplied effects, and aiming to propagate terror, *attentats* and other actions that could be categorized as "protagonism" more generally were largely responsible for the radicalization and intensification of the revolution. This was precisely the case of Corday's act.

Committed at the exact moment the recently proscribed Girondins were resorting to desperate means to prevent the Montagnards from definitively taking power, Marat's assassination was not a simple political murder. Resting on the bet that the violent death of the *Ami du People* in the middle of Paris would spread panic among the sans-culottes, reveal the Montagnards' inability to stop civil war, and offer a platform to their opponents, the knife blow was meant as a political intervention. Absolutely masterful, the act shook the young Republic for a few days. But if Corday succeeded in accelerating the course of the Revolution, she did not manage to divert it in the way she had anticipated. As often occurs in the medium term, the attack produced effects contrary to its author's intentions. The Montagnard authorities, only briefly taken unaware, quickly grasped the political advantage they could derive from the fear that spread during the summer of 1793. Inundated by demands for vengeance that followed Marat's assassination, preoccupied by the terror that threatened to put into question their enterprise of political stabilization, the Assembly and its committees focused on showing their severity, radicalizing political repression, and multiplying symbolic measures. In agreeing to "make Terror the order of the day" without this law ever being approved or hence applied, the Montagnards in power elaborated the political, legislative, and judicial fiction according to which they responded to the demands for repression coming from the *Exagérés* and held the country together. The "politics of Terror" by which the Montagnards claimed to do this, we know today, was manifested in a violent but nonetheless targeted repression aiming to instrumentalize fear rather than through a systematically planned elimination of opponents. A year later, in Thermidor year II, the Montagnards who had remained in power could easily invent a script of the French Revolution that allowed them to distance themselves from any responsibility for mass violence. This was the script recounting a deviation from the principles of 1789 toward a system of dictatorship and general repression established and directed by the Committee of Public Safety and Robespierre between the autumn 1793 and the summer of 1794. Because it would suit the interests of French and foreign counter-revolutionaries and could be used in the following century to discredit the entire revolutionary phenomenon, legitimize antidemocratic regimes and inegalitarian societies, and later to find historical precedents for totalitarianism, the fiction of the Revolution-as-Terror would take over as the preeminent script of the French Revolution. It would differentiate the French Revolution radically from her European and American sisters and prevent, at least until the comparative and transnational studies of the end of the twentieth century, an understanding of the complexity of the inter-relations among the revolutionary experiences of the modern period.[36]

The Antislavery Script

Haiti's Place in the Narrative of Atlantic Revolution

One of the great ironies of Haiti's longtime absence from the comparative canon of revolutions is that the term "revolution" has long been associated with the ideal of liberation from slavery. The theme of emancipation from human bondage is as old as Exodus and as recent as the Arab Spring. As Michael Walzer demonstrated in *Exodus and Revolution* (1986), the biblical story of the deliverance of the Jews from Egypt has often served as a symbol and rallying cry (if not always as an actual template or script) for modern campaigns against social injustice and oppression.[1] And at the height of the tensions in Tahrir Square, Cairo, that preceded the deposition of Hosni Mubarak in early 2011, a protester intoned that "[w]e prefer to be run over by tanks a hundred times than to live as slaves to Mubarak."[2] In Marxist theory, the progression from slaveholding to feudal to capitalist society describes a universally applicable and (as Martin Malia puts it) "logically phased line of social development."[3] We need not embrace even a diffuse version of this classic theory of revolution in order to see that freedom from slavery is a nearly ubiquitous refrain of revolutionary discourse, the quintessential expression of the hopes and dreams of those who purport to transform their societies.[4]

Indeed, the mantra is so ubiquitous that it raises as many questions as it purports to answer—including whether the "antislavery script" is doing any real conceptual work in these competing visions of revolution, only some of which involve actual chattel bondage. It is one thing to express revolutionary hopes in terms of antislavery; it is quite another to make abolition the very standard bearer of revolution. Saint-Domingue (Haiti as of 1804) has become the touchstone for unpacking the problematic nature of abolition in the revolutionary Atlantic world, for only there was the act of national founding expressly predicated on the negation of racialized Atlantic plantation slavery. But even there, ambiguities in the legal understanding of slavery translated into ambiguities in the process of abolition. What, indeed, does it mean, then or now, to be "free from slavery"? The answer requires that one first define the institution from which one wishes to be free. A nonexhaustive list of the conditions—some necessary, others merely sufficient—that went into the making of Atlantic chattel slavery might include: racial subordination; a claim to own individuals as property; the ability to compel another's labor; the inheritability of future generations of slaves; and a hierarchical relationship between metropole and colony.

Many of the ambiguities of the Haitian Revolution flow from the selective attention that its protagonists gave, at given points in time, to one or another of these elements. But those ambiguities were not peculiar to the revolutionary era, or to Haiti; instead, they stemmed from the complex nature of Atlantic slavery itself. Getting a handle on Haiti's place within the antislavery tradition, accordingly, requires looking beyond the familiar chain reaction of events that commences with the Seven Years' War (1754–1763) and crisscrosses the Atlantic between the 1770s and 1789.[5] The American and French revolutions alike exerted great influence on the Haitian Revolution, but (to paraphrase Tocqueville) that revolution owed less to what was done in either America or France than to what people thought at the time in Saint-Domingue.[6] And what people thought at the time in Saint-Domingue depended very much on their particular experiences of the particular kind of slave society that had been developing in this immensely profitable corner of the French empire for more than a century before the revolution began in 1789.

The eighteenth-century Atlantic world provided few if any models for the abolition of plantation slavery. Indeed, the very notion that free people of color and slaves in Saint-Domingue might have been acting out a drama first performed elsewhere has a long and troubling history. Medallions of the early French revolutionary period depicted persons of African descent above the words *moi libre aussi,* demonstrating that even sympathy for the cause of racial equality could come shrouded in condescension and a subtle form of racism.[7] The then prevalent belief that free people of color (not to mention slaves) were incapable of thinking and acting out of their own sense of political and social interests and goals has cast a long shadow over the historiography of the Haitian Revolution.

Insofar as Haiti's revolution involved a script, it derived not from prior or contemporaneous denunciations of political slavery on either side of the North Atlantic, but from experiences and understandings of slavery and racial subordination that were inscribed in the French colonial law of slavery and that preceded the outbreak of revolution in either British North America or France. To say that the law of slavery provided a script for the Haitian Revolution might itself seem to deny the extent of improvisation and innovation that took place during this period. In a colonial context that identified "innovation" in the rules pertaining to racial hierarchy and plantation labor as the worst possible form of treachery, however, tactical appeals to the authority of colonial law served an important purpose for both free people of color and slaves.

Moreover, improvisation was itself a long-standing feature of the administration of slavery in Saint-Domingue, never more so than during the revolutionary period. The dramatic metaphor takes on greater relevance when historicized. In the heat of an early modern French dramatic performance, "audience members and players might come up with interpretations that would subvert the intentions of the image makers." The spectators in the parterre (the pit just in front of the stage) regularly intervened in, and so became part of, the performance unfolding before them, and play scripts did not yet command literal adherence to a preordained text, as they would come to do in the nineteenth century.[8] In this sense, the Code Noir—a script that included some surprising plot lines for the enactment of slavery and racial hierarchy—was often liberally construed, even stretched to the breaking point, by revolutionary actors in Saint-Domingue.

The process culminated in Jean-Jacques Dessalines's 1804 Declaration of Independence, which equated liberation from slavery with total rupture with France. That conflation permitted the first of these imperatives to be obscured in the name of securing the other. And it pointed forward to the ambiguities that would come to characterize emancipation in the very nations that sought to contain Haiti's explosive precedent, above all France and the United States.

⌐

When it was not altogether absent, Haiti was often submerged in the French revolutionary story, and therefore also in the comparative sociological study of revolutions that invariably adopted the French Revolution as one of two or three primary points of comparison.[9] From Karl Marx to Thomas Piketty, the leading social scientific accounts of global economic inequality have internalized this historiographical lapse. Piketty's recent treatise argues that the French Revolution, and only the French Revolution, abolished all legal privileges and thereby established the principle of "legal equality in relation to the market." The American Revolution, says Piketty, fails this standard because it left slavery and racial discrimination intact.[10] Such facile comparisons illustrate a continuing proclivity to write Haiti out of the Western revolutionary tradition that is all the more striking when its (good) intention is precisely to draw attention to the significance of slavery. Even more difficult to accept is a recent definition of the revolutionary tradition as a strictly European phenomenon encompassing only the American Revolution among New World developments.[11]

If the irony of this perspective has sometimes been lost on students of the Atlantic revolutionary period, it could hardly have failed to impress classical republicans of the late eighteenth century who lived to see the Haitian Revolution unfold. On both sides of the Atlantic, in the years during and after the Seven Years' War, polemicists identified the overcoming of a state of political slavery as the chief object of their exertions.

The note was struck first by Whig pamphleteers in British North America. Slavery, Bernard Bailyn has observed, "was a central concept in eighteenth-century political discourse. As the absolute political evil, it appears in every statement of political principle, in every discussion of constitutionalism or legal rights, in every exhortation to resistance." Thus the Pennsylvanian John Dickinson wrote in 1768 that *"[t]hose* who are *taxed* without their own consent expressed by themselves or their representatives are *slaves."* And in 1774 John Adams, to take one other example, opined that under British rule the Americans were "the most abject sort of slaves." As Bailyn underlines, this was slavery in a very specific, eighteenth-century political sense: it denoted a state of servitude induced by corruption in the body politic that destroyed the capacity of the people for independence.[12]

The larger movement of classical republican thought in which this understanding of slavery participated is by now well charted in both the Anglo-American and French contexts (though Mary Nyquist's recent study of antityrannicism in early modern literature brings a new depth of scholarly understanding to political slavery's place in the seventeenth-century English Revolution).[13] Slavery in the sense evoked by Dickinson, Adams, and many others in British North America had a close, if not an exact, counterpart in the French pre-revolutionary pamphlet literature. The most famous example is perhaps also the most revealing of this comparison, for it was itself born of the nexus between English and French political thought of the period. Jean-Paul Marat's *Chains of Slavery* was published in London in 1774; its full title captures both the republican gist of the work and the close connection to British politics:

> a work wherein the clandestine and villainous attempts of princes to ruin liberty are pointed out, and the dreadful scenes of despotism disclosed, to which is prefixed, an address to the electors of Great Britain, in order to draw their timely attention to the choice of proper representatives in the next Parliament.

Marat was, at this time, nearing the end of a decade-long stay in Britain during the 1760s and 1770s. Occasioned by the approaching parliamentary elections of 1774, *Chains of Slavery* was an unabashed appeal to the British public to embrace the cause of the "Commonwealthmen," whom Marat saw as the inheritors of the seventeenth-century English Revolution. And like other works in the commonwealth tradition, Marat emphasized throughout the potential for the crown, through its control of places and pensions, to reduce the legislature to a state of dependence and corruption.[14]

Slavery was not exactly a state of nature, in Marat's view, since it depended on the institutions of organized society, and above all the executive power, for its existence. But it was, Marat argued, the natural fate of humanity. "It appears the common lot of mankind not to be allowed the enjoyment of liberty," he wrote in the book's opening sentence. Everywhere princes aspired to despotism, and everywhere they seemed to be prevailing, notwithstanding "the vain efforts of an unfortunate multitude to shake off oppression, and the numberless evils constantly attendant on slavery."[15] *Chains of Slavery* was republished in French in 1793, at the high-water mark of classical republican influence on French revolutionary politics, and just months before Marat's death. In that context, the work's provincial (British) origins quickly dropped out and it assumed the role of universal manifesto for the Jacobin cause.

This confluence of antislavery and Jacobinism in 1793–94 imported into classical republicanism a fateful element that was not itself a prominent theme of either *Chains of Slavery* or the Anglo-American Whig writers: the link between political revolution and violence. A *Republican Catechism* published in year II of the French revolutionary calendar concisely captures this shift. A revolution, the *Catechism* held, could be defined as none other than "a violent passage from a state of slavery to a state of liberty."[16] One clear context for such a definition of revolution ca. 1793–94 was the quest to justify the Terror as a natural and necessary response to foreign and domestic counter-revolution. The long-standing historiographical maelstrom that swirls around this problem is beyond the scope of this essay. Suffice it to say that Haiti's place in that controversy, despite long-standing and widespread associations of the Saint-Domingue Revolution with retributive racial violence, has been a very minor one. That may be in part because the political ethics of the debate over the French revolutionary terror can be mapped onto the social context of the Haitian slave revolt only with considerable awkwardness.

The exceptional case in point on both counts is Germaine de Staël, writing in 1817, near the very outset of the French revolutionary historiographical tradition. Contrasting the relative tranquility of the seventeenth-century English Revolution with the fourteen months of the Reign of Terror in France, de Staël concluded from this comparison that "no people had ever been as fortunate for a hundred years as the French people. If the Negroes of Saint-Domingue have committed even more atrocities, it is because they had been all the more oppressed." De Staël was careful to add, however, that "[i]t does not flow from these reflections that the crimes [of the Terror] merit less hatred."[17]

De Staël's interpellation of Haiti into her reading of the Terror is highly suggestive. But for most of the nineteenth century, and well into the twentieth, interpretations of the French Revolution in this period elided the Haitian Revolution where they did not overlook it altogether.[18] And while benign neglect no longer characterizes the study of Saint-Domingue, the long-standing marginalization of the colonial revolution effectively confirmed that the difference between metaphorical and Atlantic chattel slavery (and hence the difference between metropolitan and colonial antislavery) was too large to contain within the same political and analytical framework.

⮎

To be sure, this gap was not nearly as wide as a literal interpretation would have it. British imperial critics of the American revolutionaries were among the most outspoken antislavery voices of their day. Their critique avoided discussion of British imperial participation in the slave trade while exposing the hypocrisy of American invocations of political servitude against the backdrop of southern plantation slavery.[19] But the utterly instrumental nature of this critique obviated its political impact in the American colonies and elsewhere, even if it did go on to become (in Christopher Brown's view) a "foundation" of British abolitionism, notwithstanding its avoidance of the slave trade. Mary Nyquist's study of early modern antityrannicism draws some tantalizing connections between seventeenth-century English discussions of political liberty (particularly Locke and Hobbes) and England's role in the emerging Atlantic slave economy, suggesting that the former helped to legitimate the latter. But, in contrast to Dan Edelstein's exploration in this volume of the striking parallels between the events of 1649 in Britain and 1793 in France, Nyquist makes little effort to link her discussion of the English civil war to the problem of chattel slavery in the late eighteenth century.[20]

The notion that the American revolutionary understanding of antislavery could have served as a script for Saint-Domingue is problematic as an account of both the American and Haitian revolutions. Recall the essence of that understanding: the classical republican emphasis on enslavement as a process whereby the crown's control of places and pensions reduced the populace to a state of dependence on despotic power. Bailyn rightly notes that "slavery" so defined was more than "mere exclamation and hyperbole" and instead captured "a specific political condition" that Americans believed they shared with the people of France, Turkey, Russia, Denmark, and other "despotic" nations. But it is less clear that this definition of slavery "applied equally" to the enslavement of the African diaspora on New World plantations. Black plantation slavery was not simply "a more dramatic, more bizarre variation on the condition of all who had lost the power of self-determination."[21]

This is not to deny that the revolutionary movement reinforced the position of preexisting antislavery communities in British North America and generated new pressures toward the abolition of slavery in the northern colonies/states. There were indeed voices who recognized, as early as 1774, that it was difficult to "reconcile the exercise of *slavery* with our *professions of freedom*," as the Philadelphian Richard Wells exclaimed in 1774.[22] On the other hand, as George William Van Cleve notes, "there was—and could be—no uniform understanding across Revolutionary-era America of the relation between slavery and 'Revolution principles.'" Revolutionary-era denunciations of political and African American slavery, as in the Wells statement just quoted, masked "a political reality [that] was far more modest."[23] And Van Cleve demonstrates, persuasively to my mind, that the impetus toward emancipation in the North was a deeply ambivalent and qualified one that made significant concessions to the interests of southern states, most notably in the way of fugitive slave policing mechanisms. The result was the "slaveholders' union" enshrined in the 1787 Constitution.[24]

The long-standing debate over whether the Founders could have taken greater steps to limit or even abolish slavery in 1787 continues to simmer.[25] We may agree with Gordon Wood that emphasizing the revolutionary generation's failure to end slavery obscures the ultimate significance of the "revolution principles" that the Founders did articulate. But there is perhaps less to this "eventualist" defense—the notion that the American Revolution's attack on political slavery made possible the later abolition of chattel slavery—than meets the eye, at least as a way of bridging the gap between political and plantation slavery. As Alfred Young, Gary Nash, and Ray Raphael have argued, "[b]y treating liberty and equality as 'promises' to future generations, we simultaneously acquit the founders of culpability and affirm our national commitment to these high goals."[26] More problematically for the historian, we do so without then interrogating very deeply the forces that actually gave rise to abolition in the nineteenth century, whether in the United States or in Haiti.

A useful way of getting a handle on this debate is to ask why the American revolutionary emphasis on political enslavement appears to have had little or no impact on those parts of the Atlantic world that would have been especially vulnerable or receptive to such rhetoric. Jack Rakove's chapter in this volume explains part of the answer: the American revolutionaries very quickly came to subordinate revolutionary processes to the imperatives of constitutional authority. But the almost complete absence of American "revolution principles" from the prerevolutionary political scene in Saint-Domingue involved an additional and no less critical factor. The American Revolution was, in fact, a major concern of the French colonial pamphlet literature of the 1770s and 1780s, but those writers interpreted the American precedent in commercial more than political terms. Like the British colonies, the French colonies were subject to an *Exclusif* that permitted them to trade only with the mother country. The military conflicts of the Seven Years' War and the American Revolution interrupted normal trading patterns and led to a marked expansion of the long-standing illegal trade of timber and salted cod for rum and molasses between British North America and the French Caribbean colonies. The threat of famine and slave unrest encouraged French colonial administrators to turn a blind eye to the reality of this commerce, and in 1784 the monarchy followed suit by relaxing the *Exclusif* so as to essentially legalize the "Yankee-Creole" trade.[27]

In the 1784–85 pamphlet debates that swirled around this controversy, the prospect of a French colonial war of liberation modeled on the American one was not entirely absent. But it was distinctly subordinated to discussions about how best to assimilate the American example through the manipulation of trade policy. What separated commentators such as Michel-René Hilliard-d'Auberteuil, a radical thorn in the side of colonial administrators, from his opponent, Paul-Ulric Dubuisson, the former Saint-Domingue postal inspector turned pamphleteer, was a matter of emphasis within the world of colonial political economy. Hilliard-d'Auberteuil argued, in effect, that the "invisible hand" of the colonial marketplace was the best guarantee against imperial dismemberment: concede to the colonists their need to trade with the Americans, rather than rely on unenforceable prohibitions that would simply foster "a contraband so widespread that it would be seditious." Dubuisson, for his part, argued that the French Caribbean colonies were as so many "provinces of the kingdom of France, in the manner of Brittany, Normandy, and Guienne." By this he meant not that the colonial provinces ought to forgo their commercial interests in the name of loyalty to France, but rather that the metropolitan provinces ought to receive no greater priority in the national scheme of things than Saint-Domingue. Mercantilism had no place, in other words, in a world of interprovincial equality.[28]

The 1784 decree legalizing the American-Dominguan interlope trade made it unnecessary to resolve the exact legal status of the colonies in the French empire—namely, what difference it made whether Saint-Domingue was to be treated as a "colony" or a "province." This economic assimilation of the American Revolution's impact on the French Caribbean colonies, moreover, served to dampen the political implications of 1776, an effect demonstrated nowhere more clearly than in Hilliard-d'Auberteuil's somewhat mischievous treatment of the North American rebels. As a result, the American Revolution seems, overall, to have had little discernible effect on the political culture of prerevolutionary Saint-Domingue. Not surprisingly, when the time came to promulgate Haiti's own declaration of independence in 1804, Dessalines rejected an early draft that seems to have appealed to the style and language of the American declaration.[29]

⌣

If the American Revolution did not provide an actual model for the unraveling of Saint-Domingue, what of the next most obvious candidate: the French Revolution? Historians have considered many different angles on this question, including the hypothetical dead end of debating whether a Haitian slave uprising would have occurred in the absence of a metropolitan revolution. The inquiry has proven to entail the classic *question mal posée*. The French Revolution was not a "prior" event relative to the transformation of Saint-Domingue (just as the Haitian Revolution was not an "autonomous" force whose reciprocal impact on the French Revolution we can somehow isolate). The abolition of slavery in the French colonies in February 1794 — arguably the most radical act of the entire revolutionary period[30] — was an act of the French Revolution, and also of the Haitian Revolution, but above all it was the product of the interaction between these two parallel sets of events.[31]

If we break down this unwieldy question into a set of smaller inquiries, by contrast, it is possible to assess certain discrete "impacts" of the early French Revolution on Saint-Domingue and the rest of the Atlantic world. The Declaration of the Rights of Man and the Citizen, for example, was undoubtedly a force in the debates over the rights of free people of color on both sides of the Atlantic between late 1789 and early 1792. And elsewhere in the Afro-Atlantic diaspora, the example of the taking of the Bastille created a memory of popular agitation that shaped critical moments in the antislavery drama. The famous 1822 revolt of Denmark Vesey in Charleston, South Carolina, is illustrative. Himself once a slave in Saint-Domingue before his French owner returned him to his seller — a ship captain named Joseph Vesey — Denmark timed his uprising to take place on the night of Sunday, 14 July 1822. The alleged purpose and nature of the plot — to set fire to Charleston and kill off the city's white population — has become a matter of some dispute, but the links to the French and Haitian revolutionary experience seem clear enough.[32]

These and other examples notwithstanding, the framework for the revolution that eventually unfolded in Saint-Domingue is better identified not in geographic, linguistic, or national terms but rather in relation to a set of imperial political and legal dynamics, prerevolutionary in origin, that crisscrossed the Atlantic and spilled over colonial boundaries.[33] The Declaration of the Rights of Man was not the only source of egalitarian claims-making in the early revolutionary period. Free colored leaders such as Julien Raimond turned also to the 1685 Code Noir and its guarantees of equal "rights, privileges, and immunities" to those manumitted from slavery.[34] These individuals brushed the dust off of a promise that had been, by turns, long neglected or frustrated under French colonial rule, and used it to shame the National Assembly into living up to the standards enunciated more than a century earlier by Louis XIV.

As Raimond put it in his 1791 pamphlet tracing the history of racially discriminatory laws directed at free people of color — many of them enacted in the aftermath of the Seven Years' War — the Code Noir had "granted to freed persons, properly understood, the right of citizens." Strictly speaking, this statement was false, for the Code Noir said nothing about "citizenship" per se, identifying the "rights, privileges, and immunities" of freed persons with those of native-born subjects of the king. Raimond was, in other words, doing more than merely parroting the language of the Code Noir; he was updating it to fit the demands of the new revolutionary situation. For this purpose, however, it mattered little that Louis XIV's understanding of subjecthood was the product of an absolutist rather than republican culture. To the contrary, the more antiquated an appeal to the Sun King's authority would have seemed to Raimond's contemporaries, the more effective it would have been. Raimond's coup de grâce followed: "Will the National Assembly be less just than a despot?"[35]

The Code Noir's promise of civil and political rights for freed persons gave the law of slavery a logical place in the revolutionary campaign for racial equality. Somewhat less intuitive is the role that the Code Noir seems to have played in the aftermath of the 1791 slave revolt in the northern plains of Saint-Domingue. The evidence on this point is sparse, contested in its authenticity, and subject to more than one reading. Nonetheless, it appears that Jean-François and Biassou, upon whom devolved leadership of the revolt following the death of Boukman Dutty shortly after it began on the night of 22–23 August, appealed to the Code Noir's prohibitions on the torture, brutalization, and neglect of slaves in their negotiations with the representatives of the metropolitan assembly. In one letter, Jean-François and Biassou seem to have referenced these provisions as a way of articulating the grievances of insurgents fighting in their camps. They did so not as part of a demand for the abolition of slavery but rather on the assumption that something like slavery would continue, particularly given that a limited grant of freedom for Jean-François and Biassou and their inner circle was on the table. A later letter to the civil commissioners reflects a more affirmative and emphatic reading of the protections accorded slaves under royal law, along with an element of natural rights reasoning about the injustice of slavery that hearkened back to the Declaration of the Rights of Man.[36]

Strategic appeals to selected provisions of the Code Noir did not operate in a vacuum. They were part and parcel of a larger colonial concern about the prospect of slave revolt that went back to the early eighteenth century and received canonical expression in Raynal's *Histoire philosophique et politique . . . des deux Indes* (first published in 1770). Indeed, as Keith Baker's essay in this volume demonstrates, Raynal's text was one of the first works of the Enlightenment to popularize the word "revolution" itself, and it did so in the context of describing the "black Spartacus" whom Raynal warned (hoped?) would one day arise to avenge the blood of the innocent lives taken by European colonization of the New World.

In Saint-Domingue, this prospect took on a more concrete form, linked as it was to the everyday tensions and anxieties that plantation society, in all of its violence and brutality, inevitably generated at both the administrative and domestic levels. These tensions and anxieties centered on the concern that planter abuse and slave vengeance were linked in a vicious circle of violence that would one day put an end to the colonial project. The strategic ethics that animated such an administrative culture, driven as it was by the need to contain over-reaching on the part of both masters and slaves, was itself a kind of script for the Haitian Revolution, and would prove to have a profound impact on metropolitan responses to the insurgency. Ultimately, in the hands of Sonthonax, Polverel, and the French National Convention, these tactical anxieties, against the backdrop of the sequential insurgencies led by *gens de couleur* and slaves, would give rise to what we know today as the abolition of slavery in Saint-Domingue in 1793–94.[37]

Let us briefly consider some of the principal characteristics of that process, as seen through the prism of Sonthonax's August 1793 decree of general liberty in Saint-Domingue. "The regime is going to be changed," and productive work would henceforth be compensated, Sonthonax informed the insurgents, but "do not think that the liberty that you will enjoy means laziness and inactivity." All peoples "currently in slavery" were declared "free to enjoy all the rights of French citizens," even as they were made subject to a series of restrictions that implemented Sonthonax's injunction against "laziness and inactivity." In particular, "all men who do not own property and are neither in the military, nor working in agriculture, nor employed in someone's home . . . or are found to be vagrants, will be arrested and put in prison." In the new order to come, the ideal types of the warrior and the cultivator more or less exhausted the range of legitimate lifestyles. The formal terms of the Code Noir were "provisionally repealed," but whether the substance of coerced labor was repealed along with it remained very much an open question.[38]

⮑

Much of this history was subsequently effaced in the all-out violence that accompanied Haiti's war for independence in 1802–3, which saw the forced exile of Toussaint Louverture to France and his replacement by

Jean-Jacques Dessalines. The proclamation of Haitian independence on 1
January 1804 announced a new revolutionary script far more radical than
the one that had animated the contests of the 1790s. In the new order
to come, "independence" consisted of two separate but putatively overlapping imperatives. The first was the elimination of all ties to France.
The second was the end of racial domination and chattel slavery. Each of
these goals was presented in the most uncompromising of terms: "In the
end we must live independent or die," said Dessalines in his New Year's
Day address to the people of Haiti at the public square in Gonaïves.[39]
The shadows of slavery continued to haunt the Dominguan landscape, he
explained.

> Everything revives the memories of the cruelties of this barbarous people: our
> laws, our habits, our towns, everything still carries the stamp of the French.
> Indeed! There are still French in our island, and you believe yourself free and
> independent of that republic, which, it is true, has fought all the nations, but
> which has never defeated those who wanted to be free.[40]

The clear implication of this passage was that Haiti could only be free
from "the cruelties of this barbarous people" when no more identifiably
"French" individuals remained on the territory of the new nation.[41]

It was indeed a fiercely resolute warning, and one that Dessalines followed through on a few months later, between February and April 1804,
when he ordered and personally oversaw the ruthless massacre of most
whites then remaining in the colony.[42] The first Haitian national constitution, enacted in 1805, provided that "[n]o white man, regardless of his
nationality, may set foot in this territory as a master or landowner, nor will
he ever be able to acquire any property." All color distinctions were otherwise abolished, as Haitians would henceforth "only be known generically
as blacks."[43] The notion of rupture in both ideological and material or physical terms seemed absolute, and should be understood in part against the
backdrop of an ongoing and very real threat of renewed invasion by France,
not to mention the unrelenting hostility of nearly every other power in the
Atlantic world, including Jefferson's Republican administration.

And yet, in certain respects, Dessalines's regime was less radical than
it seemed, for it followed in the footsteps of Louverture's own compro-
mised and ambiguous embrace of the need to end coercive plantation
labor. Louverture's October 1800 and November 1801 labor regulations
aimed to ensure the "general liberty" of the Haitian people by guarantee-
ing continued exports of sugar and coffee, which could happen only (in
Louverture's mind) if the formerly enslaved were attached to their planta-

tions and mandated to take up the labor they had once performed as chattel property.[44] Dessalines's address on the occasion of Haitian independence alluded vaguely and awkwardly to his own variation on this revolutionary theme: "If ever you refused or grumbled while receiving those laws that the spirit guarding your fate dictates to me for your own good, you would deserve the fate of an ungrateful people." Notwithstanding such necessary compromises of the past (and those that would likely become necessary in the future), Dessalines urged his listeners to "prefer death to anything that will try to place you back in chains."[45]

Overall, the 1804 Declaration of Independence suggests that, by equating renunciation of France with actual liberation from slavery and its vestiges, Dessalines permitted himself to compromise with the second of these two goals in order to guarantee the first. By defining the meaning of "freedom from slavery" in terms of "independence or death," the Declaration privileged two critical elements of the institution of chattel slavery in Saint-Domingue over others: the ideology of racial supremacy, and French sovereign rule over the plantations as embodied in the Code Noir, one of those "laws" that "revives the memories of the cruelties of this barbarous people." Left intact, or at least unaddressed, were other components of slavery-like systems: the practice of coerced labor, and the ability of some to claim property rights in others. The first Haitian Constitution, promulgated in 1805, declared that "[s]lavery is abolished forever" while holding that "[p]roperty rights are sacred" and stating that "[a]griculture, the first, most noble, and most useful of the arts, will be honored and protected."[46]

⮌

There are reasonable and important debates to be had about what was lost, and what gained, with the coming of Haitian independence.[47] Perhaps the most famous account of the fate of Haiti's abolitionist script after 1804 is that of C. L. R. James: James's *The Black Jacobins*, first published in 1938. In an appendix to the 1963 American second edition, James posited a straight line leading "from Toussaint L'Ouverture to Fidel Castro," as the title put it, such that "[w]hat took place in French San Domingo in 1792–1804 reappeared in Cuba in 1958." A half-century later, that comparison appears less flattering to Haiti than James no doubt intended.[48]

The fact remains that, well before the United States succeeded in doing so, Haiti's 1801 and 1805 constitutions abolished slavery and racial discrimination and enacted something like equal protection of the laws: achievements that were not incorporated into the American constitution until 1865 and 1868, only to be undermined shortly thereafter by the southern back-lash against Reconstruction.[49] And the ending of slavery in the rest of the French empire itself would await 1848 and the arrival of the Second Republic. In what remains of this essay, I want briefly to consider what these subsequent abolitionist processes can tell us about the catechistic definition of revolution relative to the Haitian experience.

The antislavery script that first came to fruition in revolutionary Haiti continued to unfold in the United States of the antebellum and Civil War years.[50] The American reaction to 1804 initially took the form of denying Haiti's very existence, as Congress (with President Jefferson's support) moved to impose an embargo on trade and the movement of persons between the former French colony and the United States.[51] In other forms, however, the message of Haitian independence deeply penetrated the politics and society of antebellum America, in the North and South alike, as recent studies by Ashli White, Edward Rugemer, and Matthew Clavin have confirmed.[52] Southern strategic anxiety about a revolutionary contagion of "French negroes" joined northern prognostications of a bloody race war unfolding in the absence of gradual emancipation.

No figure better captures the tensions in these competing visions of the Haitian "threat" than Lincoln. Lincoln's path to the Emancipation Proclamation was, as James McPherson has written, a second American Revolution.[53] But it traveled by way of a complex vacillation between racism and equality, a coded commitment to "constitutional limits" on the antislavery agenda and a willingness to endure rupture for the sake of union. It also traveled through the former Saint-Domingue. While Jefferson's decision to renounce state-level ties with Haiti carried forward until 1862, the coming of war motivated Charles Sumner to open up a campaign in support of recognizing Haiti.[54] Later that year, Lincoln re-established diplomatic relations with the former French colony for the first time since the administration of the first John Adams. (In an especially fitting act of poetic justice, the post of minister resident/consul general to Haiti would eventually be held by Frederick Douglass from 1889 to 1891.)[55] Even as he embraced the cause of recognition and moved toward the wartime emancipation act, however, Lincoln was still entertaining his longtime illusion that colonization could solve the race question in the United States. On 31 December 1864, the day before the Emancipation Proclamation was issued, he signed a contract with a Charleston businessman named Bernard Kock that entailed the settlement of some five thousand African Americans to Île à Vache, off of Haiti's southern coast.[56] The venture proved (unsurprisingly) to be a fiasco, one that only the following morning's "act of justice"—a phrase that Treasury Secretary Salmon Chase persuaded Lincoln to incorporate into the Emancipation Proclamation at the last minute, so as to soften the document's otherwise emphatically strategic tone[57]—could redeem.

The close proximity, in both time and spirit, of these Haitian-American stories to the Emancipation Proclamation suggests that the Civil War witnessed a merger of Atlantic revolutionary scripts: an updating and revision of the revolutionary tradition in light of both the (first) American and Haitian insurgencies. In Lincoln's America, "revolution" had indeed proven to be a "violent passage from a state of slavery to a state of liberty."[58] But is this process accurately described as an enactment of the Founders' revolutionary-era commitment to metaphorical antislavery? The affirmative case is not so much wrong as incomplete. Alexander Tsesis has shown that the language of equality in the 1776 Declaration inspired a rhetoric of equal protection in the antebellum period that ultimately became the formal equal protection provision of the Fourteenth Amendment in 1868.[59] And Jack Balkin and Sanford Levinson have argued that the term "slavery" in the Thirteenth Amendment (declaring slavery abolished throughout the United States as of 1865) was taken from the Framers' use of the same word in the 1787 Northwest Ordinance. As of 1787, these scholars say, the term "slavery" evoked the metaphorical vision of revolutionary-era classical republicanism, which associated slavery broadly with illegitimate domination and political subordination.[60]

But if the slavery that was outlawed in 1865 and 1868 was not African American chattel slavery, as Balkin and Levinson insist, what was it? From this question flows a century and a half of still contested judicial doctrine interpreting the Thirteenth Amendment to refer only to chattel slavery – thereby excluding from that amendment's purview other coercive labor practices, such as the southern peonage regime that the Department of Justice sought to challenge in the 1940s on both constitutional and statutory grounds.[61] Balkin and Levinson write, understandably, in protest of this marginalization, which derives from the conservative ideology that a suddenly "free" society was created in 1865. But the contrarian premise that the Thirteenth Amendment evokes a metaphorical vision of slavery (and hence of antislavery) proves too much. It seeks to draw a line between the late eighteenth century and the contemporary era that effectively bypasses the second American Revolution that was the Civil War. And though debate over the character of that war persists, the notion that the Civil War was not in some central sense a war to end slavery no longer persuades.[62]

The persistence of slavery's legacies in modern American history is real, not metaphorical, even if there are many other forms of contemporary subordination that do not partake of racial inequalities.

Somewhat ironically, a variation of the Balkin/Levinson thesis might actually make better sense of the final French abolition of slavery. The 1848 emancipation was only an indirect beneficiary of the forces that resulted in the creation of the Second French Republic: the latest chapter in a still unfolding French revolutionary narrative dating back to 1789. The year 1848 witnessed the convergence of this newly radicalized republican script with Victor Schoelcher's specifically anticolonial brand of abolitionism, a cause that the moderate Alexis de Tocqueville framed as a matter of French national honor and economic self-interest.[63]

In fact, it required the threat of a preemptive slave uprising in the French West Indies to prompt the April 1848 decree by which all slaves in the French colonies were finally liberated and granted the right to vote. In bringing the curtain down on the Second French Republic a few short years later, Louis Napoleon Bonaparte retroactively limited the effect of the 1848 emancipation decree by denying the colonies representation in the metropolitan legislature.[64] The creation of this new "empire without slaves" thus recalls both the strategic pragmatism of French revolutionary abolitionism vis-à-vis Saint-Domingue and the visions of British antislavery activists of the post–Seven Years' War era.[65]

Yet for many years after 1848, the question "What is abolition?" remained a salient one in France. The revival of the Atlantic slave trade under Bonaparte after 1851 fueled a new system of indentured servitude in Martinique, Guadeloupe, and elsewhere. And the masters of the former slaves were compensated for the loss of their property.[66] Even today, the ambiguities of French abolitionism linger in public debate and legal contestation. In 2013, a descendant of Guadeloupean slaves named Rosita Destival brought suit on behalf of her grandparents, seeking reparations from the French government (as the successor to the regimes of the Code Noir) under a 2001 statute known as the Taubira law, which declared slavery a crime against humanity. Destival's claims included a retroactive demand to declare the compensation of former slave masters after 1848 unconstitutional, pursuant to a newly enacted procedure that permits French courts to review acts of the National Assembly for conformity with the French Constitution.[67] And the fourteen members of the Caribbean Community (including Haiti) are preparing to sue for reparations against France, Britain, the Netherlands, and other European governments, though it remains unclear just how the International Court of Justice would calculate damages to compensate for the many injuries inflicted by slavery.[68] What price to be paid for forced labor, for example, or for the indignities associated with racial subordination? The antislavery script lives on, quintessentially but not solely in legal form, continually soliciting original performances of an endless revolutionary plot line.

PART III

Rescripting the Revolution

Scripting the German Revolution
Marx and 1848

There have been few more famous scripts depicting the advent of revolution than the *Communist Manifesto* and other texts written by Marx and Engels in the years between 1845 and 1848. Described in a brutal, sardonic, and aggressively realist style, its formulations were accepted by generations of Marxists in the twentieth century as the classic example of the scientific class analysis made possible by "the materialist conception of history." Placed in its original context, however, in which—despite its cosmopolitan pretensions—it was intended as a set of formulations addressed to a radical German readership, the reasoning of the *Communist Manifesto* possessed less purchase on historical and political realities than the preceding "German ideology," which it was so clearly aimed to displace. The language of the *Manifesto* conjured up a largely imaginary conflict between fabricated entities, and therefore—proved to be of little, if any, explanatory value in confronting events in 1848. It was only in the twentieth century, when memories of the context, which had produced these formulations, had wholly disappeared, that these texts acquired a quasi-canonical status. They became symbolic and dramatic representations of the path to communism—a sort of communist *Pilgrim's Progress*—with an account of all the snares and delusions that might waylay or divert the progress of the unwary communist traveler.

But in order to situate these writings, it is first necessary to place them in relation to prior attempts, from 1789 onward, to situate Germany in relation to revolution and the advent of the modern world.

A Nation of Philistines

England had experienced a revolution in 1640 and again in 1688; France in 1789 and again in 1830. But nothing comparable had occurred in Germany since the time of the Reformation and the Peasants' War. The question for Marx was: Would a similar transformation engulf the states of Germanic Confederation, and could the course of such a revolution be scripted in advance? Understandably, this question increasingly preoccupied German radicals during the period of *Vormärz* (1815–48). Germany had contributed so much to the thought of the modern world. Surely this would now be matched by a comparable transformation of its political institutions. As the 1830 Revolution once again passed Germany by, the question acquired an added dispiriting dimension: perhaps the Germans were incapable of making such a revolution? For however lofty and sublime might have been the contribution of German thought to modernity, any hope of real political transformation faltered and stumbled whenever forced to confront the mundane reality of an apparently loyal and God-fearing, phlegmatic and provincial people incapable of acting out dramas of revolution, or unwilling to do so. Indeed, for radicals the situation was worse. There *had* been popular mobilization, if not popular revolt, in 1813, but it had been directed not against Germany's traditional absolutist rulers but against the French, and it had been led by the king of Prussia. For this reason, dreams about universal emancipation were repeatedly disturbed by the need to dwell upon the stubborn and persistent reality of a small-minded and parochial people. The Germans, radicals were increasingly forced to assume, were a nation of "philistines."[1]

At the time of the French Revolution of 1789 there had been no pressing need to consider the question. Kant's endorsement of the French attempt to construct a constitution based upon Reason had been widely shared by educated Germans from the thinking classes, but few assumed that a comparable upheaval was required in Germany.[2] Furthermore, as the Revolution degenerated into terror and war, Kant's admirer, Schiller, voiced the predominant reaction. For a moment, he wrote in 1795, there had seemed to be "the physical possibility of setting law on the throne, of honouring man at last as an end in himself, and making true freedom the basis of political associations." But it was "a vain hope," and the result had been either "a return to the savage state" or "to complete lethargy."[3] This distancing from the course of events in France was also reinforced by the German experience of the French occupation of the Rhineland from 1792, opposed—if not actively resisted—by all but a minority of Jacobin enthusiasts based on Mainz. Subsequent reactions to Napoleonic rule were more ambivalent. Although in retrospect, the abolition of feudalism and the reform of the law were highly valued, at the time support for these measures had been offset by the authoritarian style of Bonapartist government and the pressures of war.[4] In these circumstances, few dissented from Madame de Staël's 1807 portrayal of Germany as a land of poets and thinkers.[5]

German Philosophy and French Politics

After 1815, the association between the German and the Universal had been most powerfully articulated by Hegel. It was a discourse that made sense so long as it seemed credible that Prussia would return to the emancipatory program started in the "Reform Era." In his lectures on *The Philosophy of History* delivered in the 1820s, Hegel argued that two parallel paths could be traced in the modern history of freedom. One derived from the German Reformation, in which Luther freed religion from external authority and thus made possible the flowering of the German virtues of inward spirituality—*Innerlichkeit*—and reflective thought. This path of development culminated in the philosophy of Kant and the liberation of man from all received beliefs. The second path, that of politics, had led to the French Revolution, which despite its manifest imperfections, had produced a situation in which man's internal and spiritual freedom could now be expressed in external political and institutional form. This combination of spiritual and political freedom, Hegel believed, was now being realized in Germany. In Prussia, a rational reform program was accomplishing peacefully what the French Revolution had attempted to create by force.

But Hegel's approach had already begun to come under strain in the 1820s. The reforms once thought imminent, like the promise to summon a representative assembly, were not carried through. Instead, the government established a series of provincial diets, summoned along the lines of the traditional estates and denied any power over taxation. Similarly, the Carlsbad Decrees of 1819 severely curtailed freedom of the press, freedom of speech, and freedom of assembly. Finally, the 1830 revolutions, which delivered liberal constitutions in France and Belgium, only increased the defensiveness of political authorities in Prussia and other German states. Alarmed by the holding of a mass democratic gathering at Hambach in the Palatinate in 1832, the German Confederation, prompted by Metternich, imposed further increases in censorship and political repression.[6]

The difficulty of attempting to restate a politically progressive scenario for Germany in the light of these developments was clearly apparent in the case of Heinrich Heine. Together with other radical writers, he had been forced into exile in Paris. In his 1834 *History of Religion and Philosophy in Germany* he persisted in the attempt to develop Hegel's "remarkable parallelism" between German philosophy and the French Revolution. Thus, Kant was aligned with Robespierre, Fichte with Napoleon, Schelling with Restoration France, and Hegel with the 1830 Revolution. But by this time, and under the spell of the Saint-Simonians in Paris, Heine identified Germany's contribution to human emancipation, not as spirituality or *Innerlichkeit,* but as "sensualism" or, in philosophical terms, pantheism. In Heine's narrative, Luther was identified with the "sensualism" of everyday life. Luther's legacy bore fruit in the pantheism of Spinoza, which in turn was restated in the philosophy of the young Schelling. Here, however, the narrative broke down. Pantheism, according to Heine's argument, had completed its revolution in philosophy and was now ready to spill out into politics and everyday reality. For this reason, Germany was on the eve of its 1789, but one in which "demonic forces" would be unleashed, and "a play" would be enacted, "which will make the French Revolution look like a harmless idyll." Nevertheless, the uncomfortable truth also had to be faced, that the 1830 revolutions had passed Germany by, and, as Heine also recognized, both in Schelling and in Goethe, pantheism in actuality had produced forms of conservatism, which belied its supposed inflammatory potential. The tract, therefore, dipped despondently with Heine's admission that this pantheist apostasy "has such a depressingly paralysing effect on my feelings."[7]

The Rational State versus the Christian State

A comparable impasse was reached in the aftermath of the last major attempt to sketch out in Hegelian terms a radically progressive path for Germany—or at least for Prussia—in the *Vormärz* period, and it was outlined by Karl Marx during his brief tenure as editor of the *Rheinische Zeitung* in 1842–43. The conflict at that point was presented as one between the achievement of German philosophy—the "rational state"—and the "Christian state" based upon the fundamentalist Evangelicalism of the new Prussian king, Frederick William IV. The state, as it was portrayed in the *Rheinische Zeitung,* was republican rather than liberal; it was governed by laws rather than men, composed of citizens inspired by the civic ideals of the ancient polis rather than by the bourgeois attention to private interests.[8] It was a republicanism constructed upon the ideas of Hegel and Rousseau. Unity between individual and general will was made possible by the shared foundation of reason, which enabled each individual to prescribe the law to him- or herself. The participation of the citizenry in the formation of the general will was ensured by the existence of a free press. If the essence of the state was reason and freedom, the task of the free press was to make the existence of the state conform to its essence. What prevented the state from acting according to universal norms were, firstly, particular forms of religious consciousness and secondly, private economic interests. But Frederick William's attempt to turn Prussia into a "Christian State," it was assumed, would fail. Sooner or later "Criticism" (the Hegelian project of measuring existence by essence) would be victorious, since it was doing no more than raising to consciousness the real desires of the people.[9]

In 1843, however, the Prussian government closed down the *Rheinische Zeitung* and the rest of the opposition press. The Hegelian project of reforming the state by means of a reform of consciousness had failed. Worse still, however, had been the reaction of the people. When Charles X had attempted to muzzle the French press in 1830, there had been a revolution and the king was forced to flee. But in Prussia, and other parts of Germany, there had been no effective opposition at all. The result was to break up the Young Hegelians and to divide what was called "the Party of Movement" (*Bewegungspartei*).

How could there continue to be faith in the democratic or republican capacities of a people so timid and parochial? The situation in 1843 only reiterated what had been said about the passivity of the German people in the previous decade. At the time of the 1830 revolutions, Ludwig Börne — in Parisian exile — had mocked Hegel's celebration of the Reformation and German *Innerlichkeit*. Perhaps it was precisely that Protestant spirituality had produced "a people that despite its spiritual power and spiritual freedom, does not know how to free itself from a censor that destroys this power and this freedom."[10] Later in the same decade, others began to make analogous attacks upon "the Protestant principle" for its association with individualism and the specifically German preoccupation with privacy, individual security, and a parochial relationship with the outside world. This was a condition that radicals contemptuously entitled *Spiessbürgerlichkeit*.

In the aftermath of the government crackdown of 1843, Marx — together with Arnold Ruge, editor of the *Hallische Jahrbücher*, also suppressed around the same time — decided to leave Germany and continue radical political activity from Paris. Reacting against the radical and republican Young Hegelianism, which he had shared with Bruno Bauer, Marx adopted a form of socialism derived from the thought of Ludwig Feuerbach. According to Feuerbach, emancipation was not the product of the progress of spirit or the development of self-consciousness. It depended upon a transformation of the relations of "man to man" and was located within civil society. It was not, therefore, surprising that the Young Hegelian hope that "Criticism" would lead a movement toward the rational state in Prussia had failed. The state—even the republican state—could not be the agent of reform, since, as Marx had already learned from Proudhon, it was the creature of private property. What was needed, therefore, was not a "political" revolution but a "human" transformation of the "relations between man and man."[11]

Marx and his collaborators were now emphatic in placing no further reliance upon the German people. *War on the German conditions! By all means! They are below the level of history, beneath any criticism.*[12] There was no hope of change to be brought about by the classes of civil society in Germany. Rather, revolution would be brought about by a class outside civil society, the proletariat. This was a "class of civil society, which is not a class of civil society." It was the "*passive* element," the "*material* basis," that would act "once the lightning of thought has squarely struck this ingenuous soil of the people." For even in this scenario, the prime role accorded to German philosophy was not abandoned. Just as at the time of the Reformation, "the revolution then began in the brain of the *monk*, so now it begins in the brain of the *philosopher*." Feuerbach was the new Luther. And yet again, it was difficult to abandon Heine's "remarkable parallelism." For the philosopher was "of Franco-German parentage," and "the *day of German resurrection* will be proclaimed by *the ringing call of the Gallic cock*."[13]

Bourgeois and Proletarianism

This was the last attempt Marx made to present a specifically German path to revolution before 1848. In 1845, Marx abandoned further reference to "the philosopher" and redescribed his conception of socialism in a language that avoided normative terms and that attributed the coming revolutionary overthrow of private property to capitalist development and class struggle. Revolution in Germany was no longer related to an account of specific political groups or ideological tendencies. It was rather inferred from a putative assessment of the current state of the relationship between the forces and relations of production.

However highly stylized, the set of characters in play up until 1845 — "the Christian State," "the Philosopher," "the rational state," "the censor," "civil society," "the peasantry," the "Germans," "the Philistines," and even "the proletariat"—had still borne some relation to local realities. But once Marx moved to France, in texts running from the *German Ideology* to *the Communist Manifesto,* these were replaced by a new cast of characters and processes—most prominently "the modern state," "the class struggle," the "bourgeoisie," and the "proletariat." Although purportedly universal, these figures were more abstract and possessed less explanatory power than those they replaced, especially in relation to Germany.

In the *Communist Manifesto,* Marx combined a brilliant thumbnail sketch of the development of modern capitalism with a supposed depiction of the conflict between the classes of contemporary society. The word "bourgeois" was taken from the political debates in France during the years of the July Monarchy, and more specifically from the vocabulary of opposition journalists, especially Louis Blanc.[14] But this "bourgeois" was no longer the stodgy overfed businessman, sketched by Daumier, the coupon-clipper living off his *rentes* or the hard-hearted landlord deaf to the entreaties of poor tenants thrown onto frosty and snow-covered Parisian streets. Nor was he simply the epitome of self-centered greed and mediocrity evoked a little later by Tocqueville.[15] The "middle classes," the "bourgeoisie," the *Mittelklasse* were no longer simply local translations of "the possessing class," as they had been for Engels in 1845.[16] They had now been turned into the personification of capital itself. In the portrait found in the *Manifesto*, impersonal forces—the division of labor and the unseen hand—conceived to be at work in the expansion of exchange relations and of the progress of commercial society, were presented as stages in the formation of the collective physiognomy of a class, and by the same token, the portly representative of the once inconspicuous European middle orders was endowed with the demonic energy of capital itself. Similarly the *proletarian*, mainly thanks to Frederick Engels's *Condition of the Working Class in England: From Personal Observation and Authentic Sources*, incorporated both the "communist" militancy of the Parisian *ami du peuple*, and the mass democratic skills of the Chartist.[17]

These classes were struggling, no longer in anything as specific as "the Prussian Christian state." The arena now described was that of "the modern state." But this notion, except as a contrast to the ancient or *ancien régime* state, proved to be a more or less empty category, and as late as 1875 in his *Critique of the Gotha Programme*, Marx was still trying to provide it with corresponding content. He criticized the Social Democrats for talking vaguely about "the present state." Given their empirical diversity, the "present state" was "a fiction." But his own presumption continued to be that despite "their motley diversity of form, [modern states] do have things in common: they all stand on the ground of modern bourgeois society." "They thus also share certain essential characteristics." What were these "essential characteristics"? Marx did not specify, and as one critic has noted, the whole passage could be called "an impressive sounding tautology."[18] Marx himself seemed well aware of his failure in this area. In a letter of 1862 to his admirer Dr. Kugelmann, he claimed that he had arrived at the basic principles at least from which even others could reconstruct his system, "with the exception perhaps of the relationship between the various forms of the state and the various economic structures of society."[19]

That only left the *German*, the embarrassing and unwanted survivor from the preceding discourse on German emancipation. At first, it seemed, this difficulty might be resolved by the German proletarian. In July 1844, the Silesian weavers of Peterswaldau attacked a local firm said to be responsible for low wages and degrading working conditions. They smashed the house and works of the family and the next day reassembled in the neighboring village of Langenbielau, where panicky troops shot eleven before being driven away by an enraged crowd that proceeded to ransack another owner's house. Arnold Ruge, Marx's former ally and coeditor of the *Deutsch-französiche Jahrbücher*, argued that this was a hunger-riot, characteristic of Germans who nowhere "see beyond their own hearth and home." In reply, Marx extolled the virtues of the German proletariat "the theoretician of the European proletariat," whose revolts—in comparison with those of "French and English workers' uprisings"—possessed a "*theoretical* and *conscious* character of the Silesian revolt." Such potentiality was also to be seen in relation to the "brilliant writings" of the communist tailor William Weitling and in "the capacity for education of the German workers in general." [20] But this admiring attention did not last. Irritating personal encounters with Weitling over the following three years must have considerably dampened Marx's expectations. For German workers got no special mention in the *Manifesto*. Instead, attention to Germany was to be found only in the sneering and dismissive section of the *Manifesto* devoted to "German" or "true" socialism. There, the skepticism about political engagement, found as much among the Owenites, Fourierists, or Proudhon and his followers, as among German socialists, was treated as yet another pathological example of *Spießbürgerlichkeit*.

Marx was right to look at the period 1789 to 1848 as a series of social and political struggles of a potentially revolutionary kind. Both in France and in Britain, this was an exceptional period, because in both countries political organizations and social movements—sometimes on a national scale—sought to bring down the existing political order in the name of a *true* Republic or a *true* Constitution based upon universal manhood suffrage. But Marx's analysis misunderstood the reasons for political conflict and for the discontent of the working classes in Britain and France, and made no meaningful connection with the situation in Germany.

The antagonism in Britain and France was *not* in any immediate way related to capitalist economic development. It was not, therefore, in any meaningful sense a "class struggle" between "proletariat" and "bourgeoisie." Firstly, the emergence of this struggle can no longer be directly related to the "industrial revolution." The period 1789 to 1848 was not a period of exceptional economic growth outside a few highly localized regions, yet the conflicts tended to occur on a national or at least supraregional scale. In France, what takeoff there was occurred in the Second Empire; the 1830s prolonged eighteenth-century patterns of economic growth; industrial structures, mainly based upon the putting out system, remained little changed. Similarly, there was no exceptional growth in the population or fortunes of the middle class. In 1880, the middle class was no more substantial as a proportion of the Parisian population than it had been in 1815.[21]

Secondly, as has become clear, as much from the work of social historians in the 1960s and '70s as from the assumptions of Marx himself, major difficulties arise when attempts have been made to identify "the bourgeoisie" as a coherent political or ideological force, whether in France or in England. "The bourgeoisie" or "middle class," which Marx believed to be a real social and political actor, was never more than a rhetorical creation, and it was as a rhetorical force that it was used in different ways by governments and oppositions during the period. [22] Its invention, and celebration in France in 1830 and in England around 1832, was closely connected with the need to reform the constitution and the political system in a purportedly rational and secular way, but *without* allowing an opening to *popular sovereignty* or a *republic*, which was still greatly feared from the years of Robespierre and the Terror.[23]

It was not, therefore, the activities or strategy of a fictive "bourgeoisie," but the attempt from around 1830 to construct a political system based upon the political *exclusion* of wage earners, in Britain and France, that created the "struggle" of the "working class" and "middle class." Those excluded from the vote were defined by their lack of any property and hence their dependence on wages. In the case of France, this argument was already put forward at the time by Lorenz von Stein.[24] Conversely, however from 1848 onward, with universal suffrage in France and renewed talk of reform in England, the working class was progressively reincorporated back into the political system. Thus, the extraconstitutional significance of the "class struggle," as it had been evoked in relation to Western Europe by Marx in the *Manifesto*, faded away.

Marx and the German Revolution of 1848

In March 1848 the revolution that had started in Paris in February spread to Berlin. Back in Germany in April, Marx and his circle set up the *Neue Rheinische Zeitung* in Cologne as an "organ of democracy." Initially, events in France—and then across the countryside of Central Europe—had proceeded in close correspondence with the fantasy script of revolution harbored by Marx and other exiles across Europe. In France, Louis Philippe, like Charles X before him, had abdicated rather than risk the fate of Louis XVI. Furthermore, a republic had been declared, with a minister of labor and the declaration of a right to work. In Central Europe, Metternich fled Vienna.

In these initial moments, all sides had been surprised by the speed of events. But what soon became apparent was how unlike any preceding sequence of events 1848 would turn out to be. In France in 1789 as well, the outcome would have been very different had the king not attempted his flight to Varennes in 1791, leaving a public rejection of everything of real significance accomplished by the revolution up to that date. Nor is it likely that the king would have got himself into such a position, but for the determination of the National Assembly to reform the church. Even more decisive had been the king's inability to call upon the army to put down the disorder in the streets. Finally, the revolution would never have moved in such a radical direction from 1792 had not the revolutionary threat to the European political order led to a European war and the need to mount an armed defense of the new revolutionary order.

Before the revolution began, the confident terms in which Marx and Engels had evoked the "bourgeois revolution" belied recognition of the adventitious character of any revolution and the particular combination of local circumstances within which the opposed forces forwarding or hampering the direction of change proceed.

In Prussia, the importance of local political traditions and circumstances soon became apparent. In response to the street uprising in Berlin on 18 and 19 March, King Frederick William IV did not abandon and then bombard the city as his brother, the crown prince, advised, but in effect put himself in the hands of the city crowds. Secondly, however, although the appointment of the liberal March Ministry under Camphausen disarmed the potential rage in the street, the king made no irretrievable concession to the idea of a parliamentary monarchy. Like Louis XVIII in 1814, when he eventually issued a new constitution, it was an act of *grace*, and it was backed up by the unbroken loyalty of the army and the bureaucracy.

Marx's record on the *Neue Rheinische Zeitung* was mixed. Although the newspaper was now "an organ of democracy," the sectarianism and disproportionate ferocity, with which supposed allies on the democratic left were denounced, continued. The reporting of events abroad, especially in the multiethnic Hapsburg Empire, shared the unreflecting chauvinism of the rest of the German left. Particularly discordant in another sphere was Marx's aberrant eulogy of the workers' June insurrection in Paris, for which he was later forced to make a muffled apology.[25] This event had seriously undermined the strength of the Republic in France, and had been unanimously condemned by the French Republican left. Furthermore, it dramatically underscored the reluctance of German liberals to make common cause with democrats or republicans in Germany.

Questions concerning the precise political positioning of the Marx group in Cologne were also sometimes confused by Marx's rivalry with Andreas Gottschalk, erstwhile member of the Communist League, popular local doctor and leader of the largest group of politicized workers gathered together in the Workers' Association. Gottschalk opposed Marx's republican strategy, emphasizing in preference local workers' struggles in Cologne and arguing that like the Chartists in Britain, German socialists should not press the issue of the monarchy. It seems possible that the need to court or win away Gottschalk's supporters may have been a major calculation behind the *Neue Rheinische Zeitung*'s otherwise inexplicable decision in December 1848 to declare "the bourgeois revolution" a failure and to back social revolutionary action.[26]

But all this should not detract from the undoubted success of the newspaper in attracting a readership of five thousand from all over the Rhineland. Its great strength for most of its life was to focus on issues on which a broad spectrum of opinion in the Rhineland was united. In an overwhelmingly Catholic province, the paper was careful to avoid anticlericalism. On the other hand, it focused heavily upon the unpopularity of the Prussian state, the unacceptability of the garrisons of East Elbian Prussian troops used to quell local demonstrations, and the highhanded behavior of Prussian officials. As Jonathan Sperber has written, insofar as the paper was a success, it was because the Jacobin outlook it projected downplayed the notion of class struggle and divisive workers' issues.[27]

At its most successful, the *Neue Rheinische Zeitung* had rediscovered some of the components that had made the *Rheinische Zeitung* such a success in 1842–43. It had rediscovered ways to express its politics in a local idiom. Conversely, it also suggests that the preceding script of revolution, which was to reappear once more in the London writings of the 1850s, was to a considerable extent an expression of the pathology of exile.

Reading and Repeating the Revolutionary Script

Revolutionary Mimicry in Nineteenth-Century France

Until very recently, scholars have paid inadequate attention to the profound and wide-ranging political and aesthetic impact of nineteenth-century French revolutionary scripts. As contributors to this volume argue so convincingly, these powerful narratives, and in particular the intense enthusiasm, anxiety, and criticism they inspired, significantly influenced how revolutions were understood, imagined, and reimagined, not only during this watershed period in French history but also well beyond it, throughout the global uprisings of the twentieth and twenty-first centuries.

This chapter is divided into three sections, all of which offer evidence that what I term the "discourse of revolutionary mimicry"—that is, the predominantly negative critique that revolutionaries mindlessly imitated events and actors from a scripted and therefore inauthentic and untrustworthy past—was a decisive factor in the dramatic reconfiguration of attitudes toward French revolutionary politics that occurred after 1848. In the first section, I define the discourse of revolutionary mimicry and briefly trace its emergence and transformation during the first half of the century. Subsequently, a reading of Gustave Flaubert's 1869 novel *L'Education sentimentale* will illustrate how fears regarding the reading and repeating of revolutionary scripts existed not only in the political but also the literary sphere during the Second Empire (1852–70). Finally, I consider the political effects of this discourse upon the Paris Commune of 1871 and how it directly influenced the day-to-day decisions and actions of the Communards. Together, these analyses strongly suggest that the post-1848 discourse of revolutionary mimicry served to delegitimize unambiguously positive or romantic conceptions of "revolution," ultimately shaping not only how nineteenth-century revolutions were not only represented and judged but also how they were actually performed.[1]

Revolutionary Mimicry[2]

By the mid to late 1840s in France, the dramatic experience of the Great French Revolution had come to be regarded by many political radicals, not only as the touchstone against which the degree of success or failure of all future revolutionary action was to be judged but also as a series of events and cast of characters eminently worthy of both re-creation and emulation. There can be little doubt that a substantial number of revolutionaries-in-waiting, in fact, eagerly awaited the next upheaval, wondering hopefully whether or not it would, at long last, live up to their imagined ideal of the full glory and excitement of the period from 1789 to 1794. If the 1830 Revolution had failed to grant full political emancipation and social justice to the common Frenchman, many revolutionary hopefuls likely told themselves, the *next* one would *surely* succeed in doing so.

Yet as these men and women imagined themselves on the revolutionary stage, where did their scripts come from? Very few were old enough in 1848 to have themselves lived through the events of the Great Revolution and remembered anything about them. Nevertheless, this did little to prevent widespread exposure to revolutionary myths and histories. While these future insurgents waited impatiently for the outbreak of a revolution to call their own, the roles ascribed to them were first constructed and then transmitted primarily through visual representations (as Guillaume Mazeau's essay in this volume illustrates), theatrical performances, oral culture, and the printed text. Of these modes of transmission, there is ample evidence to suggest the predominant influence of historical models and myths of the revolution mediated through printed matter in general (such as novels, *roman-feuilletons*, and journalistic articles), and, in particular, through printed historical narratives and history textbooks. Literary scholar Roger Bellet contends, for example, that "[t]he Revolution of '93 is more than just an event: it's an event transformed, retold, mythologized by the book . . . . Books were natural vehicles for these myths [and were] especially effective in the form of 'History books.'"[3]

Indeed, the printed text did much to transform popular and official historical memory of the French Revolution. In the early years of the nineteenth century, for instance, it was in no way assured that positive representations of the Great Revolution would eventually dominate the popular imagination of mid-to-late-century political moderates and radicals. After all, as far as many were concerned during the first Napoleonic empire, and perhaps even more so during the initial reactionary phase of the Restoration, the revolutionary experiment *had failed*. From 1799 until 1848, however, narratives of the French Revolution were first modestly rehabilitated during the Restoration (1815–30) by Liberals such as Madame de Staël, Adolphe Thiers, and François Mignet; then radicalized during the July Monarchy (1830–48) by sociopolitical reformers such as Filippo Buonarotti and Felicité de Lamennais; and finally, glorified and romanticized by no less prominent historians and poets than Jules Michelet and Alphonse de Lamartine.[4]

By the mid to late 1840s, then, the notion of "revolution" had become imbued with messianic promise. Because of this influential construct, the idea of *another* revolution was increasingly viewed in a positive light, as an event to be desired, particularly in the years directly preceding 1848. It makes sense, then, that within this historical and ideological framework, the idea of revolutionary imitation or mimesis was often regarded favorably.[5] This was clear to at least one reader of Lamartine's *Histoire des Girondins* (1847), who hailed the narrative not only as "a revolution [but] a prophecy" [*une révolution [mais] un présage*).[6] Lamartine himself appears to have agreed. On the eve of the 1848 Revolution, he declared: "They are saying everywhere that [*Histoire des Girondins*] is fueling the fire for great revolutions and that it is preparing the people for future ones. May God will it!"[7]

Not long afterward, however, this optimistic faith in the belief that a new, more socially just world order was merely a cobblestone's throw away suffered a crushing blow. In the aftermath of the failed 1848 Revolution, these dreams were shattered almost immediately as the "Springtime of the people" degenerated into the violent political repression of the June Days, as the lyrical vision of class solidarity represented by Delacroix's 1830 *La Liberté guidant le peuple* so quickly transformed into Meissonier's June 1848 painting *La Barricade*, a blood-soaked image of state brutality against workers; and most painful of all, as the dream of universal fraternity, social justice, and democracy was replaced by the nightmare of historical repetition and regression of the worst kind: return to autocratic rule under Napoleon III and the Second Empire.

Almost immediately following these events, there appeared in the French public sphere a rash of strikingly similar and damning criticisms of revolutionary activism, in which revolutionary action was said to be little more than the degraded imitation and failed repetition of the French Revolution of 1789.[8] Moreover, not only was the revolution itself disparagingly represented as a pathetic tragicomic parody of both 1789 and the Jacobin Reign of Terror, but time and again, its participants and leaders were sardonically depicted as mere caricatures of past revolutionary figures, wholly unable to think for themselves or to determine their own destiny, capable only of taking cues for their actions and speech from historically predetermined scripts.

Perhaps one of the most striking aspects of this critique is that it originated from counter-revolutionaries and revolutionary allies alike. Karl Marx, for example, provides us with one of the most representative, explicit, and certainly well recognized examples of this negative discourse of revolutionary mimicry. In his oft-cited *Eighteenth Brumaire of Louis-Bonaparte* (1852), he writes:

> Hegel remarks somewhere that all events and personalities of great importance in world history occur, as it were, twice. He forgot to add: the first time as tragedy, the second as farce. Caussidière for Danton, Louis Blanc for Robespierre, the Montagne of 1848 for the Montagne of 1793–95, the Nephew for the Uncle . . . . [T]he Revolution of 1848 knew nothing better to do than parody, now 1789, now the revolutionary tradition of 1793–95 . . . . From 1848 to 1851 only the ghost of old revolution walked about.[9]

Similarly, in his *Souvenirs,* a political memoir of 1848, Alexis de Tocqueville expresses his opinion that revolutionary mimicry made not only for bad politics but for bad art as well:

> The men of the first revolution were alive in everybody's spirit, their acts and words present in everybody's memory. Everything I saw that day bore the mark of these recollections; it seemed to me that they were busy acting out the French Revolution rather than attempting to continue it . . . . And it all appeared to me a bad tragedy, performed by provincial actors.[10]

Finally, even anarchist theorist Proudhon had words no less harsh for his contemporaries:

> The monkeys of the *Montagne* (Mountain/*Montagnards*) . . . are unaware of the times in which they live. . . . Images and words from the past encumber their brain; nothing can protect them from their paralyzing magic. They wreak havoc upon their country; they spill their blood for the useless pleasure of re-enacting a warmed-over farce of 1793.[11]

For their part in the failure, therefore, revolutionaries were regarded as imitators, overidealistic dupes, and plagiarists. They were not engaging in virtuous emulation of past heroes, but naively, mindlessly, and pathetically aping them. Suddenly, in the opinion of many, France's glorious revolutionary tradition was revealed as nothing more than an empty farce.

Sentimental Education: Print Culture, Revolutionary Mimicry, and Political Failure

During this period, literary representations of revolution also became increasingly and very negatively linked to the notions of mimicry, naivete, inauthenticity, and failed repetition. For example, Gustave Flaubert's 1869 novel *L'Education sentimentale*, widely regarded as the quintessential novel of 1848 disillusionment, can also be understood as the ultimate literary expression of the dangers of revolutionary mimicry. By depicting the 1848 Revolution as a degraded copy of 1789, one badly played out by naive readers who could do nothing better than mindlessly repeat actions and words from hackneyed scripts, *L'Education* effectively discredits the event itself, its participants and the popular ideal of "revolution" as a whole. In so doing, Flaubert also presents a strikingly pessimistic and revelatory representation of the intellectual crisis of an entire generation raised not only in the long shadow of the Great Revolution but also during the culturally unsettling emergence of the modern era of mass print media.

The negative effects of widespread textual transmission are especially evident in the specific historical, political, and cultural context of the 1848 Revolution as represented in *L'Education sentimentale*. Precisely because their knowledge of the 1789 French Revolution has been mediated almost exclusively through romanticized texts and images, the main character Frédéric and many of his peers have a naive and grossly overidealized image of the event and its participants. Out of either self-interest or as a result of their textually constructed, overinflated sense of individualistic self-importance, many of the novel's characters long for another revolution, but primarily because they believe it will benefit them personally. Ultimately, this results in absurdly unrealistic and selfish expectations of what a future revolution can or should accomplish, both on personal and political levels.

For example, feminist socialists (and their sociopolitical agenda) are satirized through the unflatteringly portrayed Mlle Vatnaz, "one of those" Parisian spinsters who welcome the 1848 Revolution primarily out of personal bitterness, as the harbinger of revenge (*l'avènement de la vengeance*) upon a society that has denied them the happiness of love, a family, and fortune

(369).[12] After the revolution begins, la Vatnaz embraces and preaches an unbridled, frenetic (*effrénée*) synthesis of contemporary socialist-feminist theories in which "everything"—a new legal code, official positions, special editors, a polytechnic school, a national guard—would be created in women's interests. Fully anticipating the government's initial reluctance to support these changes, she further imagines herself with other women, heroically seizing their rights by force. She imagines "ten thousand *citoyennes*, with rifles, able to make all of the city hall tremble!" (370), in essence fulfilling their role in the great revolutionary tradition of Olympe de Gouges or the legendary women of the 1789 October Days. To help ensure the realization of these dreams, Vatnaz flatters Frédéric and heartily encourages him to pursue a seat on the National Assembly, since, she reasons, his political success would certainly benefit her own cause.

Similarly, Frédéric's career ambitions are not inspired by any real interest or desire for political engagement, but are born from "hallucinatory" visions of "the great figures of the Convention who passed before his eyes." Perhaps an even more influential factor, however, is that he finds himself completely "seduced by the clothes that the deputies were said to wear. He already imagined himself in waistcoat with lapels and a tricolor sash" (369). It is not surprising, then, that Frédéric's initial dedication to and enthusiasm for the revolution, seemingly based primarily upon egotism and vestimentary concerns, ultimately prove short-lived.

Of all the misguided characters in *L'Education sentimentale* who naively imitate mistranslated and misinterpreted models from books they have read, it is Sénécal who most strikingly illustrates the potentially ruinous personal and political effects of textually inspired revolutionary mimicry. An austere, pedantic young man, Sénécal is intransigently devoted to an alarmingly reductive brand of egalitarian socialism, one in which all forms of inequality and individualism are suppressed. Moreover, he idealizes the French Revolution to such a fanatical degree that he bases his entire persona upon mediated representations of its most radical leaders. In short, he is a sublime example of a bad copy who badly copies bad copies.

Although Sénécal claims to speak in the interests of the working class and goes to great lengths to display all the trappings of a spartan proletarian lifestyle, in reality, he is the educated son of a foreman, and therefore not a man of the people. It is also crucial to note that Sénécal's political education and revolutionary fervor are in fact of wholly abstract origin. They do not come from direct personal experience, but are transmitted to him, initially from his former schoolteacher in Lyon (the disciple of a man who modeled himself after Marat), and secondly, from the books and journals he is often represented reading or commenting upon (297).

When the reader first meets this "future Saint-Just" (72), he is reading aloud to himself from a volume of Louis Blanc that he carries with him, and joins in conversation only to disparage others and lecture them on the greatness of the revolutionary era. It is not at all surprising that Sénécal holds the French Revolution in such high esteem. In his mind, the First Republic represented no less than the ideal form of government, one he was certain would be re-established with the imminent revolution (193). Yet Flaubert leaves no doubt that Sénécal's personal conception of this anticipated ideal democratic society is not only self-serving but also a hopelessly confused conglomeration of social theories in print circulation during the years of the July Monarchy: "Each night, after his work was done, he returned to his attic room, and searched his books for ideas that would justify his dreams. He had annotated the *Social Contract* . . . . He knew Mably, Morelly, Fourier, Saint-Simon, Comte, Cabet, Louis Blanc . . . and, from mixture of all of them, he invented his own image of a virtuous democracy" (193). In addition, like Mlle Vatnaz, Sénécal does not wish for another revolution for the good of humanity, but simply because he believes it will somehow benefit him personally.

With second-rate, inexperienced actors who misunderstood their motivations and were guided by implausible, over-romanticized scripts, the 1848 remake of the French Revolution as depicted in *L'Education sentimentale* was doomed to failure. The trope of the 1848 Revolution as failed (theatrical) representation and degraded imitation or mindless repetition of the events from 1789 to 1799, one so strikingly illustrated by the observations of Tocqueville, is manifest throughout parts two and three of Flaubert's novel.[13] Political action and speech in particular are portrayed as acts of mindless imitation and empty reflex. Not long after his initial arrival in Paris, for example, Frédéric happens upon a gathering crowd on his way to class in the Latin Quarter. Intrigued, he asks a stranger if he knows the cause of the present disorder, to which the young man responds: "I have no idea . . . neither do they! It's what they do these days! What a joke!" (74). As the mob grows increasingly unruly, someone cries out: "Down with the thugs," a slogan immediately identified by the narrator as "a common insult that everyone was repeating" (78). Many years later, during the first days of the February Revolution, Frédéric again finds himself in the midst of a growing mob, where he observes a working-class woman begging her husband not to take part in the street protest. He replies that there is no decision to be made—his reaction to the outbreak of the revolution is automatic: "Leave me alone," he argues. "I did my duty in 1830, in 32, in 34, in 39! Today, they're fighting, so I have to fight, too!" (356). This intersection of the tropes of unthinking repetition and theatricality is characteristic of Flaubert's negative representation of the 1848 Revolution, a depiction that falls directly in line with those of his contemporaries Tocqueville, Marx, and Proudhon. Even as early as during the hours preceding the outbreak of the February Days, for example, Frédéric witnesses the agitated crowds grow as they march toward the Place de la Concorde. Already, he begins to see and hear the recycled costumes and musical score of the Great Revolution: just as it might in a play, *la Marseillaise* rings through the air as the demonstrators, some wearing red Phrygian bonnets, cry out seditious slogans (346–352).

The next morning, Frédéric wakes to the sound of gunfire and excitedly rushes out into the street to take in the spectacle before him: "he didn't move, he was moreover fascinated and having fun . . . . It seemed to him that he was watching a play" (357). Days later, Frédéric and his friends come across a large demonstration where they hear people singing *la Marseillaise* and observe that everything appeared to them "a most amusing and interesting spectacle" (390). It is interesting to note that neither Frédéric nor his friends are at all shocked or frightened by the (violence of the) revolution, nor does he appear immediately concerned by its destructive potential: "the wounded and dead didn't seem at all like truly injured or killed" (357). At the Tuileries Palace "there was shooting from all of the windows, bullets whistled by; blood mixed with water in the destroyed fountain" (357), and yet, he remains remarkably calm. Even the actual physical contact of stepping upon "something soft . . . the hand of a sergeant . . . face down in the gutter" or "the shock of a man, just shot in the kidneys who falls upon him" (352) does not diminish his enthusiasm.

When at last presented with the opportunity to put his political aspirations into practice, Frédéric excitedly attends a meeting of the ironically named *Club de l'Intelligence*. No other episode in the novel more scathingly assesses the 1848 Revolution as an empty, confused, textually inspired farce than the representation of this political club and its members. The inauthentic and imitative nature of the gathering is immediately revealed through the observation that most attendees came either through sheer idleness and curiosity, or were brought along by speakers for guaranteed support and applause. Moreover, there is blatant and widespread imitation of past and present revolutionary figures. In the most explicit critique of revolutionary mimicry in the novel, Flaubert writes that here "each person based himself on a model, one copying Saint-Just, the other Danton, another Marat, him over there, he was trying to look like Blanqui, who was himself imitating Robespierre" (374). The representation of the *Club de l'Intelligence* is an unsparingly damning assessment, both of the revolution itself and especially of its participants, and therefore a particularly fitting example with which to end this section. Ultimately, *L'Education* depicts 1848 as an absurd cacophony of the naive, clichéd, and selfish interpretations and desires of the petty and mindless, unable to do anything more than ape mediated representations of the words and actions of past revolutionary figures. As Flaubert's novel illustrates, then, by the end of the Second Empire, in terms of revolutionary imitation and action, once-lauded and encouraged deeds of *emulation* had become roundly condemned and derided acts of *mimicry*. It is following this remarkable discursive shift that the Terrible Year, as it came to be known, struck France.

Mimicry and Terror in the Paris Commune of 1871

During the first week of June 1871, Gustave Flaubert traveled to Paris to continue research for his novel *La Tentation de saint Antoine*. Once he was there, however, it was quite a different aspect of the capital that attracted the novelist's attention. Indeed, much about Paris at this historical moment was worthy of note. As a result of the merciless urban combat of the Commune's Bloody Week, the capital lay in a state of physical and moral ruin. Evidence of the massacre was omnipresent: personal property and national monuments had been destroyed by fire, and thousands of corpses littered the streets and lay rotting in the late spring sun. It is in reaction to this massive destruction and violence that Flaubert is reported to have commented to his close friend and traveling companion Maxime Du Camp that "none of this would have happened if they had understood *L'Education sentimentale*" ([*si*] *l'on avait compris* l'Education sentimentale, *rien de tout cela ne serait arrivé*).[14] If Flaubert did indeed voice these words (and even if they are entirely apocryphal, similar sentiments abound throughout his *Correspondance*), how should we interpret them? What exactly were the failed lessons from his work that could have, according to the writer, prevented yet another revolutionary catastrophe? How had attitudes toward revolutions and revolutionaries changed during the Second Empire? Is there evidence that the discourse of revolutionary mimicry exerted any influence on revolutionary politics after 1848?

In fact, the dramatic experience of the Paris Commune of 1871 offers unique insight into not only how late-nineteenth-century radicals regarded the issue of historical imitation but also how they understood their own role as inheritors of the French revolutionary tradition. Moreover, there is compelling evidence that the discourse of revolutionary mimicry pervaded the public political sphere during the event and was a determining factor in shaping how sociopolitical revolutions were, then and thereafter, understood, represented, performed, and judged. I contend that Communard anxieties regarding the political dangers of imitating violent past revolutionary models (or even simply being perceived as doing so) exerted a direct influence upon the day-to-day decisions and actions of the Commune, and in consequence, impeded its ability to react effectively to the Versaillais counterrevolutionary offensive that culminated in the conflict's final *Semaine sanglante* (Bloody Week) of 21–28 May 1871. This further indicates, I conclude, that Paris Communards were among the first nineteenth-century French revolutionaries to exhibit mass metadiscursive awareness of the political, philosophical, and pragmatic need to break from deep-rooted, often violent revolutionary paradigms that had dominated radical political action since 1789.[15]

Upon initial reflection, the actions of the Communards may appear to fit all too easily into familiar revolutionary patterns. Particularly during the early stages of the uprising, when the movement was still struggling to define itself politically, it seemed as if supporters of the Commune were incapable of doing anything but imitate the past. Club organizer Louis Magot from the twelfth arrondissement, for example, became known for repeating with regularity, "I want to be a second Marat," in reference to Jean-Paul Marat, one of the most radical journalists from the Revolution, infamous for his fiery prose and frequent denunciations of suspected enemies of the republic.[16] Political clubs and journals also took on names such as Club des Montagnards (Montagnard Club), Club des Amis de Robespierre (Friends of Robespierre), and L'Œil de Marat (Marat's Eye).[17] One of the most popular of these newspapers, *Le Père Duchêne* (Old Man Duchêne) was peppered with colloquialisms and expletives such as *foutre*, *bougrement*, and *grand colère* in a deliberate attempt to imitate the popular vernacular of radical Jacques Hébert's original publication.[18]

Even more prevalent than explicit acts of imitation was the widespread discursive evocation of events and participants from the Great Revolution to rally enthusiasm and inspire action. During the siege itself, in the political clubs, during official sessions of the Central Committee, on posters, and in the press, supporters of the Commune were exhorted to assume their rightful position in the glorious French revolutionary tradition, and to do so specifically by emulating the past. Prolonged applause followed the words of a speaker, for example, who proclaimed at a meeting of the Club Favié in Belleville on 7 December 1870: "It would certainly be within our rights to respond to the provocations aimed at us by marching once again on the Hôtel de Ville, and by demolishing the *Conciergerie*, just as our fathers demolished the Bastille in 89."[19] As Edith Thomas, Gay Gullickson, and Carolyn J. Eichner have shown, women, who participated actively in the clubs throughout the siege and the Commune, were not excluded in this regard.[20] Official calls to imitative action were addressed to the "citizen-nesses of Paris, female descendants of the Great Revolution."[21] Even when explicit references to 1789 were not made, writers and speakers made extensive use of verbatim rhetoric common to the early years of the French Revolution: that of a subjugated people, at last liberating themselves from "the yoke" of "abominable despotism" and "tyranny" under which they had been living.[22]

Perhaps most disturbing to the majority of the Commune's opponents, and what would ultimately prove fatal to the Commune itself, was the reappearance of explicit rhetoric from the Reign of Terror. Throughout the difficult winter of 1870–71, the spirits of the men of the Mountain were invoked time and again for inspiration and guidance. On 19 November, one club speaker declared: "What we need is a new 93. Well, we will have it," he continued, "and you can be sure that we'll find our own Robespierres and Marats."[23] Moreover, club members did not hesitate to call for a full-fledged imitation of the Terror's most violent and repressive acts. For instance, on 4 January, close to four hundred people (of whom, as police records report, at least a third were women) were in attendance at a public meeting at the *Ecole de Médecine*'s amphitheater, when a Monsieur Armand Lévy took the podium to argue: "As in 93, we must resort to desperate measures, the guillotine around the clock to make traitors' heads roll once again from the scaffold."[24] In fact, impassioned calls for *la guillotine en permanence!* as well as for *un nouveau 93* were recorded on multiple occasions in various clubs throughout Paris during the siege, suggesting that these cries had become relatively common slogans.[25]

For their part, anti-Communards were no less willing to describe and condemn the radicals' actions in terms of revolutionary imitation. Just like the 1848 Revolution before it, the Commune was frequently reduced to nothing more than a "new parody of 1793,"[26] its participants similarly de-

picted as "monkeys"[27] and mindless impersonators, capable only of mim-
icking the actions and speech of past revolutionaries. For Maxime Du
Camp, they were but "supporting actors in a drama in which they participated without really understanding."[28]

Even foreign observers such as American writer William Pembroke
Fetridge repeatedly referred to the Commune simply as "the Reign of Terror" and further reported that it "parod[ied] and even surpass[ed] all that
was most odious and grotesque in the revolution of 1793."[29] Fetridge's vir-
ulently anti-Communard account was, in fact, published in New York in
1871 and gives some indication of how the event was reported in America.

A Revolution to Call Their Own

Thinking back on the Commune from New Caledonia (to where she
and 4,586 other suspected insurgents were deported after the revolution's
violent suppression),[30] the most famous of women Communards, Louise
Michel, recalled that in the best of political clubs "one felt free, beholding
the past without overly copying '93."[31] To her mind, the event signified
no less than "the call of the Rights of Man, it was the people, master of its
destiny; . . . it was no longer 1830 or 48 . . . it was the uprising of a great
people who wishes to live freely . . . or die."[32] These recollections are especially germane to the issue of revolutionary mimicry, because the question
of how to negotiate historical emulation with the desire for self-determination was intimately tied to what distinguished the Paris Commune from
previous failed revolutions. As has been documented, it is undeniable that
many Communards consciously and willingly based their words and actions on models from the past. However, as the days of the Commune
wore on, the appearance of ideological debates over revolutionary emulation strongly indicate both a level of metacognizance regarding political
self-representation and a growing desire to create a new, progressive society, one unrestricted by the political and discursive constraints of historical
determination.

The rhetoric of *un nouveau 93* was common, perhaps even dominant,
in the political public sphere throughout the winter months of the siege,
but with spring and the official proclamation of the Paris Commune also
came new voices challenging the paradigm of historical repetition. More
precisely, it is during the campaigns for the 29 March elections that one
begins to find public declarations both celebrating the absolute novelty of
the Commune and stressing the need to pioneer social and political change,

rather than blindly copy the past. In his newspaper *Le Vengeur*, journalist and Commune member Félix Pyat praised the originality of the Parisian electorate with unmistakable enthusiasm: "Citizens, you have created a revolution without historical precedent. Your March 18 revolution has a special characteristic that distinguishes it from all others."[33] And, according to one contributor to the *Journal officiel*: All political movements that do not carry within them a new, creative idea, or that do not immediately inspire men capable of spreading and defending it, are condemned . . . to miserable failure.[34] In other words, innovation was not merely an abstract idea; it was crucial to the very survival of the revolution.

Yet another notable shift in public discourse can be detected soon after the official declaration of the Paris Commune on 28 March: the appearance of explicit calls to reject the violence of the revolutionary past. In his *profession de foi* (a written statement of belief required of all elected members of the Commune), the painter Gustave Courbet writes: "We have the open road ahead of us today. Therefore, let us abandon revenge, retaliation, violence; let us establish a new order of events that belongs to us and that comes from us alone."[35] Seemingly in response to this appeal for more peaceful social and political change, seven days later the municipal council of the eleventh arrondissement in Paris sponsored a striking public disavowal of revolutionary violence and capital punishment. Amid chants of "Down with the death penalty!" residents symbolically burned two guillotines in front of a statue of Voltaire, "to purify the quarter and to consecrate our new-found liberty."[36]

Certainly, it would be wrong to overemphasize Communards' aversion to violent action. At the very least, however, these examples do clearly indicate that a number of prominent Commune members felt strongly about actively rejecting the rhetoric of revolutionary violence, especially in relation to imitating the excesses of the 1793 Terror. Yet no other event during the uprising better illustrates recognition of the real political dangers of appearing (or actually being) slavishly tied to an outdated and repressive revolutionary model than the affair of the Comité de salut public (Committee of Public Safety).

By the end of April 1871, the Commune faced a grave military crisis: its key military defense outpost, the *Fort d'Issy* just beyond Paris's southwest perimeter, was on the verge of falling to the Versaillais troops. If this occurred, it would essentially clear the path for a direct attack and an almost certain defeat. Tensions flared when certain Commune members began openly questioning the military competence and loyalty of General Cluseret, War Delegate and commander of the National Guard, who himself was dealing with growing dissension among his officers. This situation was only further complicated by a number of bitter internal disputes that had arisen between members of the Commune over their inability to maintain political unity and local control over municipal commissions in each of the twenty arrondissements.

In response to these conflicts, rather than respond more directly to Cluseret's pleas for military reinforcements, on 28 April, Commune member (and self-identified Jacobin) Jules Miot proposed the creation of a five-man Comité de salut public. "Considering the gravity of our circumstances and the need to take quickly the most radical of measures,"[37] argued Miot, a more efficient executive governing body, one with the conviction, power, and "courage" to "make traitors' heads roll" (*faire tomber la tête des traîtres*)[38] was necessary if the Commune had any chance of survival. Not surprisingly, the proposal was met with immediate controversy, inspiring an ideological quarrel that raged for four sessions of the Commune, from 28 April to 1 May 1871, and continued more informally in newspapers and political clubs well into May.

The most remarkable aspect of this debate, however, was that for nearly everyone who voiced an opinion on the matter, the main point of contention over the "Miot proposition," as it was called, was *not* that a dictatorial committee was wholly antithetical to the socialistic and democratic ideals of the Commune (although many did express that objection as well); it concerned, rather, the political ramifications of its proposed name. While those who supported the installation of a Comité de salut public felt that the visceral terror invoked by these words was precisely the solution called for by their dire situation, opponents were adamant that by making the Commune appear to be an anachronistic caricature of the First Republic, it would ultimately cause much more political harm than good.

It is critical to consider that members of the Commune, in fact, overwhelmingly supported the idea of such a committee,[39] but nearly half, including writer Jules Vallès and Gustave Courbet, argued for the adoption of another, less politically charged name, such as the Committee for Central Control (Comité de contrôle central), Executive Committee (Comité exécutif), or the Executive Commission (Commission exécutive).[40] For many Communards, then, self-representation and discourse, at least in terms of revolutionary mimicry, were more important to the movement's survival than actual deed. After much heated debate, when the matter came down to its final vote on 1 May, the resolution to create the new *Comité* and to keep the title *salut public* passed with a large majority of forty-five in favor to twenty-three in opposition. Many of those who voted "FOR," however, did so "in spite of its name,"[41] "with great reservation,"[42] or officially conceded that the name had the unfortunate "disadvantage of being a repetition."[43] Not surprisingly, public reaction to the decision was also mixed. For example, the creation of the Comité de salut public was applauded in a number of clubs,[44] yet the newspaper *Le Rappel* expressed another opinion: "[W]e know that the new Committee of Public Safety will not be the same as the old one. Why therefore does it take the same name? The revolutionaries of '92 had their creations and titles, let us have our own. Let us be, for once, men of the present."[45]

Most revealing of all are the official statements of protest and vote abstention recorded by those members of the Commune most opposed to the new committee and its given name. Nearly all of these grounded their disapproval in critiques of the Commune's overdependence on past models and the negative political consequences of such actions. The Comité de salut public of 1871 was referred to as "an institution considered . . . as useless and it is fatal,"[46] its resurrection "a dangerous and unnecessary return . . . to a past from which we should learn, not plagiarize."[47] Still others sharply criticized what they believed to be misguided and blind faith in the remedial powers of the words themselves. Commune member Longuet, for example, stated: "Because I no longer believe in magic words or good-luck charms, I vote against it."[48]

Finally, it is Gustave Courbet's official statement that most comprehensively and coherently expresses opposition to the Comité de salut public and why rejection of it is necessary, specifically in terms of representation, language, and revolutionary mimicry:

> I would like all of the titles and words pertaining to the revolutions of 89–93 not to be used in our age. Today, they no longer carry the same significance and cannot be used with the same appropriateness and acceptance. The titles: Public Safety, Montagnards, Girondins, Jacobins, cannot be used in this socialist, republican movement. What we represent is the time that has passed from 93 to 71, with all of the ingenuity that characterizes us and that must come from ourselves. It seems to me especially evident that we look like plagiarists, and that we are re-establishing to our detriment a terror that is not of our time. Let us use words that relate to our own revolution.[49]

This was not a statement of simple protest, but one that called for revolutionaries to break decisively from the discursive constraints of the past if there was to be any hope of gaining public support, or, more important, of forging a viable future of their very own creation. Moreover, Courbet's passionate words further illustrate the complexities inherent to the deployment of the critique of revolutionary mimicry. Unlike counter-revolutionaries who attacked mimicry as an inevitable consequence of what they considered an essentially flawed political position, revolutionaries like Marx and Courbet also critiqued the phenomenon, yet from within, and not to discredit revolutionary action but to refine it.

The controversy surrounding adoption of the Comité de salut public, in essence an ideological debate over the internal and external dangers of engaging in revolutionary mimicry, was one of the major causes of the in-fighting and military confusion that plagued the last month of the Paris Commune. On 9 May, Louis Rossel, the Commune's second war delegate after Cluseret's dismissal, submitted his letter of resignation to the Comité de salut public. Throughout the letter, Rossel expresses his extreme frustration with the committee's unresponsiveness to the urgent needs of the National Guard. In his letter, he writes: "I find myself incapable of being in command when everyone deliberates, but no one obeys."[50] His successor, Charles Delescluze, was equally exasperated by the Comité, and attacked its members not only for what he rightfully considered to be fatal political indecisiveness in time of extreme military crisis, but also for their inability to learn from and make peace with the ghosts of revolutions past: "You quibble while the tricolor flag floats over Issy . . . . Your Committee of Public Safety is annihilated, crushed by the weight of historical memory."[51]

One will never know with full certainty, however, how close the Commune might have come to pioneering a truly original socialist republic. On 21 May 1871 the experiment of the Paris Commune came to a violent end as Versaillais forces succeeded in overtaking several military outposts on the western periphery of the capital. This marked the beginning of the two-month conflict's final *Semaine sanglante*, a seven-day battle during which approximately twenty-five thousand real or suspected Communards were killed in battle or summarily executed in the streets of Paris.[52] To gain a sense of the one-sided nature of this final conflict, we need only consider that in comparison to the staggering number of Communards killed, the Versaillais troops lost fewer than one thousand men.[53]

For at least a decade after the fall of the Commune, the discourse of violent revolutionary mimicry continued to influence how certain elements of the nascent Third Republic both reacted to and represented radical revolutionaries and revolutionary action. For instance, police files recorded the actions of surviving Commune members until each of their deaths. In these dossiers, special attention is paid to the activities of those known to have voted for creation of the Comité de salut public.[54] To cite another example, in a special article that appeared in the 24 February 1872 issue of the conservative newspaper *Le Figaro*, Delescluze is described in the following manner: "He had accepted, without any critical thought, all of the legends of the revolution: Robespierre was his ideal and idol; he believed in the civilizing influence of the guillotine, and imagined with naïve sincerity that he alone carried on the mission of the 'giants of 93.'"[55] Six years later, in 1879, the *Paris Journal* featured a special "Historical Documents on the Commune" section that reproduced the following police report as evidence that radical revolutionary models continued to inspire the actions of the disaffected: "On May 19th, at half past three in the afternoon, a tall young man, dressed *à la* Robespierre. . . . entered the *église de la Madeleine*. Armed and leading a battalion of *Vengeurs de Flourens*, he declared that by order of the *Comité de salut public*, the church was closed and arrested the Abbot Lamazou."[56] The existence of these representations reveals a persistent belief that even after close to one hundred years of revolutionary bloodshed, men such as Robespierre still held the power to inspire violence, to an almost compulsive degree. In other words, as antirepublican journals like *Le Figaro* and *Paris Journal* suggested to their readership, despite the horrific conclusion to the Paris Commune, a "nouveau '93" was still very much a terrifying possibility.[57] Unwavering vigilance against any recurrence of violent revolutionary imitation was, therefore, of the utmost importance. "It is to be hoped," wrote William Fetridge in the introduction to his American history of the Paris Commune, that "the people of France will never permit a repetition of the past lamentable events; and should an attempt again be made, the recollection of the destruction of property and loss of life, of the blasphemy and horror, will cause every citizen with a social position to maintain and a dollar to lose, to rise and crush the monster in its infancy."[58]

Therefore, by continuing to identify and characterize a certain type of political revolutionary as wholly unable to resist mindlessly imitating or "playing out" the destructive actions or scripts of the past, the discourse of violent revolutionary mimicry accomplished much more than simply discredit and vilify the Communards of 1871 and their attempts at socialistic reform. Ultimately, it served to help justify the early Third Republic's brutal suppression—not only of the Paris Commune, but of future revolutionary violence—as acts necessary to the preservation of order in a liberal, civilized society.[59] This, in effect, played a key role, not only in delegitimizing and harnessing the more violent strain of mass revolutionary action that had dominated France for nearly a century (one that Claudia Verhoeven suggests migrated and evolved into a more "scientific," Russian form of revolutionary terrorism) but also in paving the path necessary for the gradual acceptance of a republic gained through parliamentary politics.

"Une Révolution Vraiment Scientifique"

Russian Terrorism, the Escape from the European Orbit, and the Invention of a New Revolutionary Paradigm

> "*C'est une révolution vraiment scientifique*," as a certain Frenchman said of Russian terrorism. Understand that well, gentlemen, and don't forget it! Remember that terrorist revolution is completely moral in its aims, more reasonable, humanitarian, and consequently more ethical in the methods which it uses than mass revolution.
> —G. Tarnovski, "Terrorism and Routine" (1880)[1]

In a political cartoon that dates to the Revolution of 1905, the French and the Russian revolutionary traditions face off in personified dialogue: on the left, pointing to a guillotine with a blade on which is inscribed "1793," a brazenly feminine Marianne recommends "our little machine for tyrants"; on the right, a modest-looking Mother Russia rejects the French offer ("What for?") and asserts that it is Russia that now has the "best weapon": "little oranges" (*apel'sinchiki*), early-twentieth-century revolutionary jargon for the bombs that fill the basket she holds in her arms.[2] The Russian model thus exchanges for the spectacular executions orchestrated by the state, an assassination campaign waged by the clandestine multitude; for terror, in short, it exchanges terrorism. What this chapter seeks to explain is what made this bold exchange thinkable, or rather: when and why terrorism, or the "terrorist revolution," came, for an important segment of the radical intelligentsia, to trump the Western revolutionary script. Below, after providing background on the idea of revolution in Russia, the chapter will trace the emergence of the "terrorist revolution" in a set of political proclamations and manifestos from the mid to late nineteenth century, as well as offer some conclusions about the ways in which terrorism allowed Russians to theorize an escape from the European revolutionary orbit. It may be useful, however, to sketch out the larger argument up front.

Terrorism: A Russian Revolutionary Alternative

Terrorism, a fundamentally temporal and hyperconsciously historical violence,[3] emerged in nineteenth-century Russia for two reasons, both related to the empire's "late" modernization: first, the tension between the revolutionary script that Russians inherited from the West and the reactionary reality of their own conditions and, second, the hope that Russia could avoid both the bloody failures of the European revolutionary tradition and the structural violence of European modernity. In other words, as a form of struggle, terrorism overcompensated for the underdevelopment of the Russian revolutionary movement; it was, as Lenin said, a "symptom and sputnik" of the weakness of this movement.[4] Simultaneously, however, terrorism had more positive functions—namely, as preemptive violence meant to short-circuit time before the mistakes of the European revolutionary repertoire would be repeated in Russian history *and* as a mechanism that could catapult Russia—and eventually the rest of the world—toward an alternative modernity and a better future. Ultimately, moreover, terrorism was conceived as Russia's contribution to the world in revolt: a "new," "convenient," "just," and "truly scientific" revolution that could be used anywhere, anytime.

The (Transposed) European Revolutionary Script: "Worse than Pugachev"

For Russia's late-eighteenth-century elite, revolution was European, first of all French, and it was deeply frightening.[5] As in the case of the *Pugachevshchina* of 1773–74, homegrown Russian revolts could be terrible, but after 1789 a Europeanized freethinker like Alexander Radishchev was, in the words of Catherine the Great, "worse than Pugachev."[6] Worse, because the author of *Journey from Saint Petersburg to Moscow* (1790) and progenitor of the intelligentsia was, according to the tsarina, "full of the French madness": he disrespected Christianity, denied monarchical rights, and desired to "stir up the peasants against their proprietors and the army against its commanders."[7] In short, Radishchev's crime consisted in being modern, in being not a rebellious peasant, but a revolutionary intellectual, hence, in being a traitor and a threat to his native land.

The "worse than Pugachev" label for the intelligentsia stuck, and it received a pithy upgrade in the early nineteenth century from royalist-in-exile Joseph de Maistre, who spent the years 1803–17 at Alexander I's court in

St. Petersburg. Contemplating the future of Russian history, de Maistre famously coined "university Pugachev" (*Pougatscheff d'université*) to give voice to his greatest fear: a Russian who would succeed in setting off *"une révolution à l'européenne."*[8] Were that scenario to unfold, de Maistre wrote, "I have no words to tell you what could be feared."[9] To illustrate that he truly did not have the words, de Maistre then produced a stunned silence in the form of a twelve-dot ellipsis, followed by an adapted quotation from Virgil's *Aeneid*: "............War, horrible war! And the Neva foaming with blood" (............*Bella, horrida bella! Et multo Nevam spumantem sanguine cerno*).[10] In addition to expressing what was for de Maistre ineffable, this quotation also provides a clue about the nature of his fear, because a few lines after prophesying a river of blood, the *Aeneid*'s Sybil asserts that "the cause of all this evil . . . is once more a foreign marriage and a foreign bride."[11] As such, the real threat for de Maistre was, just as it had been for Catherine, the potentially explosive energy unleashed by the comingling of otherwise separated opposites: Europe/Russia, intellect/passion, intelligentsia/*narod,* and of course: *université*/Pugachev. Among conservatives, such was the resonance of de Maistre's "university Pugachev" that more than a century and a half later Carl Schmitt could still effectively put it to use as one of the linchpins for his *Theory of the Partisan* (1963), which features Lenin and Stalin—guilty of unlocking the gates of Acheron and flooding the continent with communism—as two of that figure's most perfect incarnations.[12]

De Maistre hit the mark not just for conservatives, however, but also for revolutionaries: we might well think of the history of the Russian revolutionary movement as a series of attempts to mold its leadership into a "university Pugachev," an intelligentsia vanguard with the popular appeal of the charismatic Cossack. And yet, from its very inception, the revolutionary movement also exhibited a kind of de Maistrian anxiety about unleashing the people's revolutionary energies. The conduct of the Decembrists during their 1825 revolt is a point in case: facing clear defeat by forces loyal to the government, these aristocratic-constitutionalist officers nevertheless did *not* call out for help from the commoners who stood watching the events on Petersburg's Senate Square.[13] To some extent, this anxiety tagged along with the thought of the revolutionary intelligentsia throughout the nineteenth century, and the quasi-aristocratic elitism that it engendered was indeed one of the factors that contributed to the development of terrorism. (This elitism among terrorists—"quasi" aristocratic because of course not all terrorists belonged to the nobility—is easily detected in their discourse, which framed the struggle with the autocracy as a "duel" and culminated in the early twentieth century with the following exclamation by Vsevolod Lebedintsev about his upcoming terrorist act: "Finally! I cannot bear it any longer! . . . Oh, how I hate this race of normal people!")[14] More important than this, however, was a set of more reasoned concerns that took shape as the intelligentsia observed the unfolding of history in the West, and these concerns had little to do with those of the conservative elite, whether European or Russian.

Russia: "Outside of Time," for Bad and for Good

"Dreadfully far" was how Lenin characterized the distance between the Decembrists and the people that winter day in 1825.[15] Dreadfully far, however, was still too close for Nicholas I, whose thirty-year reign was punctuated by policies designed to insulate the empire from foreign influences, above all of the French revolutionary kind. And so it came to be that more than a century after Peter the Great had opened up a "window to the West" and then resolved to "catch up" with said West, Petr Chaadaev's *Philosophical Letters* (1836) could *still* proclaim that Russia existed "outside of time": the empire had been left unaffected by the "history of the human spirit which has led man to the heights which he has reached today in the rest of the world."[16] To Chaadaev, what Russia's lamentable backwardness produced was a nearly unbearable lightness of being: "Look around. Don't we all have one foot in the air? We all look as though we are traveling . . . everything passes, leaving no trace outside or within us."[17]

The Philosophical Letters earned Chaadaev an insanity diagnosis from the government (he later wrote "Apology from a Madman"), but it had an "epoch making" influence on the generation of the forties, which included Alexander Herzen, Mikhail Bakunin, and Ivan Turgenev, and would become known as the classical intelligentsia.[18] When Herzen first read the *Letters*— this was during his years of exile in Vyatka (present day Kirov)—he was so stunned to see its arguments *legally* published that, "I was afraid I had gone out of my mind."[19] Chaadaev's *cri de coeur* was "a shot that rang out in the dark night" of the Nicholaevan era: "Russia's past was empty, its present insufferable, and . . . there was no future for it at all. . . . Chaadaev's *Letter* was a merciless cry of pain and reproach against Petrine Russia, which deserved the indictment."[20]

In 1847, Herzen left Russia for Europe, arriving still a passionate Westernizer: "And so I was really in Paris . . . Of that minute I had been dreaming since my childhood."[21] As befits a man of revolutionary convictions, he threw himself into the current of '48, first in Rome, with fervor, and then in Paris, more pessimistically: "Tomorrow we are going to Paris; I am leaving Rome full of animation and excitement. What will come of it all? Can it last?"[22] When it didn't last, Herzen felt himself a man scorned: his socialist dreams betrayed by the French bourgeoisie, he decisively forgot his first love—and then found his last.

It was a crucial moment in Russian intellectual history,[23] for in his despair over 1848, Herzen found new solace in an old thesis: Russia, unlike Europe, had no past, but—and this was Herzen's intervention, perhaps just as much a product of the "pathology of exile" as Marx's and Engels's *Communist Manifesto* (see Gareth Stedman Jones's chapter)—for this very reason, Russia was free, and the future belonged to the East, not the West:

> [European] liberals . . . saw the specter of socialism and became afraid; nor is this surprising, for they have something to lose, something to be afraid of. But we [Russians] are not in that position at all . . . Europe is sinking because it cannot rid itself of its cargo—that infinity of treasures accumulated in distant and perilous expeditions. In our case, all this is artificial ballast; out with it and overboard, and then full sail into the open sea![24]

In short, Herzen rethought Russia's developmental backwardness as a distinct advantage, its lightness of being as not so unbearable after all: "we are independent because we have nothing."[25] With nothing to lose, thus the radical intelligentsia could henceforth hold, Russia was free to forge ahead and into the future. Indeed, into *whatever* future, or actually, better yet, into the fullness of the present, for in Herzen's post-1848 writings, there are no prerequisites to fulfill before achieving "'progress in the future.'"[26] "There is no *libretto*," he writes in *From the Other Shore* (1850): "the path is not determined," "each historical moment is complete," and "the future does not exist."[27] That said, Herzen in fact did have a particular future in mind: it would dawn in the East, where the ancient Russian peasant commune had saved itself for centuries for the arrival of its perfect modern match, European socialism.[28] Such, for Herzen—and, indeed, for many others later, on which more below—were the happy coincidences of living in a world characterized by uneven development or, to use Koselleck's terms, the "contemporaneity of the noncontemporaneous."[29] Still, in history, Herzen held generally, "everything is *ex tempore*," and wherever "sacred unrest" would find its path blocked, "genius will pave a new one."[30]

It was this type of historical thinking that undergirded the birth of terrorism in Russia: wormhole thinking, I have called it, since what it allows subjects to do is conceive of the present as a field of boundless potentialities, a space that is lined, in effect, with tunnels of time leading to endless futures. Essentially, when the political present started to seem unbearable but the time that remained until a European-style revolution still too far off, and the prospects of such a revolution not so desirable besides, the radical intelligentsia opted for terrorism as a way of launching the new age now.

Zaichnevsky: First and Last Chance of a Eu-Russian Revolution

Before turning to terrorism proper, let us examine a proclamation that documents what was—in spite of Herzen's already published pessimism about the European path and N. V. Shelgunov's 1861 manifesto, "To the Young Generation," which was outrightly defiant of European examples[31]—the last moment when a segment of the radical intelligentsia still more or less *optimistically* imagined itself to be traveling the same historical trajectory as the states to the west: Petr Zaichnevsky's 1862 "Young Russia" (*Molodaia Rossiia*).

"Young Russia" is a violent text. In fact, it was the first manifesto to unapologetically inject violence into Russian revolutionary rhetoric. Famously, it predicts a confrontation with the "imperial party" that will have revolutionaries cry, "To the axes," and then sees these revolutionaries beating down their foes in public squares, private houses, the alleyways and boulevards of the great cities, in the countryside and in villages.[32] Because of its rhetorical violence and because it appeared four years before the first attempted assassination of the tsar in 1866, the historiography has posited this text as the precondition for the emergence of terrorism, as the "word" enabling the "act."[33] This, however, is a questionable staging, in large part because the violence that "Young Russia" promotes, although it results from an attempt to correct the mistakes of the European revolutionary script, does not, in and of itself, deviate from forms of violent struggle that are familiar to that tradition.

Except in terms of "more violence," in fact, there is not much by which "Young Russia" sets itself apart from the European tradition—nor does it mean to.[34] The name alone indicates that "Young Russia" sees itself as part of a common European struggle (cf. Mazzini's "Young Italy," *La giovine Italia*), and there is nothing "peculiarly Russian" about its demands, which include a republican-federalist political order, national independence for the empire's borderlands, an equal distribution of wealth, universal education, women's liberation, and so on. Moreover, there is every reason to think that it is Zaichnevsky's assumption of a shared historical trajectory that allows him to open the manifesto with the assertion that "Russia is entering the revolutionary period of its existence" and, near the end, to express himself so confidently on the "when" and "how" of revolution: "Soon, soon the day will come when we raise the great Red Banner of the future and, with loud cries of 'Long live the social-democratic republic of Russia,' move on the Winter Palace to exterminate its inhabitants."[35]

"To exterminate" (or "destroy," *istrebit'*) the imperial family, it is true, goes further than, say, guillotining Louis XVI after his 1792–93 trial, but by 1862 no Russian familiar with European history would have been unfamiliar with the image of a revolutionary crowd, carrying a red banner, singing slogans, and marching across the boulevard toward the center of power.

The pamphlet then goes on to speculate that while it is possible that the whole thing will blow over with the mere murder of the imperial family ("that is, some several hundreds"), it is more likely that the entire "imperial party" will come to the autocracy's defense, in which case . . . and then follow Zaichnevsky's above-cited famously violent sentences.[36] But surely this scenario, which clearly describes a civil/revolutionary war, is not actually surprising? The rhetoric might be shocking, but what "Young Russia" describes was not new: it projects onto the Eastern European future what had already happened in the Western European past.

What is new, however, is Zaichnevsky's insistence that, in order to carry out socioeconomic reforms, the "revolutionary party" should maintain a temporary "dictatorship" and that, to ensure that counter-revolutionaries do not gain a foothold in the National Assembly, elections should take place "under the influence" of the party.[37] This sounds proto-Bolshevik, but if Lenin—following Marx—learned this very lesson from the Paris Commune, Zaichnevsky, writing in 1862, of course got it from an earlier revolutionary failure: 1848.[38] Elsewhere in the manifesto, too, Zaichnevsky is very clear that European revolutionary history is Russian revolutionaries' *magistra vitae*:

> We studied the history of the West, and that lesson was not wasted on us; not only will we be more consistent than the pitiful revolutionaries of [18]48, but also than the great terrorists of [17]92; we will not be afraid if we see that to overthrow the present order we will have to shed twice as much blood as did the Jacobins during the [17]90s.[39]

"Young Russia," in sum, imagines the stages of a revolution as following a Western model, but insists on additional violence—"twice as much blood"—to ensure *deviation* from the European tradition of revolutionary failure. In other words: for success, *encore!*

Karakozov: Triggering the First Russian Revolution (mid-1860s)

It is striking that the historiography draws such a close connection between "Young Russia" and the first attempted assassination of Tsar Alexander II by Dmitry Karakozov on 4 April 1866, because the atmosphere of Karakozov's proclamation "To My Worker Friends" (*Druz'iam rabochym*) is really very different from Zaichnevsky's. True, some of the compositional elements are the same. "To My Worker Friends," for example, likewise positions the people and the imperial party as diametrically opposed forces, but in the case of Karakozov's proclamation the imperial party is *winning*. Karakozov's text even also contains, like Zaichnevsky's, the phrase "soon . . . soon," but here this temporal assessment refers to the imminent death of the people, *not* the triumphant coming of the revolution. In fact, there is no revolutionary momentum in this text at all, which is precisely why the author can write:

> It saddened and burdened me that my beloved people is perishing like this and thus I decided to annihilate the tsar-villain and die for my beloved people . . . . My death will be an example for them and inspire them. Let the Russian people recognized their main and mightiest enemy, be he Alexander II, Alexander III, and so forth, that's all the same.[40]

In other words, it is the absence of revolutionary politics in Russia that provokes Karakozov's historical intervention. And we might say, *à la* Herzen, that restless Karakozov (and restless he was), finding the path to the future blocked, paved—or blasted—a new one, and then others could follow ("Alexander II, Alexander III, that's all the same"). With this willful historical voluntarism, Karakozov is a long way away from the participants in seventeenth-century England's upheavals, who, in staging revolution as God's work, displaced their own agency to the realm of the divine (see Tim Harris's and David R. Como's chapters), but decidedly part of the tradition that began in late-eighteenth-century France, when revolution was transformed from "fact" to "act" (see Keith Baker's chapter).

But if the Russian present was so devoid of revolutionary politics, what allowed Karakozov to imagine himself as a path-breaking suicide-assassin? At least in part, it seems to have been the presence of the European revolutionary script. Although Karakozov's proclamation offers no evidence thereof, in their political discussions, Karakozov and his friends often looked westward, finding there multiple examples worthy of emulation. Petr Nikolaev, for example, found the bloodshed of the Jacobins justifiable.[41] The Carbonari, meanwhile, had impressed Viacheslav Shaganov enough to work whatever information he had about the Italian conspirators into the program he wrote up for their own organization.[42] We also know that the core of the group discussed "Fieschi, Orsini, etc.," and called these assassins "daring people."[43] Plus, importantly, they had heard rumors of a "European Revolutionary Committee," a topic that provoked debates about "the extent to which tsaricide was useful and how to commit it."[44] It wasn't *only* European, this political talk of theirs (Karakozov, for one, was heard singing a song about the seventeenth-century peasant rebel Stenka Razin not long before he attempted to assassinate Alexander II),[45] but it was *mostly* European—mostly European in a Russian context that, we know from "To My Worker Friends," was seen as not at all revolutionary. The tension between these two points produced Karakozov's act, one that would *trigger* revolution rather than *accelerate* a revolutionary process already in motion.

Finally, it is important to note, and especially so in terms of the idea of terrorism as a Russian contribution to the world in revolt, that Karakozov saw his historical intervention as part of a transnational revolutionary moment. Although he makes no mention of this in his proclamation, in his written testimonies Karakozov addressed Alexander II as follows: "Also believe, Emperor, that from time to time there will appear people, *if not in Russia then in other European states* . . . who will sacrifice their lives in order to show the people that its cause is just.[46] Thus, Karakozov saw his assassination attempt as part of a new trend that might have its origins in Russia but would certainly be reproduced across the continent. To Karakozov, indeed, and as I have argued elsewhere, it was this very reproducibility that made political assassination a viable revolutionary tactic in the age of science.[47]

Tkachev: Last Chance for the Russian Revolution (mid-1870s)

Skipping ahead a decade—across the violent Nechaev Affair and the pacifist "Going to the People" movement—we find Nechaev's comrade-in-arms Petr Tkachev, also known as the "Russian Jacobin" or the "Russian Blanquist," impatiently calling on the radical intelligentsia to introduce violence into the political process.[48] Obviously, revolution had not happened since Karakozov first shot at the tsar—neither in 1870, when Nechaev expected it, nor after the 1874 propagandist campaign in the countryside— and Tkachev now openly began to insist that, in fact, revolution happens only when a minority decides that it "does not want to wait" for the majority to understand what it needs.[49] Dismissive as he was of revolution's subjective factors, Tkachev seemed even less concerned with the objective ones: "not waiting until the course of historical events indicates the minute [for the revolution], [the revolutionary] chooses it himself."[50] What the bravado of this rhetoric obscures, though, is that in terms of timing there really wasn't very much choice involved at all, because Tkachev in fact repeatedly insisted that the revolution *must* begin now: "N o w, or very soon—perhaps—n e v e r!"[51]

As did Karakozov, Tkachev promoted voluntarist violence because he sensed that time was running out, though it is important to underline that Tkachev had a very different sense of time—compliments of capitalism. At the time that Tkachev was writing, Russia had finally, and therefore feverishly, begun to industrialize. For revolutionaries, the new economic climate created a hazy political situation: in proclamations from this period, they sometimes seem confused about the identity of their main enemy, here named the autocracy, there capitalism, here the tsar, there the bourgeoisie.[52] Tkachev understood these forces as distinct, but decidedly friendly enemies, and the more intimate they would become, the smaller the chances that Russia might escape the politicoeconomic structural violence of European modernity, a worrisome prospect that had become of increasing concern to Russian revolutionaries over the course of the 1870s. For example, when the revolutionary organization *Land and Freedom (Zemlia i Volia)* issued its first program in 1876, it also included the argument that "violent revolution" should occur post haste, "because the development of capitalism and the increasing penetration into the life of the people— thanks to the protection of the Russian government—of the various ulcers of bourgeois civilization threatens the commune with destruction."[53] Even Marx, around this time, held that if the commune were not saved, Russia would "lose the most magnificent occasion history ever presented to any people for the avoidance of all the misfortunes of the capitalist system."[54] As such, Tkachev argued, this moment, when capitalism had not irrevocably enmeshed itself with the autocracy quite yet, was the very last moment to take advantage of Russia's backwardness: through violence, revolutionaries should seize the state and use its apparatus to transform the ancient peasant commune into a modern socialist utopia. For Tkachev, therefore, terror not only triggered a short cut to one future (Russian revolution), but also a cutting-short of another (European modernity), whose history was not worth repeating.

Morozov: Inventing and Exporting the *"Terrorist Revolution"* (early 1880s)

The text to be considered in this section was written just a few years later, in 1880, which is to say, however, that it was written at a moment in Russian history that saw terrorism triumphant: numerous spies, police-men, and government officials had already been assassinated, and there was good reason to think that the revolutionary organization the *People's Will* (*Narodnaia Volia*) would succeed in its "emperor hunt" and, with a success-ful assassination, trigger a revolution.[55] Proclamations from this period, therefore, exuded both confidence and optimism about Russia's revolu-tionary future.[56] Such was the force of this moment, in fact, that as late as 1882—that is, after most members of the *People's Will* had already been arrested and their organization, for all intents and purposes, had ceased to exist—Marx and Engels could declare that Russia was now "the avant garde of the revolutionary movement of Europe."[57] In this context, Nikolai Morozov, a member of the *People's Will,* wrote "The Terrorist Struggle" ("Terroristicheskaia bor'ba"), history's first explicit argument for the devel-opment of a systematic theory and praxis of "consecutive political assassi-nation."[58]

At his time of writing, Morozov held, the "terrorist revolution" should target the tyranny of the Russian autocracy in order to create "a wide path . . . for socialist activities" (there's that path again).[59] More generally, how-ever, he thought of terrorism as a new form of struggle that could stand the test of time, so that "every new appearance of tyranny in the future will be met by new groups of people [who] will destroy oppression by consecutive political assassination."[60] That is, just as Karakozov had held, the "terrorist revolution" could be exported—even to democracies—and there was lit-tle doubt that it would be, because it was "convenient," "just," and a vast improvement on traditional revolutionary struggles: terrorism, because it only punishes the guilty, avoids "massive revolutionary movements, where people often rise against each other because of misunderstandings and where a nation kills off its children."[61] Here, in short, we thus have not only a product ready-made for export to the world in revolt, but also, importantly, a revolutionary solution to de Maistre's counter-revolutionary fear: "............War, horrible war! And the Neva foaming with blood."

Because of its practice of precise targeting, Russia's "terrorist revolution" was, as Morozov's friend G. Tarnovski wrote in his contemporaneous "Terrorism and Routine," "*une révolution vraiment scientifique*." Of course, there is some unintended irony here, for according to Tarnovski, and as the language of his quotation indicates, it was in fact a Frenchman who gave the revolutionary stamp of approval to the Russian alternative, so that at the very moment that the Russian movement declares its independence and shows its initiative, it nevertheless appeals to the French tradition for legitimacy. This, however, should not obscure the very real fact that from this point forward, there did exist—in theory and in practice—a Russian alternative. Even Trotsky, who held strong opinions about how "*vraiment scientifique*" this alternative really was (on which more below), conceded this point: "But systematic terror that sets itself the task of removing satrap after satrap, minister after minister, monarch after monarch . . . is an original product of the Russian intelligentsia."[62] And after 1880, under the label of Russian "nihilism," the terrorist revolution was indeed exported the world over: through sensationalist reporting in the mainstream media; revolutionary propaganda such as Petr Kropotkin's articles in *Le Révolté;* the literature of insiders like Sergei "Stepniak" Kravchinsky (for example, *Underground Russia* and *Career of a Nihilist*); and personal connections between increasingly transnational revolutionaries.[63] Soon enough, to give just one example, the *People's Will*'s legendary female terrorist Sofia Perovskaya was reincarnated as the Chinese "Sofya" by the nationalist revolutionary Qui Jin.[64]

Postscript: Permanent Revolution

We may now return to the Revolution of 1905, when Mother Russia so confidently asserted that the best revolutionary weapon was now a basket full of bombs. By this time, Russians had decades of experience building explosive devices, a practice taken up not long after Nechaev's and Bakunin's *Catechism of the Revolutionary* (1869) had proclaimed that the only science the revolutionary knew was the "science of destruction": "to this end, and this end alone, he will study mechanics, physics, chemistry, and perhaps medicine."[65] In this more practical sense, too, the terrorist revolution had a "scientific" dimension.

Of course, to representatives of Russia's other major revolutionary trend, Marxism, terrorism was precisely *not* scientific. As Trotsky wrote, "the revolutionary 'Narodniki' lived on phantasmagoria and a belief in miracles," where "phantasmagoria" principally meant the fabled ancient peasant commune, and "miracles," the instant revolution delivered by a political assassination.[66] Trotsky's language maps right onto Marx's and Engels's "scientific socialist" discourse on midcentury bohemian conspirators in Europe:

> They are the alchemists of the revolution, and are characterized by exactly the same chaotic thinking and blinkered obsessions as the alchemists of old. They leap at inventions which are supposed to work revolutionary miracles: incendiary bombs, destructive devices of magic effect, revolts which are expected to be all the more miraculous and astonishing in effect as their basis is less rational.[67]

Decades separate these European conspirators from their terrorist counterparts in Russia, yet the passage aptly describes at least some of the escapades of the early-twentieth-century Socialist Revolutionaries' *Combat Organization* (*Boevaia Organizatsiia*, or *BO*). The episode that comes most readily to mind is the frantic search by the notorious double agent Evno Azef—Russia's number one police spy *and* the head of *BO*—to secure funds for a "flying apparatus" with which to strike a decisive blow against enemy targets from the air.[68]

Terrorists' high hopes for such a "great moment," argued Trotsky, radically underestimated the class struggle's difficult duration.[69] Whatever Tarnovski may have believed about the relation between "terrorism and routine,"[70] Trotsky thought the first did nothing to alter the latter, describing a typical assassination in the following terms: "But the smoke of the explosion drifts away, panic subsides, the murdered minister's successor appears, life once again gets back on its old track, the wheel of capitalist exploitation turns round as before."[71] Worst of all, terrorism's historical timing was off: circa 1900, this form of struggle was appropriate enough for "the Punjab and Bengal," but in Russia, with their "bombs instead of barricades" program, terrorists looked hopelessly old fashioned next to the trending workers movement.[72] In effect, having first produced "classical" terrorists, then "epigones," and now "decadents," terrorism had already "died."[73] Early-twentieth-century terrorists were therefore little more than pathetic ghostly remainders, unaware that their pseudo-heroic struggle was "already the property of history."[74]

Nevertheless, even if he rejected terrorism on account of its faulty historical logic, Trotsky himself at this very time was cooking up what to his fellow Marxists seemed like a similarly alchemical theory of "permanent revolution." In his preface to the Russian edition of *The Permanent Revolution* (*Permanentnaia revoliutsiia*; 1930), Trotsky convincingly argues that his theory came straight out of the *Communist Manifesto* (1848),[75] but when he first put forth his ideas in *Results and Prospects* (1906), they seemed highly unorthodox to most Marxists, who at that time still expected Russia to plod along the timeline determined by the politicoeconomic "laws of history." According to Trotsky, by contrast, because of Russia's unique historical circumstances (here should resound the echoes of Chaadaev, Herzen, etc.), the victors of the Russian Revolution should be able to substitute for a long period of bourgeois democracy a temporary dictatorship of the proletariat (and here the echoes of Zaichnevsky, Tkachev, etc.), and then "go over to more and more radical social reforms and seek direct and immediate support in revolution in Western Europe," which in turn would follow revolutionary suit (and here of Karakozov and Morozov).[76] The revolution would therefore be "permanent" in the double sense, first transforming from a bourgeois into a proletarian revolution, and thence into a transnational one, eventually engulfing the whole of the globe.

Trotsky's theory obviously was not practiced as gloriously as he had hoped. Nevertheless, with the two-in-one revolution of 1917, Russia *did* escape the orbit fixed by the European revolutionary script. Compressing the bourgeois and proletarian revolutions into the span of a short year, suddenly, the last were first, and a new sun appeared in the east. That year, in 1917, events certainly outstripped experience, but they did *not* exceed expectation, because for nearly a century the radical intelligentsia had scoured revolutionary skies for wormholes that would allow Russia to deviate from the European path. Revolutionary terrorism played a decisive role in this search: accepting Russia's position "outside of time," the terrorist wing of the radical intelligentsia sought to replot the course of a revolutionary tradition that seemed to be spinning on its wheels. An anomaly when it first appeared in the mid-nineteenth century, terrorism multiplied the exceptions until they began to break the rule—and thereby helped shift the script of revolution to be able to accommodate history on the margins.

IAN D. THATCHER

Scripting the Russian Revolution

In one of his numerous arresting sentences, Marx stated that one cannot judge a period of transformation "by its consciousness." Yet surely perception is key to revolutionary change; it is precisely the "crucible of the psyche"—the ability to analyze the current situation and to outline alternatives—that determines power struggles and political outcomes.[1] As a political activist, Marx could not write human agency out of the script of revolution. There was a communist vanguard that because of its understanding of history's progression could "everywhere and in everything represent the interests of the movement as a whole" and provide the crucial guidance. Correspondingly, from the Soviet state to Cold War warriors, the root of the Russian Revolution was sought in the texts and actions of the leadership—predominantly V. I. Lenin. Even Marxists such as Leon Trotsky, renowned for their analysis of social forces underpinning revolution, argued that, ultimately, the success and failure of the Great October Socialist Revolution was dependent upon Lenin's presence or absence.

This is, however, a very narrow conception of revolution in 1917 Russia. Given that an autocracy had ruled the empire for several hundred years, in which personal rule was practiced in its absolute form, liberal as well as socialist politics were revolutionary. Oppositionist activists of differing ideological pedigree thought of themselves as historical actors playing out a script of transformation for Russia domestically and as part of an international process of world historical change. There was a specifically Russian context to this, taking into account the country's uniqueness, and also a transnational aspect in which "backward" Russia could show to the "advanced" countries the path to further progress. The "liberal script" foresaw a constitutional Russia replacing the autocracy as part of a universal move toward democracy; the "socialist script" in various versions envisioned a "Red Russia" as a constituent element of a worldwide march to communism.

Although guiding in crucial ways what we understand to be "the Russian Revolution," the main well known ideologies of revolution in Russia did not completely determine the course, content, and ultimate outcome of Russia's 1917 revolutions. A historian who focuses only upon the leaders and self-conscious revolutionaries of liberalism and socialism will omit crucial scripts. There were multiple processes of revolution, some driven by self-conscious nationality intellectuals, and others, most important, from below, by peasants, workers, and soldiers. Popular scripts directed against elites were rooted in peasant notions of "moral economy" that had radical implications for the pre-1917 order. Russian peasants stipulated that land should be given to the toilers, and subject to periodic redistribution according to need and changing circumstances. This sense of justice traveled into the factories and into the battalions in which workers and soldiers argued for their right of "control." Popular notions of moral economy developed before 1917 took on a special importance against the collapse of central state authority in conditions of world war. The absence of a central coercive state apparatus enabled the lower orders to assert their visions in 1917 with devastating political consequences.

Embroiled in a fourth year of the international conflict, over the course of 1917, and particularly by the late summer, Russia experienced meltdown in the military, in society, in the economy, and in politics. The inherent radicalism of peasant demands affected liberal as well as socialist and nationality scripts, with the effect that Russian politics stood far to the left of the mainstream of European political thought and practice of the time. Popular distrust of the propertied elites was ultimately captured by the most extreme of ideological scripts advanced by a left bloc, of which the Bolsheviks were the most prominent. This does not mean, however, that the Bolshevik script directed the play of revolution, looking over its shoulder to past experience of, for example, eighteenth-century France. Such musings were a distinctly minority pastime. Rather, the radical discourse of the extreme left script was a means adopted to express a long-standing antagonism of the peasant, worker, and soldier "oppressed" against their "bourgeois" oppressors.

There was a contradiction in this outcome. Russia was predominantly a peasant country. The peasant script was traditional and patriarchal and had little in common with the self-conscious revolutionary scripts produced in the urban centers. There was a convergence of peasant and left radical scripts in 1917 that enabled a very radical political outcome in the transfer of power to soviets and popular people's committees. There was not however a mutually acknowledged or understood unification of communist and popular programs. Multiple scripts of revolution remained to a large degree separated by background, by content, and by intended outcomes. This disparity accounts for how a radical outcome (soviet rule) contained within itself the assertion of traditional, popular peasant assumptions and practices. In Russia the "particular" dominated the "universal," and this helped to contain and isolate any potential spread of a Red Russian menace.

The Liberal Script

The key word in the general script of the February Revolution was "freedom" (*svoboda*). It was the ubiquitous term to which everyone paid homage. Journals appeared under titles such as *The Free Journal* and publishing houses began series under the banner of "The Sun of Freedom." Rallies in support of the revolution were organized as "festivals of freedom," including civic memorial services for the "freedom fighters" who had died for the cause in February. It became obligatory for important foreign visitors to pay a visit to the grave of the victims of the revolution. Places, people, war ships, buildings, and businesses changed names to align themselves with freedom. New forms of dress and address were adopted as befitting the days of freedom. "The Marseillaise" became de facto the new national anthem and was sung at all official and nonofficial public gatherings.[2] Even political parties that retained a respect for the symbols of the former regime bowed to the mood of freedom. At its VII Party Congress of 25–28 March 1917, the Constitutional Democratic (Kadet) Party, for example, renamed itself the Party of People's Freedom. But what did this freedom mean?

The liberal script in Russia stood to the left of European liberalism. The combined impact of populist demands from below and a reaction against an autocracy pushed Russian liberals leftward. From 1906 onward, when Russia's first parliament (Duma) was elected on a restricted franchise, liberals were demanding radical progressive measures such as the abolition of the death penalty and land redistribution.[3] The February Revolution of 1917 was the opportunity for the liberal script to realize itself and direct government action. The Russian Provisional Government's (RPG) first minister of justice, A. F. Kerensky, emphasized that governance of a free

Russia would be the opposite of the oppressive tsarist administration:

> The first act of the new government is an immediate amnesty. Our comrade deputies of the II and IV Dumas who were illegally exiled to the Siberian tundra will be liberated and returned to the capital with honour.
>
> Comrades, I have under my control all of the former ministers and representatives of the Council of Ministers. They will answer, comrades, for all crimes before the people, but in accordance with the law. (Cries of "Execute them!")
>
> Comrades, free Russia will not resort to the shameful means of struggle typical of the old order.[4]

Indeed, in legislation that made Russia unique among the warring liberal states, the government immediately abolished the death penalty and exile to Siberia.[5] For its supporters, the new regime was above all moral and humanitarian, setting the example to the rest of Europe in advanced democratization.[6]

Alongside a triumphalist sense of Russia leading the world in liberalism, there was also a fear that this project would flounder on the rocks of Russian "backwardness," in particular in that citizens would be blind to democratic responsibilities. Once the chains that had kept subjects in their place under the tsar had been cut, for example, would citizens observe the discipline necessary for the rule of law to take hold? Such concerns are evident in a speech of 14 April 1917 by the minister of trade and industry, A. I. Konovalov, delivered to the Moscow Stock Exchange:

> All the oppression, all the abuses that were the very foundation of the old regime are still fresh in the memory of the masses; the minds of the people are still in a state of ferment; mental equilibrium and a sober viewpoint of the future of our country, so necessary for placing our social and political life on a sound basis, are still lacking . . . . Confidence and harmony in the relations of the citizens, among themselves and towards the Provisional Government, is the basis upon which the new structure of free Russia will be erected. But the old order has left us a heritage of discord . . . . There is only one way to overcome this . . . namely, for the representatives of various groups and classes to approach one another without distrust, to openly and frankly set forth their views, and after getting mutually acquainted, combine their efforts for the common cause of all Russia.[7]

In the liberal script, citizens would have to show patience and a willingness to put the national interest above sectional grievances. There had to be a period of civil peace, in which democracy could consolidate itself. There could be no fundamental changes to the existing economic and property structures until the Constituent Assembly was elected.[8] As a responsible democracy, and as part of an alliance of democratic states, Russia should also fulfill its international obligations and pursue the war effort. Indeed, for some advocates of the liberal script this meant a fight for victory and for spoils of war in the Russian "national interest."[9]

The RPG, hard pressed for money in running the war and rebuilding the state, appealed to popular sympathy for freedom when it issued war bonds under the title "The Freedom Loan." The script here sought to re-mind citizens of the responsibilities as well as the advantages of *svoboda*:

Freedom Loan 1917: Appeal of the Provisional Government

Citizens of great free Russia. To all for whom the future of our homeland is dear we send this passionate appeal.

A powerful enemy has struck deep across our borders. It threatens to annihilate us and return the country to the old order that we have just overthrown.

Only by mobilising all our resources can we achieve the desired victory. The expenditure of many millions of roubles is needed to save the country and to build free Russia on the principles of equality and justice.

Your homeland demands sacrifice and the fulfilment of obligations.

By subscribing to the new loan you will save our freedom and preserve our national wealth.[10]

The newly won *svoboda* was, in turn, to be protected and extended via popular participation in elections. At the national and local level the four-tail suffrage was to be the organizing principle of good and accountable governance. Until free elections could be organized, power was as far as possible to be devolved to committees of responsible citizens at the local level.[11] Nationally, there should be coalition government that represented all shades of opinion. Outside the central government political parties, civic and public organizations and activists sought to flesh out and promote the liberal script.

The leading political party of the liberal script was undoubtedly the Kadets. It had established itself as the main progressive liberal party of the professions from the first Russian Revolution of 1905 and was the leading party of opposition to the autocracy in the first dumas of 1906–7. The February Revolution of 1917 was seen by many as the coming of Russia's "liberal bourgeois moment," during which the Kadet script would define the revolution's actions. This was expressed most forcefully by P. N. Miliukov:

Only a party such as ours . . . which stands above classes, can act as an arbiter among class aspirations . . . . This party guarantees that the new principles of freedom and truth will become established without unnecessary shocks, and the party will know how to combine the ideas of freedom and order.[12]

The political order envisioned in the liberal script was a democratic parliamentary republic, headed by a president elected by national representatives who would retain legislative power. The regime had to protect three basic principles: the inviolability of civil liberty and civil equality; the guarantee of complete rule by popular will; and social justice.[13] The Kadet program of 1917 sought compromise and balance. Peasants should receive more land, but only if landowners were adequately compensated. Workers should benefit from shorter working days and improved terms and conditions, but the profitability and stability of the industrial order should not be upset. Ethnic and national groups should be respected and free from oppression, but this should not undermine the integrity of the Russian empire.[14]

In an overwhelmingly peasant country, the liberals worried that the "dark peasant masses" were too ignorant to abide by the principles of the rule of law and moderation. Thus, the appeal of 12 March 1917 of the Executive Committee of the All-Russian Peasant Union was particularly welcome to the liberal script. This asked peasants to rally around the RPG and all organizations that supported it. It requested calm and respect for the freedoms and rights of others. It discouraged infringements upon landowners' property, especially while Russia was still at war: "For the good of the country let the gentry sow their own fields when they have the necessary machines and labour power." The leading Kadet and historian A. A. Kizevetter welcomed the All-Russian Peasant Union's appeal because:

> all variants of civil strife—class, party, or any other—are a mortal blow to freedom. The real importance of the appeal is in its insistence that peasants wait for the resolution of pressing social problems from the legal representatives of the people's will and not by individual acts of violence.[15]

It took much longer for the landowners to organize into a public pressure group. It was only on 20 May that the founding congress of the All-Russian Union of Landowners gathered in Moscow.[16] The documents issued here were firmly within the liberal script. Congress speeches and resolutions emphasized the urgency of improving the productivity and efficiency of Russian agriculture. This, the delegates agreed, could issue only from the incentives integral to private ownership. It was precisely the knowledge that one can pass on property as inheritance, they averred, that acted as the spur to good management and investment. Hence, the fundamental premise of Roman law: "Land belongs to the owners."[17]

The RPG has been criticized for its failure to broadly promote the liberal script of revolution—civil liberties and the separation of powers and so forth.[18] There was, however, an upsurge in pamphlet literature that sought to define and clarify the politics of freedom.[19] At the center of the liberal script lay the notion that nothing should undermine the rule of law and liberty—this was the historical justification of the Russian Revolution.

The Moderate Socialist Script

The moderate socialist script welcomed "progressive" aspects of the liberal script, but differed, however, in several important respects that acted to undermine the liberal project. For the liberal script, a republic of civil liberties and equality of all before the law was an end in itself. Moreover, for liberals the RPG was an all-national government that should reconcile competing interest groups. In contrast, the moderate socialist political parties and leaders of 1917 that controlled the soviets (and came eventually, post-July 1917, to determine the policies of the RPG), thought of liberalism as a *temporary* stage on Russia's route to socialism. At its current level of ("backward") development, Russia had to undergo a "bourgeois revolution," in which socialists had to remain in opposition. Furthermore, the RPG was as bourgeois as its revolution. It was not "above-class." This in no wise implied, however, a passive socialist script allowing the liberals to go freely about their business. Socialists had to organize in special socialist organizations—chiefly, but not exclusively, soviets—that would act as "controlling centers" of the bourgeois revolution. It fell to the socialists to guarantee that the bourgeois revolution would be as progressive as possible and the RPG would be backed only "in so far as" it adhered to a liberating mission. The "moderate" socialist script was "moderate" only in contrast to more extreme Russian scripts. It was still to the left of mainstream European labor movements. This added to Russia's "exceptionalism" in 1917. The moderate socialist script issued mainly from the Executive Committee of the Petrograd Soviet, which was dominated by the Mensheviks and backed by some Right SRs. It held political sway for much of 1917—for some historians, the question of 1917 is, Why did this script fail, rather than, Why did the Bolsheviks win?[20]

Although denying itself a right to complete executive power, the moderate socialist script envisioned a large and guiding influence over the bourgeois revolution and government policy. There was a fundamental difference between what was called "the democracy" (chiefly the parties of the soviets) and the liberal RPG. The former was elected by and responsible to the masses (that is, workers, soldiers, or peasants). The latter was "bourgeois" and defended domestic and international propertied and financial interests. Since the RPG could not be trusted to act in behalf of "the democracy," the soviets and popular committees had to exert pressure over, and try as far as possible to direct, RPG policy. Indeed, for the moderate socialists it was "the people" who had made the February Revolution, and had voluntarily ceded authority to the RPG. As the source of the tsar's overthrow and his replacement, "the democracy" had every right to hold the RPG to account: 'the Provisional Government was created by the revolution and assumed its duties with the consent of the Petrograd Workers and Soldiers . . . the people is the highest source of power and . . . to the people, represented by its elected organs, belongs the right to control all government. The Proletariat remembers this."[21]

Indeed, the Soviet intervened frequently in military, police, economic, and in foreign policy. Most famously, the Petrograd Soviet's "Order No. 1" of 1 March 1917 set the tone for the army's democratization. The rank and file were to elect representatives to the soviets and to committees that would exert control over arms; soldiers' committees should regulate relations between officers and men that should be based on mutual respect, evident in the abolition of excessively subservient forms of address such as "Your Excellency"; off-duty soldiers should enjoy full civil rights; and military orders should be obeyed only when they did not contradict soviet orders and resolutions.[22] For the Octobrist and first minister of war in the RPG, A. I. Guchkov, the Soviet's influence and control in the army was such that, whatever the moderate socialist rhetoric, real power lay with the Soviet. Guchkov, an advocate of traditional discipline, therefore resigned.

For the moderate socialists, the army's democratization was integral to creating a people's revolutionary army that would defend the "people's democracy." The former officer caste had to give way to young, promoted officers of the revolution that, far from being afraid of the men and their committees, would act in solidarity with them. The thinking here was that such an army could not be used for counter-revolutionary purposes: 'the army of revolutionary Russia is part of the revolutionary peasantry, and is at one with the working class in the soviet . . . in consolidating liberty."[23]

The most important aspect of this "liberty," in the moderate socialist script, is that it should serve a *social* as well as a political revolution. There needed to be a drastic reallocation of Russian national resources, away from the propertied elite toward the toilers and underprivileged. The measures envisioned included: universal and free education to the age of sixteen; complete secularization of the state and education; elected courts; the abolition of indirect taxation and the establishment of a progressive income tax; an eight-hour working day; two days of rest per week; the outlawing of enforced overtime and night labor; state-funded insurance; labor committees to oversee working conditions; state land to be transferred to the people's use; and the regulation of fair rents for land.[24] In July an RPG under the sway of the moderate socialist script issued a commitment to further planning in the economy, safeguards for labor, and to prepare for a land reform that would "hand it over" to the peasants.[25] Such radicalism, to repeat, made Russian politics the most left wing in contemporary Europe. The moderate socialists' internationalism saw a worldwide significance for their script, but its divergence from what was considered respectable in Europe and America limited its transnational impact and appeal.

For the moderate socialist script, a revolutionary army protecting a people's democracy at home should also be united behind a revolutionary-democratic foreign policy. Here, the moderate socialist script rejected the liberal adherence to pre-existing international commitments. Revolutionary Russia, in its conception, should reject rapacious imperialism and promote the country's defense on the basis of no annexations or indemnities, and the right of each nation to self-determination. The Soviet's "Appeal to Peoples of the World" of 27 March 1917 clashed directly with the current diplomacy of the RPG foreign minister P. N. Miliukov. If the latter worked within traditional diplomatic channels, the former addressed itself to "Comrade-proletarians, and toilers of all countries." The Soviet forced Miliukov's resignation in early May 1917. In a unique stance taken in the international relations of that time, the RPG adopted a dual strategy to attain its foreign policy goal of a democratic peace: the organization of an international socialist conference to rouse the masses from below, alongside diplomatic efforts for the Allies to declare themselves for a just end to the war. Neither strategy made any progress against Allied resistance and incomprehension. In an ironic twist that in some scholars' estimation fatally undermined the moderate socialist script, it was decided, however, that the best way in which the Russian Revolution could display its power, and thus increase its global influence, was by a successful offensive, launched with disastrous consequences in June 1917. The First All-Russian Congress of Soviets of Workers' and Soldiers' Deputies appealed to the troops: "It is not our fault that the war goes on. Your offensive, organization, and might will add weight to the voice of revolutionary Russia and its call to enemies,

Allies, and neutrals, and will bring nearer the end of the war. Our thoughts are with you, sons of the revolutionary army."[26] A population weary of war had to look elsewhere for a script that would bring the desired peace.

The Extreme Left Script

A bloc of the left-wing sections of other parties (Menshevik-Internationalists, Left SRs), Bolsheviks, and anarchists touted an extreme left script. It was the Bolsheviks, unique in their radicalism and language throughout 1917, and distinct as a political movement,[27] that reaped the most rewards.

The Menshevik-Internationalists, led by Iulii Martov, despaired at the moderate socialist concessions to the liberal script. They were against coalition with the bourgeoisie, whom they blamed for the war and its detrimental impact upon Russian society and economy. For them, there could be no genuine social revolution in coalition with bourgeois parties such as the Kadets. Russian liberals, they charged, would act like their West European counterparts and seek to establish capitalist class rule based on a propertied bourgeois minority. The Menshevik-Internationalists thought that a period of liberal domination of a bourgeois revolution was necessary, but that it would be short lived and never stable. It would be kept in check by a process of class struggle between the RPG and the Soviet, in which the latter would inevitably emerge victorious. Moreover, World War I would work to the advantage of Russian socialism, for the worldwide imperialist war would culminate in global socialist revolution. As part of a broader revolutionary movement and alliances, the future of a socialist Russia was guaranteed. It befell to Russian socialists, therefore, to keep a clear distance from liberal notions of revolution that were, in fact, reactionary. The essential task was to organize the masses into soviets, to "establish the proper *political premises* . . . to ensure and consolidate the *dictatorship of the democratic masses*."[28] The revolutionary army should pull out of the imperialist war immediately and be on guard only to defend revolutionary Russia from any imperialist attack. Internationally, there should be urgent negotiations for a general peace. Domestically the revolution should conduct a "relentless struggle" against and purge of counter-revolutionary forces. The state must take a leading role in economic management, including the sequestration of plants, especially if the factory owners were engaging in sabotage. The groundwork should be laid for a future Constituent Assembly to legislate for the confiscation of private land and its distribution to the people.[29]

Today, the Menshevik-Internationalist script has been largely forgotten and, given the indelible fact of the Great October Socialist Revolution, much historical attention has focused on the Bolshevik script and, most especially, the role of Lenin in "re-arming" the party through texts such as the "April Theses."[30] Even before Lenin's return to Russia in April 1917 from his exile in Switzerland, it was apparent that Bolshevism was writing a very radical script in the language of violent class struggle. At the time of the February Revolution, the Bolshevik Party's Russian Bureau of its Central Committee published its assessment of the Russian Revolution that remained at the core of Bolshevik thinking throughout 1917. No agreements, it insisted, could be possible with the "counter-revolutionary" RPG consisting of "representatives of the upper bourgeoisie and the nobility." Revolutionaries should agitate for the creation of a dictatorship of the proletariat and peasantry in Russia that would act as the starting point for the "revolutionary movement of the western European proletariat against their bourgeois governments." Peace would come via revolution, from below, by turning the "anti-popular imperialist war into a civil war of the peoples against their oppressors." It was imperative, the Russian Bureau insisted, that the toilers of all countries entered into direct contact, whether via their proletarian parties or fraternization in the trenches, and that armed power be captured by the masses through the formation of Red Guards. The people should then use its power to effect an immediate transfer of resources, be it in the factories or in the fields, without waiting for legitimation from above in laws of a Constituent Assembly. The Bolshevik Party's April Conference, for example, instructed the members to "support the initiative of those peasant committees which . . . are handing over the livestock and implements of the landowning nobility to the peasants."[31]

For such radicalism the Bolsheviks attracted the backing of other extreme left groups and factions, such as the anarchists, even though there remained serious differences. The anarchists used the language of socialism in their opposition to capital, but argued, for example, that "Socialism breaks the chains, but only anarchism releases us from prison." There is no reference to "revolutionary dictatorships" in anarchist scripts, only an insistence that all government is bad and based upon master-slave relations. Anarchists sought to achieve peace and order by the free association of free peoples, organized in whatever collectives were appropriate to local communities. Citizens were called upon to organize in "city, village and professional associations . . . unite in groups, in anarchist clubs. Do not let go of each other's hands, and do not let your righteous anger fade."[32] The lines between anarchist and left Bolshevik activists were nevertheless often blurred, and anarchist agitation was an important element of a left bloc that helped the Bolshevik Party to win influence and power.

The Nationalities' Scripts

The Russian Revolution, it has been pointed out, occupied "the largest physical area in which political revolution has ever occurred. The English, American (confined to the eastern seaboard) and French revolutions were storms in a teacup by comparison."[33] The fall of the autocracy fatally weakened central administrative power. Complicating and cutting across other scripts, the nationalities' scripts sought to take various degrees of autonomy rather than outright state independence, to distinct peoples and nations. The federation of the old empire may appear a reasonable and moderate demand, but in 1917 during a war, the nationalities' scripts added to the diffusion and collapse of central power.

The Russian Empire's peoples and regions were uneven in the extent to which there were well-developed national political movements. There is a lack of firm evidence about to what extent a national consciousness had taken root among ordinary citizens. There were undoubtedly national elites and intellectuals that across the Russian Empire, from the western to the eastern border, advanced similar scripts. These sought complete control over domestic policy, although military and foreign policy would continue to be conducted in partnership with Russia. National parliaments would be fully democratic, elected (like the Russian Constituent Assembly) according to the four-tail suffrage. Linguistic and cultural rights and the right to conduct government and education in the local language were paramount. To this, the Ukrainians added demands for the formation of Ukrainian national regiments within the Russian Army and set about doing that.[34]

National scripts were an integral element of the Russian Revolution. Freedom and liberation was inseparable from the redistribution of power from the central government to the nationalities. This challenged other scripts to respond. Disagreements over the "national question," therefore, lay behind several governmental crises in 1917. Most lukewarm toward accommodating this was the liberal script, for which the "preservation of the unity of the Russian State" was always paramount.[35] If Ukraine, for example, were to enjoy a large degree of autonomy, would this not act as a spur to other national movements?[36] The most enthusiastic exponent of the right to succession and autonomy was the extreme left. Lenin chided

Kerensky for trying to hold back the national movements. For him, the empire's implosion was part of a general crisis of the bourgeois state that could be resolved only by a transfer of power to the soviets.[37]

We the People

The scripts that long dominated historical work on the Russian Revolution were those either penned or perpetrated by the Russian intelligentsia and the main political parties in which they were gathered. More recently, however, a focus on the discourse of "everyday life" has thrown into doubt the extent to which a hegemony of intellectuals led and determined the political choices of ordinary citizens in the Russian Revolution. Even in the context of the supreme vanguard of Bolshevism it has been suggested that Lenin's organization borrowed from below. As well as scripting from above, the Bolshevik Party was as much led as leading, most notably in its adoption of a popular peasant land redistribution program.[38] The Russian historian of 1917 G. Gerasimenko argues that all political parties in the Russian Revolution were, in a determining sense, peripheral. The main cause of events lay in the people (*narod*),

> who day-by-day stubbornly and persistently struggled for more or less acceptable living conditions. This daily struggle for a better life impacted upon political parties and on various social bodies such as executive committees, soviets, trades unions, factory committees, and soldiers' and peasants' committees. It directly or indirectly constrained the exercise of power, from the local and regional commissars to the central government.[39]

Some citizens and social organizations supported the general rights of freedom championed in the liberal script. The Women's League for Equal Rights, for example, campaigned for the extension of civil and political rights for women. Moreover, they pressed, there had to be evidence of women's equality in female representation in the government and its various levels of administration, and in the economy via equal pay and equal rights to land for women peasants.[40] The RPG accepted that the franchise had to be universal, regardless of gender, and this made the Russian liberal script the most radical of its day. However, the numerous committees among peasants, workers, and soldiers that produced programs independently and in different contexts shared a mistrust of the elites that had for so long dominated the lives of the lower orders. The scripts of ordinary literate citizens argued that justice was on the side of the poor. The bourgeoisie was perceived as rapacious and as wrecking, and as representing domestic and international capital rather than the needs of the working majority. Thus, soldiers' letters of April 1917 contain pleas for peace because the war is seen as serving Anglo-French interests.[41] Workers' resolutions of April 1917 were also already arguing that power should be in the hands of the soviets.[42] As the industrial crisis worsened over the summer and autumn of 1917, factory committees blamed this upon capitalist and managerial sabotage and tried to keep production going and extend workers' democracy by assuming control of factories. The workers were suspicious that the bourgeoisie was engineering famine and unemployment in order to strangle a popular social revolution.[43] Peasant committees were less likely to employ terms of urban class conflict, but their traditional aspirations entailed an attack on landowners. The fundamental belief of the peasant revolution was that land should not be subject to ownership cemented in legal documents; rather it should be made available freely to those in need and willing to work the land. If the liberal script's definition of freedom (*svoboda*) entailed responsibilities as well as rights, the peasant notion of freedom was based upon *volia*, or free will through self-assertion, in which peasants had the right to impose their sense of justice. Peasant institutions from below, communes, and land committees, the villagers held, should therefore assume responsibility for control and distribution.[44]

If the scripts of "We, the People" were not written in a conscious class spirit, the division of society into a good "us" and a bad "them" both undermined liberalism and worked to the advantage of left socialism.[45] Indeed, it was the lexicon of socialism, under which numerous enemies in different contexts could be labeled "bourgeois," that came to unify disparate battles for a people's revolution.[46]

Conclusion

It is clear that the multiple scripts of the 1917 Russian Revolution were to the left of general European politics. There have been several explanations for why it was precisely the Bolshevik script that won.

There seems to be a consensus that the liberal script was the least likely to succeed. It depended, above all, on compromise and reconciliation and the belief that all citizens should be equal before the rule of law. Some scholars argue that Russian historical development prior to 1917 gave no experience or training in this form of democracy. In this sense, a liberal Russia, despite its radicalism and strong social protection, was "heavily mortgaged from the start."[47] Others focus on the circumstances and difficulties of 1917. In particular, they stress that, from the summer onward, the country was increasingly gripped by an economic crisis, expressed in shortages of key materials including basic necessities. This may have been generated by internal market price and trade disequilibria, rather than shortfalls in production,[48] but the fact remains that hunger was a very imminent and real threat for many. In these circumstances it was understandable that groups pushed for sectional above national interest. The community of democratic compromise central to the liberal script was thereby torn apart.

The shortcomings and failures of the moderate socialist script acted to further undermine the liberal script. Liberals and socialists cooperated in coalition governments that made no progress in bringing peace any nearer, and whose disagreements over social, political, and economic policy effectively paralyzed reform. At a functional level, shortages and the constant worsening of daily life pointed to the failure of the moderate socialist strategy. For the ordinary people, adequate food provision was more important than the discussions of constitutionalism and civic liberties and promised radical change of a liberal-moderate socialist revolution. The liberal and socialist politicians that formed the coalition cabinets of the RPG were a "head without a body,"[49] increasingly devoid of popular support.

Ultimately, the success or failure of Russia's political elites depended upon how successfully they could match the people's script. It was in the convergence with the people's scripts that the key to Bolshevik success is to be found. In this, the Bolsheviks borrowed as much as they gave, and often lagged behind popular demands for the transfer of power to the soviets. Nevertheless, the Bolshevik script was unique and stood out for its insistence that the demands of the popular movement, chiefly peace, bread, and land, could be satisfied in the here and now. There was no need to wait until a bourgeois Russia had enjoyed a lengthy existence and the prerequisites of socialism were firmly in place. Similarly, the surest road to end the war, in the Bolshevik script, was not through international agreement and arbitration but a unilateral declaration of peace.

It was not immediately apparent that the people and the Bolsheviks disagreed fundamentally on the meaning of the popular program. For the peasants, for example, land ownership signified the restoration of a traditional patriarchal order, something the Bolsheviks opposed as "backward." The future unraveling of these scripts was to be difficult and bloody and served to solidify Russia's isolation from general European politics. In October 1917, however, the Bolsheviks could justifiably celebrate their capture of the popular mood, expressed in joint hostility to "the bourgeoisie."

PART IV

Revolutionary Projections

JEFFREY WASSERSTROM
YIDI WU

You Say You Want a Revolution

Revolutionary and Reformist Scripts in China, 1894–2014

> Sweep away millennia of despotism in all its forms . . . Stand
> up for Revolution!   Zou Rong, 1903[1]

> If we only [think of the good things related to] American
> Independence, or only consider the French Revolution [a
> positive trend], and then follow in admiration, we are taking
> things too lightly without much consideration, which will only
> lead to failure and chaos.   Kang Youwei, 1902[2]

> Contemporary Chinese are too enthusiastic about revolution,
> too worshipful of revolution. Each and every one of us is both
> victim and carrier of that word.   Liu Xiaobo, 1994[3]

> Today, China is the least likely nation in the world to see a
> revolution, but the one that most urgently needs reform.
>   Han Han, 2011[4]

The topic of Chinese revolutionary scripts is so complex that it could easily
be the subject of a book rather than just a chapter. Such a book would need
a chapter on the 1911 Revolution, which led to the founding of the Republic of China (ROC) and to Sun Yat-sen (1866–1925), who would later found
the Guomindang (Nationalist Party), becoming that new nation's first
president. It would obviously also need a chapter on the 1949 Revolution,
the transformative struggle that culminated in the establishment of another
new state, the People's Republic of China (PRC), which throughout its history has been controlled by the Chinese Communist Party (CCP). It would
need a section on the mid-1930s through late 1940s, when the Nationalist
leader Chiang Kai-shek (1887–1975) and his arch-rival Mao Zedong (1893–
1976), whose most famous book is the subject of Alexander Cook's chapter

in this volume (which comes immediately after this one), led competing organizations that each claimed to be the true guardian of Sun's sacred tradition and disparaged the other as counter-revolutionaries. It would need a chapter on the Cultural Revolution decade (1966–76), when the "Little Red Book" that Cook discusses became such a crucial generator of revolutionary scripts in China and indeed globally.

In the pages that follow, we will not try to provide a comprehensive look at the topics just mentioned. Instead, we will content ourselves with focusing tightly on two points in time when parallel though different debates broke out over whether "revolution" or "reform" was needed to improve China's situation, and over whether any foreign event of the past—and if so, which one—provided a useful blueprint for those seeking to transform Chinese politics to follow or adapt. There are not precise starting and ending points for these debates, but 1894 and 2014 make convenient book-end dates. This is partly because, in traditional Chinese reckonings of time, sixty-year cycles have a significance much like a century, making a 120th anniversary much like a bicentennial. And partly because the war between China and Japan that began in 1894, and whose 120th anniversary has just been marked with a good deal of commentary in the PRC, ended with a defeat of Qing dynasty forces that led many Chinese intellectuals to feel that for their country to survive, some kind of dramatic shift in how it was run was needed.[5]

The first debate we will analyze began at the end of the nineteenth century, in the immediate wake of Japan's defeat of the Qing, and continued into the early years of the twentieth century. Its main participants included the first two people we have quoted above: Zou Rong, who thought that China needed a revolution like the American and French ones and spoke of the country's need to produce its own counterparts to George Washington and Napoleon Bonaparte (whom he treats simply as a symbol of revolutionary strength, rather than as a much more complex figure) and Kang Youwei, who argued that a better strategy would be to follow the lead of nearby Japan and create a constitutional monarchy.

It was during the era of this debate that the term *geming*, which is the main Chinese term for "revolution," first began to be used in its modern sense—that is, to signify a political struggle aimed at rapidly creating a completely new order and likely to involve violence. Zou used it in the title of his *Geming Jun* (The Revolutionary Army), the text we cite, which speaks of the need to "annihilate" all members of the ethnically Manchu Qing dynasty (1644–1911), so as to "cleanse" the Chinese soil of "260 years of harsh and unremitting pain" and help "the descendants of the Yellow Emperor" (that is all members of the majority Han ethnicity) "become Washingtons."

The text of Kang's we quote also includes the term *geming* in its title, but for him it is a thing to be avoided, because of the chaos and bloodshed that racked France in 1789. His commentary is called "China Only Needs a Constitution, Not a Revolution—In Answer to South and North American Businessmen," and its central thesis is that patriots should work to improve the country via nonviolent reform rather than risk traumatizing it by carrying out a violent *geming*. He favored gradual and temperate transformations that over time would remake and modernize the political order without abandoning the best things about China's traditions, including the Confucian one. In another of his most famous works, in fact, he presented Confucius as having been a champion of reform, a technique he employed to allow him to use the ancient sage as a mouthpiece for his own modernizing vision.[6]

In contrast to the case with "revolution," there was no single agreed upon term for "reform," a concept that was evoked via the use of various two-character terms, including one, *gaige*, that shares a component, *ge*, with *geming*. There was, as this linguistic overlap suggests, some common ground between revolutionaries and reformers, but there was, at that point, also one crucial difference: Zou and others in his camp thought that all monarchical forms should be jettisoned, while Kang and his allies were convinced that China should keep some kind of monarch. More than that, the latter did not denigrate the Qing as Manchu invaders, as Zou and his allies did. Not surprisingly, each group looked to different foreign models, with revolutionaries seeing inspiration and finding scripts to follow in not just the events of 1776 and 1789 but also the English ones of the 1640s, while reformers looked not just to Japan's Meiji Restoration of 1868 but also to England's so-called Glorious Revolution of 1688, an event with a strong restorationist side to it.

The second debate that interests us began roughly a century after the start of the first one and continues to this day. Centered on a related but also new kind of difference of opinion between advocates of revolution, albeit in this case one that is nonviolent in nature, and proponents of reform, this more recent turn-of-a-century debate began in the immediate aftermath of the dramatic protests and brutal massacres of April through June 1989. Simplifying the situation greatly, we can say for heuristic purposes at least that there is again a clear split that is expressed via divergent favored terms and sometimes also includes differences of opinion about foreign models. On the one side are those who place their hope for change in the coming of a Chinese counterpart to the Velvet Revolution that brought Václav Havel to power, and on the other side are those who think that change will come to China only in a more gradual manner and are skeptical of seeing something like the Central European events of 1989 play out in their own country.

Liu Xiaobo is one of the most famous new "revolutionaries," who admittedly are very different from Zou Rong and his associates in their focus on nonviolent methods for promoting change and quick to note that many bad things have been done in China in the past in the name of *geming*. Liu, the Nobel Peace Prize winner from whose essay "That Holy Word, 'Revolution'" our third opening quotation is taken, remains a prisoner of conscience as we write this in early 2015. He was incarcerated this time (he has been imprisoned before) for his leading role in the "Charter 08" online petition drive—a drive whose manifesto was strongly influenced by the Czech Charter 77 with which Havel was involved.

Representing the "reform" side now is a disparate group, ranging from middle-aged and older "liberal" professors such as Li Zehou to the young writer Han Han, who provides our final opening quotation above. They differ on many specific issues but converge around the notion that, in light of China's traumatic twentieth century, the term "revolution" should now be seen as so suspect that all scripts associated with it are not only best treated with extreme caution but discarded. Too often, they claim, struggles carried out in the name of *geming* have spiraled into violent score-settling struggles that have merely resulted in the substitution of one set of autocrats and one system of oppression for another. Liu Xiaobo would agree with them on this, but they go further, claiming that it makes more sense now to focus on moving small-scale reforms forward rather than in dreaming of a velvet or color revolution or an Arab Spring–like rising.

In examining the two debates just introduced, we will pay closest attention to the visions and arguments of those who shared the conviction that China was in urgent need of some kind of change. It is important to remember that, just as in the Russian case detailed elsewhere in this volume, there have always been in China some defenders of the status quo or proponents of modest change who stood outside of the debates we describe, sometimes disparaging both "revolution" and "reform," but in other cases appropriating one or, in more recent times, both of the words. In the mid-1890s, when our story begins, it was possible for conservatives to argue that the country needed neither reform nor revolution. In the current milieu, by contrast, the country's leaders claim that what they are doing is protecting the holy revolutionary tradition that led to the creation of a New China in 1949 *and* the bold reinvigoration of the *geming* that Deng Xiaoping ushered in under the rubric of reform. The current official vision of the entwining and shared sacrality of *geming* and *gaige* is neatly encapsulated in comments Deng made to a visiting Japanese political leader in 1985. "The reform we are now carrying out is very daring," Deng reportedly said. "But if we do not carry it out," he continued, "it will be hard for us to make progress." Then he summed up the situation as follows: "Reform is China's second revolution."[7]

China before the Debates on Revolution and Reform

> Of all the nations that have attained a degree of civilization, the Chinese
> are the least *revolutionary* and the most *rebellious*.
> —Thomas Taylor Meadows, 1856, italicized in the original.[8]

It is important, in order to place the debates to come into context, to note that China was not always a country that was thought of as a natural site for either revolutions or radical movements for reform. In the middle of the nineteenth century, even though China was rocked with insurrections that threatened to topple the Qing dynasty, Meadows and other Westerners on the scene often saw this as simply the latest proof that the Chinese were unusually "rebellious" by nature but not necessarily given to "revolutions" of the sort that had been sweeping through the Atlantic World. Chinese history, they noted, had seen many upheavals that had changed *who* held power but not how power was exercised. Riots and insurrections were commonplace, though usually confined to specific areas and focusing on specific issues, but even those rare ones that spread across wider areas and had broad goals stopped short of seeking to transform the basic structure of the political status quo, as classic revolutions do. Even the most dramatic of all traditional upheavals, the rebellions that periodically toppled dynasties, did not qualify as revolutions. The final act in the oft-followed script of these insurrections was typically the founding of a new dynasty that was much like the last one.

The rise of new dynasties, whether via rebellions (that ended with rebels becoming emperors) or conquest (the way that the Qing took power) were more restorations than revolutions: the dynastic cycle was seen as a way of periodically cleansing the political order. New dynasties typically asserted that they deserved to rule because they were able to restore order to a land that had fallen into chaos or been troubled by misrule. While every dynasty did new things—recent scholarship, for example, has shown that the Qing used Manchu script for some documents and introduced many elements into the Chinese political system that had ties to the land north of the Great Wall from which its founders came—the main thrust of the founding of new dynasties was a vision of getting a pre-existing political system back on track.

By the 1860s, when Meadows wrote, many things about China's domestic and international situation had begun to change dramatically. The Qing had been defeated in two wars with Western powers, which called into question the notion that China was not only the major power of the region but of the world. A new religion, Christianity, was making its presence felt in China, and like some earlier imported creeds, such as Buddhism, it included millenarian strains that had a revolutionary cast, since they predicted that the world was headed toward a totally transformative shift. And yet, upheavals still tended to follow familiar scripts.

The nineteenth-century upheavals that came closest to qualifying as revolutionary were linked to millenarian religious beliefs. The most important of these was the Taiping upheaval led by Hong Xiuquan, a prophet who gathered a massive number of followers by preaching a quasi-Christian creed based on hallucinatory visions he had that convinced him he was the younger brother of Jesus Christ. His forces took control of a large swath of land (roughly the size of France) and Hong announced the creation of a new country, the Taiping Tianguo (The Heavenly Kingdom of Great Peace), which would be governed on novel principles, including reverence for the Gospel and equal distribution of land among all true believers, male and female alike. Pointing above all to Hong's land reform program, which was never fully implemented, Mao and various Communist Party historians would later celebrate the Taiping effort as a precocious move to bring socialism to China, which failed as a result of its lack of a sufficiently "scientific" basis to its revolutionary strategy and the perfidy of the forces allied against it, which included not just the Qing but also, eventually, Western powers.

In the end, even though the Taiping Uprising (1848–64) had some revolutionary aspects, including a call for a turn away from traditional approaches to familial and gender relations, there was little that distinguished Hong's mode of rule from that of many rebels of the past, including those who went on to found long-lived dynasties. He behaved in his final years much like the first emperor of his own dynasty, albeit one that barely out-lasted his own death. It is possible as well to see precursors in the programs of some Taiping leaders, such as Hong Rengan, of the future ideas of radical reformers, but again only inklings.

The First Debate

> From absolute monarchy to constitution and democracy, each of these must come step by step. Disrupt this order and there is bound to be great turmoil, like what happened in France . . . . The methods of revolution . . . do not fit with China's time and space.
>
> —Kang Youwei, 1902[9]

> Kang Youwei assumes that revolution would lead to tragedy: rivers of blood would flow and numerous deaths would occur without the desired goal being reached quickly. But can a constitution be put in place without weapons? . . . In comparison between revolution and constitution, revolution is easier and establishing a constitution is harder . . . . I would rather pick the less difficult and easier path.
>
> —Zhang Binglin, 1903[10]

The ground shifted late in the nineteenth century. For a mixture of reasons, some domestic and some international, traditional political approaches, such as either attacking the ruling dynasty with an eye toward establishing a new one or pushing for small-scale reforms, were no longer the only options pursued by intellectuals and activists eager to see change occur. The government had been altering some of its strategies since the 1842 Opium War defeat, which was followed by another military loss to British and French forces in 1860, but these began to seem to some merely cosmetic in the face of such a major crisis.

The biggest development to increase the appeal of both radical reform programs and calls for revolution, as noted above, was China's loss to Japan in a war over who would have the most influence over the neighboring Korean peninsula. Even more than earlier battlefield losses to distant powers, when Japan bested China in 1895, this triggered a period of deep soul searching within the country's elite. Although some conservatives treated this loss as a fluke, which required at most simply more of the small modifications to the way the Qing governed that had already been tried—for example, increasing the supply of foreign weaponry at the dynasty's disposal, having a small number of members of the bureaucracy study foreign languages, and so forth—more and more members of the elite concluded that if a smaller country, that had long been in China's shadow, could defeat it, a big change was needed. The alternative, they claimed, was that foreign powers would continue to humiliate China and take parts of its territory (by then the number of treaty ports with foreign-run districts had grown markedly), and in the end their land might suffer the fate of being fully colonized, as had happened to nearby India. The central question became what sort of change was needed and whether any foreign country's transformation provided a template that China should follow.

Into this setting came *geming*, a potent new term—or, rather, an old term that started to be invested with a novel meaning. It was made up of two characters: a relatively uncommon one meaning stripping or skinning (*ge*) and a common one meaning mandate (*ming*), used to refer to the process by which, in traditional political thought, Heaven invested an emperor with the right to reign as its representative on earth (Tianming, heavenly mandate, was what all legitimate rulers were said to possess). The composite term *geming* had first been used more than two millennia before Japan defeated China, with its etymology usually traced back to its appearance in the classical canonical text the *Yi Jing* (*Book of Changes*). It is used there in the following passage to refer to an act in which one ruling family topples and takes the place of another: "The kings Tang and Wu overthrew the thrones of the dynasties of the Xia (2100–1600 B.C.) and the Shang (1600–1100 B.C.) in accordance with the will of Heaven, and in response to the wishes of men."[11] There is a sense of political change in this early use of the term, but there is, as in early Western uses of its kindred term "revolution" (whose root is the same as that in "revolve"), an implication of restoration, the renewal of a system in this case by a dynasty that has grown corrupt over time being replaced by one that is fresh and pure.

After its appearance in the *Book of Changes,* this term was only rarely used in China, but at least as early as the eighth century it was making its mark across the sea in Japan, with the same Chinese characters but pronounced *kakumei*.[12] In Japan, the term conveyed a sense of political transformation with continued support of a single imperial house, for in Japan, as opposed to China, the ideas of the dynastic cycle never took hold: its current emperors claims to be part of the same lineage as its earliest ones. In Japanese, a range of foreign events involving change, some leaving sovereigns in place and others deposing them, were described as acts of *kakumei.*

When the Japanese political order was revamped in 1868 in the wake of the mixture of threats and inspiring new ideas emanating from the West, this transition was called a form of *kakumei,* instead of *gaikaku,* which is reform in Japanese, and *gaige* in Chinese. In English, analysts have had to decide whether to refer to the epochal events of the time as the Meiji *Restoration* because of its creation of a constitutional system in which the emperor still had power—indeed had increased status, at least symbolically, after an era when military strongmen known as Shoguns were the true masters of the country—or to refer to it as a *revolutionary* movement because of how radically the Japanese political system was changed by the introduction of elections, a modern school system, and other new institutions borrowed wholesale or adapted from Western models. Similarly, in English, we have to decide whether to refer to the English events of 1688 as the Glorious *Revolution* or a *restoration* that revivified monarchical structures. In Japanese, there is no need to make a choice, because of the elasticity of the term *kakumei*.

When the two-character term filtered back into Chinese late in the 1800s, it took on a more specific meaning. One key figure in the term's reintroduction into Chinese was Kang Youwei's most famous protégé, Liang Qichao, who in 1898 helped his mentor in working with the liberal-minded Guangxu emperor to chart out a bold program of reforms. Known as the "Hundred Days' Reform," this program included the establishment of a modern-style university and a host of political measures modeled in part on things Japan had done in 1868. The movement was curtailed by a coup carried out by more conservative members of the Qing ruling house, including Ci Xi, usually referred to simply as the "Empress Dowager," who placed the Guangxu emperor under house arrest and drove Kang and Liang into exile.

Liang fled to Japan, where the flexible concept of *kakumei* attracted his attention as a useful way to describe the changes that he and Kang had tried to implement. Following a general pattern of the time, when novel political concepts coming into play in China were often compound terms borrowed back from Japan (words for "nation-state," "democracy," "republic," and so on had similar genealogical lineages), he began to use the term *geming* when writing about his wish to turn China into a modern polity through nonviolent methods with an altered form of imperial rule in which a constitution placed limited on the actions of the dynasty.[13] Soon, however, *geming* began to be associated more commonly with more violent visions of change, which included calls for the Han Chinese to drive the Manchus of the Qing out of China and either the ethnically Han Ming dynasty be restored to power or the dynastic system as a whole be abandoned.[14] Sun Yat-sen, a widely traveled one-time reformer who had been radicalized by his inability to gain an audience for his plans for gradual change and by his exposure to international ideas relating to politics (and who had begun to call for the Qing to be overthrown), was very pleased when a Japanese newspaper described him as leading a "revolutionary party" (*kakumei to*), instead of merely heading a rebellious organization.[15] From then on, Sun favored the use of the term *geming* to refer to antidynastic actions, and this sense of the word became its main one.

There were several other terms in play at this time that referred to dramatic shifts in political life. In the memorials that spelled out his goals for the 1898 reforms, for example, Kang had presented his program as an effort to *bianfa* (change the rules), *bianzheng* (change political institutions), and *weixin* (promote or maintain newness).[16] Kang also claimed that even the most radical parts of his reform program were in line with Confucian traditions, meaning that he was setting out to reinvigorate and modernize, not destroy, the imperial system.

Kang, like Liang, fled to Japan after the Hundred Days' Reform ended, and there he established the Protect the Emperor Society and continued to promote the idea that China's best hope lay in developing a constitutional monarchy. The competition between this group and Sun's more radical Revive China Society fostered the first great Chinese debate between backers of reform and backers of revolution. And just as *geming* traveled to Japan and then took on a new pronunciation and eventually new meanings, this debate was a mixed Chinese and Japanese affair, since each camp's flagship newspaper was a Chinese publication issued in Japan. Kang launched the first major rhetorical volley in the spring of 1902, writing the article "China Only Needs a Constitution, Not a Revolution—In Answer to South and North American Chinese Businessmen," from which the quotation that opens this section as well as an earlier one was taken. Zhang Binglin, an ally of Sun's, countered with his famous open letter to Kang, "Refuting Kang Youwei's Idea on Revolution," also quoted from at the start of this section.

The year 1903 was an important one for writings on revolution, but neither Zhang's critique of Kang nor anything Sun wrote then turned out to be the most significant text extolling the virtues of *geming*. That distinction belongs to the *Revolutionary Army*, the work by the young firebrand Zou Rong that we quoted at the start of this chapter. Zhang helped legitimate and spread word of this text, hailing it as a prophetic and inspiring one in the preface he wrote to accompany its initial print run. Zou's work is a hard-edged polemic that, as we have noted, was both fervently nationalistic and filled with calls for Chinese patriots to learn from foreign revolutionaries. Soon after its publication, Zou and Zhang were arrested on charges of sedition, and the former soon died a martyr's death in jail.

Despite the chasm that opened between reformers and revolutionaries in the late 1890s and early 1900s, it is worth stressing two commonalities between them. Both camps felt that China needed to change—and change dramatically—in order to be able to hold its own in a dangerous new world order and avoid the fate of becoming a *wangguo* (conquered nation) with an enslaved populace, the way that India, for example, was routinely described in Chinese texts of the era. And both looked for foreign models to follow in carrying out this transformation, albeit sometimes failing to have a clear understanding of just what had happened in other countries, as Zou's conflation of "Washingtons" and "Napoleons" as needed to usher in the revolution China showed. The fact that the latter proclaimed himself an emperor seemed less important to Zou, perhaps, than that both men were strong leaders and wielded power in a land that was no longer under the control of a once-hated king.

In light of this shared set of preoccupations, it is not all that surprising that some people moved from reformist to revolutionary positions and back again. Or that, especially after the 1911 Revolution led to the creation of a new Republic that quickly devolved into a divided land with different provinces under the control of individual military strongmen (the so-called Warlords), some one-time radicals tacked in a conservative direction and questioned whether the country had really been as ripe for radical transformation as they once imagined. Kang Youwei started to grow increasingly conservative after the failure of the 1898 reforms and late in his life often seemed more concerned with pointing out the problems with revolution than with describing the things that were wrong about the status quo. Sun, as already noted, started out a reformer and then became the most famous proponent of revolution. Zhang Binglin, meanwhile, agreed with Kang in 1898 that urgent reform from above was the best path to pursue, then embraced more radical stances.[17] As of 1901, he had abandoned reform in favor of revolution, ending up in 1903 among the most forceful critics of Kang.[18]

The most complicated case was Liang Qichao, who alternated between reformist and revolutionary positions over the course of his life and ended up influencing political figures of many stripes in the generations that immediately followed him. Liang wrote things that would inspire the founders of the Chinese Communist Party, including Mao, but he ultimately became skeptical that any foreign movement of radical reform or revolution provided a template that would solve China's crisis. In 1898, he had been neatly in step with his mentor in advocating a constitutional monarchy. After a worldwide tour, though, he started to believe that revolution was what China needed. But then a trip to the United States, which left him very critical of its political system, convinced Liang that China was not suited to become a democratic republic. In 1911 Liang, who had become disenchanted with the Qing, sympathized with many of the goals of the revolutionaries of that year but was against their use of violence to pursue them. Later still, he became much more conservative, moving more in line with Kang in expressing his strong distaste for the violence that accompanied the French Revolution and noting that soon after 1789, France was again run by a despot.

Zou Rong's take on the French precedent could not have been more dissimilar, as to him what was tragic was not the prospect that China would follow in France's path in moving toward a new kind of despotism, but that it had never had an episode like 1789 that swept away decrepit old forms. He argued that there were two types of revolution: barbaric ones, which were destructive and not constructive, including the Boxer Uprising, and civilized ones, which were destructive *and* constructive. He considered the French one a clear case of the latter sort of revolution, and he called for his fellow countrymen to carry out a Chinese equivalent to it.

Apart from the dichotomy between support for constitutional monarchy, on the one hand, and revolution, on the other, Kang and Liang as opposed to Zhang and Zou also diverged sharply in their attitudes toward the Manchus. In both Zhang Binglin and Zou Rong's writings, anti-Manchu sentiment is virulent. They saw the Han as members of a superior race, the Manchus as inferior, foreign, and less civilized. The revolution they envisioned would rid the country not just of outdated political forms but also usurpers who had never had the right to govern China. In contrast, Kang Youwei thought of Manchus, Mongols, and Han as members of a common race, arguing that the original distinctions between them had long ago become meaningless. Kang noted that ethnic Han held high positions within the Qing government, and he accused the revolutionaries of playing to popular prejudices against the Manchus in order to gain mass support.

The success of the 1911 Revolution, which involved the overthrow of the Manchus and the transformation of China into a republic, with the revolutionary Sun Yat-sen proclaimed its first president, altered the situation dramatically. It was a clear victory of proponents of revolution over proponents of constitutional monarchy. In the decades to come, Zhang's and Zou's works would be celebrated as revolutionary classics, while Kang's antirevolutionary tracts would be largely forgotten. For most of the rest of the twentieth century, the main debates were over what sort of revolutionary path was the right one, rather than whether *geming* or reform was best, and people at all points on the political spectrum claimed to be speaking in the name of some kind of revolutionary idea. It was only after the Mao era, during which veneration for revolution reached its apogee, that a new kind of debate with some parallels to, but also basic differences from, that of the 1890s through early 1900s broke out again.

The Second Debate

Yes to Reform, No to Revolution
—Li Zehou and Liu Zaifu, 2011[19]

I'm excited about political developments in China, and looking forward to a Jasmine Revolution. —Liao Yiwu, 2011[20]

Many new debates over reform and revolution broke out during the course of the twentieth century, but the one that interests us gained steam in the wake of the government crackdown of mid-1989. In the 1980s, in order to fill the cultural vacuum created by the Cultural Revolution, intellectuals devoured Western ideas, while also looking for and sometimes finding inspiration in other places—in the People Power struggle in the Philippines and the antiauthoritarian labor demonstrations in South Korea, for example, and in Poland's Solidarity Movement and the ideas of Gandhi. The political crisis of 1989, which left many dead in the streets of Beijing and Chengdu (both cities witnessed massacres) and many leaders of the protests centered on Tiananmen Square in jail or on the run, temporarily froze this questing "high cultural fever," as the search of the era was called. Then, in the 1990s, critical intellectuals split into many groups.[21] At first, in the cacophony of opinions, virtually no one looked to "revolution" as a way to solve existing problems. Instead, they tended to argue that the only way to bring China forward was through a step-by-step set of nonviolent reforms. What kind of reform should be prioritized became and remains the key question, though those calling for the most sweeping and swiftest sorts of reforms have sometimes linked themselves to a particular sort of new-style revolution—the kind associated with Havel's rise to power in 1989, the "color revolutions" of the very early twenty-first century, and the Jasmine Revolutions of 2011, also known as the Arab Spring.[22]

A major text of the 1990s, which can be seen in some ways as a modern day successor to Kang Youwei's arguments for reform and against militancy in 1903, was the book *Farewell to Revolution: A Critical Dialogue on 20th-Century China*. Although not an academic work, it is made up of conversations between two exiled intellectuals: Li Zehou, a philosopher, and Liu Zaifu, a literary critic. In 1992, both of these men, who were active in 1980s intellectual life in China and supporters of the 1989 protests, happened to be teaching in Colorado and began to meet frequently to discuss ideas. First they simply chatted informally as friends, but then Liu started to record and document their conversations. Their conversations ranged widely, taking up philosophical, literary, and historical topics. Because of their critical views of current Chinese politics and of the entire Chinese revolutionary tradition, as well as their identities as dissidents, the book was not surprisingly banned in the mainland.

The central argument of the book is clear from its title: Chinese activists have for too long put too much faith in revolutionary solutions. It is important to note, though, how the authors define revolution. *Geming*, in their view, specifically means "radical actions that overthrow the existing system and authority through drastic methods such as mass violence." They also note that "national revolution against foreign invasion is not included" in the category of struggles that they abhor.[23] Thus what the authors mainly disapprove of is the use of violence, and what they fear, as Kang did, is the chaos that a revolution might cause, but they do not condemn completely all events that can be classified as revolutionary struggles, leaving room, for example, for support for independence movements aimed at freeing a people from control by a foreign power. Li Zehou and Liu Zaifu both strive to do what Liu Xiaobo wanted to do in his 1994 essay quoted at the start of this chapter: take a word, *geming*, that had acquired a sacred status over the course of the last century, and demystify it. They also wanted to draw attention to the ugliness of many things done in the name of revolution and present reform as a better alternative.

In the chapter "Yes to Reform, No to Revolution," Li Zehou reevaluates some critical moments in China's past, from the Hundred Days' Reform and the 1911 Revolution to the May Fourth Movement of 1919 and the June Fourth Incident of 1989. He speaks highly of Kang Youwei, a man who he claims understood China better than Sun Yat-sen. Li conceives the 1911 Revolution as neither inevitable nor necessary, considering the historical contingency for a revolution to succeed and a promising yet gradual reform agenda. Li criticizes the May Fourth Movement—a hallowed period of intellectual ferment and patriotic fervor that has been called China's "Enlightenment" and is celebrated in official communist histories as the event that paved the way for the founding of the CCP—as a time of "too much radical emotion, not enough rational thinking," the same criticism that he levels at the Red Guards of the 1960s and the students of 1989. Li sympathized with the students but disagreed with the hunger strikes and continued occupation of the square. He feared that such uncompromising revolutionary actions were doomed to fail.[24]

The book generated a great deal of controversy in Hong Kong, on the Chinese mainland—where it has been read in smuggled in printed samizdat editions and online versions that have made their way past internet censors—and also overseas. Since the Communist Party regards itself as a revolutionary party, the negation of revolution is seen as a direct challenge to the ruling group's historical legitimacy. Consequently, some major state newspapers, including the *People's Daily,* have debunked the book as anti-Marxist and driven by a fundamental misunderstanding of history. One article mentioned that the idea of needing to say "farewell to revolution" initiated the collapse of the Soviet socialist system, which proved the importance of China steering clear of this harmful way of thinking, since the implosion of the USSR led to chaos within many of its former component states and Moscow's declining influence in the world.[25] For overseas pro-democracy dissidents like Hu Ping and Liu Binyan, the book had the opposite problem: it sounded too much like the communist narrative that celebrated Deng Xiaoping's Opening and Reform and prioritized economic growth over political democracy. These critics of *Farewell to Revolution* saw it as distressing that one-time supporters of the 1989 protests now viewed development as more important than freedom and democracy.[26]

Debates on *Farewell to Revolution* flared again in 2011, thanks to the arrival of the 1911 Revolution's centennial and the book being reprinted in its sixth edition. In an interview conducted in 2011, Li Zehou spoke of how his belief in revolution had been thoroughly shaken by the Cultural Revolution, which he thought of as being just like the French Revolution. By "farewell to revolution," he meant saying good-bye in particular to the 1911 Revolution. He even speculated that if the Empress Dowager (1835–1908) had died ten years earlier, the Hundred Days' Reform would have succeeded, and if she had died ten years later, there would have been no 1911 Revolution.[27] This time the official media did not fight back, not only because of the increasing tolerance of diverse opinions after almost two decades, but more likely because the authorities now understand the danger of violence and revolution.

Another dissident involved in the events of 1989, Liu Xiaobo, had first made a name for himself in intellectual circles by challenging Li Zehou's embrace of traditional Chinese culture during the "high culture fever." Although he would write his own criticisms of the fetishizing of the term *geming* after 1989, he had problems with *Farewell to Revolution*. He felt it overcorrected the conventional narrative and oversimplified different kinds of revolutions, foreign and Chinese alike, into one radical and violent type. He has also tended to be more skeptical of a regime as morally bankrupt as the current one being capable of reform.[28]

When it comes to his reflections on revolution, Liu Xiaobo is not drastically different from Li Zehou and Liu Zaifu. What the term "revolution" lacks in English but the Chinese term *geming* implies, Liu notices, is a sense of sacredness and righteousness that places it beyond reproach: until recently in the mainland, to say that one was against *geming* placed one beyond the pale in the way that, in the United States, saying one is against "democracy" would. Consequently, he argues, everything can be justified in the name of "that holy word," *geming*. One flaw of the 1989 movement, Liu concludes, is that even during that seemingly iconoclastic struggle, students and intellectuals like him were still carried away by a familiar sort of revolutionary righteousness and proved too ready to abandon rational debate for arguments in which each side tried to prove that they were more truly patriotic and revolutionary. He expresses the wish that the 1989 struggle will end up being seen as the last Chinese "Revolution" and that its blood and sacrifices will pave the way for lasting reform.[29]

Liu Xiaobo's subsequent frequent praise for Václav Havel and his focus on the difficulties that the Chinese Communist Party will have in carrying out needed kinds of political reforms makes it hard to categorize him neatly. Those writing suggest a belief in the potential value of some kind of nonviolent Velvet Revolution in improving China's situation. He has also, however, lamented China's lack of a moral leader capable of carrying out sweeping change, singling out Havel as an example of the sort of figure he has in mind, who has no Chinese counterpart.

In 2001, in honor of the ninetieth anniversary of the 1911 Revolution, Liu Xiaobo wrote a piece picking up on the claim in a speech by then-president Jiang Zemin describing the CCP's career as a continuation of Sun Yatsen's unfinished will. His skepticism of revolution resurfaces here, when he asserts that what makes Sun's project and the Communist Party's efforts similar is that both were rooted in the idea that grabbing power via violence was justified. Contrary to those who would argue that Sun was a virtuous revolutionary whose spirit the Communist Party only claimed to

respect, he argues that, at each turning point, Sun opted for power central-
ization and violence, leaving the legacy of a party state with one ideology
and one leader, which the CCP copied. If Sun had lived long enough to
unify China, Liu imagines, he might have become a dictator like Mao.[30]

The final texts relating to reform and revolution we will cite come from
the past few years, a time when the lives of many Chinese people might
seem to have nothing to do with *geming*, despite hundreds of local protests occurring in China on a daily basis. A small number make international headlines, while most pass by unnoticed. What has been missing
since 1989, when linked demonstrations broke out in scores of cities, has
been any protest wave that has crossed both class lines and geographical
boundaries and included large-scale rallies in the capital. In comparison to
the 1980s, people now have more stratified interests that make it difficult
to strike a chord nationwide, and the government has become more skilled
in maintaining stability via propaganda drives highlighting the need for
stability as well as through a budget for domestic security that is now larger
than that designated for maintaining an army and navy capable of responding to threats from abroad.

This might seem a time when both the authorities and ordinary people
are ready to sigh in relief that the era of "revolution" is long gone, but
that is not quite the case. The government still, periodically, presents the
Communist Party as a once and still revolutionary organization, and critics
sometimes argue that the problems with contemporary Chinese society are
rooted in the poisonous half-lives of past revolutions. Yu Hua, one of China's most famous contemporary writers and one of the most critical of authors who has not been forced into prison or exile and indeed still belongs
to the official writers association, is a case in point. In his recent writings,
he reminds us that revolutionary movements like the Great Leap Forward
and revolutionary violence like the Cultural Revolution are still with us and
capable of casting dark shadows over the present. The economic miracle of
the past thirty years that the Chinese are so proud of, he claims, has been in
part a mutation rather than simply a repudiation of past violence, with economic exploitation in a corrupt system taking the place of the persecution
of the political campaigns of Maoist times.

In his recent book *China in Ten Words*, which could not be published
on the mainland and first appeared in Chinese in Taiwan and has now been
translated into other languages, including English, *geming* is one of the
terms that is given a chapter of its own. In this chapter on "revolution" he
asserts that we can see a version of the mentality of the Great Leap For-

ward in the frenzied development mania of today, and notes that there are symbolic parallels between the Red Guards of the Cultural Revolution and businessmen of the present. Growing up as an elementary school boy during the Cultural Revolution, Yu Hua points out that Mao defined revolution as an insurrection and an act of violence and wonders whether development that can only occur via acts of oppression and that does harm to ordinary people fits into this category as well.[31]

In 2011, on the occasion of the 1911 Revolution's centennial, Yu Hua wrote an article depicting the Chinese government's ambivalent feelings toward the celebration. On the one hand, officials commemorate 1911 as a part of the communist revolutionary history leading up to 1949. On the other hand, the authorities want anything but to stir up a real revolution. Adding to the complexities of the present moment, he says, some of today's most troubling realities resemble those found in the final years of the Qing dynasty, another time when official corruption ran rampant and society was riddled with inequities. Thus the joy of celebration was overshadowed for the government in 2011 by the fear of change, the worry that they would face the same fate in the end as the Qing.[32]

The year 2011 turned out, of course, not to be just a year for commemorating and reflecting on old revolutions but also of trying to make sense of new ones. The Jasmine Revolutions—also know as the Arab Spring events—in North Africa and the Middle East were particularly important. Chinese political figures dealt with these in many ways; state-run publications, predictably, alternated between playing down their importance and warning of the likelihood that instability and violence would come in their wake. Some dissidents, such as Liao Yiwu, as noted above, saw a hopeful sign in the upheavals, suggesting that China might be the next authoritarian state to be transformed by massive protests. Still others, such as Han Han, by some account the most widely read Chinese blogger, took other positions.

Han Han fleshed out his views in a late 2011 trilogy of posts on three potentially sensitive terms: revolution, democracy and freedom.[33] As a high school dropout, he does not belong to the class of intellectuals that Chinese audiences have typically looked to for profound analysis. He has gained an important following, including among some of China's highly educated young and not-so-young people, through blog posts that are critical of or satirize the government. This makes him an admittedly unusual sort of public intellectual, which made it natural that his trilogy of posts would be scrutinized closely and generate debates.

The first two of the three posts are written in a question-and-answer form, in which he identifies himself as proreform and antirevolution, stressing that he believes neither in an old-style violent *geming* nor in a new-style nonviolence of the sort that could be led by an imaginary Chinese counterpart to Havel or driven forward by crowds like those that amassed in Tahrir Square. He reasons that in China it is almost impossible to reach a consensus among all walks of life, and the revolutionary leader is likely to become a new dictator.[34] A perfect Velvet Revolution has no chance of taking place in China, because it requires three prerequisites: a people of high quality, authorities who acquiesce, and intellectuals with charisma. China has none of these, Han claims.[35] The CCP is no longer a party or a class, but when it is as extensive as including 80 million members with 0.3 billion relatives, it becomes the people itself. Thus to change the people is to change everything. Han does not specify where the reform should start, except for mentioning that rule of law, education, and culture are the foundation.[36]

In an earlier post, Han Han pinpointed the dilemma between revolution and counter-revolution.[37] In the revolutionary era, counter-revolution was the most serious crime assigned to people who were ousted. Once the revolutionary fever is over, a counter-revolutionary label also loses its daunting effect. In fact, counter-revolution as a crime was abolished in 1997 in China. But in 2008, two university students in Shanghai reported to the local security bureau, accusing their ancient Chinese language professor of making counter-revolutionary comments in class. The students probably time-traveled backward, using language they learned in history textbooks, yet without realizing that the state had fast-forwarded its own clock. Logically, if counter-revolution is prohibited, revolution should be encouraged, yet the government wants neither. By deleting counter-revolution from the law, the state has meant to cut the incentive for revolution as well. As a result, the best way of life for the masses, as Han Han writes, is staying as they are, or in official terms, maintaining stability.

Conclusion

We have highlighted the parallels between the debates of two very different eras, focusing on the divide between reformers and revolutionaries, while also noting the key contrast that both groups in recent times have tended to emphasize the need for nonviolent methods. We will end by simply mentioning a couple of other contrasts between the two eras, which are surely due in large part to how China's place in the world has changed, how the Chinese state has changed, and to exhaustion with and the human cost of the utopian experiments carried out by Mao. In the first debate, there was a sense that China was a weak and fragile country, which needed to be strengthened and could benefit from a strong central leader, whether a "Washington" or "Napoleon" (in Zou's view) or a strengthened emperor (in Kang's). Participants in the second debate do not share their predecessors' worry over China's weakness nor put faith in visions of a strong leader—Han is skeptical of all leaders, while the figures that Liu longs to see Chinese counterparts to are not generals but proponents of nonviolent change, such as Havel, Gandhi, and Jesus. Finally, there is less self-confidence among the participants in today's debates that a secret recipe for successful transformation can be found. There is a desire for change, a sense that the Chinese people deserve to live in a more just system, but more skepticism about the existence of any foreign script or domestic blueprint that points in the right direction.

Mao's Little Red Book

The Spiritual Atom Bomb and Its Global Fallout

Half a century ago, in the midst of the Cold War, there emerged from China an alternative script for revolution with surprisingly broad influence. *Quotations from Chairman Mao* (*Mao Zhuxi yulu*), commonly known outside China as the Little Red Book, was for a time the most printed book in the world. Official editions numbered well over a billion copies in three dozen languages, not to mention untold numbers of unofficial local reprints and unofficial translations into more than fifty languages.[1] The book was a novel hybrid of two very different genres: the ancient Chinese genre of collected sayings dating back to the *Analects* of Confucius, and the modern genre of ideological primers embraced especially (but by no means exclusively) by Marxist-Leninists around the world. In addition, the book's characteristic physical form—pocket-sized, bright red, clad in sturdy vinyl—reflected its origins as an ideological field manual for soldiers of the Chinese military, the People's Liberation Army (PLA).[2] The book's contents, composed of 427 extracts from Mao Zedong's writings and speeches from 1929 to 1964 and arranged into thirty-three thematic chapters, covered an eclectic range of subjects from philosophy to warfare to art.[3]

A notable feature of this script for revolution was its versatility. Mao's Little Red Book did not present a linear, coherent argument in the style of a polemic like Marx's *Communist Manifesto*. Instead, it provided a basic grammar and vocabulary that could be adapted to diverse circumstances. After Mao's death, the Little Red Book's unsystematic presentation of fragments torn from their historical and textual contexts was dismissed in China as a vulgarization of Maoism—not to mention Marxism. During Mao's lifetime, however, his quotations were taken quite seriously. In

China and elsewhere, the quotations were adapted into many forms—from rhetoric, art, and song to talisman, badge, and weapon—and put to use for many purposes. This variety of forms and uses is explored in a volume I have edited called *Mao's Little Red Book: A Global History*. This essay will focus on just one aspect of the Little Red Book as script for revolution— namely, how its sudden and unlikely global influence reflected the circumstances of a particular historical era.

The explanation I offer here arises from a curious interpretation of the quotations' power that appeared in the foreword to the authoritative second edition of *Quotations from Chairman Mao*. The effusive foreword was credited to Lin Biao, Mao's top military man and tireless promoter of the Little Red Book. It describes how the the written script could become a material force for revolution—a weapon of mass instruction, the intercontinental delivery system for a potentially world-shattering ideological payload: "Once Mao Tse-tung's thought is grasped by the broad masses, it becomes a source of strength and a spiritual atom bomb of infinite power."[4]

Lin Biao's metaphor was an adulatory exaggeration, of course, but it should not be dismissed as only that. Through an extended exegesis, I will argue that the "spiritual atom bomb" was a coherent concept within its own Maoist intellectual context. Moreover, the metaphor was a telling symptom of several kinds of anxieties: the anxieties of the Chinese Cultural Revolution, of the Sino-Soviet split within the socialist world, of the larger Cold War between capitalism and socialism across the globe, and of humanity's confrontation with the prospect of nuclear Armageddon. In other words, Lin Biao's brief foreword to the Little Red Book arose from historical conditions specific to China, yet was also a cultural product of the global Atomic Age. In that moment of global existential crisis, when faceless technology threatened to destroy all mankind, the "spiritual atom bomb" was an alternate vision of the atomic that affirmed the primacy of the spiritual over the material.

The era of the spiritual atom bomb was brief but explosive, roughly corresponding to the height of the Cultural Revolution in China and including the global movements of 1968. The Little Red Book originated in the Chinese military under the leadership of Lin Biao, who helped to build the cult of Mao. Lin Biao incorporated the study of Maoist texts into daily drill and encouraged the emulation of moral exemplars like the model soldier Lei Feng; these practices culminating in May 1964 in the internal-use publication by the General Political Department of the PLA of *Quotations from Chairman Mao*. According to the foreword added to the reprint of

August 1965, and "in conformity with Comrade Lin Biao's instructions," the Little Red Book was to be issued "to every soldier in the whole army, just as we issue weapons." Amid the nationwide campaign to "Learn from the People's Liberation Army," this handy piece of standard issue equipment also became a prized trophy for ardent youth activists. In late August 1966, in the push that gave the Cultural Revolution its chaotic momentum, Mao approvingly reviewed throngs of young Red Guards waving Little Red Books in Tiananmen Square. The book was soon made available to the general public in order to, as Lin Biao's new foreword said, "arm the minds of the people throughout the country" with Mao Zedong Thought.[5] Mastery of Mao Zedong Thought could split the atom of the mind and unleash the power of human consciousness to destroy the old world—and create a better one in its place.

The rise and fall of the spiritual atom bomb was tied to the personal fortunes of Lin Biao. Although Lin Biao did not take an active role in creating the Little Red Book, and it is doubtful that he even wrote the foreword credited to him, his name was the corporate mark for a particular reading of Maoist ideology.[6] The appearance of the phrase "spiritual atom bomb" in PLA publications beginning in 1960 typified Lin Biao's brand of "politics in command" and his calls to structure all aspects of military affairs around Mao Zedong Thought.[7] Lin Biao had ascended to power on the strength of his unquestioned loyalty to Mao in the chairman's darkest moment, the collapse of the Great Leap Forward. Ever passive and deferential by disposition, Lin's reliable hold on the barrel of the gun proved indispensable in Mao's subsequent return to political power.[8] For while the Cultural Revolution had the appearance of a popular movement—and it's true that much of its violence unfolded in decentralized and unpredictable ways—it was Lin Biao's access to military power that secured Mao's mobilization of the masses to "bombard the headquarters" in August 1966. At key moments in Mao's attack on rivals in the power structure, which developed over the next three years, Lin Biao's loyal units protected the radical insurgents, presided over the purge of the bureaucracy, held disgruntled military commanders in check, and stepped in when internecine struggles ceased to be useful to Mao.[9] For his contributions, Lin Biao was a prime beneficiary of the Cultural Revolution, explicitly designated Mao's successor in the constitution passed by the Ninth Party Congress in April 1969. In truly dialectical fashion, however, the pinnacle of Lin Biao's rise also marked the precipice from which he fell. At the same party congress, Mao voiced annoyance with Lin Biao's insistence that the new constitution incorporate another phrase from his foreword to the Little Red Book, which stated that "Comrade Mao Zedong is the greatest Marxist-Leninist of our era. He has inherited, defended, and developed Marxism-Leninism with genius, creatively and comprehensively, and has brought it to a higher and completely new stage." The seemingly arcane debate that ensued (whether "genius" was a bourgeois concept) provided the first of several hints that the chairman's trust in his "best student" and "closest comrade-in-arms" was less than complete.[10] Even so, no one expected the revelation in September 1971, just two and a half years later, that Lin Biao had died in a plane crash allegedly fleeing the country after a failed assassination attempt on Mao. Naturally, Lin Biao's foreword to the Little Red Book was expunged, and the era of the spiritual atom bomb was over. Nevertheless, from the mid 1960s to the early 1970s in China, and somewhat later elsewhere, Lin Biao's doctrine of the spiritual atom bomb was the orthodox interpretation that introduced Mao's Little Red Book to the world.

The Foolish Old Man

Lin Biao's elevation of Mao Zedong Thought to the power of an atom bomb sounds like a foolish boast, emblematic of the belligerent irrationality of the Mao cult at the height of the Cultural Revolution. It would seem to vastly overestimate the power of ideology on the one hand, and to vastly underestimate the power of the actual atom bomb on the other. However, Lin Biao's spiritual atom bomb metaphor is so bizarre, and yet so symptomatic of its times, that it merits serious consideration on its own terms. Mao's own defense of such "foolishness" is found in "The Foolish Old Man Who Removed the Mountains" (1945), a story canonized by Lin Biao as one of the Three Constantly Read Articles in the early 1960s. "The Foolish Old Man" is one of the longest continuous passages in the Little Red Book, and also the only text to appear there in its entirety:

> There is an ancient Chinese fable called "The Foolish Old Man Who Removed the Mountains." It tells of an old man who lived in northern China long, long ago and was known as the Foolish Old Man of North Mountain. His house faced south and beyond his doorway stood two great peaks obstructing the way. He called his sons, and hoe in hand they began to dig up these mountains with great determination. Another graybeard, known as the Wise Old Man, saw them and said derisively, "How silly of you to do this! It is quite impossible for you few to dig up those two huge mountains." The Foolish Old Man replied, "When I die, my sons will carry on; when they die, there will be my grandsons, and then their sons and grandsons, and so on to infinity. High as they are, the mountains

cannot grow any higher and with every bit we dig, they will be that much lower. Why can't we clear them away?" Having refuted the Wise Old Man's wrong-headed view, he went on digging every day, unshaken in his conviction. God was moved by this, and he sent down two angels, who carried the mountains away on their backs. Today, two big mountains lie like a dead weight on the Chinese people. One is imperialism, the other is feudalism. The Chinese Communist Party has long made up its mind to dig them up. We must persevere and work unceasingly, and we, too, will touch God's heart. Our God is none other than the masses of the Chinese people. If they stand up and dig together with us, why can't these two mountains be cleared away?

This passage has been interpreted primarily as a story of perseverance, determination, and strength of will, as it concludes the chapter of the Little Red Book on "Self-Reliance and Arduous Struggle." But there are deeper meanings that surface when we answer possible objections to the application of this traditional fable to the socialist revolution in China: isn't it contrary to the logic of self-reliance to invoke external forces—the literal dei ex machina of gods and angels? Aren't such manifestations of the spiritual alien to the materialist viewpoint of Marxism-Leninism? And isn't their sudden intervention contrary to the lesson of persistence and accumulated effort? To answer, we must reinterpret "The Foolish Old Man" as Mao's followers would, from the viewpoint of Mao's interpretation of dialectical materialism and with special attention to the *mass* character of revolutionary change.

First, the agency referred to by the fable is not external. The demystified God, as Mao explains somewhat clumsily, "is none other than the masses," and the angels are their agents, the revolutionary vanguard of the Chinese Communist Party. The party cannot succeed on its own; it needs to touch the hearts of the people and enlist their support in removing the mountains. The same idea is expressed more clearly in a metaphor from the guerrilla days: the party and its army must be like fish in the water.[11] The masses are not external, but rather are the medium in which the party operates. The revolutionary force is drawn from the masses, and the masses will become the revolutionary force; without the masses the party will founder and die. Thus in his introductory remarks to the story of "The Foolish Old Man," Mao says, "We must first raise the political consciousness of the vanguard so that, resolute and unafraid of sacrifice, they will surmount every difficulty to win victory. But this is not enough; we must also arouse the political consciousness of the entire people so that they may willingly and gladly fight together with us for victory." The revolution is necessarily a mass movement.

Second, Mao's invocation of the spiritual is not necessarily contrary to the materialist outlook. The Chinese term "spiritual" (*jingshen*) here refers to phenomena with subjective existence in the human mind, as opposed to the material, which exists objectively outside of human consciousness. However, the material and the spiritual are not mutually exclusive in Maoist doctrine, but instead are dialectically intertwined by the unity of opposites. While spiritual phenomena may be ultimately reducible to manifestations of the material, nevertheless subjective thought can motivate human beings to know and change their objective conditions.[12] To explain this proposed relationship between the material and the spiritual, Mao's seminal essay on the ontology of dialectics, "On Contradiction" (1937), introduces two concepts: first, the notion of the "principal contradiction," the one whose resolution is decisive for unraveling the complex knot of secondary contradictions; and second, the notion of the "principal aspect of the contradiction," the side of the contradiction whose positive development will be decisive in its resolution. Mao points out, however, that these relationships are dialectical and dynamic: the secondary acts upon the principal, and at times may even become dominant. Therefore, concludes Mao, in the contradiction between the material and the spiritual, the material is only *generally* the principal aspect:

> When the superstructure (politics, culture, etc.) obstructs the development of the economic base, political and cultural changes become principal and decisive. Are we going against materialism when we say this? No. The reason is that while we recognize that in the general development of history the material determines the mental, and social being determines social consciousness, we also—and indeed must—recognize the reaction of mental on material things, of social consciousness on social being and of the superstructure on the economic base. This does not go against materialism; on the contrary, it avoids mechanical materialism and firmly upholds dialectical materialism.[13]

At the crucial moment of revolution, the spiritual can become decisive in the transformation of the material.

Third, sudden transformation is not contrary to accumulation, perseverance, and protracted struggle—it results *from* accumulation. Of the three basic laws of dialectics identified by Engels, one is transformation of quantity into quality. (Mao, following Stalin, sees this not as a separate law, but as a special case of the unity and struggle of opposites.)[14] The classic example is the phase change of liquid water into steam: the incremental quantitative change in temperature leads to a sudden qualitative change in form. If the masses are the water, the medium of change, then it is the agitation of myriad individual molecules that will lead to a fundamental transformation in the collective whole—in other words, a revolution.

Spiritual Fission and the Weaponization of Ideology

Lin Biao's spiritual atom bomb refers to an exceptionally powerful kind of agitation, however, and not merely to the external application of heat or kinetic energy. Fission seeks to release vast amounts of *internal* energy, by splitting from the inside, and this process is fundamental to the Maoist worldview. For Mao, the fundamental law of dialectical materialism is the unity and struggle of opposites, sometimes manifested as "two combine into one" but more often as "one divides into two." The universe is characterized by struggle: "In any given thing, the *unity* of opposites is conditional, temporary, and transitory, and hence relative, whereas the *struggle* of opposites is universal."[15] Moreover, struggle that is sufficiently violent to break nuclear bonds can release vast amounts of energy; the key to such fission is to strike at the apparently indivisible core.

Since Mao believed the division of one into two (fission) to be a "universal" phenomenon, he reasoned that it must have spiritual manifestations. For Mao, the division and transformation of human consciousness was the most important object of purposive revolutionary struggle. The preferred technique of Chinese communists was a dialectical process of criticism and self-criticism that they called "struggle-criticism-transformation." Self-criticism was employed extensively for ideological indoctrination, party discipline, and social control. During the Cultural Revolution, Maoists put great emphasis on the struggle of self against self, not only for each individual but also on a mass scale. Mao had predicted that spiritual fission on a mass scale could release tremendous material force, as in this example from 1958:

> Now our enthusiasm has been aroused. Ours is an ardent nation, now swept by a burning tide. There is a good metaphor for this: our nation is like an atom. ... When this atom's nucleus is smashed the thermal energy released will have really tremendous power. We shall be able to do things which we could not do before.[16]

Mao was not satisfied with establishing the world's most populous socialist state in 1949; he felt that socialists needed to continue the transformative revolution of self-revolution. This is why Lin Biao described the Cultural Revolution to his dismayed colleagues as "a revolution against those of us who have been engaged in the former revolutions."[17]

Lin Biao further explained this idea of waging a continuing revolution against the self in an article published in *People's Daily* at the violent height of the Cultural Revolution:

> To look at oneself according to the law of "one divides into two" means that one must make revolution against one's own subjective world as well as the objective world. Comrade Lin Biao instructs us: "We must regard ourselves as an integral part of the revolutionary force and, at the same time, constantly regard ourselves as a target of the revolution. In making revolution, we must also revolutionize ourselves. Without revolutionizing ourselves, we cannot make this revolution."[18]

The most basic fissile material of the revolution, then, is the subjective consciousness of the apparently atomistic individual, though as the story of "The Foolish Old Man" says, the process of transformation cannot be limited to the cadres. For fission to become self-sustaining, it must be concentrated on and applied to a critical mass. Thus, Lin Biao says, Mao Zedong Thought becomes a spiritual atom bomb only "once it is grasped by the masses."

It is the "grasping" of Mao Zedong Thought that allows it to be used as a weapon, says Lin Biao, and his meaning is fairly literal. Here Lin's argument invokes Engels' remarkable thesis that humans became differentiated from other animals by the dialectical coevolution of the brain and the hand through labor.[19] According to Engels, all tools and technologies—the flint ax, the iron hoe, the spinning wheel, the steam engine, the paintbrush, the camera—are extensions of this hand-brain dyad, designed to carry out human purposes. The same principle applies to that class of tools we call weapons, from the most primitive stone to the atom bomb. Without a human being to use it, the tool (which is after all merely an extension of the person) is useless. Therefore, the power of the weapon as a material object is inseparable from the subjective spiritual or ideological power of the person who wields it. In Mao's own words, "Weapons are an important factor in war, but not the decisive factor; it is people, not things that are decisive. The contest of strength is not only a contest of military and economic power, but also a contest of human power and morale. People necessarily wield military and economic power."[20]

This supposition is the basis for Mao's doctrine of "people's war." Mao's faith in the people derived in part from his belief in the historical teleology of Marxism, but it was also grounded in practical experience. In his conflicts against the vastly superior material forces of the Chinese Nationalist regime and Imperial Japan, Mao knew his rag-tag armies could not succeed, at least initially, by using standard positional warfare. Victory required the mobile tactics of guerrilla warfare, but also a long-term strategy of protracted conflict in which the enemy could be weakened through attrition and his own forces strengthened through accumulation. But the rebels could survive long enough for this to happen only at the sufferance of the local populace. Therefore, the military doctrine of people's war rests on a social proposition: the "people's army" must provide benefits that outweigh the costs of provisioning them. More than that, even, the army must be embraced by the people as a necessary part *of* the people. In the present-day parlance of insurgency and counterinsurgency, you win the war by winning hearts and minds. In the language of Mao, if the soldiers are at home like fish in the water, then the people are the sustaining medium that will eventually overwhelm and drown the enemy. People's war proved successful in the war of resistance against Japan and in the subsequent civil war against the Nationalists, so it is no surprise that Mao should return to it in his confrontation with the nuclear superpowers.

Already at the outset of the Cold War, Mao had established his view that people's war could overcome the atomic threat. Consider, for example, Mao's comments to the American journalist Anna Louise Strong in August 1946, just a year after the atomic bombing of Hiroshima and Nagasaki: "The atom bomb is a paper tiger which the US reactionaries use to scare people. It looks terrible, but in fact it isn't. Of course, the atom bomb is a weapon of mass slaughter, but the outcome of a war is decided by the people, not by one or two new types of weapon."[21] Here we have one half of the "foolish" boast, the apparent underestimation of the atomic bomb. The second half, the apparent overestimation of ideology, was introduced by Lin Biao in his famous peon to Mao, "Long Live the Victory of People's War!" (1965):

> Even if US imperialism brazenly uses nuclear weapons, it cannot conquer the people, who are indomitable. However highly developed modern weapons and technical equipment may be and however complicated the methods of modern warfare, in the final analysis the outcome of a war will be decided by the sustained fighting of the ground forces, by the fighting at close quarters on battlefields, by the political consciousness of the men, by their courage and spirit of sacrifice. Here the weak points of US imperialism will be completely laid bare, while the superiority of the revolutionary people will be brought into full play. The reactionary troops of US imperialism cannot possibly be endowed with the courage and the spirit of sacrifice possessed by the revolutionary people. The spiritual atom bomb which the revolutionary people possess is a far more powerful and useful weapon than the physical atom bomb.[22]

Mao had already stated that people matter more than weapons, and had implied that ideological weapons could overcome physical weapons, but he left it to Lin Biao to state explicitly that the people were best armed with the weapon of Mao Zedong Thought: "Military affairs are a constituent part of politics, while politics includes more things, encompasses a wider scope. What is the best weapon? It's not the airplane, not artillery, not the tank, not the atom bomb. The best weapon is Mao Zedong Thought. What is the greatest military force? The greatest military force is people, armed with Mao Zedong Thought; it's courage and fearlessness of death."[23] The Little Red Book was a weapon to be grasped by the hands of the people, so that Mao Zedong Thought could be grasped by their minds. But how could a sheaf of paper bound in vinyl be elevated to the status of an atom bomb, while the actual atom bomb was dismissed as a flimsy "paper tiger"?

Paper Tigers of the Atomic Age

Mao's supposedly cavalier attitude toward atomic weapons was a major point of contention with the Soviet Union, which withdrew its nuclear experts from China in 1960. However, Mao's negative assessment of the atom bomb was by no means based on a naive underestimation of its capacity for physical destruction. In 1955, to the consternation of his Soviet allies, Mao asserted:

> The Chinese people are not to be cowed by US atomic blackmail. Our country has a population of 600 million and an area of 9,600,000 square kilometers. The United States cannot annihilate the Chinese nation with its small stack of atom bombs. Even if the US atom bombs were so powerful that, when dropped on China, they would make a hole right through the earth, or even blow it up, that would hardly mean anything to the universe as a whole, though it might be a major event for the solar system.[24]

We may be appalled at Mao's cosmic indifference toward human life, but we cannot say he thought the atom bomb powerless.[25] Nor did Mao's bravado arise from a confident belief that atomic bombs would never be used against China. In hindsight we know not a single nuclear weapon was detonated in combat during the Cold War; but in Mao's time, nuclear war seemed like a very real possibility, and China seemed like one of the more likely targets. In the 1950s, China fought the United States to a bloody stalemate on the Korean peninsula, and the Eisenhower administration pursued a New Look policy calling for heavy reliance on nuclear weaponry as a "virtually conventional" force.[26] Yet in 1958, as the confrontation over the Taiwan Strait teetered on the brink of open war, Mao spoke of the coming atomic holocaust as an eventuality, noting insolently that it was "not a bad thing":

> We have no experience in atomic war. So, how many will be killed cannot be known. The best outcome may be that only half of the population [of the world] is left and the second best may be only one-third. When 900 million are left out of 2.9 billion, several five-year plans can be developed for the total elimination of capitalism and for permanent peace. It is not a bad thing.[27]

Socialists do not want war, said Mao, but the destruction to come will only strengthen the socialist cause. Just as World War I gave birth to the Bolshevik Revolution, and World War II to the Chinese Revolution and anticolonial movements worldwide, World War III might very well bring the global revolution to completion. Moreover, by the early 1960s, the Sino-Soviet rift had become irreparable, with Mao accusing the Kremlin of practicing revisionism or "phony" socialism. Sino-Soviet relations declined precipitously, and in 1969 border skirmishes even erupted into a brief shooting war. In the era of the Little Red Book, nuclear attack by either the United States or the Soviet Union seemed a very real possibility.

So, in Mao's entirely realistic assessment, atomic weapons could (and very possibly *would*) be used against China in the foreseeable future, and if so, the result would be massive death and destruction.[28] We need no further proof of Mao's appreciation of the atom bomb's military value than the fact that the People's Republic of China invested at great cost in a nuclear weapons program of its own. The People's Liberation Army successfully tested its first atom bomb in 1964, without Soviet assistance, becoming just the fifth nation to do so, and in 1967, China became the fourth nation to successfully detonate a thermonuclear fission-fusion device. With Mao's bold talk, the Soviets and Americans must have feared a nuclear-armed loose cannon in the East—an inscrutable "Mr. China A-Bomb"—but a 1963 RAND report correctly surmised that *the Chinese do understand the significance of nuclear warfare and are not inclined to be reckless.*[29] China entered the age of the spiritual atom bomb with a first-hand knowledge of the physical atom bomb—there can be no question of foolishness on that count—yet Mao continued to denigrate the atom bomb as a paper tiger. Nuclear weapons could destroy the world, but still they could not *win* it.

This did not mean that China could ignore the atomic threat, of course, but Mao treated the atom bomb the same as any paper tiger: tactically it is dangerous, but strategically it is vulnerable. "Despise the enemy strategically," was his mantra, "but take full account of it tactically." Beginning with the Korean War in the 1950s and continuing through the realignment of the 1970s, China made definite preparations to weather a nuclear storm. To the tactical and logistical provisions, "Dig tunnels deep, store grain everywhere," Mao added a strategic imperative: "Never seek hegemony."[30] It was this word "hegemony" that best summarized the Cold War for Mao, and it was the world order of superpower hegemony that stood to be annihilated by the spiritual atom bomb. "Mao Tse-tung's thought is Marxism-Leninism of the era in which imperialism is heading for total collapse and socialism is advancing to world-wide victory," explained Lin Biao's foreword.[31] Less than three years later, speaking on the anniversary of Russia's October Revolution and at the height of China's Cultural Revolution, Lin Biao boasted that the blast radius of the spiritual atom bomb was global: "Once Marxism-Leninism-Mao Zedong Thought is integrated with the revolutionary practice of the people of all countries, *the entire old world* will be shattered to smithereens."[32]

Three Worlds Apart

The dropping of the atom bomb at the conclusion of World War II left the globe divided into the First World of capitalism, the Second World of socialism, and a "developing" Third World, which served as the battleground of a Cold War between them. The leaders of the First and Second worlds—the United States and the Soviet Union—were supposed paradigms of capitalism and socialism, and they were "superpowers" by virtue of their nuclear arsenals. All other nations had joined one armed camp or the other, or soon would do so. This was the conventional wisdom, at least; Mao offered a different assessment. China had entered World War II with a united front between the Chinese Communist Party and Chiang Kai-shek's Nationalist Party, reasoning that the clash between socialism and capitalism must take a back seat to the fight against Japanese imperialism. Following World War II, Mao once again turned to civil war and socialist revolution in China. On a global scale, however, Mao remained convinced that for the time being the principal contradiction in the world was not between capitalism and socialism, but between imperialism and anti-imperialism.

The Sino-Soviet split added a new dimension to Mao's understanding of global imperialism. With the Soviet Union abandoning revolution at home and seeking peaceful accommodation with the capitalist world abroad, Mao spoke of three ideological worlds: capitalism, socialism, and revisionism. Even more troubling to Mao was the increasingly forceful imposition of cultural chauvinism and military domination by the revisionist Soviets over the genuinely socialist states. Now Mao began to distinguish between two types of imperialism. The "old" imperialism, which Lenin had identified as the globalization of capitalism, was clearly in decline, as waves of national liberation movements attended the postwar dissolution of the great maritime empires. However, the "new" imperialism of superpower hegemony had risen to take its place. This superpower hegemony consisted of both American capitalist imperialism and Soviet social-imperialism. Superpower hegemony was postwar imperialism par excellence, and the atom bomb its most terrible weapon. "The US and Soviet Union both have nuclear weapons," Mao stated plainly, "and they want to dominate the world."[33] Unless a third way could be found between the Americans and the Soviets, the Cold War—and possibly the world—would end with the atom bomb.

Confronted with the existential threat of nuclear war, Albert Einstein and several key Manhattan Project scientists had pleaded in 1946: "The unleashed power of the atom has changed everything save our modes of thinking, and we thus drift toward unparallel catastrophe. . . . A new type of thinking is essential if mankind is to survive and move toward higher levels."[34] The search for a third way took many forms, including the Third World movement for national liberation on its own terms, and the Non-Aligned Movement touted by Tito, Nehru, and others. But it was the spiritual atom bomb, Mao Zedong Thought, that presented itself as more than an opt-out or a political compromise—as above all a new way of *thinking*. Mao's thinking on the atomic age constellated in 1964. This was the year that Mao spoke openly of defying superpower hegemony, the year that China acquired the physical atom bomb, and the year that Lin Biao's military first issued its soldiers the Little Red Book.

Mao's unorthodox interpretation of the Cold War order revealed worlds in contradiction and susceptible to fission. The division *between* the two superpowers was obvious, delineating the two sides of the Cold War. Mao's innovation was to argue that this Cold War division was actually the manifestation of the unity of opposites. The Soviet Union and United States were dialectical poles of an underlying unity, he said, and the struggle between them was a contradiction *internal* to the world of superpower hegemony. Moreover, while the United States and Soviet Union appeared to lead two insoluble global alliances, in fact the superpowers were isolated in their hegemony, with the entire rest of the world caught between them. Mao sketched out his theory of the "intermediate zone" in January 1964 in a talk with a visiting Japanese communist:

> When we talk about intermediate zones, we refer to two separate parts. The vast economically backward countries in Asia, Africa, and Latin America constitute the first. Imperialist and advanced capitalist countries represented by Europe [and Japan] constitute the second. Both are opposed to American control. Countries in Eastern Europe, on the other hand, are against control by the Soviet Union. This trend is quite obvious.[35]

The idea of intermediate zones would be formalized some ten years later as Mao's Theory of Three Worlds, but already we see the precursors of a radical reconfiguration.[36] At the very least, common cause against superpower hegemony opened up the possibility of alliances between the old imperialist states of the capitalist world, the nonrevisionist states of the socialist world, and the oppressed nations of the Third World.

However, hegemony could not be challenged without first breaking the superpowers' exclusive hold on atomic weapons. The United Kingdom had tested its own atom bomb in 1952, drawing heavily on their wartime cooperation in the Manhattan Project, but the British remained close allies with the Americans. More significant was French acquisition of the atom bomb in 1960, by which France sought to reassert its traditional Great Power status and to announce its independence within the capitalist world.[37] Similarly, China's acquisition of the atom bomb in October 1964 safeguarded its break away from the world of Soviet revisionist socialism. Earlier in the year, when Chinese and French diplomats met to discuss the normalization of relations, Mao compared the two nations' efforts to break the thrall of the superpowers:[38]

> The US is frightening some countries, forbidding them to do business with us. The US is a paper tiger; don't take it seriously; it will break at the slightest touch. The Soviet Union is a paper tiger, too; we don't trust it at all. I'm not superstitious. Perhaps you are religious. I'm an atheist and afraid of nothing. It's not acceptable if big powers try to control us. France is a small country. China, too. Only the US and Soviet Union are big powers. Do we have to seek their approval on everything and go on pilgrimage to their land?[39]

Only an inveterate underdog like Mao could describe France and China as "small" countries, but his point was that nuclear arsenals had made the United States and Soviet Union seem "big" in a way that was qualitatively different. Expressing defiance against the superpowers in the language of religious disillusionment ("I'm not superstitious. . . . I'm an atheist. . . . Do we have to . . . go on pilgrimage?"), Mao suggests the demystification of false gods, the awakening of consciousness to alienation and exploitation, and the emboldened grasp of one's own destiny. The acquisition of the physical atom bomb in the intermediate zone secured the possibility of spiritual conversion by the Little Red Book.

The global proliferation of the Little Red Book in late 1960s and early 1970s reflected widespread disenchantment with the postwar status quo—the persistent inequalities that belied the promises of liberal capitalism, the less-than-utopian repression and drudgery of "actually existing" socialism, and the realization that Third World liberation had not allayed the poverty and violence engendered by an imbalanced world system.[40] Mao's China increasingly self-identified with the Third World, throwing in its lot with the oppressed nations of the intermediate zone. Lin Biao drew up grand visions of people's war on a global scale, with the world's hinterland surrounding and destroying its cities.[41] Third World rulers and revolutionaries for their part made mixed use of the spiritual atom bomb, whether donning its symbolic accoutrements, playing the Mao card to extract aid from China or others, engaging in dogmatic imitation, or attempting creative application of Mao's doctrines to local circumstances.[42]

Within the socialist world, the Little Red Book exacerbated the potentially explosive fissure between revolution and revisionism. Mao argued that the Soviet Union had abandoned revolution at home and abroad, and in so doing had abandoned its comrades still fighting the good fight. By early 1964 Mao could speak of generalized discontent within the socialist world against the Soviet Union:

> In fact, Khrushchev has not secured a big majority among the countries in the socialist camp. Romania has differing views; Poland can be counted as only half a supporter. Like the Americans, he wants to control others and tries to make them develop single-product economies, which is not feasible. Romania does not accept it. Cuba is quarreling with him.[43]

Only Albania would side decisively with China in the Sino-Soviet split, but heavy-handed Soviet imposition of its ideologies and institutions (and especially the invasion of socialist ally Czechoslovakia in August 1968) drew condemnation from a range of fraternal communist parties on both sides of the Iron Curtain. Moreover, while the Little Red Book was universally dismissed in the Soviet Union itself, the thoroughgoing denunciation of Maoism there provided a dress rehearsal for later dissident critiques of Soviet socialism.[44]

The Little Red Book played well to divisions within capitalist society, as well. Rocked by postwar decolonization, the waning or former imperial powers like France and Japan that constituted the more developed part of the intermediate zone exemplified the shift from old imperialism to new:

"On the one hand these countries oppress others; on the other hand they are oppressed by the United States and have contradictions with it."[45] In addition to external pressures of superpower hegemony and internal struggles between the proletariat and the bourgeoisie, the nations of the capitalist world also faced the internal effects of imperialism's external decline—economic shocks, military loss, social unrest, and political uncertainty. Moreover, groups representing oppressed minorities in the First World, such as the *Quotations*-toting Black Panthers, readily appropriated the language of Third World national liberation. As a flexible and dynamic script for revolution, the Little Red Book traveled easily from its contingent and specific origins in China to a great many different kinds of places.

Conclusion

The "spiritual atom bomb" belongs to a bygone era, the peculiar shadow of a zeitgeist long past. Nevertheless, its internal logic is still discernible to us today through the schematic plans laid out in the Little Red Book. The essential elements were a theoretical understanding of spiritual fission (Marxist dialectics), the application of dialectical analysis to a particular set of historical conditions (Mao Zedong Thought), the accumulation of a critical mass (Cultural Revolution), and the engineering of a global delivery system (the Little Red Book). Wherever deployed, the spiritual atom bomb proved a powerful fission device, initiating chain reactions of escalating violence that threatened to destroy, for better or worse, the established structures of the world order. At times it even functioned like a spiritual hydrogen bomb, a spiritual fission-fusion device that joined unlikely allies to even greater effect. However, true to Mao's doctrine of "one divides into two," such fusion events were transitory, and never sufficiently sustained to hold together the imagined socialist collective. Instead, worldwide detonation of the spiritual atom bomb produced the characteristic mushroom cloud of water vapor, fissile material, and detritus—which soon fell back to the barren, irradiated landscape, its most lasting legacy being the half-lives of human trauma. Earlier we saw the dialecticians' metaphor of revolution as the mass agitation of myriad individual particles, like the phase change of water from liquid to gas. Perhaps this explains how the builders of the bomb could have mistaken the deadly mushroom cloud as the outward manifestation of a revolution.

The Reel, Real and Hyper-Real Revolution

Scripts and Counter-Scripts in Cuban Documentary Film

Perhaps more than any other twentieth-centuryTwentieth-Century case, the simultaneous production and performance of a grand narrative among leaders and a majority of citizens played a central role in consolidating the Cuban Revolution of 1959. Militant and millenarian, this narrative was, at one level, an "elliptical morality tale" that promised equality and prosperity through unanimous and unconditional support for one leader, Fidel Castro.[1] But it was also a participatory project that rescued Cubans from a neocolonial past of constant US intervention through the empowerment of confronting and surviving US power—for decades. For most Cubans, believing in the impossible story of Cuba's liberation from US economic and political controls in the formative years of the Revolution became a means for achieving it; responding to Fidel's call—whether to the plaza for a million-person rally, to the militia, or to the ranks of voluntary labor in Cuba's cane fields—constituted a daily battle against the legacies of US imperialism, the US embargo, and exile aggressors. As Fidel and other leaders repeatedly explained in televised speeches, radio addresses, and dozens of mass rallies over the course of 1959, Cuba's revolution was fundamentally a moral one whose exceptional nature, commitment to true liberation, and inevitable victory over underdevelopment could not be denied.

In the summer of 1960, repeated standoffs with the United States over Cuba's still relatively moderate reforms and expansion of trade with the Soviets led to widescale nationalization. Amid the government's sudden and surprising shift in ideology, citizens' participation in the revolutionary script of redemption and total unity authored by Fidel and other guerrilla leaders in the early months of the Revolution thus became intrinsic to the rapidly unfolding series of events that it was intended to explain. By the fall of 1960, government control over all media and Cuba's universities was well established and command over public discourse shifted almost exclusively to leaders, especially Fidel Castro. Soon the idea that virtually *all* of Cuba's internal problems were caused by direct or indirect pressures from the United States became the universal backdrop to the everyday national drama that citizens carried out on a global stage . Through mass organizations such as government-controlled labor unions and neighborhood surveillance groups known as Committees for the Defense of the Revolution [CDRs], citizens verbally and mentally defended the Revolution from the criticism of local "*desmoralizadores* [demoralizers]," "*negativos*," and other doubters who questioned the value or direction of communist policies and state programs. Through persuasion, shouting matches, and direct intimidation on the street, in the workplace and in classrooms, citizens defeated what Fidel called "the cowards who want to destroy the combative morale of the people and raise the flag of surrender before imperialism."[2] By the late 1960s, intolerance of dissent reached unprecedented proportions. Even articulating key social concerns such as post-1959 racism or questioning the quality and nature of peasant liberation was equated with an insidious form of counter-revolution defined legally as "*diversionismo ideológico* [ideological diversionism]." Far from immune, Cuba's vanguard youth and Communist Party militants were the citizens most often targeted for this new category of political crime.[3]

Indeed, the grand narrative of redemption through a "moral revolution" that citizens and leaders authored in the early months of the 1959 came to rely on a certain silent logic that every textual and visual representation of Cuba's reality by intellectuals, filmmakers, and writers was supposed to employ. This logic defined the Revolution as an *unending* event, a triumph over US power that beat the odds and continued to beat them, no matter how high they became. Among Cuba's average citizens and intellectuals, consciousness of this logic necessitated a constant reiteration of the attending conditions of triumphalism and euphoria in all forms of media and, by extension, of public discourse. Touting "the good" rather than "the bad" rendered taboo any recognition of negative conditions caused by government shortcomings or widespread popular resistance to communist economic policy. Sheila Fitzpatrick's observation of this aspect of life in the Soviet Union could apply to Cuba as well: "Writers and artists were urged to cultivate a sense of 'socialist realism'—seeing life as it was becoming, rather than life as it was. . . . But socialist realism was . . . not just an artistic style. Ordinary citizens also developed the ability to see things as they were becoming and ought to be, rather than as they were."[4] Images and image-making were central to Cubans' apprehension of the enormity of what they were collectively experiencing. At a simple level, people did not realize what participation in a mass rally of more than a million people meant until they went home and saw images of the rally on television or in newspapers and magazines. Images did not just convey information. As José Quiroga puts it, "The photograph had a duty to perform: it was a document and, as such, it contained a certain kind of *knowledge* that would be used to produce more *knowledge* in turn."[5]

Critical to explaining imagery's importance to struggles over the grand narrative is the idea that images—photographic, imaginary, personal—played a central role in placing Cubans outside the mundane circumstances of their daily lives and into the "hyper-reality" of the Revolution—that is, a utopia caught in the process of becoming. Like hyper-real spaces in any society, hyper-realities of state-orchestrated mass rallies and routinized volunteer labor projects convinced participants that the euphoria, the happiness, the sense of justice, the pride of unity and self-righteousness that the experience generated were emblematic of reality—that is, the rest of society external to the hyper-real experience. One authenticated the other, even though they were not the same; that authentification showed that the values of the hyper-real experience should not be contested.[6]

Ironically, long before Cuba's guerrilla leaders embraced communism-Communism, Cuba's historic Communist Party, known as the PSP [Partido Socialista Popular], identified imagery and filmmaking as primary instruments of political radicalization. Since the late 1930s, PSP communistsCommunists who would become Fidel's key advisors and cabinet members in 1961, devoted much of the party's resources to the making of documentary films on the same themes and subjects that after 1959, Cuba's state film industry, ICAIC, would also promote. This coincidence was no accident: as early as January 1959, PSP militants whose communist affiliation was publicly unknown gained positions in state programs for educating Cuba's new, mostly illiterate peasant army through the use of films and a technique called "*cine-debate*", a form of ideologically guided viewing. Three months later, many of the same militants moved directly from their positions as cultural instructors of the Rebel Army to found ICAIC.

Led by long-time communist and Fidel's college friend, Alfredo Guevara, ICAIC's most important founders were all communist militants who eventually became world-famous directors, including Manuel Pérez, Tomás Gutiérrez Alea, Santiago Alvarez, and Julio García Espinoza.[7] Much as the PSP had done before 1959, ICAIC founders viewed film as uniquely capable of disarming an audience of its fears, prejudices, and ideological convictions. Film was necessarily central to the building of socialism as a result. For directors like Gutiérrez Alea and ICAIC president Alfredo Guevara, the goal was to represent reality in a "responsible" way.[8] One did this by showing only "those aspects of reality that satisfied political and entertaining ends" simultaneously.[9]

In order to bolster its reputation and justify a state monopoly on filmmaking, ICAIC administrators soon created the fiction that Cuba had had no film industry prior to 1959, qualifying the previous period as Cuba's dark age or "*prehistoria*".[10] They also attempted to elide public memory of several Cuban films about rural poverty and the struggle against the dictator that were made without PSP collaboration, although all of these films were box office hits.[11] In the wake of repeated standoffs over national sovereignty with the United States and the triumph of Cuban forces over the CIA-directed invasion at the Bay of Pigs April 1961, ICAIC intensified its interest in producing solidly didactic documentaries that followed a simple storyline of revolutionary redemption and popular obedience to Fidel Castro's leadership.

In May 1961, a scandal erupted over ICAIC's confiscation of the short documentary film *P.M.* Made by two young filmmakers who had barely reached their twenties, *P.M.* featured no narration and focused instead on mostly black revelers getting drunk, dancing and talking in live street scenes, working-class bars, and other night spots in Old and Centro Havana. *P.M.* was shot in the unrehearsed style of free cinema that Alfredo Guevara condemned on ideological grounds.[12] Because of the film's cutting edge approach and the fact that it was made by his younger brother Sabá, Guillermo Cabrera Infante, the host of a nationally televised version of *Revolución*'s literary magazine, *Lunes*, broadcast *P.M.* in May 1961. When its makers subsequently sought ICAIC approval to exhibit the film in a privately owned movie house in Havana, ICAIC immediately confiscated the film, leading to a firestorm of controversy among revolutionary intellectuals. Accused of depicting Cuban culture in counter-revolutionary terms, the defenders of *P.M.* found and interviewed its real-life protagonists: every one of them identified as a revolutionary and many were *milicianos*, members of the state-organized militias. Nonetheless, ICAIC returned the film only on the condition that it never be shown again.[13] For its defense of *P.M.* and related reasons, *Lunes de Revolución* was soon shut down altogether.[14] *Bohemia* fired its film critic, Nelson Almendros, for giving *P.M.* a positive review and attempting to make a free-style documentary himself.[15] The incident marked a crucible for intellectuals and intellectual production in Cuba.

Looking specifically at films produced by communist filmmakers of ICAIC that were nonetheless *censored* by ICAIC's founders in the formative period of the 1960s allows us to understand why images mattered as much as texts, if not more so, to the building of socialism in revolutionary Cuba. Importantly, the power of film to disarm an audience of its fears, political prejudices, and ideological convictions could cut both ways. Ambivalent, ambiguous, or parodic films could generate or confirm alternative stories. These stories formed counter-narratives—*counterscripts*—that made citizens primary protagonists of the Revolution, effectively inviting them to question state policies, propose their own, and thereby undermine the grand narrative and the authority of leaders in the privacy of people's heads. Indeed, the genre of documentary films became a primary focus of ICAIC efforts in the mid- to late 1960s, because documentaries when made "responsibly," as Gutiérrez Alea put it, bound together otherwise bifurcated political realities: the reality of a society struggling with the strain of achieving perfection, total unity (what Fidel called "*apoyo absoluto*"), through the repression of conflict; and the hyper-reality of a citizenry that denies all strain and all conflict as quintessential to the perfecting process. Reality— what is—and hyper-reality—what *should* be—are made one. Paradoxically, the future utopia could only survive and flourish if citizens engaged in regular displays of aspiration toward it as well as a day-to-day discourse that *denied* the existence of any obstacle impeding its triumph. Thus, not only did "authentic" filmic representations of the Revolution *require the denial of all local conflict* but they also required a *denial of the need to deny conflict* as foundational to the building of a truly classless society.

In fulfilling these goals, possibly no other ICAIC filmmaker failed as consistently or as miserably as the black filmmaker Nicolás Guillén Landrián. Despite his family's deep roots as pioneers of communism in Camagüey province and the fact that his uncle, Nicolás Guillén, was Cuba's poet laureate and then president of UNEAC, the state union of artists and writers, all but a handful of Guillén Landrián's fifteen films were banned. Assigned to document evidence of the transformative presence of the Revolution in citizens' lives and consciousness, Guillén Landrián did the opposite: his films interrogated their subjects as much as their spectators, asking what (and who) actually constituted "the Revolution." Did liberation through total unity really exist? What does total unity mean, and what does it cost? Could constant repetition of a revolutionary script in slogans, rallies, and a formulaic press truly reignite the euphoria felt by people in the Revolution's early years? In asking such questions, Guillén Landrián put on display for public inspection not only the grand narrative of the Revolution but also his own role as a revolutionary filmmaker. Understanding why his superiors at ICAIC found Guillén Landrián's work so threatening requires exploring how ICAIC expected the films of its documentary filmmakers to behave. By way of background and comparison, it is therefore to the perspective and filmic gaze of Santiago Alvarez, ICAIC's most celebrated director, that we now turn.

Santiago Alvarez and the Disciplinary Function of Documentary Film in the Cuban Revolution

In late 1960s Cuba, finished documentary films supported and produced by ICAIC were supposed to conform to the following goal: no aspect of Cuban life should exist outside the frame of the Revolution; all aspects of life were (and should be) deliberately politicized. That most ICAIC documentaries assumed this posture was clear. After watching over forty documentaries in 1967, Theodor Christensen, a foreign director who had served as an ICAIC advisor in the early 1960s, remarked, "It is a principle: the presence and vigor of the revolution controlled the structure and message of documentaries. . . . a belief surged that the revolution provided structure, nourished the imagination and was in itself the very guarantee of the vital presence of reality. Belief worked! The Revolution worked! The films worked!"[16] Christensen's comments speak to ICAIC's goal of depicting what several of its founding directors, especially Tomás Gutiérrez Alea, called a "responsible" version of reality. Like the state press, documentaries were supposed to convey what citizens ought to know and think was true. Beyond this, documentaries were understood to carry information through emotional and sensory means; they could, therefore, serve to restrain unruly thoughts about the contradictory and disappointing aspects of revolutionary life. While films made in the late 1960s illustrate this imperative more than others, in doing so, they also reveal the *indiscipline* of citizens themselves, a fact which ironically undermined the absolute truth of the grand narrative as a whole.

By the late 1960s, Cuban intellectuals had come to grips with Fidel's oft-cited 1961 maxim, "all within the Revolution, nothing without." After 1965, the combination of re-education camps, a wave of purges of students and faculty at the universities on charges of "ideological diversionism," the sanctioning of rising stars in the music world such as Silvio Rodríguez, and an unexpected March 1968 raid of Carlos Franqui's museum of contemporary art by G2 had left indelible scars on the hearts and minds of the Revolution's once vibrant theatrical, literary, and artistic communities. As novelist Edmundo Desnoes put it in 1969 while addressing an intimate group of Latin American intellectual radicals, many of whom had sought exile in Cuba from right-wing regimes: "I think that we should recognize that many of us have been responsible for creating an illusion, the illusion that an absolute freedom to express oneself freely existed in Cuba, without recognizing the demands of a society in revolution. . . . [W]hen foreign artists and intellectuals visited us, we created that illusion, we repeated that in Cuba there was unconditional freedom to express problems, to give opinions. That is relatively false within the Revolution."[17] Allegoric of the very conditions Desnoes described, the meeting of Latin American intellectuals where he made his remarks actually took place in Havana; however, its transcript was only widely published and made available in Mexico.

Then famous for his collaboration with Tomás Gutiérrez Alea on the feature film *Memorias del Subdesarrollo,* Desnoes was no stranger to themes of alienation or doubt. Like his 1961 novel of the same title, *Memorias* represented a sine qua non pursuit of the meaning of the Revolution's truth for Sergio, a man consumed by individual doubts, all of which are rendered irrelevant to the national struggle by the end of the film.[18] Importantly, the pivotal scenes in the film that propel Sergio toward a broader political consciousness are filmed documentary sequences of the interrogation of unrepentant *batistiano* torturers captured after Playa Girón, ostensibly witnessed by Sergio on television or in newsreels. These documentary sequences serve to "suffocate" Sergio's internal world of doubts (and those that Sergio might share with viewers) by subsuming them in the past and assigning a negative judgment to them.

For director Gutiérrez Alea, *Memorias*, like his other films of the 1960s, constituted what he called "responsible" filmmaking in a revolutionary context. One of the only directors to explain how revolutionary filmmakers should make movies in the early period of the Revolution, Gutiérrez Alea maintained that directors had not only to take sides (*tomar partida*) with the Revolution but also to consciously *ignore* aspects of society still disconnected from it; to do otherwise (as the makers of *P.M.* did) was to "hide or disfigure" reality itself.[19] In this way, politically "responsible" filmmakers helped to remake society by portraying it much as early literacy manuals and state magazines such as *INRA* had: as *already* remade. More than photography, film was uniquely endowed with the power to convince because the collective focus on the "massive enveloping screen" in a dark theater made audiences passive, open vessels into which values, ideas, and politically subjective narratives could be poured.[20]

Yet, while Gutiérrez Alea's *Memorias* relies on the imperative of disciplining Sergio (as well as viewers like Sergio) to make its point, the film's artistry also humanizes both, effectively undermining the imperative itself. By contrast, Santiago Alvarez, ICAIC's most famous documentary filmmaker of the time, rendered no such ambivalence in his films. A pioneer in the production of weekly newsreels for Cuban movie houses, Alvarez depicted current events and documentary subjects in an equally unapologetic, ideological fashion. According to Alvarez himself, little distinguished "revolutionary journalism" from documentary. Most of his own documentaries arose from his newsreels, reflecting unwavering narratives of certainty and "a single line of argument."[21]

Alvarez's documentaries achieved this by invoking unambiguous emotional responses and relying on sloganistic screen scripts that relied on simple principles of "good" or "bad." Combining footage shot in the observational mode with still photo montage, captions, and images that reference other archival films, Alvarez's early documentaries of the 1960s focused on the bravery of Cuba's masses and the heroism of its militias in the face of common crisis.[22] By the mid-to-late 1960s, Alvarez's films denouncing US racism and the imperialist war in Vietnam were more famous than his works on Cuba.[23] Like Gutiérrez Alea, Alvarez used archival footage to produce filmic "memories" that bridged the present day with the hyper-real future through selective, triumphalist assessments of the Revolution's past.[24] However, the same characteristics that made many of Alvarez's finished documentaries compelling instruments of persuasion undermined this effect in the theater.

No other film reveals this better than *Despegue a las 18.00 (Take-off at 18.00)*, a documentary written, edited, and directed by Alvarez. Ostensibly a report on the mobilization of workers in Oriente Province for the Quincena de Girón, the film addresses viewers with a series of captions that interpret the film for them: "YOU ARE GOING TO SEE / A FILM THAT IS / DIDACTIC / INFORMATIVE / POLITICAL / AND . . . / PROPAGANDISTIC . . . / ABOUT A PEOPLE / IN REVOLUTION / ANX-

IOUS . . . /DESPERATE . . . /TO FIND A WAY OUT OF /AN AGO-NIZING /HERITAGE . . . /UNDERDEVELOPMENT." Consequently, the titles give way to images of the demolition of an old-fashioned live-stock building with a thatched roof followed by a set of new titles: "IF BLOCKADED /COMPLETELY /WHAT WOULD WE DO? /STOP PRO-DUCTION? /FOLD OUR ARMS?" The film then turns to examining the expressions and gestures of citizens looking forlorn and exhausted as they stand in an unmoving ration line. As eerie music displaces the sounds of their voices, a large-print caption suddenly appears on screen, declaring: "NO HAY [There is none]."

Posted on signs in storefronts, cafeterias and ration centers, the phrase "NO HAY" had become synonymous with the material hardships that Cu-bans faced and the general absence of any discussion of these hardships in the state press. Apparent to any Cuban watching the film in 1968, "NO HAY" would have referred to the lack of food one expected to get at a ration center or store; it also referred to items that a store normally sold: for example, a citizen in the 1960s regularly encountered this sign when entering a shoe store that was open for business but had no shoes to sell. "NO HAY" not only announced that whatever product or ration s/he was expecting to purchase was unavailable but that the government would give no explanation as to why: then, as now, everyone was to assume that the US embargo was to blame. However, the film's timing (it was made only a month after the Ofensiva Revolucionaria began) suggests that Alvarez had a clear objective in mind: silencing very real public frustrations with the ubiquitous "NO HAY." Only weeks before the film's release, the UJC's *Alma Mater* had voiced these frustrations in a caricature denouncing the "NO HAY" sign at state lunch counters and cafeterias.[25]

Clearly anticipating that viewers would assume the standard meaning of "NO HAY," the film spends several frames ensuring that audiences develop and hold onto this meaning. Scenes of tired, unsmiling old folks, decidedly unenthusiastic women and bored children appear to invite identification with the drudgery of their everyday lives. Then, suddenly, Alvarez ruptures the audience's understanding of the phrase "NO HAY" by castigating view-ers for having thought in such terms in the first place. Shifting from the im-age of an old couple pathetically shrugging their shoulders as they wait for bread, the film reproduces 1961 archival footage of a government crew top-pling the imperial eagle from the monument in Havana that honored the *USS Maine*. The captions then reveal *what the audience should have thought* when they read the title "NO HAY" minutes earlier: "THERE IS NO IL-

LITERACY / THERE IS NO PROSTITUTION / THERE IS NO UNEM-
PLOYMENT / THERE ARE NO VAGRANTS / THERE ARE NO HOME-
LESS / THERE ARE NO LOTTERIES / THERE IS NO POLIO / THERE
IS NO MALARIA." The film then climaxes with a speech by Fidel. The
Revolution, he explains, calls on Cubans "to work like animals so that they
will no longer work like animals." Punctuating his point, images of emiser-
ated indigenous people in other parts of Latin America illustrate what
working like an animal means in any country but Cuba.

If one ignores the film's immediate historical context and fails to recognize the significance of the sign "NO HAY," it is easy to assume a very
different meaning for Alvarez's film.[26] However, rather than being an effective piece of deliberate propaganda, it can also be read an unintention-
ally ironic, antieuphoric portrait of despair. *Despegue a las 18.00* is as much
an effort to co-opt the empathy that this portrait generates as a vehicle for
inverting its meaning. Once "reminded" of what *else* has disappeared from
Cuba besides most foods and basic goods—illiteracy, prostitution, and
unemployment—the film demands that viewers feel grateful and conform
to what they *already* have rather than lament what they lost. By characterizing itself as "propagandistic" at the beginning, Alvarez attempts to
convince a national audience of the merits of socialist sacrifice by *correct-
ing* their gaze. If haggard faces and shabby clothes like the ones featured
in *Despegue a las 18* would have implied injustice and political neglect at
the beginning of the Revolution, now they were metaphors for the hostility of US policy toward Cuba and witnesses to its effects. Poverty is
reimagined as evidence of national defiance rather than the failure of (or
resistance to) communist economic policy.[27] Indeed, even the film's title
Take-off at 18.00 betrays itself: a reference to the economic takeoff ensured
by labor mobilizations for production that started every day at 6 a.m. in
the campo, it is meant to co-opt audience doubts as to whether the battle against underdevelopment succeed. Instead, the title underscores this
doubt as the rewards Fidel promises for "working like animals" remain far
from tangible.

Like all of Alvarez's movies, *Despegue a las 18:00* was widely seen in Cuba
and abroad.[28] How the unintended ambiguity of this film might have affected Cubans' private attitudes might never be known. Nonetheless, placing *Despegue* into the larger panorama of documentary films underscores a
great irony: despite the fact that in the late 1960s, the state controlled the
interpretive frame of the Revolution better than ever before, creating films
that credibly reflected the hegemony of this frame—rather than the ambi-

guity of revolutionary life—had become more difficult rather than easier to achieve.

This was particularly obvious in the work of Nicolás Guillén Landrián, an intellectual whose black identity, youth, and deep family roots in the pre-1959 PSP propelled him to explore the question of what (and who) actually constituted "the Revolution."". Assigned to explore the *presence* of the Revolution in citizens' lives by ICAIC, Guillén Landrián enlisted spectators in assessing (rather than receiving) its meaning. In Guillen Landrián's films, the camera intentionally places the hyper-real itself on display and interrogates the rituals and expressions of belief that made it up. What does total unity mean and what does it cost? Is total inclusion in the Revolution truly liberating if the terms of inclusion are dictated by the state? In answering these questions filmically, Guillén Landrián argued for the authority of the masses and emphasized that collective freedom would never be achieved through contradictory means. As a result, Guillén Landrián's work served as an allegory for the many hidden layers of a revolutionary palimpsest written through the resistance and persistence of citizens themselves.

"Clashing with the Context": Nicolás Guillén Landrián's Filmic Attack on Induced Euphoria

Unlike Santiago Alvarez, who expected audiences to "learn" proper revolutionary perspectives from his films, Guillén Landrián, better known as "Nicolasito," deliberately interrogated the hierarchical relationships of power that the genre of documentary film (and, by extension, the revolutionary state) created when it interpreted people's lives and history for them. In his films, the relationship between the present day and the hyper-real is a troubled one: neither a scene of triumph nor an opportunity for triumph, reality seems an uncertain factor in every historical equation. As Manuel Zayas, a documentary filmmaker himself and an expert on Guillén Landrián, contends, "Alvarez, who knows everything, *teaches*; Nicolasito, who doubts, *reveals*."[29]

Trained by Joris Ivens and Theodor Christensen, acclaimed foreign filmmakers who spent more than a year in Cuba working with the documentary division at ICAIC, Guillén Landrián deliberately engaged audiences with ambiguous scenes. He also inserted ironic, often contradictory titles to parody rather than parrot the slogans and official discourse that pocked citizens' everyday landscape. Thus, many of his films such as *Barrio Viejo* (1963) and *Los del Baile* (1965) featured black Cubans engaging in rituals of the Afro-Cuban religion of Santería, dance, and urban street life,— all activities that, for ICAIC censors, symbolized the past and reified "backward" or contradictory identities. At the time, ICAIC directors not only expected its directors to depict citizens engaged in "productive" processes such as militia duty, labor, or political instruction but they were supposed to make agents or institutions of the state a primary focus. Thus, *Barrio Viejo* and *Los del Baile* were banned and never publicly screened.

A similar fate befell almost all of Guillén Landrián's documentaries, including *Ociel del Toa* (1965), a film that won the coveted and highly prestigious Valladolid Film Festival's Espiga de Oro prize as well as *Reportage* (1966). Indeed, upon their completion, Guillén Landrián was arrested by G2, interrogated at its headquarters in Villa Marista, and sentenced to two years of hard labor at a prison camp for ideologically diversionary communistsCommunists on the Isle of Pines. A year and half later, Guillén Landrián was treated with electroshock therapy at the military hospital of Havana's former Camp Columbia and placed under house arrest until 1968. In an apparent act of rage over his unjust imprisonment, the filmmaker had doused with gasoline the chickens he was supposed to feed and set them on fire.[30] Three months before his death in 2003, Guillén Landrián explained his arrest to Manuel Zayas in these terms: "In my anxiousness to achieve a position within the film industry, I dared to make things that were not well looked upon, because, at the time, all cinema was expected to be about the Cuban people and, at the very least, [made] with euphoria and I just didn't have it."[31] Guillén Landrián's assessment helps explain what made his early films abhorrent to authorities and why his post-"rehabilitation" productions of 1968–72 also failed to conform to ICAIC's standards and show any political remorse. Guillén Landrián wanted, as he explained years later, to make his work original and personal, based on "immediate and plausible themes."[32] Yet, the task of doing so in dialogue with official discourse often proved challenging. Simply put, Guillén Landrián never managed to link the real with the hyper-real.

Close inspection of Guillén Landrián's originally problematic films, *Ociel del Toa, Retornar a Baracoa,* and *Reportaje,* reveal why. On the one hand, they represented the Revolution's triumphs as incomplete: all three used images of Cubans in isolated eastern settlements to show what life was like for them after 1959 "without being too optimistic.""[33] As ICAIC's on-and-off director García Espinosa told him repeatedly, Guillén Landrián "refused to follow the approved script" for each of his documentaries, leaving both him and his work under political suspicion.[34] Moreover, Guillén

Landrián reiterated many images from these banned films in his 1968–69 productions: effectively, accumulated evidence of the Revolution's incompleteness (and the injustice that Guillén Landrián suffered) never went away.

In this and other ways, Guillén Landrián reframed the Revolution through his documentaries by pointing out and thereby questioning the obvious: that an official discursive frame for interpreting reality actually existed and that it informed how citizens reacted and acted within the Revolution. By the same token, his subjects' endorsement of official discourses through their words and activities often backfired. In Guillén Landrián's films, displays of euphoria are clearly induced—often by the director himself—a fact that then destabilizes all narratives, grand or otherwise, including that of the Revolution and the documentary's own.

For example, *Ociel del Toa* focused on a sixteen-year-old *miliciano* with a third-grade education who tows a *cayuca*, or dug-out river raft, to communities with no roads. In this respect, little has changed with the coming of the Revolution; ending the peasants' isolation is mostly a political affair. Emphasizing this, the screen says: "Food, clothes, the teachers . . . . It's hours with one's feet in the water. One's feet in the water . . . . It's good that people should see this in Havana." Subsequent images show the coexistence of revolutionary reality with still-vibrant relics of the past: Ociel and his fellow peasants attend a dance, a (technically illegal) cockfight, an educational assembly called by the Revolution's mass organizations and religious services at a Protestant church. Guillén Landrián then conveys these apparent contradictions in practical terms: "The girl who sells sodas at the assembly wants to be a Communist but she goes to church with her aunt. But she goes to Church with her aunt. . . . On Sunday night, there is nothing to do. And the Church fills with guajiros [peasants]." Indeed, virtually every aspect of these peasants' lives subverts standard discourses about the Revolution's impact on peasants: once isolated, religious, and prone to gambling before the Revolution, so they apparently remain. Worse yet, they— like the film's "star," Ociel—claim to be loyal revolutionaries.

Like *Ociel del Toa,* Guillén Landrián's other films about isolated communities showed the transformations wrought since 1959 but also revealed the contradictory persistence of the past. *Retornar a Baracoa,* a clearly favorable report, focuses on a town that remained accessible only by sea for more than three hundred years. While the film features state projects such as the building of a radio station, a high school, an airport, and a park, the images and voices of loyal residents leave viewers feeling that all this still might be too little. Indeed, Guillén Landrián ends his film with a decidedly realistic, rather than euphemistic, euphoric, or hyper-realistic on-screen assessment: *"Baracoa es una cárcel con parque* (Baracoa is a prison with a park)."[35]

Yet, despite the counternarratives his films told, Guillén Landrián maintained throughout his life that he never meant the content or images of his work to be disloyal. What made his works so problematic was the thought process that they invoked in audiences. In sharp contrast with Alvarez, on-screen narrations fixed audiences' attention on revolutionary images without fixing these images' meaning. Guillén Landrián also ended many of his films ambiguously, with the phrase "FIN PERO NO ES EL FIN (The end but there is no end)." The viewer is forced to wonder where the ending (of a film, the Revolution, or any spectacle) lies. In tapping the viewer's thoughts, these documentaries recognize the viewer's own internal narrative and ask from where it might arise.

The question of where narratives come from is particularly central to Guillén Landrián's banned 1965 film *Reportage* and the subsequent films of the late 1960s that reiterated much of its imagery. Showing hundreds of peasants engaged in a mock funeral of "Don IG Norancia [Sir IG Norance]," *Reportage* haunts the viewer by directly questioning the credibility of one of the Revolution's most common public rituals: mock funerals. Since 1960, mock funerals, in effigy, of US politicians, of newly nationalized foreign companies, and of Cuba's formerly independent press had become common. However, unlike any mock funeral in Havana, *Reportage*'s participants march in silence, carrying poorly written signs, and weep (rather than dance), as if in mourning—ironically, for the death of their own ignorance! After a number of similarly parodic scenes (of a political rally in which all participants look bored; of a state-sponsored community dance in which only one peasant smiles), the film ends with a black screen reading: "Report: An informative genre that emerged in the Nineteenth Century that today has enormous importance: in general, it provides a vivid account of an event or reality that is studied and exposed."

Given the fact that the only "audience" of these films had been Guillén Landrián's accusers and interrogators, recycling multiple scenes from them for subsequent films *Coffea Arabiga* (1968) and *Desde la Habana: !1969!* endowed later documentaries with an internal tension: unbeknownst to most viewers, each of these documentaries represented *more than one reality at once*, that of the actual film and that of repressed/selectively remembered films made earlier. Effectively, Guillén Landrián created a secret counternarrative that made these films unavoidable reflections of their maker's own consciousness. This strategy acquires special significance when one considers the fact that both *Coffea Arabiga* and *Desde la Habana* engaged the Revolution's grand narratives as none of Guillen Landrián's work had previously done.

Meant to demonstrate the director's ideological rehabilitation, *Coffea Arábiga* was one of only two ICAIC works to focus on Fidel Castro's high-profile pet project to make Cuba a leading exporter of coffee (the other was a newsreel by Santiago Alvarez). Initially well received, *Coffea Arabiga* was promoted in posters designed by Raúl Oliva and selected as ICAIC's official entry for the International Short Film Festival in Oberhausen, East Germany.[36]

Filmed in 1968, *Coffea Arábiga* celebrated a mass mobilization of volunteers to plant coffee in El Cordón de la Habana, a newly created "green belt" that displaced thousands of small farmers who had previously grown native fruit for sale.[37] Although El Cordón de la Habana remains the poor cousin of the infamous Ten Million Ton Harvest of 1970 in the history and memory of that period, it was promoted on a similar scale at the time.[38]

According to Ismael Suárez de la Paz, a founding member of Fidel's Economic Planning Commission, Fidel first dreamed of transforming Cuba into a coffee powerhouse in 1963 when a visiting communist from Colombia, Tarcisio Ciabato, suggested that *café caturra* could be grown on state farms under direct sun with minimal labor and other inputs. As the principal aide in Fidel's many pet projects, Suárez de la Paz acquired the seeds of this variety in Mexico and directed the work of twelve thousand workers in San Andrés de Caibaunabo, the first agricultural station to cultivate it. For reason of age, health, or gender, those who did not make good candidates for cutting cane in the key harvests of 1968–70 worked in coffee and, as Suárez de la Paz remembers, this meant that most volunteers were women.[39]

For most of its running time, *Coffea Arábiga* focuses on these volunteers, surprising audiences with filmic and printed images of women doing typically "masculine" tasks such as crop fumigation. Punctuated by upbeat music and scenes of hard-working, often smiling, workers, Guillén Landrián peppered the film with official discourse, including the voice and poetry of his uncle and UNEAC president, Nicolás Guillén, reciting a famous 1958 poem that imagines Cuba as an alligator rising from the sea.[40] "If yesterday it was heroic to combat in the Sierra and the Llano, today it is heroic to transform agriculture," a billboard reads. As images explain parasitic blights on coffee, a light-hearted rumba elicits ironic humor. Substituting "Cubans" for Fidel in a reiteration of a 1960 revolutionary cheer, the screen reads: "*¡Cubanos, seguros, a los Yanquis dáles duro!* [Cubans, sure of themselves, whip those Yankees hard!]."

By contextualizing images in ways he had never done before, Guillén Landrián's *Coffea Arábiga* also insisted discussing race and confronting antiblack prejudice such that it need not be a taboo. He also argued that black culture was historically infused with revolutionary goals. For example, images of black women dancing in a Santería ritual accompany scenes of an abandoned coffee plantation as the screen reminds viewers that coffee was first cultivated in Cuba by African slaves. In fact, the film relies on titles to make fun of the taboo on discussing race, even when it pertains to slavery, and corrects the audience's racist shock. "The blacks on coffee plantations were the main source of labor," one screen reads. Subsequent screens flash: "The Blacks / *What?!* / *The Blacks?!!* / Yes!!" Through this and other scenes, Guillen Landrián portrayed the Revolution as an inversion of the historical exploitation and marginality of blacks, depicting slaves as the intellectual authors and heroes of Fidel's contemporary *Plan Café*.

Describing *Coffea Arábiga* as a labor of love, Guillén Landrián later recalled that he dared to make the documentary because everything he had heard about Fidel's *Plan Café* told him that it was going to be one of the Revolution's great achievements: purposefully, he embedded evidence of his own propensity to doubt in the film in order to expose its falsity.[41] Unfortunately, Guillén Landrián's intended self-criticism backfired when the *Plan Café* soon showed itself to be one of the greatest economic disasters of the Revolution thus far.

Anxious to replace the coffee that imprisoned and relocated anticommunist small farmers of the Escambray mountain range had once supplied, Fidel repeatedly ignored his own advisors' warnings that café caturra would not flourish in Cuba's hot climes as predicted by "the theories of bourgeois Mexican economists."[42] Moreover, the coffee plan's reliance on unskilled volunteers and sky-high goals ignored basic problems of how the saplings would grow: when transferring the saplings in polyester nylon bags for planting in the field, volunteers tended to bend the root because adjusting each sapling in its hole took more time. "As long as the little sapling was growing in the fertilized material of its bag, it seemed to work well in the Cordón," Suárez de la Paz explains. "But after a while, it failed miserably! Then, began the insanity of getting people to plant the coffee in their backyards. So they destroyed their home gardens, they uprooted everything to grow coffee; then they turned to planting alongside highways—everywhere! The focus moved to El Escambray. On one single afternoon, as I remember, 275,000 volunteers were mobilized to plant coffee. And you know what? . . . All that got us not even a *quintal*. Nowhere, not in El Escambray, not in El Cordón de la Habana, nowhere. It produced nothing."[43] The only evidence in the state press of the plan's massive failure was silence: after daily reports in *Granma* on the planting process in the spring of 1968, no figures or estimates were given of a harvest at all. Guillén Landrián was guilty—before the fact—of having taken so much notice.

Previously embraced as an ode to Cubans' idealism, *Coffea Arabiga*'s didactic use of irony and metaphors for Cubans' struggle to free themselves from colonialism suddenly embodied ridicule, counter-revolution, and treason. Once innocuous scenes became subversive. One such scene showed a woman (played by Guillén Landrián's first wife, Dara Kristova) repeating in Bulgarian the scientific account of how coffee seeds grow that she had ostensibly heard over Radio Cordón.[44] Meant to invoke the revolutionary idea that productive work outside the home set women free, the camera followed this on-the-spot "interview" with Kristova at a bus stop on Havana's Calle Línea with close-ups of her face. Accompanying these close-ups, a song by Diana Ross and the Supremes blares, "Set me free, why don't you, babe? Get out my life, why don't you, babe?" In the context of *El Plan Café*'s failure, however, Guillén Landrián's celebration of women as workers morphed into an intentional critique of the Revolution's exploitation.

Even more problematic in the new context of *El Plan Café*'s defeat was Guillén Landrían's choice of an ending. In the last minutes of the film, Fidel Castro is seen climbing the speaker's mount to address a mass rally at his usual spot in the Plaza of the Revolution. Echoing Fidel's own frequent admonitions to the roaring crowds that attended mass rallies, the screen reads, "just a minute / please / in order to finish." At that point, a Beatles song replaces what would normally be Fidel's speech. Viewers see the dirtied, weathered palms of an old man, looking like those of a worker or possibly a beggar. Appearing on screen is a Spanish translation of the lyrics from the Beatles' "The Fool on the Hill," a song about an idealistic man who never stops dreaming: *Todos creían que era un tonto / el hombre sobre la colina veía / la tierra girar y el sol caer*. The lyrics reminded viewers that early skeptics and counter-revolutionaries had once used *tonto* as well as *bobo* [Spanish words for "fool"] to describe Fidel and all those who supported confrontation rather than acquiescence to the United States.[45]

However, the soaring voice of John Lennon does *not* match the film's translation of his words at all, a point that made its political implications—post–*Plan Café*—very easy to attack. "Day after day," said the soundtrack, "Alone on a hill, / The man with the foolish grin is keeping perfectly still / But nobody wants to know him, / They can see that he's just a fool, / And he never gives an answer, / But the fool on the hill, / Sees the sun going down, / And the eyes in his head, / See the world spinning 'round." Ostensibly, the English version of the song unites the image of the open, hard-worked hands to the idealism of Fidel as he defies all odds. Yet, months after its release, officials no longer saw it that way. In one of many conversations about showing this film to his class on Cuban cinema at the University of Havana in the early 1990s, now deceased ICAIC historian Raúl Rodríguez remarked to me, "The reality of Plan Café made a fool of Fidel. That wasn't Nicolasito's fault. He might have thought he was a fool all along but his film never showed that. On the contrary. The problem was that Nicolasito's film became a prophecy: it was supposed to show Fidel as an idealist who would win, but circumstances made the film show Fidel as a lunatic and fanatic."[46] While none of these scenes mattered at the time that ICAIC promoted the film at home and abroad, the failure of the state's latest mass project made discussing that project (let alone criticizing it) taboo. Suddenly, *Coffea Arábiga* was a film that ridiculed the Revolution and concluded with a treasonous portrait of Fidel. Betrayed by ICAIC, Guillén Landrián ended up on the wrong side of history.

Nonetheless, it was Julio García Espinoza's and Alfredo Guevara's opposition to Guillén Landrián's subsequent films that finally silenced his cinematic voice and all memory of it in Cuba for years. After he made *Coffea Arábiga*, Guillén Landrián made *Desde la Habana: ¡1969!*, a film that relied heavily on repetition of the same images and sounds in order to invoke the mental process that the state's incessant echoing of its own official images and sounds produced. Once again, the film's initial impression is not dissidence but an ambiguous endorsement of how constant repetition of a historic truth transforms that truth into a something greater, a myth that is part of the self. Perhaps for these reasons, *Desde la Habana: ¡1969!* was considered Guillén Landrián's most subversive film. Steeped in visual and verbal repetitions, it is a film that points out the oppressive effect of inescapable propaganda on daily existence; yet the film also seems to require multiple viewings in order for its own (hidden?) message to be understood. Not surprisingly, ICAIC never released *Desde la Habana*, citing it and Guillén Landrián himself as equally *"incoherente con el contexto* [clashing with the context]."[47] This negative evaluation grew only worse with the completion of *Taller Línea y 18*, a film about a bus repair shop in Vedado whose workers are shown *avoiding* rather than embracing election to Communist Party ranks in factorywide assemblies.[48]

By disarticulating the script of a hyper-real political performance from the performance itself, Guillén Landrián dissected the bonds linking the real and the hyper-real on film: the effect was to sabotage (from ICAIC's perspective) the documentary's purpose and invert its role as the state's most powerful media ally. This definitive shift in ICAIC's assessment of Guillén Landrián's work and motivations quickly led to what he called *folie*, or total insanity.

The word describes as much ICAIC's treatment of him as the politically induced results of Guillén Landrián's subsequent internment in Cuban mental hospitals. "The paradox is that there really was no true political confrontation on my part," the filmmaker wrote to Manuel Zayas in 2003, "only a mute and complicit consent with all of that disaster. As I already said, my friend, *folie*."[49] After several more treatments in mental hospitals, Guillén Landrián descended into political and cultural obscurity. Officials went so far as to accuse of him of promoting the assassination of Fidel and other state officials through his films.[50] Until he was finally allowed, in 1988, to leave Cuba for Miami, where he became a visual artist, Guillén Landrián reportedly lived for many years as a part-time vagrant who wandered Havana's streets, hallucinating, paranoid, and alone. When Guillén Landrián eventually made *Downtown* (2001), an award-winning documentary about being homeless in Miami, he described the tragedy of his own condition in more ways than one.

Reel vs. Real in Making a Hyper-Real Revolution

ICAIC banned Nicolás Guillén Landrián's documentaries because they destabilized the Revolution's grand narrative of redemption and national liberation through total unity; his work demonstrated how the power of documentary film, like the power of the state, lay in framing reality as a dramatic spectacle in which citizens were invited to participate and observe but not direct or control. In films like *Ociel del Toa* and especially *Coffea Arabiga*, the filmic reel trumped the real and betrayed the hyper-real Revolution. Like Fidel addressing real-life rallies and mass mobilizations for labor, the dynamic of power that positioned documentary filmmakers as supreme organizers of knowledge (and viewers as recipients of knowledge) did not always legitimate the grand narrative; it could jeopardize its viability easily and intentionally. As ICAIC's leading official filmmakers such as Santiago Alvarez realized, stability was fundamental to the grand narrative of the Revolution and therefore the survival of Cuba's communist state because adhering to its scripts and obeying its self-appointed directors limited how citizens could discuss their reality and openly contest it on their own, self-authored terms. In the radicalized context of the 1960s, adopting official discourse as a public sign of personal loyalty had become an effective way to generate the appearance of political homogeneity and conformity to Community Party mandates, even if they did not exist. Ironically and brilliantly, Nicolás Guillén Landrián's complex visual representations of the Revolution not only undermined the success of this process by *documenting* it; they also actively tested its validity by subverting the passive role in observing and assessing reality that the communist state assigned to citizens.

Writing on the Wall

1968 as Event and Representation

The year 1968 was a decisive moment in the mutation of an older model of modern revolution toward seemingly new nonrevolutionary scripts of social change that emerged in the late twentieth century. In spite of its many internal variations, that older model had gradually developed between 1790s France and 1940s China, with the Russian Revolution of 1917 as a decisive turning point, through a slow accretion of by-now familiar elements, including confident philosophies of history and historical rupture, Promethean voluntarism, national and international horizons of action, paradoxes of democratic representation (for example, tensions between minority leadership and mass inclusion), the development of factions and then parties, and vicissitudinous violence. In 1968—a symbolic year that points toward a larger era—such elements were decisively pushed to the limit or undermined, opening the way for thorough-going reevaluations of the inheritance of modern revolution and the development of new modes of interpersonal, institutional, civil-social, and global social action. Immanuel Wallerstein, for instance, is largely correct to see in 1968 the widespread decomposition of nineteenth-century national and social antisystematic "Old Left" movements centered on the acquisition of state power and their subsequent replacement by disparate minority groups caught between immediate claims-making and unresolved strategic questions of what to do and how to do it.[1] It is for this reason that "the sixties" have been known as a moment of "revolution in the revolution" when that social and political form was itself radically transformed.[2] To be sure, declarations of turned pages and postrevolutionary postscripts have themselves long been part of the modern revolutionary tradition. Nevertheless, self-consciousness about the repetitions written into the scripts of revolution themselves took on particular urgency in the late twentieth century, as evidenced in part by the disintegration of the Marxist paradigm and by postmodern rhetoric that affirmed distinctiveness while rejecting novelty.

The year 1968 was recognized at the time as a pivotal year. Waves of explosive events signaled upheaval and crisis. In dramatic, sweeping transformations that stretched from daily life to international state relations, many people around the world saw revolutions in the making, a prospect that inspired hope in some and fear in others. The global scale of this ferment was truly original. While the very novelty of 1968 paradoxically connected it to other moments of supposed revolutionary rupture (all revolutions are *new*), the unprecedented magnitude and simultaneity of events that year demonstrated their multiplicity, indeterminacy, and even antiscriptural qualities. Indeed, "1968" represents more than a twelve-month period; it stands for the sixties as a whole, emblematizing an age of sustained cultural reordering, social conflict, and political crisis whose effects and meanings are still debated today. If scenarios of modern revolution were fundamentally transformed between the 1950s and the 1970s, we are still grappling with the scripts/antiscripts revealed by that era's events and representations. Fifty years later we remain contemporaries of "1968." In what follows, I focus on one famed setting of that crowded year—France in May and June— where the writing of revolution involved recycling material from the reservoirs of national history and also reflecting on the meaning of *events* themselves. I then turn to the broader historical representations of 1968 and the sixties, for the scripts of revolution cannot be detached from subsequent depictions of what happened at that time and what it meant.

I.

The revolutionary scripts of 1968 can initially be approached by focusing on one of the most iconic sites of this "first global rebellion": the French *événements* of May and June.[3] What began in early May as a spontaneous protest over university disciplining of student activists had by the end of the month become the largest general strike in French history. The political crisis culminated on 29 May when President Charles de Gaulle abruptly disappeared overnight before returning the next day to reassert his authority. Popular imaginations in France and around the world latched onto images of young people setting up barricades in the Latin Quarter student district and occupying the Sorbonne until mid-June. Around-the-clock general assemblies led to flourishing talk, militancy, playfulness, and imagination. The ethos of "May '68" expressed the values and experiences of spontaneity, immediacy, multiplicity, and openness. The events in themselves and as one instance of global ferment exemplified what Gerald J. DeGroot has called the "kaleidoscopic" sixties.[4]

Revolution found literal inscription on the walls of the Latin Quarter through ephemeral graffiti—"It is forbidden to forbid"; "Be realistic, demand the impossible"; "Underneath the paving stones, the beach"—and posters—"Beauty is in the streets" (the image of a young woman throwing a paving stone); "May '68: Beginning of a long struggle" (a factory with a revolutionary flag). Irreverently ludic and politically charged, such anonymous, iconic scripts of "May '68" captured the spirit of critique and social action with a sound-bite lucidity that lent itself to replication, amplification, and transmission within France and around the world, not least via television. At the same time, as Victoria H. F. Scott has shown, in spite of their seemingly authentic handmade quality, the tens of thousands of posters produced by Beaux-Arts students borrowed liberally from placard styles flourishing in the contemporaneous Chinese Cultural Revolution— large-character notices (*Dazibao*) and instructional cartoons (*Manhua*).[5] Graffiti and posters also built on earlier traditions of experimental cultural avant-gardism, a phenomenon Lionel Trilling allegedly dismissed at the time as "modernism in the streets"—a move that contributed to a paradigmatic shift to postmodernism.[6]

Protagonists in 1968 acted out and on other historical playbooks as well. Street protest had long been part of the vernacular of French politics: the challenge of the constitutive "people" to constituted authority, frequently from the left but occasionally from the right. Demonstrations and street battles in 1968, if often bloody, typically operated according to theatrically performative codes familiar to demonstrators and police alike: thrown rocks, tear gas, billy clubs, and alternating charges toward opposing lines. Pierre Vidal-Naquet noted at the time the curious fact that, with the exception of a demonstration on 1 June, weekends had "remained sacrosanct" and thus quiet during the events.[7] Symbolically, nowhere was the injection of past revolutionary form into the present more apparent than at the site of the barricade. Activists dug up paving stones, removed sidewalk grates, pulled down trees, and overturned cars in order to erect protective barriers in their clashes with police. Barricades served the dual symbolic function of demarcating "liberated" space and of connecting with earlier moments in France's revolutionary past.

Citation of other revolutionary moments (1830, 1848, 1871) by various actors during the "year of the barricades" was often deliberate and self-conscious.[8] On 15 May 1968, a poster hung prominently at the Sorbonne declared anachronistically, "For the first time since 1848, someone's using a vacuum cleaner here."[9] By the end of the year, J. M. Trevelyan's quip that 1848 was the turning point in European history that "did not turn" was evoked to explain the "failure" of 1968.[10] In the mid-1960s Mao Zedong had explicitly cited the Paris Commune of 1871 as a model for the Chinese Cultural Revolution, itself feeding *événements* in France. On the other hand, when a series of bombings struck Paris in late 1968, the government invoked a nineteenth-century security law originally passed to deal with the Communards.[11] The minister of the interior beginning in late May 1968, Raymond Marcellin, compared his task of restoring order to that of Louis-Eugène Cavaignac, the general who had suppressed the revolution of 1848. To Raymond Aron, who assumed a position analogous to Alexis de Tocqueville's consternated liberalism during 1848, the events of May–June 1968 threatened to endanger republican institutions. The "angry" radical students Aron met in Germany in January of that year resembled "their militant counterparts of 1930 and 1931" he had encountered forty years earlier.[12] Indeed, scripts from France's post- and prerevolutionary past were recycled more generally. French protestors applied the term "fascist" to state power and social conformism, taunting the riot police (the Compagnie républicaine de sécurité) with jeers of "CRS-SS," and chanting "We are all German Jews" when the Franco-German-Jewish student leader, Daniel Cohn-Bendit, was refused re-entry into France. Recalling a deeper past still was an infamous graffiti tag at the Sorbonne defacing a classical painting with a phrase adapted from the radical cleric Jean Meslier (1664–1729): "Mankind will not be happy until the last bureaucrat [instead of *autocrat*] has been strung up by the guts of the last capitalist [instead of *priest*]."[13]

The scripting of revolution in France during May–June 1968 included literal writing on the walls in the form of graffiti and poster art; choreographed street protests, including the revival of practices such as the barricade that recalled key moments in France's revolutionary past, such as 1848 and 1871; and the recitation and acting out—by both protestors and the "forces of order"—of rhetorical positions recycled from France's recent and distant past. A final type of script to mention touches on what Michel de Certeau called in May 1969 the "instruments of thought and of action that [May–June 1968] brought forth."[14] The prominent cultural and political role of intellectuals in France in the 1960s and 1970s made them uniquely situated to theorize the meaning of "1968," especially with respect to questions of language and representation, subjectivity, power, and history. Several generations of thinkers and scholars around the world have since been shaped directly and influenced indirectly by French "'68 thought."[15] To some extent, the very existence in the twenty-first century of a volume on the "scripts of revolution" demonstrates the continuing currency of ideas about language and revolution that can be traced to France in the years before and after 1968. Ideas can thus serve as indexes of broader historical phenomena.

One telling example of the revolutionary scripts of the French events of May–June 1968 pertains to contemporaneous reflection on the category of "the event" itself by thinkers such as Henri Lefebvre, Claude Lefort, Michel de Certeau, and Roland Barthes. Underscoring how "May '68" had reinjected political possibility into a stagnant situation, Lefebvre observed that "events belie forecasts . . . to the extent that events are historic, they upset calculations. . . . Because of their conjectural nature, events upset structures which made them possible."[16] In early July, Lefort wrote, "Everyone tries to name the event that has shaken French society, tries to relate it to the familiar and foresee its consequences. . . . Some would like to dam up the breach . . . in vain." The events had been unforeseen; they swiftly revealed the essential fragility of structures and systems otherwise taken as predictable and unassailable. The spontaneity of the students, their rejection of leaders, hierarchy, and discipline, had enabled "an indeterminate possibility" to be "reborn"; the "audacity [to] intervene in a concrete situation *here* and *now*" revealed the promise of "a power . . . of those without power."[17]

Later in the year, de Certeau also echoed Lefebvre's and Lefort's views of the events as unexpectedly revealing new possibilities: "The event cannot be dissociated from the options to which it *gave place*; it is that space constituted by often surprising choices." May–June 1968 had been a "*symbolic revolution*" in which "speech [played] the decisive role." "Last May," he quipped, "speech was taken the way, in 1789, the Bastille was taken." Playing on the link between event and "advent," de Certeau stressed the priority of experience and practice in determining what "May '68" had meant and what it could mean:

> An event is not what can be seen and known about its happening, but what it becomes (and, above all, for us). This option is grasped only in risk, not by observation. It is therefore clear that what happened last May has become for many an inaugural or revealing event. . . . The *event* engages the *structure*. The whole order is at stake and, first of all, it seems to me, a system of representation, what

grounds both knowledge and politics . . . . *[I]nterpretation* could still be the sign of *events* . . . . The solution . . . is in union . . . based on the new structuring called forth by the event.[18]

The impact and "afterlives" of the events were to be determined in part in fights over their representation and meaning.[19] Events surprised, disrupted structures, opened possibilities, and pointed toward unconditioned futures; in other words, they took the form of antiscripts, hence the emphasis in 1968 on spontaneity, immediacy, multiplicity, and openness. In this respect, it is striking the degree to which Lefebvre's, Lefort's, and de Certeau's reflections on "the event" rehearsed remarks Cohn-Bendit had made in a famous interview with Jean-Paul Sartre published on 20 May 1968. There, the student leader had emphasized the challenge of the student revolt to French society as a whole (not just the state), the creation of a "breach" that exploded "the myth that 'nothing could be done,'" the replacement of outmoded vanguardism by "an active minority functioning as a permanent leaven," the sudden and potentially self-organizing freeing of "speech," and the sense of a fleeting "experiment [that] allows a glimpse of a possibility."[20]

Less sanguine about the events' possibilities than these voices was Roland Barthes, who in his December 1968 essay "Writing the Event," analyzed the discursive scripts and representational systems that had framed both circumstances and experiences earlier that year. "To describe the event," he began, "implies that the event has been written." The events had involved different kinds of speech: "live" radio, student communiqués/press conferences, and performances such as "wild" slogans and graffiti, students' "missionary" appeal to workers, and "functionalist" talk of reform. Although Barthes seemingly agreed with de Certeau when he wrote that "the crisis *was* language," he parted company with him when he asserted that wild speech was harmlessly ineffectual and that missionary and functionalist speech expressed the moment's structural ambiguity in ways that tended to facilitate recuperation. Barthes extended this analysis to the symbolic economy of May–June 1968, noting the "striking phenomenon" that protagonists on all sides held to an "almost unanimous adherence to one and the same symbolic discourse." Competing appeals to red flags, black flags, or tricolor flags, for example, all took shape within a sociohistorical field possessing a steady-state consistency. His position resembled that of an anthropologist: "The symbolic system under which an event functions is closely linked to the degree of this event's integration within the society of which it is both the expression and violation: it is also formed by a homogeneous set of rules, a commonly acknowledged recourse to these rules . . . almost all played the same symbolic game." One could cheer or jeer when cars were overturned to make barricades, but one could not avoid the power of the barricade-as-symbol within French culture and history. In short, all graffiti requires the wall on which it is painted.[21] In contrast to Barthes, Margaret Atack has noted that the figurative "writing" of May–June 1968 as "text" also involves rewriting as much as mediation, the present and future of its utopian discourse as much as the return of earlier revolutionary forms. Its "hall of mirrors" quality *continues* to embrace diverse experiences, spectacle, theatricality, a "new politics," and manifold elements best rendered and conveyed by literature and film.[22]

The point of this detour through French theories of the event written in 1968 is to illustrate the pressures placed on revolutionary scripts that year. Between historical citation and recycling (barricades, 1848 and 1871, antifascism) and free, wild speech (perhaps more fittingly exemplified by speak-outs and general assemblies than the dried ink of graffiti and poster art), tensions over revolution as structure and antistructure become clear. Insofar as "the events" embodied a sense of rupture and *novum*, they conformed to earlier models of modern revolution. Nevertheless, emphasis on the unanticipated and surprising aspects of the "explosion" (or *irruption*, as Lefebvre's book was originally titled) and on immediate, fleeting improvisation stripped of leaders and programmatic goals intensified the experience of rupture as an end in itself. The sense that the events had surged forth and been produced by "an *objective situation*," as Cohn-Bendit put it, reinforced the view articulated by theorists of the event that no one was in charge of "May '68" and that *being in charge* ran precisely counter to the spirit of the moment.[23] Tensions could thus be noted between, on one hand, the voluntarist agency of multitudinous social actors and, on the other, irruptive and transcendent "events" somehow mysteriously irreducible to intentions.[24] The events were presumed not to obey a script: they were antiscriptural and antistructural in an antiauthoritarianism directed against both Gaullist society and the French Communist Party (the latter embodying the structural repetitions of an ossified and unimaginative "revolutionary tradition").

And yet, as Barthes pointed out, on another level it was not so easy to escape structure: everyone played an assigned part in the script of revolution, like pieces on a chessboard bound by rules and space. Jacques Lacan, too, opined that structure wins out against attempts to flee it when he notoriously remarked to his students on 3 December 1969: "What you aspire to as revolutionaries is a new master. You will get one."[25] More was at work in these criticisms than conservational impulses. As the enthusiasts of the event themselves were aware, developing new structures adequate to the events posed particularly thorny challenges. De Certeau had gestured toward the "solution" of a "new structuring called forth by the event," but he had stopped short, treating "interpretations as a function of the event and [inscribing] the event into the register of our theoretical apparatus."[26] Neither making interpretation depend on events nor reducing the latter to pre-existing apparatuses seemed to answer the challenge of articulating a "new structuring." At stake was the question of whether or not the antiscript of "May '68" could become a new script for social action and social order, and if so, how. Wallerstein later highlighted precisely this dilemma when, as we saw above, he observed how the era's antisystematic movements ceased aspiring to state power. A powerful and unresolved triangulation could thus be discerned among transcendently irruptive events, immanent volitional agency, and structure/antistructure. In subsequent years the script/antiscript standoff of "1968" and the continued pursuit of antinomian voluntarism helped lead to an overcoming of the modern revolutionary inheritance (especially through the late-twentieth-century collapse of Marxism) and the foregrounding of nonrevolutionary scripts of emancipatory social action.[27]

Nevertheless, it is difficult to draw such large lessons from what is in effect a narrow case. In having focused on factors like graffiti and ideas, there is something exceedingly limited in the above treatment of "May '68." We now know much more about the breadth and depth of the "'68 years" in France—for example, the significance of worker insubordination and immigrant mobilization.[28] Iconicity can provide entry and insight but never fully bodied historical comprehension. There was anyway something inward looking about the French events of May–June 1968 themselves (debates about De Gaulle, the Fifth Republic, and the French Communist Party; the attempt to build bridges between students and workers, recalling long-term dilemmas of French socialism)—a fact replicated today in the tendency of French scholarship on 1968 still to focus above all on domestic circumstances.[29] The French experience only begins to scratch the surface of "1968." Even my own treatment has been unable to keep non-French elements from seeping in: the Chinese Cultural Revolution, cultural modernism, 1848 throughout Europe, twentieth-century Germany, and so forth. Today for the better, it is increasingly impossible to talk about 1968 with respect to one country or "1968" without reference

to the general era. While there are other scripts of the moment to consider—Brian Moore's 1971 novel, *The Revolution Script*, about radicalism
and crackdown in Canada;[30] psychedelic fonts or the screenplays of popular films in the United States[31]—I will now turn to historiographic representations of 1968 since that year posed and continues to pose questions
about the adequacy of representations and interpretations to events. As de
Certeau maintained: "The event thus shakes the structure of *knowledge* just
as it shakes that of *society*."[32]

II.

In a superb short discussion of 1968 written ten years later, the historian
Eric Hobsbawm declared that the meaning of this "signpost" date derived
not only from the swarm of significant worldwide events that crowded
the calendar between January and December but also from ongoing circumstances that coursed through that year: the Chinese Cultural Revolution, conflict in the Middle East and Nigeria, and above all "symptoms of
breakdown" in the international postwar order. The diverse events of 1968
around the world, sharing a "dramatic character" and "certain unexpected-
ness," transpired in three zones: the West, the anti-imperialist Third World,
and the communist bloc, symbolized respectively by France, Vietnam, and
Czechoslovakia.

In 1968 postwar economic prosperity in the West showed the first signs
of downturn but also the crisis of a young generation caught in contradictions among material affluence, relative freedom, high expectations, and
awareness of worldwide social problems. Hobsbawm followed others in
noting that young people in the sixties were "the first since the generation of 1848 . . . to turn to the left en masse." Outside the West, anticolonial struggles had been underway before 1968 and continued afterward. In
Latin America, the 1959 Cuban Revolution, Peru and Mexico in 1968, and
then early-1970s leftwing governments in Chile and Argentina troubled
American power especially. It was the Vietnamese Tet Offensive in January–February 1968, however, that dramatized "the essential weakness of
the American position." Finally, the "socialist world" expanded during the
1940s–70s. The pluralization of "different national roads of development
under socialism" evidenced an international critique of the preeminence
of the Soviet model, itself under the internal pressures of de-Stalinization
since 1956. Yet experimentation in Yugoslavia and China led all the same to
upward concentrations of power, and democratic socialist reform efforts in

Czechoslovakia during the Prague Spring of 1968 were put down by Soviet and Warsaw Pact force in August of that year.

Behind this global variety, Hobsbawm observed two unifying trends: first, 1945 as a caesural date everywhere; second, "the political role of students, professional people, and intellectuals" whose "major function" was to serve as a "spark" for broader movements. On their tenth anniversary, the events of 1968 appeared to Hobsbawm to have been a turning point in the West more than in the postcolonial and socialist spheres, where the year seemed part of longer processes. In the West, 1968 "announced the period of global capitalist crisis and political complexity" still underway as he wrote in 1978. Evoking the Babylonian prince who had the prophet Daniel translate a cryptic message on his palace wall that foretold his preordained demise, Hobsbawm concluded, "In 1967, Belshazzar was enjoying himself at his feast. In 1968 the writing appeared on the wall, announcing the end of the feast. And it has ended."[33] This kind of graffiti differed markedly from that found in Paris in May–June 1968.

Hobsbawm's account is instructive for the way it condenses elements regularly found in interpretations of 1968. Evaluations of that year and its consequences always appear on decennial anniversaries. Hobsbawm additionally highlighted familiar tensions in representations of "1968": between that calendar year and broader time periods, iconic hot spots and geographical range, dramatic turning points and larger trends, high politics and social movements, and beginnings and endings. More precisely, he foregrounded how the question of the scripts of revolution cannot be dissociated from either the times and spaces of "1968" or the positions of antiestablishment actors. Some who called themselves revolutionaries in the years before and after 1968, while identifying with older meanings of the term, transformed the scripts of revolution in substantial ways.

Today there is wide acceptance of the temporal and spatial spans of "1968"—that is, appreciation for broadened periodization of that year as part of the "long sixties" as well as for places beyond familiar "epicenters."[34] Even if all years are in some sense eventful, and despite the fact that "1968" does not hold any appreciable meaning in large parts of the world, it is nonetheless true that "the year that rocked the world" was indeed dramatically action-packed.[35] Beyond happenings Hobsbawm named—the Chinese Cultural Revolution, the Tet Offensive, the Prague Spring and its suppression—other notable incidents included the assassinations of Martin Luther King, Jr. and Robert Kennedy, violence at the Democratic National Convention in Chicago, the removal of António de Oliveira Salazar from power in Portugal, the beginning of the Troubles in Northern Ireland, and the massacre of student demonstrators in Mexico City. There were also significant social protests and upheaval in Brazil, Egypt, England, Italy, Jamaica, Japan, Senegal, Serbia, Spain, Turkey, and West Germany, among other places. Yet "1968" obviously never refers only to 1968. We have already seen attempts to link that year to earlier moments in the history of revolution (for example, 1848, 1871). More pervasive has been the tendency to view 1968 as a pivotal moment in postwar history, serving as a synecdoche for the sixties as a whole and emblematizing the age of which it was part. That era can be defined differently, for instance, beginning in 1954, 1956, or 1960 and ending in 1974, 1978, or 1981. It is undoubtedly significant that the year 1968 fell precisely midway between the end of World War II and the collapse of the Soviet Union.

In the same way that the *when* of 1968 was more prolonged than the date itself suggests, as the previous global examples map out, the *where* of '68 was also more extensive than often indicated by focus on prominent places like Paris, Prague, Chicago, Mexico City, and Tokyo. My own discussion of France above, together with my examination of the West that follows, suffers from a selective myopia that neglects the globality of 1968. Interpretive choices can betray events. The global turn in the study of the sixties that broke through in the early twenty-first century has reflected a return to perceptions and experiences rooted in the era itself that had been minimized during the 1970s–90s, when national and personal representations predominated. Hobsbawm's 1978 description of the three global zones of 1968 was in this sense noteworthy. We continue to relearn more about the supranational—regional and transnational—as well as, in related ways, the subnational and local dimensions of "1968."[36] The point is that reflection on the scripts of revolution in 1968 must contend with the extended duration of their enactments and the vast scale of their stagings. The meanings of 1968/"1968" emerge at the intersection of middle-term historical forces and protagonists' multifarious perceptions and experiences.

Portrayals of the sixties at the time and since have insisted on the overlap of causal factors and substantive content; in other words, the link between the *why* and *what* of "1968." In general, the sixties marked a transitional chapter in postwar world history involving an interwoven set of circumstances, social facts, and large-scale changes that Hobsbawm had partially referenced. The Cold War shifted from high tension epitomized by the 1962 Cuban Missile Crisis to détente by the early 1970s, a process enabled by regional pressures such as the Sino-Soviet split, de-Stalinization, and the limits of American containment strategy in Vietnam. Young people on both sides of the Iron Curtain rejected the stakes of atomic jeopardy, and as Jeremi Suri has argued, elites in the United States, Eastern Europe, or China shared analogous anxieties as they confronted domestic protest.[37] The postwar demographic boom, skyrocketing university enrollments, and the expansion of popular media culture, especially music and film, meant that in large parts of the world young people experienced self-consciousness about their generational identity and numerical power. Wherever televisions existed, they gave people a shared sense of belonging instantaneously to imagined global communities, making them viscerally aware of far-off economic disparity and war, and thus consequently attuned to social conflicts near at hand. The unprecedented economic boom in the postwar West called attention to differences between haves and have nots around the world; peaceful cultures of plenty contributed to rebellious youth cultures by raising expectations and senses of possibility as well as fostering guilt and disaffection with materialism (inversely, such rebellions could be seen as the tantrums of spoiled children). All the same, Hobsbawm accurately pointed to "the end of the feast," a reversal signaled by the sterling and gold crises of 1967–68 and fully underway by the Oil Crisis of 1973. In addition to antibipolarity, demographic explosion and youth culture, and economic boom and decline in the West, the sixties were also shaped by the epoch-making world-historical forces of anticolonialism and decolonization. From Latin America to Africa and the Middle East to Southeast Asia—the great symbol of the era was indeed Vietnam—challenges to European power and then the Cold War order propelled the tremors of revolutionary change around the globe. Third Worldism was a byword for internationalist ideologies such as Maoism and Castroism that reinforced imagined global communities and, as Cynthia A. Young, Quinn Slobodian, and others have shown, fed Western militancy.[38]

Such settings and scenes shape scripts. Contemporaneous perceptions of this "transnational moment of crisis and opportunity" included worldwide senses of cultural ferment, social conflict, radical political change, and global realignment that inspired "exhilaration" in some while causing distress over looming chaos in others.[39] The mainspring of social action in the sixties was indeed youth (the *who*), not only as a demographic reality but above all as individual and shared identities that gave rise to oppositional and constructive projects, antiestablishment stances dovetailing with future-oriented visions. One found rebels with causes and those without, as embodied by two notable figures of 1955 America: Jim Stark, the irreverent and aimless character played by James Dean in Nicholas Ray's *Rebel without a Cause*, and the forty-two-year-old Rosa Parks, who launched the Civil Rights Movement by refusing to give up her seat on a bus in Montgomery, Alabama. These paragons represented positions inherited in subsequent decades by countercultural actors and political radicals. Such stances could be seen as distinct—the difference in the United States between "freaks" and "rads" or in France between "the party of desire" (*les désirants*) and "neo-Leninism." Or, they intermingled—personal and interpersonal rebellion overlapping with revolutionary political transformation (cultural revolution or "the personal is political").[40]

The countercultural foregrounded quotidian experience and experimentation, alternative lifestyles, and immediate liberation. Self-fashioning via hairstyles, dress, music, drug use, "dropping out," sexual promiscuity, and so forth embodied antiestablishment performances. Hippies and communes recalled earlier intentional communities from the utopian socialist and anarchist traditions.[41] Nonconformism could be a kind of conformism, but the generalization of "adversary culture," in spite of the anxiety it provoked among an older generation, reflected the popularization of older visions of expressionist liberation previously confined to minor avant-garde and bohemian circles.[42] The tremendous informalization of authority relationships, for instance, between parents and children, teachers and students, could be read as a symptom of modernization. Countercultural turbulence did not have the same effects everywhere. In Eastern Europe tokens of American capitalism such as blue jeans and Hollywood movies often served a critical function, while Western European radicals were typically more suspicious of American culture. The counterculture had less traction in Third World countries in the process of anticolonial insurgency or postcolonial national self-formation.[43] Nevertheless, emblematizing the global scale of the counterculture was the sexual revolution, a phenomenon that involved the convergence of social facts, such as the widespread availability of birth control, and volitional acts that ran the gamut from sexual frankness to social movements based on gender and sexuality.[44] We are still grappling today with the infinite scripts unleashed by the counterculture and sexual revolution of the sixties.

Overestimating the importance of the counterculture, however, can obscure the significance of sixties political radicalism.[45] No matter the influential salience of cultural rebellion, the political is not only personal and intersubjective; it involves structures, institutions, and states. Beyond long hair and pot, therefore, antiauthoritarianism manifested itself through mass antimilitarism, anticapitalism, and antibureaucracy. Such negatory stances leaned on positive emancipatory criteria like peace, fairness, equality, social justice, diversity, and freedom. Taking many forms, radical politics in the sixties employed languages and tactics borrowed from older progressive and revolutionary social traditions (suffragism, labor, Trotskyism), shared with contemporaneous movements within imagined global communities (Third Worldism), and invented to speak to immediate circumstances (second wave feminism). Familiar debates were replayed about the relative merits of revolution versus revolt, radical action versus reform, organization versus spontaneism, and violence versus nonviolence. Many radicals in the '68 years embraced the terms of revolution: global unrest signified that a "new world was being born," a world beyond war, inequality, and arbitrary traditions and directed by "people power." The sense that large-scale changes were underway made revolution seem less a future prospect than a present reality. The presentism of "1968" both reinforced the experience of immediate contestation and created high expectations of political transformation that, if disappointed, could lead to either deeper radicalization or disillusionment. Protestors and state authorities alike took social unrest and the prospects of revolution seriously.[46] Nevertheless, the conquest of state power in most places unrealistic, "revolution" was redirected toward concrete goals such as ending the war in Vietnam and institutional contestation as well as symbolic oppositional protest and global emancipatory longings.

Although a cynic could note that the year of the barricades was closer in time to Claude-Michel Schönberg's musical *Les Misérables* (1980) than to, say, the Paris Commune of 1871, nevertheless languages and tactics drawn from historical revolutionary repertoires contributed productively to mass political movements seeking to make states and institutions accountable to people and to challenge explicit and subtle forms of oppression and injustice in the name of emancipation, fairness, and peace. To be sure, not all social movements of the era claimed to follow revolutionary scripts. Activists in the Soviet bloc found themselves challenging regimes that claimed the revolutionary mantle of 1917, a dynamic that played out in more subtle ways in England and the United States, whose revolutions lay far in a foreclosed past. Another example of radicalism without revolution was the civil disobedience of the early Civil Rights Movement in the United States, a decidedly reformist campaign compared with the ensuing revolutionary black nationalism of Malcolm X and then the Black Panthers. And yet, Martin Luther King, Jr., too, eventually called for a "revolution in values."[47]

Indeed, the *fundamental dilemma of tracking revolutionary scripts in the years before and after 1968 is that the era witnessed sea changes in the meaning of revolution itself.*

Two prominent markers of this transfiguration were the emergence of the New Left in the 1960s and the New Social Movements of the 1970s. Breaking with the social-democratic and Marxist "Old Left" emphases on labor and the working class, the New Left diversified the sites and types of emancipatory contestation.[48] American and West German experiences were noteworthy: the Students for a Democratic Society (1960), the Sozialistische Deutsche Studentenbund (1961), and the Berkeley Free Speech movement (1964) followed the Civil Rights and peace movements in insisting on citizen-led renewals of democracy through critique and social action.[49] The Port Huron Statement (1962) by the Students for a Democratic Society captured the New Left's sense of personifying a generation "bred in comfort" and yet "looking uncomfortably" upon realities of racism, the threat of atomic destruction, chaos in international relations, poverty, and so forth, realities that challenged their faith in the democratic principles on which they had been raised. Faced with complex social problems, a lack of clear alternatives, and a "yearning" to act, the collective authors of the Port Huron Statement detailed the humanistic "values" that ought to guide individuals and society: belief in every person's capacity for reason, freedom, love, and independence; relationships based on fraternity, honesty, interdependence; and nonviolent "participatory democracy." Students were uniquely situated to combat pervasive "apathy," and universities had the potential to become prominent sites for "social criticism."[50] The New Left had a broad amplitude, ranging in 1964, for example, from Herbert Marcuse's call for a "Great Refusal" of unnatural and dehumanizing capitalism to Jacek Kuron's and Karol Modzelewski's *Open Letter* to the Polish Communist Party in which they appealed for multiple political parties, an end to censorship, the right to strike, and abolishing the political police.[51] Anticapitalism and antibureaucracy were resonant positions that cut across geopolitical divides.

As in other times of heightened social conflict and protest, sixties radicalism accelerated and intensified through escalatory dynamics between, on the one hand, antiestablishment proponents of transformation and, on the other, establishment actors defending existing systems (some establishment figures—politicians, religious leaders—sympathetically identifying with the forces of change).[52] By 1968, the scale and intensity of protest movements around the world made visions formulated a few years earlier, such as the

Port Huron Statement and *Open Letter*, seem comparatively modest. Everywhere, American militarism and the Vietnam War galvanized radical action as potent symbols of Cold War intractability, economic disparity, and postcolonial possibility.[53] The International Vietnam Congress brought activists from around the world to Berlin in February 1968.[54] In the United States, unable to achieve nonviolently their goal of ending the Vietnam War (the attempt to levitate the Pentagon in October 1967 having failed), and in the wake of bloody confrontations in Chicago in August 1968, some young protestors tried to "bring the war home" by embracing violence as a tactic. The Weather Underground emerged in 1969 from a splinter faction of the Students for a Democratic Society. In Germany, Italy, and Japan, too, the perceived ineffectiveness of mass movements likewise spawned violent far-left extremism and outright terrorist campaigns.[55] Not coincidentally, perhaps, these had been the Axis powers of World War II. Guerrilla warfare tactics advanced by anticolonial figures like Mao Zedong, Ho Chi Minh, Fidel Castro, Che Guevara, and Carlos Marighella, and mediated by groups like the Black Panthers and the Popular Front for the Liberation of Palestine, were vainly implemented in relatively stable democratic industrial societies. By the early 1970s, the New Left had splintered, pulled apart by countervailing forces that included state repression (dramatically in Czechoslovakia and Mexico, more subtly in the United States),[56] self-immolating terrorism, and counterculture depoliticization.

The fracturing of New Left politics had worthwhile consequences as well. In the late 1960s and 1970s New Social Movements emerged that were organized around specific identities and agendas: age, gender, sexuality, race, ethnicity, disabilities, psychiatry, prisons, immigration, and the environment.[57] These developments intersected with countercultural emphases on everyday life and arose smoothly from the democratic ethos of the New Left in which autonomy, self-management, and diversity were principal values. Struggles against sexism, racism, and homophobia, for example, expressed the cultural-political sensibility of the personal-as-political, but they also enabled marginalized social groups to represent their interests in the public sphere. Indeed, civil-social mobilization by such groups expanded the notion and experience of what politics could mean (power infuses all social relationships), and it often pointed in reformist directions by making states and institutions the addressee of particularist demands. The proliferation of the New Social Movements also helped undermine certain revolutionary traditions, notably Marxism, whose sweeping philosophies of history and social analyses were shelved in favor of critical positions that were more "specific" and less "universal" and that proposed "micropolitics" and "molecular revolution" in lieu of grand projects of total transformation.[58]

What Hobsbawm had called the "signpost" year of 1968 indeed lay at the heart of a broader period characterized by crisis and complexity around the world and not only in iconic centers. Long-term revolutionary traditions and medium-term historical circumstances and forces were the necessary preconditions for social actors' positions. Those actors, youth and students but also intellectuals and liberal professionals (today, the creative classes), broke with earlier revolutionary templates, not least by overcoming the Old Left's fixation on working-class agency. From the counterculture to the political radicalism of the New Left, and through the dispersive fragmentation of the latter either into ineffectual violence or innovative civil-social mobilization, the sixties concluded by inscribing new types of nonrevolutionary contestatory social action.

III.

What then of scripts of revolution and 1968? Those scripts cannot be divided from representations of events that emerged in the sixties and since: the comedy of world-historical aspirations, the tragedy of disappointed hopes and fragmentation, the irony of unintended consequences and creativity. If the "beginning of a long struggle" sensibility of 1968 was almost immediately shadowed in the 1970s by a sense of "the beginning of the end"—the close of a chapter in postwar history if not a much longer age of revolution—at the same time, new forms of social, cultural, and political action emerged in the 1950s–70s that have proved durably influential for the past fifty years. These forms may have drawn from the well of revolutionary tradition, but they contributed to the expansion of nonrevolutionary styles of engagement.

The events of "1968" lay between and thus relayed two other notable scenes of postwar history: 1950s–60s anticolonialism and the end of Soviet communism in 1989–91. The untold story of sixties revolution remains how in many places anticolonial insurgency and postcolonial optimism passed into instability, civil war, authoritarianism, neocolonialism, and restrained development. Beyond their own boundlessly complex history in themselves (which I have avoided), projects of postcolonial self-determination, in playing both sides of the Cold War or rejecting the First and Second worlds together, as did the Non-Aligned Movement, powerfully affected young radicals in the West. Imagining themselves as part of global revolutionary communities facilitated criticism of their own societies, although the appeals of Third Worldism diminished as knowledge of horror in China and Cambodia spread in the 1970s. Self-criticism was evidenced in the Soviet sphere as well, post–1956 de-Stalinization opening fissures in the Iron Curtain. Until Czechoslovakian "normalization" in 1968, the reform of revolutionary-communist societies looked feasible to some. Yet in the face of intractable economic and state systems, in the 1970s the chief casualty of the moment was the notion of revolution itself. Self-criticism, in other words, itself drawn from revolutionary lexicons, helped undermine revolution as a viable historical project. Suspicions of totalizing ideologies and philosophies of history did characterize the postmodern moment in the West during the last decades of the twentieth century when the blocked repetitions of revolutionary scripts were widely noted. The emergence of human rights in the 1970s West and the persistent effects of Eastern-bloc dissidence into the 1980s were basic symptoms of this paradigm shift.[59]

And yet, the overcoming of the modern revolutionary inheritance, particularly visible in the late-twentieth-century collapse of Marxism, did yield new scripts of emancipatory social action. In some sense, "revolution happened." The informalization of authority relationships and the sexual revolution, for example, took place. As thinkers like Lefebvre, Lefort, and de Certeau had observed, events surprise, disturb, and open. To return to an earlier point, we can now see how the triangulation among transcendent events, volitional agency, and structure/antistructure played out in some ways in the decades after 1968. The events irrupted and then passed away; kept alive in memory, they came to play a role in leftist imagination analogous to that played by the Paris Commune for the European left until 1917. But finding structures adequate to the events of 1968 has proved elusive, not least in terms of representational ambiguities yielding tremendous interpretive plurality. Suspicion toward structures has become a new orthodoxy with many faces. So too, outlasting the ephemeral events of 1968 have been new traditions of political voluntarism. One of the basic revolutionary scripts transfigured in the 1950s–70s involved a politics of the will that led back through the twentieth century to Marxism-Leninism. In short, what Vladimir Lenin had denounced in 1920 as the "infantile disorder" of leftism—anarchic spontaneity, diversity, reformism—won the day against unitary, disciplined, hierarchical, party-oriented, and violent intentional projects.[60] Revolution in a Leninist sense "failed" in 1968, but it was a productive failure. The models of voluntarist, antinomian social action that emerged in the late twentieth century—from the New Social Movements and dissidence to 1989 and alter-globalization—were less Promethean than their antecedents. To be sure, politicizing or problematizing representation itself, as some partisans of the event are wont to do, walks an ambiguous line between effective antisystematic evasion and ineffectual powerlessness. To claim, as alter-globalization movements have in an explicit link to 1968, that "another world is possible" is to reject accommodation to existing states of affairs as natural or permanent but also perhaps to avoid the ambiguities, complications, and imperfections of building that new world. Pre-1968 scripts of revolution are to be avoided at all costs. Post-1968 social action reaches for a nontotalizable totality of interventions: from the personal and interpersonal to the institutional and civil-social to the state, humanity in general, and the environment. It rejects hierarchy and is leaderless, along the lines Cohn-Bendit had described in May 1968. It foregrounds values the New Left and the New Social Movements had expressed: nonviolence, participation, rights, fairness, equality, diversity, and freedom.

Many scripts of "1968" have been emphasized over the past fifty years. Inaugural in France, for example, it was "the year the dream died" in the United States.[61] Already in the 1970s, attempts were made to separate the redeemable aspects of sixties mobilization from its associated chaos and violence.[62] Narratives of success or failure in the sixties fed into later culture wars between those who championed post-traditional liberation and those who worried over moral disintegration. After 1989, the genre of justificatory personal memoire was succeeded by more judicious accounts that treated 1968 as a turning point in the recently concluded Cold War. In the late 1990s, national accounts began slowly to give way to local, regional, and global treatments that have illustrated the diversity and complexity of the sixties. Critics have consistently pointed out that the anticapitalism of many '68ers ironically helped pave the way for a "new spirit of capitalism" conducive to postindustrial service, information, and finance economies.[63] As had been the case for Hobsbawm in 1978, decennial anniversaries still occasion extensive reflection on 1968. This "past that does not want to go away" maintains a surprising currency and influence, as evidenced by controversies over 1968 during 2007–8 national elections in France and the United States.[64] Debates about the history and memory of 1968 thus generally convey a sense that the sixties "remain urgently with us"—hence the ongoing difficulty of separating the events of "1968" from their representations.[65]

Today, 1968 resonates in its multiplicity and globality. Beyond the imagined global communities constructed at the time by television and internationalist ideologies, we now are piecing together a globalism on the ground—real circulations and relationships whose contemporaneity speaks to us: Martin Luther King, Jr., touring the newly independent Ghana in 1957; the shah of Iran's 1967 visit to West Germany sparking violent protests; Columbia University students demonstrating at the New York offices of the German publisher Springer in April 1968 in response to the attempted assassination of the German radical Rudi Dutschke; the Czech writer Václav Havel witnessing student strikes at Columbia University in May–June 1968; Daniel Cohn-Bendit giving his name to the authorities upon arrest as "Kuron-Modzelewski"; graffiti in the Latin Quarter that read "Solidarity with the African-American people"; the French writer Jean Genet visiting the Black Panthers and attending the August 1968 Democratic Convention in Chicago; West German students denouncing the arrival of tanks in Prague that same month; a slogan shouted in East Germany, "Freedom for Vietnam—Freedom for Czechoslovakia."[66] The whole world is still writing.

Scripting a Revolution

Fate or Fortuna in the 1979 Revolution in Iran

Purposes mistook,
Fall'n on the inventor's heads
—*Hamlet*

Revolutions are as much political carnivals as they are mere Machiavellian scripts. They are no less the unintended consequence of "social engineering"—the dream of all historicist narratives of history—as they are sudden radical breaches brought about by the cunning, or genius, of a revolutionary mastermind. They are more akin to that rare meteorological phenomenon called the "perfect storm"—an unusual confluence of political, social, psychological factors that all but pulverizes the status quo and steers the ship of state toward the unknown "bank and shoal" of time. Hannah Arendt has argued that before the modern age, and the incumbent rise of such notions as human agency in shaping politics, the word "revolution" was in English bereft of historical or political connotations. Revolutions in those days referred only to movements of stars; in Persian, too, the word for revolution—*Engelah*—had no political connotations before the advent of the modern age. It referred to changes in mood, or material composition; it sometimes even denoted vomiting. Only in the last two centuries and the prevalence of ideas about popular will and popular sovereignty has the word "revolution" taken on its new, sociopolitical meaning.

The movement that overthrew the shah and brought Khomeini to power in 1979 has been called one of the most consequential revolutions of twentieth century—some arguing that only the 1917 Bolshevik Revolution was more traumatic in its after-shocks. About 11 percent of the total 38 million population of Iran at time participated in the revolution, compared with 7 and 9 percent in the French and Russian revolutions.[1] Slogans of the day were unmistakably democratic as well. Anywhere between 38 and

50 percent of the slogans were directed against the shah, while about 16 to 30 percent favored Khomeini personally. At best, 38 percent asked for an Islamic Republic (and none for a clerical regime).[2]

Two narratives, one secular in appearance, and the other teleological in approach, have argued that the events in Iran in 1979 were a fully scripted revolution. The Persian malady of conspiracy theories, attributing every major event in the modern history of the country to some pernicious or pious but pervasive force—God, the British, the Freemasons, the communists, the "Zionist-American" conspiracy, and more recently the "velvet revolution" conspiracy—has added poignancy to these narratives.[3]

Belief in conspiracy theories is, as Richard Hofstadter has argued, founded on a "paranoid style of politics" and exaggerated suspicions and fantasies.[4] They posit and produce a passive citizenry, willing to accept that forces outside society—someone else's "script"—shape and determine the political fate of the community.[5] A truly enfranchised citizenry, cognizant of its rights and responsibilities, is a prerequisite for democracy, but conspiracy theories absolve citizens of any role in or responsibility for their own action and their society's fate, and place all the blame on the "Other."[6] The anticolonial rhetoric of the left in Iran, with its tendency to place all the blame on the "Orientalist" or "imperialist" West, helped nurture this "nativist" tendency—one that foregoes self-criticism and responsibility, opting instead to blame the Other.[7]

Such conspiracy theories are, in a sense, the secular, albeit humiliated, articulation of the messianic proclivity found not only in Shiism but also in pre-Islamic Persian thought. In Shiism, the messiah, or Mahdi, represents Allah's will, and his bloody and apocalyptic return will bring salvation. It is, in other words, the ultimate revolution in human affairs, the real "end of History." The argument that the 1979 Revolution in Iran was a part of a divine script for History is a critical component of this messianic surmise. When societies partially secularize—as Iran did in the Pahlavi era (1925–79)—and yet citizens are deprived of political agency and free access to information, then their messianic desires easily transubstantiate into conspiracy theories—at once ridding the population of responsibility for their own fate, but also positing some "script" for any serious change.

Khomeini and his allies have often argued that their victory—as indeed all of History—is part of a divine script. All history has been, in their view, planned in the timeless eternity of Sacred Time. The Islamic Revolution was but a moment of this divine design. Only with Allah's grace, they say, and only in light of His wisdom, the shah, and his mighty army, and his mightier American supporters could be defeated. Even three decades after the revolution, clerical supporters of the regime never tire of repeating the mantra that divine designs and sacred scripts have been key reasons why the regime has survived. More than once, they have claimed that nocturnal visits from the Mahdi to the Leader (first Khomeini and then Khamenei) provide plans and guidance on how to manage the affairs of the state. On the eve of the revolution, for example, a rumor spread through the capital like a wild fire claiming that a silhouette of Khomeini has appeared on the moon; it is a heavenly affirmation of the victorious contours of the Islamic Revolution, presaging divine determinism—a "scriptural Script"—of Islam's victory.

On the other hand, the shah, whose overthrow ended monarchy in Iran, and heralded the rise of radical Islam in the country and the region, claimed more than once that the revolution against him was nothing but a script masterminded by outside conspirators. Sometimes the scribes of this concocted script were, in his mind, the communists, sometimes Western oil companies, and sometimes, remarkably, a collusion of the two. He argued that to "understand the upheaval in Iran . . . one must understand the politics of oil." He goes on to claim that as soon as he began to insist on a fair share of oil wealth for Iran, "a systematic campaign of denigration was begun concerning my government and my person . . . it was at this time that I became a despot, an oppressor, a tyrant . . . . This campaign began in 1958, reached its peak in 1961. Our White Revolution halted it temporarily. But it was begun with greater vigor in 1975 and increased until my departure."[8] What he failed to understand was that in fact it was the democratic aspirations of the Iranian people, as well as the strange confluence of often competing "Scripts"—from the sacred Shiite script to the dream (or nightmare) of a Bolshevik revival in Iran—that begot that movement. Indeed, the shah fancied himself a revolutionary, and had clearly laid out his "script" for what he called the "Shah and People Revolution." Ultimately, the social and economic policies of the sixties and seventies conducted under the banner of this revolutionary script—his version of Authoritarian modernization, with the monarch as the mastermind and vanguard of the script—helped created the urban working and middle classes and the new technocratic strata that united to overthrow him. He dismisses nearly every opposition to his rule as a tool of Western governments, or of communists, to bring pressure on him.[9]

In a meeting with the shah in October of 1978, the British ambassador offered a surprisingly frank and insightful analysis of the essential elements of the shah's aborted "script" and why, as a result, Iran was in turmoil and the regime in crisis. The shah, Anthony Parsons said, "had kept the country under severe discipline for 15 years while he had pursued his policy of rapid modernization. It was inevitable that when this discipline was relaxed, there would be a violent release of popular emotion. Thanks to the fact that the modernization program had ridden rough shod over the traditional forces in Iran, and thanks to the inequalities of wealth and appalling social conditions for the urban poor which had resulted from the boom, it was not surprising that this wave of emotion had become a wave of opposition."[10] In an earlier meeting, Parsons referred to the "massive influx into the cities from the rural areas," creating a "rootless urban proletariat of dimensions hitherto unknown in Iran." They had nothing to look forward to, and "in this state of mind, it was natural for them to turn back to their traditional guides and leaders, the religious hierarchy."[11]

The shah ignored the task of socializing this new urban class into the ethos of modernity. Nor was he willing to share power with them or the burgeoning middle classes. According to a CIA profile of the shah, he believed democracy "would impede economic development" in Iran.[12] In his "script" for what he called "The Shah and People Revolution," he would deliver social and economic improvements in the lives of the people but would himself determine when the democratic component of the script would be allowed to take root. In other words, he overdetermined the economic elements of the script he had for modernizing Iran—he wanted to help change the very fabric of life, yet keep intact the structure of despotic power. In a sense, long before the Chinese model of offering economic liberalization in lieu of democracy became a subject of curiosity and theoretical contemplation, the shah was, albeit inadvertently, trying to walk down the same path.

This shah's "majestic failure,"[13] some believed, was not just the result of an incongruent, historically untenable script, but also at least partially the result of the chasm that separated the shah's persona from his personality. He was, in the words of the Ann Lambton, the eminent British scholar, "a dictator who could not dictate,"[14] a weak and vacillating man who pretended to have the authoritarian disposition of his charismatic father. Another diplomat described him as a Hamlet-like character. He went from arrogant dismissal of his opponents to paralysis in the face of their strength. In 1978, faced with the first signs of massive discontent, the shah shrugged it off, claiming dismissingly that the cooks in his army could defeat the opposition. According to the CIA, the shah had a concept of "himself as a leader with a divinely blessed mission to lead his country from years of stagnation . . . to a major power, supported by a large military establishment."[15] But then, virtually overnight, he went from this haughty disposition to abject submission to not only the advice from American and British ambassadors, but also the advice of innumerable political figures, some from the ranks of the hitherto stymied opposition, who were invited to the court and offered him advice on how to contain the wrath of the people.

The anomalies of this script seem more remarkable when understood in the context of the monarchy's history at the moment he ascended the throne in 1941. By then, for more than a century, the institution of Iranian monarchy had been clearly in a historic crisis. In Europe, the crisis had been even older. In Iran, since mid-nineteenth century every king, save one, had been either assassinated or forced to live his last years eating "the bitter bread of banishment." The sole exception to this tragic pattern, the only king who died in Iran and peacefully, was Mozzafer-al Din Shah, who, not coincidentally, was the potentate who signed the decree marking the victory of the 1905–7 constitutional revolution. In Europe, too, the only monarchies that have survived what scholars have called the first, second, and third waves of democracy were those willing to accept a simply ceremonial role for the king.[16]

The last Iranian reminder of monarchy's institutional crisis was the fate of the shah's own father, who was forced to abdicate and died in exile, forlorn and heartbroken. It was a clear indication of the shah's concept of power that in spite of this historic crisis, and in spite of the fact that to celebrate twenty-five hundred years of monarchy in Iran, he commissioned twenty-five hundred books chronicling the accomplishments of his regime, he did not even once try to commission a serious substantive book that offered a convincing argument on either the merits of monarchy for the modern age, or the necessity for his style of authoritarianism—treatises that would try to answer the question of why monarchy is the best regime for Iran in the twentieth century and why authoritarianism the sole structure of power that can realize the social changes he envisioned. The failure to foster such an argument reveals the shah's strangely premodern "divine right" conception of power. His first memoir was called *Mission for My Country,* and in it he unabashedly made the claim that his rein was divine in origin, and his decisions divine in inspiration.[17] He claimed that Shiite saints saved his life three times. It was, he believed, simply "natural" for Iranians to accept his absolutist power—one he believed also enjoyed Allah's anointment.

In contrast, during the age when the British monarchy was experiencing a similar crisis, rooted in the political challenge of modernity, British kings and queens either wrote themselves or commissioned others to write virtually hundreds of monographs, essays, and books in defense of monarchy.[18] James I himself wrote dozens of treatises arguing why monarchy is the best system possible for England. The shah, in stark comparison, never articulated a theory about how and why monarchy can survive in the modern age. Moreover, in spite of evidence that in modern societies, monarchies survive only as a symbol of national unity in an otherwise democratic polity, the shah insisted on rapidly modernizing Iran while at the same time insisting that only his authoritarian rule could bring about the requisite changes in the country. He wagered on what he believed was a monarchist spirit ingrained in Iranian culture, and when he lost his bet, he blamed foreign scripts for the revolution. The script he wrote for the revolution he championed eventually begot the very forces that refused to accept his continued stewardship of the society.

By the time the shah realized he had been wrong in his assessment of this *Geist*, when he finally understood the incongruence of his script, the armed forces were in disarray, its generals were in despair, and the opposition was emboldened by what they perceived was the West's new critical disposition toward the shah. The concessions the regime had already made further encouraged the opposition. As is often the case with revolutionary movements, every concession by the beleaguered regime only fed the emboldened opposition's appetite for more, and in a vicious circle that ends with the collapse of the status quo, every concession also undermined the regime's cohesion and ability to survive. Compounding this process was the fact that in a gesture of appeasement the shah ordered the arrest of some of his staunchest allies—for example, his prime minister of thirteen years, Amir Abbas Hoveyda[19]—while freeing virtually all the almost four thousand political prisoners in the country. While the latter brought discipline, militancy, and experience to the ranks of the opposition, the arrest of regime stalwarts disheartened the royalist ranks. Champions, guardians, and enforcers of the old scripted "revolution from the top" were in disarray, while myriad advocates of new scripts and blueprints were every day more emboldened in their aspirations for engineering a new future for Iran.

While the shah had believed he could use the promise of economic incentives and a rising standard of living to induce the moderate middle classes into accepting his authoritarian modernization, scholars and diplomats commonly believed that, in reality, it was the power of the military and the increasingly Procrustean demands of SAVAK—the Persian acronym for the country's security and intelligence organization—that ensured the shah's ability to survive. Now the military was in disarray and its leaders either increasingly doubted the shah's capacity for leadership, or on rare occasions were seeking to make a "deal" with the opposition. By the end of 1978, the number of deserters in the military was also rapidly rising. The stories of alleged "betrayal" by generals were also aplenty. Surely by the time the shah's fall seemed imminent, some of his generals, sometimes encouraged by the US embassy, tried to make their peace with the opposition.

But all too many royalists, including the shah, have concocted fantastic conspiracies that posit that a foreign scripted "revolution" overthrew the shah. They claim, for example, that charismatic officers, such as a one-time commander of the Iranian Air Force, were killed a few years before the revolution, lest they come to the shah's support and disrupt the scripted revolution.[20] In other words, the script had been at least several years in the making. Accusations against General Hussein Fardust, for fifty years one of the shah's closest friends and confidants, were easily the most fantastic of these allegations.[21] He has been accused of everything from working with foreign intelligence agencies to secretly cooperating with Khomeini to overthrow the shah. The myth of fully scripted revolutions—whether sacred or profane—invariably needs not just an omnipotent architect but also a master villain, a Rasputin. And General Fardust became the perfect foil, the Rasputin incarnate, for this script. President Carter's decision to send General Huyser to Iran without telling the shah has added fuel to the royalist rage against America's alleged role in creating this script and neutralizing the military.[22]

In spite of the role his own policies had in the creation of the crisis, the shah felt betrayed not just by the West but also by the people of Iran. The authoritarian system the shah had established placed him as the sole "decider" for nearly every major economic, political, and military decision in the country. As a report by the State Department's Bureau of Intelligence and Research made clear, "the Shah is not only king, he is de facto prime minister and is in operational command of the armed forces. He determines or approves all important governmental actions. No appointment to an important position in the bureaucracy is made without his approval. He personally directs the work of the internal security apparatus and controls the conduct of foreign affairs, including diplomatic assignment. No promotion in the armed forces from the rank of lieutenant up can be made without his explicit approval. Economic development proposals—whether to accept foreign credit or where to located a particular factory—are referred to the Shah for decision. He determines how the universities are administered, who is to be prosecuted for corruption, the selection of parliamentary deputies, the degree to which the opposition will be permitted, and what bills will pass the parliament."[23] In 1978 his failing health, caused by the onset of cancer, his deteriorating mood, brought about by his sense of abandonment by his allies and by the people of Iran, and finally the indecisions that he had shown all his life when faced with a crisis all combined to render him incapable of making any decisions. As a result, the entire machinery of the state came to a grinding halt. The shah felt that the West's decision to allow Iran to fall into the hands of what he called a group of "Marxists, terrorists, lunatics and criminals" was a betrayal that far exceeded "the giveaway at Yalta."[24]

By the time the United States and England had decided that the shah was not likely to survive—by the time they realized that their script of fighting a communist revolution through alliance with authoritarian allies was no longer working—they both decided that, in the words of the British prime minister, they "should start thinking about reinsuring."[25] When they began to "reinsure" and tried to establish ties with leaders of the opposition, the only force they found that could, in their judgment, keep the country from chaos or falling into the Soviet orbit was Khomeini and his coterie of clerics. Khomeini's ability to assume such a position was, to no small measure, the unintended consequence of the shah's own warped script for the "controlled revolution" he espoused.

In the months leading to the collapse of the shah's regime, Khomeini had grabbed the mantle of a populist leader and instead of espousing his own true intentions—namely, the realization of what he believed were the contours of a Divine Script for Iran—he took on the ideological guise befitting the leader of a democratic movement. He outmaneuvered all his allies: some in the left believed him to be a Kerensky. He will, they surmised, will be a useful tool to use against the shah and then can easily be dislodged. In fact, the real Khomeini was—in his steely determination and his ability to offer, dependent on exigencies of the moment, minimalist and maximalist scripts for change—more akin to Lenin. Many took solace in the assumption that Khomeini's zany ideas were ill fitted to the complexities of Iranian society; he could never, they assumed, create a Sharia-ruled society in Iran. Still others were mesmerized by his charisma, and a final group was co-opted by the promise of a share of power after the revolution. In reality, most democrats believed that "the ascending of mullahs" will be a "passing phase . . . as they are not equipped to handle complex affairs."[26] Iranian democrats, as well as the Marxists, were children of modernity and both imbued with the spirit of Enlightenment. To them, religion was either an "opium of the masses" or at best a relic of a bygone era when revelation ruled reason. Modernity, both Marxist and liberal democratic paradigms of History assumed, had ushered in the age of reason, and pushed what remained of religion to the private sphere.[27] Science and rationality would, advocates of modernity surmised, eclipse revelation and superstition.

But Khomeini and his cohorts not only proved adept at handing "complex affairs" but also had elaborate designs of re-establishing the age of revelation and dismissing as flawed the rule of reason in human affairs, particularly in the realm of law and jurisprudence.

From his first book in Persian, written in the aftermath of the fall of Reza Shah, to the collection of his sermons on an Islamic government, compiled by his students in Najaf in the late sixties, Khomeini had offered the essential outlines of a script to the changes that would usher in his mind the only genuine form of government is the absolute rule of the jurist who rules not in the name of the people and for the goal of democracy but for implementing Islamic Sharia.[28] He called the theory *Velayat-e Faqih*, or the rule of the jurist. Even in the annals of Shiite history, Khomeini's view was a minority, espoused by only a handful of ayatollahs.[29] In reality, the top Shiite clerics of Iran had, in 1905, sided with the constitutionalists, and the top clergy at the time, Ayatollah Nai'ni, had argued that before the return of the Twelfth Imam (now in Occultation), democracy is the best form of government. A minority of clerics in 1905 sided with Ayatollah Nouri, who advocated the establishment of an Islamic state, according to Allah's sacred script, and according to Sharia.[30] In the months leading to the revolution, however, Khomeini never referred to his own concept of *Velayat-e Faqih*. The fact that the shah and his SAVAK had banned Khomeini's books for decades made them unavailable to Iranian readers or critics.

In the months before the revolution, Khomeini exhibited exemplary discipline and not only did not refer to *Velayat-e Faqih* but repeated more than once that the next government after the shah would be democratic and that the clergy would have no role in any of its political institutions. There will be freedom for all, and coercion on none, he promised more than once. He could certainly find passages in the *Qur'an* to support this liberal proposition. For long, now, it has been known that *Qur'anic* verses have different dispositions. While some scholars have divided the verses into four distinct phases and categories, it is more commonly agreed that these verses can be divided into two groups: those composed while the prophet was in the city of Mecca, where he had few followers, and the verses are tolerant in attitude and poetic in tone. Those composed in Medina, where Mohammad was the head of state, were stern in disposition and tone. In Paris, Khomeini opted more for Meccaean verses. He quoted the verse in the *Qur'an* that conjures Jefferson's views on religious freedom: "There is no coercion in matters of faith."[31] Khomeini even claimed in an interview on 7 November 1978 that "personal desire, age and my health, and do not allow me to personally have a role in running the country." On the same day, he told the German *Die Spiegel* that "our future society will be a free society, and all the elements of oppression, cruelty and force will be destroyed." A few days earlier, on 25 October, he had said, "the ranking Shiite religious clergyman do not want to govern in Iran themselves," promising at the same time that women will "be free . . . in the selection of their activities, and their future and their clothing."[32] At the same time, unbeknownst to much of the world, in Tehran he had already appointed a few trusted clerics—nearly all his students in earlier years—to a covert "Revolutionary Committee" that managed the day-to-day affairs of the movement against the shah. In short, instead of openly articulating a "divine design," or sacred script, in the months before the revolution, Khomeini used a combination of guile, dissimulation—what Shiites call *Taqiyeh*, or useful lies in the service of the faith and the faithful—and steely resolve to master the otherwise inchoate democratic coalition that helped topple the shah. His other allies, each with an imagined script of their own, emphasized only those aspects of Khomeini's carefully crafted words and messages that confirmed their own designs and desires for the future of Iran.

About six months after Khomeini's return home, contrary to his Paris promises, the US embassy in Tehran reported that he and a handful of clerics in Qom were "now making decisions on all matters of importance including public security, the press, commerce and the military."[33] In Iran, seeing the fractured, feuding, and relatively weak democratic forces, and realizing how quixotic the different Marxist groups were in trying in realize in Iran their version of a Chinese, Russian, Cuban, or even Albanian model of socialism, Khomeini gradually laid bare the true nature of his envisioned script of creating a theocracy. Using a militant anti-Americanism as a motto to neutralize or co-opt many among the radical forces of the Iranian left—foremost among them the Soviet-backed Tudeh Party and the Maoist Ranjbaran Party—and finally, using the chaos and crisis caused by

Saddam Hussein's decision to attack Iran and the occupation of the American embassy by his ardent student supporters, Khomeini used a pliant Constituent Assembly to pass not the promised democratic constitution but a new one founded on his ideas about *Velayat-e Fagih*. It was a constitution in which he was granted more despotic powers than arguably any despot in any constitutional government, and certainly more than the shah he had just replaced. It was, in the words of one scholar, "the constitution of the hierocratically oriented Islamist camp, the product of a social stratum which, in the decades of modernization had been forced to relinquish more and more of its positions of power and were, after the revolution able to expand a scarcely hoped for historical chance not only to retrieve lost ground but to realize not ever dared to speak of openly in bygone centuries."[34] Before long, Khomeini introduced the concept of *Maslahat* (expedience)—allowing him, or his successor to trump divine laws of Sharia, if the expedience of the Islamic regime demanded it. The new script, in other words, was no longer simply realizing divine laws but followed—and has been following—anything expedient for the preservation of the postrevolutionary status quo. Surprising as these developments were to many, the fact that change was inevitable in Iran in the 1970s was in retrospect hard to ignore.

As early as 1958, the CIA and the State Department were convinced that unless something drastic was done in the realms of politics and economy, Iran was heading toward a revolution. In September of 1958, the National Security Council met to discuss a new "Special National Intelligent Estimate" which claimed that the shah's regime "is not likely to last long." It was decided that the United States must work hard to "convince the Shah that the most immediate threat to his regime lies in internal instability rather than external aggression."[35] He must, in other words, reduce his "preoccupation with military matters," and focus more on social development. The shah was to be pressed for prompt, "meaningful, political, social and economic reforms." The main opposition to the shah was said to be "the growing educated middle class" discontent with "Iran's antiquated feudal structure and the privileges of the ruling classes."[36] They were further angered by the corruption of the military, political, and civil service authorities, including members of the royal family and the shah himself. It was further decided that should the shah resist these proposed changes, the United States should take immediate steps toward "developing appropriate contacts with emerging non-communist groups."[37] Unless there was a controlled revolution toward democracy and a market economy from the top, the US was convinced, a radical revolution from the bottom, one that might benefit the Soviet Union, would be inevitable. As early as 1966, the State Department's Bureau of Intelligence and Research "pointed to basic difficulties for the Shah . . . . It appears likely that the Shah will confront a choice between allowing greater participation in government or seriously risking a fall from power."[38] Much the same language was used in 1978 to describe why the shah fell.

The changes the shah brought about, beginning in 1961—the "controlled revolution" urgently encouraged by the Kennedy administration— altered the economic and political face of Iran and the foundations of the shah's basis of support. A market economy replaced the semifeudalism of the postwar years. While these changes were, in themselves, enough to help create new urban and middle classes, the sudden rise in the price of oil in the late sixties and early seventies only accelerated the process. The shah had long believed that unless he led such a "controlled revolution," chaos and radicalism would be unavoidable. For long, the CIA had concluded that "Mohammad Reza Pahlavi is incapable of taking necessary actions to implement" such needed changes.[39] In reality, the shah proved more than capable of bringing about the necessary economic components of these changes. But the more he succeeded in the economic component of this controlled scripted revolution, the more he was unwilling to accept what had been all along the political correlate of these changes—namely, sharing power with moderate forces.

When the State Department talked of middle-class and moderate opposition to the shah, they meant more than any group the National Front, created by Mossadeq in 1949. Although the United States was involved in the overthrow of the Mossadeq government in 1953—for many the "original sin" of US policy in Iran—from the late fifties, the US policy changed and it began to see Mossadeq's followers as the harbingers of democracy and political reform in Iran. From 1959 the shah was under pressure from the United States to reconcile with this group. In 1978, on the eve of the revolution, those pressures reached new heights.

But the secular National Front leadership ultimately decided against making peace with the shah, first in 1962 and then again in 1978. In 1962 the memory of 19 August 1953 and the fall of Mossadeq were fresh on their minds. Their leader, Dr. Mossadeq, was still under virtual house arrest and barred from taking part in politics. Although they were ostensibly representatives of Iran's moderate middle class, the leaders of the National Front preferred the puritan politics of uncompromising opposition to the shah over the pragmatic realism of unity with a weakened shah. In fact, in 1978 the National Front leadership not only refused to form a national unity government but also blocked and succeeded in defeating efforts by two of their own leaders—Gholam-Hussein Sadiqi and Shapour Bakhtiyar—who saw clerical despotism on the horizon and were ready to form a secular coalition government that would avert the revolution. Karim Sanjabi, the presumptive leader of the National Front in 1978, decided to defer leadership of the movement to Khomeini. When he traveled to Paris, on his way to a convention of socialist parties of the world, he met with Khomeini and abdicated all pretense of leading an independent secular movement. In a communiqué he issued after his meeting with Khomeini (a statement Khomeini refused to sign, lest the august secular leader develop delusions that he was on par with the ayatollah), he accepted not only Khomeini's leadership but also the increasing role of Islam in shaping the ideology of the movement. Upon his return to Tehran, Sanjabi told the shah "that no solution would work without a green light from Khomeini," and the ayatollah would no longer accept anything short of the shah's abdication.[40] In the National Front's imagined script, Khomeini needed them to run the machinery of state, and inexorably the power of the bureaucracy they would manage would afford them the ability and power to push aside Khomeini from the helm. They hoped that Khomeini would be Gandhi, whereas the Ayatollah had Savonarola on his mind.

The failure of the National Front to realize their goals was not entirely the fault of their zeal for puritan politics. The shah, too, had been for years adamantly opposed to the idea of reconciliation. Even in 1978, faced with the end of his dynasty, he was less than enthusiastic about forming such a coalition. In June 1978, in a private meeting with British officials, in describing his decision to liberalize he went on "vitriolic denunciations of the old National Front" and made it clear that they were beyond "the lines of political acceptability."[41] Later on, when he had no choice but to seek—indeed beseech from a much weakened position—a coalition with some of these leaders, he refused to abide by the key demands of the two leaders who had, independently of each other, agreed to form a coalition. The first was Gholam Hussein Sadiqi, who had predicated his willingness to form a cabinet on the condition that the shah stay in Iran. The shah refused, telling Sadiqi that the Americans "want me out."

The shah also undermined the chances of survival of the second leader, Shapur Bakhtiyar, who actually did form such a government. It was clear that his survival depended to no small measure on his ability to keep the military together and on his side. But the shah rejected the requests of the one man who was, possibly, in a position to achieve that critical goal. His name was Fereydoon Jam. He was a charismatic officer, a one-time brother-in-law of the shah, and for a while the chairman of Iran's Joint Chiefs of Staff. He was forced to resign when he showed too much independence. In late 1978, he was asked to return to Iran from his sinecure as Iran's ambassador to Spain. He was now the top candidate to assume the post of minister of war in the new coalition cabinet. He met with the shah and demanded the operational command of the armed forces. Although the shah was already planning to leave Iran, he in fact "stubbornly insisted not only [on] retaining his role . . . of commander-in-chief . . . but also on controlling the military budget."[42] Jam left Iran in disgust. It took the military thirty-six days before it turned against Bakhtiar and made peace with the mullahs who seemed poised to take over the reins of power.

In spite of Iran's rapid economic growth, by 1975 not only members of the bazaar—the traditional heart of trade in Iran and a source of support for democratic change in modern Iran, and by then increasingly disgruntled and economically marginalized by Iran's new emerging industrial and financial bourgeoisie—but even members of that emergent modern industrialist class were disgruntled with the status quo. A speech to the senate by Gassem Lajevardi, a scion of one of the most important industrialist families in Iran and at the time himself a senator, embodied this disgruntlement. What Lajevardi discretely demanded was more democracy and rule of law as a way to guarantee long-term stability to Iran.[43]

The speech was important from a different perspective. There was an unwritten contract between the shah and Iran's entrepreneurial class, particularly those in modern sectors. They would not engage in politics and accept the shah's absolute leadership; in return they could count on the government's probusiness policies. For two decades, buoyed by rising oil prices, the covenant worked. Iran witnessed impressive socioeconomic growth. Iran was in fact among the fastest growing developing economies in the world. But the covenant came back to haunt the regime and the entrepreneurial class when the system went into a crisis. The entrepreneurs, in 1978, were either critical of the shah or politically inactive, impotent, and unable to successfully defend the regime or their own investments. To what extent did the shah's constant conjuring of revolutionary rhetoric make the idea and concept of revolution an accepted part of the Iranian political discourse? How much did his grandiose promises of rising standards of living, of surpassing Germany and Japan, fuel the population's rising expectations and contribute to the classical J-curve of expectations rising faster than the government's ability to satisfy them?[44] In other societies, the word "revolution" brings to mind cataclysmic changes. By 1978, the word had been a constant part of Iran's political vocabulary for almost two decades.

During his days of power, the shah had followed a political scorched earth policy, eliminating or curtailing not just his radical opponents but even moderate critics. Prudent moderates, advocating reform and democracy, as well as radical advocates of change from every political persuasion were shunned or barred from politics. The shah believed that the clergy— with the few exceptions of Khomeini supporters—were his reliable allies in the fight against communists or secular nationalists. His scorched earth policy left the clergy and their vast nimble network of organizations an opportunity to grow, and dominate the public domain. Moreover, Assadollah Alam, the powerful court minister for more than a decade before the revolution, constantly reminded the shah that in 1963, when Alam was the prime minister, he had successfully "deracinated" radical clergy like Khomeini. Alam had used the might of the military to suppress the 5 June 1963 uprising of Khomeini supporters—an event considered by many scholars as the dress rehearsal for the 1979 Revolution. Alam convinced the shah that those clerics still left in Iran after Khomeini's exile in 1964 had no choice but to support the shah and were not "important enough" to pose a threat.[45] The more the moderate clergy were ignored, the easier it became for Khomeini and his radical allies to gain and consolidate hegemony over religious forces in Iran.[46] As a result, when the regime went into a crisis in 1977, the clerical network, led by Khomeini, gradually emerged as the sole alternative to the shah.

Ironically, in 1973, as Iran's economy was rapidly growing, for a fleeting moment the shah realized that maybe the time for some political change had arrived. He asked to meet with Mehdi Samii—one of Iran's most respected technocrats, with extensive connections among the country's moderate political forces—and some of the leaders of the National Front. The shah told Samii of his worries about the future, and about the "problem of transition"—particularly after his death—and asked Samii to form a new political party that would indeed succeed in soliciting the support of the Iranian educated middle classes. For almost five months Samii met regularly with the shah, discussing and setting out the parameters of what the new party would be allowed to do. It would have been a loyal opposition party, a centrist party with hints of social democratic ideas in its proposed platform. But then the price of oil suddenly quadrupled, and in Samii's words, "suddenly His Majesty changed his mind, and pulled the plug on the party."[47] Instead of facilitating the creation of such a centrist democratic party, the shah opted for the disastrous idea of a one-party system. All other parties were dismantled in favor of the new Rastakhiz (resurgence) Party. The new Resurgence was a stillborn monster and an immediate source of discontent, even ridicule. Some think that the idea came to him from Sadat in Egypt; others point the finger to a group of five, mostly American-trained technocrats who suggested the one-party system based on Huntington's prescription for political development in developing countries.[48] Whatever the source, the idea was a political liability and added to the already brewing sense of discontent. It was, in a sense, the shah's effort to complete the political component of the script he had imagined for his revolution: he would use authoritarianism to introduce modernization, and he would use a centrist party, composed of technocrats but beholden to him, to control the "problem of transition" he knew was on the horizon. Yet the curse of oil changed his mind, leading him to opt instead for a one-party system. Moreover, his misguided effort to use the one-party system to solve this problem of transition and political participation could not have come at a worse time.

Not long after the creation of the party, the Carter administration came to power, ending the Nixon-era ban on pressuring the shah to democratize. Moreover, in the last years of the Nixon administration and for nearly much of the Ford administration, Iran and the United States were fighting a quiet war of diplomacy on the price of oil. Eventually, the US made a covert pact with Saudi Arabia to stabilize the price of oil. Some scholars have even claimed that the vagaries of oil prices precipitated the fall of the shah.[49] Just as Iran's revenues failed to reach the projected rise, the Carter administration resumed pressure on the shah to democratize and liberalize. The timing could not have been more inauspicious: the shah was sick and the economy was in a downturn. The normal instabilities that accompany any authoritarian regime's attempt to democratize only augmented the effects of the economic crisis. By 1978, Iran's "GNP growth in real terms dropped to 2.8 Percent." This recessionary slowdown was exacerbated by unusually high inflationary rates. Like much of the West, Iran too faced the strange hybrid phenomenon of "stagflation." Some in the US Congress began to worry about Iran's budgetary priorities (and the fact that in line with the shah's views, precedence was given to matters military over social needs). These anxieties led to ideas to "link Iran's human rights performance with arms transfer."[50] It is hard not to be tempted to ask what might have happened in Iran if the Congress had developed such a matrix a decade earlier, when Nixon had given the shah his now famous "carte blanche" to buy any non-nuclear weapon system he desired. But in 1978, such a matrix was just one more indication to the Iranian opposition that the shah's position was precarious and vulnerable. The shah's deteriorating emotional and physical condition along with these other factors combined to create the perfect storm that was the revolution.

Even this unusual constellation of stars might not have guaranteed the revolution's victory. In the last two years of his rule, in each moment of crisis, the shah made arguably the worst possible choice. He showed weakness when he was supposed to be strong, and he feigned power when he in fact had none. The reason for this remarkable series of errors was not tactical but strategic, rooted in his view that the whole revolution was a conspiracy of outside forces—a misguided but masterfully planned foreign script. He changed his mind about who masterminded the script but never wavered in the belief that it was the causal root of the revolution. Even in his last book, *Answer to History,* written in exile and long after he had been "un-kinged," he argues, with surprising certainty, that it was a conspiracy of Western and communist forces that overthrew him.

When the shah sought for the domestic sources of the revolution, he had a myopic vision. He concluded that he should have exercised more authoritarianism and not less. "Today, I have come to realize that the events of 1978–9 are attributable in part to the fact that I moved too rapidly in opening the doors of the universities, without imposing more severe preliminary selection. The entrance exams were too easy."[51] He calls the students "spoiled children" who helped wreak havoc on Iran.

In short, then, a complicated combination of factors—the shah's myopic vision, his scorched earth policy, his decision to use religion as a bulwark against communism, his vacillations in times of crisis, the oppositions' delusions about the role of religion in modern times and about their own ability to realize their revolutionary scripts, and finally Khomeini's ability to hide his true intentions in the months before the fall of the shah—helped to determine the contours of the 1979 Revolution. Instead of searching for one "Script," we are faced with myriad scripts, some aborted, some begetting unexpected consequences, and some falling prey to their own utopian illusions-turned-nightmares (as when they praised as revolutionary the work of Khomeini-appointed Islamic courts that summarily executed hundreds of members of the ancient regime, only to feel the devastating consequences of these courts themselves a few months later when they were used against the opposition.) In thinking about a complex historic event like the Islamic Revolution of 1979 in Iran, then, we might be better served if we heed Tom Stoppard's advice when he says, "the unpredictable and the predetermined unfold together to make everything the way it is."[52] His brilliant *Coast of Utopia*, with its account of Russian intellectuals' voyage on their way to a revolution and their shipwreck and salvage, could, with minor changes, be read as a prehistory of the illusions and dangers of Iranian social engineers, of every political hue, bent on forcing their scripts on the contours of life.[53]

The Multiple Scripts of the Arab Revolutions

Introduction

The early days of the Arab uprisings awakened not only an assumedly "passive" Arab public but also the imaginations of observers and scholars of the region who had long internalized the "fact" of authoritarian durability in the region.[1] The very term used to describe the uprisings—the "Arab Spring"—captures the universally positive and future-oriented assessment of the events.[2] With the Reign of Terror of the French Revolution and the violent revolutions of the twentieth century that resembled it replaced in the historical imagination by the relatively peaceful, popular, and sovereignty-restoring revolutions in Eastern Europe of the end of the century, this euphoria was understandable. In fact, as many scholars have pointed out, not only did the claims of Arab revolutionaries appear similar—initial calls for reform turned into demands for the overthrow of the regime and establishment of democracy—but in some cases they were in direct contact with Eastern European revolutionaries, adopting their script and protest methods.[3]

While they may be useful, I argue that these comparisons with previous popular revolutions obscure distinct features of the Arab revolutions. As in the Eastern European revolutions, "popular sovereignty" and "democracy" remained the preferred concepts of revolutionaries of all stripes, but just weeks—and often days—after the revolutionary unrest began in each country, different parties became convinced that their own understanding of these terms was fundamentally different from that of their corevolutionaries. In reality, no revolutionary group had a coherent ideology in terms of a programmatic plan for a future political system, and different groups within the Arab Uprisings had distinct and usually incompatible values, such as secularism, moderate Islamism, and Salafism.[4] In the absence of ideological coherence concerning what it was that the revolution should achieve, Arab revolutionaries set aside these differences (in fact, mentioning them was tantamount to betraying the revolution) for one of the few aspects on which they all agreed: the overthrow of the regime and the rejection of paternalistic personification of the state in one man.

This chapter proceeds in three parts. First, I briefly discuss the historical meaning(s) of revolution in order to establish the context for comparison with the Arab Uprisings, drawing on previous work that examines the role of ideology and the goals of historical revolutionary movements.[5] While practically no revolution has occurred without its ideology being fraught with contradictions, many of these ideological fights occurred *within* a largely shared revolutionary worldview. Additionally, revolutions tended to represent either: (a) a relatively brief period of revolt in the name of popular sovereignty followed by the consolidation of a new regime that signaled the end of the revolution (such as the Eastern European revolutions), or (b) the beginning of an arduous and ambitious project of social and political transformation without an end in sight (such as the French Revolution after 1792, the communist revolutions of the twentieth century, and many of the Middle Eastern regimes since the 1950s).[6] In the second part, I look more closely at the recent Egyptian and Yemeni revolutions and argue that while they appear similar to the first type, ideological fights *between* different revolutionary groups over visions of the future political system suggest that "genuine popular sovereignty" is not necessarily a shared demand as it was in Eastern Europe, and a system that would support it has yet to be achieved. Finally, I consider how, despite these contradictions, the failure for any single revolutionary group to claim revolutionary authority over others may make it possible for genuine popular sovereignty to succeed inadvertently. I therefore conclude that in this situation, discord is a valuable antidote to utopian excess or potential for a French-style millenarian revolution.[7]

The Historical Meaning(s) of Revolution

As for most studies of social phenomena, the alleged causes of revolutions are multiple and subject to constant dispute.[8] However, whether the focus is on structural, economic, social, organizational, or more "subjective" and ideological causes, there is one aspect of the study of revolution that has been very consistent: current political theories of revolution have a terrible track record at predicting when a revolution will occur. In fact, revolutionaries themselves are often caught by surprise by the timing of a revolution, when their tiny opposition suddenly mushrooms into a crushing majority.[9] Nevertheless, periods prior to a revolution are often preceded by either an overt and widespread "revolutionary culture"—as was the case with the outright revolutionary struggles of the Bolshevik and other communist revolutions—or select groups within countries try to capture social dissatisfaction or incite protest through various clandestine activities, as was the case with the French and Eastern European revolutions. In other words, the *timing* of the revolution may come as a complete surprise to actors and observers alike, but in retrospect it is possible to identify an uncrystallized revolutionary consciousness that needed a particular spark to switch from the level of conception to that of voluntative action.[10]

The political idiom in French discourse prior to the revolution of 1789 was replete with references to Locke, Sidney, Gordon, Hutcheson, and other social contract theorists whose work was associated with questions of classical republicanism, debates about the role of government, and discussions of the rights of man and rights of resistance.[11] While the role of these thinkers as a direct cause of the development of a revolutionary consciousness can be debated, their influence is clear in the vocabulary of the revolutionaries, such as in the "Declaration of the Rights of Man and of the Citizen" adopted by the French National Constituent Assembly.[12] Echoing Locke, the second article of the treatise codifies specifically the "natural and imprescriptible rights of man" and "resistance to oppression."[13] This does not mean, however, that this particular political discourse represented the entirety of the political vocabulary in the period leading up to the revolution. Such discourse had occupied French political space for decades prior to the upheaval, and when the revolution started the intellectual competition over which vision of government would dominate was fought predominantly within the confines delimited by it. The French debate, then, was not whether the "natural rights of man" or his "right of resistance" were legitimate claims, but rather which political system—representative or direct democracy—was best suited to achieve those goals. It could be argued, in fact, that this singular obsession with the achievement of the "natural rights of man"—which are, by definition, universal and cannot be fulfilled only in part—abetted the transformation of the concept of revolution during the course of the French Revolution from achievement of popular sovereignty (a discrete event) in its initial stages to unrestrained government authority over future political and social transformations (an ongoing effort) after 1792.[14]

The twentieth-century successors of the French Revolution—the communist revolutions—began as self-consciously ambitious processes that would require decades, and even generations, to achieve. Also, like the French Revolution, these revolutions were preceded by decades of political discourse charged with ideological debate. This time, however, discussion constellated not around the "rights of man" in the Lockean tradition, but different interpretations of Marx's theories of politics and economics and various ways of achieving a proletarian utopia. The details of these ideological debates are beyond the scope of this chapter, but it suffices to point out that these revolutions as well were preceded by a rich political culture that dictated to a large extent the nature of the revolutionary government that followed the overthrow of the old regime.

Finally, even though the electrifying collapse of the Eastern European regimes of 1989 "astonished even the most seasoned political observers," the type of regime that was called for as a replacement for the communist revolutionary governments came as no surprise.[15] In the ubiquitous Cold War between the United States and the Soviet Union, the two ideological visions of each empire were mutually exclusive, and where one won, the other lost. In this context, the obvious alternative to the communist regimes in Eastern Europe was popular sovereignty through a democratic government. This alternative was not only theoretical, however, for outbreaks of democratic protests were not uncommon in some East European countries and dissidents within and outside of these countries condemned communist regimes.[16] In a 1979 essay Václav Havel criticized Eastern European regimes as weak and argued that their replacement through an "explosion of civil unrest" or collapse from within was imminent.[17] Meanwhile in Poland, the Solidarity movement—a trade union that for years was demanding political pluralism and that had become a veritable force by the beginning of 1989—won all of the contestable seats in the Polish parliament.[18] Of course, the events that followed and the timing of the uprisings against the regimes surprised both Havel and the leaders of Solidarity, but they still represented the main alternative to communism that would shape the new regimes that were soon established.

This has been a cursory review of very complex phenomena that have spurred an enormous literature in the humanities and social sciences, and the previous chapters have discussed the role of ideology in each of these revolutions in detail. However, this brief discussion highlights the role of leadership and revolutionary ideology prior to these revolutions and their effect on the type of regime that was created. All of these cases fit the narrow definition of revolutions as "a mass-supported seizure of political power that aims to transform the social and political order."[19] Regardless of the eventual success or failure of the particular revolutionary goals, their character and content were influenced by revolutionary scripts that had their roots in both previous revolutions and in the intellectual traditions of their times.

This is not to suggest that revolutions must by necessity start with a revolutionary intention, or that purposive revolutionary movements are the only way to an eventual revolution. Rather, a more evolutionary model of revolutions is often more appropriate: the French Revolution began as calls for reform of the monarchy, and ended with the king's execution and the establishment of a republic. Similarly, Eastern European revolutions started out as calls for reform that were transformed in the course of the uprisings into real revolutionary movements that demanded the complete transformation of the political system. Because of this, Skocpol and Hobsbawm, among others, explicitly reject the idea of ideological leadership—or what Skocpol calls the "purposive image of how revolutions develop."[20] This perspective, however, ignores the fact that even in those cases when participating masses were not directly "organized or ideologically inspired by avowedly revolutionary leaders and goals," their revolutionary vocabulary was nonetheless greatly influenced by the political discourse of the time and previous revolutionary movements.[21] An absence of intentional leadership does not necessarily mean the absence of a predominant and influential ideology. Moreover, the revolutionary leadership that developed and the regime that was later created had to legitimize its political authority by appealing to this political discourse as offering solutions to the problems of the masses. This does not imply a successful solution to these problems, but simply an attempt to couch those problems and their solutions in revolutionary language.

Thus, while each of these revolutions had to reconcile contradictions within their respective revolutionary ideologies, the competition was predominantly *within* the confines of a larger revolutionary worldview. Just as the French revolutionaries debated how best to achieve a social contract based on the rights of man, communist revolutionaries debated how best to achieve the dictatorship of the proletariat: these were debates about the means, and less so about the ultimate ends, of the revolution. Some of these ideologies started out defining a utopian vision of social and political transformation that would require generations to be fulfilled (such as communist revolutions); others were more temporally limited in their revolutionary timeframe, and once a new regime associated with popular sovereignty was achieved, the revolution officially ended (such as the Revolution of 1688, France in 1830, the European revolutions of 1848, Germany in 1918, and most recently the Eastern European revolutions of 1989 and the Color Revolutions of the twenty-first century). Two revolutions, however, started out as mass rebellions aiming to restore popular sovereignty, but in their course evolved millenarian dimensions that lengthened their timeframe until the achievement of some ideal social and political state (the French Revolution of 1789, which started the millenarian script, and its latest and updated reincarnation in the Iranian Revolution of 1979).

The Arab revolutions are often compared to the 1848 revolutions and the Eastern European revolutions of 1989, and are described as shifting away from the millenarian model. As I will argue below, this is only partially correct. A closer analysis of the revolutions in Yemen and Egypt shows how the mass uprisings initially began as calls for "popular sovereignty" and "democracy," but in later stages those words masked vast differences between different revolutionary groups, some of which can even be classified as millenarian. The recent Arab revolutions can be best described as uprisings *against* personalistic regimes rather than *for* a particular type of regime. There was, in an important sense, no shared revolutionary worldview, despite similar tactics and vocabulary across the region. Nevertheless, the ideological debates *between* vastly different worldviews of Arab revolutionary groups and the failure of any one of them to claim revolutionary authority may serve as an antidote for the millenarian model.

The Scripts of the Arab Revolutions

What makes the Arab Uprisings so remarkable is the fact that for decades Middle Eastern regimes were considered the most durable bastions of authoritarianism in modern history. Yet in many ways the uprisings have been a long time coming. From Michael Hudson's *Arab Politics* published in 1979 until the first protests in Tunisia, there was little confidence in both scholarship and on the ground in the legitimacy of any of the Arab regimes.[22] Nevertheless, mass discontent only rarely generates a popular uprising against the political status quo, and Arab regimes seemed to have perfected a sophisticated mechanism that ensured their durability.[23] Elections, distributive politics, patrimonial networks, a repressive apparatus, and intertwined civil-military relations ensured the longevity of many of these regimes.[24] All of these are important factors not only for regime durability but also in explaining how, once the revolutions started, ideological and social cohesion were hard to achieve.

The Arab regimes were—and those that remain still are—mostly creations of the 1950s–1960s, following military coups that overthrew the monarchies of Iraq, Egypt, and Libya. The militaries that took over used a combination of socialist ideologies specific to the region, Baathist ideologies, and their respective social and political practices in order to buttress their regimes.[25] As a result, the so-called authoritarian bargain was struck between the new regimes and the publics, which laid down the social contract and engineered the expectations of generations of Arab publics. Central to this bargain was the expectation that the state would provide "equitable and universal access to basic necessities like food, shelter, education, and health care."[26] Additionally, the state would also provide guaranteed employment at livable wages. In short, the state and the personalistic leader often at its helm became a behemoth on which most sections of society were entirely dependent. Despite the fact that only three countries transformed from monarchies to republics, this social contract rippled through the rest of the Arab regimes, all of which adopted a similar bargain.

The turn toward economic liberalization in the late 1980s and early 1990s cracked this social safety net. Regimes, forced through international institutions to diminish the state, invented new ways of maintaining their power and insulating themselves from the shock of potential (and actual) protests.[27] Most of these regimes created smaller, and deeper, bargains with the military and business communities, providing larger privileges to ever decreasing sections of society.[28] These changes left many Arabs, especially those born after the beginning of the erosion of the authoritarian bargain, with very few prospects for the future. It is no surprise, then, that Arab revolutions started out as "youth revolutions": this vaguely defined group was able to turn their daily grievances into socially and regionally shared critiques of the regimes.

Meanwhile, starting in the 1990s the region experienced an Islamist revival. Islamist parties that were persecuted—and yet politically manipulated by the regimes—started filling the gaps left by the withdrawal of the state. Islamist organizations started providing social services mixed with a degree of proselytism in most Arab states. As a result, the degree of religiosity and support for these parties increased, as was evidenced through both an increase in social conservatism and the improved performance of these parties on the political stage.[29] The particular "brands" of Islam, meanwhile, proliferated. The Muslim Brotherhood in various countries was no longer the sole bearer of the Islamist flag, as Saudi-funded Salafi groups increased their presence even in more traditionally liberal countries in the region.[30]

At a minimum, then, Arab countries in 2010 experienced the following conditions: severe economic stagnation following decades of sluggish growth and the financial crises of 2008; increasingly unresponsive and corrupt regimes; a growing Islamist population; and a large, young, and well-educated middle class. Additionally, many of these countries, including two that experienced revolutionary uprisings (Syria and Yemen) were also divided along sectarian and tribal lines. While many of these divisions were engineered and exacerbated by the regimes in their attempts to divide and conquer their own populations, they became even more real the longer the uprisings continued.

What political ideology would appeal to such a large number of disparate groups, none of which had concrete boundaries, but most of which held a deep-seated distrust of the others? In such a context, the lowest common denominator among the revolutionary groups was their agreement on overthrowing the existing regimes. In significant ways, this was the script of the Arab revolutions, embodied in the chant sung in every country where protests took place: "The people want the overthrow of the regime!" There were no calls for *Liberté, Egalité, Fraternité,* as during the French Revolution; no calls for the universal rights of workers, as during the communist revolutions; nor simply calls for "democracy," as during the Eastern European revolutions. As I will argue below, however, beyond this minimalist yet powerful demand, each group had its own vision of what the revolution was and what it ought to achieve. These differences have only become larger almost three years after the start of the revolutions in 2011, which has resulted in near constant instability in most of these countries. While I examine the Egyptian and Yemeni scripts in particular, these conclusions apply to the other Middle Eastern revolutions.

The Egyptian Script

Following an idiosyncratic event in Tunisia—the self-immolation of a street vendor, which epitomized social grievances shared across the Middle East—protests spread from a small town to the capital city of Tunis. After the Tunisian president's departure on 14 January, Egyptian opposition groups such as the April 6 Youth Movement, which were tolerated by the Mubarak regime and had experience in protest organization, began to organize small protests and to mobilize against the regime through social media. This group was especially relevant in the initial stages of the Egyptian protests, and since its inception it had been trained by Serbian youth movement activists from Otpor, a civic group working toward a democratic revolution in Serbia (and previously Yugoslavia) from 1998 to 2003.[31] Both the tactics of April 6 (social media, local associations with labor) and their goals (democratic transition) were strikingly similar to those of Otpor. The April 6 Movement extended their association to other independent youth activists, such as the organizers of the Facebook page "We Are All Khaled Said," which had become a medium for political opposition to Hosni Mubarak's regime, and together they planned a major protest on 25 January, a holiday celebrating Egyptian police.[32]

The initial demands of the protesters were the end of the Emergency Law, which had been in existence since Nasser's presidency, freedom of speech and elections, and an end to corruption. Prior to the major protests of 25 January, the word "revolution" was not mentioned in public gatherings or the proclamations of any of the involved groups. However, following the appearance of hundreds of thousands of protesters in Tahrir Square on 25 January, which took both protest organizers and the regime by surprise, protesters started chanting "the people want the overthrow of the regime." In this sense, Skocpol is correct to emphasize the evolutionary dynamic wherein protest movements transform unbidden into revolutions, but not in her rejection of the role of ideology and leadership in these events.[33] Many of the people participating in protests may have been drawn by their individual grievances, but the only imaginable alternative to the Mubarak regime for the youth activists and protesters was a democratic one.

In examining the French Revolution, Edelstein writes: "come the Revolution, everything changes."[34] Everything was indeed changed after the first day the word "revolution" was uttered in Tahrir Square. What began as a protest and calls for reform was transformed into a veritable revolutionary movement, complete with individuals willing to sacrifice their lives for a mission they considered vital and a renewed confidence in their abilities and chances of success. During the first three days of protest, Egyptian youth groups were leading the revolutionary protests and determining the vocabulary of the revolution.

Enter the Muslim Brotherhood, and everything changed yet again. The Brotherhood's belated but vastly important participation in the revolution changed the meaning of the revolution. Whereas the revolution had called for the overthrow of the regime *and* its replacement with a democratic one, the entrance of the Muslim Brotherhood and other Islamists created the perception among the non-Brotherhood groups that the only thing they could agree on was to overthrow the regime. There was enormous suspicion about the real intentions of the Muslim Brotherhood, including the often-cited fear that their goal was the establishment of an Islamic caliphate. Despite mutual distrust, revolutionaries of all groups agreed to pool their efforts and to set aside differences in order to form a united front against the Mubarak regime.[35] There is much speculation as to the "true" motives and ideology of the Muslim Brotherhood and the compatibility of a devout and internally authoritarian group with liberal democracy, but a more important fact during the revolution itself was the subjective perception of the Muslim Brotherhood on the part of revolutionary groups.[36] Youth activists were under the impression that *they* were the ones to determine the course of the revolution, only to realize later on that the Brotherhood machine was slowly taking over the reins of the revolution.[37] For them, that meant that the future of Egypt could look more like a theocracy than the democracy they were demanding.[38] Each group's subjective understandings of one another matter more than any evidence of their true intentions that could be put forth.

Once Mubarak stepped down on 11 February 2011, the Supreme Council of the Armed Forces (SCAF) under General Tantawi took the reins of Egypt and made various constitutional declarations, including one that gave itself seemingly unconstrained powers.[39] While popular support for the SCAF rarely fell below 70 percent and the institution had initially been entrusted with revolutionary authority and legitimacy, the military shared none of the revolutionaries' views about the future of Egypt.[40] Instead, in the months that followed they entrenched themselves and further cemented their power and interests through unilateral constitutional changes. Egyptian "liberals"—a term that encompasses Nasserists and secularists as well as religious individuals—as well as the Muslim Brothers, felt that their revolution had been hijacked by the military.

All of the groups' visions for the future of Egypt (either those they professed or were accused of holding) represent vastly different worldviews. Like the political resistance during the French Revolution, the Egyptian uprising can best be described "as form of 'self-defense': it was a *reactive* right to be invoked in response to" regime corruption and repression.[41] However, unlike the French Revolution and those that followed it, emphasis on this reactive right and insistence on overthrowing the regime was the only coherent part of the Egyptian revolutionary script. Differences between revolutionary worldviews (real and perceived) meant that the revolutionary script could refer to the establishment of a democratic regime, a utopian ideal of an Islamist state, or Nasserist socialism.

Nevertheless, with the euphoria of successfully ousting Mubarak not yet subsided, in the initial months post-revolution there was much hope that these different views would be productively brought together into a democratic system: after all, these are precisely the types of issues that democratic mechanisms are designed to handle. But Egypt needed to simultaneously elect a parliament, design a constitution, elect a president, and reform the state, and the very order with which those events would take place would empower different actors and result in (potentially) vastly different types of regimes. Early elections could empower the Brotherhood, already used to running for office, whereas an early constitution draft could further entrench the power of the military. Without a broad agreement among the elites on the rules of the transition and the nature of the future Egyptian state, agreeing on a sequence of events that would follow Mubarak's ouster became a deeply divisive debate that further exacerbated the differences and fears of each group. It is no surprise, then, that the frequent elections in the thirty months from Mubarak's ouster up to the 3 July 2013 coup failed to deliver authoritative outcomes and instead deepened group divisions.

The Muslim Brotherhood won the various rounds of elections for the two houses of parliament in late 2011 and early 2012 fairly easily, but the results satisfied no one. Non-Islamists felt their fear of an Islamist majoritarianism deepening; Islamists discovered that with the constitutional declarations after coming to power, SCAF had essentially made parliament impotent; and, finally, even the SCAF was not satisfied with the results, as they realized that the power they had given themselves was only temporary and bound to vanish as soon as a new president was elected.

With only a few months in parliament, the Brotherhood further antagonized the non-Islamist revolutionaries by appointing a predominantly Islamist constitutional assembly, which began giving key constitutional articles a particularly Islamic cast and giving a greater role to Sharia (Islamic law) than the previous constitution. So deep was the distrust of many "liberals" for the Brotherhood that when the presidential elections rolled around in May and June 2012, many decided to vote for Ahmed Shafiq—the last prime minister of Egypt under the Mubarak regime and someone whose election would signal a counter-revolutionary move—for president.[42] Others split their vote between Adel Moneim Abul Ftouh (a former Muslim

Brother backed by the Salafis) and Hamdeen Sabahi (a late-comer to the elections and self-professed Nasserist). These candidates represented either the old Mubarak regime, a Muslim Brotherhood that was not considered prodemocracy by revolutionaries, or the old Nasserist ideology. For the latter group, which represented the third largest revolutionary block, the revolution was not so much about a move forward toward a more democratic regime, but rather a move *backward* toward a system similar to Nasser's that Mubarak had betrayed through his failed economic liberalization and corruption.

Mohammad Morsi won the presidential elections by a narrow margin, but as soon as the elections were over, Egyptians woke up to conflicts deepened, rather than assuaged. The Supreme Constitutional Court rushed out a ruling that declared the existing lower house of parliament unconstitutional, while the military issued yet another constitutional declaration that robbed the not yet sworn-in president of much of his powers and carved a larger role for the military. Immediately upon coming to power, Morsi attempted to reverse these changes: he failed at reinstating the parliament but managed to issue a constitutional declaration that not only removed the previous declarations by the military but rendered his own powers virtually unchecked. In reality, his powers were rather limited as the military remained powerful, the courts vastly hostile, and the Interior Ministry— Mubarak's repressive arm—almost entirely out of the president's authority.

With non-Islamists continuing to remain outside of the constitutional assembly, the forming constitution was predictably Islamist, which was predictably criticized by independent media, which was itself subsequently repressed by an ever-more authoritarian presidency. Arguments—sometimes based on nothing more than rumors or misinterpretations—that the judges were planning to dissolve the constitutional assembly and reverse Morsi's constitutional declaration curtailing the power of the military circulated frequently within the Morsi government. In an atmosphere of deep distrust, it remains unclear—it probably always will—how much of Morsi's fears were based on facts and how much they were overblown, but one thing does seem clear: his acting on such fears made them come true. Morsi tried to preempt potential acts against him by issuing another constitutional declaration that removed the issue of the constitutional assembly from judicial review: this move essentially made him the most powerful and untouchable president in Egyptian history, even though such powers would be invalidated the moment a new constitution was voted on.

Following this declaration, large protests took place outside the presidential palace in December 2012, with Muslim Brotherhood members protecting the palace and punishing protesters in an extrajudicial fashion. Despite anti–Muslim Brotherhood sentiments reaching an all time high, the new constitution was voted on and approved. In the first months of 2013, the Brotherhood continued both its practice of rewarding its supporters and harshly repressing its opponents. In response, on 30 June millions of Egyptians marched in the streets nationwide to demand an immediate end to Morsi's presidency, as they felt that future elections were meaningless as long as the president and the Brotherhood-dominated upper house of parliament set the rules of the game. The military rewarded them on 3 July by forcibly deposing Morsi, arresting him and his top aides, shutting down Islamist broadcasters, severely restricting the political role of the Brotherhood, and threatening other measures that would have effectively destroyed the Brotherhood. Morsi, through his unilateral moves in attempting to preempt a possible judicial or military infringement on his power, essentially willed to happen what he feared most.

The discussion after the military took power was whether this was an antidemocratic military coup, another revolution, or a corrective to the earlier revolution to steer it back onto its original course. From a legal standpoint, this had significant implications for the politics of Egypt and the legitimacy of the military move and its continued power grabbing. But if we are asking whether this was a corrective to the original revolution, the very idea that there was an "original revolution" could hardly be more devoid of meaning. Each group had either vastly different ideas of what the revolution should bring, or they had no specific idea other than obtaining and maintaining power. As a result, alliances were soft, amorphous, and shifted continually: the "liberals" and the Brotherhood worked together against Mubarak and then the SCAF; once the Brotherhood came to power, these same "liberals" joined with a military that had repressed them violently; and now that the military's power was getting more entrenched by the day, both the Brotherhood and the "liberals" were once again against the military—but not necessarily together in their revolt. The "liberals" have been the constant losers in this game, predominantly because they are made up of so many different groups with opposing or incoherent visions. Whereas the various revolutionary movements in the weeks prior to Mubarak's overthrow were joined together by a reactionary antiregime rhetoric, the so-called liberals are joined together by an almost universal anti-Brotherhood, and sometimes antimilitary, rhetoric. Ironically, they have been the force that has sparked antiregime protests in all the early stages—both to overthrow Mubarak and to overthrow Morsi—but they cannot build upon what they destroy, because they have neither coherence nor any institutional or formal sources of power. Without an agreement on a prescriptive plan for a future Egyptian state, politics has evolved into a game of musical chairs where at least one of the players is left standing and plotting for the next round.

While it may be possible to point to the start of a particular revolution, it may be nearly impossible to point to its end. This will be particularly hard in the case of Egypt, when the revolution means many different things to its participants. It seems premature, therefore, to propose analytical narratives of the Egyptian revolution when, whatever it stands for, it is still continuing. Nevertheless, events so far point to a revolution that was highly reactionary and without a shared coherent script in terms of a programmatic vision of a future political system and renewed social contract. What was, furthermore, an initial uprising in order to restore popular sovereignty (d)evolved into a power grab by two major centers of power (the military and the Muslim Brotherhood)—the first of which lacks a vision for Egypt and is concerned with maintaining and increasing its own power, while the second may or may not have an ideological vision for which popular sovereignty is subordinate to the establishment of an Islamist state.[43] And both are rejected by a disparate group of "liberals."

The Yemeni Script

The Yemeni revolution developed more slowly than the Egyptian one, yet its revolutionary script is even less coherent and the aftermath of the ouster of President Ali Abdullah Saleh possibly less certain. In important ways, the Yemeni revolution went through stages similar to those of its Egyptian counterpart. The first groups to take to the streets were young and well-educated and generally agreed on replacing the Saleh regime with a constitutional democracy. Similarly, the Islah Party—an Islamist party that is itself a coalition of Muslim Brothers, Salafis, and conservative businessmen—joined the revolution after university students were already settled in Change Square in Sana'a. Unlike the Egyptian Islamists, however, Islah was deeply connected to the Saleh regime despite being part of the opposition. In fact, Islah was more deeply embedded in Saleh's patrimonial network than Saleh's own party (the General Congress Party). Islah was able to counterbalance the president and had sufficient independent finances to be able to put real pressure on the president.[44] Islah's participation in protests was, therefore, seen by many as opportunistic.[45] Since

Yemen's unification, Islah has shown itself to be very adaptable to the needs of political power-sharing and has often reinvented itself and its positions accordingly.[46] Its participation in the revolution, therefore, was seen by youth activists as simply more of the same politics that had obtained under Saleh's regime.

Yemen's revolution took a different turn when the second most powerful man in Yemen—General Ali Mohsen—defected on 18 March 2011, together with the twelve brigades under his command. His defection was explained as being a result of regime brutality against protesters, but given the well-known fact that Ali Mohsen was the architect of much more brutal attacks in northern Houthi regions of Yemen for seven years, his self-professed solidarity with the revolution was viewed with great suspicion.[47] In reality, General Mohsen already had a difficult relationship with Saleh over the latter's decision to name his own son his successor, as well as other political moves Saleh had made to strengthen his own family to the detriment of General Mohsen's interests. General Mohsen's defection made it possible for the protesters to be protected by real firepower against regime repression, but it also transformed the revolution from demands for a democratic state to simply overthrowing the Saleh regime.

In addition to these three groups—Islah, the various revolutionary youths, and General Ali Mohsen—northern Zaydi Shi'a groups (called Houthis) and southern Hiraaki separatists represented the largest revolutionary groups in Yemen. The Houthi group—so-called after their leader, Al Houthi, who aimed at a Shi'a revival in Yemen—demanded the overthrow of the regime and equal rights for the Shi'a, in addition to having a vague ideological stance against Western liberalism and Israel.[48] The Hiraaki movement, meanwhile, represents one of the strongest oppositions to the very experiment of a united Yemeni state; they demand secession from Yemen, citing repression and intentional economic underdevelopment. They called not only for overthrowing the Saleh regime but also for a referendum on the question of secession. Popular sovereignty for them required a reconsideration of the very nature of the state and the nation.

Despite these differences, these five often conflicting groups—who had clashed with each other not only at the discussion table but also on the battlefield—set aside these differences in order to form a united front against the Saleh regime. Tellingly, a new political party (Al Watan), which had its origins in Change Square in May 2011, kept its intentions secret until Saleh officially stepped down in order to avoid fissures in the revolutionary movement.[49] All revolutionary groups engaged in self-conscious efforts not to discuss their visions for the future of Yemen for the same reason. The devil lies in the details, and in this case those details could unravel the entire uprising. This intentional and temporary glossing over of differences masked the fact that these different groups had vastly different understandings of what the revolution ought to achieve beyond overthrowing President Saleh.

In November 2011, the Gulf Cooperation Council (GCC) brokered a deal that would remove Saleh from power. The deal had several components, the first of which was the election of a new president, followed by a national dialogue with participants from various groups, in order to provide a more detailed transition and reform plan. In February 2012, Abdu Rabu Mansour Hadi ran uncontested and subsequently replaced President Saleh. Part of the reason Saleh stepped down without a fight was that, according to the GCC roadmap, he would remain immune from domestic prosecution, and the military balance of power in the country was such that neither side—neither Saleh nor his opponents—were sure of victory.

The former opposition bloc, called the Joint Meeting Parties—a five-party alliance that includes Islah, the Yemeni Socialist Party, the Nasserist Popular Unity Party, as well as two small Zaydi parties—dominates the current transitional government. President Hadi has managed limited, but difficult, military reforms, but official power in the country still remains split between Saleh's bloc, the current president, General Ali Mohsen, and an important tribe under the leadership of the Ahmar family. Outside of the capital Sana'a, however, power has devolved into the hands of various regional groups or tribal leaders. This is a precarious balance of power, but it is precisely the fact that no single group is able to dominate the capital, let alone the national scene, that holds a civil war at bay.

This is also the reason that a national dialogue was deemed necessary before the country could move forward into national parliamentary elections. The national dialogue started in March 2013 and was supposed to end in September 2013, but it continued until January 2014. The dialogue brought together 565 delegates from across the country in order to address the most pressing issues, with security sector reform, the constitution-writing process, the question of southern secession, and the northern rebellion being the most fundamental. In many ways, then, Yemen seems to have succeeded where Egypt failed: in bringing together opposing actors to discuss and compromise on their own visions for the future of Yemen.

Yet most Yemenis and participants themselves see this dialogue as an empty gesture and a rubber stamp that cannot address their most serious disagreements, but is acting only as a delay that aids the further entrenchment of the current power centers. While the Houthis sit at the dialogue table, their soldiers in the north of the country keep gaining more territory and fighting with various Sunni (including Islah) followers. Any question of serious security sector reform threatens to disturb the balance of power between the two most powerful men—Saleh's son and General Ali Mohsen—and is seen as a potential spark of civil war. Southerners feel that the Hiraak representatives are not speaking for them, and that the question of secession is not being addressed. One side or the other has rejected various alternatives to secession, including types of federalism that give different degrees of autonomy to the south. In late November 2013, the Hiraak representatives withdrew entirely from the dialogue, leaving the future of Yemen uncertain.

Yemen has changed dramatically since the start of the revolution, and new actors, such as the Houthis, the opposition "youth" groups, and the Hiraakis—who were not significant players on the national stage—are now playing a role. But in many other ways, the rules of the game have remained the same, as official and military power still remains in the hands of old actors within Saleh's regime. Everyday politics itself is progressing much as it did in Saleh's days, with clientelist networks being used to balance groups against each other, and institutions being filled only with loyalists. In that sense, very little has changed in Yemen.

Therefore, what started as a movement with seemingly democratic ideals by a group of idealistic, fragmented, and disgruntled youth was soon hijacked by existing political entities that used the revolution to further their own interests. There is little in the political debate in Yemen today that focuses directly on the ideological underpinnings of the future Yemeni state: while every group pays lip service to democracy, the negotiations are ultimately based on how to make sure to give as little as possible to others while maintaining as much as possible for one's own group.

No Victor, No Vanquished

The Middle East revolutions that succeeded did so only partially in their efforts to overthrow the regime—presidents may have departed, but old regime figures continue to play musical chairs in their attempt to retain power.[50] In these (unfinished) Arab revolutions the fundamental change does not lie in the changing nature of institutional power or the advance of a democratic political system, but in the transformation of entire communities and the expected relations between state and society in the most profound sense. Groups that have never had any political power and that were marginalized for decades (or, in the case of Yemen, for centuries) are now putting pressure on governments to fulfill their demands. Further, the legitimacy of one-man rule is irreparably eroded. In fact, Arab revolutions were among the few ideologically leaderless revolutions. This is not to say that there was no organizational leadership, but rather that no group put forth ideological leaders who could speak for the revolution as whole. The Arab revolutions have no Robespierre, Lenin, Mao, or Havel. They stand as vehement rejections of power concentrated in the hands of any one man, and so leaderless revolutions were almost the only logical conclusion. When Mohammad Morsi—a man greatly lacking in charisma—was selected as the Egyptian Brotherhood candidate for president, the popular reaction even among his detractors was that his lack of charisma made him a more acceptable candidate because he posed no danger of becoming another Mubarak, Saleh, Qadafi, or Hafez Al Assad. The rejection of this type of authoritarian model is itself a great transformation of these revolutions.

This rejection, however, arose from many different ideological positions. Following decades of opposite and parallel social developments—a growth of both liberal and conservative sections of society—popular sovereignty was bound to be interpreted in fundamentally different ways by these groups. What began as youth movements reacting to repressive regimes and demanding freedom of speech and participation became broader and less specified movements once other groups joined the revolution. These revolutions may have started out as the Eastern European revolutions did, but the ideological fights between different groups made it impossible for them to end in similar ways: quick and effective transitions of power to a leadership that could legitimately claim revolutionary authority.

In that sense, the meaning of revolution evolved much as it did during the French Revolution—in other words, away from popular sovereignty. This latter comparison, however, also ends here: the Arab revolutions have not shifted toward a millenarian model. Whereas three years into the French Revolution the leadership shifted their focus from popular sovereignty to a permanent revolution as an end in itself, this was achieved largely as a result of their being imbued with revolutionary authority in the early years. The Arab revolutions have not produced legitimate revolutionary leadership; whichever group is currently holding power in the immediate postrevolutionary period has more detractors than it has supporters. For revolutions to result in French-style millenarianism, the positing of either a final settlement (as in communist revolutions) or a permanent revolution is necessary in order for the revolution to gain a certain religious quality related to millenarianism. The vast ideological discord between revolutionary groups, coupled with the sense of empowerment and the inability of any one group to claim revolutionary authority, makes it difficult to envision any of the Arab uprisings evolving into either a French-style millenarian revolution, or a utopian, universalist revolution like those of the twentieth century.

The danger of a retrenchment of authoritarianism in the short term is real, since the tools of power remain in the hands of the old elite. However, the deep ideological divisions between revolutionary groups and personal aspirations of some revolutionary actors may ensure enough balance of power and pressure on the governments that popular sovereignty is a likely—if de facto—outcome in the long run. In that sense, the immediate failures and long-term successes of the 1848 revolutions may yet be replicated in the Arab world.

DAVID A. BELL

Afterword

In their introduction to this volume, Keith Michael Baker and Dan Edelstein posit two distinct approaches to the history of revolutions. The first approach derives from the social sciences, and belongs to the grand Western tradition of trying to discern impersonal, predictable patterns of human behavior. It accords particular importance to social and economic conditions, and to the ways self-interested states behave under these conditions. This approach has been taken in many different directions, with great subtlety and sophistication, but in most of its incarnations it retains a clear, visible affiliation with the version most famously developed by Karl Marx.

The second approach—the one that the editors themselves advocate, and have set forth as the basis for this volume—has, by contrast, a hermeneutic basis. Rather than looking to the material structures in which revolutions took place, it examines how revolutionaries understood what they were doing: how they interpreted the social, cultural, and political contexts in which they operated, and how their ideas shaped and gave meaning to their actions. As Baker memorably wrote in justification of this approach, a quarter of a century ago: "The action of a rioter in picking up a stone can no more be understood apart from the symbolic field that gives it meaning than the action of a priest in picking up a sacramental vessel . . . . All social activity has an intellective dimension that gives it meaning, just as all intellectual activity has a social dimension that gives it point."[1]

It is worth noting that these social scientific and hermeneutic approaches are not just the invention of modern scholars, deriving from two distinct intellectual traditions (ones that have consciously opposed each other since the days of Wilhelm Dilthey). Both are deeply inscribed in the histories of revolutions themselves. As early as the 1790s, revolutionaries in France were describing the events taking place around them *both* as the product of impersonal, predictable, quasi-natural forces, *and* as the result of changes in what we would now call political culture. Antoine Barnave, not long before his 1793 execution, wrote a book explaining the French Revolution by reference to the rise of "industrial property," which in his view had led inexorably to the political ascendancy of the common people.[2] In addition, as the historian Mary Ashburn Miller has argued, the idea of revolution as a natural phenomenon akin to natural calamities formed a staple element of revolutionary rhetoric.[3] The revolutionaries liked nothing better than to compare the events they were living through to volcanic eruptions, earthquakes, lightning strikes, and floods, all of which, to use a favorite word from the period, possessed "irresistible" force, putting them beyond ordinary human control. As Miller further notes, these analogies were informed by the natural sciences of the day, which treated this type of violent natural event as an inevitable, pressure-releasing restoration of natural equilibrium, through processes that could be scientifically measured and predicted.

Yet at the same time, as many historians have stressed, nothing was more common in the 1790s than to attribute the origins and progress of the revolution to "philosophy," which was held to have given French people new ways of seeing the world around them, and new political ideals to strive toward.[4] Moreover, as Keith Michael Baker has long argued, the French Revolution marked the moment at which the word "revolution" itself came to mean an act of organized, collective political will. This new meaning eclipsed the older one of a sudden, uncontrollable upheaval: as Baker succinctly puts it, a shift took place from "revolution as fact" to "revolution as act."[5] Henceforth, the word signified an extended process that could be driven forward, indefinitely, by the conscious intentions of its actors.

As many of the essays in this volume make clear, the tension between seeing revolution in terms of impersonal structural change, and seeing it in terms of conscious political will, has remained a central one throughout modern history. It has been especially strong in the Marxist tradition. The *Communist Manifesto* stands, in one sense, as the great embodiment of this tension, and therefore as a remarkably paradoxical piece of work. It deployed all the immense rhetorical skill Marx and Engels were capable of to persuade men and women to carry out an action—revolution—that its own animating theory suggested would come about by itself, without help, thanks to the iron laws of historical change. Later in the history of Marxist revolutionary movements, as several other essays here remind us, revolution became associated not just with the will of a particular social group but also with the will of a single, virtually superhuman individual: the great revolutionary leader (Lenin, Stalin, Mao, Castro . . .). Needless to say, Marxist revolutionaries, being politicians, rarely let themselves be troubled by the potential contradictions between scientific and voluntaristic theories of revolution. If a few Russian Marxists valiantly declined to fight for proletarian revolution in 1917, on the grounds that Russia had not yet reached the appropriate stage of history, others simply adjusted the theory, or ignored it altogether. Trotsky deftly reconciled scientific Marxism with the nascent Lenin cult by writing: "It was the will of history to cast a figure in which our entire hard and great Epoch is reflected . . . . This is Lenin, the greatest man of our Revolutionary epoch."[6]

In short, the revolutionary tradition itself provides ample source material for both of the approaches that Baker and Edelstein describe. And as Baker and Edelstein admit in their introduction, both still have a useful role to play. Yet when it comes to the comparative study of revolutions, scholars over the past century have opted overwhelmingly for the social scientific approach alone. The reasons for this choice have been, if anything, over-determined. Thanks to the prestige of Marxism and the *Annales* school of historical studies, this approach overshadowed hermeneutic ones for much of the twentieth century. Among scholars ideologically committed to revolutionary movements, the ability to pronounce such movements "inevitable" and "irresistible" also served obvious political uses, both in attracting followers and also in justifying violence as the unavoidable price of inexorable progress. Most importantly, perhaps, comparative historical study by its nature demands the reduction of potentially incommensurate phenomena to uniform categories. This is a procedure central to the social sciences, but not to hermeneutic criticism.

The heyday of the social scientific study of revolution, however, occurred nearly half a century ago. Since the publication in the 1960s and 1970s of major works by Barrington Moore, Charles Tilly, and Theda Skocpol, it has declined markedly in popularity, despite Steve Pincus's recent efforts to press it into service to explain the Glorious Revolution of 1688.[7] And again the reasons have been overdetermined. The 1970s and 1980s marked a general resurgence of hermeneutic approaches with the "linguistic turn," and a concomitant crisis of social scientific models of explanation in many different domains.[8] This shift took place alongside, and in inextricable connection to, the crisis of communism. As communist regimes around the world collapsed, it became virtually impossible to see socialist revolutions, even with their corruptions and imperfections fully acknowledged, as belonging to any sort of scientifically determined forward march of history. "Late capitalism," a term in common use since the 1950s, if not before, seemed to be coming no closer to the end-point the term implied. In France, the former communist François Furet published a seminal book that cast the radical French Revolution—and by extension all violent social revolutions—not as an historical inevitability but as an historical pathology, born out of an illiberal political culture.[9] Furet did not come to his insights out of an engagement with the linguistic turn, but others more influenced by the turn—notably Keith Michael Baker—profited greatly from them, seeing in them a demonstration of how language shapes political action.[10]

Since the 1980s, the cultural history of individual revolutions has become an academic boom industry, with important work carried out by many of the contributors to this volume. This work, heavily hermeneutic in nature, has placed new emphasis on revolutionary language and imagery, on the intellectual background of revolutionary actors, on revolutionary emotions, and on the way meanings evolved in the heat of revolutionary conflict. Overall, it has gone very far toward recuperating the side of revolutions that the social scientific approach largely neglected. As Baker and Edelstein point out, this work also entailed a shift in chronological emphasis from the outbreak of revolutions to their most intense phases.

But, perhaps not surprisingly, this major and now long-lived shift initially generated very little genuinely new reflection on what different modern revolutions have had in common. As just noted, hermeneutic approaches tend, by their nature, to seek to grasp singular historical moments in all their complexity, rather than to engage in the work of comparison. As a result, rather than moving in a hermeneutic direction, the comparative study of revolutions simply withered. This was the case even though revolutions themselves have, throughout history, consciously and incessantly appropriated each other's language and imagery, and proudly situated themselves within a broader revolutionary "tradition." Most famously, many Russian revolutionaries looked back to the French experience as a matrix for their own, openly wondering which of their factions was the Girondins, and which the Montagne; which of their leaders was Robespierre, and which one Bonaparte.[11]

The present volume has now very effectively stepped into the breach. It has done so by focusing attention precisely on the way revolutions have invoked each other, and, more generally, on the way what Baker called "revolution as act" depended on a vision of how that act *should* proceed ("a certain number of actions, to be executed in a certain order," as Baker and Edelstein put it). In other words, it has focused on the way revolutions have followed—while also changing, adapting, and even subverting—scripts. The editors assembled an exceptionally broad and talented group of historians, and gave them an exceptionally well defined charge. They were not just to reflect in general terms on the cultural history of the revolutions they specialized in but also to examine these revolutions in terms of "scripting."

To be sure, the concept of political "scripting" can, as the editors themselves note, be applied to a very wide range of historical phenomena. Well before the age of revolutions, European monarchies had developed an impressively large and stable repertoire of "scripts," notably in the great royal rituals of coronations, formal entries, and funerals. In our own times, no Western political figure has been as intensely "scripted" as Queen Elizabeth II: for constitutional monarchs, the slightest deviation from the letter of the script can potentially ignite a constitutional crisis. Similarly, in early modern Europe, the history of ancient Greece and Rome offered a seemingly inexhaustible stock of scripts that proved surprisingly easy to adapt to a world of Christian monarchies. The French Enlightenment raised the concept of "emulation" to new heights as the most reliable means of stimulating political virtue, and the period's cultural productions sometimes seemed like an endless procession of virtuous *exempla*.[12]

Have political revolutions in fact possessed a distinct, recognizable set of scripts? Inevitably, perhaps, the essays collected here challenge and complicate the editors' initial proposal that revolutionary scripts consist above all of a self-conscious modeling of revolutionary actions on those of revolutions past. Some of the actors and thinkers quoted in the book effectively rejected the idea of scripts altogether, as in the case of Alexander Herzen, and his dictums that, in history, "there is no libretto . . . . everything is *ex tempore*" (from the essay by Claudia Verhoeven). In some cases (notably, the nineteenth-century French ones discussed by Dominica Chang), an overly faithful appropriation of older language and imagery turns out to have been counterproductive, by appearing to important segments of the potential "audience" as little more than sterile mimicry. In other cases, explicitly "revolutionary" scripts were quickly superseded by and subsumed into others (constitutionalism, for the Americans in Jack Rakove's essay; terrorism, for the nineteenth-century Russians in Verhoeven's). Several of the essays point to the way revolutionary scripts themselves assimilated much older ones with roots in classical antiquity (civil war, for David Armitage; tyrannicide, for Guillaume Mazeau). And several others (especially

Ian Thatcher's and Silvana Toska's) explicitly discuss revolutions as a site of collision and quasi-anarchic contestation between "multiple scripts" that assigned vastly different roles to such actors as revolutionary parties and the popular masses. The essay dealing with France's most recent brush with revolutionary energies (Julian Bourg's, on 1968) strikingly identifies as its "chief casualty . . . the notion of revolution itself"—at least in the sense of unitary, disciplined revolutionary projects. As its author notes, the apparent collapse of coherent revolutionary scripts in the 1960s in fact contributed not insignificantly to the birth of poststructuralism, with its suspicion of all "metanarratives," and therefore to the broader return to hermeneutic approaches that helped produce the present volume.

Given the huge variety of ways in which "scripts" turn out to have functioned (or not) in revolutionary situations, it clearly does not make sense to take the concept too literally. We cannot reduce the manifold ways in which revolutionaries have invoked past revolutionary experience to a set of distinct scripts that past revolutions could choose among, in the manner of theatrical companies deciding which play to perform. But the essays in the volume do suggest some importance common features of "scripting" in the revolutions they examine.

The first of these is that in practice, the invocation of past experience functions less as a set of instructions to be followed step by step ("first, seize the Bastille . . .") than as a set of appeals to the emotions. Of the essays, it is the one that focuses on a filmmaker (Lillian Guerra's, on Cuba) which most explicitly discusses the role of emotion in revolution. But long before the invention of film, revolutionary cultural impresarios, going back at least to Jacques-Louis David in France, consciously designed their productions so as to elicit intense emotional responses from audiences. What is it, after all, that drives men and women to break faith with a previous source of political authority, and to embrace a new, revolutionary one? Pure reasoning as to the best form of government is not necessarily absent from the process, but it nearly always requires a strong emotional response as well. The philosophers of the European Enlightenment understood this point very well. Consider the famous passage from Locke's *Second Treatise* quoted by Keith Michael Baker in his essay: "But if a long train of Abuses, Prevarications, and Artifices, all tending the same way, make the design visible to the People, and they *cannot but feel what they lie under, and see, whither they are going*, 'tis not to be wonder'd, that they should then rouze themselves" (emphasis added). Or to quote Montesquieu: "There are certain truths which it does not suffice to persuade people of; you have to make people feel them."[13] It is also worth recalling that no less an expert on the history of revolutions than Eric Hobsbawm, reflecting on his own experiences as a teenage communist in Weimar Germany, wrote that "next to sex, the activity combining bodily experience and intense emotion to the highest degree is the participation in a mass demonstration at a time of great public exaltation."[14]

The importance of emotions to revolutionary scripts comes across explicitly in many of the essays in this book. Keith Baker's essay points to the way, by 1789, the word "revolution" could induce "fears of cataclysmic social collapse." Guillaume Mazeau emphasizes how the emotions generated by the assassination of Jean-Paul Marat accelerated the move toward the Terror in France. The Russian revolutionaries in Claudia Verhoeven's essay lived amid an overheated, overflowing cauldron of emotions, lurching constantly between wild hope to bleak despair as they moved to embrace a program of terrorism that "trumped" older revolutionary scripts. It would be useful, as programs of research develop beyond this book, for future students of revolutionary scripts to bring the burgeoning historiography of the emotions to bear explicitly on the subject.[15]

A second point concerns the way that "revolution" came to signify, for its partisans, a suspension of ordinary, constitutional political rules. Maximilien Robespierre laid out this idea systematically in his *Report on the Principles of Revolutionary Government* in 1794. He insisted that revolutionary regimes, compared with constitutional ones, needed to operate with "extraordinary means," while constrained by "less uniform and less rigorous rules," in order to deal with "stormy, fast-moving circumstances."[16] Ever since, the adjective "revolutionary"—born, as Baker notes, at this very historical moment—has connoted a departure from ordinary political rules and practices. Numerous essays in the book bear out this point. Edelstein highlights the extraordinary moment in the French Revolution when the National Convention voted to suspend the constitution it had just approved, and proclaimed the French government "revolutionary until the peace." Ian Thatcher notes that in 1917, not just the extreme left but also moderate socialists saw the need for the revolutionary "soviets" to assume powers that until then had inhered in constitutional institutions. The Parisian wall slogans of 1968, discussed by Julian Bourg, called for a suspension of ordinary rules of all kinds: "Imagination has taken power." And Abbas Milani discusses how, upon coming to power in Iran in the late 1970s, the Ayatollah Khomeini introduced the principle of *Maslahat* (expediency) that allowed him to over-rule even divinely dictated Sharia law in the name of preserving the revolutionary Islamic Republic. It is tempting to call the idea of a state of exception the foundation of all revolutionary scripts.

As Edelstein further points out in his essay, the suspension of ordinary constitutional rules can create a vacuum of legitimate authority. In whose name are revolutionaries wielding power? While they may claim to represent the nation, or a particular social class, or even a religious confession, the ordinary procedures for establishing legitimate representation no longer obtain. The result, Edelstein argues, is that the revolutionaries end up investing "revolution" itself with authority, turning it into what he has elsewhere characterized as a "mythic" figure.[17] To extend Baker's formula, we might call the development a shift from "revolution as act" to "revolution as agent." And it has clearly taken place in many revolutions besides the French. Jeffrey Wasserstrom and Yidi Wu note in their essay on twentieth-century China the way that the concept of *geming* (revolution) there took on qualities of sacredness, with Liu Xiaobo calling it a "holy word."

Finally, it is worth noting one particular group whose importance to the elaboration of revolutionary scripts is highlighted in virtually every essay in this volume: intellectuals. A "script," after all, is a relatively sophisticated object, whose elaboration requires a degree of historical knowledge, and a certain grasp of political philosophy. The number of world revolutionary leaders who deserve the label of serious intellectual is long: Adams and Jefferson, Sieyès and Robespierre, Lamartine and Louis Blanc, Lenin and Trotsky. University students—a category that includes many aspiring intellectuals—have played a key role in revolutionary upheavals from Paris in 1830 to the Middle East today. Yet for the reasons discussed above, comparative studies of revolution have devoted less attention to this common factor than they have to such subjects as class structure, population pressure, and international competition. They have made relatively little use of the sociology of intellectual life that stretches from Max Weber and Karl Mannheim to Seymour Martin Lipset and Pierre Bourdieu and beyond.[18]

In fact, well over half the essays in this volume could be given the subtitle "A Case Study in the History of Revolutionary Intelligentsias." Intellectuals have been the compilers, the interpreters, and the guardians of revolutionary scripts. We do not need, in the social scientific manner, to treat them as a self-conscious and potentially self-interested social group (in Bourdieu's well-known phrase, "a dominated fraction of the dominant class") to acknowledge that they have played a crucial role in virtually every modern revolution.[19] To be sure, the process of compiling, interpreting, adapting, changing, and subverting scripts has by no means been the work of intellectuals alone. From the common soldiers of the New Model Army and the French revolutionary sans-culottes, to the crowds in Tahrir Square in 2011, non-intellectuals have shown a happy capacity to subvert the elegant exhalations of the seminar room and editorial office. But the revolutions studied in this book would have looked very different if intellectuals had not found ways to make revolutionary scripts not just persuasive, but urgent and compelling to millions of people—an observation that brings us back to the problem of revolutionary emotions. Departing from the sociological tradition, it would be interesting to pose the question of how the professions to which the intellectuals belonged—professor and priest, lawyer and journalist—shaped their self-image in revolution, and their sense of their own role within the scripts they elaborated.

These quick observations on some of the features shared by the revolutionary scripts discussed in this book have obviously been anything but exhaustive. And the fact that, in making them, I have perhaps offered more questions than conclusions about the materials collected in these pages should not be taken as a criticism. As already noted, this book is very much a venture into terra incognita, one of the first serious attempts (perhaps *the* first) at a comparative history of revolutions from a cultural and hermeneutic point of view, as opposed to a social scientific one. Single-authored comparative work along these lines is still vanishingly scarce.[20] It is in the nature of a pioneering volume like this one, that the more successful it proves, the more quickly other scholars will come to challenge and overturn the hypotheses it presents. And in that sense, perhaps, in keeping with the Silicon Valley terminology its Stanford editors deploy in the Introduction, this book itself might be thought of, quite honorably, as "Scripting Revolution 1.0."

Contributors

DAVID ARMITAGE is the Lloyd C. Blankfein Professor of History at Harvard University, where he teaches intellectual history and international history. Among his fourteen books to date are, as author, *The Declaration of Independence: A Global History* (2007), and *Foundations of Modern International Thought* (2013); as coauthor, *The History Manifesto* (2014); and, as coeditor, *The Age of Revolutions in Global Context, c. 1760–1840* (2010) and *Pacific Histories: Ocean, Land, People* (2014).

KEITH MICHAEL BAKER is the J. E. Wallace Sterling Professor in the Humanities and Professor of Early Modern European History and (by courtesy) French at Stanford University. He received his M.A. from Cambridge University and his Ph.D. from University College, London. Before moving to Stanford, he taught for many years at the University of Chicago, where he served for almost a decade as coeditor of the *Journal of Modern History*. Baker has held a Guggenheim Fellowship, has been named Chevalier dans l'Ordre des Palmes Académiques, and is an elected member of the American Academy of Arts and Sciences and of the American Philosophical Society. He is a former President of the International Society for Eighteenth-Century Studies. His many publications include *Condorcet: From Natural Philosophy to Social Mathematics* (1975), and *Inventing the French Revolution* (1990).

DAVID A. BELL is Sidney and Ruth Lapidus Professor in the History of North Atlantic Revolutions at Princeton University, and the author, most recently, of *The First Total War: Napoleon's Europe and the Making of Warfare as We Know It* (Boston, 2007).

JULIAN BOURG is Associate Professor and Core Moderator at Boston College. He received his Ph.D. from the University of California, Berkeley. His first book, *From Revolution to Ethics,* won the 2008 Morris D. Forkosch book prize from *the Journal of the History of Ideas.* He serves on the editorial board of *Modern Intellectual History* and is the past recipient of a Mellon Postdoctoral Fellowship in Interdisciplinary Studies at Washington University in St. Louis, a Fulbright Fellowship, and a Charlotte Newcombe Fellowship from the Woodrow Wilson Foundation. His continuing interests include French theory, especially the thought of Michel Foucault; the relationship between ethics and aesthetics; and twentieth-century French Catholic intellectuals.

DOMINICA CHANG is Associate Professor of French and Francophone Studies at Lawrence University. She earned a bachelor's degree in French language and literature from University of Wisconsin-Madison, a master's degree in French studies from Middlebury College, and a Ph.D. in Romance languages and literatures from the University of Michigan. Her research interests include nineteenth-century French studies, literary history and historiography, print culture, film studies, and language pedagogy.

DAVID COMO is Associate Professor of Early Modern British History at Stanford University. He received his Ph.D. from Princeton University, and is the author of *Blown by the Spirit: Puritanism and the Emergence of an Antinomian Underground in pre-Civil-War England* (Stanford, 2004). His research covers such topics as early modern British history, Puritanism, politics, the English Revolution, and the history of print.

ALEXANDER C. COOK is an Assistant Professor of History at the University of California, Berkeley. He received his Ph.D. from Columbia University and has previously held positions at Stanford University and Brown University. His research interests include cultural, intellectual, legal, and political history of twentieth-century China. His forthcoming book, *The Cultural Revolution on Trial: Mao and the Gang of Four,* is under contract with Cambridge University Press.

DAN EDELSTEIN is Professor of French and (by courtesy) History at Stanford University. He has published two books, *The Terror of Natural Right: Republicanism, the Cult of Nature, and the French Revolution* (2009), and *The Enlightenment: A Genealogy* (2010), both with the University of Chicago Press. His current research interests include natural law theory, the comparative study of revolutions, and digital humanities.

MALICK GHACHEM is an Associate Professor of History at the Massachusetts Institute of Technology and a Senior Scholar at the University of Maine School of Law. He holds undergraduate and law degrees from Harvard University and a Ph.D. in history from Stanford. He is the author of *The Old Regime and the Haitian Revolution* (Cambridge University Press, 2012) and numerous articles in the fields of French colonial and American legal history.

LILLIAN GUERRA is currently Associate Professor of Cuban and Caribbean History at the University of Florida, having previously taught at Bates College and Yale University. She received her Ph.D. from the University of Wisconsin-Madison, and is the author of three books, *Popular Expression and National Identity in Puerto Rico* (University of Florida Press, 1998), *The Myth of José Martí: Conflicting Nationalisms in Early Twentieth-Century Cuba* (University of North Carolina Press, 2005), and *Visions of Power in Cuba: Revolution, Redemption and Resistance, 1959–1971* (University of North Carolina Press, 2012). She has also contributed chapters to many scholarly collections and published articles in journals such as *The Hispanic American Historical Review*, *Social History*, and *Cuban Studies*.

TIM HARRIS received his BA, MA, and Ph.D. from Cambridge University and was a Fellow of Emmanuel College from 1983 before moving to Brown University in 1986. A social historian of politics, he has written about the interface of high and low politics, popular protest movements, ideology and propaganda, party politics, popular culture, and the politics of religious dissent during Britain's Age of Revolutions. He edits the book series *Studies in Early Modern Cultural, Political and Social History* for Boydell Press and is on the editorial board of the journal *The European Legacy*.

GUILLAUME MAZEAU is a lecturer in modern history at the Université Paris 1 Panthéon-Sorbonne. He is a member of the Institut d'Histoire de la Révolution française and a member of the editorial board of the *Annales historiques de la Révolution française*. He is the author of *Corday contre Marat. Les discordes de l'histoire* (Corday against Marat: The Discords of History) (Artlys, 2009), and *Pour quoi faire la Révolution* (The Revolution, What For?) (Agony, 2012, in collaboration with Jean-Luc Chappey, Bernard Gainot, Frederick Regent, and Pierre Serna). His work focuses on the history of collective mobilization and violence, as well as practices and visual culture in times of revolution.

ABBAS MILANI is the Hamid and Christina Moghadam Director of Iranian Studies at Stanford University and a Professor (by courtesy) in the Division of International, Comparative, and Area Studies. His expertise is in United States–Iran relations and Iranian cultural, political, and security issues. He previously taught at Tehran University's Faculty of Law and Political Science, where he was also a member of the Board of Directors of the University's Center for International Relations. He also served as the Chair of the Political Science Department at the Notre Dame de Namur University, and has been a Research Fellow at the University of California, Berkeley's Middle East Center and the Hoover Institution at Stanford.

JACK RAKOVE is the William Robertson Coe Professor of History and American Studies and Professor of Political Science and (by courtesy) Law at Stanford University, where he has taught since 1980. His principal areas of research include the origins of the American Revolution and Constitution, the political practice and theory of James Madison, and the role of historical knowledge in constitutional litigation. He is the author of six books, including *Original Meanings: Politics and Ideas in the Making of the Constitution* (1996), which won the Pulitzer Prize in History, and *Revolutionaries: A New History of the Invention of America* (2010), which was a finalist for the George Washington Prize. He is a member of the American Academy of Arts and Sciences, the American Philosophical Society, and a past president of the Society for the History of the Early American Republic.

GARETH STEDMAN JONES is Professor of the History of Ideas at Queen Mary, University of London. He received a BA from Lincoln College, Oxford, and a D.Phil. from Nuffield College, Oxford. He has been Director of the Centre for History and Economics at Cambridge since 2001, as well as Professor of Political Science and History, Cambridge University, where he is also a Fellow of King's College, and was an Alexander von Humboldt Stiftung Fellow at the Goethe University, Frankfurt. His publications include the books *An End to Poverty?* (Columbia University Press, 2005), *Languages of Class: Studies in English Working Class History, 1832–1982* (Cambridge, 1983), *Outcast London* (Oxford, 1971), and *Religion and the Political Imagination* (coedited with Ira Katznelson, Cambridge, 2010). His research interests include Modern European political thought; political, intellectual and economic history of Europe from the time of the French Revolution; and Victorian London.

IAN D. THATCHER is Professor in History and Head of the School of English and History at the University of Ulster, Coleraine. From 2012 to 2014 he was Research Director at the Helsinki Collegium for Advanced Studies, University of Helsinki. A graduate of the then Institute of Soviet and East European Studies, University of Glasgow, he has published widely on the Russian Revolution and on Russia from the late imperial period to the collapse of communism.

SILVANA TOSKA is a doctoral candidate in international relations and comparative politics in the Department of Government at Cornell University. She is currently a visiting scholar at Harvard University. Prior to starting the doctoral program, Silvana did graduate work at Georgetown and Oxford universities in Arab and African studies. She works on the spread of revolutions, revolution and war, and gender.

CLAUDIA VERHOEVEN is Associate Professor in the History Department at Cornell University. She received her Ph.D. in 2004 from UCLA and was Assistant Professor of Modern European history at George Mason University from 2006 to 2009. She is the author of *The Odd Man Karakozov: Imperial Russia, Modernity, and the Birth of Terrorism* (Cornell University Press, 2009), and has more recently published a series of chapters and articles examining terrorism's temporality. She is also the coeditor of *The Oxford Handbook of the History of Terrorism* and "Cultures of Radicalization: Discourses and Practices of Political Violence and Terrorism," a special issue of the *Social Science History Journal*.

JEFFREY WASSERSTROM is Professor of Chinese History at the University of California, Irvine. He received his Ph.D. from the University of California, Berkeley. His books include *Student Protests in Twentieth-Century China: The View from Shanghai* (Stanford, 1991), and *China in the 21st Century: What Everyone Needs to Know* (Oxford, 2010). He is a Fellow of the Asia Society, the Editor of the *Journal of Asian Studies*, and the Asia Editor of the *Los Angeles Review of Books*. He is also a regular contributor to a wide range of general-interest periodicals, including the *New York Times*, the *Wall Street Journal*, and *The Times Literary Supplement* (London).

YIDI WU is a history Ph.D. candidate at the University of California, Irvine. Her interests include student activism and social movements in modern Chinese history. Her dissertation focuses on Chinese students' reactions between the Hundred Flowers and the Anti-Rightist Campaigns of

1957. She has coauthored with Jeffrey Wasserstrom an annotated bibliography of the 1989 People's Movement for the Oxford Bibliographies, and her chapter on the Yan'an Rectification Campaign is part of a 1943 book project, edited by Joseph Esherick and Matthew Combs, to be published by Cornell University Press.

Notes

Baker and Edelstein: Introduction

1. Wael Ghonim, *Revolution 2.0, The Power of the People Is Greater than the People in Power: A Memoir* (Boston, 2012), 293–94. This brief discussion by Ghonim draws on Keith Michael Baker, "Revolution 1.0," *Journal of Modern European History* 11 (2013): 187–88.

2. Keith Michael Baker, "A Script for a French Revolution: The Political Consciousness of the Abbé Mably," in *Inventing the French Revolution: Essays on French Political Culture in the Eighteenth Century* (Cambridge, 1990).

3. Most notably Jack A. Goldstone, *Revolution and Rebellion in the Early Modern World* (Berkeley, CA, 1991).

4. See Barrington Moore, *Social Origins of Dictatorship and Democracy* (Boston, 1966), xv–xvii. The subtitle of Moore's book, *Lord and Peasant in the Making of the Modern World*, is also telling.

5. Theda Skocpol, *States and Social Revolutions: A Comparative Analysis of France, Russia, and China* (Cambridge, 1979), 25. Compare with Marx, e.g., in *The German Ideology*, in *The Marx-Engels Reader*, ed. Robert Tucker (New York, 1978), 164–65. Skocpol herself highlights this Marxist genealogy (25).

6. See notably William Sewell, "Ideologies and Social Revolutions: Reflections on the French Case," *Journal of Modern History* 57 (1985): 57–85; and Martin Malia, "High Social Science and 'Staseology,'" in *History's Locomotives: Revolutions and the Making of the Modern World* (New Haven, CT, 2006), 302–16.

7. This distinction can be seen in Skocpol's use of nineteenth-century Prussia and Japan as "counter-points" to her thesis about the origins of revolution in France and China; see *States and Social Revolutions*, 99–111.

8. Marx, *The German Ideology*, part I, section D, 5 (emphasis added).

9. See, in this volume, the discussion by Silvana Toska of the "stagnation thesis."

10. Steven Pincus, *1688: The First Modern Revolution* (New Haven, CT, 2009), 41.

11. Similar criticisms have been leveled by sociologists themselves: see notably John Foran, "Theories of Revolution Revisited: Toward a Fourth Generation?" *Sociological Theory* 11, no. 1 (1993): 1–20.

12. Goldstone, *Revolution and Rebellion*, 459.

13. Crane Brinton famously suggested that all revolutions experience a "Terror" phase, followed by a "Thermidorean reaction," on the French model: see *The Anatomy of Revolution*, rev. ed. (New York, 1965), chs. 7 and 8. See also Lyford Edwards, *The Natural History of Revolution* (Chicago, 1927).

14. For Goldstone, this corresponds to "phase two" of the Revolution: it occurs when "the Old Regime state has lost the initiative and either collapses or struggles among the host of contenders who seek to establish a new monopoly of authority; this phase is marked by efforts to mobilize supporters, rapid-fire legislation and creation of economic and political structures, and often by civil war and a 'reign of terror.'" In *Revolution and Rebellion*, 417–18.

15. "If the Reign of Terror was an inherent part of the process of revolution, so too military rule was its inevitable conclusion." See ibid., 431–32.

16. As David Bell has shown, the war against Austria and Prussia (later joined by Britain) was not in the slightest preordained, but rather the result of a deliberate strategy on the part of a prowar faction among the Jacobins, led by Brissot: see Bell, *The First Total War: Napoleon's Europe and the Birth of Warfare as We Know It* (Boston, 2007).

17. See, for instance, his argument that "it is very difficult to deny that if France were to enter the modern world through the democratic door *she had to pass* through the fires of the Revolution, including its violent radical aspects." Moore, *Social Origins of Dictatorship and Democracy*, 105 (emphasis added).

18. See Arno Mayer, *The Furies: Violence and Terror in the French and Russian Revolutions* (Princeton, NJ, 2000), 256.

19. See, notably, Stanley Aronowitz, *The Crisis in Historical Materialism: Class, Politics, and Culture in Marxist Theory* (Minneapolis, MN, 1990).

20. On Bernstein, see notably Peter Gay, *The Dilemma of Democratic Socialism: Eduard Bernstein's Challenge to Marx* (New York, 1952). On the reception of Marx in the late nineteenth century, see James H. Billington, *Fire in the Minds of Men: Origins of the Revolutionary Tradition* (New York, 1980). For Lenin, see *What Is to Be Done?*, in *Essential Works of Lenin* (New York, 1987), and below. In *The German Ideology*, Marx argued that "if these material elements of a complete revolution are not present . . . then, as far as practical development is concerned, it is absolutely immaterial whether the *idea* of this revolution has been expressed a hundred times already." *Marx-Engels Reader*, 165.

21. See R. R. Palmer, *The Age of Democratic Revolution*, 2 vols. (Princeton, NJ, 1959–64); Eric Hobsbawm, *The Age of Revolution: Europe, 1789–1848* (1962); Jacques Godechot, *Les Révolutions: 1770–1799* (Paris, 1963).

22. See David Armitage and Sanjay Subrahmanyam, eds., *The Age of Revolutions in Global Context, c. 1760–1840* (Basingstoke, UK, 2010); and see also Suzanne Desan, Lynn Hunt, and William Max Nelson, *The French Revolution in Global Perspective* (Ithaca, NY, 2013), 2 (quotation).

23. Armitage and Subrahmanyam, "Introduction," *The Age of Revolutions in Global Context*, xix.

24. Desan, Hunt, and Nelson, "Introduction," in *The French Revolution in Global Perspective*, 5.

25. Benjamín Vicuña Mackenna, *The Girondins of Chile: Reminiscences of an Eyewitness*, trans. John H. R. Polt (Oxford, 2003), 19. Thanks to Jorge Myers for this reference.

26. For a critique of the "diffusionist" model (in which ideas about revolution stem only outward from Western capitals), see Samuel Moyn and Andrew Sartori, "Approaches to Global Intellectual History," in *Global Intellectual History* (New York, 2013).

27. David Bell, "Questioning the Global Turn: The Case of the French Revolution," *French Historical Studies* 37, no. 1 (2014): 1–24.

28. See Rachel Hammersley, *The English Republican Tradition and Eighteenth-Century France: Between the Ancients and the Moderns* (Manchester, 2010).

29. See David Armitage, "What's the Big Idea? Intellectual History and the *Longue Durée*," *History of European Ideas* 38, no. 4 (2012): 493–507.

30. See John Lynch, *The Spanish American Revolutions, 1808–1826* (New York, 1986).

31. This scholarship is discussed and analyzed in Parts I and II of this volume.

32. For an introduction to *Begriffsgeschichte*, see Melvin Richter and Michaela W. Richter, "Introduction: Translation of Reinhart Koselleck's 'Krise,'" in *Geschichtliche Grundbegriffe*," *Journal of the History of Ideas* 67, no. 2 (2006): 343–56.

33. See Reinhart Koselleck, "Historical Criteria of the Modern Concept of Revolution," in *Futures Past: On the Semantics of Historical Time*, trans. Keith Tribe (New York, 2013), 43–57; and Neithard Bulst, Jörg Fisch, Reinhart Koselleck, and Christian Meier, "Revolution, Rebellion, Aufruhr, Bürgerkrieg," in *Geschichtliche Grundbegriffe: Historisches Lexikon zur politisch-sozialen Sprache in Deutschland*, 8 vols. (Stuttgart, 1984), 5: 653–788.

Harris: Did the English Have a Script for Revolution?

Acknowledgment: I am grateful to the Andrew W. Mellon Foundation for funding an extended period of research leave at the Institute for Advanced Study in Princeton, during which time I was able to undertake much of the research and writing of this article.

1. British Library, Add. 27,419, f. 43; Trinity College Dublin MS 716, fol. 80. From Peter Heylyn, *Cosmographie in Four Bookes* (London, 1652), 118 (which has slight variations in wording). The adage appears to have predated the seventeenth-century rebellions. In October 1632, Dr. Conyers of Braintree, Essex, was brought before King's Bench and committed to prison for saying "that as the Emperor is king of kings, the king of Spain king of men, and the French king king of asses, so the king of England is king of devils": David Cressy, *Dangerous Talk: Scandalous, Seditious, and Treasonable Speech in Pre-Modern England* (Oxford, 2010), 180.

2. James Howell, *Twelve Several Treatises, of the Late Revolutions in These Three Kingdomes* (London, 1661), 118.

3. R. C. Richardson, *The Debate on the English Revolution*, 3rd ed. (Manchester, 1998), 87.

4. Perez Zagorin, *The Court and the Country: The Beginning of the English Revo-*

lution (London, 1969), 13; J. R. Western, *Monarchy and Revolution: The English State in the 1860s* (London, 1972), 1; V. F. Snow, "The Concept of Revolution in Seventeenth-Century England," *Historical Journal* 5, no. 2 (1962): 167–74.

5. Christopher Hill, "The Word 'Revolution' in Seventeenth-Century England," in *For Veronica Wedgewood These: Studies in Seventeenth-Century History*, ed. Richard Ollard and Pamela Tudor-Craig (London, 1986), 134–51 (quotations at 139, 151). See also Ilan Rachum, "The Meaning of 'Revolution' in the English Revolution (1648–1660)," *Journal of the History of Ideas* 56 (1995): 195–215.

6. See the valuable corrective provided by David Cressy, *England on Edge: Crisis and Revolution, 1640–1642* (Oxford, 2006), 17–24 (quotations at 18–19). For a reassessment of the use of the term "revolution" in the later Stuart period, see Tim Harris, *Restoration: Charles II and His Kingdoms 1660–1685* (London, 2005), 32–37.

7. *Oxford English Dictionary*; Henry Ellis, ed., *Original Letters Illustrative of English History*, 2nd series, 4 vols. (London, 1827), I: 289–90; *State Papers Published Under the Authority of His Majesty's Commission: King Henry the Eighth. Part IV: Correspondence Relative to Scotland and the Borders, 1513–1534* (London, 1836), 458n3.

8. Pierre Boaistuau, *Certaine Secrete Wonders of Nature*, trans. Edward Fenton (London, 1569), 88v.

9. Cited in Hill, "The Word 'Revolution' in Seventeenth-Century England," 138.

10. John Davies, *Historical Relations*, 3rd ed. (Dublin, 1666), 12.

11. Philemon Holland, *A Learned, Elegant, and Religious Speech* (London, 1622), 5.

12. John Gadbury, ed., *The Works of the Most Excellent Philosopher and Astronomer, Sir George Wharton* (London, 1683), 387.

13. Richard Cox, "A Letter . . . Containing a Brief Account of the Transactions . . . since 1653," in *Hibernia Anglicana*, 2nd ed. (London, 1692), 3.

14. Sir George Mackenzie, *Memoirs of the Affairs of Scotland from the Restoration of King Charles II* (Edinburgh, 1821), 5, 113.

15. Thomas Hobbes, *Behemoth*, ed. Paul Seaward (Oxford, 2010), 389.

16. F[olger] S[hakespeare] L[ibrary], X.d.29 (3), fol. 42.

17. The National Archives, Public Record Office SP 29/1, fol. 69.

18. TNA, PRO SP 29/1, fol. 90.

19. TNA, PRO SP 29/1, fol. 72.

20. See, for example, *A Lively Pourtraict of our New-Cavaliers . . . in a Compendious Narrative of Our Late Revolutions* (London, 1661); David Lloyd, *Never Faile; Or, That Sure Way of Thriving under all Revolutions . . . from 1639 to 1661* (London, 1663).

21. "The King's Declaration," *Journal of the House of Lords* (London, 1767–1830), 11: 7; Rachum, "The Meaning of 'Revolution' in the English Revolution (1648–1660)," 213–14.

22. John Paterson, *Post Nubila Phoebus* (Aberdeen, 1660), 6.

23. Nicholas French, *The Bleeding Iphigenia* (London, 1675), sigs. ******r–v, *******3v.

24. Folger Shakespeare Library, G.a.2, 43.

25. Hill, "The Word 'Revolution' in Seventeenth-Century England," 141–45; Rachum, "The Meaning of 'Revolution' in the English Revolution (1648–1660)," 200–202.

26. *London Gazette*, no. 1713, 17–20 April 1682.

27. FSL, X.d.433, 7.

28. *The State-Prodigal His Return* (London, 1689), 1, 3.

29. *The Present Conjuncture; In a Dialogue between a Church-Man and a Dissenter* (London, 1689), 3.

30. *The Records of the Parliaments of Scotland to 1707*, ed. K. M. Brown et al. (St. Andrews, 2007–14), 1693/4/121. Compare Keith Michael Baker's chapter, below.

31. William Leigh, *Great Britaines, Great Deliverance, from the Great Danger of Popish Powder* (London, 1606), sigs. C4v–D.

32. Anthony Maxey, *The Churches Sleepe* (London, 1606), sigs. A6v, B1–v, B2r–v.

33. E[dward] R[eynolds], *Eugenia's Teares for Great Brittaynes Distractions* (London, 1642), 45–46.

34. Quentin Skinner, *The Foundations of Modern Political Thought*, 2 vols. (Cambridge, 1978). For the early-seventeenth-century English context, see J. P. Sommerville, *Royalists and Patriots: Politics and Ideology in England, 1603–1640* (London, 1999).

35. Peter Donald, *An Uncounselled King: Charles I and the Scottish Troubles, 1637–1641* (Cambridge, 1990), 188.

36. See in particular his *Observations upon Some of His Majesties Late Answers and Expresses* (London, 1642). For Parker more generally, see Michael Mendle, *Henry Parker and the English Civil War: The Political Thought of the Public's "Privado"* (Cambridge, 1995).

37. Harris, *Restoration*, 156–61, 199–200; Tim Harris, *Revolution: The Great Crisis of the British Monarchy, 1685–1720* (London, 2006), 83–84, 286–88, 358–59; Mark Goldie, "The Revolution of 1689 and the Structure of Political Argument," *Bulletin of Research in the Humanities* 83 (1980): 473–564.

38. *An Information to all Good Christians Within the Kingdome of England* (Edinburgh, 1639), 4–5, 7.

39. Margaret Judson, *The Crisis of the Constitution: An Essay in Constitutional and Political Thought in England, 1603–1645* (New Brunswick, NJ, 1949), 19.

40. Harris, *Revolution*, esp. chap. 6; Mark Goldie, "The Political Thought of the Anglican Revolution," in *The Revolution of 1688*, ed. Robert Beddard (Oxford, 1991), 102–36.

41. Johann P. Sommerville, ed., *Political Writings: King James VI and I* (Cambridge, 1994), 183.

42. Harris, *Revolution*, 243–48, 268.

43. David Owen, *Herod and Pilate Reconciled* (Cambridge, 1610), 43–44.

44. Sommerville, ed., *Political Writings*, 80, 83.

45. FSL, V.a.478, fol. 99.

46. FSL, X.d.29, fols. 30v–31.

47. Charlwood Lawton, *Jacobite Principles Vindicated* (London, 1693), 23. For a fuller discussion of the themes explored in the preceding paragraphs, see Tim Harris, *Rebellion: Britain's First Stuart Kings* (Oxford, 2014), chap. 1.

48. John Morrill, ed., *The Scottish National Covenant in Its British Context* (Edinburgh, 1990); Harris, *Rebellion*, 370–71.

49. Goldie, "The Revolution of 1689 and the Structure of Political Argument"; Harris, *Revolution*, esp. chap. 8.

50. The word radical comes from the Latin *radix*, meaning root.

51. The literature is vast. The fullest recent surveys are Michael Braddick, *God's Fury, England's Fire: A New History of the English Civil Wars* (London, 2008), and Harris, *Rebellion*.

52. Mark Goldie, "The Roots of True Whiggism 1688–94," *History of Political Thought* 1 (1980): 195–236.

53. John Locke, *Two Treatises of Government*, ed. Peter Laslett (Cambridge, 1964), II, paras. 223, 225.

54. Harris, *Revolution*. Compare Steven C. A. Pincus, *1688: The First Modern Revolution* (New Haven, CT, 2009).

Como: God's Revolutions

1. François Guizot, *Histoire de la Révolution Angleterre*, 2 vols. (Paris, 1826–27); S. R. Gardiner, *The First Two Stuarts and the Puritan Revolution* (London, 1876).

2. Lawrence Stone, *The Causes of the English Revolution* (New York, 1972); Conrad Russell, *The Causes of the English Civil War* (Oxford, 1990), 8; for a particularly extreme example of this revisionist impulse, see Alastair MacLachlan, *The Rise and Fall of Revolutionary England: An Essay on the Fabrication of Seventeenth-century History* (Basingstoke, UK, 1996).

3. Ilan Rachum, *"Revolution": The Entrance of a New Word into Western Political Discourse* (Lanham, MD, 1999). An earlier attempt to chart the use of the word in English may be found in Vernon Snow, "The Concept of Revolution in Seventeenth-century England," *Historical Journal* 5, no. 3 (1962): 167–74; for discussions in the wake of the revisionist challenge, see Christopher Hill, "The Word 'Revolution,'" in Hill, *A Nation of Change and Novelty: Radical Politics, Religion and Literature in Seventeenth-century England* (London, 1990), 82–101; David Loewenstein, *Representing Revolution in Milton and His Contemporaries: Religion, Politics, and Polemics in Radical Puritanism* (Cambridge, 2001), 9–10; Tim Harris, *Restoration: Charles II and His Kingdoms, 1660–1685* (London, 2005), 32–38.

4. See, e.g., Snow, "The Concept of Revolution in Seventeenth-century England," 172–74.

5. Bellièvre to "Monsieur" [presumably Brienne], 22 June 1647, Archives du Ministère des Affaires Etrangères, Paris: Fonds de la correpondence politique—Angleterre (origines-1871). vol. 55 (1647), fol. 232r: "qu'on nevoitpoint, dans l'histoire qu'il soit arrivé desemblable revolution, ny qu'ils ait jamais eu de Prince plusballotté que C'est auiourdhuy le Roy de la G.B."

6. Rachum, *"Revolution,"* 71: "l'Histoire de la plus estrange révolution qui soit jamais arrivée dans le monde."

7. Snow, "The Concept of Revolution in Seventeenth-century England," 169–70; Rachum, *"Revolution,"* 1–100.

8. Rachum, *"Revolution,"* 16–79.

9. Two editions followed in 1645, in Geneva and Bologna; as well as in 1647 (Geneva) and in 1648 (Bologna).

10. [Allesandro Giraffi], *Relatione Delle Rivolutioni Popolari Successe nel Distretto, e Regno di Napoli* (Padua, 1648), 7.

11. For early descriptions of the rising, see *The Moderne Intelligencer*, 12–19 Au-

gust 1647, 4–5; *The Moderate Intelligencer*, 12–19 August 1647, 1216–17. These newspapers, which handled foreign news, carried periodic updates in the weeks that followed.

12. Calls for the execution of the king were first made explicit in *Regall Tyrannie discovered: Or, A Discourse, shewing that all lawfull (approbational) instituted power by God amongst men, is by common agreement, and mutual consent* (London, 1647), although the idea had been hinted at in earlier pamphlets. The Levellers and their ideological innovations, together with their relationship to the development of a European tradition of revolution, receive more detailed scrutiny in Dan Edelstein's essay, below.

13. Bodleian Library, Oxford, Nalson MS. 15, fol. 87r.

14. Allyn B. Forbes, ed., *Winthrop Papers*, 6 vols. (Boston, 1929–), 5: 207.

15. See, e.g., *A Discourse: wherein is examined, what is particularly lawfull during confusions and revolutions in government* (London, 1648), sig. *3r, 3.

16. See D. R. Woolf, "Howell, James (1594?–1666)," *Oxford Dictionary of National Biography* (Oxford, 2004; online edn, 2008).

17. See Eric W. Allen, "The International Origins of the Newspapers: The Establishment of Periodicity in Print," *Journalism Quarterly* 7, no. 2 (June 1930): 307–19, which demonstrates, for instance, that Luca Assarino, early popularizer of the term "revolution," was the publisher of one of the first Italian periodical newspapers; Folke Dahl, *Dutch Corantos, 1618–1650* (The Hague, 1946); Joad Raymond, *The Invention of the Newspaper: English Newsbooks, 1641–1649* (Oxford, 1996); Joad Raymond, ed., *News Networks in Seventeenth Century Britain and Europe* (London, 2006).

18. J. H. Elliot, *The Revolt of the Catalans* (Cambridge, 1963); H. G. Koenigsberger, "The Revolt of Palermo in 1647," *Cambridge Historical Journal* 8, no. 3 (1946): 129–44.

19. Rachum, *"Revolution,"* 37–39, gestures at such a line of interpretation. For the debate on a seventeenth-century "General Crisis," see Trevor Aston, ed., *Crisis in Europe, 1560–1660* (New York, 1967); although largely discarded by historians after 1970, elements of the interpretive framework arguably migrated into the work of revisionist historians of England, who were keen to emphasize the structural similarities that beset England and other European composite states such as Spain. See, for example, Conrad Russell, "Parliamentary History in Perspective, 1604–1629," *History* 61 (1976); for an account that incorporates and builds on this attempt to place England in a broadly European context, and that emphasizes shared structural features, see Jonathan Scott, *England's Troubles: Seventeenth-Century English Political Instability in European Context* (Cambridge, 2000). More recently, growing interest in world history has led to the suggestion of an even broader, global crisis of the seventeenth century; for an interesting attempt to assimilate the events described here under this interpretative umbrella, see Geoffrey Parker, "The Crisis of the Spanish and Stuart Monarchies in the Mid-Seventeenth Century: Local Problems or Global Problems," in *British Interventions in Early Modern Ireland*, ed. Ciaran Brady and Jane Ohlmeyer (Cambridge, 2005), 252–79.

20. The National Archives, Public Record Office, SP 18/35, fols. 287r, 291r, 317r.

21. Hill, "The Word 'Revolution,'" 90. Hill names the writer as Henry Marten,

and does not cite his source; the document is to be found in Marten's papers but is not in his hand: Brotherton Library, Leeds University, Marten-Loder MS. vol. 93 (Political and Miscellaneous, vol. II).

22. David Norbrook, "A Republican Verse Manifesto, 1653: John Ward's 'The Changes,'" *Seventeenth Century* 13, no. 2 (Autumn 1998): 185–211.

23. For another, similar example from around the same moment, see the letter by unnamed radical Puritans who wrote to Cromwell with a remonstrance "in such a criticall tyme, and under such a revolution as this," calling for the "reformation and redress" of the "pressures and grievances which are oppressive to this nation," and anticipating that "the day of reformation doth beginn to dawne." J. Nickolls, *Original Letters and Papers of State, Addressed to Oliver Cromwell* (London, 1743), 89.

24. See Rachum, *"Revolution,"* 88–91; Wilbur Cortez Abbott, ed., *The Writings and Speeches of Oliver Cromwell,* 4 vols. (Cambridge, MA, 1937–47), 3: 592.

25. For a useful recent survey of the complexities of the constitutional maneuvers during this period, see Patrick Little and David L. Smith, *Parliaments and Politics during the Cromwellian Protectorate* (Cambridge, 2007).

26. Thomas Birch, ed., *A Collection of the State Papers of John Thurloe,* 7 vols. (London, 1742), 4: 774. Of course, even here there may be a qualification hidden in the use of the word: the Portuguese deposition of Philip IV and his replacement by John IV was described as a restoration, and Longland's use may have absorbed this sense of return within it. It should also be noted that Longland was writing from Tuscany, arguably the etymological birthplace of the term. Local influence should not be discounted.

27. See Little and Smith, *Parliaments and Politics during the Cromwellian Protectorate,* 12–48, 102–26, 183–91. For an interesting use of the word "revolution" to describe a feared political insurrection against the authority of the army, see p. 109.

28. For a recent and extensive examination of the turmoil, see Ruth Mayers, *1659: The Crisis of the Commonwealth* (Woodbridge, UK, 2004).

29. *To the Parliament of the Common-wealth of England, &c. The Humble Petition and Representation of Divers Well-affected of the County of South-hampton* (London, 1659).

30. R. Fitz-brian, *The Good Old Cause Dress'd In It's Primitive Lustre, and Set Forth to the View of All Men. Being a short and Sober Narrative of the great Revolutions of Affairs in these later times* (London, 1659), 2, 15.

31. Ibid., 10.

32. *An Essay toward Settlement upon a sure foundation for God in this perillous time* (London, 1659).

33. *A Testimony to truth, agreeing with an Essay for Settlement upon a sure Foundation* (London, 1659); for another casual use of the term, by a Quaker of a rather different political orientation, see George Bishop, *Mene Tekel, Or, The Council of Officers of the Army* (London, 1659), 5.

34. *To the Right Honourable The Lord Maior, Aldermen, and Common-Councel of the City of London. The Humble Petition and Remonstrance of several Inhabitants and Citizens of the said City* (London, 1659); *The Free-Mens Petition* (London, 1659).

35. The National Archives, Public Record Office, SP 18/219/36, fol. 54r. This petition was more ambiguous than the other two, invoking the language of "the good Old Cause" and parliamentarian zeal in a way that suggested it was not the work

of straightforward supporters of the Stuarts. For a discussion, see Ann Hughes, *Politics, Society and Civil War in Warwickshire, 1620–1660* (Cambridge, 1987), 332.

36. *Edinburghs Joy for his Majesties Coronation in England* (London, 1661), 7.

37. For Locke's use of the word, and for the ways in which the phrase was used after 1689, see Keith Baker's essay below.

Armitage: Every Great Revolution Is a Civil War

1. Keith Michael Baker, "Revolution 1.0," *Journal of Modern European History* 11 (2013): 189; Keith Michael Baker, "Inventing the French Revolution," in *Inventing the French Revolution* (Cambridge, 1990), 203, 223; Dan Edelstein, "Do We Want a Revolution without Revolution? Reflections on Political Authority," *French Historical Studies* 35 (2012): 269–89; compare Alain Rey, *"Révolution," Histoire d'un mot* (Paris, 1989); William H. Sewell, Jr., "Historical Events as Transformations of Structures: Inventing Revolution at the Bastille," in *Logics of History: Social Theory and Social Transformation* (Chicago, 2005), 225–70.

2. François Furet, "The Revolutionary Catechism," in *Interpreting the French Revolution*, trans. Elborg Forster (Cambridge, 1981), 83.

3. Karl Marx, *The Eighteenth Brumaire of Louis Bonaparte* (1852), in *Karl Marx: Selected Writings*, ed. David McLellan (Oxford, 1977), 300.

4. David Armitage, *Civil War: A History in Ideas* (New York, 2016).

5. Reinhart Koselleck, "Historical Criteria of the Modern Concept of Revolution," in *Futures Past: On the Semantics of Historical Time*, trans. Keith Tribe (New York, 2004), 46–49; on the conceptual continuities between "revolution" and "civil war," see Neithard Bulst, Jörg Fisch, Reinhart Koselleck, and Christian Meier, "Revolution, Rebellion, Aufruhr, Bürgerkrieg," in *Geschichtliche Grundbegriffe. Historisches Lexikon zur politisch-sozialen Sprache in Deutschland*, ed. Otto Brunner, Werner Conze, and Reinhart Koselleck, 8 vols. (Stuttgart, 1972–97), 5: 653–788, esp. 712–14, 726–27, 778–80.

6. Nicole Loraux, *The Divided City: On Memory and Forgetting in Ancient Athens*, trans. Corinne Pache and Jeff Fort (New York, 2002), 107–8, 197–213; Clifford Ando, *Law, Language, and Empire in the Roman Tradition* (Philadelphia, 2011), 3–4.

7. Cicero, *De officiis*, I. 86, in *On Duties*, ed. M. T. Griffin and E. M. Atkins (Cambridge, 1991), 34 ("apud Atheniensis magnae discordiae, in nostra re publica non solum seditiones sed etiam pestifera bella civilia").

8. Cicero, *De imperio Cn. Pompei*, 28, in *Political Speeches*, trans. D. H. Berry (Oxford, 2006), 119.

9. Appian, *The Civil Wars*, trans. John Carter (Harmondsworth, UK, 1996) 32–33 (I. 59–60).

10. Paul Jal, *La guerre civile à Rome. Étude littéraire et morale* (Paris, 1963); John Henderson, *Fighting for Rome: Poets and Caesars, History and Civil War* (Cambridge, 1998); Brian Breed, Cynthia Damon, and Andreola Rossi, eds., *Citizens of Discord: Rome and its Civil Wars* (Oxford, 2010).

11. Tacitus, *Historiae* (I. 2), in *Histories, Books I–III*, trans. Clifford H. Moore (Cambridge, MA, 1925), 5.

12. Lucan, *Bellum civile* (2, 223–34), in *Civil War*, trans. Susan H. Braund (Oxford, 1992), 27.

13. Algernon Sidney, *Discourses Concerning Government* (London, 1698), 172.

14. Appian, *The Civil Wars*, 4 (I. 6); [Appian,] *An Auncient Historie and exquisite Chronicle of the Romane warres, both Civile and Foren* (London, 1578), title page.

15. Augustine, *The City of God against the Pagans*, ed. R. W. Dyson (Cambridge, 1998), 132, 929 (III. 23, XIX. 7).

16. Peter Burke, "A Survey of the Popularity of Ancient Historians, 1450–1700," *History and Theory* 5 (1966): 135–52; Paul Seaward, "Clarendon, Tacitism, and the Civil Wars of Europe," *Huntington Library Quarterly* 68 (2005): 289–311; Freyja Cox Jensen, "Reading Florus in Early Modern England," *Renaissance Studies* 23 (2009): 659–77; Jensen, *Reading the Roman Republic in Early Modern England* (Leiden, 2012), 56–73; Thomas Hobbes, *Behemoth*, ed. Paul Seaward (Oxford, 2010), 52; *Statutes of the University of Oxford Codified in the Year 1636 under the Authority of Archbishop Laud*, ed. John Griffiths (Oxford, 1888), 37; Nicholas Phillipson, *Adam Smith: An Enlightened Life* (London, 2010), 18.

17. Arnaldo Momigliano, "Ancient History and the Antiquarian," *Journal of the Warburg and Courtauld Institutes* 13 (1950): 294; Jean Marie Goulemot, *Le règne de l'histoire. Discours historiques et révolutions XVIIᵉ–XVIIIᵉ siècles* (Paris, 1996), 127–56.

18. Sven Trakulhun, "Das Ende der Ming-Dynastie in China (1644). Europäische Perspektiven auf eine 'große Revolution,'" in *Revolutionsmedien—Medienrevolutionen*, ed. Sven Grampp et al. (Konstanz, 2008), 475–508.

19. Baker, "Inventing the French Revolution," 207–9.

20. Gabriel Bonnot de Mably, *Des Droits et des devoirs du citoyen*, ed. Jean-Louis Lecercle (Paris, 1972), 66 (my translation); Keith Michael Baker, "A Script for a French Revolution: The Political Consciousness of the Abbé Mably," in Baker, *Inventing the French Revolution*, 94.

21. Sir Robert Filmer, *Patriarcha: Or the Natural Power of Kings* (London, 1680), 54, 55–56, 58.

22. Sidney, *Discourses Concerning Government*, 121.

23. Ibid., 187–89, 193, 196–99.

24. Thomas Paine, *Common Sense* (1776), in *Collected Writings*, ed. Eric Foner (New York, 1995), 18–19.

25. Sir William Blackstone, *Commentaries on the Laws of England*, 4 vols. (Oxford, 1765–69), 4: 435.

26. Edmund Burke, *Reflections on the Revolution in France* [1790], ed. J. G. A. Pocock (Indianapolis, 1987), 26–27 (quoting Livy, *Histories*, 9.1.10) (my emphasis).

27. Edmund Burke, *A Letter from the Right Hon. Edmund Burke . . . to Sir Hercules Langrishe . . . on the Subject of Roman Catholics of Ireland* (London, 1792), 41. My thanks to Richard Bourke for this reference.

28. Compare Pier Paolo Portinaro, "Introduzione: Preliminari ad una teoria della guerra civile," in Roman Schnur, *Rivoluzione e guerra civile*, ed. Portinaro (Milan, 1986), 3–49; Paolo Viola, "Rivoluzione e guerra civile," in *Guerre fratricide: Le guerre civili in età contemporanea*, ed. Gabriele Ranzato (Turin, 1994), 5–26.

29. *Civil War; a Poem. Written in the Year 1775* (n.p., n.d. [1776?]), sig. A2ʳ; David Hartley, *Substance of a Speech in Parliament, upon the State of the Nation and the Present Civil War with America* (London, 1776), 19; John Roebuck, *An Enquiry, whether the Guilt of the Present Civil War in America, Ought to be Imputed to Great Britain or America* (n. p., n.d. [1776?]); William Henry Drayton, *A Charge, on the Rise of the American Empire* (Charlestown, SC, 1776), 2, 8, 15.

30. François Guizot, *Histoire de la révolution d'Angleterre* [1826], quoted in J. C. D. Clark, *Rebellion and Revolution: State and Society in England in the Seventeenth and Eighteenth Centuries* (Cambridge, 1986), 37.

31. The original epigram runs: "Treason doth neuer prosper? What's the Reason? / for if it prosper none dare call it treason": Sir John Harington, *Epigrams*, III. 43, in *The Epigrams of Sir John Harington*, ed. Gerard Kilroy (Farnham, 2009), 185.

32. Karl Marx and Friedrich Engels, *The Communist Manifesto* [1848], in *Selected Writings*, 230.

33. V. I. Lenin, *The Military Programme of the Proletarian Revolution* [1916], in *Collected Works*, 45 vols. (Moscow, 1960–70), 23: 78.

34. Josef Stalin [1928], quoted in Alfred J. Rieber, "Civil Wars in the Soviet Union," *Kritika* 4 (2003): 140.

35. See, for example, Wim Klooster, *Revolutions in the Atlantic World: A Comparative History* (New York, 2009), 11–44; Maya Jasanoff, *Liberty's Exiles: American Loyalists in the Revolutionary World* (New York, 2011), 21–53; Alan Taylor, *The Civil War of 1812: American Citizens, British Subjects, Irish Rebels, and Indian Allies* (New York, 2010); Jean-Clément Martin, *La Vendée et la Révolution* (Paris, 2007); David Andress, *The Terror: Civil War in the French Revolution* (London, 2005); Manuel Lucena Giraldo, *Naciones de rebeldes: Las revoluciones de independencia latinoamericanas* (Madrid, 2010); Tomás Pérez Vejo, *Elegía criolla: Una reinterpretación de las guerras de independencia hispanoamericanas* (Mexico City, 2010).

36. Pace Pierre Serna, "Toute révolution est guerre d'independance," in *Pour quoi faire la Révolution*, ed. Jean-Luc Chappey (Marseille, 2012), 19–49; Pierre Serna, "Every Revolution Is a War of Independence," in *The French Revolution in Global Context*, ed. Suzanne Desan, Lynn Hunt, and William Max Nelson (Ithaca, NY, 2013), 165–82.

Baker: Revolutionizing Revolution

Note: This chapter is an abbreviated and slightly revised version of my article "Revolution 1.0," *Journal of Modern European History* 11 (2013): 187–219. To my regret, that article was written before I learned of the work of Ilan Rachum, *"Revolution": The Entrance of a New Word into Western Political Discourse* (Lanham, MD, 1999), which covers much of the same ground. My thanks go to David Bell, Dan Edelstein, Daniel Gordon, Jack Rakove, and Caroline Winterer for their helpful comments.

1. *Early Books on Line Text Creation Partnership (EEBO-TCP)*, Word Index (Phase I), available at quod.lib.umich.edu/e/eebo.

2. Hannah Arendt famously argued that the astronomical meaning of "revolution" was the conventional one until the end of the eighteenth century. See Arendt, *On Revolution* (London, 1963), 40.

3. The aspect of the Glorious Revolution as a Dutch invasion and conquest is well brought out by Jonathan Israel, "The Dutch Role in the Glorious Revolution," in *The Anglo-Dutch Moment: Essays on the Glorious Revolution and Its World Impact* (Cambridge, 1991), 105–62; and Lisa Jardine, *Going Dutch: How England Plundered Holland's Glory* (New York, 2008).

4. John Locke, *Second Treatise of Government,* §223. Here, as in other quotations, any italics are to be found in the original. As Peter Laslett established in his edition of the *Two Treatises of Government* (Cambridge, 1960), the *Second Treatise*

was in all probability composed in 1679–81 during the Exclusion Crisis. The standard reference for discussion of Locke's use of "revolution" is Vernon F. Snow, "The Concept of Revolution in Seventeenth-Century England," *Historical Journal* 5 (1962): 167–90.

5. Locke, *Second Treatise of Government,* §225.

6. James Dupont, *Three Sermons preached in St. Maries Church in Cambridg, upon the three Anniversaries of the Martyrdom of Charles I, Jan 30, Birth and Return of Charles II, May 29, Gun-powder Treason, November 5* (London, 1676), 50.

7. *The Mystery and Methods of His Majesty's Happy Restauration laid open to Public View by John Price Doctor of Divinity one of Albemarle's Chaplains, and Privy to all the Secret Passages, and Particularities of that Glorious Revolution* (London, 1680).

8. On the politics of the synchronization of the date of William's landing with the date of the Gunpowder Plot (and the fortunes of a competing alternate date, 4 November), see James Richard Redmond McConnel, "The 1688 Landing of William of Orange at Torbay: Numerical Dates and Temporal Understanding in Early Modern England," *Journal of Modern History* 84 (2012): 539–71.

9. Samuel Freeman, *A Sermon preached before the honorable House of Commons at St. Margaret's Westminster on Wednesday the Fifth November, 1690* . . . (London, 1690), 16. A contemporary diarist offered a more worldly picture of this, "the greatest revolution that was ever known." Noting that "politick frauds is and always has been in action in all kingdoms, revolutions, and nations, which is sufficient licence for their lawfulness," he observed that "in this time of our revolution wee had many a strange story of long popish knives, gridirons, and instruments of torture . . . with supposititious letters, speeches, and such like, to irritate the people and encourage them to obey the revolution." Rumors of Irish soldiers disbanded by James II, he reported, had everyone up in arms and resolved to fight but unable to find the enemy. See *The Diary of Abraham de la Pryme,* Publications of the Surtees Society, vol. 54 (Durham, 1870), 14–15.

10. On this theme, see Rachum, *"Revolution,"* 80–100; J. P. Kenyon, *Revolution Principles: The Politics of Party, 1689–1720* (Cambridge, 1977).

11. See http: //artfl-project.uchicago.edu/content/ecco-tcp.

12. Note that collocation analyses typically begin by eliminating approximately one hundred of the most frequently used words in the language (e.g., "the," "and," "of").

13. See http: //quod.lib.umich.edu/e/evans/.

14. Rachum, *"Revolution,"* 140. The fact that this term does not show up in the ECCO database (as a result of an imaging error in the initial microforms on which it is based) points to the need for caution in interpreting these data.

15. See, for example, *A Letter concerning the Union, with Sir George Mackenzie's Observations and Sir John Nisbet's Opinion upon the same Subject* ([Edinburgh?], 1706), 20 ("all honest Revolutionists must be against them [the Jacobites]"); Conyers Place, *The True English Revolutionist, or The Happy Turn Rightly Taken* (London, 1710); *The Revolution and Anti-Revolution Principles Stated and Compar'd, the Constitution Explain'd and Vindicated, And the Justice and Necessity of Excluding the Pretender.* . . . *By the Author of the Two Disswasives against Jacobitism* (London, 1714), 14, 27–28 ("Revolutionists" vs. "Anti-Revolutionists"); *A Vindication of the Honour and Justice of His Majesty's Government. Being some Remarks upon Two Treasonable*

Papers. . . . Wherein is discover'd the present Endeavours of the jacobites, to create fresh Disturbances, and raise a new Rebellion (London, 1717), 43.

16. Further evidence on this point is offered in Baker, "Revolution 1.0," 195–97.

17. Thomas Bradbury Chandler, *A Friendly Address to all Reasonable Americans, on the Subject of our Political Confusions* (Boston, 1774; New York, 1774), 50 ("the projected revolution"), 52 ("the aim of the revolution they propose"); *What think ye of the Congress now?* (New York, 1775), 31 ("till a complete political revolution is effected"), 37.

18. Casca, *The Crisis: Number XXIV* (New York, 1775), 203 ("another glorious and necessary revolution"); *The Crisis: Number XXVI* (New York, 1775), 220 ("another Revolution").

19. *An Essay upon Government. Adopted by the Americans: Wherein the Lawfulness of Revolutions, are demonstrated in a Chain of Consequences from the Fundamental Principles of Society* (Philadelphia, 1775), 113.

20. Peter Whitney, *American Independence Vindicated. A Sermon delivered September 12, 1776. At a Lecture appointed for publishing the Declaration of Independence* (Boston, 1776), 48.

21. *The Genuine Principles of the Ancient Saxon, or English Constitution. Carefully selected from the best Authorities. With some Observations, on their peculiar fitness, for the United Colonies in general, and Pennsylvania in particular. By Demophilus* (Philadelphia, [1776]), 40; Benjamin Rush, *Observations upon the Present Government of Pennsylvania* (Philadelphia, 1777), 3.

22. David Ramsay, *An Oration on the Advantages of American Independence . . . , on the second anniversary of that glorious aera* (Charleston, SC, [1778]), 14; Thomas Paine, *The American Crisis. Number V* (Lancaster, PA, 1778), 83.

23. *Observations on the American Revolution, published according to a Resolution of Congress, by their Committee. For the consideration of those who are desirous of comparing the conduct of the opposed parties, and the several consequences which have flowed from it* (Philadelphia, 1779).

24. Phillips Payson, *A Memorial of Lexington Battle, and of Some Signal Interpositions of Providence in the American Revolution. A Sermon preached at Lexington, on the nineteenth of April 1782* (Boston, [1782]), 6.

25. Pierre Richelet, *Dictionnaire français* (Geneva, 1680), 2: 316; Antoine Furetière, *Dictionnaire universel* (The Hague, 1690), 3: 418; *Dictionnaire de l'Académie française, dédié au Roi,* 1st ed. (Paris, 1694), 2: 406; *Dictionnaire de l'Académie française, dédié au Roi,* 2nd ed. (Paris, 1717), 2: 512 and later editions; *Encyclopédie, ou Dictionnaire raisonné des sciences, des arts et des métiers, par une société de gens de lettres . . . ,* 17 vols. (Paris, 1751–65), 14: 337; *Dictionnaire universel français et latin,* 3 vols. (Trevoux, 1704), 3 (s.v. *revolution*) and later editions. Translations from the French are my own unless otherwise stated.

26. But see below for some uses of "happy" to describe revolutions in politics and government that do not appear in the ARTFL database, which has its origins in a dictionary project skewed toward literary texts by recognizable authors. It is unfortunate that evidence from ARTFL cannot yet be supplemented by more advanced searches in the Goldsmiths-Kress Collection digitized in *The Making of the Modern* World database.

27. This connotation of the term gave rise to an entire genre of political writ-

ing devoted to the *Histoire des révolutions* . . . of various countries. See Jean-Marie Goulemot, *Le règne de l'histoire: discours historiques et révolutions. XVIIe–XVIIIe siècle* (Paris, 1996).

28. *Dictionnaire de l'Académie française*, 5th ed. (Paris, 1798), 2: 499.

29. "Discours préliminaire," *Encyclopédie*, 1: xxxviii, xx.

30. "Encyclopédie," *Encyclopédie*, 5: 637.

31. Voltaire, *Essai sur les moeurs*, ed. René Pomeau, 2 vols. (Paris, 1963), 2: 915. See also G. Mailhos, "Le mot 'révolution' dans l'*Essai sur les moeurs* et la *Correspondance* de Voltaire," *Cahiers de lexicologie* 13 (1968), 84–93; Baker, *Inventing the French Revolution. Essays on French Political Culture in the Eighteenth Century* (Cambridge, 1990), 213.

32. M. J. A. N. Caritat de Condorcet, *Discours de reception à l'Académie française, le 21 février 1782*, as translated in Baker, *Condorcet: Selected Writings* (Indianapolis, IN, 1976), 7, 22.

33. Voltaire to Chauvelin, 2 April 1764, in Theodore Besterman, ed., *Voltaire's Correspondence* (Geneva, 1953–65), letter 10968.

34. [Jean-Paul Rabaut Saint-Etienne,] *Le triomphe de l'intolérance* (1779). For this, and other examples of "happy revolutions" see Rolf Reichardt, *Reform und Revolution bei Condorcet. Ein Beitrag zur späten Aufklärung in Frankreich* (Bonn, 1973), 338–42 (Rabaut quotation, p. 339).

35. Jacques Peuchet, "Discours préliminaire," in *Encyclopédie méthodique: Jurisprudence,* vol. 9, *Police et municipalités* (Paris, 1789), lxiv; fuller quotations in Baker, *Inventing*, 216.

36. On the reorientation toward the future in Enlightenment thinking, see the classic essays by Reinhardt Koselleck, *Futures Past: On the Semantics of Historical Time,* trans. Keith Tribe (Cambridge, MA, 1985); François Hartog, *Régimes d'historicité* (Paris, 2003).

37. Jean-Jacques Rousseau, *Emile, ou De l'éducation,* in *Oeuvres completes,* ed. Bernard Gagnebin and Marcel Raymond, 5 vols. (Paris, 1959–95), 4: 468–69; as translated in *Emile,* trans. Allan Bloom (New York, 1979), 194.

38. [Simon-Nicolas-Henri Linguet], *Annales politiques, civiles, et littéraires du dix-huitième siècle,* 8 vols. ("London," 1777–80), 84, 104; for a fuller discussion, see Baker, *Inventing*, 216–17.

39. Guillaume-Thomas Raynal, *Histoire philosophique et politique des établissements et du commerce des Européens dans les deux Indes,* 7 vols. (The Hague, Gosse fils, 1774), 4: 226–27. My thanks to Mary Ashburn Miller for help in locating this edition. An English translation appeared in five volumes (London, T. Cadell, 1776); quotation at 3: 466.

40. *Histoire philosophique et politique . . . ,* 10 vols. (Geneva: Pellet, 1781), 6: 139.

41. For the most useful general introduction to the history, bibliographical complications, and reception of the *Histoire philosophique et politique,* and recent work on it, see now the critical edition edited by Anthony Strugnell et al. (Ferney-Voltaire, 2010–), 1: xxvii–lii.

42. Ibid., 23.

43. Ibid., 24.

44. *Histoire philosophique et politique . . . ,* 6 vols. (Amsterdam, 1770), 6: 425.

45. *Révolution de l'Amérique par M. l'abbé Raynal, Auteur de l'Histoire philosophique et politique des établissements et du commerce des Européens dans les deux*

Indes (London, chez Lockyer David: Holbourn, 1781), 3. Translations from the French are my own, though I have also consulted the English translation published simultaneously under the same imprint.

46. Ibid., 9.

47. Ibid., 7–8.

48. Ibid., 25.

49. See Thomas Paine, *Letter to the Abbé Raynal, on the Affairs of North America: in which the Mistakes of the Revolution of America are Corrected and Cleared Up* (Philadelphia, 1782). The plagiarism was actually the work of Diderot, who drafted some of the most eloquent passages of the *Histoire philosophique et politique* on the American Revolution. These and other contributions are translated in Denis Diderot, *Political Writings,* ed. John Hope Mason and Robert Wokler (Cambridge, 1992), 169–214.

50. *Révolution de l'Amérique,* 74–85.

51. Ibid., 151.

52. Ibid., 28, 61, 66, 72, 82, 126, 129, 144.

53. Ibid., 145–46.

54. Baker, *Inventing,* 218–23. This analysis owed much to Pierre Rétat, "Forme et discours d'un journal révolutionnaire: Les *Révolutions de Paris* en 1789," in *L'Instrument périodique: La fonction de la presse au XVIIIe siècle,* ed. Claude Labrosse, Pierre Rétat, and Henri Duranton (Lyon, 1986), 139–78.

55. William H. Sewell, Jr., "Historical Events as Transformations of Structures: Inventing Revolution at the Bastille," in *Logics of History: Social Theory and Social Transformation* (Chicago, 2005), 225–70; Mary Ashburn Miller, *A Natural History of Revolution* (Ithaca, NY, 2011); Dan Edelstein, "Do We Want a Revolution without Revolution? Reflections on Political Authority," *French Historical Studies* 35 (Spring 2012): 269–89.

56. The 1798 edition of the *Dictionnaire de l'Académie française* retained conventional eighteenth-century definitions of "revolution." But its *Supplément contenant les mots nouveaux en usage depuis la révolution* added verb and adjectival forms expressing the radical transformation of the term since 1789. "Révolutionner. v.act. Mettre en état de révolution; introduire les principes révolutionnaires dans . . . Révolutionner un État"; "Révolutionnaire. s.m. Ami de la révolution"; "Révolutionnaire. adjective des 2 gen. Qui appartient à la révolution, qui est conforme aux principes de la révolution, qui est propre à en accélérer les progrès, etc. *Mesures révolutionnaires. Gouvernement révolutionnaire;*" "Contre-révolution. s. f. Seconde révolution en sens contraire de la première, et rétablissement des choses dans leur état precedent"; "Contre-révolutionnaire. sub. masc. Ennemi de la Révolution, qui travaille à la renverser, etc. On a dit aussi adjectivement, *Projet, action, discours contre-révolutionnaire,*" *Dictionnaire de l'Académie française,* 5th ed., 2 vols. (Paris, 1798), *Supplément,* 2: 775. On this edition of the dictionary, see Joshua Lobert, "Between Monarchy and Republic: The Dictionary of the Académie Française during the French Revolution, 1762–1798" (Ph.D. dissertation, Stanford University, 2011).

Rakove: Constitutionalism

1. Benjamin Rush, *Address to the People of the United States,* originally published under the pen-name Nestor in the Philadelphia *Independent Gazetteer,* 3 June 1786;

later appeared in the inaugural issue of the *American Museum* magazine, January 1787. It is reprinted in John Kaminski et al., eds., *The Documentary History of the Ratification of the Constitution*, 26 vols. (Madison, WI, 1976–), 13: 45–49 (quotation at 46).

2. Kaminski, *The Documentary History of the Ratification of the Constitution*, 44–45. Rush thus echoes Rousseau's famous point, not as a criticism of representative government but to identify its proper characteristics.

3. Ibid., 46–47. Indeed the role of the post office in fostering citizenship is often discussed in recent scholarship for the early American republic. See, in particular, Richard R. John, *Spreading the News: The American Postal System from Franklin to Morse* (Cambridge, MA, 1995). On the idea of a national university, see George Thomas, *The Founders and the Idea of a Natiobal University: Constituting the American Mind* (New York, 2014).

4. Christian Fritz, *American Sovereigns: The People and America's Constitutional Tradition before the Civil War* (New York, 2008). In fact, a reference to the Algerine Constitution does appear at www.trivia-library.com. For a representative example of what might be called (speaking generationally) the neo-neo-progressive voice of historiography, see two works by Woody Holton, *Forced Founders: Indians, Debtors, Slaves, and the Making of the American Revolution in Virginia* (Chapel Hill, NC, 1999), and *Unruly Americans and the Origins of the Constitution* (New York, 2007)

5. The classic statements belong to Bernard Bailyn, *The Ideological Origins of the American Revolution*, enl. ed. (Cambridge, MA, 1992), 272–301; and Gordon Wood, *The Creation of the American Republic, 1776–1787* (Chapel Hill, NC, 1969), 46–124.

6. Adams to Mercy Otis Warren, 16 April 1776, in *Papers of John Adams*, 16 vols., ed. Robert Taylor et al. (Cambridge, MA, 1977–), 4: 124.

7. Jefferson to Thomas Nelson, 16 May 1776, in *The Papers of Thomas Jefferson*, 40 vols., ed. Julian Boyd et al. (Princeton, 1950–), 1: 292.

8. A good example of this is John Dickinson to William Pitt, 21 December 1765, in Edmund S. Morgan, ed., *Prologue to Revolution: Sources and Documents of the Stamp Act Crisis, 1764–1766* (Chapel Hill, NC, 1959), 118–22.

9. Jack N. Rakove, *The Beginnings of National Politics: An Interpretive History of the Continental Congress* (New York, 1979), 3–20. I return to this theme in the opening pages of *Revolutionaries: A New History of the Invention of America* (Boston, 2010).

10. John Adams to James Warren, 9 April 1774, in *Papers of John Adams*, ed. Taylor, 2: 83.

11. As P. J. Marshall suggests, the idea that resort to Parliament might correct the defects of other assertions of legal authority appears to have been a tempting remedy that British officials periodically considered for India as well as America, yet the reservations against deploying it typically outweighed the advantages. P. J. Marshall, *The Making and Unmaking of Empires: Britain, India, and America c. 1750–1783* (Oxford, 2005).

12. Thus in late July 1775, Adams spoke of "the present critical situation of affairs, when a revolution seems to be in the designs of providence," while in early October he mused again "That a great Revolution in the affairs of the world, is in the womb of Providence, Seems to be intimated very Strongly, by many Circumstances." John Adams to Josiah Quincy, 28 September 1775 and 6 October 1775, in

Letters of Delegates to Congress, 1774–1789, 26 vols., ed. Paul H. Smith (Washington, DC, 1976–2000), 1: 676; 2: 128.

13. North Carolina Delegates to the North Carolina Committees, 19 June 1775, ibid., 1: 514.

14. Rakove, *Revolutionaries*, 27–49. For more detailed treatments, see Richard D. Brown, *Revolutionary Politics in Massachusetts: The Boston Committee of Correspondence and the Towns, 1772–1774* (Cambridge, MA, 1970); and Bernard Bailyn, *The Ordeal of Thomas Hutchinson* (Cambridge, MA 1974).

15. Samuel Adams to Samuel Cooper, 30 April 1776, in *Letters of Delegates to Congress, 1774–1789*, ed. Smith, 3: 601.

16. Robert Morris to Silas Deane, 5 June 1776, ibid., 4: 147.

17. Pauline Maier, *From Resistance to Revolution: Colonial Radicals and the Development of American Opposition to Britain, 1765–1776* (New York, 1972).

18. Ibid., 139.

19. This is the theme I pursue in *Revolutionaries*, which argues, among other things, that many of the most active patriot leaders after 1774 spent the previous few years preoccupied with the usual personal affairs—meaning primarily the pursuit of property—with little expectation that a revolution lay just over the horizon.

20. Benjamin Woods Labaree, *The Boston Tea Party* (New York, 1964), 70–73.

21. Bailyn, *Ideological Origins of the American Revolution*, 94–143.

22. Rakove, *The Beginnings of National Politics*, 88–110.

23. For one version of this story, see Rakove, *Revolutionaries*, chap. 2.

24. Lawrence Stone, "Theories of Revolution," *World Politics* 18 (1966): 159–76.

25. Richard Ashcraft, *Revolutionary Politics and Locke's Two Treatises of Government* (Princeton, NJ, 1986). That view seems to be endorsed in a number of passing references to Locke in Steven Pincus, *1688: The First Modern Revolution* (New Haven, CT, 2009).

26. By which I mean, moving from the adoption of the first state constitutions in 1776 through the ratification of the federal Constitution in 1788 and its initial amendments by 1791.

27. As again in the case of Jephthah, an intriguing source for Locke's notion of the "appeal to heaven" that has curiously received less attention than it might deserve. But see Samuel Moyn, "Appealing to Heaven: Jephthah, John Locke, and Just War," *Hebraic Political Studies* 4 (2009): 286–303; and Andrew Rehfeld, "Jephthah, the Hebrew Bible, and John Locke's *Second Treatise of Government*," *Hebraic Political Studies* 3 (2008): 60–93.

28. For this question in a slightly different but not unrelated context, see Richard P. McCormick, "The 'Ordinance' of 1784?" *William and Mary Quarterly* 50 (1993): 112–22.

29. Rakove, *The Beginnings of National Politics*, 64–67.

30. The best accounts are Wood, *The Creation of the American Republic*, 306–43; and (I hope) Rakove, *Original Meanings: Politics and Ideas in the Making of the Constitution* (New York, 1996), 94–130.

31. See Jefferson's key discussion in *Notes on the State of Virginia*, Query XIII, points 4 and 5, in Merrill Peterson, ed., *Thomas Jefferson: Writings* (New York, 1984), 245–51.

32. "Later laws contradicting earlier ones abrogate them." Compare Rakove, *Original Meanings*, 96–102.

33. Concord resolutions of 21 October 1776, reprinted in Jack Rakove, *Declaring Rights: A Brief History with Documents* (Boston, 1997), 74.

34. The classic account and relevant sources are found in Oscar Handlin and Mary Handlin, eds., *The Popular Sources of Political Authority: Documents on the Massachusetts Constitution of 1780* (Cambridge, MA, 1966).

35. John Adams to John Penn (ante March 27, 1776), *Papers of John Adams*, 4: 79. In revised form, this letter was the basis for Adams's pamphlet *Thoughts on Government* (Philadelphia, 1776)

36. For discussion of the idea of a convention, see Rakove, *The Beginnings of National Politics*, 325–29, 368–80. On popular ratification, see Madison, *Vices of the Political System of the United States;* and Madison to George Washington, 16 April 1787, in Jack N. Rakove, ed., *James Madison: Writings* (New York, 1999), 73–74, 83.

37. By far the best study of this process is the recent book by Pauline Maier, *Ratification: The People Adopt the Constitution, 1787–1788* (New York, 2010), which does an especially nice job of explaining how the procedures for ratification were worked out in each state (but particularly the populous states where the Constitution was most sharply contested).

38. Bruce Ackerman, *We the People, Vol. 1: Foundations* (Cambridge, 1991), 41–42.

39. Madison to Edward Everett, 28 August 1830, in *James Madison,* ed. Rakove, 848.

Edelstein: From Constitutional to Permanent Revolution

Note: This essay is an expanded and revised version of my article, "Do We Want a Revolution Without Revolution? Reflections on Political Authority," *French Historical Studies* 35, no. 2 (2012): 269–89. Copyright, 2012, Society for French Historical Studies. All rights reserved. Republished by permission of Duke University Press. Both essays are from a book project on revolutionary authority.

1. Quoted in Geoffrey Robertson, *The Tyrannicide Brief: The Story of the Man Who Sent Charles I to the Scaffold* (New York, 2006), 149, 155–56.

2. See *Sharp's Dictionary of Power and Struggle* (Oxford, 2012), s.v. "Revolution," 257. A political scientist known for his work on nonviolent resistance, Sharp gained prominence for his gurulike status among revolutionaries in Serbia and the Middle East.

3. This definition of revolutions as conflicts between rival forms of authority is therefore to be distinguished from Charles Tilly's theory of "multiple sovereignty." Tilly's theory assumes that revolutions are over as soon as one side vanquishes the other and brings about "the reimposition of routine governmental control throughout the subject population." See *From Mobilization to Revolution* (New York, 1978), 217. But this assumption flies in the face of revolutionary history, most of which takes place well after the initial seizure of power.

4. While closely identified with Trotsky, the concept of a permanent revolution should in fact be traced back to Marx. See *Witnesses to Permanent Revolution: The Documentary Record*, ed. Richard B. Day and Daniel Gaido (Leiden, 2009); and

Edelstein, "Revolution in Permanence and the Fall of Popular Sovereignty," in *The Scaffold of Sovereignty*, ed. Zvi Ben-Dor Benite, Stefanos Geroulanos, and Nicole Jerr (New York, forthcoming).

5. William H. Sewell, "Historical Events as Transformations of Structures: Inventing Revolution at the Bastille," in *Logics of History: Social Theory and Social Transformation* (Chicago, 2005), 225–70 (quotation at 236); author's italics. See also Samuel Huntington, *Political Order in Changing Societies* (1968; repr., New Haven, CT, 2006), 265; and James Billington, *Fire in the Minds of Men: Origins of the Revolutionary Faith* (1980; repr., New Brunswick, NJ, 1999), 20–21.

6. See for instance Lally-Tollendal's speech of 9 June, *Archives parlementaires de 1787 à 1860* [hereafter *AP*], ed. M. J. Mavidal et al., 127 vols. (Paris, 1862–), 8: 83; or Mirabeau's remarks on 27 June, 8: 168.

7. See notably Pauline Maier, *American Scripture: Making the Declaration of Independence* (New York, 1998).

8. See William Henry Drayton, *A Charge, on the Rise of the American Empire* (Charlestown, SC, 1776), 11; text available through the *America's Historical Imprints* database. This expression did not really catch on until 1779, when the Continental Congress (of which Drayton was then a deputy) published its *Observations on the American Revolution* (Philadelphia, 1779), 122; available online through *America's Historical Imprints*. My thanks to David Armitage for first calling this text to my attention. The authorship of the *Observations* is usually attributed to Gouverneur Morris, who served on many committees with Drayton.

9. Locke, *Second Treatise*, §§229 and 232. For a more nuanced view, see Maier, *American Scripture*, 72, 87.

10. See Quentin Skinner, *The Foundations of Modern Political Thought*, vol. 2 (Cambridge, 1978).

11. Ibid. 2: 239; on the radical Calvinists more generally, see 321–35.

12. Hence, while many of Locke's ideas bear a strong resemblance to those put forward by the Levellers, there is no evidence that he was aware of (or had read any of) their writings. He appears to have "come to [his] conclusions by a different route and in response to different problems." See Julian Franklin, *John Locke and the Theory of Sovereignty* (Cambridge, 1978), 126.

13. See "De l'Amitié," *Essays*, I, chap. 28. Note, however, that Montaigne offers a more favorable view of his friend's treatise in "De l'institution des enfants." On *De la servitude volontaire*, see the excellent article by Nannerl Keohane, "The Radical Humanism of Étienne de La Boétie," *Journal of the History of Ideas* 38, no. 1 (1977): 119–30; and Murray N. Rothbard's introduction to *The Politics of Obedience: The Discourse of Voluntary Servitude*, trans. Harry Kurz (Auburn, AL, 2008), which is also the best available English translation of this test. Curiously, La Boétie's *Discours* is not discussed in Skinner, perhaps because of its perceived lack of originality.

14. Emmanuel Joseph Sieyès, *Qu'est-ce que le Tiers Etat?* (Paris, 1789).

15. See Anthony Pagden, ed., *The Languages of Political Theory in Early-Modern Europe* (Cambridge, 1990).

16. Many historians of this event have made similar claims: see, for instance, Perez Zagorin, who noted how, with the Levellers, "we perceive the germ of a political doctrine new to Europe which, by its appeal to reason and natural right, would

at a later day help to remould the institutions of the Western peoples," in *The Court and the Country: The Beginning of the English Revolution* (New York, 1970), 17. Of course, as we have just seen, the Leveller arguments were hardly "new to Europe." See also Laurence Stone, *The Causes of the English Revolution*, 2nd ed. (New York, 1996); John Morrill, *The Nature of the English Revolution* (Harlow, 1993); and more recently, Clive Holmes, *Why Was Charles I Executed?* (London, 2006), chap. 8.

17. See esp. Martin van Gelderen, *The Political Thought of the Dutch Revolt, 1555–1590* (Cambridge, 1992). As Martin Malia notes, however, this revolt did not bring about significant constitutional changes in the Dutch States: see *History's Locomotives: Revolutions and the Making of the Modern World* (New Haven, CT, 2006), 127–29.

18. See Holmes, *Why Was Charles I Executed?* On ancient constitutionalism, see John Pocock's classic study, *The Ancient Constitution and the Feudal Law* (Cambridge, 1957).

19. *The Parliamentary History of England* (London, 1807), 2: 374.

20. See Max Weber, *Economy and Society: An Outline of Interpretive Sociology*, ed. Guenther Roth and Claus Wittich; trans. Ephraim Fischoff et al., 2 vols. (Berkeley, 1978), esp. 1: 50–51.

21. Alan Cromartie has argued that the measures taken by Parliament in 1640–42 amount to a "constitutionalist revolution," but we are still far here from a modern understanding of "constitutional," since (a) Parliament's changes were not ratified by popular vote; and (b) Parliament's authority to amend the ancient constitution was severely questioned, as the controversy surrounding the Grand Remonstrance would underscore. See *The Constitutionalist Revolution: An Essay on the History of England, 1450–1642* (Cambridge, 2006).

22. See notably Pauline Gregg, *King Charles I* (Berkeley, CA, 1984), 340–42.

23. See *A Declaration of the Lords and Commons Assembled in Parliament* (London, 1642), 15 [Early English Books Online, henceforth abbrieviated EEBO], emphasis added.

24. See notably G. E. Aylmer, ed., *The Levellers in the English Revolution* (Ithaca, NY, 1975); on the Puritan roots of this movement, see David Como, "Radical Puritanism, c. 1558–1660," in *The Cambridge Companion to Puritanism,* ed. J. Coffey and P. Lim (Cambridge, 2008), 241–58.

25. *An Arrow Against All Tyrants and Tyranny* (n.p., 1646), 3–4 [EEBO]. For an interesting discussion of natural right, see also William Ames, "Conscience with the Power and Cases Thereof," in *Puritanism and Liberty*, ed. A. S. P. Woodhouse (Chicago, 1951), 187–91.

26. See Michael Mendle, ed., *The Putney Debates of 1647: The Army, the Levellers and the English State* (Cambridge, 2001).

27. For these quotations, and a more developed exposition of this opinion, see John Lilburne, *London's Liberty in Chains Discovered* (London, 1646) [EEBO], 6. My thanks to David Como for this reference, and for his invaluable assistance in sorting through Leveller ideas.

28. In Andrew Sharp, ed., *The English Levellers* (Cambridge, 1998), 116.

29. See, notably, Jon Elster and Rune Slagstad, eds., *Constitutionalism and Democracy* (Cambridge, 1988); see also Jan-Erik Lane, *Constitutions and Political Theory* (Manchester, 1996).

30. "That the people of England being at this day very unequally distributed by counties, cities and boroughs for the election of their deputies in parliament, ought to be more indifferently proportioned according to the number of the inhabitants," in *English Levellers*, ed. Sharp, 93–94.

31. *The Case of the Armie Truly Stated* (1647), in *Puritanism and Liberty*, ed. Woodhouse, 433. A more detailed description of constitutional procedure can be found in the 1649 *An Agreement of the Free People of England*, in *English Levellers*, ed. Sharp, 168–78.

32. On "rights provisions," see Cass Sunstein, "Constitutionalism and Democracy: An Epilogue," in *Constitutionalism and Democracy*, ed. Elster and Slagstad, 327–28. See also Michael Kent Curtis, "In Pursuit of Liberty: The Levellers and the American Bill of Rights," *Constitutional Commentary* 8 (1991): 359–93. Available at Social Science Research Network: http: //ssrn.com/abstract=956931.

33. See notably Bernard Schwartz, *The Great Rights of Mankind: A History of the American Bill of Rights* (Lanham, MD, 2002), 15–18.

34. *An Act Declaring and Constituting the People of England to be a Commonwealth and Free-State* (London, 1649) [EEBO].

35. See Blair Worden, *God's Instruments: Political Conduct in the England of Oliver Cromwell* (Oxford, 2012), chap. 7.

36. Robertson, *The Tyrannicide Brief*, 193.

37. Vile, *Constitutionalism and the Separation of Powers*, 2nd ed. (Indianapolis, 1998), chap. 3.

38. See Jack Rakove, *The Beginnings of National Politics: An Interpretive History of the Continental Congress* (New York, 1979).

39. In French, "jusqu'à ce que la Constitution du royaume soit établie et affermie sur des fondements solides" (*AP*, 8: 138). This was the famous Tennis Court Oath of 20 June 1789. The Third Estate had proclaimed itself a National Assembly, and invited the other two estates to join it, three days before.

40. See Keith Baker, "Fixing the Constitution," in *Inventing the French Revolution* (Cambridge, 1990), 252.

41. *AP*, 8: 312 (31 July 1789).

42. *AP*, 53: 158–65 (quotation at 160), my italics.

43. Robespierre had defended the storming of the Bastille in similar terms: "is there anything more legitimate than to rise up against a horrid conspiracy to destroy the nation?" *AP*, 8: 253 (20 July 1789).

44. *AP*, 53: 164.

45. *AP*, 53: 160–61 (for all quotations in this paragraph).

46. *AP*, 53: 390–92 (13 November 1792). I analyze the role of jusnaturalist theories played in the king's trial in *The Terror of Natural Right: Republicanism, the Cult of Nature, and the French Revolution* (Chicago, 2009), chap. 3.

47. Quotations from this paragraph are taken from *AP*, 54: 74–77 (3 December 1792).

48. "Rapport sur les principes de morale politique," in Œuvres de Maximilien Robespierre, ed. Société des études robespierristes, 10 vols. (Ivry, 2000), 10: 357.

49. *AP*, 76: 313–17.

50. I examine these debates in *Terror of Natural Right*, chap. 4.

51. *AP*, 76: 318n.

52. On the "natural republicanism" of the Jacobins, see my *Terror of Natural Right*, chap. 5. On the utopian socialists, see notably Frank Manuel, *The New World of Henri Saint-Simon* (Cambridge, MA, 1956); and Billington, *Fire in the Minds of Men*.

53. See *The Class Struggles in France* [1850], in *The Class Struggles in France: From the February Revolution to the Paris Commune* (Chippendale, AU, 2003), 106.

54. Lenin, "On Constitutional Illusions," in *Toward the Seizure of Power, Part I* (n.p., 1932), 62–75.

55. I explore the afterlife of the Jacobin script in "Revolution in Permanence and the Fall of Popular Sovereignty," forthcoming.

Mazeau: Scripting the French Revolution

1. Claude Mossé, *L'Antiquité dans la Révolution française* (Paris, 1989).

2. Robert R. Palmer, *The Age of Democratic Revolutions: A Political History of Europe and America, 1760–1800* (Princeton, NJ, 1959); Jacques Godechot, *Les Révolutions: 1770–1799* (Paris, 1963).

3. Annie Jourdan, *La Révolution française, Une exception française?* (Paris, 2004).

4. For the body of works, see *Brochures sur les fêtes en l'honneur de Marat et Le Peletier*, French Revolution Research Collection, Gallica.

5. Clifford D. Conner, *Jean-Paul Marat and the Scientific Underground of the Ancien Régime* (New York, 1993); Clifford D. Conner, *Jean Paul Marat Scientist and Revolutionary* (Atlantic Highlands, NJ, 1997); Olivier Coquard, *Jean-Paul Marat* (Paris, 1993); Guillaume Mazeau, "Marat ou la naissance d'un héroïsme républicain (1789–1793)," in *Héros et héroïnes de la Révolution française*, ed. Serge Bianchi (Paris, 2012); Ian Germani, *Marat, Hero and Antihero of the French Revolution* (Lewinston, 1992).

6. "Portrait de l'Ami du Peuple, tracé par lui-même," *Journal de la République française* 98 (14 janvier 1793).

7. Guillaume Mazeau, *Corday contre Marat. Deux siècles d'images* (Versailles, 2009).

8. Alain Chevalier, preface to ibid.

9. Guillaume Mazeau, "L'assassinat de Marat: une réponse au déclassement nobiliaire," in *Noblesses et révolution*, ed. Philippe Bourdin (Rennes, 2010).

10. Jean-Clément Martin, *Contre-Révolution, révolution et nation en France, 1789–1799* (Paris, 1998), chap. 1: "Au début était la Contre-Révolution."

11. Coquard, *Jean-Paul Marat*.

12. *Scrutateur Universel*, CLXCV (14 juillet 1793).

13. Articles cited by Jacques de Cock and Charlotte Goëtz, eds., *Jean-Paul Marat. Œuvres politiques*, tome X, juin–juillet 1793, Bruxelles, Pôle Nord, 1995, 1717.

14. Guillaume Mazeau, *Le bain de l'histoire. Charlotte Corday et l'attentat contre Marat (1793–2009)* (Seyssel, 2009), chap. 3.

15. T. Corneille, *Le comte d'Essex*, 1678, acte IV, scène III. AN AE II 38 (Armoire de fer and Musée de l'Histoire de France).

16. Cited by Jacques Guilhaumou, *1793. La Mort de Marat* (Bruxelles, 1989), 57–58.

17. Peter McPhee, *Robespierre, A Revolutionary Life* (New Haven, 2012).

18. *Les Chaînes de l'Esclavage* (Paris, 1792), 6.

19. *Journal de Marseille*, 20 juin 1793; J. De Cock, "La santé de l'Ami du peuple," in De Cock and Goëtz, eds., *Jean-Paul Marat*.

20. Stanis Perez, *La santé de Louis XIV. Une biohistoire du Roi-Soleil* (Seyssel, 2007).

21. Mona Ozouf, *La fête révolutionnaire* (Paris, 1976).

22. Mazeau, *Le Bain de l'histoire*, 159.

23. *Adresse de la Société républicaine de Chaumont à la Convention nationale*, 18 juillet 1793, AN C 266, d. 582.

24. Arlette Farge, *Dire et mal dire. L'opinion publique au XVIIIe siècle* (Paris, 1992).

25. Marcel Morabito and Daniel Bourmaud, *Histoire constitutionnelle et politique de la France (1789–1958)* (Paris, 1993), 108–11.

26. Michael Walzer, *Régicide et Révolution. Le procès de Louis XVI* (Paris, 1989), 81.

27. Mazeau, *Le Bain de l'Histoire*, chap. 2.

28. AN F7 4385, Comité de Sûreté Générale, 24, *Lettre de Genève du 19 juillet 1793 de Jean-Pierre Marat, membre du club révolutionnaire genevois*; *Discours pour la fête funèbre de Marat et le Peletier de la section de Brutus, par Charlemagne fils*, 15 septembre 1793; Marie-Hélène Huet, *Rehearsing the Revolution : The Staging of Marat's Death* (Berkeley, 1992).

29. Dan Edelstein, *The Terror of Natural Right: Republicanism, the Cult of Nature, and the French Revolution* (Chicago, 2009).

30. Reinhardt Koselleck, *Le futur passé. Contribution à la sémantique des temps historiques* (Paris, 1990); Jean-Marie Goulemot, *Discours, histoire et révolutions* (Paris, 1975).

31. Pierre Serna, "Radicalités et modérations, postures, modèles théories. Naissance du cadre politique contemporain," *Annales historiques de la Révolution française*, no. 3 (2009): 3–19.

32. Mazeau, *Le bain de l'histoire*, chap. 3.

33. Jean-Clément Martin, *Violence et Révolution. Essai sur la naissance d'un mythe national* (Paris, 2006); Michel Biard, *Les politiques de la Terreur* (Rennes, 2009); Guillaume Mazeau, "La 'Terreur,' laboratoire de la modernité," in *Pour quoi faire la Révolution*, ed. Jean-Luc Chappey et al. (Marseille, 2012).

34. Haïm Burstin, "Le 'protagonisme' comme facteur d'amplification de l'événement: le cas de la Révolution française," dans *L'Evénement* (1983), PUA, 1986, 65–75.

35. Guillaume Mazeau, "Violence politique et transition démocratique: les attentats sous la Révolution française," in *La Révolution française*, available at http://lrf.revues.org/380, accessed 14 August 2012.

36. Jourdan, *La Révolution française*.

Ghachem: The Antislavery Script

Acknowledgment: Thanks to audiences at the Montreal French Atlantic History Seminar, the University of Pennsylvania Legal History Workshop, the NYU Atlantic History Workshop, and the Brandeis-Mellon Sawyer Seminar on "Rethinking the Age of Revolution" for helpful comments on earlier drafts of this essay. I am also indebted to Jeff Ravel and Joseph Miller for conversations that stimulated my thinking on this subject.

1. Michael Walzer, *Exodus and Revolution* (New York, 1986).

2. Quoted in Omar Ashour, "Egypt's Revolution: Two Lessons from History," *Sada* (7 February 2011), available at www.carnegieendowment.org/2011/02/07/egypt-s-revolution-two-lessons-from-history/6be5.

3. Martin Malia, *History's Locomotives: Revolutions in the Making of the Modern World*, ed. Terence Emmons (New Haven, CT, 2006), 3.

4. Compare Orlando Patterson, *Freedom*, vol. 1, *Freedom in the Making of Western Culture* (New York, 1991), ix (noting that freedom is "the catchword of every politician").

5. A perspective often identified with the work of R. R. Palmer, *The Age of the Democratic Revolution: A Political History of Europe and America*, 2 vols. (Princeton, NJ, 1969–70). See Allan Potofsky, "The One and the Many: The Two Revolutions Question and the 'Consumer-Commercial' Atlantic, 1789 to the Present," in *Europe and America in the Age of the Democratic Revolutions*, ed. Manuela Albertone and Antonino De Francesco (New York, 2009), 29.

6. I am here adapting a statement that Tocqueville makes in book III, chapter 1 of *The Ancien Régime and the French Revolution*, trans. Arthur Goldhammer, ed. Jon Elster (New York, 2011), 133.

7. For an example of these caricatures, see the 1790 medallion by Simon-Louis Boizot available at http://jcb.lunaimaging.com/luna/servlet/detail/JCB~1~1~2921~4660006: Moi-Libre-aussi.

8. Jeffrey Ravel, *The Contested Parterre: Public Theater and French Political Culture, 1680–1791* (Ithaca, NY, 1999), 6–7, 83 (quotation).

9. Palmer's *The Age of the Democratic Revolution* is frequently cited in this context. As Lynn Hunt has observed, Palmer's work should be understood and appreciated as an important intervention into the debates of its own scholarly time. Lynn Hunt, preface to "Robert Roswell Palmer: A Transatlantic Journey of American Liberalism," *Historical Reflections/Réflexions historiques* 37, no. 3 (Winter 2011): v–viii. For a reading of the revolutionary era that absorbs the recent rise of Haiti as an historical actor, see, e.g., Wim Klooster, *Revolutions in the Atlantic World: A Comparative History* (New York, 2009).

10. Thomas Piketty, *Capital in the Twenty-First Century*, trans. Arthur Goldhammer (Cambridge, MA, 2013), 30. This is to say nothing of the author's archaic (and related) characterization of the French Revolution as "the 'bourgeois' revolution par excellence."

11. Malia, *History's Locomotives*, 1–2.

12. Bernard Bailyn, *The Ideological Origins of the American Revolution*, enl. ed. (Cambridge, MA, 1992), 232–34. Cf. F. Nwabueze Okoyo, "Slavery as the Nightmare of the American Revolutionaries," *William and Mary Quarterly* 37, no. 1 (Jan. 1980): 3–28 (arguing that chattel rather than political slavery was at stake in the American Whig pamphlets).

13. Mary Nyquist, *Arbitrary Rule: Slavery, Tyranny, and the Power of Life and Death* (Chicago, 2013). For the Anglo-American classical republican context, see J. G. A. Pocock, *The Machiavellian Moment: Florentine Political Thought and the Atlantic Republican Tradition* (Princeton, NJ, 1975). Both Pocock and Bailyn built upon the earlier findings of Caroline A. Robbins, *The Eighteenth-Century Commonwealthman* (Cambridge, 1961). For the French context, see Keith M. Baker, "Transforma-

tions of Classical Republicanism in Eighteenth-Century France," *Journal of Modern History* 73 (2001): 43–44; Keith M. Baker, "Political Languages of the French Revolution," in *The Cambridge History of Eighteenth-Century Political Thought*, ed. Mark Goldie and Robert Wokler (New York, 2006), 643.

14. See Rachel Hammersley, "Jean-Paul Marat's *The Chains of Slavery* in Britain and France, 1774–1833," *Historical Journal* 48, no. 3 (2005): 642–46.

15. Jean-Paul Marat, *The Chains of Slavery* (London, 1774), 1.

16. *Catéchisme révolutionnaire, ou l'histoire de la Révolution française, par demandes et par réponses: à l'usage de la jeunesse républicaine, et de tous les peoples qui veulent devenir libres* (Paris, 1793–94), 3; also quoted in Michel Vovelle, *La mentalité révolutionnaire: Société et mentalités sous la Révolution française* (Paris, 1985), 103. On the connection of classical republican rhetoric to the Terror, see Baker, "Transformations of Classical Republicanism in Eighteenth-Century France."

17. Germaine de Staël, *Considérations sur la Revolution française*, ed. Jacques Godechot (Paris, 2000), 303–4.

18. But see Jean Jaurès's *Histoire socialiste de la révolution française* (1901–7), which, alone among the great early-twentieth-century French narratives, devotes considerable attention to the Saint-Domingue Revolution.

19. Christopher Leslie Brown, *Moral Capital: Foundations of British Abolitionism* (Chapel Hill, NC, 2006), 105–53.

20. Nyquist, *Arbitrary Rule*, chaps. 8–10, epilogue.

21. Bailyn, *The Ideological Origins of the American Revolution*, 234. See also Gordon S. Wood, *The American Revolution: A History* (New York, 2002), 127.

22. Quoted in Bailyn, *The Ideological Origins of the American Revolution*, 239. See also Peter A. Dorsey, *Common Bondage: Slavery as Metaphor in Revolutionary America* (Knoxville, TN, 2009).

23. George William Van Cleve, *A Slaveholders' Union: Slavery, Politics, and the Constitution in the Early American Republic* (Chicago, 2011), 45. See also David Brion Davis, *The Problem of Slavery in the Age of Revolution, 1770–1823*, new ed. (New York, 1999), 255–62 (discussing the limits of American revolutionary ideology).

24. Ibid., chaps. 2–4.

25. For a sympathetic reading, see Gordon S. Wood, *The Radicalism of the American Revolution* (New York, 1991), 186–87; Wood, *The American Revolution*, 57. For a more critical perspective, see Van Cleve, *A Slaveholders' Union*; and Gary Nash, *Race and Revolution* (Madison, WI, 1990), chap. 2.

26. Alfred F. Young, Gary B. Nash, and Ray Raphael, eds., *Revolutionary Founders: Rebels, Radicals, and Reformers in the Making of the Nation* (New York, 2011), 4.

27. For the details of this history, see Malick W. Ghachem, "Sovereignty and Slavery: Haitian Variations on a Metropolitan Theme," Ph.D. dissertation, Stanford University, 2002, chap. 3.

28. Ibid., 191–206.

29. David Armitage, *The Declaration of Independence: A Global History* (Cambridge, MA, 2007), 115. No actual manuscript reflecting this initial draft has survived the passage of time, but a portion seems to have been preserved and appears in Gaétan Mentor, *Les fils noirs de la veuve: Histoire de la franc-maçonnerie en Haïti* (Port-au-Prince, 2003), 168–69. See David Geggus, "La declaración de independen-

cia de Haiti," in *Declarando Independencias: Textos fundamentales*, ed. Alfredo Ávila et al. (Mexico City, 2013). Julia Gaffield's very recent discovery of an original print of the final declaration in the British National Archives gives one reason to hope that the earlier draft, believed to have been composed by a free person of color named Jean-Jacques Charéron, may eventually be found. For Gaffield's discovery, see http: //today.duke.edu/showcase/haitideclaration/juliasdiscovery.html.

30. Compare Laurent Dubois, *Avengers of the New World: The Story of the Haitian Revolution* (Cambridge, MA, 2004), 154, 170.

31. Compare Potofsky's essay "The One and the Many," which describes the Haitian Revolution as a "future revolution" relative to that of France, and one whose "immediate origins must be found in the same sense of inequality or injustice as well as the promise of universal human rights" (at 32; internal quotations omitted). Stated at this level of generality the thesis proves too much, for the origins of nearly all revolutions must then be traced to the French Revolution, and then further back in time to the American Revolution, and so on.

32. David Brion Davis, *Inhuman Bondage: The Rise and Fall of Slavery in the New World* (Oxford, 2008), 222–23.

33. I have developed this argument elsewhere and will only briefly summarize the main lines of argument here. See Malick W. Ghachem, *The Old Regime and the Haitian Revolution* (New York, 2012).

34. Code Noir (1685), arts. 57 and 59.

35. Julien Raimond, *Observations sur l'origine et le progrès du préjugé des colons blancs contres les hommes de couleur* (Paris, 1791), 27–28. See also Ghachem, *The Old Regime and the Haitian Revolution*, 240–41.

36. The two letters in question—dated 22 December 1791 and July 1792, respectively—are discussed in Ghachem, *The Old Regime and the Haitian Revolution*, 276–85.

37. I am here summarizing the argument of Ghachem, ibid., chaps. 3–6.

38. The 29 August 1793 decree appears in English translation in Laurent Dubois and John D. Garrigus, *Slave Revolution in the Caribbean, 1789–1804: A Brief History with Documents* (Boston, 2006), 122, 124–25.

39. Dessalines himself gave a short address to the assembled crowd in Creole. His secretary, Louis Boisrond-Tonnerre, then read, in French, the longer speech that is known today (somewhat misleadingly) as the Haitian Declaration of Independence. A separate act announced the independence of Haiti proper, and a third document made Dessalines governor-general of Haiti for life.

40. Address of Jean-Jacques Dessalines at Gonaïves, 1 January 1804, in Dubois and Garrigus, *Slave Revolution in the Caribbean*, 188–89.

41. Dessalines went on expressly to threaten with death any French persons who dare "approach our coast" and set "profane" foot in Saint-Domingue, thereby "soil[ing] the land of liberty." Ibid., 189.

42. See Davis, *Inhuman Bondage*, 168.

43. The 1805 Haitian Constitution, arts. 12 and 14, in Dubois and Garrigus, *Slave Revolution in the Caribbean*, 192–93.

44. Claude Moïse, *Le projet national de Toussaint Louverture et la Constitution de 1801* (Montreal, 2001). This fine volume reprints Louverture's October 1800 and November 1801 labor regulations at 131–57.

45. Address of Dessalines to the People of Haiti (1 January 1804), in Dubois and Garrigus, *Slave Revolution in the Caribbean*, 191.

46. The 1805 Haitian Constitution, in ibid., 192, 196.

47. See the essays in Julia Gaffield, ed., *The Haitian Declaration of Independence: Creation, Context, and Legacy* (Charlottesville, VA, 2015).

48. C. L. R. James, *The Black Jacobins: Toussaint L'Ouverture and the San Domingo Revolution*, 2nd ed. (New York, 1963), 391.

49. Davis, *Inhuman Bondage*, 167.

50. It is certainly possible to trace many other genealogies. See David Patrick Geggus and Norman Fiering, eds., *The World of the Haitian Revolution* (Bloomington, IN, 2009); David Barry Gaspar and David Patrick Geggus, eds., *A Turbulent Time: The French Revolution and the Greater Caribbean* (Bloomington, IN, 1997); David Patrick Geggus, ed., *The Impact of the Haitian Revolution in the Atlantic World* (Columbia, SC, 2002); and Ada Ferrer, *Freedom's Mirror: Cuba and Haiti in the Age of Revolution* (New York, 2014).

51. Dubois, *Avengers of the New World*, 303. As Julia Gaffield's work shows, this embargo was not watertight even as to American merchants, and in the Caribbean trade with Haiti continued as it had for decades under French colonial rule. See Julia Gaffield, "Haiti and Jamaica in the Remaking of the Early Nineteenth-Century Atlantic World," *William and Mary Quarterly* 69, no. 3 (2012): 583–613.

52. Ashli White, *Encountering Revolution: Haiti and the Making of the Early Republic* (Baltimore, MD, 2010); Edward Barlett Rugemer, *The Problem of Emancipation: The Caribbean Roots of the American Civil War* (Baton Rouge, LA, 2008); Matthew J. Clavin, *Toussaint Louverture and the American Civil War: The Promise and Peril of a Second Haitian Revolution* (Philadelphia, 2010).

53. James M. McPherson, *Abraham Lincoln and the Second American Revolution* (New York, 1992), 23–42.

54. Dubois, *Avengers of the New World*, 303.

55. Eric Foner, *The Fiery Trial: Abraham Lincoln and American Slavery* (New York, 2010), 222; Dubois, *Avengers of the New World*, 305.

56. Foner, *The Fiery Trial*, 239–40. Only about four hundred African Americans were actually transported to the island at the end of the day, and most returned to the United States within a very short period.

57. Ibid., 241.

58. *Catéchisme révolutionnaire*, in Vovelle, *La mentalité révolutionnaire*, 103.

59. Alexander Tsesis, *For Liberty and Equality: The Life and Times of the Declaration of Independence* (New York, 2012), chs. 4–10.

60. Jack M. Balkin and Sanford Levinson, "The Dangerous Thirteenth Amendment," *Columbia Law Review* 112 (2012): 1459–1500.

61. See Risa Goluboff, *The Lost Promise of Civil Rights* (New York, 2007).

62. But see Gary Gallagher, *The Union War* (Cambridge, MA, 2012) (distinguishing between a war fought to end slavery and a war fought to preserve the union that had the effect of ending slavery).

63. See Seymour Drescher, *Dilemmas of Democracy: Tocqueville and Modernization* (Pittsburgh, PA, 1968), 161–62.

64. Seymour Drescher, *Abolition: A History of Slavery and Antislavery* (New York, 2009), 281–82.

65. See Christopher L. Brown, "Empire without Slaves: British Concepts of Emancipation in the Age of the American Revolution," *William and Mary Quarterly* 56, no. 2 (1999): 273–306.

66. Drescher, *Abolition*, 282.

67. See Mathieu Olivier, "Une descendante d'esclaves dépose plainte contre l'État pour crime contre l'humanité," *Jeune Afrique*, 8 January 2013, www.jeuneafrique.com/Article/ARTJAWEB20130108183220/.

68. See Laurent Dubois, "Confronting the Legacies of Slavery," *New York Times*, 28 October 2013.

Stedman Jones: Scripting the German Revolution

1. For an impressively broad analysis of this question, see Warren Breckman, "Diagnosing the "German Misery': Radicalism and the Problem of National Character, 1830–1848," in *Between Reform and Revolution: German Socialism and Communism from 1840 to 1990*, ed. David E. Barclay and Eric Weitz (New York, 1998), 32–61.

2. "Immanuel Kant, "On the Common Saying: "This May Be True in Theory, But It Does Not Apply in Practice,"" in *Kant's Political Writings*, ed. H. Reiss (Cambridge, 1970), 61–93; see also Jacques Droz, *L'Allemagne et la Révolution Française* (Paris, 1949).

3. Friedrich Schiller, *On the Aesthetic Education of Man*, ed. Elizabeth M. Wilkinson and L. A. Willoughby (Oxford, 1982), 25.

4. See Michael Rowe, *From Reich to State: The Rhineland in the Revolutionary Age 1780–1830* (Cambridge, 2003).

5. Madame De Staël cited "one of the most distinguished of their writers," Jean Paul Richter, "L'empire de la mer c'était aux Anglais, celui de la terre aux Français, et celui de l'air aux Allemands." Madame De Staël, *De l'Allemagne* (Paris, 1860), 18. On the shift away from politics among the early Romantics, see Frederick C. Beiser, *The Romantic Imperative: The Concept of Early German Romanticism* (Cambridge, MA, 2003).

6. On the character of democratic nationalist sentiment in the *Vormärz* period, see Hagen Schulze, *The Course of German Nationalism: From Frederick the Great to Bismarck, 1763–1867* (Cambridge, 1991).

7. Heinrich Heine, *On the History of Religion and Philosophy in Germany*, ed. Terry Pinkard (Cambridge, 2007), 111, 116; see also Harold Mah, "The French Revolution and the Problem of German Modernity: Hegel, Heine and Marx," *New German Critique* 50 (Spring–Summer 1990): 3–20.

8. The importance of republican themes in the thought of the Young Hegelians has been brought out by Douglas Moggach; see Moggach, "Introduction: Hegelianism, Republicanism and Modernity," in *The New Hegelians: Politics and Philosophy in the Hegelian School* (Cambridge, 2006), 1–24.

9. See Gareth Stedman Jones, Introduction to *The Communist Manifesto* by Karl Marx and Friedrich Engels (London, 2002), 90–99.

10. Cited in Breckman, "Diagnosing the "German Misery,"" 39. Börne considered that the passivity of Shakespeare's *Hamlet* could be attributed to the time he spent studying German philosophy at the University of Wittenberg. Ibid., 39. Ludwig Börne, a democratic writer and a lapsed Jew, went into exile in Paris at the same time as Heine. He was one of the heroes of the young Friedrich Engels, especially be-

cause of his attack on the anti-French German nationalism of Wolfgang Menzel, in his 1837 *Menzel der Franzosenfresser*. Heine fell out with him and denounced him after his death in *Ludwig Börne: eine Denkschrift* (1840), which Engels regarded as "despicable."

11. On the political implications of Feuerbach's philosophy, see especially Warren Breckman, *Marx, The Young Hegelians and the Origins of Radical Social Theory: Dethroning the Self* (New York, 1999); and see also Warren Breckman, "Ludwig Feuerbach and the Political Theology of the Restoration," *History of Political Thought* 13, no. 3 (Autumn 1992): 437–61.

12. Karl Marx, Introduction to "Contribution to the Critique of Hegel's Philosophy of Law," *Marx/Engels Collected Works* [hereafter *MECW*], 50 vols. (London, 1975), 3: 177.

13. Ibid., 187.

14. The regime of Louis Philippe, in particular its chief spokesman, Guizot, claimed that it represented *la classe moyenne*, a class without privileges and open to the talented from all classes. See Adeline Daumard, *Les Bourgeois et la Bourgeoisie en France depuis 1815* (Paris, 1987), 44–51; Pierre Rosanvallon, *Le Moment Guizot* (Paris, 1985), passim. The Saint-Simonians played an important part in initially defining the 1830 Revolution as "bourgeois" and underlining its pejorative character. See Shirley Gruner, "The Revolution of July 1830 and the Expression 'Bourgeoisie,'" *Historical Journal* 11, no. 3 (1968): 462–71. From the Saint-Simonians, this terminology spread to the rest of the left. The journalistic work of Louis Blanc was particularly important. See, for example, Louis Blanc, *Révolution Française: Histoire de dix ans, 1830–1840*, 5 vols. (Paris, 1841–44). Blanc characterized "the social history of the bourgeoisie" as "the banking interest enthralling industry and commerce; individual credit profiting the strong, injuring the weak; in a word, the reign of competition tending inevitably to overthrow small fortunes, and to undermine those of middle standard and all this for the purpose of arriving at a real financial feudality . . . an oligarchy of bankers." "From 1815 to 1830," Blanc continued, "the bourgeoisie busied itself only with completing its domination. To turn the elective system to its own advantage, to seize on the parliamentary power and render it supreme after having achieved its conquest, such was for fifteen years the work prosecuted by liberalism." Louis Blanc, *The History of Ten Years 1830–1840*, 2 vols. (London, 1845), 1: 27, 33.

15. Alexis de Tocqueville, *Recollections*, trans. George Lawrence (London, 1970), 52, 92.

16. Friedrich Engels, "The Condition of the Working Class in England," *MECW*, 4: 304. For international comparisons, see Manfred Riedel, "Burger," in *Geschichtliche Grundbegriffe*, ed. Otto Brunner et al. (Stuttgart, 1972), 1: 672–725; Reinhart Koselleck, Ulrike Spree, and Willibald Steinmetz, "Drei bürgerliche Welten? Zur vergleichenden Semantik der bürgerlichen Gesellschaft in Deutschland, England und Frankreich," in *Bürger in der Gesellschaft der Neuzeit*, ed. Hans-Jürgen Puhle (Göttingen, 1991), 15–58; Reinhart Koselleck and Klaus Schreiner, *Bürgerschaft: Rezeption und Innovation der Begrifflichkeit vom Hohen Mittelalter bis ins 19 Jahrhundert* (Stuttgart, 1994); Jürgen Kocka, "Das Europäische Muster und der deutsche Fall," in *Bürgertum im 19 Jahrhundert: Deutschland im europäischen Vergleich*, 3 vols. (Göttingen, 1995), 1: 9–76; Pamela M. Pilbeam, *The Middle Classes in Europe, 1789–1914: France, Germany, Italy and Russia* (Basingstoke, UK, 1990).

17. See *MECW,* 4: 295–597.

18. See John M. Maguire, *Marx's Theory of Politics* (Cambridge, 1978), 203.

19. *MECW,* 41: 435; and see my discussion in "The Young Hegelians, Marx and Engels," in *The Cambridge History of Nineteenth Century Political Thought*, ed. Gareth Stedman Jones and Gregory Claeys (Cambridge, 2011), 579–85.

20. Karl Marx, critical marginal notes on the article "The King of Prussia and Social Reform by a Prussian," *MECW* 3: 201–2; on the elaboration of the myth of the weavers' uprising, see Christina von Hodenberg, *Aufstand der Weber: die Revolte von 1844 und ihr Aufststieg zum Mythos* (Bonn, 1997), 111, 137–51.

21. Daumard, *Les Bourgeois et la Bourgeoisie en France depuis 1815*, 85–93.

22. In the case of France during the July Monarchy, see the discussion in Sarah Maza, *The Myth of the French Bourgeoisie: An Essay on the Social Imaginary, 1750–1850* (Cambridge, MA, 2003).

23. See Gareth Stedman Jones, "The Rise and Fall of 'Class Struggle': England and France, 1789–1850," unpublished.

24. Lorenz von Stein, *Der Socialismus und Communismus des heutigen Frankreichs: ein Beitrag zur Zeitgeschichte*, 2nd ed. (Leipzig, 1848), 447–48. See also Stedman Jones, Introduction to *The Communist Manifesto,* 27–39.

25. *MECW,* 7: 144–64.

26. *MECW,* 8: 154–79; on the rivalry between Marx and Gottschalk in Cologne in 1848–49, see Dieter Dowe, *Aktion und Organisation: Arbeiterbewegung, sozialistische und kommunistische Bewegung in der preußischen Rheinprovinz 1820–1852* (Hannover, 1970), part 2; Jonathan Sperber, *Rhineland Radicals: The Democratic Movement and the Revolution of 1848–1849* (Princeton, 1993), part 2.

27. Sperber, *Rhineland Radicals*, 490.

Chang: Reading and Repeating the Revolutionary Script

Note: Portions of this chapter were first published in Chang, "'Un nouveau '93': Discourses of Mimicry and Terror in the Paris Commune of 1871," *French Historical Studies* 36, no. 4 (Fall 2013): 629–48. Copyright, 2013, Society for French Historical Studies. All rights reserved. Republished by permission of Duke University Press.

1. My argument is built upon the seminal work of scholars such as François Furet, Keith M. Baker, Lynn Hunt, and Roger Chartier, all of whom have greatly enriched the field of revolutionary studies by examining the significance of competing discourses, public opinion, political symbolism, identity formation, and (self-) representation during the French Revolution. See Keith M. Baker, *Inventing the French Revolution* (Cambridge, 1990); Roger Chartier, *Les Origines culturelles de la Révolution française* (Paris, 1986); François Furet, *Penser la Révolution française* (Paris, 1978); Lynn Hunt, *Politics, Culture, and Class in the French Revolution* (Berkeley, 1984).

2. Current scholars in the humanities often (and understandably) associate the term "mimicry" with the important work of postcolonial theorist Homi K. Bhabha. See, in particular, his *Of Mimicry and Man* (New York, 1994). My own use of "mimicry," however, does not occur in a multicultural or postcolonial context and should be read more generally as the pejorative representation of historical imitation.

3. Roger Bellet, "Mythe jacobin et mythe révolutionnaire chez Jules Vallès de 93 à la Commune de Paris," in *Mythes et Révolutions*, ed. Yves Chalas (Grenoble, 1990), 229.

4. For primary texts, see Filippo Buonarotti, *La Conspiration pour l'égalité dite de Babeuf* (Brussels, 1828); Alphonse de Lamartine, *Histoire des Girondins* (Paris, 1847); Felicité de Lamennais, *Paroles d'un croyant* (Paris, 1834); François Mignet, *Histoire de la Révolution française depuis 1789 jusqu'en 1814* (Paris, 1824); Germaine de Staël, *Considérations sur la Révolution française* (Paris, 1818); Adolphe Thiers, *Histoire de la Révolution française* (Paris, 1823–27). For more about this process of rehabilitation between the years 1799 and 1830, see, for example, André Jardin and André-Jean Tudesq, *Restoration and Reaction, 1815–1848*, trans. Elborg Forster (Cambridge, 1983); Edgar Leon Newman, "Republicanism during the Bourbon Restoration in France, 1814–1830," Ph.D. dissertation, University of Chicago, 1969; George Weill, *Histoire du parti républicain en France, 1814–1870* (Paris, 1928); and Stanley Mellon, *The Political Uses of History: A Study of Historians in the French Restoration* (Stanford, CA, 1958). For studies on the romanticization and radicalization of these representations, especially those that appeared to serve as a call to revolutionary action, see, in particular, Lionel Gossman, *Between History and Literature* (Cambridge, 1990); Hayden White, *Metahistory: The Historical Imagination in Nineteenth-Century Europe* (Baltimore, MD, 1973); and Edgar Leon Newman, "The Historian as Apostle: Romanticism, Religion, and the First Socialist History of the World," *Journal of the History of Ideas* 56 (1995): 239–61.

5. It is also notable that imitation of historical events and persons was, as Chateaubriand observed, a common practice of the "original" French Revolutionaries, who proudly copied the symbols, rituals, rhetoric, and even clothing of the Roman Republic to legitimate their actions and foster popular support. See François-René de Chateaubriand, *Mémoires d'outre-tombe*, ed. Maurice Levaillant, 4 vols. (Paris, 1948–49).

6. Letter to *La Presse*, 4 April 1847, cited in Fernand L'Huillier, *Lamartine en Politique* (Strasbourg, 1993), 152.

7. Letter to Ronot, 20 March 1847, cited in ibid., 156.

8. Because the charge of revolutionary mimicry did exist before 1848, post-1848 depictions of this phenomenon are thus less notable for their complete novelty than for the fact that so many of them appeared so suddenly after the 1848 Revolution, for their incisive illustrative value, and because they are made by critics of rather diverse political ideologies.

9. Karl Marx, *The Eighteenth Brumaire of Louis-Bonaparte*, in *Karl Marx: Selected Writings*, ed. David McLellan (Oxford, 1990), 300–301.

10. Alexis de Tocqueville, *Souvenirs* (Paris, 1942), 82.

11. P.-J. Proudhon, *Les Confessions d'un Révolutionnaire: pour servir à l'histoire de la Révolution de février* (Paris, 1929), 13.

12. Gustave Flaubert, *L'Education sentimentale* (Paris, 1985). All citations from *L'Education* are taken from this French edition. Unless otherwise noted, English translations are mine. Regarding feminism in France during the mid-nineteenth century, see Felicia Gordon, *Early French Feminisms, 1830–1940* (Cheltenham, UK, 1996); and Claire Moses, *Feminism, Socialism, and French Romanticism* (Bloomington, IN, 1993).

13. Two recent studies, Susan Maslan's *Revolutionary Acts* and Paul Friedland's *Political Actors*, examine how metaphors of theatricality—as well as actual theatrical representations—were crucial to how the French Revolution of 1789 was both un-

derstood and performed. See Susan Maslan, *Revolutionary Acts: Theater, Democracy, and the French Revolution* (Baltimore, MD, 2005); and Paul Friedland, *Political Actors: Representative Bodies and Theatricality in the Age of the French Revolution* (Ithaca, NY, 2002).

14. Maxime Du Camp, *Souvenirs littéraires* (Paris, 1883), 2: 474.

15. Historians such as Mona Ozouf and James Livesey have previously examined the discourse of Terror during the French Revolution and the Revolution of 1848. More recently, Dan Edelstein, Patrice Gueniffey, Jean-Clément Martin, and Sophie Wahnich have all presented compelling challenges to our current understanding of revolutionary violence and the ideological origins of the Terror. However, no one, to my knowledge, has yet provided an analysis of how the discursive association between revolutionary action and inexorable violence functioned, especially on a metacognitive level, immediately preceding and during the Paris Commune of 1871. See Dan Edelstein, *The Terror of Natural Right: Republicanism, the Cult of Nature, and the French Revolution* (Chicago, 2009); James Livesey, "Speaking the Nation: Radical Republicans and the Failure of Political Communication in 1848," *French Historical Studies* 20, no. 3 (Summer 1997): 459–80; Patrice Gueniffey, *La Politique de la Terreur: Essai sur la violence révolutionnaire 1789–1794* (Paris, 2000); Jean-Clément Martin, *Violence et révolution: Essai sur la naissance d'un mythe national* (Paris, 2006); Mona Ozouf, "War and Terror in French Revolutionary Discourse (1792–1794)," *Journal of Modern History* 56, no. 4 (December 1984): 579–97; and Sophie Wahnich, *La Liberté ou la mort: Essai sur la Terreur et le terrorisme* (Paris, 2003).

16. Cited in Martin Phillip Johnson, *The Paradise of Association: Political Culture and Popular Organizations in the Paris Commune of 1871* (Ann Arbor, MI, 1996), 261.

17. See Gustave Molinari, *Les Clubs rouges pendant la siège de Paris* (Paris, 1871). The most recent study of political clubs during the Commune is Johnson, *The Paradise of Association*. For a comprehensive overview of newspapers published during the Commune, consult Firmin Maillard's, *Histoire des journaux publiés pendant le siège et sous la Commune, 4 septembre 1870 au 28 mai 1871* (Paris, 1871).

18. Jacques Hébert's *Le Père Duchesne* was first published in 1790 and remained one of the most popular publications of the French Revolution until its creator's execution in 1794. These colloquialisms can be loosely translated by versions of "damn," "bloody," or "hell."

19. Cited in Molinari, *Les Clubs rouges pendant la siège de Paris*, 131. Although the veracity of primary sources such as personal testimonies and police spy records must always be questioned, this is particularly true with documents from the Paris Commune, since the majority of these reports come from observers who show a clear bias against the uprising. Therefore, a variety of primary sources have been consulted. Firsthand accounts such as Molinari's *Les Clubs rouges pendant la siège de Paris* and Paul Fontoulieu's *Les Églises de Paris sous la Commune* (Paris, 1873) have proven accurate when such verification is possible, and are generally accepted as reliable sources by major historians of the Paris Commune such as Jacques Rougerie and Stewart Edwards.

20. See Carolyn J. Eichner, *Surmounting the Barricades: Women in the Paris Commune* (Bloomington, IN, 2004); Gay Gullickson, *Unruly Women of Paris: Images of the Commune* (Ithaca, NY, 1996); and Edith Thomas, *Les Pétroleuses* (Paris, 1963).

21. *Le Journal officiel de la République française*, 11 April 1871.

22. From posters reproduced in Firmin Maillard, *Affiches, professions de foi, documents officiels, clubs et comités pendant la Commune* (Paris, 1871), 52, 63, 71, 103–4. See also, in particular, the 19 March 1871 issue of the *Journal officiel*.

23. Cited in Molinari, *Les Clubs rouges pendant la siège de Paris*, 96.

24. Taken from police records at the Archives de la Préfecture de Police (hereafter referred to as APP) in Paris, carton BA 364–63.

25. Cited in Molinari, *Les Clubs rouges pendant la siège de Paris*, 161; also in police observation records stored at the Bibliothèque historique de la ville de Paris in Paris, Ms. 1083, 29 December 1870 and 4 January 1871.

26. APP, carton BA 365–1.

27. Cited in Molinari, *Les Clubs rouges pendant la siège de Paris*, 274.

28. Maxime Du Camp, *Les Convulsions de Paris* (Paris, 1889), 4: 115.

29. William Pembroke Fetridge, *The Rise and Fall of the Paris Commune in 1871; with a full account of the bombardment, capture, and burning of the city* (New York, 1871), 454.

30. Jacques Rougerie, *Paris Libre 1871* (Paris, 1971), 257.

31. Cited in Johnson, *The Paradise of Association*, 123.

32. Louise Michel, *Souvenirs et aventures de ma vie* (Paris, 1983), 27.

33. Reprinted in Maillard, *Affiches, professions de foi, documents officiels, clubs et comités pendant la Commune*, 125–27. Interestingly, despite his praise of the Commune's novelty, Pyat was one of the staunchest supporters of the Comité de salut public of 1871.

34. *Journal officiel*, 25 March 1871. The *Journal officiel* became the official organ of the Paris Commune beginning 20 March 1871. In spite of the newspaper's title and the fact that it was responsible for reprinting the official declarations and meeting minutes of the Commune, many of its articles were written by anonymous contributors. Therefore, the opinions expressed in them, unless explicitly stated as such, cannot be considered to be official views of the Paris Commune.

35. Reprinted in Maillard, *Affiches, professions de foi, documents officiels, clubs et comités pendant la Commune*, 214.

36. As reported in the *Journal Officiel de la République française*, 10 April 1871. Another eyewitness report of this appears in Catulle Mendès's *Les 73 journées de la Commune* (Paris, 1871), 139–40.

37. *Procès-Verbaux de la Commune de 1871* (hereafter referenced as *PVC*), 2 vols., ed. G. Bourgin and G. Henriot (Paris, 2002), 1: 556.

38. *PVC*, 1: 586.

39. See *PVC* for a transcript of the 30 April 1871 vote on the issue, 1: 573–89.

40. In a preliminary vote on the name of the new committee, out of sixty-two members, twenty-eight preferred "Comité exécutif," while thirty-two voted for "Comité de salut public." See *PVC*, 2: 21.

41. Official statement of Eugène Pottier, 1 May 1871, *PVC*, 2: 34.

42. Official statement of Francis Jourde, 1 May 1871, *PVC*, 2: 34.

43. Official statement of Edouard Vaillant, 1 May 1871, *PVC*, 2: 36.

44. As translated by Edwards, *The Paris Commune 1871*, 227.

45. *Le Rappel*, 3 May 1871, cited in ibid., 229.

46. *PVC*, 2: 27.

47. *PVC*, 2: 26.

48. *PVC*, 2: 36

49. *PVC*, 2: 36–37.

50. *PVC*, 2: 309.

51. *PVC*, 2: 299–303.

52. This figure, cited on page 346 of Edwards, *The Paris Commune 1871*, is based upon the cited research of M. Winock and J.-P. Azéma, *Les Communards* (Paris, 1964). It must be noted, however, that these casualty figures have recently come under renewed scrutiny by historian Robert Tombs. See "How Bloody Was the Semaine Sanglante? A Revision," paper presented at the 57th Annual Meeting of the Society for French Historical Studies, Charleston, SC, 12 February 2011, available at www.h-france.net/Salon/Salonvol3no1.pdf.

53. As cited in Edwards, *The Paris Commune 1871*, 346.

54. APP, carton BA366–3.

55. *Le Figaro*, 24 February 1872.

56. *Paris Journal*, 1 September 1879. The *Vengeurs de Flourens* was a military battalion formed in 1871, named in honor of fallen Communard Gustave Flourens.

57. It is important to remain mindful of the highly partisan nature of the press in nineteenth-century France. Nevertheless, these citations illustrate the deployment of the discourse of terrorist revolutionary mimicry in the decade following the Paris Commune. For much more detailed information about specific journals during this period, refer to Claude Bellanger, et al., *Histoire Générale de la presse française* (Paris, 1969), esp. tomes II and III.

58. Fetridge, *The Rise and Fall of the Paris Commune*, 22.

59. For a recent study of violence and radical revolutionary politics in late-nineteenth-century France (and especially as an illustration of how revolutionary action evolved after the Paris Commune), see John Merriman, *The Dynamite Club: How a Bombing in Fin-de-Siècle Paris Ignited the Age of Modern Terror* (Boston, 2009). See also Claudia Verhoeven's essay in this volume.

Verhoeven: "Une Révolution Vraiment Scientifique"

1. Walter Laqueur, ed., *Voices of Terror: Manifestos, Writings and Manuals of Al Qaeda, Hamas, and Other Terrorists from around the World and throughout the Ages* (New York, 2004), 86.

2. International Institute of Social History (IISH), Partija Socialistov-Revoljucionerov (Rossija) Archives, PSR, "Commemoration and History," 596. The cartoon is part of an album of Narodnaia Volia– and PSR-related photographs and caricatures that was put together by V. S. Minachorjan after 1930. The caricatures are not dated, but their content makes it clear that they date to the Revolution of 1905-7.

3. For terrorism as a temporal violence, see my "Time of Terror, Terror of Time: On the Impatience of Russian Revolutionary Terrorism," in "Terrorism in Imperial Russia: New Perspectives," special issue, *Jahrbücher für die Geschichte Osteuropas* 58 (2010): 2, 254–73; "Oh, Times, There Is No Time (But the Time That Remains): The Terrorist in Russian Literature, 1863–1913," in *Terrorism and Narrative Practice*, ed. Thomas Austenfeld, Dimiter Daphinoff, and Jens Herlth (Munster, 2011);

and *The Odd Man Karakozov: Imperial Russia, Modernity, and the Birth of Terrorism* (Ithaca, NY, 2009), passim.

4. V. I. Lenin, "The Present Situation in Russia and the Tactics of the Workers' Party," in *Collected Works* (hereafter *CW*) (Moscow, 1965), 10: 112–19; *Polnoe sobranie sochinenii* (hereafter *PSS*) (Moscow, 1960), 12: 180. Originally published in *Partiiniye Izvestia*, no. 1, 7 February 1906.

5. For an overview of the reception of the French Revolution in Russia, see Dmitry Shlapentokh, *The French Revolution in Russian Intellectual Life 1865–1905* (Westport, CT, 1996).

6. These words were reported by Catherine II's private secretary, Aleksandr Vasil'evich Khrapovitsky. Cited in Roderick Page Thaler, Introduction to *A Journey from Petersburg to Moscow*, by Alexander Nikolaevich Radishchev, trans. Leo Wiener (Cambridge, MA, 1958), 11. The original reads: *Sk[azyvat'] iz[voli]la, chto on buntovshchik, khuzhe Pugacheva*. See Khrapovitsky's entry for 7 July 1790: *Dnevnik A. V. Khrapovitskogo s 18 Ianvaria 1782 po 17 Sentiabria 1793 goda* (Moscow, 1901), 199.

7. Radishchev, *A Journey from Petersburg to Moscow*, 239.

8. Joseph de Maistre, "Letter to Cavalier de Rossi 15 (27) August 1811," *Lettres et Opuscules Inédits du Comte J. de Maistre*, 5th ed. (Paris, 1869), 1: 267.

9. Ibid.

10. Ibid. The original reads: *[B]ella, horrida bella, et Thybrim multo spumantem sanguine cerno* ("War, horrible war, and the Tiber foaming with blood"). *The Aeneid of Virgil Books 1–6*, ed. R. D. Williams (New York, 1972), 86–87.

11. Ibid., 93–94.

12. See Carl Schmitt, *Theorie des Partisanen. Zwischenbemerkung zum Begriff des Politischen*, 3rd ed. (Berlin, 1992), 57–59.

13. For a quick, lively discussion of the Decembrist revolt, see Avrahm Yarmolinsky, *Road to Revolution: A Century of Russian Radicalism* (New York, 1962), 44–63, esp. 48–52.

14. L. G. Praisman, *Terroristy i revoliutsionery, okhranniki i provokatory* (Moscow, 2001), 291.

15. Lenin, "In Memory of Herzen," *CW*, 18: 25–31; "Pamiati Gertsena," *PSS*, 21: 261. Originally published in *Sotsial-Demokrat*, no. 26, 8 May (25 April) 1912.

16. Petr Chaadaev, "Filosoficheskie pis'ma (1829–1830). Pis'mo pervoe," *Polnoe sobranie sochinenii* (Moscow, 1991), 1: 321.

17. Ibid., 322.

18. "Epoch making" is Martin Malia's description of Chaadaev's *Letters*: *Alexander Herzen and the Birth of Russian Socialism* (New York, 1961), 60.

19. Alexander Herzen, *My Past and Thoughts: The Memoirs of Alexander Herzen*, trans. Constance Garnett (Berkeley, 1973), 293.

20. Ibid.

21. Ibid., 323.

22. Ibid., 324. This translation of the passage adopts the one found in Isaiah Berlin, "Russia and 1848," in *Russian Thinkers* (New York, 1978), 3–4.

23. On 1848 as a "turning point" in Russian intellectual history and its importance for Herzen and the development of Russian populism, see Isaiah Berlin, "Russia and 1848," 1–21, esp. 1–4.

24. Alexander Herzen, *Sobranie sochinenii v tridtsati tomakh* (Moscow, 1955), 5: 13–14. The translation here is mostly from Berlin, "Russia and 1848," 3–4.

25. Ibid., 233.

26. Alexander Herzen, *From the Other Shore*, trans. Moura Budberg, and *The Russian People and Socialism: An Open Letter to Michelet*, trans. Richard Wollheim (London, 1965), 37; Herzen, *Sobranie*, 6: 34. The scare quotes around "progress in the future" appear in the original.

27. Herzen, *From the Other Shore*, 39, 38, 35, and 34; Herzen, *Sobranie*, 6: 36, 35, 32, and 31.

28. For a detailed discussion of Herzen's intellectual development during the late 1840s and early 1850s, see Malia, *Alexander Herzen and the Birth of Russian Socialism*, chaps. 15–16; Shlapentokh, *The French Revolution in Russian Intellectual Life*, 104–20.

29. Reinhart Koselleck, *Futures Past: On the Semantics of Historical Time*, trans. Keith Tribe (Cambridge, MA, 1985), 279.

30. Herzen, *From the Other Shore*, 39; Herzen, *Sobranie*, 6: 36.

31. See N. V. Shelgunov, "K molodomu pokoleniiu," in *Revoliutsionnyi radikalizm v Rossii: Vek deviatnadtsatyi*, ed. E. L. Rudnitskaia (Moscow, 1997), esp. 98–100.

32. "Molodaia Rossiia," in *Revoliutsionnyi radikalizm v Rossii*, ed. Rudnitskaia, 149.

33. See, for example, O. V. Budnitskii, *Terrorizm v rossiiskom osvoboditel'nom dvizhenii. Ideologiia, etika, psikhologiia* (vtoraia polovina IXI-nachalo XX v.) (Moscow, 2000), 30.

34. This is not meant to suggest that there are no very violent European manifestos prior to Zaichnevsky's. See, for example, Karl Heinzen's 1849 "Murder," reprinted in Laqueur, *Voices of Terror*, 57–67.

35. "Molodaia Rossiia," 149.

36. Ibid.

37. Ibid.

38. See Zaichnevsky's analysis of 1848 in ibid., 148. For Lenin on the lessons of the Paris Commune, see *State and Revolution* (Washington, DC, 2009), 37–58; *Gosudarstvo i revoliutsiia*, *PSS*, 33: 36–56.

39. "Molodaia Rossiia," 146.

40. "Druz'iam rabochim," Godudarstvennyi arkhiv rossisskoi federatsii (hereafter GARF), f. 272, op. 1, d. 10, ll. 4–5.

41. Trial testimony, Petr Nikolaev, *Pokushenie Karakozova: Stenograficheskii otchet po delu D. Karakozova, I. Khudiakova, N. Ishutina, i dr.*, ed. M. M. Klevenskii and K. G. Kotel'nikov. Seriia Politicheskie protsessy 60–80 gg., ed. V. V. Maksakov and V. I. Nevskii (Moscow, 1928–30), 1: 220 and 2: 334.

42. Trial testimony, Viacheslav Shaganov, *Pokushenie Karakozova*, 1: 190–92

43. Trial testimony, Petr Ermolov, *Pokushenie Karakozova*, 1: 218.

44. Trial testimony, ibid., 1: 73.

45. Written testimony, Dmitry Ivanov, GARF f. 272, op. 1, d. 13, ll. 30b-4.

46. Written testimony, Karakozov, GARF f. 95, op. 1, d. 163 T. 1, l. 780b. Emphasis mine.

47. See Verhoeven, *The Odd Man Karakozov*, 147–49.

48. Note the following titles of books on Tkachev: Robert C. Williams, *Petr Nikitich Tkachev: Russian Jacobin Thought from 1861–1882* (Cambridge, UK, 1960); Deborah Hardy, *Petr Tkachev: The Critic as Jacobin* (Seattle, 1977); E. L. Rudnitskaia, *Russkii blankizm* [Russian Blanquism] (Moscow, 1992). For an overview, see Franco Venturi, "Tkachev," in *Roots of Revolution: A History of the Populist and Socialist Movements in 19th Century Russia*, trans. Francis Haskell (London, 2001), 389–428.

49. P. N. Tkachev, From the Brochure "Zadachi revoliutionnoi propagandy v Rossii (Pis'mo v radktsiiu zhurnala *Vpered!*)," April 1874, in *Revoliutsionnyi radikalizm v Rossii*, ed. Rudnitskaia, 330.

50. Ibid., 331.

51. Ibid., 332.

52. For example, in "A Death for a Death," written by Sergei "Stepniak" Kravchinsky after his 4 August 1878 assassination of the chief of the gendarmerie and head of the secret police in Saint Petersburg, General Nikolai V. Mezentsev, the author, after enumerating Mezentsev's countless crimes, suddenly addresses Russia's administrators as follows: "You are the representatives of power; we—the opponents of every form of enslavement of one individual by another, hence you are our enemies and between us there can be no reconciliation. You must be destroyed and you will be destroyed. But . . . [our] real enemies are—the bourgeoisie, who at present hide behind your back, even though they hate you because you tie their hands, as well." "Smert' za smert' (Ubiistvo Mezentseva)," in *Revoliutsionnyi radikalizm v Rossii*, ed. Rudnitskaia, 402.

53. "Programma 'Zemli i Voli,'" in *Revoliutsionnoe narodnichestvo. Semidesiatykh godov XIX veka*, vol. 2, *1876–1882 gg.*, ed. S. S. Volk (Moscow, 1965), 28.

54. "Letter K. Marx to the Editor of 'Otechestv. Zapisok,'" in *Narodnaia volia v dokumentakh i vospominaniiakh*, ed. A. V. Iakimovaia-Dikovskaia et al. (Moscow, 1930), 238.

55. On the *People's Will*, see Venturi, "Narodnaya Volya" and "1st March 1881," in *Roots of Revolution*, 633–720.

56. See, for example, "Proklamatsiia N. K. Mikhailovskogo," *Letuchii Listok*, no. 1, April 1878, in *Revoliutsionnoe narodnichestvo*, 55–57; "Proklamatsiia 'Zemli I voli,' 'Pokushenie na zhizn Drentel'na,'" 13 March 1879, in *Revoliutsionnoe narodnichestvo*, 81–82; "Proklamatsiia 'Ot Ispolnitel'nogo komiteta' po povodu pokusheniia na Aleksandra II," 22 November 1879, in *Revoliutsionnoe narodnichestvo*, 221–22; "Proklamatsiia Ispolnitel'nogo komiteta po povodu vzryva v Zimnem dvortse," 7 February 1880, in *Revoliutsionnoe narodnichestvo*, 223–24; and N. A. Morozov, "Znachenie politicheskikh ubiistv," "Listok 'Zemli i voli,'" nos. 2–3, 22 March 1879, in *Revoliutsionnyi radikalizm v Rossii*, ed. Rudnitskaia, 413–15.

57. "K. Marx and F. Engels about Russia," Iz Pred. Kommunistich. Manifesta 1882 g.—"Narodn. Volia," nos. 8–9, 5 February 1882, in *Narodnaia volia v dokumentakh i vospominaniiakh*, 241.

58. Nikolai Morozov, "The Terrorist Struggle," in Laqueur, *Voices of Terror*, 79.

59. Ibid., 77–78.

60. Ibid., 79.

61. Ibid., 77.

62. Leon Trotsky, "Krakh terrora i ego partii (K delu Azefa)," in *Sochineniia*

(Moscow, 1926), 4: 346. First published in *Przeglad Socyal-demokratyczny*, May 1909.

63. See, for example, "The Spirit of Revolt," in *Kropotkin's Revolutionary Pamphlets: A Collection of Writings by Peter Kropotkin*, ed. Roger N. Baldwin (New York, 1970), 34–43; Sergei Stepniak Kravchinsky, *Underground Russia: Revolutionary Profiles and Sketches from Life* (London, 1883) and *Career of a Nihilist* (New York, 1899). For the best example of work on the transnational movements of revolutionary culture during the "age of early globalization," see Benedict Anderson, *Under Three Flags: Anarchism and the Anti-Colonial Imagination* (London, 2007), which includes a treatment on the influence of Russian "nihilism" on global revolutionary repertoires.

64. Gotelind Müller, "China and the 'Anarchist Wave of Assassinations': Politics, Violence, and Modernity in East Asia around the Turn of the Century," in *The Oxford Handbook of the History of Terrorism*, ed. Carola Dietze and Claudia Verhoeven (Oxford, forthcoming in 2015). Online publication date February 2014.

65. Nechaev and Bakunin, "Catechism of the Revolutionist," in Laqueur, *Voices of Terror*, 71; "Katekhizis revoliutsionera," in *Revoliutsionnyi radikalizm v Rossii*, ed. Rudnitskaia, 244.

66. Leon Trotsky, *Permanent Revolution and Results and Prospects*, trans. John G. Wright and Brian Pearce (New York, 1970), 45.

67. Marx and Engels, review of Chenu, *Les Conspirateurs* (Paris, 1850); and de la Hodde, *La Naissance de la République* (Paris, 1850), published in *Neue rheinishcne Zeitung* (1850), reprinted in *Die neue Zeit* 4 (Stuttgart, 1886), 555–56, 552, 551, cited in Walter Benjamin, "Convolute V: Conspiracies, Compagnonnage," in *The Arcades Project*, trans. Howard Eiland and Kevin McLaughlin (Cambridge, MA, 2002), 606.

68. See Praisman, *Terroristy i revoliustionery, okhranniki i provokatory*, 244.

69. Trotsky, "Krakh terrora," in *Sochineniia*, 4: 348.

70. "Routine" in Tarnovski's "Terrorism and Routine," refers to the "routine of word games," "status quo," and "conventional morality"; terrorism, by contrast, is "new and unprecedented." See Laqueur, *Voices of Terror*, 83, 84, and 85.

71. Trotsky, "Terrorizm," in *Sochineniia*, 4: 367. First published in German in *Der Kampf*, November 1911.

72. Trotsky, "Krakh terrora," in *Sochineniia*, 4: 350 and 348

73. Trotsky, "Revoliutsionnaia romantika i Azef," *Sochinenii*, 4: 361; "Krakh terrora," 350. "Revoliutsionnaia romantika i Azef" was first published in *Die Neue Zeit*, May 1909.

74. Trotsky, "Krakh terrora," in *Sochineniia*, 4: 351.

75. See Trotsky, *The Permanent Revolution and Results and Prospects*, 131; *Permanentnaia revoliutsiia* (Izdatel'stvo "Granit," 1930), 13. Trotsky might have added that Marx and Engels even provided explicit arguments for Russia's role in the forging of a European revolution, though that would have meant acknowledging that they still believed in the "phantasmagoria" of the Narodniki. For example, in 1882, Marx and Engels wrote: "If the Russian revolution gives a signal to the revolution of the proletariat in the West and, thereby, both support each other, then the existence of communal landownership in Russia can serve at the starting point of communist

development." "K. Marx and F. Engels about Russia," in *Narodnaia volia v doku-mentakh i vospominaniiakh*, 241. In the same vein, Engels later recalled the following about the late 1870s, this time not mentioning the commune and thus actually coming closer to Trotsky's own views: "The fall of tsarism seemed close—Revolution in Russia should have deprived the European reaction of its strongest support, its great reservist army, and thus give a new powerful push to the political movement of the West and, besides that, create for it more favorable circumstances of the struggle." "Engels o Rossii Kontsa 1870-ykh gg.," in *Narodnaia volia v dokumentakh i vospominaniiakh*, 235.

76. Trotsky, *The Permanent Revolution and Results and Prospects*, 31.

Thatcher: Scripting the Russian Revolution

1. For an analysis of the importance of intellectual and cultural perceptions on the politics of the Russian Revolution in 1917 see, for example, John Keep, "1917: The Tyranny of Paris over Petrograd," *Soviet Studies* 20, no. 1 (1968): 22–35.

2. For an excellent account of the ways in which the revolution was embodied in its symbols, see Orlando Figes and Boris Kolinitskii, *Interpreting the Revolution: The Language and Symbols of 1917* (New Haven, CT, 1999), 30–70.

3. See Ian D. Thatcher, "The First State Duma, 1906: The View from the Contemporary Pamphlet and Monograph Literature," *Canadian Journal of History* 46, no. 3 (Winter 2011): 531–61.

4. Cited in V. V-ii, *A. F. Kerenskii* (Petrograd, 1917), 37. See also H. J. White, "Civil Rights and the Provisional Government," in *Civil Rights in Imperial Russia*, ed. Olga Crisp and Linda Edmondson (Oxford, 1989), 287–312.

5. For the "freedom acts" see Robert Paul Browder and Alexander F. Kerensky, eds., *The Russian Provisional Government, 1917: Documents* (Stanford, CA, 1961), 1: 196–98, 199–200, 207–8, 210.

6. V-ii, *Kerenskii*, 44. See also Prince G. E. L'vov's comments cited in Rex A. Wade, *The Russian Revolution, 1917* (Cambridge, 2005), 61.

7. A. J. Sack, *The Birth of Russian Democracy* (New York, 1918), 258–60.

8. See, for example, the pamphlet *Chego trebovat ot Vremennago Pravitel'stva?* (St. Petersburg [*sic*], 1917), issued by the "Friends of Freedom," which asserted that the RPG had only two tasks: (i) to ensure that the Constituent Assembly be elected freely and fairly on a four-tail suffrage; and (ii) that order and peace be maintained until the Constituent Assembly should meet.

9. This was true, above all, of the leading Kadet and first foreign minister in the RPG, P. N. Miliukov. See, for example, L. P. Morris, "The Russians, the Allies and the War, February–July 1917," *Slavonic and East European Review* 50, no. 1 (1972): 29–48.

10. This appeal was widely circulated and printed. It was signed by all ministers and was dated 27 March 1917. This has been translated from *Solntse Rossii*, no. 367(9), April 1917. The various responsibilities of different groups of citizens (bourgeois, workers, civil servants, communication workers, and such like) to support the liberal script are listed in M. Borisov, *O Podderzhke Vremennago Pravitel'stva* (Petrograd, 1917).

11. See Daniel T. Orlovsky, "Reform during Revolution: Governing the Prov-

inces in 1917," in ~~*Reform in Russia and the USSR*~~, ed. Robert O. Crummey (Urbana, IL, 1989), 100–125.

12. Cited in Thomas Riha, *A Russian European: Paul Miliukov in Russian Politics* (Notre Dame, IN, 1969), 308.

13. Fedor Fedorovich Kokoshkin, *Respublika* (Petrograd, 1917), 5–6.

14. For an excellent account of the politics of the Kadets see William G. Rosenberg, *Liberals in the Russian Revolution: The Constitutional Democratic Party, 1917–1921* (Princeton, NJ, 1974).

15. Cited in N. E. Khitrina, *Agrarnaia politika Vremennogo Pravitel'stva v 1917g.* (Nizhnii Novgorod, 2003), 29.

16. For an account of the Russian elites in 1917, see Matthew Rendle, *Defenders of the Motherland* (Oxford, 2010).

17. Cited in Khitrina, *Agrarnaia politika Vremennogo Pravitel'stva*, 117–18.

18. Daniel T. Orlovsky, "The Provisional Government and Its Cultural Work," in *Bolshevik Culture: Experiment and Order in the Russian Revolution*, ed. Abbott Gleason, Peter Kenez, and Richard Stites (Bloomington, IN, 1985), 39–56.

19. See, for example, I. Iashunskii, *Chto Takoe Respublika?* (Petrograd, 1917); Ia. M. Magaziner, *Respublika, eia sushchnost i vazhneishiia demokraticheskaia formy* (Petrograd, 1917).

20. See, for example, Ziva Galili and Albert P. Nenarokov, "The Mensheviks in 1917," in *Critical Companion to the Russian Revolution, 1914–1921*, ed. Edward Acton, Vladimir Iu. Cherniaev, and William G. Rosenberg (London, 1997), 267–80; Rex A. Wade, *The Russian Search for Peace February–October 1917* (Stanford, CA, 1969).

21. "Dual Government," *Izvestiia*, no. 27, 11 April 1917, in Frank Alfred Golder, *Documents of Russian History, 1914–1917* (New York, 1927), 319.

22. "Order No. 1, March 1, 1917," in *Russia in War and Revolution, 1914–1922: A Documentary History*, ed. Jonathan W. Daly and Leonid Trofimov (Indianapolis, IN, 2009), 48–50.

23. Keep, "1917," 29.

24. I. Rybakov, *Demokraticheskaia respublika. Chto ona dast rabochim i krestianam* (Odessa, 1917).

25. "Declaration of the Provisional Government," 21 July 1917, in Golder, *Documents of Russian History*, 467–69.

26. Cited in Louise Erwin Heenan, *Russian Democracy's Fatal Blunder: The Summer Offensive of 1917* (New York, 1987), 55–56.

27. This is not to deny divisions within the Bolshevik script over key policies such as the pace and nature of revolutionary change. Nevertheless the Bolsheviks were less disunited than other parties.

28. N. N. Sukhanov, *The Russian Revolution 1917* (Princeton, NJ, 1984), 104.

29. See, for example, "Martov's Resolution, 17 July 1917," in *The Mensheviks in the Russian Revolution*, ed. Abraham Ascher (London, 1976), 102–3.

30. This argument was put most forcibly by Leon Trotsky, *History of the Russian Revolution, Volume 1* (London, 1967), in ch. 16: "Rearming the Party," and in app. II. For a contrary view, see, for example, Lars T. Lih, "The Ironic Triumph of Old Bolshevism: The Debates of April 1917 in Context," *Russian History* 38 (2011): 199–242.

31. The Bolshevik script has been summarized largely from the relevant docu-

ments contained in Ralph C. Elwood, *Resolutions and Decisions of the CPSU*, vol. 1, *The Russian Social Democratic Labour Party, 1898–October 1917* (Toronto, 1974), 196–205, 217–25, 249–61.

32. "A Proclamation by the Petrograd Anarchists' Club, May 1917," in *Competing Voices from the Russian Revolution*, ed. Michael C. Hickey (Santa Barbara, CA, 2011), 223–24.

33. Roger Pethybridge, "The Significance of Communications in 1917," *Soviet Studies* 19, no. 1 (1967): 112.

34. For documents on the nationality question, see Browder and Kerensky, *The Russian Provisional Government*, 317–433.

35. "The Kadet Policy on the National Question," in Browder and Kerensky, *The Russian Provisional Government*, 317.

36. Such concerns were most evident in the liberal script. See, for example, P. N. Miliukov, *The Russian Revolution*, vol. 1, *The Revolution Divided, Spring 1917* (Gulf Breeze, FL, 1978), 110–33.

37. Browder and Kerensky, *The Russian Provisional Government*, 382–83.

38. See the excellent discussion in John Eric Marot, "Class Conflict, Political Competition and Social Transformation: Critical Perspectives on the Social History of the Russian Revolution," *Revolutionary Russia* 7, no. 2 (1994): 111–63; Steve Smith, "Rethinking the Autonomy of Politics: A Rejoinder to John Eric Marot," *Revolutionary Russia* 8, no. 1 (1995): 104–16; William G. Rosenberg, "Autonomous Politics and Locations of Power: Social History and the Question of Outcomes in 1917: A Response to John Marot," *Revolutionary History* 9, no. 1 (1996): 95–113; and John Eric Marot, "Political Leadership and Working-Class Agency in the Russian Revolution: Reply to William G. Rosenberg and S. A. Smith," *Revolutionary Russia* 9, no. 1 (1996): 114–28.

39. Grigorij A. Gerasimenko, *Narod i vlast' 1917* (Moscow, 1995), 5.

40. "A Resolution by the Moscow Chapter of the League for Women's Equal Rights, 6 March 1917," in Hickey, *Competing Voices from the Russian Revolution*, 167–68.

41. Mark D. Steinberg, *Voices of Revolution, 1917* (New Haven, CT, 2001), 117–19.

42. Ibid., 95.

43. See, for example, S. A. Smith, *Red Petrograd: Revolution in the Factories, 1917–18* (Cambridge, 1983), 180–81. This brilliant study concludes (p. 259) that: "It was the organised working class, not the Bolshevik party, which was the great power in society—more powerful than even the capitalist class, as its success in resisting redundancies suggests."

44. Steinberg, *Voices of Revolution*, 239–40, 242–44; Hickey, *Competing Voices from the Russian Revolution*, 155–57.

45. There are numerous excellent case studies that illustrate how a liberal script lost out to a socialist script, and how the language of socialism came to embody the common language of social justice. See, for example, Michael C. Hickey, "Discourses of Public Identity and Liberalism in the February Revolution: Smolensk, Spring 1917," *Russian Review* 55 (1996): 615–37; and William G. Rosenberg, "The Democratization of Russia's Railroads in 1917," *American Historical Review* 86, no. 5 (1981): 983–1008.

46. This is most apparent from Figes and Kolinitskii, ~~*Interpreting the Revolution,*~~ and collections that followed this ground-breaking study. See, for example, the editorial commentary in Steinberg, *Voices of Revolution.*

47. W. E. Mosse, "The February Regime: Prerequisites of Success," *Soviet Studies* 19, no. 1 (1967): 108.

48. Norman Stone states: "The First World War provoked a crisis of economic modernization, and Bolshevik revolution was the outcome," *The Eastern Front 1914–1917* (Harmondsworth, UK, 1998), 285–86.

49. Graeme J. Gill, *Peasants and Government in the Russian Revolution* (London, 1979), 170.

Wasserstrom and Wu: You Say You Want a Revolution

1. Tsou Jung (Zou Rong), *The Revolutionary Army: A Chinese Nationalist Tract of 1903*, trans. John Lust (Paris, 1968), 58.

2. Kang Youwei, "Da nanbei meizhou zhuhuashang lun zhongguo zhike xing lixian buneng xing geming shu" [China Only Needs a Constitution, Not a Revolution—In Answer to South and North American Businessmen], May 1902, in *Kang Youwei quanji* [Kang Youwei's Collected Works] (Beijing, 2007), 6: 314.

3. Liu Xiaobo, "That Holy Word, 'Revolution,'" in *Popular Protests and Political Culture in Modern China*, 2nd ed. Elizabeth J. Perry and Jeffrey N. Wasserstrom (Lanham, MD, 1994), 309–24.

4. Han Han, *This Generation: Dispatches from China's Most Popular Literary Star (and Race Car Driver)*, ed. and trans. Allan Barr (New York, 2012), 237.

5. On PRC discussions of the 120th anniversary of the war, see Chris Buckley, "China's Leaders Draw Lessons from the War of 'Humiliation,'" *Sinosphere: Dispatches from China* (blog), *New York Times*, 28 July 2014, available at http://sinosphere.blogs.nytimes.com/2014/07/28/chinas-leaders-draw-lessons-from-war-of-humiliation; see also Jeffrey Wasserstrom, "Marking Time in China and the West—A New Year's Post," *China Blog* (blog), *Los Angeles Review of Books*, 27 January 2014, available at http://blog.lareviewofbooks.org/chinablog/marking-time-china-west-new-years-post/.

6. Kang Youwei, *Kongzi Gaizhi Kao* [A Study of the Reforms of Confucius] (1897; repr. in Minguo congshu, Shanghai, 1992).

7. For Deng's phrasing, see "Reform Is China's Second Revolution," billed as an excerpt from a talk with Susumu Nikaido, vice president of the Liberal Democratic Party of Japan, 28 March 1985, accessed via *People's Daily's* website at http://english.peopledaily.com.cn/dengxp/vol3/text/c1360.html.

8. Thomas Taylor Meadows, *The Chinese and Their Rebellions* (London, 1856), 25. The next sentence in this text reads: "Speaking generally, there has been but one great political revolution in China, when the centralized form of government was substituted for the feudal, about 2,000 years ago."

9. Kang Youwei, *Kang Youwei quanji*, 314, 321.

10. Zhang Binglin (Zhang Taiyan), "Bo Kang Youwei lun geming shu" [Refuting Kang Youwei's Idea on Revolution] (1903), in *Zhang Taiyan quanji* [Zhang Binglin's Collected Works] (Shanghai, 1982), 4: 178–80.

11. *The Book of Changes*, trans. James Legge (Toronto, 1986), 254.

12. Noguchi Takehiko, *Oodo to kakumei no aida* [Between the Ways of Kingship and Revolution] (Tokyo, 1986), 5.

13. On the flow of political terms between China, Japan, and the West, see Lydia Liu, *Translingual Practice: Literature, National Culture, and Translated Modernity—China, 1900–1937* (Stanford, CA, 1995).

14. Chen Jianhua, "Chinese 'Revolution' in the Syntax of World Revolution," in *Tokens of Exchange: The Problem of Translation in Global Circulations*, ed. Lydia Liu (Durham, NC, 1999), 368.

15. Ibid., 363–64.

16. Chen Jianhua, "World Revolution Knocking at the Heavenly Gate: Kang Youwei and His Use of Geming in 1898," *Journal of Modern Chinese History* 5, no. 1 (June 2011): 89–108.

17. Chen Jianhua, "Chinese 'Revolution' in the Syntax of World Revolution," in *Tokens of Exchange*, 363.

18. Michael Gasster, *Chinese Intellectuals and the Revolution of 1911: The Birth of Modern Chinese Radicalism* (Seattle, WA, 1969), 194–95.

19. This is the title of one of the sections their coauthored book, *Gaobie geming* [Farewell to Revolution], 6th ed. (Hong Kong, 2011).

20. Quoted in Philip Gourevitch, "Liao Yiwu Unbound," *News Desk* (blog), *New Yorker*, 6 July 2011, available at http://www.newyorker.com/online/blogs/news-desk/2011/07/liao-yiwu-leaves-china.html.

21. For major intellectual debates in the 1990s, see Wang Chaohua, "Minds of the Nineties," in *One China, Many Paths*, ed. Wang Chaohua (New York, 2003), 16–19.

22. Liu Xiaobo is a complicated case here. On the one hand, we have found no example of him calling for any kind of revolution, even a Velvet one. He has, however, lamented China's lack of a moral leader capable of carrying out sweeping change and flags the Velvet Revolution's leader Havel as an example of the sort of figure he has in mind. See, for example, his 13 January 2000 "Letter to Liao Yiwu," translated in Liu Xiaobo, *No Enemies, No Hatred: Selected Essays and Poems*, ed. Perry Link, Tienchi Martin-Liao, and Liu Xia (Cambridge, MA, 2012), 286–89. There is none of Zou Rong's belief in the cleansing power of violence in Liu's writings (he also cited Gandhi and Jesus as models), but his wish for a Chinese Havel resonates with the call for Chinese Washingtons and Napoleons in *The Revolutionary Army*.

23. Li and Liu, *Gaobie geming*, 28.

24. Li Zehou, "Yao gailiang buyao geming" [Yes to Reform, No to Revolution], in ibid., 287–305.

25. Gu Fang, "Ping gaobie geming" [Comments on Farewell to Revolution], in ibid., 434.

26. Hu Ping, "Ping Li Zehou Liu Zaifu duihualu" [Comments on the Dialogues between Li Zehou and Liu Zaifu], *Gaobie geming*, 464–81.

27. Li Zehou, "Gaobie xinhai geming" [Farewell to the 1911 Revolution], an interview with Ma Guochuan, August 2011, available at http://www.21ccom.net/articles/lsjd/lsjj/article_2011092045683.html.

28. Liu Xiaobo, "Xiegei Wang Yuanhua xiansheng de zaitian zhi ling" [Writ-

ing to Mr. Wang Yuanhua's Soul in Heaven], 2008, available at http://www.chinese-thought.org/zttg/wangyuanhua/005695.htm.

29. Liu, "That Holy Word, 'Revolution,'" 309–24.

30. Liu Xiaobo, "Sun Zhongshan de yichan yu zhonggong de mianhuai" [Sun Yat-sen's Legacy and CCP's Tribute], 2001, available at https: //docs.google.com/a/uci.edu/document/d/1kQQMGDu17–7BEFFbt2ZNffwwG-C1lS-Xn8ff7h27sMU/preview?pli=1.

31. Yu Hua, *China in Ten Words*, trans. Allan Barr (New York, 2011), 113–41.

32. Yu Hua, "Fear of Dragons," trans. Allan Barr, *New York Times*, 7 October 2011, available at http://www.nytimes.com/2011/10/08/opinion/08iht-edyu08.html?_r=2.

33. Han Han, *This Generation*, 231–47.

34. Han Han, "Speaking of Revolution," *This Generation*, 233–34.

35. Han Han, "Speaking about Democracy," in ibid., 239.

36. Ibid., 242–43.

37. Han Han, "What Do You Do If It's Too Downbeat?" in ibid., 222.

Cook: Mao's Little Red Book

Note: A version of this essay was published as the introduction to Alexander C. Cook, ed., *Mao's Little Red Book: A Global History* (New York, 2014). Reprinted with the permission of Cambridge University Press. That volume resulted from a collaborative project examining the global production, circulation, and appropriation of the Little Red Book, with scholars presenting original research based on work in at least a dozen languages, including Chinese, English, French, German, Russian, Spanish, Italian, Serbo-Croatian, Albanian, Bengali, Swahili, and Bambara.

1. By comparison, the entire population of the world in the early 1970s did not exceed 4 billion people. See http://www.census.gov/population/international/data/idb/informationGateway.php.

2. For a history of the compilation of various editions, see Daniel Leese, *Mao Cult: Rhetoric and Ritual in Mao's China* (New York, 2011), 108–27.

3. On the distribution of quotations by source, see Stuart Schram, ed., *Quotations from Chairman Mao Tse-tung* (New York, 1967), xiv–xvii. For linguistic analysis, see John De Francis, *Annotated Quotations from Chairman Mao* (New Haven, CT, 1975).

4. Lin Biao, foreword to the Second Chinese Edition (16 December 1966). Full text of the official English translation is available at http://www.marxists.org/reference/archive/lin-biao/1966/12/16.htm. A rousing choral version of the foreword, composed by Tang Ke and Sheng Mao and performed by the China Railway Art Troupe in 1968, can be heard at http://www.youtube.com/watch?v=Chgz-2meXKdo.

5. The previous foreword addressed to the army had said "to arm the minds of all our commanders." General Political Department, Foreword to the Reprint of the First Edition (1 August 1965). For a word by word comparison of the forewords to the first and second editions, see Schram, *Quotations from Chairman Mao Tse-tung*, xxxi–xxxiii. Schram, the foremost Western interpreter of Mao in the postwar era,

was a polymath and polyglot who had assisted the Manhattan Project before turning to the study of politics. "Having worked on the bomb," his widow explained in his obituary, "he wanted to study more of human beings." William Yardley, "Stuart R. Schram, Nuclear Physicist and Mao Scholar, Dies at 88," *New York Times*, 21 July 2012.

6. It was common practice among Chinese communist ideologues, including Mao, to read speeches and issue public documents edited, compiled, or written by others. Daniel Leese dispels the myth of Lin Biao as architect of the Little Red Book in *Mao Cult*, 109. On Lin Biao's plagiarism of himself or others in the foreword, see Schram, *Quotations from Chairman Mao Tse-tung*, xxv–xxvi.

7. See, for example, the Army Day (1 August) 1960 editorial in *PLA Daily*. On "politics in command," see Henry Yuhuai He, *Dictionary of Political Thought in the People's Republic of China* (Armonk, NY, 2001), 457–60.

8. Characterization of Lin Biao based on Frederick C. Teiwes and Warren Sun, *The Tragedy of Lin Biao: Riding the Tiger during the Cultural Revolution, 1966–1971* (Honolulu, HI, 1996), 1–18.

9. Roderick MacFarquhar and Michael Schoenhals, *Mao's Last Revolution* (Cambridge, MA, 2006).

10. Ibid., 285–336.

11. Mao Zedong, "On Guerilla Warfare" (1937), available at http://www.marxists.org/reference/archive/mao/works/1937/guerrilla-warfare/ch06.htm.

12. Mao developed his philosophical position through an active but nevertheless fairly orthodox reading of the basic texts of the Soviet New Philosophy of the 1930s. See Nick Knight, *Marxist Philosophy in China: From Qu Qiubai to Mao Zedong, 1923–1945* (Dordrecht, The Netherlands, 2005), especially 171–95.

13. Mao Zedong, "On Contradiction" (1937), in *Selected Works of Mao Zedong*, vol. 1, available at http://www.marxists.org/reference/archive/mao/selected-works/volume-1/mswv1_17.htm. The latter half is excerpted in Schram, *Quotations from Chairman Mao Tse-tung*, chap. 22.

14. See discussion in Slavoj Žižek, *Žižek Presents Mao: On Practice and Contradiction* (London, 2007), 11, 181.

15. Mao Zedong, "Talk on Questions of Philosophy," 18 August 1964, in *Selected Works of Mao Zedong*, vol. 9. Žižek likens Mao's view to Adorno's theory of negative dialectics. *Žižek Presents Mao*, 11.

16. Mao Zedong, "Speech at the Supreme State Conference," 18 January 1958, in *Selected Works of Mao Zedong*, vol. 8.

17. Lin Biao, "Directive on the Cultural Revolution" (13 September 1967), in China Problems Research Center, *Selected Works of Lin Piao* (Hong Kong, 1970), 152.

18. "Look at One's Self in the Light of Dividing One into Two," *People's Daily*, 19 July 1968, reproduced in *People's China: Social Experimentation, Politics, Entry onto the World Scene, 1966–1972*, ed. David Milton, Nancy Milton, and Franz Schurmann (New York, 1974), 202–5.

19. Frederick Engels, "The Part Played by Labour in the Transformation of Ape to Man" (1876), available at http://www.marxists.org/archive/marx/works/1876/part-played-labour/index.htm.

20. Mao Zedong, "On Protracted War," May 1938, in *Selected Works of Mao Zedong*, vol. 2. Excerpted in Schram, *Quotations from Chairman Mao Tse-tung*, chap. 12.

21. Mao Zedong, "Talk with the American Correspondent Anna Louise Strong" (1946), in *Selected Works of Mao Zedong*, vol. 4.

22. Lin Biao, "Long Live the Victory of People's War! In Commemoration of the 20th Anniversary of Victory in the Chinese People's War of Resistance against Japan," 3 September 1965, available at http://www.marxists.org/reference/archive/lin-biao/1965/09/peoples_war/ch08.htm. The authorial attribution to Lin Biao is again questionable; see Teiwes and Sun, *The Tragedy of Lin Biao*, 27.

23. Lin Biao, "Dui yijiuliuliu nian quanjun gongzuo tichu de wu xiang yuanze" [Five Principles Addressed to the All-Army Work Conference of 1966], 18 November 1965, in *Lin Biao wenxuan* [Selected works of Lin Biao] (Hong Kong, 2011), 413.

24. Mao Zedong, "The Chinese People Cannot Be Cowed by the Atom Bomb," 28 January 1955, in *Selected Works of Mao Zedong*, vol. 5.

25. See also Slavoj Žižek, "Mao Zedong: The Marxist Lord of Misrule," in *Žižek Presents Mao*, 9–10, 27–28.

26. John Wilson Lewis and Xue Litai, *China Builds the Bomb* (Stanford, CA, 1988), 16–19.

27. Mao Zedong, "Speeches at the Second Plenum of the Eighth Party Congress: Second Speech," 17 May 1958, in *Selected Works of Mao Zedong*, vol. 8. See also Chen Jian, *Mao's China and the Cold War* (Chapel Hill, NC, 2001), 189–90.

28. For a discussion of how Mao's view evolved over time, see Shu Guang Zhang, "Between 'Paper' and 'Real Tigers': Mao's View of Nuclear Weapons," in *Cold War Statesmen Confront the Bomb*, ed. John Lewis Gaddis et al. (Oxford, 1999), 194–215.

29. "Mr. China A-Bomb" from "South of the Mountains to North of the Seas: Excerpts from American Journalist Edgar Snow's Interview with Mao Tse-tung," 9 January 1965, in *Selected Works of Mao Zedong*, vol. 9. RAND assessment from Alice Langley Hsieh, *Chinese Nuclear Force* (Santa Monica, CA, 1963), 15 (italics in original). On American nuclear Orientalism, see Hugh Gusterson, "Nuclear Weapons and the Other in the American Imagination," in *People of the Bomb: Portraits of America's Nuclear Complex* (Minneapolis, MN, 2004), 21–47.

30. See, for example, "Let Us Clearly Unite and Clearly Distinguish between Ourselves and the Enemy," 4 August 1952, in *Selected Works of Mao Zedong*, vol. 5. The United States and other Cold War belligerents made similar plans to weather an attack.

31. The ordering of the phrases suggests a two-stage revolution, first anti-imperialist (antihegemonic), then socialist (antirevisionist).

32. Lin Biao, "Speech at Peking Rally Commemorating the Fiftieth Anniversary of the October Revolution," 7 November 1967, in *Selected Works of Lin Piao*, 172.

33. "There are Two Intermediate Zones," part II, excerpt from talk with Kikunami Katsumi, Politburo member of the Japanese CP, 5 January 1964, in *Mao Zedong on Diplomacy* (Beijing, 1998), 387–89.

34. Open telegram from Albert Einstein et al., as quoted in *The New York Times*, 25 May 1946, 13.

35. "There are Two Intermediate Zones," 387–89.

36. See Yang Kuisong, "Zhong-Mei hejie guocheng zhong de Zhongfang bian-zou: Mao Zedong sange shijie lilun tichu de Beijing tanxi" [A Variation on the Chinese Side during Sino-American Reconciliation: An Analysis of the Background of Mao's Three Worlds Theory], in *Cuiruo de lianmeng: Lengzhan yu Zhong-Su guanxi* [Fragile Alliance: The Cold War and Sino-Soviet Relations] (Beijing, 2010), 457–81.

37. Philip H. Gordon, "Charles De Gaulle and the Nuclear Revolution," in *Cold War Statesmen Confront the Bomb*, 216–35.

38. Jeremi Suri, *Power and Protest: Global Revolution and the Rise of Détente* (Cambridge, MA, 2003), 73–79.

39. Talk with French National Assembly Delegation, 30 January 1964, in *Mao Zedong on Diplomacy*, 398.

40. The various contributions to our volume, *Mao's Little Red Book: A Global History*, will address the following issues in historical detail.

41. Lin Biao, "Long Live the Victory of People's War!"

42. See Alexander C. Cook, "Third World Maoism," in *Critical Introduction to Mao*, ed. Timothy Cheek (Cambridge, 2010), 288–312.

43. Mao Zedong, "Statement," 17 January 1964, in *Mao Zedong on Diplomacy*, 393.

44. Elizabeth McGuire, "The Book That Bombed," conference paper presented at University of California, Berkeley, 21 October 2011.

45. Mao Zedong, "Statement," 393.

Guerra: The Reel, Real, and Hyper-Real Revolution

Note: This essay is drawn from the much larger work by Lillian Guerra, *Visions of Power in Cuba: Revolution, Redemption, and Resistance, 1959–1971* (Chapel Hill, NC, 2012).

1. José Quiroga, *Cuban Palimpsests* (Minneapolis, MN, 2005), 11.

2. Fidel Castro, "Cuba se mantendrá firme y victoriosa," *ANAP* 2, no. 8 (August 1962): 13.

3. Lillian Guerra, "Gender Policing, Homosexuality and the New Patriarchy of the Cuban Revolution," *Social History* 35, no. 3 (August 2010): 268–89; Guerra, *Visions of Power in Cuba*, esp. chaps. 4, 7, and 8.

4. Sheila Fitzpatrick, *Everyday Stalinism: Ordinary Life in Extraordinary Times: Soviet Russia in the 1930s* (New York, 1999), 9, 34–39, 42–47.

5. Quiroga, *Cuban Palimpsests*, 95. Examples include the many images of impoverished peasants featured prominently in the glossy, *Life*-like magazine *INRA*. Although the photos were taken between 1960 and 1962, the peasants' obvious wretchedness was supposed to be representative of the pre-1959 past, even though they were actually photographed in the revolutionary present.

By the late 1960s, images showing peasants and urbanites wearing ragged or worn clothes were not supposed to illustrate the same thing that they had in 1959; interpreting such images, for instance, as signs of government neglect or economic mismanagement of resources was unthinkable, a counterrevolutionary taboo. These images were to reflect national resistance to imperialism and evidence of the evils of the US embargo.

6. Jean Baudrillard, ~~Simulacra and Simulation~~, trans. Sheila Faria Glaser (Ann Arbor, MI, 1994), 12–15. As Umberto Eco has argued, imperial societies like the United States designed hyper-realities like Disney World as a place of "total passivity." Disney World "not only produces illusion, but—in confessing it—stimulates the desire for it." Eco, *Travels in Hyperreality*, trans. William Weaver (San Diego, CA, 1986) 44, 48.

7. For a longer discussion of ICAIC's early mission, see Guerra, *Visions of Power in Cuba*, 162–64.

8. Tomás Gutiérrez Alea, "Hacia un cine nacional," *Cine Cubano* 1, no. 1 (October–November 1960): 173; Alfredo Guevara, "Realidades y perspectivas de un nuevo cine," *Cine Cubano* 1, no. 1 (October–November 1960): 3–4

9. Victor Martín Borrego, "Conversaciones con nuestros cineastas: Tomás Gutiérrez Alea," *El Caiman Barbudo* (June 1979): 13.

10. José Miguel García Ascot, "Nacimiento de un cine," *Nueva Revista Cubana* 1, no. 3 (October–December 1959): 210; Raúl Rodríguez, *Cine silente en Cuba* (Havana, 1992).

11. These films include *Jocuma* (1955), *Sierra Maestra* (1958), and *De la tiranía a la libertad* (1959) directed by Eduardo Hernández of Noticuba; director Eddy Palmer's *Gesta Inmortal* (1959), produced by Cuban Color Films. See *Revolución*, 28 January 1959, 19; Arturo Agramonte, *Cronología del cine cubano* (Havana, 1966).

12. Alfredo Guevara, "Transcripción. Intervenciones en el Consejo de Dirección del ICAIC," in *Tiempo de fundación*, ed. Camilo Pérez Casal (Madrid, 2003), 95.

13. Nicholas Wollaston, *Red Rumba: A Journey through the Caribbean and Central America* (London, 1962), 179–85.

14. Carlos Franqui, *Retrato de familia con Fidel* (Madrid, 1981), 261–73; Heberto Padilla, *Self-Portrait of the Other: A Memoir*, trans. Alexander Coleman (New York, 1990), 50–54; Linda Howe, *Transgression and Conformity: Cuban Writers and Artists after the Revolution* (Madison, WI, 2004), 24–25.

15. Nestor Almendros, *A Man with a Camera*, trans. Rafael Phillips Belash (New York, 1984), 38–39; Wollaston, *Red Rumba*, 184.

16. Theodor Christensen, "Estructura, imaginación y presencia de la realidad en el documental cubano," in *Cuba: Una revolución en marcha*, ed. Francisco Fernández-Santos and José Martinez (Madrid, 1967), 343.

17. Roque Dalton et al., *El Intelectual y la sociedad* (Mexico City, 1969), 26–27.

18. John Mraz, "Memories of Underdevelopment: Bourgeois Consciousness/Revolutionary Context," in *Revisioning History*, ed. Robert A. Rosenstone (Princeton, NJ, 1997), 104; 106–9.

19. Tomás Gutiérrez Alea, "El Free Cinema y la objetividad," *Cine cubano* 1, no. 4 (December–January, 1960–61): 38–39.

20. Tomás Gutiérrez Alea, "Hacia un cine nacional," *Nueva Revista Cubana* 1, no. 1 (April–June 1959): 173; Guevara, "Realidades y perspectivas de un nuevo cine," 3–4.

21. Michael Chanan, *Santiago Alvarez* (London, 1980) 7–8.

22. See *Ciclón* (1963); *Escambray* (1961). For descriptions of all of Alvarez's works of the 1960s, see "Annotated Alvarez Filmography" in Chanan, *Santiago Alvarez*, 31–45.

23. Examples include *Now* (1965), *Hanoi Martes 13* (1967), *LBJ* (1968), and *79 Primaveras* (1969).

24. See *Cuba 2 de Enero* (1965) and *Abril de Girón* (1966), films equating the armed defense of the Patria at Playa Girón with present-day military parades and mass rallies as well as volunteer labor in agriculture. See also *Segunda Declaración de la Habana*, a film on the million-plus rally of February 1962, which appeared for the first time in 1965.

25. Tanatos, untitled cartoon, *Alma Mater*, 31 August 1967, 11.

26. See Michael Chanan, *Cuban Cinema* (Minneapolis, MN, 2004), 240–43.

27. Quiroga, *Cuban Palimpsests*, 81–83.

28. Chanan, *Santiago Alvarez*, 43.

29. Manuel Zayas, "Nicolás Guillén Landrián: Muerte y resurrección," *Cinémas d'Amérique Latine* 18 (2010): 1–35.

30. Ibid., 13; Manuel Zayas, "Mi correspondencia con Nicolás Guillén Landrián," *Encuentro en la red. Diario independiente de asuntos cubanos,* 22 July 2005, 2–3, available athttp://arch1.cubaencuentro.com/entrevistas/20050722/54b1f-f4a6a60816ffca3713ab8f19e92.html; *Nicolás: El fin pero no es el fin (primera parte),* directed by Jorge Egusquiz Zorrilla and Victor Jiménez (1999).

31. Lara Petusky Coger, Alejandro Ríos, and Manuel Zayas, "Entrevistas. El cine postergado," *Encuentro en la red. Diario independiente de asuntos cubanos*, 26 August 2005, 2, available athttp://arch1.cubaencuentro.com/entrevistas/20050827/74540a9e00385c591a45bac12d946245.html.

32. Zayas, "Mi correspondencia con Nicolás Guillén Landrián," 2.

33. Ibid., 3.

34. Ibid., 3–4.

35. Ibid., 12.

36. Personal communication with Raúl Rodríguez, October 1996; email communication with Manuel Zayas, 16 September 2007.

37. *Noticiero No. 402: Amarrando el cordón*, directed by Santiago Alvarez (1968); "Antes nos deslojaban . . . hoy nos fabrican viviendas gratuitas!" *Juventud Rebelde*, 6 January 1968, 8.

38. *Granma* offered daily news from El Cordón and statistics on plantings. "Sucedió en el cordón" and "Gran siembra de primavera en el Cordón de la Habana," *Granma*, 3 June 1968, 4; "Sembraron café en Wajay turistas franceses," *Granma*, 31 May 1968, 5.

39. Filmed interview with Ismael Suárez de la Paz, 12 August 2008, San Juan, Puerto Rico.

40. The poem is "Un largo lagarto verde" [A large green lizard].

41. Coger, Ríos, and Zayas, "Entrevistas," 4.

42. Filmed interview with Suárez de la Paz.

43. Ibid.

44. Email correspondence with Manuel Zayas, 16 December 2007.

45. Cuban humorist Enrique Nuñez Rodríguez refers to this practice in *Oyé como lo cogieron* (Havana, 1991), 61.

46. Personal diary entry, Havana, 22 June 1996.

47. Quoted in Coger, Ríos, and Zayas, "Entrevistas," 4.

48. Ibid., 5.

49. Quoted in Zayas, "Nicolás Guillén Landrián," 4.

50. Coger, Ríos, and Zayas, "Entrevistas," 6; *Nicolasito: El fin pero no es el fin.*

Bourg: Writing on the Wall

1. Immanuel Wallerstein, "1968, Revolution in the World-System: Theses and Queries," *Theory and Society* 18, no. 4 (July 1989): 431–49; "New Revolts against the System," *New Left Review* 18 (November–December 2002): 29–39. The events of 1989 and the Arab Spring belie Wallerstein's downplaying of state power.

2. Régis Debray, *Revolution in the Revolution?: Armed Struggle and Political Struggle in Latin America*, trans. Bobbye Ortiz (New York, 1967).

3. Wolfgang Kraushaar, "Die erste globale Rebellion," in *1968 als Mythos, Chiffre und Zäsur* (Hamburg, 2000).

4. Gerard J. DeGroot, *The Sixties Unplugged: A Kaleidoscopic History of a Disorderly Decade* (Cambridge, MA, 2010).

5. Victoria H. F. Scott, "Silk-Screens and Television Screens: Maoism and the Posters of May and June 1968 in Paris," Ph.D. dissertation, SUNY Binghamton, 2010, chap. 2.

6. Morris Dickstein, *Gates of Eden: American Culture in the Sixties* (New York, 1977), 266.

7. Pierre Vidal-Naquet, "Outline of a Revolution," in *The French Student Uprising, November 1967–June 1968*, ed. Alain Schnapp and Vidal-Naquet, trans. Maria Jolas (Boston, 1971), 44.

8. David Caute, *The Year of the Barricades: A Journey through 1968* (New York, 1988).

9. Eric Wentworth, "Cacophony of Leftist Voices Enlivens Talk-in at Sorbonne," *Washington Post*, 16 May 1968, A16.

10. William Shannon, "The Year That Failed to Turn," *New York Times*, 30 December 1968, 30. On 26 June 1968, Hannah Arendt wrote to her old friend Karl Jaspers: "It seems to me that the children of the next century will once learn about 1968 the way we learned about 1848." Cited in Martin Klimke and Joachim Scharloth, "1968 in Europe: An Introduction," in *1968 in Europe: A History of Protest and Activism, 1956–1977*, ed. Klimke and Scharloth (New York, 2008), 7.

11. John Bryan Starr, "Revolution in Retrospect: The Paris Commune through Chinese Eyes," *China Quarterly* 49 (January–March 1972): 106–25; Cheng Tche-se, "Les grandes révélations de la Commune de Paris," *Pékin Information* 15–18 (11 April–2 May 1966); "France Enlists 1871 Law to Halt Bombings: Police to Check Cars, Explosives Dealers," *Boston Globe*, 10 December 1968, 2. The one hundredth anniversary of the Commune in 1971 occasioned international memorialization through press reports, conferences, books, song collections, and even a Soviet postage stamp.

12. On Marcellin, see Julian Bourg, *From Revolution to Ethics: May 1968 and Contemporary French Thought* (Montreal, 2007), 61–65; Raymond Aron, *The Elusive Revolution: Anatomy of a Student Revolt*, trans. Gordon Clough (New York, 1969), 11 (on Tocqueville), 145 (on angry students).

13. Vladimir Fisera, ed., *Writing on the Wall, May 1968: A Documentary Anthology* (New York, 1978), 27.

14. Michel de Certeau, *The Capture of Speech and Other Political Writings*, ed. and intro. Luce Giard, trans. and afterword Tom Conley (Minneapolis, MN, 1997), 62.

15. The term was misleadingly used by Luc Ferry and Alain Renault, *La Pensée 68: essai sur l'anti-humanisme contemporain* (Paris, 1985); *French Philosophy of the Sixties: An Essay on Antihumanism*, trans. Mary Schnackenberg Cattani (Amherst, MA, 1990).

16. Henri Lefebvre, *The Explosion: Marxism and the French Revolution*, trans. Alfred Ehrenfeld (New York, 1969), 7.

17. Claude Lefort, "Le désordre nouveau," in Edgar Morin, Jean-Marc Coudray [Cornelius Castoriadis], and Claude Lefort, *Mai 1968: la brèche* (Paris, 1988), 37, 49–50, 62. The last phrase anticipated Václav Havel's 1978 "The Power of the Powerless," in *Open Letters: Selected Writings, 1965–1990* (New York, 1992).

18. De Certeau, *The Capture of Speech and Other Political Writings*, 3, 5–6, 11, 20, 23, 26, 30, 39.

19. Kristin Ross, *May '68 and Its Afterlives* (Chicago, 2002).

20. Daniel Cohn-Bendit, interview by Jean-Paul Sartre, 20 May 1968, in *The Global Revolutions of 1968*, ed. Jeremi Suri (New York, 2007), 134, 137–38, 140.

21. Roland Barthes, "Writing the Event," in *The Rustle of Language*, trans. Richard Howard (New York, 1986), 149–53. In *Writing Degree Zero* (1953), Barthes had criticized socialist realism and Stalinism as the reflux of nineteenth-century petit-bourgeois realism, preferring instead the "neutral" writing of Albert Camus. See the excerpt published as Barthes, "Writing and Revolution," *Yale French Studies* 39 (1967): 77–84.

22. Margaret Atack, *May 68 in French Fiction and Film* (Oxford, 1999), 1–8.

23. Cohn-Bendit, interview by Jean-Paul Sartre, 136.

24. Martin Jay, "Historical Explanation and the Event: Reflection on the Limits of Contextualization," *New Literary History* 42 (2011): 557–71; "Historicism and the Event," in *Against the Grain: Jewish Intellectuals in Hard Times*, ed. Ezra Mendelsohn et al. (New York, 2013).

25. Jacques Lacan, *Le Séminaire de Jacques Lacan*, vol. 17, *L'Envers de la psychanalyse, 1969–1970*, ed. Jacques-Alain Miller (Paris, 1991), 239; Stephen Frosh, "Everyone Longs for a Master: Lacan and 1968," in *1968 in Retrospect: History, Theory, Alterity*, ed. Gurminder K. Bhambra and Ipek Demir (Basingstoke, UK, 2009).

26. De Certeau, *The Capture of Speech and Other Political Writings*, 18, 39.

27. On antinomianism and 1968, see Bourg, *From Revolution to Ethics*, 6–7, 340–42.

28. Xavier Vigna, *L'insubordination ouvrière dans les années 68: essai d'histoire politique des usines* (Rennes, 2007); Daniel A. Gordon, *Immigrants & Intellectuals: May '68 & the Rise of Anti-Racism in France* (Pontypool, UK, 2012).

29. Philippe Artières and Michelle Zancarini-Fournel's 850-page edited volume, *68: une histoire collective, 1962–1981* (Paris, 2008), is mostly about France.

30. Brian Moore fictionalized the 1970 "October crisis" in Canada when two officials were kidnapped by the Front de libération du Québec and the government responded by evoking the severe War Measures Act. Moore, *The Revolution Script* (New York, 1971).

31. While the top-three-grossing American movies between 1965 and 1974 con-

tinued to appeal to innocence, tradition, and sentimentality—*The Sound of Music* (1965), *The Bible in the Beginning* (1966), and *Love Story* (1970)—the number of such films involving revolution, rebellion, generational conflict, race relations, sexual explicitness, and antiwar feeling is instructive—from *Doctor Zhivago* (1965) to *The Graduate* and *Guess Who's Coming to Dinner* (1967) to *Butch Cassidy and the Sundance Kid*, *Midnight Cowboy*, and *Easy Rider* (1968) to *M.A.S.H.* (1970). The decade also saw films that appeased fears of social conflict by appealing to extralegal police authority—*Dirty Harry* (1971)—nostalgia—*The Godfather* (1972) and *American Graffiti* (1973)—and escapist disaster—*The Poseidon Adventure* (1972) and *The Towering Inferno* (1974).

32. De Certeau, *Culture in the Plural*, ed. and intro. Luce Giard, trans. and afterword Tom Conley (Minneapolis, MN, 1997), 89.

33. Eric Hobsbawm, "1968—A Retrospect," *Marxism Today* (May 1978): 130–36. Daniel 5:1–31.

34. Arthur Marwick, *The Sixties: Cultural Revolution in Britain, France, Italy, and the United States, c. 1958–c. 1974* (Oxford, 1998), 7; Philip Gassert and Martin Klimke, "Introduction: 1968 from Revolt to Research," *Bulletin of the German Historical Institute*, supplement 6 (2009): 13.

35. Mark Kurlansky, *1968: The Year That Rocked the World* (New York, 2004).

36. The editors of a 2013 collection on the Third World in the global sixties could still justifiably complain that "the Third World remains *terra incognita* in the scholarship on the 1960s": Samantha Christiansen and Zachary A. Scarlett, "Introduction," in *The Third World in the Global 1960s*, ed. Christiansen and Scarlett (New York, 2013), 2; Gassert and Klimke, "Introduction," 13–14, highlight monographs on local experiences in Heidelberg (Katja Nagel), Philadelphia (Paul Lyons), and Lawrence, Kansas (Rusty L. Monhollon).

37. Jeremi Suri, *Power and Protest: Global Revolution and the Rise of Détente* (Cambridge, MA, 2003).

38. Cynthia A. Young, *Soul Power: Culture, Radicalism, and the Making of a U.S. Third World Left* (Durham, NC, 2006); Quinn Slobodian, *Foreign Front: Third World Politics in Sixties West Germany* (Durham, NC, 2012).

39. Gerd-Rainer Horn, *The Spirit of '68: Rebellion in Western Europe and North America, 1956–1976* (Oxford, 2007), 4; Paul Berman, *A Tale of Two Utopias: The Political Journey of the Generation of 1968* (New York, 1996), 9.

40. Michael Seidman, *The Imaginary Revolution: Parisian Students and Workers in 1968* (New York, 2004), 7.

41. Timothy Scott Brown, *West Germany and the Global Sixties: The Anti-Authoritarian Revolt, 1962–1978* (Cambridge, 2013), and "A Tale of Two Communes: The Private and the Political in Divided Berlin, 1967–1973," in *Between Prague Spring and French May: Opposition and Revolt in Europe, 1960–1980*, ed. Martin Klimke et al. (New York, 2011).

42. Lionel Trilling, *Beyond Culture: Essays on Literature and Learning* (New York, 1965), xv.

43. Christiansen and Scarlett, "Introduction," 9; Jeffrey L. Gould, "Solidarity under Siege: The Latin American Left, 1968," *American Historical Review* 114, no. 2 (April 2009): 348–75.

44. Lessie Jo Frazier and Deborah Cohen, ed., *Gender and Sexuality in 1968: Transformative Politics in the Cultural Imagination* (New York, 2009).

45. Suri sees political radicalism as marginal and as having reinforced the status quo ante. Jeremi Suri, "The Rise and Fall of an International Counterculture, 1960–1975," *American Historical Review* 114, no. 1 (2009): 49, 53, 57.

46. See excerpts from the insightful September 1968 CIA report *Restless Youth* in Suri, ed., *The Global Revolutions of 1968*, 216–38.

47. Martin Luther King, Jr., "Beyond Vietnam: A Time to Break Silence," 4 April 1967, available at http://mlk-kppo1.stanford.edu/index.php/encyclopedia/documentsentry/doc_beyond_vietnam.

48. C. Wright Mills, "Letter to the New Left," *New Left Review* 5 (September–October 1960): 18–23.

49. Martin Klimke, *The Other Alliance: Student Protest in West Germany and the United States in the Global Sixties* (Princeton, NJ, 2011).

50. Students for a Democratic Society, "The Port Huron Statement (1962)," in Suri, ed., *The Global Revolutions of 1968*, 40–50.

51. Herbert Marcuse, *One-Dimensional Man: Studies in the Ideology of Advanced Industrial Society* (Boston, 1991), 63; Jacek Kuron and Karol Modzelewski, *A Revolutionary Socialist Manifesto/An Open Letter to the Party* (London, 1975), 60–70.

52. The Paris chief of police in 1968, Maurice Grimaud, recounts his sympathies for the protestors in his *En mai, fais ce qu'il te plaît* (Paris, 1977).

53. Japanese student revolt was fueled by outrage at the U.S.-Japan military alliance. William Marotti, "Japan 1968: The Performance of Violence and the Theater of Protest," *American Historical Review* 114, no. 1 (2009): 97–135.

54. Tariq Ali, *Street Fighting Years: An Autobiography of the Sixties* (London, 2005), 239–46.

55. Jeremy Varon, *Bringing the War Home: The Weather Underground, the Red Army Faction, and Revolutionary Violence in the Sixties and Seventies* (Berkeley, CA, 2004); Karrin Hanshew, *Terror and Democracy in West Germany* (Cambridge, 2012); Marco Briziarelli, *The Red Brigades and the Discourse of Violence: Revolution and Restoration* (New York, 2014).

56. Seth Rosenfeld, *Subversives: The FBI's War on Student Radicals and Reagan's Rise to Power* (New York, 2012).

57. Alain Touraine, *The Voice and the Eye: An Analysis of Social Movements*, trans. Alan Duff (Cambridge, 1981).

58. Michel Foucault and Gilles Deleuze, "Intellectuals and Power," in Foucault, *Language, Counter-Memory, Practice: Selected Essays and Interviews*, ed. and intro. Donald F. Bouchard, trans. Bouchard and Sherry Simon (Ithaca, NY, 1977); Felix Guattari, "The Micro-Politics of Fascism" and "Molecular Revolution and Class Struggle," in *Molecular Revolution: Psychiatry and Politics*, trans. Rosemary Sheed (Harmondsworth, UK, 1984). Eastern European dissident initiatives such as Charter 77 in Czechoslovakia paralleled the New Social Movements in making civil society the privileged arena for engagement and "the power of the powerless." "Charter 77—Declaration (1 January 1977)," in Suri, ed., *The Global Revolutions of 1968*, 284–89; Ágnes Heller, "The Year 1968 and Its Results: An East European Perspective," in *Promises of 1968: Crisis, Illusion, and Utopia*, ed. Vladimir Tismaneannu (Budapest, 2011).

59. Samuel Moyn, *The Last Utopia: Human Rights in History* (Cambridge, MA, 2010); Barbara J. Falk, *The Dilemmas of Dissidence in East-Central Europe: Citizen Intellectuals and Philosopher Kings* (Budapest, 2003)

60. Vladimir Lenin, *"Left-Wing" Communism: An Infantile Disorder: A Popular Essay in Marxian Strategy and Tactics* (New York, 1940).

61. Jules Witcover, *The Year the Dream Died: Revisiting 1968 in America* (New York, 1997).

62. The following is indebted to Martin Klimke, "Revisiting the Revolution: 1968 in Transnational Cultural Memory," in *Memories of 1968: International Perspectives*, ed. Ingo Cornils and Sarah Waters (Oxford, 2010).

63. Thomas Frank, *The Conquest of Cool: Business Culture, Counterculture, and the Rise of Hip Consumerism* (Chicago, 1997); Luc Boltanski and Eve Chiapello, *The New Spirit of Capitalism*, trans. Gregory Elliott (London, 2005).

64. Klimke, "Revisiting the Revolution," 27.

65. Jeremy Varon et al., "Time Is an Ocean: The Past and Future of the Sixties," *The Sixties* 1, no. 1 (June 2008): 2; Robert Gildea, James Mark, and Annette Warring, ed., *Europe's 1968: Voices of Revolt* (Oxford, 2013).

66. Christiansen and Scarlett, "Introduction," 1, 4; Edmund White, *Genet: A Biography* (New York, 1993), 521–44, 560–68; Carol Fink et al., "Introduction," in *1968: The World Transformed*, ed. Fink et al. (Cambridge, 1998), 17–22.

Milani: Scripting a Revolution

Note: This is a much-revised version of the paper read at the Stanford Conference on Scripting Revolutions. Parts of this paper have earlier been published in my book on the shah. I am grateful to the organizers of the conference for their invitation and their patience.

1. Charles Kurzman, *The Unthinkable Revolution in Iran* (Cambridge, MA, 2004).

2. Two different studies, one by Mohmmad Mokhtari, and the second by Mehdi Bazorgan, the first a poet and the second the first prime minister of the IRGC, come up with slightly different percentages about the content of the slogans. For a discussion of the two studies. See Mohsen Milani, *The Making of the Islamic Revolution*, 2nd ed. (Boulder, CO, 1999), 136.

3. The first attempt to study conspiracy theories from a scholarly perspective was undertaken by Hamid Ashraf, "The Appeal of Conspiracy Theories to Persians," *Princeton Papers* 5 (Winter 1997): 57–88.

4. Richard Hofstadter, "The Paranoid Style in American Politics," *Harper's*, November 1964, 77–86. The seminal essay was later republished as a part of a book, in *The Paranoid Style in American Politics and Other Essays* (Cambridge, MA, 1996).

5. For conspiracy theories as a form of political participation, see Jon W. Anderson, "Conspiracy Theories, Premature Entextualization, and Popular Political Analysis," *Arab Studies Journal* 4, no. 1 (Spring 1996): 96–102. For a brilliant depiction of what engagement in conspiracies theorizing, particularly about the British, does to the fabric of life and political thought in an average middle-class family in Iran, read the now classic novel *My Uncle Napoleon*. Written by Iraj

Pezeshkzad and translated into English by Dick Davis (first published by Mage and then by Modern Library Paperbacks, the book was also made into one of Iran's most acclaimed television series. There is now a small library of books and articles written about who and why the novel was written—many seeing a British hand in its publication!

6. For a thorough discussion of conspiracy theories in Iran, read Houchang E. Chehabi, "The Paranoid Style in Iranian Historiography," in *Iran in the 20th Century: Historiography and Political Culture*, ed. Touraj Atabki (London, 2009), 155–205; for a psychological approach to this proclivity, see Marvin Zonis and Joseph Craig, "Conspiracy Thinking in the Middle East," *Political Psychology* 15, no. 3 (1994): 443–59.

7. For a description of the nativist tendency in Iran as well as the Othering process, see Mehrzad Boroujerdi, *Iranian Intellectuals and the West* (Syracuse, NY, 1996), 1–76.

8. Mohamad Reza Pahlavi, *Answer to History* (New York, 1980), 93–97.

9. Ibid., 146.

10. Public Record Office (PRO), "Iranian Internal Situation, 12 October 1978," PREM 16/1719.

11. PRO, "Iranian Internal Situation, 16 September 1978," PREM 16/1719.

12. CIA, Mohammad Reza Pahlavi, Shah of Iran, 23 October 1978. I obtained a copy through a Freedom of Information Act request.

13. Marvin Zonis, *Majestic Failure: The Fall of the Shah* (Chicago, 1991). Zonis used psychological theories to argue that the men and women the shah relied on for his Selfhood were all gone by the time of the revolution.

14. PRO, "Letter by ACI Samuel to Foreign Office, July 18, 1955," FO 371/114810.

15. CIA, Profile of the Shah, Freedom of Information Act Request.

16. See, for example, Samuel P. Huntington, *The Third Wave: Democratization in the Late Twentieth Century* (Norman, OK, 1991).

17. Mohammed Reza Pahlavi, *Mission for My Country* (London, 1962). More than once, he claims divine protection and revelation. In later years, he repeated these claims, suggesting that many of his decisions are made after divine inspiration.

18. For a discussion of some of the theories developed in Europe in legitimizing monarchy, see Ernst H. Kantorowicz, *The King's Two Bodies: A Study in Mediaeval Political Theology* (Princeton, NJ, 1957).

19. I have written at length about these decisions and their aftermath. See *The Persian Sphinx: Amir Abbas Hoveyda and the Riddle of the Iranian Revolution* (Washington, 2000).

20. General Mohammad Khatam is central in this conspiracy script. Although he died in a gliding accident, and though he was implicated in massive financial malfeasance, advocates of the conspiracy believe that his death was no accident but fully scripted. In the chapter on Mohmmad Khatam in my *Eminent Persians: The Men and Women Who Made Modern Iran, 1941–1979* (Syracuse, NY, 2008), I have offered a sketch of his life and death.

21. He was alleged to have been working with Khomeini for many years. The

regime published two volumes of damaging material on the shah that it claimed to be the general's prison memoirs. For a brief account of his life, see my *Eminent Persians*, the chapter on General Fardust.

22. As is evident even from the rather lengthy title of his book, there is a sharp difference between Huyser's perception of the purpose of his mission and that of the shah and the general. See General Robert E. Huyser, *Mission to Tehran: The Fall of the Shah and the Rise of Khomeini Recounted by the US General Who Was Secretly Sent at the Last Minute to Prevent It* (New York, 1986).

23. NSA, Bureau of Intelligence and Research, Department of State, "Studies in Political Dynamics in Iran," Secret Intelligence Report #13, no. 603.

24. William Shawcross, *The Shah's Last Ride* (London, 1989), 99.

25. PRO, "30 October 1978, Prime Minister's office to Foreign Ministry," PREM 16/1719.

26. NSA, "Ambassador Foroughi, September 17, 1979."

27. For Iran's encounter with modernity and the influence of its ideas on intellectual discourse, see my *Lost Wisdom: Rethinking Modernity in Iran* (Washington, 2002). I have also written about these ideas in two books in Persian: *Tajadod va Tajado Setizi dar Iran* (*Modernity and Its Foes in Iran*, published in Iran and now in its ninth printing), and *King of Shadows* (published in Los Angeles, and still, after seven years, waiting to clear the censors!).

28. For a collection of Khomeini's books, see *Islam and Revolution: Writings and Declarations of Imam Khomeini*, trans. Hamid Algar (Berkeley, CA, 1981). For a brief biographical sketch of his life and intellectual development, see the chapter on Khomeini in my *Eminent Persians*.

29. For a brilliant exposition of this history, see Mehdi Haeri Yazdi, *Hekmat va Hokumat* (London, 1995).

30. For a brief overview of these two versions of Shiism, see my "New Democrats," *New Republic*, 15 July 2009, 17–19.

31. *Qur'an*, 2:256.

32. All quotations are from Jalal Matini, "The Most Truthful Individual in Recent History," *Iranshenasi* 14, no. 4 (Winter 2003).

33. US Embassy, Tehran, "Moves toward Government Unification, 8/3/79," in *Asnad-e Laneye Jasusi* [Documents from the Den of Spies], vol. 16 (Tehran, n.d.).

34. Asghar Schirazi, *The Constitution of Iran: Politics and State in the Islamic Republic of Iran*, trans. Jon O'Kane (London, 1997), 293.

35. US Department of State, "Statement of US Policy toward Iran," *Foreign Relations of the US, 1958–1960* (Washington, 1993), 613.

36. Ibid., 606.

37. Ibid., 613.

38. NSA, no. 369, "Political Internal Issues."

39. CIA, "Stability of the Present Regime in Iran: Secret Special National Intelligence Estimate," 1958/08/25, NSA, no. 362. Much the same sentiment is reflected in another NIE: see "The Outlook for Iran: Secret National Intelligence Estimate NIE 36–40," NSA, no. 385.

40. PRO, "Tehran to Foreign Office, 19 December 1978," PREM 16/1720.

41. PRO, "Tehran to Foreign Office, 6 July 1978," FCO 8/3184.

42. George Ball, *Issues and Implications Of the Iranian Crisis, Seeley G, Mudd Manuscript Collection*, Princeton Library, 3.

43. A copy of his speech was given to me, courtesy of Senator Lajevardi.

44. James Davies, "The J-Curve of Rising and Declining Expectations as a Case of Some Great Revolutions and a Contained Rebellion," in *Violence in America*, ed. Hugh Davis Graham and Ted Robert Gurr (New York, 1969). For a brief discussion of the curve in relation to Iran's revolution, see, for example, Mohsen Milani, *Iran's Islamic Revolution: From Monarchy to Islamic Republic* (Boulder, CO, 1988), 16.

45. Alam recounts other episodes in the fifth volume of his memoir. I have discussed the letters and the response, and how the government's decision to ignore them strengthened Khomeini. See my "Alam and the Roots of the Iranian Revolution," in *King of Shadows* (Los Angeles, 2005) 46–79.

46. NSA, no. 2048, "Religious Leaders Fear Departure of the Shah," 1/9/1969.

47. Mehdi Samii has kindly provided me with his notes, taken at the time of his meetings with the shah. They are a remarkable document in the honesty of their discussion.

48. I have written at some length about the origins of the one-party idea in *The Persian Sphinx*, 275–87.

49. For a detailed account behind the scenes, see Andrew Scott Cooper, "Showdown in Doha: The Secret Deal That Helped Sink the Shah of Iran," *Middle East Journal* 62, no. 4 (Autumn 2008).

50. "A Brief Overview of the US-Iran Relations," NSA, 27. The report was prepared in the early eighties; it displays no author or other indications about who commissioned it.

51. Pahlavi, *Answer to History*, 116.

52. Tom Stoppard, *Arcadia* (London, 1993), 47.

53. Tom Stoppard, *The Coast of Utopia: Voyage, Shipwreck, Salvage* (New York, 2007).

Toska: The Multiple Scripts of the Arab Revolutions

1. On the paradigm of authoritarian resilience that dominated Middle Eastern studies for the past two decades, see Dan Brumberg, "The Trap of Liberalized Autocracy," *Journal of Democracy* 13, no. 4 (2002): 56–68; Thomas Carothers, "The End of the Transition Paradigm," *Journal of Democracy* 13, no. 1 (2002): 5–23; Holger Albrecht and Oliver Schlumberger, "Waiting for Godot: Regime Change without Democratization in the Middle East," *International Political Science Review* 25, no. 4 (2004): 371–92; Steven Heydemann, "Upgrading Authoritarianism in the Arab World," Brookings Institution Analysis Paper, no. 13 (2007), available at www.brookings.edu/,/media/Files/rc/papers/2007/10arabworld/10arabworld.pdf.

2. Marc Lynch, who coined the term "Arab Spring," rejected it soon after the revolutions started hanging in the balance in favor of the more neutral—and measured—term "Arab Uprisings." Marc Lynch, *The Arab Uprising: The Unfinished Revolutions of the New Middle East* (New York, 2012).

3. Valerie Bunce, Sharon Wolchik, and David Patel, "Fizzles and Fireworks: A Comparative Perspective on the Diffusion of Popular Protests in the Middle East

and North Africa," in *The Arab Uprisings in Comparative Perspective,* ed. Marc Lynch (forthcoming).

4. Sune Hougball, "Reflections on Arab Ideology after the Uprisings," *Jaddaliya,* 23 March 2012, available at www.jadaliyya.com/pages/index/4764/reflections-on-ideology-after-the-arab-uprisings.

5. See Keith Baker, "Enlightenment and Revolution in France: Old Problems, Renewed Approaches," *Journal of Modern History* 53, no. 2 (June 1981): 281; Keith Baker, "A Script for a French Revolution: The Political Consciousness of the Abbee Mably," *Eighteen-Century Studies* 14, no. 3 (1981): 235; Dan Edelstein, "Do We Want a Revolution without a Revolution? Reflections on Political Authority," *French Historical Studies* 35, no. 2 (2012): 270.

6. For the former see David Bell, "Why We Can't Rule out an Egyptian Reign of Terror: A Historian's Look at Revolution and Its Discontents," *Foreign Policy,* 7 February 2011, available at www.foreignpolicy.com/articles/2011/02/07/why_we_cant_rule_out_an_egyptian_reign_of_terror; for the latter, see Edelstein, "Do We Want a Revolution without a Revolution?"

7. Bell, "Why We Can't Rule out an Egyptian Reign of Terror."

8. For a review of the literature on the causes of revolutions, see Theda Skocpol, *States and Social Revolutions: A Comparative Analysis of France, Russia and China* (Cambridge, 1979) 3–33; see also James C. Davies, "Toward a Theory of Revolution," *American Sociological Review* 27 (February 1962): 5; Ted R. Gurr, *Why Men Rebel* (Princeton, NJ, 1970); David Snyder and Charles Tilly, "Hardship and Collective Violence in France, 1830 to 1960," *American Sociological Review* 37 (October 1972): 520; and Charles Tilly, Louise Tilly, and Richard Tilly, *The Rebellious Century: 1830–1930* (Cambridge, 1975).

9. Timur Kuran, "Now out of Never: The Element of Surprise in the East European Revolution of 1989," *World Politics* 44, no. 1 (1991): 13.

10. Baker, "Enlightenment and Revolution in France," 285.

11. For a discussion of the role of these authors in prerevolutionary political discourse, see Baker, "A Script for a French Revolution," 241–42.

12. Edelstein, "Do We Want a Revolution without a Revolution?"

13. John Locke, as quoted in ibid., 276.

14. Ibid., 272.

15. Kuran, "Now out of Never," 7.

16. Ibid., 9–17.

17. Ibid., 8.

18. For an informative account of Poland's political transformation, see Elie Abel, *The Shattered Bloc: Behind the Upheaval in Eastern* Europe (Boston, 1990).

19. Kuran, "Now out of Never," 13.

20. Skocpol, *States and Social Revolutions,* 17; see also Eric Hobsbawm, *The Age of Revolution: 1789–1848* (London, 1996).

21. Skocpol, *States and Social Revolutions,* 17.

22. Michael Hudson, *Arab Politics: The Search for Legitimacy* (New Haven, CT, 1979).

23. For a discussion on the grievances for revolutionary onset, see Gurr, *Why Men Rebel*; for its critique, see Skocpol, *States and Social Revolutions*; Snyder and

Tilly, "Hardship and Collective Violence in France"; and Kuran, "Now out of Never."

24. See Lisa Blaydes, *Elections and Distributive Politics in Mubarak's Egypt* (Cambridge, 2010); April Longley Alley, "The Rules of the Game: Unpacking Patronage Politics in Yemen," *Middle East Journal* 64, no. 3 (2010): 385–406; and April Longley, "Shifting Light in the Qamariyya: The Reinvention of Patronage Networks in Contemporary Yemen," Ph.D. dissertation, Georgetown University, 2008.

25. For a discussion of the early developments of the Arab states, see Kanan Makiya, *Republic of Fear: The Politics of Modern Iraq* (Berkeley, CA, 1998); and Raymond A. Hinnebusch, *Authoritarian Power and State Formations in Ba'athist Syria* (Boulder, CO 1989).

26. Ariel Ahram, "State-Breaking and the Crisis of Arab Authoritarianism" (unpublished, 2011); for an analysis of the authoritarian bargain, see also Tarik Yousef, "Development, Growth, and Policy Reform in the Middle East and North Africa since 1950," *Journal of Economic Perspectives* 19, no. 4 (2004); Steve Heydemann, "Social Pacts and the Persistence of Authoritarianism in the Middle East," in *Debating Authoritarianism: Dynamics and Durability in Non-Democratic Regimes,* ed. Oliver Schlumberger (Stanford, CA, 2007). For an excellent history of the region's political-economic transition since the 1950s, see Alan Richards and John Waterbury, *A Political Economy of the Middle East* (Boulder, CO, 2007); and Stephen King, *The New Authoritarianism in the Middle East and North Africa* (Bloomington, IN, 2009).

27. For a discussion of the active protest movements in Egypt under Mubarak, see Blaydes, *Elections and Distributive Politics in Mubarak's Egypt,* chap. 3.

28. See Blaydes, *Elections and Distributive Politics in Mubarak's Egypt*; and Bassam Haddad, *Business Networks in Syria: The Political Economy of Authoritarian Resilience* (Stanford, CA, 2012).

29. For an analysis of the changing role of Islamists in Middle Eastern politics, see notably Sameer Shehata, ed., *Islamist Politics in the Middle East: Movements and Change* (New York, 2012); and Shadi Hamid, "Arab Islamist Parties: Losing on Purpose?" *Journal of Democracy* 22, no. 1 (2011): 68–88.

30. Shehata, ed., *Islamist Politics in the Middle East,* introduction.

31. Bunce, Wolchik, and Patel, "Fizzles and Fireworks."

32. See Mona El Ghobashy, "The Praxis of the Egyptian Revolution," *Middle East Research and Information Project (MERIP)* 41 (2011), doi: MER258.

33. Skocpol, *States and Social Revolutions,* 17.

34. Edelstein, "Do We Want a Revolution," 270.

35. Spokesperson for the April 6 Movement, interview with author, July 2011.

36. For an analysis of the Brotherhood's ideology, see Shehata, *Islamist Politics in the Middle East,* chaps. 4, 6, and 7.

37. Spokesperson for the April 6 Movement, interview with author, July 2011.

38. In light of recent events—the Brotherhood president Mohammad Morsi recently appointed avowedly Islamist ministers and judges and has adopted an increasingly Islamist rhetoric, and curtailed media freedom significantly—"liberals" feel both defeated and vindicated. Defeated, because the revolution is no longer related to notions of popular sovereignty, but rather it is slowly replaced by an Is-

lamist script. Vindicated, because their warnings and boycott of the elections seem justified in retrospect. For a list of recent Morsi appointments and constitutional changes, see Robert Springborg, "Egypt's Cobra and Mongoose Become Lion and Lamb?" *Foreign Policy,* 14 August 2012, available at http://mideast.foreignpolicy. com/posts/2012/08/14/egypts_cobra_and_mongoose_become_lion_and_lamb.

39. While for many revolutionaries and analysts the revolution was incomplete because the current regime in Egypt is still in the hands of many of the same individuals and the bureaucracy remains intact, as per the narrow definition of revolutions outlined above and the assertion that the uprisings represent a vast social transformation, the fall of Mubarak is here examined as the overthrow of an old regime through a revolution.

40. El Ghobashy, "The Praxis of the Egyptian Revolution."

41. Edelstein, "Do We Want a Revolution without Revolution?" 276.

42. For election results of the first and second round of the presidential elections, see reporting by Matthew Weaver, "Muslim Brotherhood's Mohammed Morsi Wins Egypt's Presidential Race," *Guardian Online,* 24 June 2012, available at www.guardian.co.uk/world/middle-east-live/2012/jun/24/egypt-election-results-live.

43. Despite its having been in the public eye for decades, the Brotherhood remains rather mysterious. Analysts disagree on the extent and rigidity of their ideology. See, for example, Shehata, ed., *Islamist Politics in the Middle East*; and Steven Cook, *The Struggle for Egypt: From Nasser to Tahrir Square* (Oxford, 2011).

44. Abdul Ghani Al-Iryani, political analyst and cofounder of "Democratic Awakening" movement, interview with author, August 2012. See also the International Crisis Group Report, "Yemen: Enduring Conflicts, Threatened Transition," *Middle East Report* 125 (July 2012), available at www.crisisgroup.org/en/regions/middle-east-north-africa/iraq-iran-gulf/yemen/125-yemen-enduring-conflicts-threatened-transition.aspx.

45. Personal interview.

46. Abdul Ghani Al-Iryani, interview with author, August 2012.

47. Houthi spokesperson in Sana'a, Yemen, personal interview with author, 6 August 2012.

48. Houthi spokesperson in Sana'a, Yemen, personal interview with author, 6 August 2012. While "Death to America, Death to Israel" is the official slogan of Houthis, this has seen by many of them as a strategic mistake at labeling themselves under the influence of the Iranian government, which supplies them with weapons and cash. Many Houthis are far less interested in this international dimension of their ideology, but their interpretation of Zaydi Islam can often be exclusive of other Islamic sects (as are those sects toward the Zaydis) and in many ways as religiously conservative as the Salafis.

49. Hussam Al Sharjabi, cofounder of Al Watan Party, Yemen, interview with author, 30 July 2012.

50. Marina Ottaway, "The Presidents Left, the Regimes are Still There," Carnegie Endowment Paper, February 14, 2011, available at http://carnegieendowment. org/publications/?fa=442627.

Bell·Afterword

1. Keith Michael Baker, *Inventing the French Revolution: Essays on French Political Culture in the Eighteenth Century* (Cambridge, 1990), 13.

2. Antoine Barnave, *De la révolution et de la constitution*, ed. Patrice Gueniffey (Grenoble, 1988).

3. Mary Ashburn Miller, *A Natural History of Revolution: Violence and Nature in the French Revolutionary Imagination, 1789–1794* (Ithaca, NY, 2011).

4. See for instance Roger Chartier, *The Cultural Origins of the French Revolution*, trans. Lydia G. Cochrane (Durham, NC, 1991), 87–89; Jonathan I. Israel, *Democratic Enlightenment: Philosophy, Revolution, and Human Rights, 1750–1790* (Oxford, 2011), 808–21.

5. In addition to the essay in this volume, see also Keith Michael Baker, "Inventing the French Revolution," in *Inventing the French Revolution*, 203–23; and Keith Michael Baker, "Revolution 1.0," *Journal of Modern European History* 11, no. 2 (2013): 187–219.

6. Quoted in Benno Ennker, *Die Anfänge des Leninkults in der Sowjetunion* (Cologne, 1997), 38.

7. Steve Pincus, *1688: The First Modern Revolution* (New Haven, CT, 2009). For the works by Tilly, Moore, and Skocpol, see Baker and Edelstein's discussion in the Introduction.

8. On this shift, see, above all, William Sewell, *Logics of History: Social Theory and Social Transformation* (Chicago, 2005), esp. 22–80.

9. François Furet, *Penser la Révolution française* (Paris, 1978).

10. In addition to Baker, *Inventing the French Revolution*, see Lynn Hunt, *Politics, Culture and Class in the French Revolution* (Berkeley, CA, 1984). On Furet, see Christophe Prochasson, *François Furet: Les chemins de la mélancolie* (Paris, 2013).

11. See Dimitry Shlapentokh, *The French Revolution and the Russian Anti-Democratic Tradition: A Case of False Consciousness* (New Brunswick, NJ, 1997).

12. Jean-Claude Bonnet, *Naissance du Panthéon: Essai sur le culte des grands hommes* (Paris, 1998); David A. Bell, *The Cult of the Nation in France: Inventing Nationalism, 1680–1800* (Cambridge, MA, 2001), 107–39.

13. Montesquieu, *Lettres persanes* (Paris, 1831), 22.

14. Eric Hobsbawm, *Interesting Times: A Twentieth-Century Life* (New York, 2003), 73.

15. See, as a starting point, the historians and works referenced in Jan Plamper, "The History of Emotions: An Interview with William Reddy, Barbara Rosenwein and Peter Stearns," *History and Theory* 49, no. 2 (2010): 237–65.

16. Maximilien Robespierre, *Rapport sur les principes du gouvernement révolutionnaire* (Paris, n.d. [1794]), 3.

17. Dan Edelstein, "Do We Want a Revolution without Revolution? Reflections on Political Authority," *French Historical Studies* 35, no. 2 (2012): 269–89.

18. For a good introduction, see Jerome Karabel, "Towards a Theory of Intellectuals and Politics," *Theory and Society* 25, no. 2 (1996): 205–33.

19. Pierre Bourdieu, "The Intellectual Field: A World Apart," in *In Other Words:*

Essays Towards a Reflexive Sociology, trans. Matthew Adamson (Stanford, CA, 1990), 140–49 (quotation at 145).

20. See, though, for one excellent recent example, Nathan Perl-Rosenthal, "Corresponding Republics: Letter Writing and Patriot Organizing in the Atlantic Revolutions, circa 1760–1792," Ph.D. dissertation, Columbia University, 2011.

Index

CPSIA information can be obtained
at www.ICGtesting.com
Printed in the USA
LVHW031920191121
703843LV00010B/812

9 780804 796163